Management Control Systems

The Robert N. Anthony/Willard J. Graham Series in Accounting

Management Control Systems

Robert N. Anthony
Ross Graham Walker Professor Emeritus of Management Control

John Dearden
Herman C. Krannert Professor of Business Administration

both of the Graduate School of Business Administration Harvard University

Norton M. Bedford
Arthur Young Professor of Accounting University of Illinois

Fifth Edition

IRWIN

Homewood, Illinois 60430

Case material of the Harvard Graduate School of Business Administration is made possible by the cooperation of business firms who may wish to remain anonymous by having names, quantities, and other identifying details disguised while basic relationships are maintained. Cases are prepared as the basis for class discussion rather than to illustrate either effective or ineffective handling of administrative situations.

ISBN 0-256-02961-X
Library of Congress Catalog Card No. 83–82134

Printed in the United States of America

6 7 8 9 0 K 1 0 9 8 7

Preface

This fifth edition of our book follows closely the format of the fourth. All of the text, however, has been rewritten to incorporate new findings from the literature and observations from practice. The first four chapters and Chapter 9 are almost entirely new. New cases have been added in many chapters, and several cases included in the fourth edition have been deleted. Also contributing to the fifth edition is a new co-author, Professor Norton M. Bedford.

The book continues to focus on the subject of management control. It does not deal extensively with topics such as cost accounting and budgeting procedures, which are discussed in separate accounting courses. Instead, its focus is on newer topics, not usually discussed in such courses—topics such as the control of discretionary costs, profit centers, and the programming process.

The book is designed for a one-semester course for students who have had a course in management accounting and who wish to study management control in greater depth. Few of the cases require a detailed knowledge of accounting or finance, and many of them have been used successfully in management education courses in which many of the participants have had no formal accounting courses.

Most of the cases have been used at the Harvard Business School. Many have also been used at other institutions. All have been selected for their interest and value as a basis for class discussion. They are not necessarily intended to illustrate either correct or incorrect handling of management problems. As in all cases of this type, there are no right answers. The educational value of the cases comes from the practice the student receives in analyzing management control problems and in discussing and defending his or her analysis before the class.

ACKNOWLEDGMENTS

The course from which the material in this book was drawn was originally developed at the Harvard Business School by the late Ross

G. Walker. We wish to acknowledge his pioneering work in the development of both the concepts underlying the course and the methods of teaching these concepts. We thank the following members or former members of the Harvard Business School faculty who have contributed much to the development of this book: Francis J. Aguilar, Robert H. Caplan, Charles J. Christenson, Russell H. Hassler, Regina E. Herzlinger, Robert A. Howell, Gerard G. Johnson, F. Warren McFarlan, Richard F. Vancil, and John R. Yeager. In addition, we wish to acknowledge the assistance provided us by Robert H. Deming, James S. Hekimian, John Mauriel, Chei-Min Paik, and Jack L. Treynor.

We appreciate the comments and suggestions of Professors Kenneth A. Sinclair, of Lehigh University, and Srinivasan Umapathy of Boston University.

Authors of cases other than those copyrighted by Harvard University are as follows:

Case 4–3, Pierce-Irwin Corporation, Gerald Wentworth, Stanford University, copyright © by the Board of Trustees of Leland Stanford University; Case 7–8, Quality Metal Service Center (A), V. Govindarajan and Darryl Raimer, Ohio State University, copyright 1983; Case 7–9, Ballwin Oil Corporation, M. Edgar Barrett; Case 8–3, Diversified Products Corporation, William Rotch, University of Virginia, copyright © by the University of Virginia; Case 8–6, Schoppert Company, Dwight Ladd, copyright © by IMEDE, Management Development Institute; Case 8–7, Quality Metal Service Center (B), V. Govindarajan and Darryl Raimer, Ohio State University, copyright 1983; Case 9–1, Quaker Oats Company, Richard F. Vancil; Cases 10–2 and 11–10; Case 12–2, Galvor Company, copyright © by IMEDE; Case 12–3, Binswanger & Steele, Inc., J. Sterling Livingston; Case 12–4, Performance Rating of Divisional Controllers, adapted from an article by Frank J. Tanzola, reprinted by permission of *The Financial Executive;* Case 14–3, Universal Data Corporation, M. Edgar Barrett, adapted with permission from an article in May–June 1977 *Harvard Business Review,* copyright © 1977, by Harvard University; Case 17–1, Northeast Research Laboratory (B), Richard T. Johnson, Stanford University; Case 17–2, Star Industrial Contractors, Inc., was written by William H. Lucas and Hema V. Rao of Southern University, copyright © 1983 by Southern University, adapted by permission from William H. Lucas and Thomas L. Morison, "Management Accounting for Construction Contracts," *Management Accounting,* November 1981; Case 17–4, Sonic Aircraft Corporation, was prepared by Professor John E. Setnicky, University of Southwestern Louisiana, and is copyright © 1982 by Professor Setnicky.

Except as otherwise noted, all cases in this book are copyrighted by the President and Fellows of Harvard College, and we appreciate their permission to reproduce them here. We owe an even greater debt to the many businessmen who cooperated with us in the preparation of these cases and to the administration of the Harvard Business School for supporting our efforts in case collection and the development of this course.

Robert N. Anthony
John Dearden
Norton M. Bedford

Contents

Management Control Systems

PART ONE

An Overview

CHAPTER 1

The Nature of Management Control

To start, we shall describe the nature of control and management control in particular. Control is a broad concept applicable to people, things, situations, and organizations. In organizations, it includes both management control and other planning and controlling processes. Also, we shall distinguish between the control function and other functions of management. The chapter concludes with an overview of the management control structure and the steps in the management control process.

We shall use the following six terms to introduce the subject of control. They will be defined more precisely later on.

1. *Strategy*—A broad, general, long-term plan of action that governs organization policy formulation and programs for action.
2. *Policy*—A broad rule or set of rules that guides and governs actions throughout an organization.
3. *Programming*—The development and selection of a set of programs to be carried out.
4. *Control*—Guiding a set of variables (machines, people, equipment) toward an objective or goal.
5. *Management control*—All methods, procedures, and devices, including management control systems, that management uses to assure compliance with organization policies and strategies.
6. *Management control system*—An organized systematic process and structure that management uses in management control.

These terms are related to each other in organizations in the following manner. The first thing management needs to do when forming or changing an organization is to determine what the organization should do and how it should do it. The result of this strategic planning is a set of goals for the organization and various *strategies* for attaining the goals. The strategies developed include both *policies* to guide ways of acting and broad *programs* of activities to pursue goals. When these decisions have been completed, though they are reexamined continuously, management needs some way to assure that people in the organization do what they are supposed to do. *Control* is the process used to do this. It aims to assure that people in organizations do what management wants them to do. The management role in control is called "management control"; and the system used to do such things as collect and analyze information, evaluate it, and use it and other devices to control activities is a *management control system*.

With the foregoing introductory general framework of organizational control as background, we shall now consider the fundamental notions underlying management control and illustrate the universality of the concept of control.

THE NATURE OF CONTROL

Most of us think we have our lives under reasonable control. We guide ourselves to reach goals or objectives and correct our actions when we stray from the path to our goals. The driver strives to keep the automobile under control to reach a destination on time, to stay on the road, to avoid an accident, or to gain some other goal. Using various mechanical control devices, such as an accelerator, a steering wheel, and a brake pedal which respond to the driver's direction, the automobile is guided to perform as the driver wishes. These same control devices are used to correct the movements of the automobile when it drifts from the desired speed or slips to the side of the road. Should the driver let the automobile go out of control, undesirable things happen.

In a similar manner, an organization of managers and workers must be motivated and guided to do the things its leaders want it to do and must be corrected when it departs from the pursuit of management goals. Just as the automobile driver must keep the automobile under control, management must keep an organization under control so it will do the things it is supposed to do. If management loses control and the organization goes out of control, undesirable things happen to many people. The control devices used in business are many and much more complex than those used to control an automobile, primarily because control of an organization is a much more complicated process. Routine control devices include physical barriers to prevent inventory slippage; authorization forms for ordering or using equipment; inspirational leadership; and others processes, among which is a formal management control system. We shall lead up to a discussion of control in organizations by first describing the control process in simple situations.

Introductory Control Situations

Underlying all control processes is the idea of directing a variable, or set of variables, to a goal or objective, whether that variable is an individual, a machine, or an organization. In an organization, people are the variables to be directed, guided, or motivated to pursue goals and those doing the directing represent management. While management performs other functions, the management control function pervades an organization. Control systems also are used in nonorganization situations, but any control system has at least these four components:

1. An observation device that detects or observes and measures or describes the activities or other phenomena being controlled. The term for this component may be *observor,*, *detector,* or *sensor.*
2. An assessing device that evaluates the performance of an activity or organization, usually relative to some standard or expectation of what should be, and identifies out-of-control activities and conditions. The term for this component is *evaluator, assessor,* or *selector.*
3. A behavior modification device for altering or changing performance if the need for doing so is indicated. This component may be called a *director, modifier,* or *effector.*
4. A means of transmitting information among the other devices. This component's term is *communication network.*

The transmission of information from the detector through the selector to the effector is termed *feedback.*[1]

Collectively, these components may be structured as a *system,* because they are a set of interrelated processes serving a common purpose. The interrelationship is that each component of the system affects and is affected by other components. The bare bones of all control systems are diagrammed in Exhibit 1–1.

EXHIBIT 1–1 Essential Components of a Control System

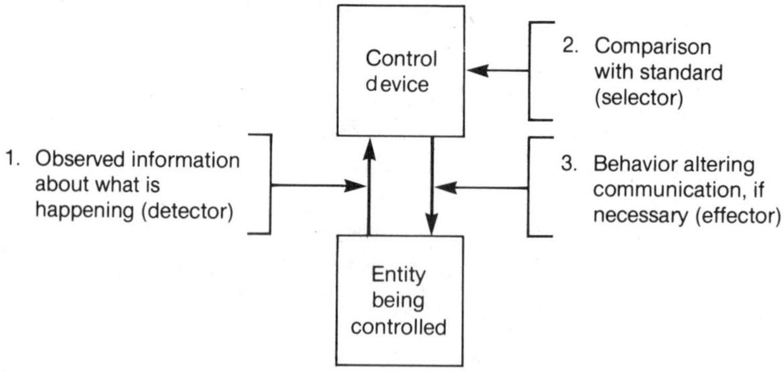

[1] For a more complete discussion, see Norbert Weiner, *Cybernetics* (New York: John Wiley & Sons, 1948). Cybernetics is defined as "control and communication in man and machine."

The control system functions in multiple forms and for various purposes, as illustrated by three representative examples: an electrical control system—a thermostat for room temperature control; a biological control system—a human body for body temperature control; and a mental control system—a brain and sensing organ for human behavior control.

Thermostat. The thermostat connected to a furnace is a control system that contains the components listed above: (1) the thermostat has a thermometer (detector), which measures the current temperature in the room; (2) the thermostat compares this measurement with a preset standard of the desired temperature (selector); and (3) if the current temperature is below the preset standard, the thermostat signals the furnace to turn on and to send heat to the room, and when the temperature reaches the preset standard, the thermostat signals the furnace to shut off (effector).

Electrical circuits are used to transmit the observed information in the form of electrical impulses from the thermometer to the assessor part of the thermostat and then convey instructions from the thermostat to the furnace.

Body temperature. Most mammals are born with a built-in standard of desirable body temperature. In humans, it is 98.6°F. Control of body temperature is achieved using the four components in the following manner: (1) sensory nerves scattered throughout the body (detectors) measure the current temperature and transmit information about it to the hypothalamus center in the brain; (2) the hypothalamus compares information on current body temperature with the standard of 98.6° (selector); and (3) if this comparison indicates that the current temperature is significantly above the standard, the hypothalamus activates devices (effectors) to reduce it (panting, sweating, opening of skin pores) or, if the current temperature is significantly below the standard, the hypothalamus activates devices (effectors) to increase it (closing of skin pores, shivering).[2] The control process in this self-regulating system for maintaining a relatively stable internal temperature is called "homeostasis." If the system is functioning properly, it automatically corrects for deviations from the desired state.

Although the control system for body temperature uses the same components as the thermostat for the control of room temperature, there are two important differences that make an understanding of the body temperature control system more difficult than an understanding of the thermostat. First, the system is more complicated: sensors are scattered all through the body, the hypothalamus acts on both plus and minus deviations from normal, and the actions that it motivates involve

[2] S. A. Richards, *Temperature Regulation* (London: Wykeham Publications, 1973).

a variety of muscles and organs. Second, although we know what the hypothalamus does, we do not really understand exactly how it works.

Human behavior. Consider an automobile driver on a highway where the speed limit is 55 mph. The driver functions as a control system that acts as follows: (1) the eye (detector) observes the speed as stated on the speedometer and communicates this speed to the brain (or perhaps the sense of speed is communicated by a general perception of movement); (2) the brain (assessor) compares the current speed with the limit of 55 mph; and (3) if this comparison indicates that the speed is too fast, the brain (effector) may or may not direct the foot to ease up on the accelerator.

Although this control system has the same essential components as the other two, it has an additional complication: we cannot state with confidence what, if any, action the brain will direct if actual speed exceeds 55 mph. Some people obey the speed limit, and therefore, will ease up on the accelerator; others act only when the actual speed consistently exceeds 55 mph; and still others obey the speed limit at certain times, but not at other times. In these circumstances, although a control system exists and functions reasonably well, we cannot predict specifically, solely from the characteristics of the system, what will happen when the brain receives information about the automobile's speed. Control is not automatic; and to use well this type of control system, we need to know, at a minimum, something about the personality of the driver.[3]

Control in Organizations

Control systems for organizations use the same essential components as the electrical, biological, and mental control systems just described. But the selection of the best observing, assessing, and behavior altering devices requires consideration of the following conditions before establishing an organizational control system:

1. The environment, both external (degree and nature of competition, developments in the industry, government policies, and general economic and social conditions) and internal (top management support for control standards, degree of emphasis on formal control throughout the organization, and types of internal activities), in which the organization exists and acts.

[3] These examples are arranged in order of increasing complexity. Systems theorists point out that the universe consists of a hierarchy of systems, each higher level system being more complicated than systems of lower levels. One list is: atoms, molecules, crystals, viruses, cells, organs, organisms (e.g., human beings), groups (e.g., teams), organizations, societies, and supranational organizations. See L. von Bertalanffy, "General Systems Theory," *Yearbook of the Society of General Systems Research,* 1956.

2. The extent of the tendency of the organization, or parts of it, to go out of control. This tendency is related to the character of employees, span of managers responsibilities, structure of the organization, quality of organization leadership, extent to which employees know their jobs, nature of the production process, sensitivity of organization to external events, and a host of similar considerations.
3. The inventory of feasible control devices and techniques available to observe, assess, and alter the various organization tendencies to fail to attain goals. This includes both specific devices and coordinated and compatible sets of devices that function as a control system for the whole organization.

The *control system* in the organization, like the brain of the automobile driver, directs and guides the organization to the desired goals. It does this by collecting information about the actual state of the organization, comparing it with the desired state, and initiating action to alter organization performance, if necessary. Different types of systems are needed for different actions. Control systems for some parts of an organization are almost as automatic as the thermostat. Examples are the process controls in a petroleum refinery, the control of the flow of electricity through a distribution network, and the production controls on an automated assembly line. Such control systems, and others having similar characteristics, are called "task control systems."

Control of the organization as a whole, however, is much more complicated than any of the preceding examples. It requires a *management control system,* the term implying that organization control is exercised through managers. Several conditions make management control a complicated control system:

1. The organization is comprised of various departments, divisions, and groups, each with some degree of autonomy, which requires that the control system coordinate, motivate, and correct errors and irregularities so the managers of these units operate to attain overall organization goals, rather than their independent goals.

2. The standards used for assessing organization performance are not preset by external conditions. To a major degree organization goals are established by organization leadership. Planning is involved in determining both the goals and the process the organization should use to meet them. The latter, in particular, connects planning so closely to control that for many purposes both may be viewed as one process.

3. Management control includes both formal and informal controls. The formal detectors of most of what is happening in an organization provide essential information for correcting major variations from standards; but those happenings that various managers see, sense, hear, and correct immediately without formal control signals are also

part of the control system. In addition, over and above the corrective control processes, are formal and informal motivation controls that encourage managers and workers to want to maintain the organization on track toward established goals.

The informal control systems, sometimes reflected in unwritten organization policies, have been referred to as the organization control environment or its culture. Operations researchers use the term *black box* to describe an operation whose exact nature cannot be observed. An informal management control system is similar to a black box that includes processes for motivating managers to take desired actions and preventing and correcting employees and suborganization units from taking inappropriate actions.

CONTROL PROCESS

The three phases of the management control process are *planning* action, *execution* of action, and *evaluation* of action that occur before, during, and after the action or event, respectively. All three phases are applied at different levels in an organization, which may range from top management to the smallest operating unit.

We have mentioned two types of planning and control processes that are found in organization: management control and task control. In this section, we add a third process, *strategic planning,* and discuss differences among the three of them. Our purpose is to establish the boundaries of the subject area of interest to us: management control systems. The following descriptions of the three types are brief but adequate to differentiate them from management control:

1. *Strategic planning* is the process of deciding on the goals of the organization, and the formulation of broad strategies to be used in attaining these goals. This process uses methods quite different from those used for management and task control.
2. *Management control* is the process by which management assures that the organization carries out its strategies.
3. *Task control* is the process of assuring that specific tasks are carried out effectively and efficiently.

Obviously, we do not mean to imply that these three processes can be separated by sharply defined boundaries; one shades into another. Strategic planning sets the guidelines for management control, and management control sets the guidelines for task control. The three processes are distinct, however, and those who design and use planning and control systems will make costly errors if they fail to take into account both the common characteristics and the differences among the processes.

Management Control

Management control is primarily a process for motivating and inspiring people to perform organization activities that will further the organization's goal. It is also a process for detecting and correcting unintentional performance errors and intentional irregularities, such as theft or misuse of resources.

Process. Management control includes a management control system composed of a structure—organizational arrangements, authorities, responsibilities, and information constructs—for facilitating the exercise of control and a process or set of actions which take place to assure that the organization operates to realize its goals.

Managers. Management control is a process for managers. They use it in their interaction with one another and with subordinates. It is a people-oriented process. Line managers are the focal points in management control. They make the plans for attaining goals, and they are the persons who must influence others and whose performance is measured. Staff people collect, summarize, and present information that is useful in the process, and make calculations that translate management judgments into the format of the system. Such a staff may be large in numbers; indeed, the control department is often the largest staff department in a company, but the significant decisions are made by the line managers.

Since it focuses on people and plan implementation, psychological considerations are dominant in management control. Such activities as communicating, persuading, exhorting, inspiring, and criticizing are an important part of the process.

Goals. The goals[4] of an organization are set in the strategic planning process. They are normally timeless and last indefinitely, although information obtained during the management control process may lead to a change in goals. After organization goals are in place, the strategic planning process may be used to develop strategies in the form of ways of achieving goals. While developing programs to implement strategies, it frequently occurs that broad company-wide policies, such as the well-published policy of assuming the customer is always right, applicable to all strategies, can be formed. Parts of the implementing programs used to operationalize strategies may be reduced to annual budgets for management control in a particular year.

The goals, strategies, and policies are taken as given in the management control process. Management control aims to implement strate-

---

[4] In this book we use the word *goals* for the broad, overall aims of the organization, and *objectives* for the more specific statements of planned accomplishments in a given time period. Some people use these two words interchangeably, and others reverse the meanings given above. The words *target* and *aim* are also used as synonyms for either word. Confusion can result if these differences in intended meaning are not understood.

gies and is concerned with the actions of managers and employees in their efforts to achieve organization goals.

Efficiency and effectiveness. Management control uses task control to assure efficient and effective performance at the task level. By effectiveness, we mean accomplishment or how well an organization unit does its job of producing an output of products or services or the extent to which the unit produces intended or expected results. *Efficiency* is used in the engineering sense of economy—as the amount of input used per unit of output. The most efficient organization unit is the one which produces a given quantity of outputs with a minimum consumption of inputs, or the most output with given inputs.

Effectiveness is always related to the organization's goals. Efficiency, per se, need not be related to goals. An efficient organization unit is one which does whatever it does with the lowest consumption of resources; but if what it does, its output, does not accomplish organization goals, the unit is ineffective.

Assurance. Senior managers use a management control system to detect out-of-control situations, and to assure themselves that the organization carries out its strategies effectively and efficiently. The assurance process is important to managers primarily because, when they are acting as managers, they do not themselves do the work. Their function is to assure that the work gets done by others; and when they cannot observe the work being done by others, they need constant assurance from the management control system that it is done.

Characteristics of management control systems. Management control includes both actions to guide and motivate efforts to attain organization goals and actions to detect and correct ineffective and inefficient performance. Different management control systems are needed for different situations, but all seem to possess the following characteristics:

1. Management control systems focus on programs and responsibility centers. A program is a product, product line, research and development project, or similar activity that the organization undertakes to achieve its goals. A responsibility center is an organization unit headed by a responsible manager.

The relationship between a *program* (the horizontal flow) and responsibility *center* (the vertical flow) is presented in Exhibit 1–2 which reveals that work on a program may involve several responsibility centers. For example, manufacturing product X (a program) may have components made in departments A, B, and C and be assembled in D (responsibility centers).

2. The information processed in a management control system is of two general types: (a) *planned data,* in the form of programs, budgets, and standards; and (b) *actual data,* on what has or is actually

EXHIBIT 1–2 Relationship between Programs and Centers

Responsibility Centers

Programs	A	B	C	D	Costs
X	$1,000	$2,000	$ 500	-0-	$3,500
Y	2,000	2,000	3,000	1,000	8,000
Z	800	-0-	700	-0-	1,500
Costs	$3,800	$4,000	$4,200	$1,000	$13,000

happening, both inside the organization and in the external environment.

3. A management control system is a *total organization system* in that it embraces all aspects of organization operations. It functions to help management maintain all parts of the operation in balance with one another, and operate the organization as a coordinated whole.

4. Management control systems are usually built around a *financial structure,* where organization resources and activities are expressed in monetary units. Monetary valuation is the common denominator that can be used to combine and classify the heterogeneous resources and activities of an organization into categories that can be used to compare the performance of various organization units. Nonmonetary measures, such as minutes per operation, number of employees, and reject and spoilage rates, may also be used to extend the scope and quality of the management control system.

5. The planning aspects of the management control system tend to follow a definite pattern and timetable. In budget preparation, which is an important activity in the management control process, certain steps are taken in a predetermined sequence at certain dates each year: dissemination of guidelines, preparation of original estimates, transmission of these estimates up through the several echelons in the organization, review of these estimates, final approval by top management, and dissemination back through the organization. The procedure to be followed at each step in this process, the dates when the steps are to be completed, and even the forms to be used can be, and often are, set forth in a policies and procedures manual. This same rhythmic process

is used in other areas of the management control system: feedback reports and coordination information.

6. A management control system is a *coordinated, integrated system* where data collected for different purposes are reconciled for comparison purposes, over time and organization units. In particular, data on actual performance are structured in the same way as planned data—that is, defined and measured consistently—to permit valid comparisons of actual with planned performance. While it may be useful for some purposes to think of the management control system as a set of interlocking subsystems, such as programming, budgeting, accounting, and reporting systems, better organization-wide coordination may be effected by thinking of the management control system as a single system.

Strategic Planning

The word *strategic* means an act of great value or importance to an organization. The term *strategic planning* refers to the explicit process of developing organization-wide statements of policy, strategies, and goals so communicated that various parts of the organization function as a unified whole to attain them. Program statements indicate what products or services the business will produce. Policy and strategy statements indicate how to combine and employ resources, and goals indicate what the organization wants to do. Strategic planning is a process for the formulation of long-range activities that spans both goal establishment and guiding policies and strategies for reaching the goals. Changes in such long-range strategic plans change the character and direction of an organization. Strategic planning includes plans for the acquisition and disposition of major facilities, divisions, or subsidiaries; the markets to be served and distribution channels for serving them; the organization structure; research and development activities; sources of long-term capital; and dividend policy.

Once the strategic planning decisions and statements are in place, it becomes the function of management control to assure that these policies and strategies are carried out. When the organization performs as it has been directed by the policies and strategies, the organization is said to be "under control." When it does not, it is "out of control."

Distinctions between Management Control and Strategic Planning. Briefly, here are some ways the strategic planning process differs from the management control process. First, the management control process takes the strategies as given and develops a system for implementing them.

The second distinction is that the strategic planning process is essentially *irregular,* whereas management control is a continuous fairly systematic process. Broad problems, sensed opportunities, and bright ideas are the inspiration for strategic planning, and they do not spring forth according to any set timetable. In contrast, observations about what is now happening in the organization, comparisons of actual performance with planned performance, and the altering of behavior—the essentials of management control—are regular and continuous.

Third, as previously noted, strategic planning is a *process* of becoming aware of significant and relevant environmental developments in the economy, government, industry, and competition, and of determining what the organization should be doing to seize opportunities and avoid problems; but it is unrealistic to describe this as a *system*. In fact, an attempt to develop a system for strategic planning could easily stifle its essential element of creativity.

Fourth, strategic planning emphasizes the development of competitive strategies for outperforming other companies;[5] the exploitation of technological developments; and adapting the organization to the conditions for survival and growth which the environment imposes on it. For example, universities may develop strategies for developing faculties better then their competitors or ways of adjusting educational programs to technological developments. Management control and the data used in it aim to influence managers to take action that will lead to the desired results. Much of the information useful for the development of various strategies is derived from external sources. In contrast, most of the information for management control is developed internally in the form of economic and psychological measures that can be used to inspire, guide, and correct the actions of managers.

Both management control and strategic planning involve senior management, but other managers are more involved in management control than in strategic planning. The pressures of everyday activities do not allow middle managers the necessary time for strategic planning, and they usually are knowledgeable about only their part of the organization, and strategic planning requires a broad company-wide background. Middle managers may, of course, make strategic plans for their own segment of the organization; and the use of a decentralized organization structure fosters the tendency for divisions to set up separate staffs to gather external facts and make analyses that provide background material for strategic decisions at all levels. But, essentially, strategic planning is a senior management responsibility.

The management control process and the strategic planning process tend to overlap at times; but the types of analytical tools used, types of thinking required, and the sources of information differ and need to be

[5] For an examination of methods for developing competitive strategies in a business, see Michael E. Porter, *Competitive Strategy* (New York: Free Press, 1980).

EXHIBIT 1–3 Some Distinctions between Strategic Planning and Management Control

Characteristic	*Strategic planning*	*Management control*
Focus of plans	One aspect at a time	Whole organization
Complexities	Many variables	Less complex
Communication of information	Relatively simple	Relatively difficult
Purposes	Show expected results	Lead to desired results
Persons primarily involved	Staff and senior management	Line and senior management
Number of persons involved	Small	Large
Mental activity	Creative; analytical	Administrative; persuasive
Source discipline	Economics	Social psychology
Planning and control	Planning dominant	Emphasis on different type of planning and control
Time horizon	Tends to be long	Tends to be short
End result	Policies and programs	Action within policies and programs
Appraisal of the job done	Extremely difficult	Much less difficult

explicitly differentiated. Other differences between management control and strategic planning are summarized in Exhibit 1–3.

At times, it may appear that task plans (schedules, inventory levels, and the like) are derived directly from strategic plans and merely surface as part of the management control process of coordinating organization activities for both the short-term and long-term success of the organization. This tendency must be avoided, and task plans need to be an aspect of management control. With due regard for the dangers of oversimplification, we may structure the relationships among strategic planning, management control, and task control as starting with strategic planning to establish goals and adopt strategies (policies and long-range programs) for reaching the goals. Management control to implement these strategies is then initiated by developing plans and means of assuring that they are carried out. Simultaneous with management control processes, task control implements the detailed work to achieve organization goals. Strategic plans and tasks plans do need to be coordinated for organization control. An overemphasis on task planning and control, to the neglect of strategic plans, for example, may provide short-run temporarily success at one level of organization activity at the cost of long-run disaster for the whole organization. The management control system is involved in performance and aims to motivate attainment of both task and strategic plans; but the methods of task control differ from the management control used for assuring compliance with strategies.

Task Control

Task control refers to the detailed control of individual work and procedures. The system consists of three interrelated parts:

1. An identification of points and activities in such areas as schedules, inventory levels, and other tasks where departures from task plans are likely to occur. These will depend upon the degree of task control judged necessary.
2. A selection of control techniques and methods appropriate for each identified area, point, or activity to prevent or correct departures from plans. Different techniques and methods are used for different situations.
3. Constant review to assure that the system is adequate for control and that employees do not override the control system.

To understand the nature of the areas, points, and activities to which task control is applicable, we need to introduce the idea of *scheduled* activities. *Scheduled activities* take the form of a specific action to be taken to perform a task within a given situation. This does not mean that tasks are so routine that they can be scheduled in detail and be automated and performed mechanically. But it does suggest that the task is performed according to a somewhat standard process, such as having the legal department perform legal tasks.

Each act in the process of performing a task represents a possible area, point, or activity that may be used to evaluate the performance of the task for control purposes. For example, a task may be behind schedule if a selected activity or point in the activity is performed at a time later than the scheduled or planned time. Or a task may be evaluated as being inefficiently performed if the quality of the task output, at some preselected point, is below the quality required by the task plan. *Task control* includes the process of correcting or preventing variation of the scheduled activities from their objectives, procedures, or sequential steps. Scheduled activities are sometimes referred to by such titles as standard operating procedures and structured operations. A fundamental understanding of the notion of scheduled activities may be grasped by examining the terms *outputs* and *inputs* and noting the relationship between them.

Outputs and inputs. *Outputs* are the goods or services created by a unit or an organization. *Inputs* are the resources and services the unit consumes. Every organizational unit does something and, therefore, has outputs of some type, whether or not they are clearly definable or readily measurable. In a manufacturing business, outputs are goods. In a school, the service output is education; in a hospital, it is patient care; and in government, it is service to the public.

Every unit—division, department, activity—within an organization has outputs. In the production plant, the outputs are goods. In other units, such as personnel, transportation, sales, engineering, and administration, outputs are services. It is difficult to measure the quantity or quality of the outputs of many organizations; however, for every unit and every organization, they exist.

Inputs are the resources and services used to create the outputs. It is a management task to seek the optimum relationship between outputs and inputs. In simple situations, the inputs are so closely related to the outputs that control treats the relationship between the inputs and outputs as linear. An example is the situation in which the input of raw material resources becomes a physical part of the finished good output. Control centers on producing the outputs at the time needed and in the desired quantities with minimum inputs.

In many situations inputs are not directly related to outputs, as illustrated by the indirect relationship between an input of advertising and an increase in sales output. There is a perceived relationship, but it is not a constant direct relationship. The increase in sales output from an additional dollar of advertising input may vary significantly over time and under different situations. Managers seek, for control, to determine the long-run optimal constant relationship between outputs and the indirectly related inputs; but, practically, they quickly turn to means of controlling inputs and outputs separately. Task plans may be developed for the timing, amount, nature, and type of an advertising input within a year using subjective judgment about the output (effectiveness) of different types of advertising. Task control of inputs also includes efforts to assure that the timing, amount, nature, and type of the advertising each month within the year is according to plan. The term *discretionary costs* identifies the type of input for which there is no reasonably objective way of ascertaining the optimum standard output quantity to be expected from the inputs. Management's subjective judgment, a part of the management control process and possibly reflected in the annual budget, is needed to establish the "right" amount of discretionary costs to be permitted in a given situation. Costs whose optimum amounts for given outputs can be estimated objectively are called "engineered costs."

Scheduled activities. In some situations, an optimum relationship between outputs and inputs of a responsibility center can be estimated within reasonable limits. Even though it is unrealistic to imply that an exact relationship can be determined, inasmuch as new and better ways of doing things are constantly being developed, the "optimum" amount of inputs at a point in time, or the optimal combination out of all *known* combinations, can be defined as the combination that will produce the desired output at the lowest cost. If the optimum combination input-output relationship for a given activity can be predetermined, the inputs to be used in a given situation can be scheduled or described. Task control is directed to such activities.

Distinction between management control and task control. To make clear the distinction between task control and management control, we will illustrate each. Certain features of inventory management lend themselves to task control. If the demand for an inventory item, the cost of storing it, its production cost and production time, and the loss involved in not filling an order are known, then the optimum inventory level and optimum production or procurement schedule can be developed. Even though these four factors cannot be known precisely, reasonable estimates can be made and inventory levels and production schedules can be calculated based on the estimates. An inventory control system using rules derived from such calculations is a *task control system.*

To illustrate management control, consider the legal department of a business where it is not possible to measure the quality, or even the quantity, of the legal service that constitutes the output of this department. There is no means of determining the amount of service the department should render or the optimum amount of costs that should be incurred. Management judgments on the "right" amount of service, the "right" amount of cost, and the "right" relationship between service actually rendered and cost actually incurred on a project are strictly subjective. Yet the legal department, as a part of the whole organization, must be controlled. Lacking a means of task control, the chief counsel must operate the legal department within the framework of policies prescribed by top management; the type of control necessary in his situation is *management control.*

Examples of activities that are susceptible to task control are automated plants, such as oil refineries and power-generating stations; direct production operations of manufacturing plants; production scheduling; inventory control; and order processing and similar paperwork activities.

Examples of activities for which management control is necessary are the total operation of most manufacturing plants, which includes judgments based primarily on organization policies for attaining organization goals. Specific activities typically included are: employees' benefits and welfare programs, training, and supervision; most advertising, sales promotion, pricing, and similar marketing activities; most aspects of finance; most aspects of research, development, and design; the work of staff units and all types; and the activities of top management.

Management control and task control have certain common features. Both need an internal control environment that supports cooperativeness, efficiency, competence, honesty, and belief in the organization. The rigor needed for both vary with the internal uncertainties and opportunities for going astray from the pursuit of organization goals. Both require the use of different control devices or techniques in different ways according to the environment and uncertainties in which the organization performs. And both have to be reviewed frequently to assure that they do encourage managers and workers to perform efficiently and effectively and to correct irregularities.

Beyond these broad similarities, management control differs from the task control in at least the following respects.[6] First, management control is used to control the whole organization, whereas each task control procedure is designed specifically for the needs of one unit of the organization. Management control functions from a set of strategies. Task control functions from a set of procedures and rules derived from management control.

The techniques which management control uses for evaluation are seldom precise, which makes it somewhat difficult to provide assurance that actions are proceeding as desired. In contrast, the procedures and rules to be followed in task control may provide precise numerical objective standards for evaluating performance and a higher degree of assurance that actions are or are not proceeding as desired.

Management control, being people-oriented, is directed more toward assisting managers to attain organization strategies than in correcting performance to conform with some fixed standard of performance. A task control system, being more concerned with specific actions, uses more *rational* and more precise performance standards frequently developed from a set of logical rules. At times these standards can be programmed into a computer and, if it is less costly to do so, task control can function as a computer control system.

Management control largely controls *people*; task control largely controls *things*. In management control, psychological considerations are dominant. The management control system does not directly or by itself result in action without human intervention. By contrast, the end product of an inventory control system can be an action order, such as a decision to replenish a certain inventory item, based entirely on calculations from formulas incorporated in the manual or computerized task control system.

In developing a task control system, analogies with mechanical, electrical, and hydraulic systems may be useful, and such related terms as *feedback, network balancing,* and *optimization* are relevant and appropriate. It is reasonable, for example, to view certain task control systems as analogous to the operations of a thermostat. These simple analogies do not serve well as models for management control systems, however, because the success of these control systems is highly dependent on their impact on people, and people are not like thermostats or furnaces.

---

[6] See R. K. Mautz and James Winjum, *Criteria for Management Control Systems* (New York: Financial Executives Research Foundation, 1981) for a distinction between accounting control and management control.

Whereas the formal management control system is ordinarily built around a financial structure and uses financial measures for control, task control data are often nonmonetary. They may be expressed in such terms as labor-hours, number of items, or pounds of waste. Further, since each task control procedure is designed for a limited area of application, such as the operation of a single production department, it is feasible to use different measurement bases, selecting whichever is most appropriate for each area.

The information used in a task control system or systems may frequently relate to individual transactions: a production order for one lot, a purchase order for one item of inventory, or a requisition for one maintenance job. Much of the information in a management control system consists of summaries of transactions: production costs for a month, the status of groups of items in inventory, and maintenance costs in total.

Data used in a task control system are immediate and, often, in real time (reported as the event is occurring), whereas data used in a management control system are often summaries of past activities. Computer specialists who do not recognize the need for a distinction between the information needs of the two types of control systems sometimes suggest a system that will display to the management the current status of every individual activity in the organization. This *should not* be done because it would overload management with detailed information not needed for management control.

Task control uses exact data, whereas management control uses summaries and approximations. Because material is ordered and scheduled in specific quantities and employees are paid the exact amount due them, a task control system needs exact information; but data in management control reports can be rounded to thousands or millions of dollars.

The formal management control system is only a part of the management control process. For example, the organization structure itself is a control device by which duties and responsibilities are assigned to people according to their qualifications. A decentralized organization is a type of control structure.

The success of the management control process depends on the qualifications of managers; yet personnel selection, placement, and promotion, normally outside any formal management control system, are used to assure that only managers with sound judgment, adequate knowledge, and an ability to influence others are assigned responsibility for guiding and directing the organization to its goals.

In task control, the formal system itself is more important. Except in fully automated operations, it is an exaggeration to say that the system is the process; but it is not much of an exaggeration. Some task control systems compare actual performance with planned performance and state what action should be taken; the system makes the decisions. Management vigilance is required, of course, to detect an unforeseen foul-up in the operation or a change in the underlying conditions or assumptions on which the control technique is constructed, and to initiate any necessary corrective action. Management may also seek ways to improve the technique. In general, however, the degree of management involvement in task control is small, whereas in management control it is large.

Exhibit 1–4 suggests in general terms the relationship among strategic planning, goals, policies, management controls, the management control system, and other planning and control functions.

EXHIBIT 1–4 General Relationships among Planning and Control Functions

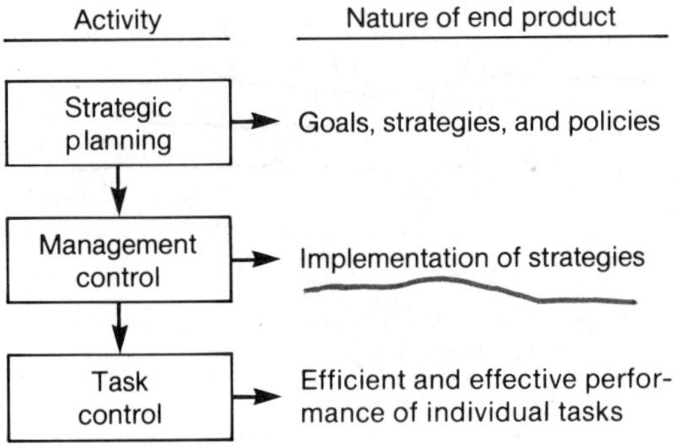

Most organizations function as suggested by Exhibit 1–4. They decide what they plan to do (goals), and they do have means of reaching the goals (strategies). Implementing the strategies involves developing general policies, such as a policy of doing only quality work, and programs, such as programs for distributing a product. The policies and programs indicate what the organization leaders want the organization to do. It is the responsibility of management to see that the programs are accomplished. They do this by using both formal and informal management controls. While Exhibit 1–4 does not reveal it well, management controls may also influence strategies when it is discovered that strategies need to be modified.

Exhibit 1–4 suggests that management control implements strategies which involve the three activities of making task plans and fostering task evaluations; motivating and assisting people, using budgets and other means to carry out programs within policy guidelines; and exercising judgmental control, using such devices as financial report comparisons and trends to correct performance as appropriate.

Distinctions between management control and internal accounting control. The notion of internal accounting control for public accounting reports has been used for many years in business organizations. Its scope of activities and the number of people employed has expanded significantly in recent years, because it has been used by some organizations as a substitute for management control as well. Today, the internal auditor is very much a part of the control process used by large organizations. Traditionally, the accounting control system emphasized precautionary measures to curb errors (unintentional mistakes) and irregularities (intentional undesirable acts). To assure that errors and irregularities that result in departures from organization plans are minimized, internal accounting controls include:

1. A means of assuring that transactions are executed only as authorized by management.
2. A means of assuring that all such transactions are recorded to permit, as a minimum, the preparation of appropriate financial reports and to maintain accountability for resources.
3. A means of assuring, by a periodic physical examination and count of organization resources, that the accounting recorded accountability for organization resources is correct.
4. A means of assuring that access to resources, such as supplies and merchandise, and use of resources, such as tools and machinery, is only by documented management authority.

Management control is more positive-oriented. It aims to encourage, assist, and motivate managers and workers to implement organization strategies and to follow organization policies in the process. It places less emphasis on the discovery and correction of errors and irregularities.

Internal auditors have supported efforts to develop and integrate internal accounting control with management planning until accounting and auditing control is integrated as part of the management control process. Doing this might require an external auditor to audit not only compliance with accounting standards but also the efficiency and effectiveness of organization planning, coordinating, and performing. Other efforts have been made to confine internal accounting control to task control.

Distinctions between task control and internal accounting control. Many of the techniques used in task control systems are also used in internal accounting control systems. Both systems use feedback information, which is compared to standards of desired performance. But the traditional accounting control system functions primarily to *safeguard assets* and to check the *accuracy and reliability* of the accounting data to be used in the annual financial reports. It treats, as management or administrative control, managerial efforts to promote organization efficiency and effectiveness and its efforts to encourage implementation of organization strategies.

EXHIBIT 1–5 Some Distinctions among Management, Accounting, and Task Controls

Characteristic	*Management control*	*Accounting control*	*Task control*
Focus of activity	Whole operation	Errors and irregularities	Single task or transaction
Scope	Broad and inclusive	Corrective action	According to specific rules
Purpose	Describe management opportunities	Describe accounting and auditing responsibility	Describe specific performance relative to specific standard
Nature of structure	Psychological	Systematic	Rational
Nature of information	Integrated; financial; approximations acceptable; future and historical	Articulated model; objective financial data; historical	Tailor-made to the operation; often nonfinancial; precise
Persons primarily involved	Management	Accountants	Supervisors
Source discipline	Psychology	Economics	Engineering
Time horizon	Weeks, months, years	Months, quarters, year	Day to day

Internal accounting controls normally use financial measure, whereas task controls may use nonfinancial types of measures as well. The notion of "accounting control" has authoritative senior management support, has been clearly articulated, and is widely used for the preparation of public financial statements on the organization and its activities. The differences among management control, accounting control, and task control are summarized in Exhibit 1–5.

OTHER MANAGEMENT PROCESSES

An old classification of the functions of management, which is still used, is that of Fayol: planning, organizing, coordinating, and controlling.[7] Current descriptions of management may expand that a little, but essentially Fayol's functions are valid today.

There is a danger that a summary description of management control, to relate it to the totality of management, may create the impression that management control is the whole of management. This is obviously not the case; management control is only a part of management. For example, we have noted the management function of strategic planning; and we have noted that managers must make judgments on hiring, assigning responsibilities, creating an environment for effective work, and other people-oriented activities. These are not part of management control, though management control may provide information for dealing with them.

Finally, managers do not spend all their time in the management function itself. The sales manager may close a deal with an important customer. The production manager may "get his hands dirty" with some problem in the plant. The financial vice president may personally negotiate credit arrangements. For these reasons this discussion of management control is by no means a discussion of the whole process of management, nor is it a description of all that managers do.

OVERVIEW OF MANAGEMENT CONTROL SYSTEMS

A system consists of a *structure or design* of relationships among things and a *process* or set of activities that the system does. The structure of a management control system will be described in terms of the units in an organization and the nature of the information that flows among these units. The process will be explained in terms of what managers do with this information.

---

[7] Henry Fayol, *Industrial and General Administration*, trans. J. A. Coubrough (Geneva: International Management Institute, 1929). Originally published in 1916.

Structure

The management control structure is described later in more detail. Broadly, that description focuses on various types of responsibility centers. A *responsibility center* is an organization unit headed by a responsible manager. Each responsibility center has inputs and it has outputs. Responsibility centers are classified according to the degree to which these inputs and outputs are measured in monetary terms and for which a center manager is responsible.

In an *expense* center, inputs are measured in terms of money costs; but outputs are either not measured—or not measured in terms of money—and the center manager is responsible primarily for expense control. In an *engineered expense center,* the costs are scheduled as described earlier. In a *discretionary expense center,* costs are not scheduled; they can be varied at the discretion of the managers involved. Most staff departments in an organization are discretionary expense centers.

In a *revenue center,* revenues are measured in monetary terms that are not matched with expenses, and the manager of the unit is responsible primarily for revenue maximization. Sales offices are an example.

In a *profit center,* both revenues and the expenses associated with earning those revenues are measured and matched to calculate profit, which is the unit manager's responsibility.

In an *investment center,* both the profit—as measured as in a profit center—and the investment, or capital, used in that responsibility center are measured. Then the center profit is related to the investment.

Process

Much of the management control process involves informal communication and interactions among managers and workers. Informal communication occurs by means of memoranda, meetings, conversations, and even by such signals as facial expressions. Although these informal activities are of great importance in management control, they are not amenable to a systematic description. In addition to the informal controls, most companies also have a formal management control system, which includes the following interrelated phases of programming (Program Selection), budgeting, operating and measurement, and reporting and analysis as revealed in Exhibit 1–6.

As indicated in Exhibit 1–6, each activity leads to the next. They recur in a regular cycle and collectively they constitute a "closed loop." These four phases are described briefly below, and later in greater depth.

Programming. Programming is the process of selecting specific programs for organization actions. The programs that are the result of

EXHIBIT 1–6 Phases of Management Control System

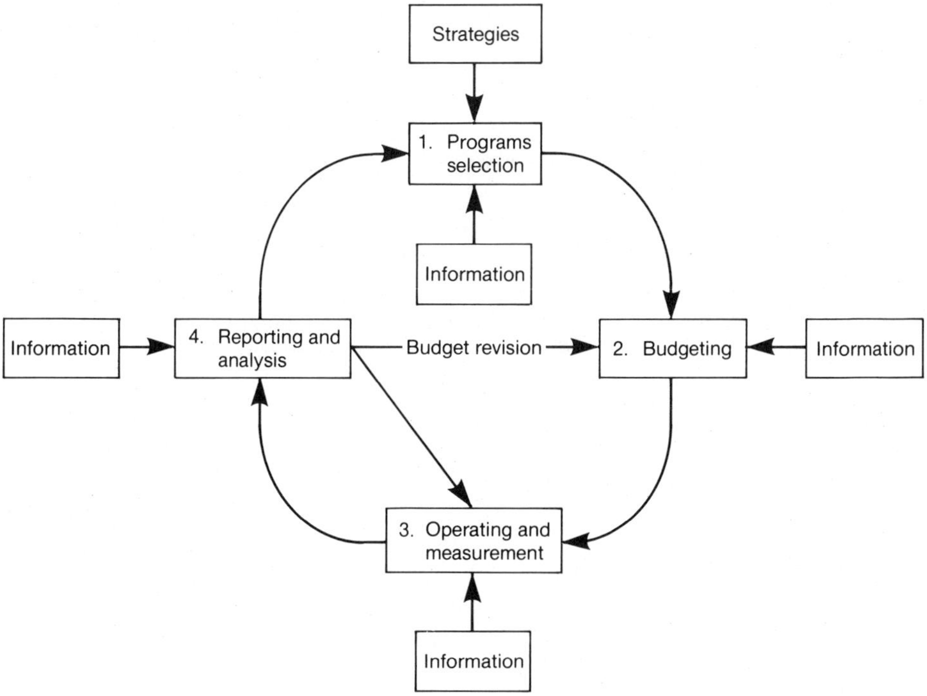

the programming process show which, when, and what amounts of resources will be used on each program. Programs indicate activities than an organization will undertake to implement its strategies. In a profit-oriented company, each principal product or product line is a program. Various research and development projects may be programs. The essence of a program for either business or nonbusiness organizations is a set of actions that leads to the production or distribution of a good or service output using resources from one or more units of the organization.

Budgeting. An organization's operating budget is its plan of actions, usually expressed in monetary terms, for a specified period, normally one year. In the budgeting process, the budget is typically constructed by aggregating division and department budgets, which are the responsibility of the division or department manager. As part of this process, each program is translated into activities that correspond to responsibilities of the manager of each responsibility center for the time period. Each manager is charged with executing a program or some part of one. Although means of implementing strategies are initially developed as programs, in the budgeting process the programs are translated into duties of responsibility centers. The process of developing a budget is essentially one of negotiation between the manager of a responsibility center and a superior to determine what the manager will do, and in what manner. The end product of these negotiations is an approved statement of the revenues and expenses expected during the budget year for each responsibility center and for the organization as a whole.

Operating and measurement. During the period of actual operations, records are kept of resources actually consumed, expressed in terms of costs, and of revenues actually earned. These records are so structured that cost and revenue data are classified both by programs and by responsibility centers. Data classified according to programs are used as a basis for future programming, and data classified by responsibility centers are used to measure the performance of responsibility center managers. For the latter purpose, data on actual results are reported in such a way that they can be readily compared with the plan as set forth in the budget.

Reporting and analysis. The management control system serves as a communication device. The information that is communicated consists of both accounting and nonaccounting data, generated within the organization and in the environment outside the organization. This information keeps managers informed about what is going on, to ensure that the work done by the separate responsibility centers is coordinated.

Reports are also used as a part of control. Some are derived from analyses that develop plans and compare actual performance with planned performance, with explanations for variance between them. Based on these formal reports, and also on information received through informal communication channels, managers decide what, if any, action should be taken. They may decide, for example, to change the plan as set forth in the budget, and this leads to a new planning process. This justifies showing the phases shown in Exhibit 1–6 as a closed loop, with each phase leading to the next.

SUGGESTED ADDITIONAL READINGS

Donald, A. G. *Management, Information, and Systems.* New York: Pergamon Press, 1979.

Duffy, Neil M. *Information Management: An Executive Approach.* New York: Oxford University Press, 1980.

Eilon, S. *Management Control.* New York: Pergamon Press, 1979.

Newman, W. H. *Constructive Control.* Englewood Cliffs, N.J.: Prentice-Hall, 1975.

Mautz, R. K., et al. *Internal Control in U.S. Corporations: The State of the Art.* New York: Financial Executives Research Foundation, 1980.

Rowe, A. J. *Strategic Management and Business Policy: A Methodological Approach.* Reading, Mass.: Addison-Wesley Publishing, 1982.

Simon, Herbert A. *The New Science of Management Decision*. Rev. ed. New York: Prentice-Hall, 1977.
Stonich, P. J., ed. *Implementing Strategy: Making Strategy Happen*. Cambridge, Mass.: Ballinger Publishing, 1982.
Wilson, R. M. S. *Management Controls and Marketing Planning*. London: Heinemann, 1979.

CASE 1–1
Stewart Box Company*

Stewart Box company was a well-established manufacturer of paperboard cartons and boxes which were sold primarily as packages for consumer products. The cartons were manufactured in the company's carton factory. The raw material for the carton factory was paperboard, which was manufactured in the company's paperboard mill adjacent to the carton factory. The plant complex also included a 60,000-square foot warehouse where finished orders were stored pending delivery. The company had approximately 425 employees in 1979. Robert Stewart, the president, was also a large stockholder.

The company marketed its products within a radius of about 500 miles from its factory which was located in a fairly small town. It had seven sales engineers, who were compensated on the basis of a nominal salary, plus commission. In the marketing organization were six other persons, including three who prepared price quotations for prospective customers, according to specifications obtained from the customers. The company had an excellent reputation for product quality and customer service.

The paperboard and carton industry was characterized by strong competition because of the potential overcapacity that existed in most plants. Because of this overcapacity, competition for large orders was particularly keen, and price cutting was common. Stewart met this competition by designing special boxes to customer specifications, by actively catering to its customers' wishes, and by strict adherence to promised delivery dates.

The production process required that the paperboard mill operate continuously on three shifts for maximum efficiency, but the carton factory operated an average of only one and one-half shifts per day.

A partial organization chart is shown as Exhibit 1. The paperboard mill and the carton factory were profit centers. In the carton factory were 10 production departments, each consisting of a printing press or a group of similar presses and associated equipment and each headed by a foreman. There were five service departments, which performed

* This case was prepared by R. N. Anthony, Harvard Business School.

EXHIBIT 1 Organization Chart

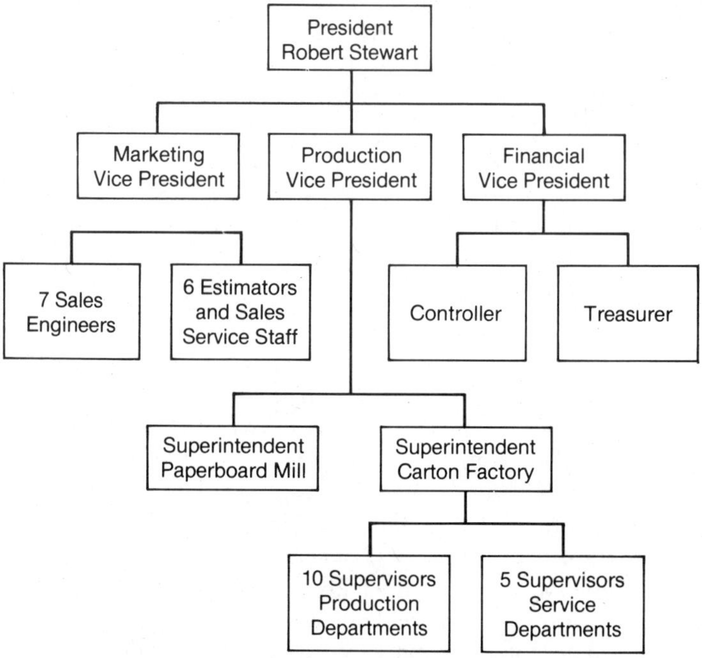

functions such as ink manufacture, quality control, and warehouse storage; each was headed by a supervisor. Each of these 15 departments was an expense center. The 10 production departments were production cost centers, and the five service departments were service cost centers.

ACCOUNTING SYSTEM

The company had a job cost accounting system, using standard costs. The board mill was a single cost center, operating a single paperboard manufacturing machine. A rate per machine-hour was established annually, which combined direct labor and manufacturing overhead costs. Manufactured paperboard was charged to the carton factory at a transfer price that includes standard cost plus a standard return on the assets employed in the board mill. The profit component of this charge was subtracted from the inventory amounts as shown on the financial statements (because generally accepted accounting principles do not permit a profit allowance to be included in inventory).

In the carton factory, each order was a job. The job was costed at the standard cost of the materials used on the job, a standard rate per press hour for the time that the job used on presses, and a standard rate per direct labor-hour for other operations. These rates included both labor and factory overhead costs and were estimated annually. The system also collected actual labor and overhead costs for each responsibility center.

PROGRAMMING

The company had a five-year plan, which it revised annually. The management team (president, vice presidents, and superintendents) spent a total of about two days each summer discussing and agreeing on this revision. In 1979, for example, the sales estimates for 1980–84 indicated that the capacity of the warehouse would become inadequate by 1981. This led to an investigation of alternative warehousing arrangements, and a decision to build a larger warehouse and to tear down the existing one. The capital required for this warehouse was significant, and it was decided to borrow part of the cost and to finance the remainder from funds generated by operations.

As an aid in deciding on proposed capital acquisitions, the company calculated the net present value and a profitability index whenever the available information was sufficiently reliable to warrant a formal analysis. About 85 percent of the proposals in terms of numbers, but less than 50 percent in terms of dollar magnitude, were in this category. Exhibit 2 is an example of the numerical part of such an analysis. (The accompanying explanation is omitted.) It is for the replacement of a printing press which was so old and worn that maintenance and operating costs were high. The decision was made to acquire this press in 1979, and the $20,000 cost was included in the capital budget for 1980.

EXHIBIT 2 Analysis of Proposed Printing Press

	Tax calculation	*Present value calculation*
Annual cash inflows:		
Saving in maintenance costs		$ 2,000
Saving in direct labor costs		6,200
Saving in power		1,000
Saving in supplies		500
Annual pretax cash inflow	$9,700	9,700
Less: Depreciation* $20,000 ÷ 10	2,000	
Additional taxable income	7,700	
Additional income tax 50% × $7,700		3,800
Annual aftertax cash inflow		5,900
Present value of cash inflows ($A_{10/10\%}$ = 6.145)		22,400
Investment in press installed		20,000
Net present value		$ 2,400
Profitability index $22,400/$20,000		$1.12

* For simplicity in this illustration straight-line depreciation is used. The company actually used sum-of-the-years'-digits depreciation for income tax purposes.

Over a period of about five years the company conducted a review of each facet of its operations. For production operations, it usually hired a consulting firm expert in carton manufacturing methods to conduct this review. For marketing and general administrative functions, it used the management services division of the firm of certified public accountants that audited its financial statements.

BUDGET PREPARATION

The controller was responsible for the mechanics of the annual budgeting process. He saw to it that the sales staff prepared sales estimates. These were discussed at length in a meeting attended by Mr. Stewart, the marketing vice president, and the controller. After final sales estimates were agreed upon, the controller communicated these estimates to heads of responsibility centers as a basis for their budget preparation.

Some budget items were stated as a fixed amount per month, others were stated as variable amounts per unit of output, and still others were stated as a fixed amount per month plus a variable amount per unit of output. For the production departments, output was measured in terms of machine-hours or direct labor-hours; and for the service departments, it was measured in terms of an appropriate measure of activity, such as pounds of ink manufactured.

Each responsibility center head discussed his proposed budget first with the controller (who had had long experience in the industry and hence could point out discrepancies or soft spots), and, in the case of the carton factory, with its superintendent. Mr. Stewart then discussed the proposed budgets for the board mill and the carton factory with the superintendents of these profit centers. He discussed the marketing budget with the marketing vice president. From these discussions, an approved budget emerged. It consisted of a master budget showing planned revenues and expenses at the estimated sales volume, a variable budget for each responsibility center showing the fixed amount per month and the variable rate per unit of output for each significant item of expense, a purchasing budget, and a cash budget. Standard unit costs and overhead rates were revised if necessary, so that they were consistent with the approved budget.

PRODUCT PRICING

Pricing was a crucial element in the company's marketing tactics. Prices were prepared by the company's estimators for each bid or order, on the basis of sales specifications and the appropriate standard cost elements as shown in tables the company had developed for this purpose. To the calculated amount of total factory costs, there were added allowances for selling and administrative expenses, sales com-

EXHIBIT 3 Price Estimate

PREPARATORY COST	Production per Hours	Rate	Unit	Material Cost		Mfg. Cost	
Original Plates	F. or E.						
Electros 9¾ x 9¼		18.94	28	530	32		
Wood				15	99		
Rule				34	09		
Composing							
Die Making	(3)	4.85	41.8			202	73
Make-Ready—Ptg.	2 x	12.80	30.0			384	00
Make-Ready—C. & C.	11.55	11.25	15.8			177	75
Total Preparatory Cost				580	40	764	48
QUANTITY COST							
Board 65,005 (3¾)	171.00+25			5557	93		
Board (32,5025)				25	00		
Ink		.37	300	111	00		
Ink 30"		.75 .15	300 231	328	95		
Cases Corrugated	700	.30	1429	428	70		
Cellulose Material							
Board, Storage, & Handling		1.87				60	78
Cutting Stock							
Printing		} 22.766					
Cut and Crease		}				813	09
Stripping	.933-4	.178+	120			391	60
Cellulose							
Auto Gluing		.562	.466+	11.24		477	24
Hand Gluing							
Wrapping or Packing		6.503				92	93
Inspection							
Total Quantity Cost				6451	58	1835	64
Total Preparatory Cost				580	40	764	48
Total Cost to Make				7031	98	2600	12
Selling & Commercial		45+8	(% + $)			1178	05
Material Forward						7031	98
Shipping 56+		7.25+	2 60,287			220	54
Freight and Cartage		.40				241	15
Total Cost						11271	84
Profit		20%				2254	37
Total Selling Price						13526	21
Finished Stock Price							
Commission & Discount		4%				541	05
Total Selling Price						14067	26
Selling Price per M—Calculated						28	14
Selling Price per M—Quoted						30	60

missions, cash discounts, and a profit margin. These allowances were expressed as percentages, and were based on the budget. A sample price estimate is reproduced as Exhibit 3.[1] The price calculated in the estimate was often adjusted for quotation purposes. It might be lowered to meet competitive conditions, or it might be increased because the design work on the order was judged to be particularly good, or for other reasons. In Exhibit 3, the calculated selling price came to $28.14 per thousand boxes, but the actual quotation was increased to $30.60.

Estimators of several companies met regularly under the auspices of a trade association to price sample boxes according to their own formulas. Based on these meetings, Mr. Stewart concluded that while most of his competitors were shaving prices below formula, Stewart's quoted prices were higher than the calculated estimate about 65 percent of the time, and lower 15 percent of the time. "It all depends on the competition, and on your assessment of the whole situation," he once said.

On some occasions, the company departed from its normal pricing practices. This usually happened when orders for cartons were not in sufficient volume to keep the board mill working at capacity. On these occasions the company took orders for paperboard at prices below full cost, in order to keep the board mill busy. Such contribution pricing was not used often, however.

REPORTS

Each month an income statement was prepared (Exhibit 4). It was constructed so as to focus on the performance of the two profit centers. Also, a spending report was prepared for each of the 15 expense centers in the carton factory. An example is given in Exhibit 5.

In addition, Mr. Stewart received a variety of other reports on a regular basis. The *internally generated* reports were as follows:

1. Balance sheet, monthly.
2. Selling, general and administrative statement, monthly.
3. Overdue accounts receivable, monthly.
4. Overdue shipments, monthly.
5. Inventory size, monthly.
6. Raw materials shrinkage report, monthly.
7. Cash and securities listing, monthly.
8. Actual sales, weekly, with a monthly comparison of actual and budgeted sales.
9. Carton factory production, monthly. This included operating hours statistics and efficiency percentages.

---

[1] Many of the abbreviations and terms in this form are peculiar to the company. The purpose of Exhibit 3 is only to illustrate the form used in preparing a price estimate. An understanding of its details is not necessary for this purpose.

EXHIBIT 4

STEWART BOX COMPANY
Income Statement
($000 omitted)

	December 1979		12 months 1979	
	Actual	*Variance**	*Actual*	*Variance**
Board Mill:				
External sales	$ 52	$ 12	$ 344	$ 38
Transfers to carton factory	168	16	1,970	130
Total revenues	220	28	2,314	168
Cost of goods sold	169	(16)	1,831	(154)
Gross margin	51	12	483	14
Volume variance		15		34
Other variances		(13)		(14)
Selling and administrative expenses	30	(4)	374	(6)
Board mill profit	21	10	109	28
Carton Factory:				
Sales	666	22	7,968	248
Standard cost of goods sold	492	(18)	5,664	(130)
Gross margin	174	4	2,304	118
Manufacturing variances		16		40
Selling expenses	50	(5)	552	(12)
Administrative expenses	12	1	143	7
Carton factory profit	112	16	1,609	153
Company:				
Total factory and mill profits	133	26	1,718	181
Corporate expenses	52	2	457	18
Nonoperating income (loss)	(4)		(12)	2
Income before income tax	77	28	1,249	201
Income tax	38	(13)	617	(96)
Net income	$ 39	$ 15	$ 632	$ 105

* ( ) = unfavorable.

10. Outstanding orders (backlog) weekly.
11. Machine production report, daily.
12. Quality control report, monthly.

Mr. Stewart examined the reports illustrated in Exhibits 4 and 5 carefully. If there were important departures from plan, he discussed them with the manager responsible. Other reports were prepared primarily for the use of some other executive, and Mr. Stewart received only an information copy. He might or might not glance at these reports in a given month, but he was certain to do so if he suspected that trouble might be brewing in the area covered by the report.

Mr. Stewart also paid close attention to several *external* reports he received regularly from the industry trade association. They showed current economic trends, the probable effects of these trends on different segments of the paperboard carton industry, and sales orders, ac-

EXHIBIT 5 Spending Report, Department 14 (two-color Meihle printing presses)

	December 1979		12 months 1979	
	Actual	*Variance**	*Actual*	*Variance**
Labor—pressmen	$ 5,885	$(107)	$ 81,057	$ (647)
Labor—helpers	2,074	(46)	28,978	(235)
Press supplies	373	120	3,279	146
Repairs	1,472	(604)	8,562	120
Power	484	66	6,369	322
Other controllable overhead	242	52	3,444	461
Total controllable costs	10,530	(519)	131,689	167
Departmental fixed cost	2,426	—	29,112	—
Allocated costs	3,352	—	40,224	—
Total costs	$16,308	—	$201,025	—
Volume variance		(340)		1,012
Total variance		($859)		$1,179

* ( ) = unfavorable.

tual sales, production volume, and other related statistics for all members of the association.

Questions

1. The following questions relate to Exhibit 4 and the December 1979 amounts:
   a. A transfer price was used in connection with *two* items. What are these two items?
   b. Assuming that inventory levels did not vary in December, what was the actual cost of goods manufactured in the carton factory?
   c. Why is the assumption in question *b* necessary to answer that question?
   d. What is the budgeted amount of corporate expenses?
   e. In December, was activity in the board mill above or below the standard volume?
2. The following questions relate to Exhibit 5 and the December amounts:
   a. What was the actual cost of labor—pressmen?
   b. What was the budgeted amount of total controllable cost?
   c. What amount of total controllable cost was applied to products?
   d. Why do no amounts appear in the spending variance column for departmental fixed costs and allocated costs?
3. As his assistant, write a memorandum calling Mr. Stewart's attention to matters you think he should note when he reads Exhibit 4.
4. Do the same with Exhibit 5.
5. What do you regard as the particularly strong points of the system described in this case? What are its weak points? Can you suggest ways of overcoming these weaknesses?

CHAPTER 2

Control and Organizational Behavior

We stated previously that control systems applied to human beings are complicated because we cannot be certain how an individual will react to a disclosure that performance is not according to plan. While the thermostat will always react to shut off the furnace when it senses that the temperature is too high, we cannot know how the manager of a division will react when notified that costs are exceeding budget.

As a consequence of the variability in the human response to control system signals, those who develop or use management control systems need to understand why and how individuals behave in organizations. Clearly, it does not do much good to design and implement a management control system if no one pays any attention to it. And people are not going to pay any attention to it if there is no incentive to do so, or if the system attempts to direct the organization in a direction management does not want it to go. Likewise, a control system that attempts to motivate a division manager by providing a reward of prestige, when the manager really wants more money, is not going to be a howling success.

In this analysis, we describe certain behavioral related characteristics of organizations and the behavior of people in general and their behavior in organizations. Both organization characteristics and the behavior of people as they interact in an organization influence the design and use of management control systems. Since the controller of an organization is responsible for developing these systems, we shall discuss the function of the controller.

Familiarity with an organization and the process by which it functions is necessary if management is to develop and use well a management control system to make the organization do what management wants it to do. Just as the driver of an automobile needs to be familiar with an automobile and its operations to guide and direct it, management needs to know how the organization of people responds to different control signals and devices. And like the automobile driver, management does not need to know the details of the multitude of mechanical processes underlying the functioning of either the organization or the automobile.

An understanding of an organization appropriate for the development and use of management control systems starts by distinguishing between a macro view of the organization and the micro features of the organization. The first is the essence of organization theory, which is associated with the performance of the organization. The second refers to organization behavior, which emphasizes the performance of managers. The two differ in that factors beyond the control of the manager are not considered in controlling managers. To nail this distinction down, ask yourself when it is possible for an organization to perform well even though a manager performs poorly or when an organization may fail even though the manager's performance is excellent.

Once the distinction between organization performance and manager performance is reasonably clear, we need to say a little about the distinction between group behavior and individual behavior to develop an understanding of the organization that will enable us to develop and use a management control system to guide the people composing the organization.

With the objective of understanding an organization and its functioning in mind, we will open this chapter with a brief examination of various theories of people behavior in organizations and then consider a few theories of an organization.

ORGANIZATION BEHAVIOR

What is an organization? What does it do? Why does it do it? Let us start with some theories of how people behave in organizations and then relate them to the tasks of practitioners. We do this to establish a base that can be used to develop management control systems.

Definition of an Organization

An organization is a group of people working together to attain certain goals. Organizations arise when people join together for some reason, whether an impromptu organization to defend against a fire or flood or a formal business organization to enhance their economic well-being. Stated more directly, organizations are people functioning in goal-seeking systems. Work is divided among people and then that divided work is coordinated to achieve organization goals. This notion of an organization is well established. Fully 45 years ago, Chester Barnard defined an organization as a system of consciously coordinated activities of two or more persons.[1] Current definitions add little

[1] C. Barnard, *The Functions of the Executive* (Cambridge, Mass.: Harvard University Press, 1938), p. 73.

to that definition when they recognize an organization as a going concern performing differentiated functions through rational coordination of goal-directed activities by a collection of people.[2]

About what an organization of people does, we can say it acquires resources and uses them, hopefully in an efficient way, to produce an output of goods and services. By behavior of an organization, we mean the process by which members of the organization do these things.

Theory of Organization Behavior

There are many theories of how and why people behave in organizations. A brief discussion of two will be sufficient to appreciate the need to know how people behave before developing and using management control systems.

Need hierarchy theory.[3] The proposition that people have multiple needs and wants so structured in a hierarchy that as one need is met the individual moves to satisfy a higher level of needs was proposed several years ago. At any one time individuals will want to satisfy different needs and these needs determine human behavior. The hierarchy of human needs ranges from basic physical needs, such as sex, food, and sleep, to psychological needs for better food, prestige and status, and comforts of life.[4] This theory implies that management control systems should be based on individual interest in satisfying needs, which differ over time and conditions and among individuals. Senior management has different needs and wants than junior managers. The management control system must be designed with these needs in mind if people are to be directed toward organization goals in an efficient and effective manner.

Achievement motivation theory.[5] A second theory of manager behavior in organizations holds that individuals are influenced by a desire for *success* (achievement), a search for *power*, and a need for *affiliation*. The theory implies that the reward and penalty structure of the management control system must be based on these motives.

---

[2] See A. A. Etzioni, *A Comparative Analysis of Comparative Organizations* (New York: Free Press, 1975) for the essence of this view.

[3] Abraham Maslow is closely associated with the development of this theory. For more information about it, see A. H. Maslow, *Motivation and Personality* (New York: Harper & Row, 1970).

[4] Various authorities structure the hierarchy in greater or less detail and recognize their overlapping nature to a greater or less degree. For an extension of Maslow's structure, see C. P. Alderfer, *Existence, Relatedness, and Growth: Human Needs in Organization Settings* (New York: Free Press, 1972).

[5] David McClelland conceived and developed achievement motivation theory and John Atkinson extended it. See D. C. McClelland, J. W. Atkinson, R. A. Clark, and E. L. Lowell, *The Achievement Motive* (New York: Appleton-Century-Crofts, 1953, and Irvington Publishers, 1975). For extensions, see J. W. Atkinson and J. O. Raynor, *Motivation and Achievement* (Washington, D.C.: V. H. Winston & Sons, 1974).

ORGANIZATION THEORY[6]

If we are going to develop and implement a management control system for an organization, we are going to need to know a little more about an organization than merely the behavior of people in it. We are going to have to know something about the technology the organization is using, how it is structured, what goals it has, the type of people involved, and how it reacts to the environment.

We have already indicated that an organization is a collection of people (workers and managers) working together to attain certain goals. While we don't need to know how to put that collection together to design a management control system, we do need to know how management is structuring and operating the elements—people, material resources, and money—of an organization to design an effective management control system.

Like organization behavior, there are many organization theories. We will describe two types, those having a closed internally oriented systems perspective and those having an open externally oriented systems perspective, because they require different types of management control systems.

Internally Oriented Organization Theories

Some theories treat entire organizations as independent entities that function without excessive concern for the external environment. These theories assume organizations use hierarchial decision making and responsibilities with projects, programs, and functional components. Internally oriented organization theories underlie many present-day management control systems. Bureaucratic organizations are frequently internally oriented organizations with rational, logical ordering of rules and regulations, supported by hierarchical authority for enforcement, that formally guide the functioning of the organization so it attains specified goals. Internally oriented organizations seem to follow Douglas McGregor's Theory X, which holds that in dealing with people, management should treat them as passive elements to be directed,

---

[6] The distinction between organization behavior and organization theory is somewhat artificial; the former refers to micro-level analysis of individual and small group behavior within an organization (see the writings of such authors as John B. Atkinson, Jay Galbraith, Frederick Herzberg, Edward E. Lawler, Abraham H. Maslow, David C. McClelland, Douglas McGregor, Lyman W. Porter, Ben F. Skinner, and Victor H. Vroom for the theoretical base of *organization behavior*) while the latter deals with relationships among groups, the organization structure and the relation of the organization to the environment (see the writings of such authors as Warren G. Bennis, Alfred D. Chandler, Henry Fayol, Paul R. Lawrence, Rensis Likert, Jay W. Lorsch, Ralph M. Stogdill, Herbert A. Simon, J. D. Thompson, and Max Weber for *organization theory* concepts).

motivated, controlled, and modified to fit the needs of the organization.[7]

The grid type of organization is frequently an internally oriented organization. Vertically, the organization is multi-level structured in hierarchical form, with delegation of various authority and responsibility to managers at different levels. Superimposed on the vertical structure is a horizontal structure of the programs the organization must undertake to realize organization goals.

The foregoing introductory theoretical description of internally oriented organization illustrates one type of manager behavior to which a management control system must adapt. An externally oriented organization requires another adaptation of the management control system. The application of management control systems to different types of manager responsibilities, motivations, and authorities will be discussed later.

Externally Oriented Organization Theory

In contrast to the view that the organization is a unified independent entity that can be guided with little regard to its impact on external parties is the open-system theory of organization-induced behavior. This theory views the organization as a group of independent parts that interrelate. Further, it holds that the whole organization interrelates with its environment. We will discuss this theory by reviewing two types of open-system oriented organization: general systems organizations and management systems organizations.

The open-general systems organization is based on general systems theory.[8] It assumes there is a continuous relationship between the environment and the organization. It also assumes that a decentralized organization or its equivalent will permit the local manager to adapt to changes in the local environment when such facilitates the realization of organization goals.

Important characteristics of the general systems type of organization include an emphasis on multiple organization goals and closely interrelated functioning of decentralized subunits.

A management systems organization[9] is designed to motivate managers to coordinate and unify strategies and individual behavior. In an

---

[7] For more on the bureaucratic theory of organizations, see M. Weber, *The Theory of Social and Economic Organizations*, trans. A. Henderson and T. Parsons (New York: Free Press, 1947). See the early part of H. Simon, *Administrative Behavior*, 3d ed. (New York: Free Press, 1976) for an introduction to administration or management organization theory.

[8] See L. Bertalanffy, *General Systems Theory: Foundations, Development and Applications* (New York: Braziller, 1968) for the foundations of this organization theory.

[9] See J. D. Thompson, *Organizations in Action* (New York: McGraw-Hill, 1967) for the development of the designed organization idea.

externally oriented organization, the strategy formation process and the needs of people involved vary with the uncertainty associated with joining different types of each together. The greater the uncertainty, the greater the amount of information that must be used to assure efficient and effective performance.

The management control system appropriate for this type of organization theory typically generates and disseminates a great deal of information. We will discuss the nature, quality, and quantity of information involved later.

Let's make a mental note to keep these theories in mind, plan to study them more at a later time, and take a look at the types of organizations now used.

TYPES OF ORGANIZATIONS

Although organizations come in all sizes and shapes, they can be classified into three general categories: (1) a functional organization, in which each manager is responsible for a specified function, such as production; (2) a divisional organization, in which each divisional manager is responsible for almost all of the functions involved in producing and distributing each division's group of product or line of products; (3) a matrix organization, in which there are two organization structures, one arranged by function and the other by programs.

Functional Organizations[10]

The functional form of organization was one of the first attempts to divide managerial work in a manner similar to that used to divide up labor work, to obtain the advantages of specialized work in large-scale production. It involves the notion of a specialized manager who can bring specialized knowledge to bear on decisions related to the function. Collectively, these specialized functions may be gathered together in higher level categories to overcome both the tendency to extend too far a manager's span of control and the tendency for uncoordinated functions to suboptimize their operations.

Functional organizations have the potential of greater efficiency, because they use specialized managerial inputs and functional responsibility centers at lower levels. Also the quality of supervision and technical services, such as engineering and quality control, is likely to be better when highly specialized workers and managers are joined in the performance of some specialized function for the organization.

A disadvantage of a functional organization structure is that the

[10] For the origin of the functional form of organization, see Frederick W. Taylor, *The Principles of Scientific Management* (New York: Harper & Row, 1911).

effectiveness of the separate functions cannot be determined unambiguously. If one functional manager is responsible for manufacturing a product and another manager is responsible for marketing the product, it may be quite difficult, or impossible, to identify the portion of the joint output that is attributable to each manager. Further, in a functional organization, top management must plan and coordinate the activities of the functional units and resolve disputes among their managers, which may make top management control more difficult.

In terms of organization behavior theory, functional organizations provide a means for individuals to satisfy their need for esteem and respect resulting from their specialized knowledge, which may ease the motivation aspects of the management control system. In terms of organization theory, however, the functional organization has the tendency to cause workers to lose sight of the common organization goals, particularly the closed-system organization. This imposes on the management control system the task of opening up the functional areas through information disclosure to give the organization an ability to coordinate itself along the lines suggested by open-system management organization theory.

Divisional Organizations

For control purposes, a division in a decentralized organization can be treated almost as if it were an independent entity. Subject to senior management approval, the division manager can develop a strategy for the particular business, finding a competitive niche for it that may be different from the strategy being pursued by other division managers with different product lines. Tactically, a product division can also be more responsive to current customer needs. The division manager has the authority to change the production schedule in response to the request of an important customer; in a functional organization, such a request would have to flow up from the sales manager to senior management and then down to the production manager, which may be time consuming. Moreover, divisions may be excellent training grounds for young managers, by fostering enterpreneurship and increasing the number of centers of initiative in a corporation.

Division managers are responsible for and control the main profitability elements of divisions. They can be held accountable for their division's results; but they should not be held accountable, under the management control system, for activities and conditions that they cannot control. The chief executive makes the decision that controls the divisions, which can take various forms, of which withholding essential materials for divisional operation may be an extreme form. To the extent that certain activities and conditions are beyond the control of the division manager, they are the responsibility of other executives.

Division managers do, of course, set up functional responsibility centers within the division. The control task for these divisional functional centers is similar to that for a whole company that is functionally organized except that it is on a smaller scale.

In terms of organization behavior theory, divisional organizations provide a means for the management control system to emphasize control of managers by separating items controllable and not controllable by managers. But it must do this more as a motivational effort, before the manager acts, than in a corrective sense, after the manager acts. The concept of feedforward information on expectations, rewards and penalties rather than feedback information needs to be emphasized.

The divisional organization form is more open-system oriented, which emphasizes the divisional manager responsibility of being aware of the local external forces impinging on organization activities. This leads to a management control system that is oriented to external data bases and the use of profit centers and investment centers for control, in contrast to the cost centers and revenue centers used in a functionally structured organization.

Matrix Organizations

In a matrix organization, referred to previously as the grid structure, responsibility centers are arranged by functions, and program responsibility is superimposed on it, which may or may not include various projects. A project is any task or group of tasks involved in reaching a specified end objective, such as producing a new product, preparing an advertising campaign, or building a new plant. It cuts through the functional organization, obtaining service from many functions. A program is an ongoing set of activities set up for a specific purpose. The program manager has to use personnel, material, and services from the various functional units to accomplish the objective. A project because it is terminated when the objective is achieved, may or may not be carried out in a similar manner.

Shipyards provide examples of a matrix organization. The basic organization structure is a functional one by shops—plumbing shop, electrical shop, machine shop, and so on—but each ship overhaul is a separate project within a program of building ships. The ship project manager calls on the functional shops for the resources required for the job. If these resources are personnel, they work under the supervision of the project manager while assigned to the project. If a functional shop furnishes material or services, responsibility for the cost, quality, and timely delivery of these items is primarily that of the shop manager; but responsibility for the quantity, ordering time, and type of use is that of the project manager. In most instances, responsibility must be shared between them, according to predetermined rules.

Research organizations, construction companies, manufacturers of aircraft, and other companies producing a variety of somewhat similar products or services that require different functional services traditionally have used a matrix organization. More recently, some companies have attempted to use it for all types of projects. In most of these companies, teams are created for various special purposes, and the workings of these teams are equivalent to projects.

In a related form of the matrix organization, product managers are responsible for the overall profitability of a product line; but the functional organization units actually produce and market the product lines. Product managers are responsible for the profitability of the product line, but do not have line authority over the functional units, which do the actual production and marketing of the products. This part of the matrix organization is called the "transaction" dimension. Since functional units provide resources to product managers, they are called the "resource" dimension.

The management control problems in a matrix organization are more difficult than those in the other two types. Planning must mesh the requirements of the programs and projects with the resources that are available in the functional units. Coordination involves so scheduling the activities of the several units that projects are completed on time and personnel are not idle. Control is particularly difficult when profitability is the joint responsibility of several managers.

Implications for Organization Design

While ease of control is a factor, it is not the only criterion used in designing the structure of an organization. Efficiency and effectiveness are overall criteria. A functional organization may be efficient because the larger functional units provide economies of scale, but a divisional organization may provide a means of adjusting quickly to local environment changes and be more effective. The divisional organization requires a somewhat broader type of manager than the specialist who manages a function. The different types of organizations suggest that different management control systems are needed for different types of managers. For example, a functional organization may need a management control system with frequent feedback on performance, information on technical changes, and generally short-term control feature; whereas a divisional organization that does not structure itself for function control may need a more flexible management control system, where emphasis is placed on output information and return on investment measures. More complex management control systems are needed for matrix organization; but the advantage of the matrix organization is that it not only guides the production of the project but also permits personnel with similar skills to have a home base in a functional unit whose manager is responsible for developing these skills.[11]

Because of the seemingly clear-cut nature of the assignment of profit responsibility in a divisional organization, designers of a management control system may be inclined to recommend such an organization structure without giving appropriate consideration to other criteria for a good organization design. For example, because it may be possible to attract higher-quality specialized technical employees to an organization-wide function, where efficiency is the main source of profit, a functional organization may be more appropriate.

Contingency Theory

There are three approaches that management may take to control an organization: the *traditional approach,* which emphasizes organizing, planning, and controlling; the *systems approach,* which emphasizes the use of groups of people for dealing with management problems and decisions; and the *behavioral approach,* which emphasizes the motivation, the prediction, and the control of people. The contingency theory approach makes it possible to use all three management approaches; it also provides a structure that fits all organizations.

As organization charts indicate, an organization consists of a number of units. These units are arranged in a hierarchy, in the sense that the managers of some units report to the managers of higher level units. A hierarchy exists in all sizeable organizations, not only in the United States and other capitalist societies but also in the Soviet Union, China, and other Socialist societies. The number of these separate units, their nature, the way they relate to each other, and the number of levels in the hierarchy vary in different organizations. Our concern attaches to the factors that govern the selection of the most appropriate organization design in a given situation to pursue a given goal, and to the means of adapting management control systems to different organization designs.

Contingency theory is a broad concept. As applied to organization design, this theory states that the number and nature of the organization units and the degree of their authority to act is contingent on the environment in which the organization exists. The question is, What are the characteristics of the environment that make a difference? One version of contingency theory describes the relationship between the

[11] For an excellent discussion of the complex factors that must be considered in making a basic change in organization structure, see Alfred D. Chandler, *Strategy and Structure* (Cambridge, Mass.: MIT Press, 1962).

organization and its environment in terms of *differentiation and integration*.[12] The more complex and uncertain are the environmental influences, the more the organization needs to differentiate and specialize, creating more units performing different functions, with each unit relating to a relatively small sector of the environment. This need for differentiation is a function of uncertainties and fluctuations in environmental influences, such as changes in specialized technology, consumer tastes, and competitive pressures. It differs for each organization. A company that manufactures cement needs less differentiation than a company whose products are influenced by developments in electronics.

The more the number of organization units, the more these units are independent in a decentralized organization, and the more there is an associated increase in the variety of functions they perform, the greater the need for *integration* of the work of the separate units. Managers of separate units must work together to achieve organization goals. The more specialized each unit, the more likely that their managers will view problems differently, and this makes more difficult the task of resolving conflicts for the general good of the organization. Integration may be accomplished by departments created for that purpose, by cross-functional teams, by meetings of managers, and by a careful delineation of responsibilities. This requires that senior management be kept well informed and be sensitive to major changes in the environment of each unit. This is facilitated by the flow of information through an appropriate management control system.

Overall, we may say an organization's structure should fit its environment; that is, its degree of differentiation is consistent with the complexity of its environment; and its integration is appropriate for this degree of differentiation. Implications of this are that there is no one best way to organize and no one best management control system. Integration is accomplished through the management control system, and the nature of that system depends on the degree of differentiation in a particular company.

MANAGEMENT BEHAVIOR

We have described organization behavior largely in terms of people behavior, particularly as they function as managers. We have noted that complicated organizations with many parts tend to make human behavior more complicated—and as every mother knows, it is complicated enough without any complicated organization. Also, we have

[12] See Paul R. Lawrence and Jay W. Lorsch, *Organization and Environment* (Homewood, Ill.: Richard D. Irwin, 1969), and Richard Vancil, *Decentralization: Managerial Ambiguity by Design* (Homewood, Ill.: Dow Jones-Irwin, 1979).

noted that, in an organization, control occurs through the interactions of human beings, and the behavior of human beings is not well understood. From this it follows that the optimum control techniques in an organization are also complicated and not well understood.

Fundamental Concepts

An organization is "in control" when it is doing what management wants it to do. To do that, people in the organization must understand what management wants them to do. This information takes several forms, ranging from detailed budgets to broad policies. Constantly telling people in an organization what is to be accomplished requires an extraordinary amount of work, often creates frictions when people don't understand why things are to be done, and, frequently, there are communication failures. For these reasons, management control systems that tell people in an organization what to do normally are human-behavior-oriented. The telling takes the form not of telling someone what to do, but telling them what senior management wants the organization to accomplish. This gives workers and subunit managers a sense of freedom in their efforts to have the organization accomplish its goals.

Organization goals are determined by senior management, and management wants all operating managers to work to achieve these goals.[13] To have operating managers perform as desired, senior management must use a management control system to motivate, teach, and inspire operating managers. To do this, the control system should recognize the behavior difference in people. For one thing, managers differ in their ability to carry out responsibilities. Management ability depends partly on innate traits and partly on their education, experience, and suitability for the assigned job. The designer of a management control system must accept the fact that these differences exist, and that it is impossible to predict exactly the response of individual managers to stimuli provided by the management control system.

Because control is achieved through the actions of managers, management control systems in organizations differ from mechanical (thermostat) or biological (human body) control systems in two other important ways. First, operating managers may not fully understand what top management wants them to do; this is the problem of *goal perception*. Second, they may, or they may not, react in the way that top management wants them to react; this is the problem of *motivation*.

[13] For simplicity, we shall refer to senior management and operating managers as if there were only two management levels in an organization. Although most organizations have several levels, similar considerations apply with respect to each of them.

Goal Perception

In order to work toward the goals of the organization, operating managers must know what these goals are. They receive information through various channels. In part, the information is conveyed by budgets and other *formal* documents. In part, it is conveyed by conversations and other *informal* means. The result of multiple inputs of information often is ambiguous messages—and managers who do not know what senior management wants done. An organization is complicated; and the actions that should be taken by one part of it to accomplish the overall goals cannot be set forth with absolute clarity, even under the best of circumstances. Furthermore, the messages received through the various information channels may conflict with one another, or managers may interpret them in different ways. For example, the budget mechanism may convey the impression that managers are supposed to make current profits as high as they can, whereas other sources may indicate that it is desirable to reduce current profits to increase future profits. Overall, operating managers' perceptions of what they are supposed to do are vastly less clear-cut than the message that the furnace receives from the thermostat.

An effective management control system can do much to reduce the amount of ambiguous and conflicting information that the manager receives. Clarity, preciseness, some redundancy for assurance, sensitivity to human behavior patterns, and comprehensive communication channels are essential characteristics of such a control system.

The Informal Organization

An important cause of erroneous perceptions of desired actions is the existence of an informal organization alongside the formal organization. The lines on an organization chart depict the formal organization; that is, the formal authority and responsibility relationships of the several managers. The organization chart may show, for example, that the production manager of Division A reports only to the general manager of Division A. In actuality, however, the production manager of Division A may communicate with various other people in the organization: other managers in Division A, managers in other divisions, and managers and staff people at headquarters. In extreme situations, the production manager may pay very little attention to messages received from the division manager. This tends to happen when the production process is highly technical and the production manager is evaluated more on production efficiency than on overall performance. Moreover, the goals of the various sources of information in the supplementary informal organization may not be consistent with the goals of the formal organization. To such a supplemental informal structure, the formal management control system must adapt and use it as a supplement to the formal system. The relationships that constitute the informal organization are not shown on the organization chart. They are nevertheless important in understanding the realities of the management control process.

Strength of perception. A management control system will not be effective unless senior management creates an environment conducive for its use. In various ways, senior management signals the degree of importance that should be attached to the control process—by the amount of time devoted to the process, by the speed and vigor of its reaction to reports that it receives, and, in general, by its attitude toward control. Management control systems must give consideration to the fact that the perceptions developed by operating managers involve understanding not only how they are supposed to help attain organization goals but also how strongly senior management wants a certain course of action. An organization in which senior management disregards control is seldom managed well. Nor does senior management's attention only to feedback reports on past performance, which aim to provide information to correct the recurrence of the past mistakes in the future, provide a sufficient indication of the importance of the management control system. The strength of the operating managers' perceptions of senior management's directives, as transmitted through the management control system, depends heavily on before-the-fact information about rewards, goals, assistance techniques, and other indications of the importance of the control system.

Functional fixation. Many erroneous perceptions arise from functional fixation; that is, the tendency of people to interpret directives and terms according to accustomed definitions, even though a different definition is intended in the control system currently being used. Functional fixation is a very real problem. Managers may, because of their background, assume that a term has a different meaning from that intended, even though a different definition is explicitly given; they may not read or comprehend the definition. Greater emphasis in management control reports on terminology is one means of reducing the impact of functional fixation.

Motivation

Information in reports does not by itself lead to action. Action depends on how managers react to it. Managers react to information in different ways. Their reactions depend on their motivation, whether that motivation is keeping a job, being promoted, given a salary increase, gaining prestige or influence, or being idle. Motivation occurs within the individual; it is inner-directed. External stimuli can influence a person's motivation, but the motivation and inclination to act reflect the person's reaction to these management control stimuli. As a basis for understanding motivation, we describe briefly the relationship between individuals and the organization of which they are a part.

Personal goals. All people in an organization become participants in an organization because they believe that by doing so they can achieve their *personal* goals. We have noted that an individual's personal goals can be expressed as needs, some of which are material and some are psychological. Money earned on the job can provide for themselves and their families. But people also need to have their abilities and achievements recognized; they need to feel secure; and they may need a feeling of power and prestige.

These personal needs can also be classified as either extrinsic or intrinsic. *Extrinsic needs* are satisfied by the actions of others. Examples are money received from the organization and praise received from a superior. *Intrinsic needs* are satisfied by the attitudes people have about themselves. Examples are a feeling of achievement, of competence, or a clear conscience.

The relative importance of these needs varies with different persons, and their relative importance to a given individual varies at different times. For some people, earning a great deal of money is a dominant need; for others, monetary considerations are much less important. Some people attach much importance to the need to exercise discretion; others to the need for achievement, and these persons tend to be the leaders of the organization.[14] The relative importance that individuals attach to their own needs is heavily influenced by the attitudes of their colleagues and of their superiors. A management control system should provide for the harmonization of personal goals with organization goals.

Expectancy theory. How do people behave so as to satisfy their needs? A number of psychologists have answered this question on the basis of an *expectancy theory* model of motivation. This theory states that the motivation to engage in a given behavior is determined by (1) a person's beliefs or "expectancies" about what outcomes are likely to result from that behavior; and (2) the attractiveness the person attaches to those outcomes, in terms of their ability to satisfy the person's needs. For example, a person who has a high need for achievement and who is not a good player of card games will probably not join a bridge club whose members are skilled card players. However, another per-

---

[14] McClelland argues there is a relationship between the strength of the achievement motivation of the leaders of an organization and the success of that organization, and that a similar relationship helps to explain why certain countries have a rapid economic growth at certain times while others do not. See David McClelland, *The Achieving Society* (New York: Irvington Publishers, 1961), and David C. McClelland and David G. Winter, *Motivating Economic Achievement* (New York: Free Press, 1969).

son, no better at playing bridge than the first, might be motivated to join the bridge club because of having a high need for social contacts. The first person has a low expectancy that playing bridge with the club's members will satisfy the need for achievement, while the second person feels there is a good chance that affiliating with the group will help satisfy the social need. A third person, who is a superb bridge player and is somewhat introverted, may decline an invitation to join the bridge club because neither winning more bridge games nor socializing with the other players is important to that person.

Incentives. The solution to the management problem of motivating people to behave in a way that furthers the goals of the organization relies on the concept of organization incentives in relation to personal expectancies. Individuals are influenced both by positive incentives and by negative incentives. A *positive incentive,* also called a "reward," is an outcome that results in increased satisfaction of individual needs. A *negative incentive,* also called a "punishment," is an outcome that results in a decrease in the satisfaction of personal needs. People join organizations to satisfy their needs. Reward incentives are inducements to better satisfy those needs that they cannot obtain without joining. Organizations dispense rewards to participants who perform in agreed-upon ways. Research on incentives tends to support the following:

1. If senior management signals by its actions that it regards the management control system as important, operating managers will react to it. If senior management pays little attention to the system, operating managers also are likely to pay it little attention.
2. Individuals tend to be more strongly motivated by the potential to earn rewards than by the fear of punishment, which suggests that management control systems be reward-oriented.
3. A personal reward is situational. Monetary compensation is an important means of satisfying certain needs; but, beyond the satisfaction level, the amount of compensation is not necessarily as important as nonmonetary rewards, though it can be an indication of how a person's achievement and ability are regarded.
4. Incentives appealing to the inherent personal motivation of people depend on individuals receiving reports (feedback) about their performance; without such feedback, people are unlikely to obtain a feeling of achievement or self-realization or to sense corrective actions needed to satisfy some of their basic needs. Providing this information is sometimes a difficult task. But the optimal frequency of feedback is related to the "discretion" time between performance of the task and detection of inadequate performance. At lower levels in the organization, this span may be only hours; for senior management, it may be months or more. In general,

however, the effectiveness of incentives diminishes rapidly as time elapses between an action and the reward for it. People need to know, on some fairly regular basis, how their superior regards their performance.

5. Beyond a certain point, adding more incentives only adds more pressure and accomplishes nothing. This optimum point is far below the maximum amount of pressure that conceivably could be exerted. Motivation is weakest when the person perceives an incentive as being either unattainable or too easily attainable. Motivation is strong when the objective can be attained with some effort and when the individual regards its attainment as important in relation to personal needs.
6. Of particular significance to management control systems, research suggests the incentive provided by a budget or other statement of objective is strongest when managers participate actively in the process of arriving at the budgeted amounts.
7. Objectives, goals, or standards are likely to provide strong incentives only if the manager perceives them to be fair and feels committed to attaining them. The commitment is strongest when it is a matter of public record; that is, when the manager has explicitly agreed to them.
8. Managers tend to accept reports of performance more willingly and to use them more constructively when they regard the reports to be fair. They are inclined to learn better ways of doing things only when they personally recognize the inadequacies of their present behavior.

Types of incentives. There are many types of incentives. Praise for a job well done can be a powerful reward. Most people regard monetary rewards as extremely important, which may include a bonus based on a comparison of planned and actual results. Rewards carry both positive and negative incentives. Negative incentives include not receiving a bonus if there is a bonus system and the employee is eligible; not receiving a pay increase, or receiving a smaller one than peer employees received; not being promoted if the person expected promotion; and, in more extreme cases, pay cuts, demotions, suspensions, and being discharged. As this partial list indicates, punishments often take the form of not receiving a reward, rather than explicit penalties such as demotions.

Rewards and punishments are highly personalized. Management might feel it is punishing an employee by not promoting this person; but if the employee feels undeserving of the promotion, or does not have a high need for achievement, the employee may not perceive it as punishment. Similarly, a $25,000 bonus may not be satisfying if the recipient feels a $35,000 bonus is deserved, even though senior management views the $25,000 bonus as a handsome reward. Since individuals differ in their needs and in their reactions to incentives, an important function of any manager is to attempt to adapt application of the management control system to the personalities and attitudes of the individuals supervised.

Role of managers. The processes that influence employee behavior vary not only among individuals but also according to the environment at the time the employee is performing and the internal state of the individual. The internal state of the individual varies with the memory recall of the individual at the time of action. The manager needs to be aware of individual employee responses to incentives in different situations, and adapt the management control system as needed.

The role of the manager involves the use of informal controls as well as formal control methods. For example, since employees are responsible to their managers, those managers should provide praise, corrective assistance, criticism, and other forms of incentives that are appropriate to motivate each employee. Staff people should not be directly involved in these motivation activities. The managers are the focal points in management control. Staff people collect, summarize, and present information that is useful to managers in the management control process. However, the significant decisions and control actions are the responsibility of managers.

Goal Congruence

We noted previously that individuals have personal goals. Organizations also have goals. An effective management control system must so harmonize these two sets of goals that both are satisfied by a common action. This is done by assuring that one set of goals can be satisfied only by meeting the other set of goals. This makes the goals congruent. Organizational goals are actually the goals of senior management. Establishing congruence of these goals with those of other participants in the organization sometimes involves a shift from primary to secondary goals of individuals.[15]

The extent of the difference between organizational goals and personal goals suggest the difficulty of the management control system task. The primary responsibility of the management control system is to assure actions that are in the best interests of the organization; but it should encourage goal congruence as far as is feasible. The closer the goals are joined, the better the management control system. As McGregor stated:

[15] See V. H. Vroom, *Work and Motivation* (New York: John Wiley & Sons, 1964) for an analysis of the process by which an individual relates primary preferences to secondary goals.

> . . . conditions could be created such that the members of the organization perceived that they could achieve their own goals best by directing their efforts toward the success of the enterprise.[16]

Perfect congruence between individual goals and organizational goals does not exist. Therefore, it is important to ask two separate questions when evaluating a management control system:

1. What action does the management control system motivate people to take in their own perceived self-interest?
2. Is this action in the best interests of the organization?

For example, a proposal that the management control system for a company include a measure of the degree to which the company maintains a balanced portfolio of products (stable, well-accepted products; growing and expanding products; and innovative and future-oriented products) should consider the two questions. In answer to the first question, if inquiry revealed that managers were interested in money rewards that could be obtained by three accepted yet different types of activities, the management control system might provide that managers be paid a bonus on the basis of performance in the three activities: new products introduced, increases in sales over last year's performance, and overall cash flow for the year. If these three activities also met organization goals, the second question would be answered and the management control system might put different weights on each of the activities, after discussion with the managers, to assure that the company maintains a life-cycle group of products (introduction, growth, stability, decline, and removal).

Cooperation and Conflict

The lines connecting the boxes on an organization chart imply that the way organizational goals are attained is that senior management makes a decision and communicates that decision down through the organizational hierarchy to managers at lower levels of the organization who then implement it. Because this ignores the personal goals of individuals, it is not the way an organization actually functions.

The fact is that each operating manager reacts to instructions from senior management in accordance with how those instructions affect his or her personal needs. Also, usually more than one manager is involved in carrying out senior management plans, so the interactions among managers also affect how well plans are implemented. For example, although the manager of the maintenance department may be

---

[16] Douglas McGregor, *The Human Side of Enterprise* (New York: McGraw-Hill, 1960).

assigned responsibility for assuring that the maintenance needs of the production departments are satisfied, the needs of one department may be slighted if there is friction between the maintenance manager and a production manager. More importantly, many actions that a manager may want to take to achieve personal goals could have an adverse effect on other managers and on overall profitability. For example, managers may argue about which of them is to get the use of limited production capacity or other scarce resources, or about potential customers that several managers want to solicit, unless the management control system provides instructions in advance. For these and many other reasons, conflict exists within organizations, and management control systems should help to minimize them.

The work of the organization will not get done unless its participants work together with a certain amount of harmony, so there is need for cooperation in organizations. Participants must realize that, unless there is a reasonable amount of cooperation, the organization will dissolve, and the participants will then be unable to satisfy any of the needs which motivated them to join the organization in the first place.

An organization attempts to maintain an appropriate balance between the forces that create conflict and those that create cooperation. Some conflict is desirable. Conflict results in part from the competition among participants for promotion or other forms of need satisfaction; such competition is, within limits, healthy. A certain amount of cooperation is also obviously essential; but if undue emphasis is placed on engendering cooperative attitudes, the most able participants will be denied the opportunity of using their talents fully. The management control system must help maintain the appropriate balance between conflict and cooperation within the organization.

Organizational Climate

As noted above, perceptions about an organization's goals and about decisions that a manager should take to achieve these goals come not only from the formal control system but also through the informal organization. Both the formal and informal structure combine to create what is called the organizational climate. As defined by Andrews:

> The term "climate" is used to designate the quality of the internal environment which conditions in turn the quality of cooperation, the development of individuals, the extent of members' dedication or commitment to organizational purpose, and the efficiency with which that purpose becomes translated into results. Climate is the atmosphere in which individuals help, judge, reward, constrain and find out about each other. It influences morale—the attitude of the individual toward his work and his environment.[17]

[17] Kenneth R. Andrews, *The Concept of Corporate Strategy* (Homewood, Ill.: Dow Jones-Irwin, 1971), p. 232.

Organizational climate has important influences on motivation. The attitude of the chief executive officer toward control is an important ingredient of that climate. The nature of the management control process in a given organization is also affected by the "style" of the top management. Some chief executive officers rely heavily on reports and other formal documents; others prefer conversations and informal contacts. The formal system must be consistent with senior management's preferences. It follows that if a new senior management, with a different style, takes over, the system should change correspondingly.

By its very nature, climate cannot be described concretely. Some alternative characteristics of different "climates" are:

1. A focus on results versus a focus on following the rules, which suggests a management control system that uses profit centers for the former and a cost center for the latter.
2. An emphasis on individual accomplishment versus being a member of the team, which means the management control system should provide individual specific performance criteria for the former and organization performance standards for the latter.
3. Encouragement of initiative and risk-taking versus "not rocking the boat," which suggests that the reward system should provide large bonuses for profits on new ventures to encourage initiative and rewards for meeting the budget to encourage stability.
4. The relative importance of participatory management versus authoritarian management.[18]

Types of Control

One way of summarizing the foregoing comments on motivation is indicated in Exhibit 2–1. Three types of control are present. There is, first, the formal control mechanism that is administered through regular organization channels, and which is the most clearly visible type of control simply because it is manifested in budgets, reports of performance, and other documents. Second, there are the controls associated with the informal organization. Third, there are the controls associated with the intrinsic goals of the manager as an individual. All these controls should be working in the same direction, but in the real world this ideal never is fully achieved.

Variations in Controls

As we noted previously in discussing contingency theory, the general nature of control that is appropriate in a given situation varies according to the nature of the work, the type of organization, the

[18] Adapted from an unpublished paper by Professor Robert H. Caplan.

EXHIBIT 2–1 Control in Organizations

	Types of control				
Controls administered by	*Direction for controls deriving from*	*Behavioral and performance measures*	*Signal for corrective action*	*Reinforcements or rewards for compliance*	*Sanctions or punishments for noncompliance*
Formal organization	Organizational plans, strategies, response to competitive demands	Budgets, standard costs, sales targets	Variance	Management commendation Monetary incentives, promotions	Request for explanation
Informal group	Mutual commitments, group ideals	Group norms	Deviation	Peer approval, membership, leadership	Kidding Ostracism, hostility
Individual	Individual goals, aspirations	Self-expectations, intermediate targets	Perceived impending failure, missed targets	Satisfaction of "being in control" Elation	Sense of disappointment Feeling of failure

Source: Adapted from Gene W. Dalton and Paul R. Lawrence, eds., *Motivation and Control in Organizations* (Homewood, Ill.: Richard D. Irwin, 1971). © 1971 by Richard D. Irwin, Inc.

environment, and the individual manager. Three dimensions of the situation are important in developing and using management control systems:

1. The amount of management discretion.
2. The amount of interdependence.
3. The time span of performance.

Management discretion. The work done by an organization unit can be located along a scale, with routinized production or clerical operations at one end, and creative and unspecifiable activities, such as research, at the other. For activities at or near the routine end, specific performance standards can be established, and rewards can be related to how actual performance compares to these standards. For activities at the other end of the scale, a broad management control system may be needed because specific standards are not feasible; indeed, an attempt to impose them would likely have dysfunctional consequences.

Interdependence. Organization units can also be located along a scale according to their degree of independence from, or interdependence with, other units. To the extent that the work of the whole organization requires that individual units cooperate closely with one another, management control systems that focus on the performance of an individual unit can be dysfunctional.

Time span. Finally, to reinforce our previous discussion, different management control systems are needed for different organization units, according to the time span between the initiation of action and results. When the time span is short, performance measurement can be, and should be, frequent, and actual performance can be compared with short-run standards. When the time span is long, any measurement of interim performance should be regarded as being highly tentative.

FUNCTION OF THE CONTROLLER

The *controller* may be the person responsible for the design and operation of an organization's formal informational systems; although in some organizations a person with the title of *informative systems manager* may be largely responsible for the function, and the controller may be responsible only for accounting systems. In other organizations, a person with the title of financial vice president may have overall responsibility for information systems, and the controller, who then typically has responsibility for only the accounting part of this area, reports to the financial vice president. In still other organizations, the controller functions as part of the management decision-making team and adds to the organization's information system his responsibility for internal control practices and the management control system.

Despite the variations in practice, it is useful conceptually to think of a function that has to do with information systems, including management control systems, and of a controller as a person who is responsible for that function.

Controller Responsibilities

The controller has different responsibilities in different companies. In many companies, this includes responsibility for the design and operation of all systems for processing the recurring and quantitative information that relates to resources, personnel, materials, services, and money. In most companies, the controller is directly responsible for the design and operations of programming, budgeting, and accounting systems. Collectively, these are called financial systems because most of the information flowing through them is stated in monetary terms.

In more recent years, the use of management control systems has increased and the controller has assumed the staff and advisory function associated with them. In some instances, this has resulted from an expansion of the internal accounting control system work. In others, managements have not adopted organization-wide management control systems, and the controller has assumed responsibility for such systems as part of various internal control systems.

The degree of the controller's responsibility for these different types of systems varies. For systems specific to a certain function, such as the personnel records of the industrial relations department, or the materials control and production scheduling systems in a factory, the functional specialist has primary responsibility. The controller's responsibility with respect to such systems is to ensure, as far as possible, that systems throughout the organization are efficient and compatible with one another; this means that one system provides information for another, that unnecessary duplication is eliminated, and that common terminology is used in all systems.

In addition to the design and operation of various types of information and control systems, the controller may perform any or all of the following functions:

1. Prepare financial statements and financial reports to government agencies and to other external parties.
2. Prepare tax returns.
3. Prepare and analyze reports on financial performance.
4. Assist managers by analyzing and interpreting reports, by analyzing program and budget proposals, and by consolidating the plans of various segments into an overall annual budget.
5. Use internal audit and accounting control procedures, assure the

validity of information, establish adequate safeguards against theft and defalcation, and perform operational audits.

6. Develop controller personnel and participate in the education of management personnel in matters relating to the controller function.[19]
7. Provide for cash management, insurance, and similar activities for protecting assets.

Relation to Line Organization

The controller function is a staff function. Although the controller is usually responsible for the design and operation of the system whereby control information is collected and reported, the use of this information in actual control is the responsibility of line management. In addition to responsibility for processing information, the controller may also be responsible for developing and analyzing control measurements, and for making recommendations for action to management. Moreover, the controller may police adherence to limitations on spending laid down by the chief executive, control the integrity of the accounting system, and be responsible for safeguarding assets from theft and fraud.

design operation

The controller does not make or enforce management decisions. The responsibility for control runs from the president down through the line organization, not through the controller, who is a staff officer.

The controller does make some decisions. In general, these are decisions that implement policies decided on by line management. For example, a member of the controller organization often decides on the propriety of the expenses listed on a travel voucher.

The Divisional Controller

Many companies are organized into divisions, each headed by a manager who has considerable autonomy, and each with a controller. Divisional controllers inevitably have a divided loyalty. On the one hand, they owe some allegiance to the corporate controller, who is presumably responsible for the overall operation of the control system. On the other hand, they owe allegiance to their division managers, since controllers are responsible for furnishing staff assistance to their managers. In some companies, the division controller reports to the division general manager, and has what is called a "dotted line" rela-

[19] Incidentally, the spelling "comptroller" is also used. This spelling originated with an error made some 200 years ago in translating from French to English; but the erroneous spelling has become embedded in dozens of federal and state statutes and in the bylaws of many companies, and it is therefore difficult to eradicate. Comptroller is pronounced exactly the same as controller.

tionship with the corporate controller; that is, the corporate controller is responsible for specifying the ground rules within which the control system must operate, and he must participate in decisions relating to compensation and other personnel actions regarding division controllers—but the division manager is the controller's boss. In other companies, division controllers report directly to the corporate controller; that is, the corporate controller is their boss, as indicated by a "solid line" on the organization chart. A study by Sathe of 129 large corporations reported concerns about each of these relationships.[20]

> On the one hand, if the division controller is made responsible primarily to the division general manager, a variety of concerns are voiced:
>
> > "We do not know everything going on down there. There is probably some fat hidden in the divisional budget, but we can't be sure because the divisional controller does not report directly to us." (corporate staff executive)
> >
> > "If you will pardon the expression, controllers reporting directly to the general manager are nothing more than whores. They cannot stand up and challenge the manager." (corporate financial executive)
> >
> > "Our concern is: are division controllers losing their objectivity because they report directly to the division general manager?" (general auditor)
>
> On the other hand, if the primary reporting relationship of the division controller is to the corporate controller, the division controller may be regarded as a "spy from the front office" rather than a trusted aide by division management. The following comments are indicative of the concern:
>
> > "If division controllers reported directly to me, there is a danger they would become isolated from division management." (corporate controller)
> >
> > "Reporting relationship is not a trivial matter. If the division controller did not report to me, I'd find someone else to get the job done." (division general manager)

The trend seems to be in the direction of having a solid-line relationship between the division controller and the corporate controller. Although only 21 of the 129 firms that Sathe studied had such a relationship in 1977, four of these had made the shift from the dotted-line relationship within the preceding three years, and an additional 14 companies planned to do so within the following year.

Even in companies in which the division controller's primary loyalty is to the division manager, it is expected that division controllers will not condone or participate in the transmission of misleading infor-

---

[20] Vijay Sathe, *Controllership in Divisionalized Firms: Structure, Evaluation, and Development* (New York: American Management Association, 1978), pp. 20–21.

mation or the concealment of unfavorable information; their overall ethical responsibilities should not countenance such practices.

The specific responsibilities of a divisional controller are suggested by the following list of criteria that have been used in evaluating their performance:

1. *Accounting and financial reporting.* Timeliness and accuracy of regular reports submitted to division management and corporate controller's office. Does the controller meet schedules and deadlines, and are the reports accurate and reliable?
2. *Knowledge of division operations.* Comprehensive but detailed understanding of division operations. Can the controller explain accounting reports, reflecting an in-depth comprehension of trends and reasons for specific results? Does the controller's overall understanding of operations and current conditions result in anticipating and predicting the effect of operational decisions and directions?
3. *Performance against objectives.* Has the controller accomplished the objectives agreed to for the period under review?
4. *Compliance with policy.* Attitude and cooperation in complying with corporate policies. Does the controller understand the necessity of and reasons for policies? Does the controller seek compliance by other managers and fulfill all responsibilities in assuring overall compliance by the division?
5. *Management contribution.* Influence and effect on the division management group. Is the controller respected and viewed by the division president and other key executives as an important and essential factor in the overall management of the business? Does the controller have a significantly positive impact on management decisions and operations?
6. *Accounting knowledge.* Does the controller have sufficient training and experience to be considered reasonably expert in most accounting areas. If not sufficiently competent in certain areas, does the controller seek appropriate assistance and thus expand accounting knowledge?
7. *Integrity and professionalism.* As the chief financial and control executive of the division, does the controller recognize and accept responsibility to the corporation and to the standards of integrity implicit in his or her role? Does the controller exercise a degree of independence and professionalism in reporting and advising line management and the corporate controller of conditions and circumstances that might otherwise be ignored or not reported?
8. *Cooperativeness.* Attitudes and performance in responding to corporate requirements and requests. Does the controller re-

spond positively to requests for regular and special information by the corporation and assist other divisions and corporate staff in improving overall accounting and control programs and procedures?

9. *Organization and staff.* What is the quality and performance of the controller's subordinates and staff? Is the controller developing a professional competence in the organization and also developing subordinates for promotion within the company?
10. *Initiative and drive.* Has the controller initiated constructive changes and improvements in controller operations? In other divisional functions over which he or she has a direct or indirect control responsibility, does the controller take an aggressive and positive position with regard to improving the overall operational control and procedures of the division?

SUGGESTED ADDITIONAL READINGS

Argyris, Chris, and **Shon, D. A.** *Theory in Practice: Increasing Professional Effectiveness.* San Francisco: Jossey-Bass, 1974.

Atkinson, John W., *Personality, Motivation and Action.* New York: Praeger Press, 1983.

Barnard, Chester I. *The Functions of the Executive.* Cambridge, Mass.: Harvard University Press, 1938.

Becker, Selwyn W., and **Neuhauser, Duncan.** *The Efficient Organization.* New York: Elsevier–North Holland Publishing, 1975.

Carver, C. S., and **Scheier, M. F.** *Attention and Self-Regulation: A Control-Theory Approach to Human Behavior.* New York: Springer-Verlag, 1981.

Chandler, Alfred D., *Strategy and Structure.* Cambridge, Mass.: MIT Press, 1962.

Cyert, Richard M., and **March, James G.** *A Behavioral Theory of the Firm.* Englewood Cliffs, N.J.: Prentice-Hall, 1963.

Dalton, Gene W., and **Lawrence, Paul R.,** eds. *Motivation and Control in Organizations.* Homewood, Ill.: Richard D. Irwin, 1971.

Herbert, Theodore T. *Dimensions of Organizational Behavior.* New York: Macmillan, 1981.

Hofstede, G. H. *The Game of Budget Control.* Assen, Netherlands: van Gorcum, 1967.

Hopwood, Anthony. *Accounting and Human Behavior.* Englewood Cliffs, N.J.: Prentice-Hall, 1976.

Lawrence, Paul R., and **Lorsch, Jay W.** *Organization and Environment.* Homewood, Ill.: Richard D. Irwin, 1969.

Lorsch, Jay W., and **Morse, John J.** *Organizations and Their Members: A Contingency Approach.* New York: Harper & Row, 1974.

March, James G., and **Simon, Herbert A.** *Organizations.* New York: John Wiley & Sons, 1958.

Miles, Robert H. *Macro Organization Behavior.* Glenview, Ill.: Scott, Foresman, 1980.

Miner, John B. *Theories of Organization Behavior.* Hinsdale, Ill.: Dryden Press, 1980.

Mintzberg, H. *The Nature of Managerial Work.* New York: Harper & Row, 1973.

Sathe, Vijay. *Controller Involvement in Management.* Englewood Cliffs, N.J.: Prentice-Hall, 1982.

Schiff, M., and **Lewin, A. Y.,** eds. *Behavioral Aspects of Accounting.* Englewood Cliffs, N.J.: Prentice-Hall, 1974.

Schlesinger, L. A.; Eccles, R. G.; and **Gabarro, J. J.** *Managing Behavior in Organizations.* New York: McGraw-Hill, 1983.

Scott, W. R. *Organizations: Rational, Natural, and Open Systems.* Englewood Cliffs, N.J.: Prentice-Hall, 1981.

Simon, Herbert A. *Administrative Behavior.* 2d ed. New York: Macmillan, 1957.

Skinner, B. F. *Beyond Freedom and Dignity.* New York: Appleton-Century-Crofts, 1971.

Staw, Barry. *Psychological Foundations of Organization Behavior.* Glenview, Ill.: Scott, Foresman, 1983.

Steers, Richard M. *Introduction to Organization Behavior.* Santa Monica, Calif.: Goodyear Publishing, 1981.

Swieringa, R., and **Moncur, R.** *Some Effects of Participative Budgeting on Managerial Behavior.* New York: National Association of Accountants, 1975.

Tannenbaum, Arnold. *Control in Organizations.* New York: McGraw-Hill, 1968.

Vancil, Richard. *Decentralization: Managerial Ambiguity by Design.* Homewood, Ill.: Dow Jones-Irwin, 1979.

CASE 2–1
Rendell Company*

Fred Bevins, controller of the Rendell Company, was concerned about the organizational status of his divisional controllers. In 1975 and for many years previously, the divisional controllers reported to the general managers of their divisions. Although Mr. Bevins knew this to be the general practice in many other divisionally organized companies, he was not entirely satisfied with it. His interest in making a change was stimulated by a description of organizational responsibilities given him by the controller of the Martex Corporation.

* This case was prepared by R. N. Anthony, Harvard Business School.

The Rendell Company had seven operating divisions; the smallest had $10 million in annual sales, and the largest over $100 million. Each division was responsible for both the manufacturing and the marketing of a distinct product line. Some parts and components were transferred between divisions, but the volume of such interdivisional business was not large.

The company had been in business and profitable for over 50 years. In the late 1960s although it continued to make profits, its rate of growth slowed considerably. James Hodgkin, later the president, was hired in 1970 by the directors because of their concern about this situation. His first position was controller. He became executive vice president in 1973 and president in 1974. Mr. Bevins joined the company as assistant controller in 1971, when he was 33 years old. He became controller in 1973.

In 1970, the corporate control organization was primarily responsible for (1) financial accounting, (2) internal auditing, and (3) analysis of capital budgeting requests. A budgetary control system was in existence, but the reports prepared under this system were submitted to the top management group directly by the operating divisions, with little analysis by the corporate control organization.

Mr. Hodgkin, as controller, thought it essential that the corporate control organization plays a more active role in the process of establishing budgets and analyzing performance. He personally took an active role in reviewing budgets and studying divisional performance reports, and hired several young analysts to assist him. Mr. Bevins continued to move in the same direction after his promotion to controller. By 1975, the corporate organization was beginning to be well enough staffed so that it could, and did, give careful attention to the information submitted by the divisions.

Divisonal controllers reported directly to the divisional general managers, but the corporate controller always was consulted prior to the appointment of a new division controller, and he also was consulted in connection with salary increases for divisional controllers. The corporate controller specified the accounting system to which the divisions were expected to conform, and the general procedures they were to follow in connection with budgeting and reporting performance. It was clearly understood, however, that budgets and performance reports coming from a division were the responsibility of that division's general manager, with the divisional controller acting as his staff assistant in the preparation of these documents. For example, the divisional general manager personally discussed his budget with top management prior to its approval, and although the divisional controller usually was present at these meetings to give information on technical points, his role was strictly that of a staff man.

Most of the divisional controllers had worked for Rendell for 10 years or more. Usually, they worked up through various positions in the controller organization, either at headquarters, in their division, or both. Two of the divisional controllers were in their early 30s, however, and had only a few years' experience in the headquarters controller organization before being made, first, divisional assistant controller and then divisional controller.

Mr. Bevins foresaw increasing difficulties with this relationship as the corporation introduced more modern control techniques. For one thing, he thought the existing relationship between himself and the divisional controllers was not so close that he could urge the development and use of new techniques as rapidly as he wished. More important, he thought that he was not getting adequate information about what was actually happening in the divisions. The divisional controller's primary loyalty was to his division manager, and it was unreasonable to expect that he would give Mr. Bevins frank, unbiased reports. For example, Mr. Bevins was quite sure that some fat was hidden in the divisional expense budgets, and that the divisional controllers had a pretty good idea as to where it was. In short, he thought he would get a much better idea of what was going on in the divisions if reports on divisional activities came directly from controllers working for him rather than for the divisional manager.

Mr. Bevins was therefore especially interested in the controller organization at the Martex Company as he learned about it from E. F. Ingraham, the Martex controller, when he visited that company.

Until his visit to Martex, Mr. Bevins had not discussed the organization problem with anyone. Shortly thereafter, he gave William Harrigan, his assistant controller, a memorandum describing his visit (see the appendix) and asked for Mr. Harrigan's reaction. Mr. Harrigan had been with Rendell for 25 years, and had been a divisional controller before going to headquarters in 1972. Mr. Bevins respected his knowledge of the company and his opinion on organizational matters. Mr. Harrigan was accustomed to speaking frankly with Mr. Bevins. The gist of his comments follows.

> I don't think the Martex plan would work with us; in fact, I am not even sure it works at Martex in the way suggested by the job descriptions and organization charts.
>
> Before coming to headquarters, I had five years' experience as a divisional controller. When I took that job, I was told by the corporate controller and by my general manager that my function was to help the general manager every way I could. This is the way I operated. My people got together a lot of the information that was helpful in preparing the divisional budget, but the final product represented the thinking and decisions of my general manager, and he was the person who sold

it to top management. I always went with him to the budget meetings, and he often asked me to explain some of the figures. When the monthly reports were prepared, I usually went over them, looking for danger signals, and then took them in to the general manager. He might agree with me, or he might spot other things that needed looking into. In either case, he usually was the one to put the heat on the operating organization, not me.

We did have some problems. The worst, and this happened several times a year, was when someone from the corporate controller's office would telephone and ask questions such as, "Do you think your division could get along all right if we cut $X out of the advertising budget?" Or, "Do you really believe that the cost savings estimate on this equipment request is realistic?" Usually, I was in complete agreement with the data in question and defended them as best I could. Once in a while, however, I might privately disagree with the "official" figures, but I tried not to say so.

Questions of this sort really should be asked of the general manager, not of me. I realize that the head office people probably didn't think the question was important enough to warrant bothering the general manager, and in many cases they were right. The line is a fine one.

The business of the division controller's being an "unbiased source of information" sounds fine when you word it that way, but another way to say it is that he is a front office spy, and that doesn't sound so good. It would indeed make our life easier if we could count on the divisional controllers to give us the real lowdown on what is going on. But if this is to be their position, then we can't expect that the general manager will continue to treat his controller as a trusted assistant. Either the general manager will find somebody else to take over this work unofficially, or it won't get done.

I think we are better off the way we are. Sure, the budgets will have some fat in them, and not all the bad situations will be highlighted in the operating reports, and this makes our job more difficult. But I'd rather have this than the alternative. If we used the Martex method (or, rather, what they claim is their method), we can be sure that the divisional controller will no longer be a member of the management team. They'll isolate him as much as they can, and the control function in the division will suffer.

Questions

1. What is the organizational philosophy of Martex with respect to the controller function? What do you think of it? Should Rendell adopt this philosophy?

2. To whom should the divisional controllers report in the Rendell Company? Why?

3. What should be the relationship between the corporate controller and the divisional controllers? What steps would you take to establish this relationship on a sound footing?

4. Would you recommend any major changes in the basic responsibilities of either the corporate controller or the divisional controller?

APPENDIX
Notes on Martex Controller Organization

Mr. Ingraham, the corporate controller, reports directly to the president and has reporting to him all division controllers and other accounting, data processing, and analysis groups. The Martex Company's descriptions of responsibility and organization charts are included herein (Exhibits 1, 2, 3, and 4), and indicate the structure and function of the organization.

EXHIBIT 1 Position Descriptions from the Martex Management Guidebook

Controller

The trend of modern business management is to change the basic concept of the controller's position from that of an administrative function concerned largely with accounting detail to that of an important position in management as it relates to the control of costs and the profitable operation of the business as a whole.

The more our business becomes diversified with operations scattered throughout the United States, the greater is the need for an officer to whom the president delegates authority with respect to those factors affecting costs and profits in the same manner as he may delegate authority to others in strong staff positions.

In our vertical type of organization there is great need for an appointed officer whose responsibility it is to establish budgetary standards of operations and objective percent of profit on sales targets for each of the operating divisions and domestic subsidiaries. He shall also establish budgetary standards of operation for staff functions in line with divisional and overall company profit objectives. When the standard of operations or profit target is not attained, the controller has the right and the responsibility within his delegated authority to question the failure and recommend changes to accomplish the desired result.

The controller shall work with the various divisions of the company through divisional controllers assigned to each major operating division and staff function. It is not intended that the controller take the initiative away from the division managers, since the responsibility for efficient operations and profits is assumed by the managers. However, the controller and his staff should have the right and the responsibility to expect certain operating results from the division head; and when a difference of opinion occurs as to the reasonableness of the demand for results, the matter should then be referred by either party to the president.

Along with the foregoing, the following responsibilities are an es-

Exhibit 1 (*continued*)

sential part of the position and apply to the corporation and its subsidiaries:

1. The installation and supervision of all accounting records.
2. The preparation, supervision, and interpretation of all divisional and product profit and loss statements, operating statements, and cost reports, including reports of costs of production, research, distribution, and administration.
3. The supervision of taking and costing of all physical inventories.
4. The preparation and interpretation of all operating statistics and reports, including interpretation of charts and graphs, for use by management committees and the board of directors.
5. The preparation, as budget director, in conjunction with staff officers and heads of divisions and subsidiaries, of an annual budget covering all operations for submission to the president prior to the beginning of the fiscal year.
6. The initiation, preparation, and issuance of standard practice regulations and the coordination of systems, including clerical and office methods relating to all operating accounting procedures.
7. Membership of the controller or his designated representative in all division and subsidiary management committees.

He shall be responsible for the selection, training, development, and promotion of qualified personnel for his organization and their compensation within established company policy. He shall submit to the president an organization plan for accomplishing desired objectives.

The controller may delegate to members of his organization certain of his responsibilities, but in so doing he does not relinquish his over-all responsibility or accountability for results.

Treasurer and assistant treasurers

Subject to the rules and regulations of the Finance Committee, the treasurer is the chief financial officer and generally his functions include control of corporate funds and attending to the financial affairs of the corporation and its domestic and foreign subsidiaries wherever located. More specifically the duties and responsibilities are as follows:

Banking: He shall have custody of and be responsible for all money and securities and shall deposit in the name of the corporation in such depositories as are approved by the president all funds coming into his possession for the company account.

Credits and collections: He shall have supervision over all cashiers, cash receipts, and collection records and accounts receivable ledgers. He shall initiate and approve all credit policies and procedures.

Exhibit 1 ***(continued)***

Disbursements: He shall authorize disbursements of any kind by signature on checks. This includes direct supervision over accounts payable and payroll departments and indirect supervision over all receiving departments for the purpose of checking on the accuracy of invoices presented for payment. He shall maintain adequate records of authorized appropriations and also determine that all financial transactions covered by minutes of management and executive committees and the board of directors are properly executed and recorded.

General financial reports: He shall prepare and supervise all general accounting records. He shall prepare and interpret all general financial statements, including the preparation of the quarterly and annual reports for mailing to stockholders. This also includes the preparation and approval of the regulations on standard practices required to assure compliance with orders or regulations issued by duly constituted governmental agencies and stock exchanges.

He shall supervise the continuous audit (including internal controls) of all accounts and records and shall supervise the audit and procedures of Certified Public Accountants.

Taxes: He shall supervise the preparation and filing of all tax returns and shall have supervision of all matters relating to taxes and shall refer to the general counsel all such matters requiring interpretation of tax laws and regulations.

Insurance property records: He shall supervise the purchase and placing of insurance of any kind including the insurance required in connection with employee benefits. He shall be responsible for recommending adequate coverage for all ascertainable risks and shall maintain such records as to avoid any possibility that various hazards are not being properly insured. He shall maintain adequate property records and valuations for insurance and other purposes and, if necessary, employ appraisal experts to assist in determining such valuations and records.

Loans: He shall approve all loans and advances made to employees within limits prescribed by the Executive Committee.

Investments: As funds are available beyond normal requirements, he shall recommend suitable investments to the Finance Committee. He shall have custody of securities so acquired and shall use the safekeeping facilities of the banks for that purpose. As securities are added or removed from such vaults or facilities, he shall be accompanied by an authorized officer of the Corporation.

Office management: He will be responsible for the coordination of all office management functions throughout the company and its domestic subsidiaries.

Financial planning: He shall initiate and prepare current and

Exhibit 1 (*concluded*)

long-range cash forecasts, particularly as such forecasts are needed for financing programs to meet anticipated cash requirements for future growth and expansion. He shall arrange to meet sinking fund requirements for all outstanding debenture bonds and preferred stock and shall anticipate such requirements whenever possible.

He shall have such other powers and shall perform such other duties as may be assigned to him by the board of directors and the president.

The treasurer shall be responsible for the selection, training, development, and promotion of qualified personnel for his organization and their compensation within established company policy. It is expected that since he will have to delegate many of the duties and responsibilities enumerated above, he shall confer with and submit to the president an organization plan and chart.

The treasurer may delegate to members of his organization certain of his responsibilities together with appropriate authority for fulfillment; however, in so doing he does not relinquish his over-all responsibility or accountability for results.

The treasurer is a member of the Finance, Retirement, and Inventory Review Committees.

EXHIBIT 2 Organization Chart, Division A, January 1, 1975

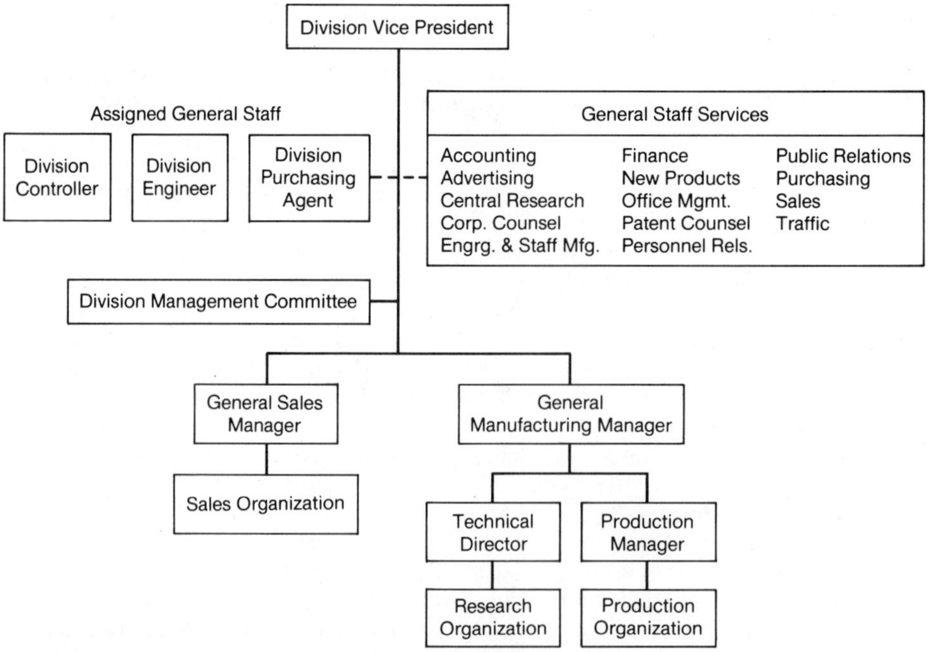

Note: Various levels on the chart do not necessarily indicate relative importance of positions.

EXHIBIT 3 Organization Chart of Controller's Division, January 1, 1975

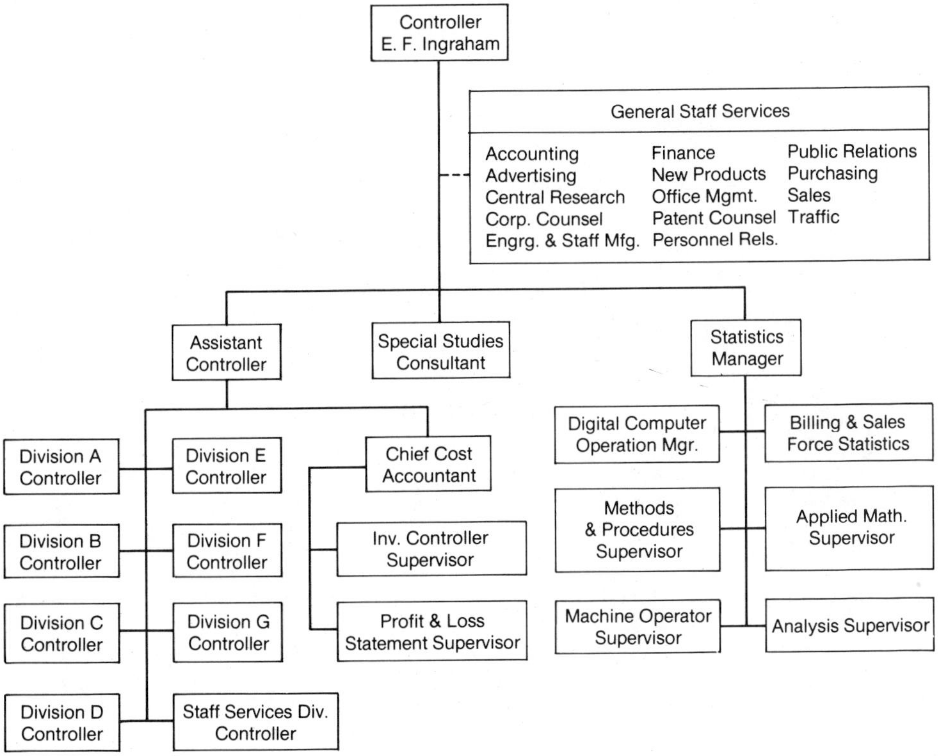

The controller's organization is charged with the responsibility of establishing cost and profit standards in the corporation and of taking appropriate action to see that these standards are attained. It reviews all research projects, and assigns names and numbers to them in order to coordinate research activities in the various divisions and their central research. The organization also handles all matters involving cost and profit estimates.

The present size of divisional controllers' staffs ranges from 3 to 22. Division controllers are not involved in preparing division profit and loss statements; these are prepared by a separate group for all divisions and the corporation.

LINE-STAFF RELATIONSHIPS

A division manager has no staff of his own, not even a personal assistant. He receives staff assistance from two sources.

First, he has some people assigned to him from the general staff—typically, a controller, an engineer, and a purchasing agent.

All division management and all the corporate staff are located in the corporate headquarters building. However, the "assigned staff"

EXHIBIT 4 Organization Chart of Treasurer's Division, January 1, 1975

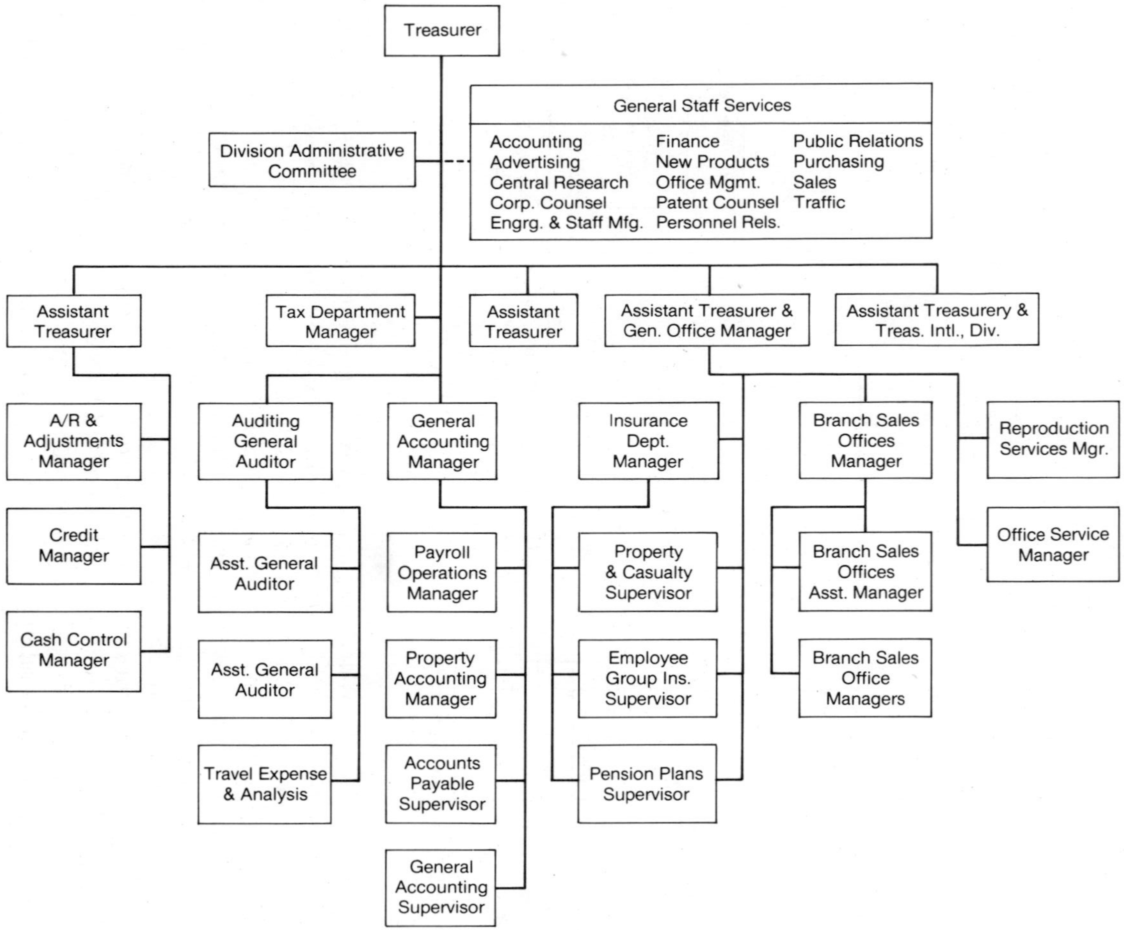

Note: Various levels on the chart do not necessarily indicate relative importance of positions.

are located physically with their staff colleagues; for example, a divisional controller and his assistants are located in the controller's section of the building, not near his divisional manager's office.

Second, the division can call on the central staff to the extent that the manager wishes. The divisions are charged for these services on the basis of service rendered. The central staff units are listed in the General Staff Services box of Exhibit 2.

DIVISION MANAGER-CONTROLLER RELATIONSHIP

The success of the Martex controller organization and its relations with divisional managers appears to be largely the result of managers' and controllers' having grown up with the arrangement and accepting it long before they arrived at their managerial positions.

Some additional factors that appear to contribute to their successful relationship are the following:

1. A uniform and centralized accounting system.
2. Predetermined financial objectives for each division.
   a. Growth in dollar sales.
   b. A specified rate of profit as a percent of sales.
3. Profit sharing by managers and controllers.

ACCOUNTING SYSTEM

The controller's division has complete control of the accounting system. It determines how and what accounts will be kept. The controller's division has developed an accounting system that is the same for all divisions. Mr. Ingraham pointed out that no division had a system perfectly tailored to its needs, but he believes that the disadvantages to the divisions were more than offset by having a system uniform over all divisions and understood by all concerned. Mr. Ingraham indicated it was likely that if Martex divisions were free to establish their own accounting systems, every division would have a different one within two years, and interpretation by corporate management would be difficult, if possible at all.

The accounting system appears to provide a common basis for all divisional financial reports and analyses, and it aids in maintaining the bond of confidence between division managers and controllers.

DIVISION OBJECTIVES

The corporation has established two financial objectives for each division. These are *(a)* growth in dollar sales, *(b)* a specified rate of profit as a percent of sales.

These objectives are determined in advance by recommendations of the controller's division with the advice and counsel of divisional managers. The objectives are long range in nature; the target profit rate has been changed only three times since 1950.

The particular percentage of sales selected as the target profit rate is based on several factors, among which are (1) the patentability of products, (2) a desired rate of return on investment, (3) the industry's margin of profit, and (4) the industry's rate of return on investment. These factors and others determine the profit rate finally selected.

Within limits, attainment of these financial objectives represents the primary task required of division general managers by corporate management.

PROFIT SHARING

Divisional managers receive about 75 percent of their total compensation from profit sharing and stock options. Divisional controllers receive about 25 percent of their compensation from profit sharing—half from a share in divisional profits, and the other half from corporate profits.

DIVISION MANAGERS' VIEW OF THE SYSTEM

Mr. Ingraham indicated that divisional managers like to have divisional controllers report to the corporate controller because (1) it gives them an unbiased partner armed with relevant information, (2) the controller is in a better position to do the analysis needed for decision making, and (3) when cost reports are issued there is little or no argument about them among affected parties.

CASE 2–2
Tanner Corporation*

As a consequence of an unfortunate incident that had occurred recently in the Process Systems Division of Tanner Corporation, John Bentwood, chairman of the audit committee of the board of directors, was considering whether he should support a proposed change in the committee's relationship with divisional management. This change was

* This case was prepared by R. N. Anthony, Harvard Business School.

designed to increase the committee's ability to find out what was going on in the company.

Tanner Corporation was a large, diversified company organized into 31 operating divisions. The company was well established, had operated profitably for many years, and had expanded steadily, both through internal growth and through acquisitions. In 1975 its sales revenue was approximately $900 million. Its board of directors had 12 members; 9 were outside directors, plus Seth Remick, the president (who was also chairman); the executive vice president; and the financial vice president, Spencer Brody.

THE AUDIT COMMITTEE

The Audit Committee of the board was created in 1972. At that time, there was a general movement to set up such committees in publicly held corporations. Its impetus came in part from recommendations made by the New York Stock Exchange, the Securities and Exchange Commission, the American Institute of Certified Public Accountants, and the major public accounting firms. The recent tendency for the Securities and Exchange Commission and the courts to increase the responsibilities of boards of directors for overseeing corporate affairs, and the fines and other penalties levied on board members that were found not to exercise the appropriate amount of diligence, were also important stimuli. A Conference Board survey showed that about 45 percent of 504 manufacturing companies had audit committees in 1973, compared with less than 20 percent in 1967.[1] In the formal board minutes that established the Audit Committee, its purpose and functions were given as follows:

> The Audit Committee will be comprised of not less than three nor more than five nonmanagement Directors. Its purpose is to assist the full Board of Directors in fulfilling the board's fiduciary responsibilities with respect to the corporation's accounting, internal control, and reporting practices.
>
> The Audit Committee's activities on behalf of the board shall include, but not be limited to, the following:
>
> 1. Recommend the selection, each year, of the independent auditors for the company.
> 2. Review with financial management and the independent auditors the proposed auditing program for the ensuing year and suggest changes in emphasis or scope as necessary. This will encompass both the independent and internal audit programs.
> 3. Review with financial management and the independent auditors,

[1] *Corporate Directorship Practices: Membership and Committees of the Board, Report No. 588* (New York: Conference Board, 1973), p. 62.

both together and separately, the results of the audits, including the audited financial statements, with particular attention to:

a. The conformance of the statements to generally accepted accounting principles.

b. The full disclosure of all material matters affecting the company's operations and financial condition, and their fair presentation.

c. The scope and effectiveness of the audit activity.

4. Review with the independent auditors their recommendations for improvements in internal control, and assure that appropriate action is taken in response to these recommendations.
5. Report at least annually to the full board on the above matters.

These functions were believed to be fairly typical of those of audit committees in general.

In 1975, the committee consisted of four members:

John Bentwood, chairman, partner in a managing consulting firm, and a certified public accountant with long experience in accounting and control systems.

Francis Dube, a lawyer whose firm had no connection with the company.

Guay Hamel, executive vice president of a large manufacturing company.

George Spring, senior vice president of Tanner Corporation's principal commercial bank.

Hamel had been elected to the board in 1973 and became a member of the Audit Committee in 1974. The other three members had been directors for many years and were original members of the Audit Committee.

Prior to the establishment of the Audit Committee, there had been no formal channel of communication between the board and members of management other than the president; that is, the agenda for board meetings was set by Remick, and although issues were presented to the board by various members of management, each issue was accompanied by Remick's recommendations. In some cases the board voted against his recommendations, and in other cases, proposals were sent back for further study. In Bentwood's opinion, these differences were simply differences of judgment among men of goodwill; that is, they did not indicate friction between the board and management.

Although the only formal channel between the board and management was through the president, board members had many informal contacts with members of management, and Remick encouraged such contacts. Bentwood said:

> Of course, at every board meeting we meet management people, not only the inside board members, but also those who are presenting proposals to us, and we get to know these people in the luncheons and

> other activities that are associated with board meetings. Also, we make a trip at least once a year during which we visit several divisions, observe what is going on as carefully as we can, and form impressions about the many management people that we meet.

As can be seen from the minute quoted above, the formation of the Audit Committee created two new formal channels of communication. First, the committee was authorized to meet privately with the independent public accountants. Such meetings were held annually, and the engagement partner of the public accounting firm was asked specifically whether he had any relevant comments beyond those which were contained in the usual "management letter," that is, the letter setting forth the public accountant's observations on the adequacies of the company's control system and recommendations for improving it. In no case did the partner bring up topics other than those contained in the management letter, but he did indicate certain topics that he thought should be emphasized. For example, the 1974 letter suggested that internal audit activity devoted to computer-based systems should be stepped up, and the partner stressed the importance of this. The partner also made complimentary remarks about the cooperation his firm received from the financial management organization and the competence of that organization.

The second new formal channel of communication was between the Audit Committee and the financial vice president. The committee met two or three times a year with Brody, who was usually accompanied by members of his staff. There was no thought of excluding the president, and Remick usually did attend part of each meeting. Remick was not present most of the time, however, stating that the matters to be discussed did not involve him.

PROCESS SYSTEMS DIVISION

In 1971 Tanner Corporation acquired a small company whose management had developed new technology for automating production processes in a variety of chemical companies. The Process Systems Division was an outgrowth of this acquisition. The division developed a general approach to process automation for a given industry, with heavy emphasis on special purpose computers, and it then adapted this general approach to the needs of specific companies on a contract basis. It built many of the components required for the new system, adapted other components, and purchased still other components. Usually, the contract with the Process Systems Division required that it install the system and make it ready to operate. Most contracts were for at least $100,000, and some were much larger.

In the first year, customers were hard to find, but after a few successful installations, sales volume increased. It doubled in 1973 over

1972 and more than doubled again in 1974. Because of development costs and the relatively expensive professional organization that the division assembled, overhead costs were high. In 1974, for the first time, the division reported a profit, but it was a relatively small percentage of sales. Sales volume continued to increase in 1975, and in that year a sizable profit was expected. Actual reported performance for the first six months of 1975 exceeded these expectations.

In July 1975, however, Brody, the financial vice president, received a letter from an accountant in the Process Systems Division who recently had been discharged on grounds of incompetence. The ex-employee alleged that division management was furnishing false reports to the corporation. The letter contained so many specifics that Brody decided to have the matter looked into, and he sent a member of the internal audit staff to investigate. Within a week, the internal auditor reported that it was indeed likely that a serious problem existed, but that intensive work was required to measure its magnitude.

Brody immediately called in the public accountants to make a special audit of the division. He also reported the existence of the problem to the Audit Committee, and they in turn reported it to the board of directors. Throughout the investigation that followed, the board was kept fully informed.

By September, the investigation had uncovered the facts summarized below. The division had been audited by the internal auditors in September 1974, in accordance with the regular audit program in which some divisions were assigned to outside auditors and others to internal auditors. That audit included an attempt to validate the inventory, but the cost accounting system was found to be so unreliable that it was not feasible to make a good check against the physical inventory. At that time, the internal auditors called attention to the system defects, acknowledged that these were probably caused by the fact that the system had not kept up with the rapid growth of the division, and recommended improvements.

Sometime in 1974, control over the work-in-process inventory records had been lost. A job cost record was established for each component of each contract, but not all the material, parts and other costs of the component were recorded on these records. When the components were billed to the customer, the job cost record was used as the basis for calculating cost of goods sold, but since costs on this record were incomplete, cost of goods sold was understated and gross margin was correspondingly overstated. The total effect of correcting this error was to wipe out the division's reported profits for 1974 and to change the results for 1975 from an expected profit of $1 million to a loss of $1 million, on sales volume of $10 million.

A careful examination of the economics of the division led to the conclusion that selling prices for contracts already written were too low, and that the advantages of the new system to the customer were not sufficiently great to permit prices to be increased to a point where a satisfactory return on investment could be earned.

The division was therefore discontinued. This was done by completing the backlog of contract work. During the phase out period it was possible to reduce fixed costs so substantially that the eventual net loss on the whole operation was relatively insignificant.

AUDIT COMMITTEE REACTIONS

Members of the Audit Committee discussed the implications of this incident at length, both in formal meetings and informally. Dube and Spring were of the opinion that although there was clearly a breakdown in the control system, it was primarily attributable to the rapid growth in the division's activities. They pointed out that the failure to charge all costs to the job cost cards seemed to have started either shortly before or shortly after the 1974 audit, and in any event was not prevalent enough at the time of that audit to be a matter that the auditors reasonably could be expected to detect. They also pointed out that as soon as corporate management learned of the problem, it took prompt action and kept the Audit Committee and the board fully advised.

Hamel, the new member of the board, felt differently. Here is a systems breakdown that corporate management didn't know about until an ex-employee spelled it out for them, he said. Furthermore, by hindsight, we can see that the inventory reported by the division was growing at a rate that was out of line. (Others replied that it was easy to see this by hindsight, but that at the time, the inventory growth was regarded as a commendable attempt to stockpile components and parts to fill the huge backlog of orders.) Admittedly, the final outcome in this case had practically no effect on profits, Hamel said, but there may be other more serious problems somewhere in the corporation that we have no inkling of. The board is responsible.

Hamel thereupon suggested to his colleagues that it might be a good idea to add the following sentence to the stated functions of the Audit Committee: "In carrying out its responsibilities, the Audit Committee may meet privately with the independent auditors, with internal auditors and with other employees, and can undertake such additional analysis as it deems necessary." His thought was that the Audit Committee would meet annually and privately with the manager of internal audit (who reported to the financial vice president), and that it would publicly encourage communication of relevant information from any corporate employee to the Audit Committee.

Spring was strongly opposed to this proposal, on three grounds. First, he said, the internal audit manager would not report anything to the Audit Committee that he had not already discussed with the financial vice president; if he did, he should be fired for disloyalty. Second, the very idea conveyed an implication of distrust of management that was distasteful to him. Third, he envisioned the possibility that the Audit Committee would be deluged with crank letters that it was unequipped to handle. Dube tended to agree with Spring.

As of the end of 1975 Hamel's suggestion had been discussed only within the committee. Bentwood felt that if a formal proposal along the lines suggested by Hamel were made, it probably would be accepted by Remick and Brody; to oppose such a proposal could be regarded as tantamount to an admission that there was something to hide. He also felt that they would feel hurt by such a proposal, and that it might lead to tension between management and the board. Based on years of contact, Bentwood had a high regard for both the ability and the integrity of Remick and Brody. He was, however, mindful of the new responsibilities that boards of directors were asked to assume, and the possibility of SEC or stockholder suits if at any time the board did not act with diligence.

Questions

1. What is the cause of the problem in Tanner Corporation? Why wasn't it picked up earlier?
2. What should be done to lessen the likelihood of a recurrence of this event? Do you think Hamel's solution is workable?
3. What is the role of the people specifically charged with the audit function: internal and external auditors, and the audit committee of the board of directors?

CASE 2–3*
International Telephone and Telegraph Company

In early 1968 Herbert C. Knortz, comptroller of the International Telephone and Telegraph Corporation, appointed an ad hoc committee to develop a procedure for critically examining the effectiveness with which various functions within the comptroller's area of responsibility were being carried out. Four months of full-time effort by the five-member committee led to the development of a "Comptrollership Rating Manual" for the formal review of comptrollership activities at ITT.

* This case was prepared by Vijay Sathe, Harvard Business School.

EXHIBIT 1 Comptroller's Organization at Headquarters

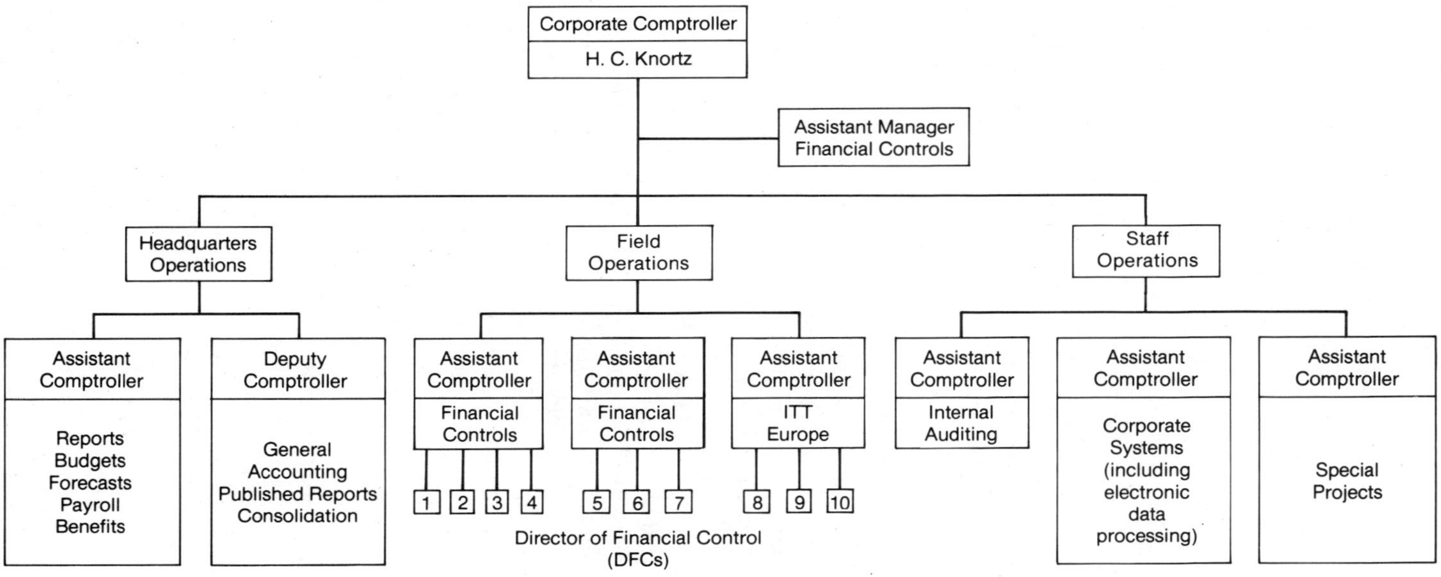

Corporate Comptroller
H. C. Knortz
Assistant Manager Financial Controls
Headquarters Operations
Field Operations
Staff Operations
Assistant Comptroller
Reports Budgets Forecasts Payroll Benefits
Deputy Comptroller
General Accounting Published Reports Consolidation
Assistant Comptroller
Financial Controls
Assistant Comptroller
Financial Controls
Assistant Comptroller
ITT Europe
Assistant Comptroller
Internal Auditing
Assistant Comptroller
Corporate Systems (including electronic data processing)
Assistant Comptroller
Special Projects
1 2 3 4 5 6 7 8 9 10
Director of Financial Control (DFCs)

EXHIBIT 2 Comptrollership Activities in Field Units

Comptrollership activity	*Percent of unit comptroller's staff performing the activity**
General accounting	45%
Cost accounting	20
Budgets and forecasts	4
Internal audit	2
Data processing	13
Systems and procedures	6
Treasury	5
Other	5
Total	100%

* The breakdown shown is an approximate percentage based on numbers for all field units combined.

The underlying goal of the manual was "to assist in the establishment within each operating unit of the ITT system a professional comptrollership function which could be objectively rated best in the industry." This case describes the comptrollership evaluation procedure in 1977 which evolved from that earlier effort.

In 1977 ITT employed approximately 400,000 people worldwide and about 23,000 of these were engaged in comptrollership activities. The organization of the 325 people in the comptroller's headquarters staff is shown in Exhibit 1. The scope of the comptrollership function at the 240 field units reporting to ITT headquarters varied greatly depending upon the diversity of the unit's operations, the duration of time that the unit had been in the ITT system, and the relative size of the unit. A list of the comptrollership activities performed at these units together with the approximate distribution of employees across activities for all units combined is shown in Exhibit 2.

REPORTING SYSTEM FOR UNIT COMPTROLLERS

The performance of the comptrollership function at each unit within the ITT system was monitored and reviewed by 10 directors of financial control (DFCs). Seven were located in ITT's world headquarters in New York and the remaining three were based in ITT's European headquarters in Brussels. Each DFC was responsible for between 20 and 30 field units.

For each of the 240 units within the ITT system, an effectiveness score was computed for each of 30 areas of comptrollership responsibility. A listing of the specific areas evaluated is shown in Exhibit 3.

For each of these areas, the unit comptroller answered between 30 to 60 "Yes–No" type questions directed at how well activities in the particular area were being performed. For the 30 areas combined, the unit comptroller answered 1,600 questions. This self-evaluation accounted for 75 percent of the scores assigned to the unit. The other 25 percent was determined by answers to five questions for each of the 30 areas by the director of financial control responsible for monitoring the activities of the unit. Thus, the DFC answered 150 questions for each of the 20 to 30 field units under his jurisdiction.

To illustrate the computational procedure, consider questionnaire no. 28, "Unit Comptroller's Interface with Unit Management and Director of Financial Controls" (use Exhibit 3). The specific questions answered by the unit comptroller and the DFC in order to determine the effectiveness with which this function was being performed for a given field unit are shown in Exhibit 4. A hypothetical example show-

EXHIBIT 3 List of Specific Comptrollership Areas Evaluated

Questionnaire no.	*Comptrollership area*
1	Intercompany Accounting
2	Fixed Asset Accounting
3	Budgets and Forecasts
4	Personnel Expense Reporting
5	Cost Accounting
6	Cost Reduction Programs
7	Headquarters Reporting Requirements
8	Capital Expenditures
9	Payables
10	Management Development and Other Personnel Practices
11	Credit and Collections
12	Receivables and Billing
13	Inventory Controls
14	Cash Management and Controls
15	Scrap Accounting and Controls
16	Payroll
17	Tax Accounting
18	Responsibility Accounting and Flexible Budgeting
19	Accounting for Engineering Costs and Expenses
20	Contract Accounting
21	Debt Management and Foreign Exchange
22	Insurance Administration
23	Comptroller's Monthly Operating and Financial Review
24	Auditing
25	Product/Business Planning
26	Financial Analyses and Managerial Reports
27	Systems and Data Processing
28	Unit Comptroller's Interface with Unit Management and Director of Financial Controls
29	Accounting and Control of Marketing and A&G Expenses
30	Installation Cost Accounting

EXHIBIT 4

ITT COMPTROLLERSHIP RATING MANUAL	SUBJECT: UNIT COMPTROLLER'S INTERFACE WITH UNIT MGMT. & DIRECTOR OF FINANCIAL CONTROLS	QUESTIONNAIRE NO. 28
		PAGE NO. 1 OF 4
	AFFECTS: ALL COMPANIES	EFFECTIVE DATE September 23, 1968

	YES	NO
1. Does your unit General Manager hold regular weekly staff meetings?	___	___
2. Do you participate regularly in those staff meetings?	___	___
3. Do you participate with the unit General Manager in periodic reviews held with group management?	___	___
4. Do you regularly review "The Comptroller's Monthly Letter" with the General Manager prior to release?	___	___
5. Does the General Manager routinely brief you on "The Manager's Monthly Letter"?	___	___
6. Are you or a member of your staff presently assigned to a unit level "task force" or special project by the General Manager?	___	___
7. Are all projections of financial data, applicable to your unit, coordinated by the Comptroller's Department?	___	___
8. Are all publications pertinent to the actual results of your unit's operations coordinated by the Comptroller's Department?	___	___
9. Prior to publication, do you discuss all Comptroller's Department reports and correspondence on matters sensitive to your unit with the unit General Manager?	___	___
10. Have you formally reviewed with the General Manager and/or all other department heads within the past 12 months, the format, content, timeliness, and degree of detail included in all recurring internal financial reports?	___	___
11. Does your current internal financial reporting system provide each department head and the unit General Manager with the current and projected financial status of his areas of responsibility?	___	___
12. Are you responsive to requests for special reports from the General Manager and other department heads?	___	___
13. Do you regularly participate in the staff meetings of other departments?	___	___
14. Do you regularly discuss the financial results of each department with the responsible department head?	___	___
15. Do you keep the unit General Manager apprised of the volume and content of the Comptroller's Headquarters reporting requirements?	___	___

EXHIBIT 4 ***(continued)***

INTERNATIONAL TELEPHONE AND TELEGRAPH CORPORATION

SUBJECT: UNIT COMPTROLLER'S INTERFACE WITH UNIT MANAGEMENT AND DIRECTOR OF FINANCIAL CONTROLS	QUESTIONNAIRE NO. 28
	PAGE NO. 2 OF 4

	YES	NO
16. Have you developed an internal distribution of Headquarters reports that are of special interest to local management?	___	___
17. Do you regularly make presentations to the General Manager and his staff concerning the in-depth financial status of your unit?	___	___
18. Do you use appropriate visual aids in these presentations?	___	___
19. Do you encourage the active participation of nonfinancial management in these presentations?	___	___
20. Do you use trade publications or other media pertinent to your unit's product lines and specific industry, to develop your knowledge of your unit's position in its particular area of endeavor?	___	___
21. Did your department within the last year participate in a formal review of your unit's market position?	___	___
22. Has your department within the last year participated in a formal review of proposed new products?	___	___
23. Do you advise your Director of Financial Controls of major problems in your unit when they occur rather than wait for "The Comptroller's Monthly Letter"?	___	___
24. In the past six months, have you notified your Director of Financial Controls of all significant revisions to forecasts prior to their being released by the unit?	___	___
25. During the past six months, have your monthly Comptroller's letters been sufficiently comprehensive and informative so as to keep the requests for clarification from the Director to an acceptable minimum?	___	___
26. Do you supply your Director with extracts from memos issued by the members of unit management which will have an impact on unit profitability?	___	___
27. Do you keep your Director advised of all significant unit projects in which your department is involved?	___	___
28. Do you periodically review the reports issued to your Director with him to determine their continuing significance?	___	___
29. Do you periodically review your internal reporting requirements with your Director?	___	___

EXHIBIT 4 *(continued)*

INTERNATIONAL TELEPHONE AND TELEGRAPH CORPORATION

SUBJECT: UNIT COMPTROLLER'S INTERFACE WITH UNIT MANAGEMENT AND DIRECTOR OF FINANCIAL CONTROLS	QUESTIONNAIRE NO. 28
	PAGE NO. 3 OF 4

	YES	NO
30. Do you keep your Director advised of your manpower requirements?	___	___
31. Do you discuss your future manpower needs with your Director prior to incorporating them into a final budget?	___	___
32. Do you discuss open positions with your Director in order to determine required specifications for candidates?	___	___
33. Do you advise your Director of openings when they occur to obtain his assistance in finding suitable candidates?	___	___
34. Do you request your Director to interview job candidates for supervisory level positions in your department?	___	___

Unit ______________________

Comptroller's signature ______________________

EXHIBIT 4 ***(concluded)***

INTERNATIONAL TELEPHONE AND TELEGRAPH CORPORATION

SUBJECT: UNIT COMPTROLLER'S INTERFACE WITH UNIT MANAGEMENT AND DIRECTOR OF FINANCIAL CONTROLS	QUESTIONNAIRE NO. 28
	PAGE NO. 4 OF 4

* *

TO BE RATED BY THE DIRECTOR OF FINANCIAL CONTROLS:

To assess the qualitative performance of the function being rated by this questionnaire, the Director of Financial Controls is requested to score the unit Comptrollership function to the following:

	Score		
	0	2	5
1. Rapport with General Manager.			
2. Effectiveness in dealings with General Manager.			
3. Rapport and effectiveness in dealings with other members of unit management.			
4. Rapport with Director.			
5. Keeping Director advised of all significant problems.			

EXHIBIT 5 Illustration of the Procedure Used to Compute a Unit's Rating

QUESTIONNAIRE NO. 28

UNIT NUMBER________

PART I - Responses from unit comptrollers

Number of "no" responses or responses rejected by directors of financial controls (A)	Total applicable questions in questionnaire* (B)	Score $\frac{B - A}{B} \times 75 =$
4	34	66

PART II - Responses from directors of financial controls

Question	Point value assigned†
1.	5
2.	5
3.	5
4.	2
5.	2

Total 19

Total rating (Part I and Part II) 85

Comments (use additional pages if required):

Signed________________
Director of Financial Controls

Notes

* If certain questions are not applicable to the unit, they can be deleted with the DFC's concurrence.

† 0 = Not acceptable, 2 = Minimum acceptable, 5 = Satisfactory

ing how a numerical score was determined for a unit on questionnaire no. 28 is included as Exhibit 5. A perfect evaluation (score of 100) was possible only if the unit comptroller could answer "Yes" to every question and the DFC gave a score of "5" for each of the five items.

The ratings achieved for each of the 30 areas evaluated for comptrollership effectiveness formed the basis for establishing a re-rating timetable and for initiating action programs. The ratings were interpreted as follows:

Rating	Evaluation and action	Next rating in	Color code
90 and above	Satisfactory	2 years	Blue
80–89	Acceptable	1 year	Green
70–79	Requires improvement—action program should be initiated	6 months	Yellow
Under 70.	Unacceptable—action program must be initiated	3 months	Red

It was the DFC's responsibility to initiate the required action programs and provide each unit comptroller under his jurisdiction with the appropriate questionnaire in accordance with the re-rating timetable. The color codes were used in constructing a "comptrollership grid" to provide a convenient overview of how effectively the 240 units within the ITT system were performing in the 30 specific areas of comptrollership responsibility. A schematic of the grid is shown in Exhibit 6. The

EXHIBIT 6 Schematic of "Comptrollership Grid"

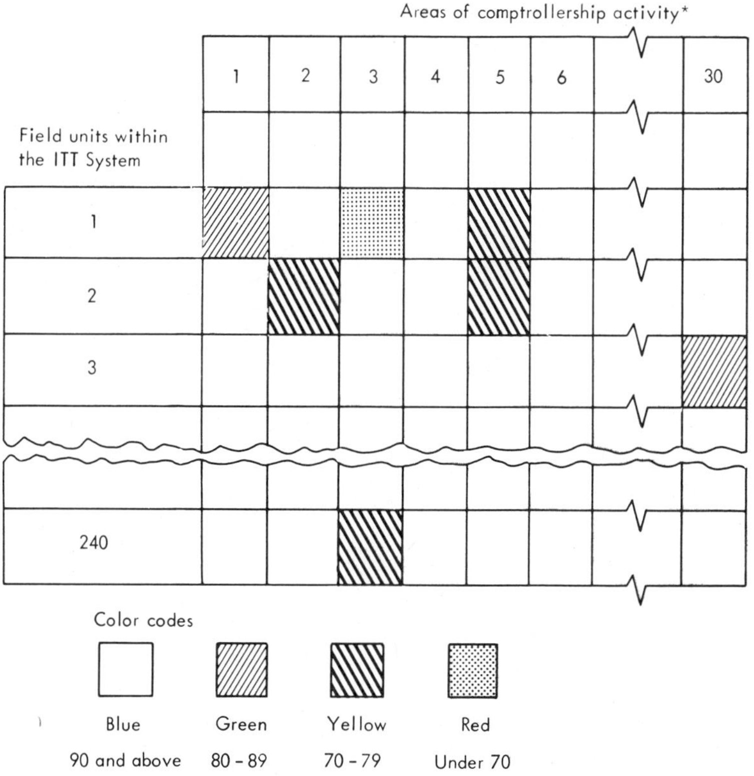

* See Exhibit 3 for a listing of the areas.

various units of the ITT system were grouped by area and product line and a glance across the grid revealed the performance of any unit in any specific area of controllership responsibility.

It should be noted that the grid revealed how well a particular comptrollership *activity* was being performed in a given unit and did not necessarily refer to the performance of the unit's *comptroller*. For example, it was not unusual for a unit newly acquired by ITT to have an initial yellow or red rating in several areas. This did not automatically imply that the unit's comptroller was ineffective, because it could take one or two years to get the unit's comptrollership function "up to speed" in some instances. Indeed, one measure of the unit comptroller's effectiveness was the time it took him to do so, given the unit's "situation complexity." Examples of high situation complexity included a bad business environment, inadequate staff, multiplant operations, high technology business, or the requirement of dealing in government contracts or foreign currency transactions. For units that had been in the ITT system for some time, unit comptrollers were evaluated using regular ITT personnel evaluation forms, but the unit's comptrollership effectiveness did account for 10 to 15 percent of the individual's total rating.

Questions

1. List the strong and weak points of this rating system.
2. What types of companies should use such a system? What types should not?

CHAPTER 3

Goals and Strategies: A Management Control View

Recall that organizations need goals in the form of statements indicating what they want to do to provide purpose for members of the organization. Without broad, stable, and ongoing goals, managers and workers have no way of knowing what to do or even why they should do anything. Goals can be pursued in different ways and approached by different paths. To coordinate organization activities in pursuit of goals, organizations develop strategies to indicate the path organization management wants followed to achieve goals. Strategies used to indicate the paths to be followed include policies, general guides for acting, such as assuming the customer is always right, and programs of activities for realizing goals, such as producing a certain type of product. The process of selecting goals and developing programs involves strategic planning.

The process of strategic planning is not well developed in many smaller organizations. For some, it is merely an ad hoc process of guessing or having a feeling that certain ends are desirable and that these should be pursued. For others, strategic planning is an informal brainstorming process to arrive at a desirable future state for the organization. This sporadic process may or may not include consideration of means the organization should use to reach its goals.

Beyond the sporadic are those managements that systematically and regularly review organization policies and strategies for achieving goals in the light of current conditions. In the process of review, adjustments of existing strategies and substitutions of alternative strategies are considered. This process of strategic planning includes the collection of information on threats to present organization policies and strategies, and on opportunities available in the prevailing environment. The review considers strategies individually and by groups in terms of such factors as possibility, feasibility, and practicality.

At the extreme, some organizations develop elaborate methods to gather external information on possible future developments in society, governments, industry, and technology. That collection process is followed by an extended analysis to determine opportunities for the organization and ways of countering threats. Using this external information, senior management identifies possible goals and strategies for the organization. The organization strategic planners might also develop a number of broad programs by which the organization can reach its goal. For example, one strategy might be to produce a product that meets a minimum standard of quality at a low price, and to advertise extensively. Another strategy might be to produce a high-quality product initially and sell it at a high price and then gradually reduce price to enter the mass market after the quality characteristic is well established.

Whichever process of strategic planning the organization uses—from the "feeling" level to brainstorming and flashes of genius to the formal systematic level—external information and an inventory of organization resources represent the type of information most useful for the process.

While doubts exist about the effectiveness of all broad types of strategic planning—and some contend that none are worth the effort involved—it is certainly clear that an organization must decide in some way what it will do. The strategic planning processes by which these types of decisions are made vary from organization to organization and from environment to environment to such an extent that it is inappropriate to suggest one process as the best type of strategic planning for all organizations.

The outputs of the strategic planning process are largely organization strategies, because goals are stable and long lasting. The strategies are intended to guide development of the organization by providing a common base from which people throughout the organization can plan. The steadfastness and dependability of the organization strategies foster efficient and effective performance throughout the organization. But changes in the environment inevitably force changes. For this reason, strategic planning should include continuous review of strategies and a continuous search for new strategies.

We have indicated previously that strategies take the form of *policies* (general overall guides for action) and *programs*, and have noted that these form the base for various types of management control and management control systems. For an organization to develop effective management controls, it must have clear policies and realistic programs, and these, in turn, depend upon well communicated unambiguous goals. The management control process is concerned with the attainment of goals through the implementation of strategies. To the extent possible, a management control system should be tailor-made to fit the particular strategies of each organization, and managers should know how the strategies influence the management control process. System designers must ensure that the management control system is consistent with, and leads to, the organization goals—whatever they might be. In view of the necessary close relationship of strategies to management controls, it seems desirable to examine methods of establishing strategies and means of communicating them to those responsible for management controls. Let's start by distinguishing goals and strategies.

GOALS

Organization goals come in different forms, and some conflict with each other. These conflicts need to be resolved in some way so the organization can function as a coordinated whole. When the conflicts among goals are so extensive that the organization cannot operate as a unified whole, consideration should be given to the separation of the organization into two or more organizations until coordinated goals can be established for each entity. For an organization to exist, there must be a common set of shared beliefs among organization leaders that can be communicated to workers about the desired state the organization wants. For an existing organization, there may be a need to review organization goals from time to time; but seldom should changes in goals be made, for to do so upsets things throughout the organization. Nevertheless, goal changes may have to be made when the conditions of survival and growth imposed by a changed environment demand them.

Goals Distinguished from Objectives

We use the term *goals* to mean broad, fairly timeless statements of what the organization wants to achieve; and we use the term *objectives* for more specific statements of ends, the achievement of which is contemplated within a specific time period. Our use is consistent with the underlying meaning of these terms; but more importantly, our meaning of objectives is consistent with its meaning in "management by objectives," a phrase used in both business and government control systems. Let us keep in mind that goals precede strategies in the strategic planning process, while objectives are used in the management control process. Essentially, goals and objectives both specify ends sought, but they differ with respect to the time period and the degree of specificity. Strategies refer to means of attaining goals, while more detailed plans are the means used to attain objectives.

In developing management control systems, which are directed to goal achievements, we need to emphasize the distinction between goals and objectives. To confuse the two ends could misdirect the flow of control information to different levels of management and might motivate senior management to save the tree and lose the forest. Goals are stated without reference to a time period, whereas objectives are

Goals- Time Period
objectives - Specific Date

intended to be accomplished by a specified date—sometimes in one year and sometimes in five years or longer. For example, a goal of government might be to improve health. To attain the goal the government might establish objectives for medical education, research, insurance programs, construction of health care facilities and the like, each of which is to be attained by a certain time, and each of which is intended to contribute toward the goal.

While goals are stated in general terms that provide purpose for organization activities, objectives are stated in rather specific terms, preferably in such a way that there is some measurable basis for determining the extent to which they have been achieved. For example, an objective of McDonald's may be to open X number of additional fast-food outlets next year. Or a company may set as an objective the attainment of $Y million sales volume five years from now. If objectives are stated in this way, periodically the management control system can measure the degree of their attainment. If objectives are vague or ill defined, no system can measure their attainment.

Profitability as a Goal

Profitability is sometimes suggested as a goal, and earning a profit is an important goal of most businesses, but this term is too vague to be particularly useful for management control. Shareholders invest money in a business, and expect a return on the investment. Profit is generally accepted as a measure of this return. Presumably, the higher the profit, the better off the business has performed for the shareholders. It follows, in a general way, that a goal of the business should be to earn as high a profit for the shareholders as is feasible. This is a more specific statement than that of "earning a profit." We should make it even more specific by allowing for the fact that the desirable amount of profit is related to the amount of investment. This leads to a statement that relates profit to investment.

For management control purposes, among others, two important observations need to be made about this relationship between profit and investment. First, profit and revenue (from output) do not necessarily flow together; and it does not follow that the higher the revenues of the business, the better the business has performed for the shareholders. Additional revenues do not automatically generate additional profit for the shareholders. Second, it does not even follow that a higher profit percentage of sales means the business has performed better for the shareholders. Neither measure takes into account the amount of shareholders' investment employed in generating the profit.

Cost

Revenues, dollars of profit, and return on sales are not desirable statements of business goals. Other things being equal, of course, it is desirable to have more revenues or more profit rather than less, and to have a higher profit margin rather than a lower one. Other things are not equal and, barring special situations, an objective of a business should seldom be to increase revenues if the increase requires a more than offsetting increase in expenses. Such an objective would conflict with the goal of a higher return on investment. Similarly, an objective should seldom be to increase profit or profit margin if the increase requires a more than offsetting increase in investment. Normally, the objectives of increasing revenues, dollars of profit, or profit margin are sound if, but only if, they do not decrease the return on investment below the rate that could be earned elsewhere.

It is useful to think of the economics of a business in terms of the following equation:

$$\frac{\text{Revenues} - \text{Expenses}}{\text{Revenues}} \times \frac{\text{Revenues}}{\text{Investment}} = \text{Return on investment}$$

which is expressed in money terms, for example, as:

$$\frac{\$10{,}000 - \$9{,}500}{\$10{,}000} \times \frac{\$10{,}000}{\$4{,}000} = 12.5\%$$

In this equation, the first term reveals the *return on revenue;* the profit of $500 and the revenue of $10,000 yield a 5 percent return on revenues. The second term, called *capital turnover,* shows the number of revenue dollars generated annually by each dollar of investment, thus indicating that the capital turnover is 2.5 times ($10,000 ÷ $4,000). Then return on revenues times capital turnover equals return on investment:

$$5\% \times 2.5 = 12.5\%$$

The equation suggests that, in the analysis of profitability as a goal, two basic activities should be kept in mind. First, the business must earn an adequate profit on the average dollar of sales revenue; and second, its sales volume must be adequate to produce an acceptable capital turnover. A business should try to increase its revenues if it can do so with less than a corresponding increase in expenses; it should try to reduce expenses if this can be done without decreasing revenues; and it should add to its investment if there is an appropriate increase in profits. All elements in the equation are related to one another, and in developing a strategy to pursue the profitability goal, it is wrong to focus on one element without considering the others.

Qualifications. Several qualifications should be mentioned to the foregoing analysis of profitability as a goal and of strategies developed to pursue the goal. Regardless of the logic of the analysis, some managements consciously strive to make their companies bigger, to increase revenue without much concern for the effect of growth on profits. Sheer size is considered to be a measure of success in such companies. If the name of the game is growth in sales, the management control system should be so constructed that it is consistent with that goal.

In some companies, the dominant goal is growth in reported earnings per share of common stock. This goal is similar to, but not necessarily identical with, return on investment. For example, earnings per share will tend to increase without a corresponding increase in its return on investment if a company increases its capital, without changing the number of shares outstanding, by retaining a relatively large fraction of its earnings. In companies that seek growth in earnings per share, the management control system should reveal the impact of the additional investment on earnings per share.

Some companies state their financial goal in terms of shareholder wealth, or the market price of their stock. The organization's success in pursuit of this goal is frequently measured in terms of both earnings per share and the price/earnings multiple. The price/earnings multiple measure presumes to reflect, among other things, an indication of investors' prediction of growth in earnings per share and the stability of that growth. Management control systems in companies that use such measures should endeavor to reveal information on the several variables that are presumed to affect stock prices as an aid to managements in controlling the company.

Some managements are less willing to take risks than others, and this difference in the degree of risk aversion leads to differences in their actions, so the return-on-investment measure should be qualified by revealing management's attitude toward risk.[1]

Social goals are another qualification to the profitability goal. The fact is that the task of deciding on the goals of a business organization in today's cultural, political, and economic environment is complex. While it seems so now, but may not have been so then, goals were more economics-oriented in the past than now. Today's cultural environment, being composed of the attitudes, beliefs, and values of society, seems to be having an increasing impact on organization goals. In particular, the organizations want to help develop the nation, contribute to the community, and be a good place for employees to work. As a result, for example, personal goals of organization employees have become a fact to be considered in identifying organization goals. As noted previously, personal goals include individual pursuit of dignity, influence, leisure, money, prestige, security, and job satisfaction; and the personal goals, as well as political and other social goals, may conflict with such organization economic goals as growth, efficiency,

---

[1] For discussion of the implications of this point, see John Lintner, "The Impact of Uncertainty on the 'Traditional' Theory of the Firm," in J. W. Markham and G. F. Pananek, eds., *Industrial Organization and Development* (Boston: Houghton Mifflin, 1970), pp. 238–65.

stability, industry leadership, and profitability. Some reconciliation of the multiple desires occurs in selecting organization goals.

As a result of the cultural environment, and its reflection in the political environment, most business organizations pursue both social and economic goals. Articulating the social goals in a manner that can be recognized in the management control system is difficult because such goals as behaving ethically, being a responsible member of a community, and contributing to the development of the nation are not clear and precise. Some companies treat social goals as intermediate or way points along the road to the long-term economic goal of organization profit or shareholder wealth. These organizations pursue the social goal of being a responsible member of a community because it is considered a means toward the long-run goal of a higher return on investments. As the intermediate way points to profitability, social pursuits are not organization goals but are more like strategies used to attain the goal of a profit return. On the other hand, the pursuit of the social goal of providing employment, hiring minorities, attaining a short-term profit at a sacrifice of long-term profit, when identified as a separate goal by organization leadership, have a significant impact on the design and structure of the management control system.

Still another qualification to the profitability goal, when expressed as the return on investment, is that the term *investment* is defined in several ways. It has been used to refer to *shareholder investment*. For many purposes, it is more useful to think of investment as the total capital supplied to the business, which includes debt capital supplied by creditors as well as the equity capital supplied by shareholders. There are advantages to the use of the broader definition in management control systems. The sum of debt capital and equity capital represents the capital employed, and return on capital employed is a fundamental performance measure in many management control systems. Lumping both types of capital together makes it possible to disregard the mix of debt and equity capital of different companies, and the mix is not relevant in most business decisions, except for financing decisions.

Focusing on capital employed implies that capital is the important resource that should govern the company's decisions. This disregards the importance of human resources: the men and women that the company has hired, trained, and formed into a team. Few management control systems take into account the capital value of these human resources, but there is increasing interest in finding feasible ways of doing so.

Although return on investment or capital employed is frequently expressed as a percentage, a conceptually better way of expressing it is by the number called *residual income,* which will be explained later.

Profit maximization as a goal. Some writers, although agreeing with the idea that a dominant goal of a company is return on investment, state this goal more specifically than we have. They say that the goal is to maximize the return on investment, and have in mind a conceptual framework that is much more specific than the notion, "the more profits, the better." They assume businesses set their selling prices and make related output decisions by analyzing the difference between marginal revenue and marginal cost at various volume levels, as proposed in economic theory.

There is little evidence to support the conclusion that business leaders actually behave in the way that the profit maximization model assumes, primarily because businesses do not have satisfactory marginal cost and marginal revenue data. They cannot develop specific information to reveal the shape of the cost and demand curves for their products, or the effects on profits of various amounts of spending on such activities as research and development. Direct contradiction of the profit maximization goal, involving marginal cost/marginal revenue pricing in any meaningful sense, is revealed by the General Motors Corporation pricing policy, described in a case accompanying this chapter, where full costs, including historical depreciation, are used in arriving at its selling prices.

Satisfactory return on investment as a goal. An alternative to the profit maximization goal is the satisfactory return goal. It takes two forms.

According to one view, organizations pursue many goals, of which more profit is one. Since some goals conflict with others, some balance of them must be made to arrive at a combination that yields a satisfactory realization of them all without maximizing the return of any one goal. This is difficult and involves the question of how much profit an organization should trade off for more of some other goal.

The other form of the satisfactory return on investment goal assumes that the purpose of a business is to use its resources as efficiently as possible in supplying goods and services to its customers, and that the business will compensate equitably the shareholders who supply the capital used to obtain these resources. This implies that managers invest in projects that are likely to yield at least a satisfactory return on investment, even though a global search for investment opportunities might turn up some opportunities that are better than those that have been accepted. The concept also suggests that selling prices are set so that, on the average, they will recover full costs plus a satisfactory return on investment, even though a different pricing policy might possibly produce even more profit (but then again, it might produce less). Finally, it suggests that management performance is measured against a standard of satisfactory results under the prevailing circumstances, rather than against a standard that purports to measure the maximum profits attainable.

Most managers select a satisfactory return on investment goal in accordance with their perception of the investment opportunities in their industry. They are not sure that this perception is correct, but they are not unduly concerned about this fact. Although management has neither the time nor the ability to explore all possible alternative courses of action, management nevertheless must make decisions. Because of this limitation, management's acts are said to represent *bounded rationality,* as contrasted with complete rationality. Although the satisfactory return model seems less precise than the profit maximization model, the evidence suggests that it is a better reflection of what happens in the real world.[2]

Goals in Nonprofit Organizations

Nonprofit organizations do not have profitability as a goal. They pursue other ends. Universities exist to educate students and to add knowledge. Hospitals seek to help patients get well. Governmental units provide fire protection, assist those in need, and try to ensure domestic tranquility. In general, the goal of a nonprofit organization is to provide service.

Goals cannot be clearly

Precisely stated

In most nonprofit organizations, goals cannot be clearly and precisely stated; and measurement of the degree to which they have been attained is difficult. Because of the absence of the seemingly clear-cut focus provided by some type of profitability goal, the management control process is more difficult in a nonprofit organization than in a profit-oriented company. Even so, the evidence is that nonprofit organizations with systematic management control systems perform better than those without them.

Statement of Goals

A statement about profitability (along the lines discussed above) and a statement about growth express the main economic goals of many organizations. In addition, although often unstated, an organization has the fundamental goal of survival and, therefore, will not knowingly adopt strategies that are so risky that they threaten its very existence. The organization also has social goals, although they may be difficult to formulate in meaningful words.

The list of goals is desirably short. The more numerous they are, the greater the possibility that one criterion of goal success will conflict with another when a proposed strategy is being discussed, and this conflict will hamper resolution of the issue.

Some companies state a long list of goals, some of which are little more than platitudes; and a serious attempt to analyze proposed strategies in terms of these multiple criteria can be frustrating. When the list

---

[2] For further discussion of this topic, see Robert N. Anthony, "The Trouble with Profit Maximization," *Harvard Business Review,* November 1960, pp. 126–34.

is long, the tendency develops to disregard many of the stated goals when proposed strategies are being analyzed and actions planned.

Externally Motivated Goals or Strategies

There is some fuzzy thinking about the notion of externally imposed or motivated goals. Obviously, a profession, the law, or other external force may limit the type of goals an organization may pursue—or may even encourage the selection of certain goals. But these are not externally imposed goals. Goals are selected by management. Even a statement of organization purpose that is set forth in the articles of incorporation, by which an organization is legally formed, does not reveal goals. The fundamental reason for the existence of articles of incorporation, or their equivalent, is to place boundaries or limits to the scope of an organization's activities. These limits may serve the two functions of providing an environment that encourages stable goal setting activities or of fostering some nation-wide coordination and control of economic activity, but they do not set goals.

The second function of the notion of externally imposed limits refers to the process where senior management develops policies that guide goal selection within an organization to coordinate activities throughout the organization.

Industry charters. Within an industry, each company presumably tries to find the best niche for itself; the term for this is *positioning*. While the impact of these industry influences depends on the personality and ability of the organization's chief executive officer, survival of the organization requires that it accept them. Within them, the company can develop goals and strategies that aim at any part of the market: geographic, price, or other. It can develop strategies for manufacturing or buying what it sells, seeking a dominant market share, maintaining a steady market share, or milking a market at the expense of market share. It may develop a strategy to distribute through distributors or wholesalers, catalogs, commission agents, its own salespersons, or its own retail stores. It can invest heavily in research and development, rely on outside sources for new product ideas, or copy products introduced by innovating companies. Whatever list of strategies is developed, some will have characteristics of goals and others will border on routine statements of means of attaining some goal. Some may be strategies for maximizing return on investment.

Division charters. Divisional charters take on characteristics of senior management strategies, but may be assigned the role of a goal by a division for developing divisional strategies. In our view, thinking of goals as organization targets and of viewing management control as an organization-wide process, a management control system should treat divisional charters as strategies regardless of whatever actions and terms the divisions might use.

Whatever a charter is called, it is constructed so that, within the boundaries of the whole company, specific charges of authorities, responsibilities, and scope are established for each division or other principal operating unit. These divisional charters are an important factor in the management control process for they set limits to divisional planning. In some companies, divisions are permitted to grow and to extend their activities without regard to a specific charter. When this happens, programs of two or more divisions may overlap in an undesirable way. Two divisions may compete against one another in the same market. Or, one division may be counting on orders from another division to fill its production capacity, without knowing that the other division has made plans to obtain its products from another source. Without guidance, an important market segment may be overlooked by all the divisions. Under certain circumstances, competition among the divisions is sound practice. For example, the various car divisions of General Motors Corporation compete vigorously with one another. The point is not that such competition should be eliminated, but rather that it should be carried on knowingly and as a part of the overall strategy of the corporation.

Although divisional charters are set by senior management, divisional managers usually participate actively in the process. For various reasons, Division A may wish to invade the territory assigned to Division B, and the Division A manager will argue vigorously the case for doing so. Because the manager of Division B usually does not want his own boundaries to be constricted, he will likely oppose such a move, and senior management must then decide. This decision often leads to a change in the charter to a division. Indeed, if charters are not reevaluated from time to time, unfortunate consequences can ensue.

Charters also exist for units within divisions. The charter for each lower-level unit in the organization are constrained by the guidance furnished by the higher-level unit of which it is a part.

STRATEGIES

Strategies take many forms; but typically, a strategy will indicate the types of goods or services to be sold, the resources and technology to be used in production, the method of coordination of efforts and plans to be used to perform efficiently and effectively, and types of actions to be taken. A strategy includes both strategy formulation and strategy implementation. *Strategy formulation*—the selection of a long-term method of performing or competing—aims to provide a pathway to success in attaining organization goals. *Strategy implementation* refers to carrying out the formulated strategy. Statements of strategy are expressed in the form of organization "policies" and as organization "programs."

Strategies may be classified as functional strategies, such as *marketing strategies, production strategies, or even combined strategies.* Illustrative strategies are:

Production strategy	*Marketing strategy*	*Combined strategy*
1. Programs to utilize capacity	1. Programs to develop competitive edge over competition	1. Programs to coordinate total organization operation
2. Programs to improve employee performance	2. Programs for developing customer loyalty	2. Programs to develop and sell new technologically advanced products

Relevance to Management Control

We previously described the thermostat as a control system. The thermostat is set at a desired temperature level by the person who wants temperature controlled. When actual temperature deviates from this desired state, the thermostat can react in only one way: it can cause the furnace to be turned on or off. Organizations differ from these characteristics of a thermostat. Rather than having a desired state, or goal, that is set entirely by some outside force, the organization sets its own goals within the constraints of the external environment. Rather than being limited to a simple on-off action as a way of achieving its goals, the organization can select strategies from a wide variety of possible courses of action. The management control process seeks to ensure that the strategies are carried out. Although the process does not involve the formulation of strategies, management control requires that the programs required to implement strategies be clearly identified. Information obtained in the management control process also may at times indicate the need to change strategies. Although the components of strategies can be classified in various ways, for management control purposes it is important to distinguish the action programs for implementing strategies from policies which merely guide actions.[3]

Policies. Strategies include broad policies that govern corporate activities. These policies are essentially constraints within which functional and subordinate managers are expected to operate. They include promotion, transfer, compensation, retirement, and other personnel policies; dividend, debt structure, short-term borrowing, and other financial policies; capital investment criteria; quality levels and other

[3] For an examination of the function of management systems in decentralized operation, see Richard F. Vancil, *Decentralization: Managerial Ambiguity by Design* (Homewood, Ill.: Dow Jones-Irwin, 1979), pp. 73–97.

product policies; and policies regarding discrimination, pollution, and other social issues. The formulation of policies that are specific enough to be more than platitudes, yet broad enough so they do not unduly restrict the operating manager, is a difficult task.

Programs. Companies compete with each other; and they adapt to a constantly changing social, economic, and technological environment. Keeping in mind organization goals and policies, managements evaluate their relative strength (resources and abilities), their performance record, and the environment, and develop organization programs for action that will enable the organization to attain corporate goals. Programs may join together projects, functional units, and responsibility assignments into plans for organization action. The programs include means of outperforming competition, assuring employee and customer support, and producing and selling efficiently and effectively. Overall, they cover all the organization as a whole will do and how it will do it.

STRATEGIC PLANNING

The strategic planning process may be used at two time periods. First, when the organization is formed, it is used to select goals and strategies. Subsequently, it is used to select policies and broad programs for action.

Overview of Strategic Planning

An entrepreneur who is starting a business to make a profit has a wide range of possible strategies. By contrast, a company that is a going concern must formulate new strategies that may conflict with some already existing. We can illustrate the essence of the process by referring to Exhibits 3–1 and 3–2.

Exhibit 3–1 is a diagram of a stable, going company. This company has various resources, uses them to produce outputs, and attains its

EXHIBIT 3–1 Diagram of a Stable Company

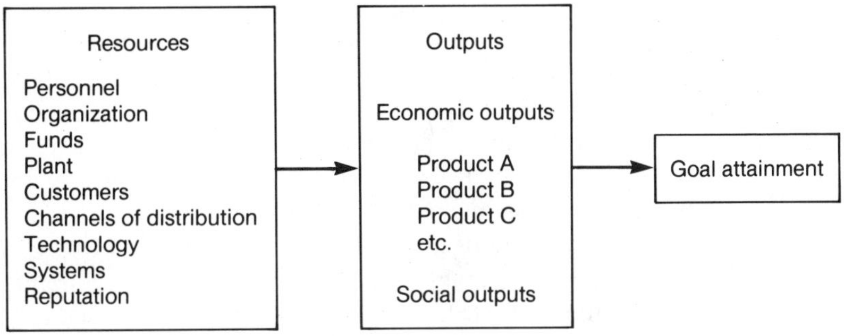

EXHIBIT 3–2 The Strategic Planning Process

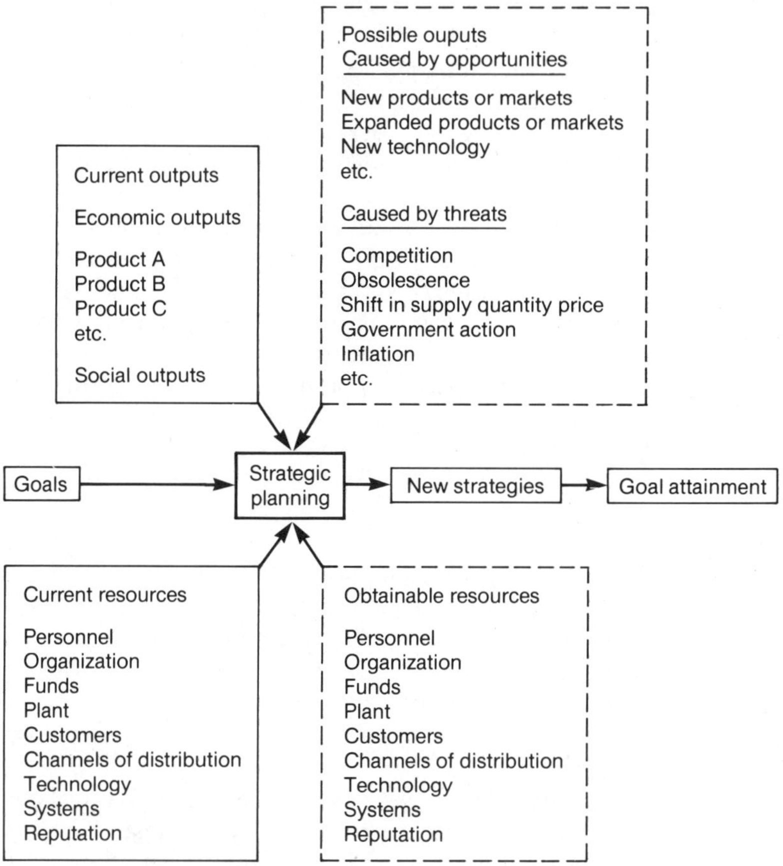

goals. The resources include its personnel, organization structure, funds, physical plant, and body of customers, channels of distribution, technology (for manufacturing, marketing, and administering), systems, and reputation. In addition to using these resources to produce and distribute products to customers, the organization also uses its resources to produce social outputs, such as contributions to the communities in which it operates. The first type of output generates profits that attain the company's economic goal, and the second type leads to other results that attain the company's community service goals. All of this work is carried on according to the set of policies and programs that constitute organization strategies. In the absence of changes in its external environment, the company could operate indefinitely in this fashion and the life of management should be somewhat placid.

This model of a stable company is rarely, if ever, found in the real world. In the real world, the outside environment changes, and these changes require changes in strategies. They lead to the process diagrammed in Exhibit 3–2, which illustrates that for the going concern the strategic planning process starts from a base of current outputs and current resources, the same as in Exhibit 3–1. Then perturbations in a stable situation imply a need for new outputs. These perturbations may be caused by perceived opportunities, such as new products or markets, or newly developed technology. They may also be caused by threats to the existing situation that arise from actions of competitors, obsolescence of products or of technology, shifts in consumer tastes, shifts in sources of materials or in the price of materials, inflation, and other factors.

In the strategic planning process, the company reacts to these opportunities and threats. It reviews its currently available resources and considers additional resources that it may be able to obtain. These considerations are bounded by the prevailing goals of the organization. From these considerations emerge one or more new strategies that change policies or programs for using efficiently and effectively the available and obtainable resources to produce the outputs most likely to achieve the company's goals.

Formulating Strategies

Thinking about strategy is an important senior management activity. Andrews says that the strategist considers four questions simultaneously: What might we do? What can we do? What do we want to do? What should we do?[4]

A few companies have developed systematic approaches to the formulation of strategy. General Electric Company, for example, once developed a model that incorporated the principal factors that, according to its studies, governed return on investment; and it used that model both to search out strategic opportunities at the corporate level and, also, to analyze strategies proposed by division managers.[5] Aguilar describes companies that systematically reexamine their environment as a basis for making changes in strategy.[6] Many companies do not make systematic strategic studies. Instead, when an opportunity or a threat is identified, it is studied, and the study may lead to a change in strategy. Strategies are also reexamined when a new management takes over. Some of the possibilities originate at corporate headquar-

---

[4] Kenneth R. Andrews, *The Concept of Corporate Strategy* (Homewood, Ill.: Dow Jones-Irwin, 1971), p. 41.

[5] Sidney Schoeffler, Robert D. Buzzell, and Donald F. Heany, "Impact of Strategic Planning on Profit Performance," *Harvard Business Review*, March–April 1974, pp. 137–45.

[6] Francis J. Aguilar, *Scanning the Business Environment* (New York: Macmillan, 1967).

ters; others originate when a division perceives an opportunity that is outside its existing charter.

The evaluation and selection of alternative strategy proposals is difficult. It involves, initially, examining information on the external environment of the organization in a search for opportunities that the organization might pursue. Sensing the opportunities that may be available may be by individual insight or through group discussion; but information on the environment and changes in it is the base for the development of new strategies. Most companies require that alternative strategy proposals be developed in some detail, with policies and programs suggested, to provide a basis for evaluating the feasibility of the strategy.

Evaluating alternative new strategy proposals are first examined in terms of the extent that they contribute to the realization of organization goals. Some companies occasionally review and clarify goals at the same time if significant changes have taken place in the environment. For example, in 1982, General Electric started emphasizing "share of the market" goals. Whatever organization goals prevail, feasible proposed new strategies are evaluated relative to the goals. There are significantly different views about other criteria that may be used for further evaluation on proposed strategies. Below are two illustrative alternative sets of additional evaluation criteria that might be used for strategy selection, Criteria Set A[7] and B[8]:

Criteria Set A	*Criteria Set B*
1. Is the return on investment increased?	1. Does the strategy fully exploit all environmental opportunities?
2. Is the risk of losing scarce resources decreased?	2. Is the strategy consistent with corporate competence and resources?
3. Will the strategy increase company growth?	3. Is the level of risk feasible in economic and personal terms?
4. Will the strategy contribute to social welfare?	4. Is the strategy appropriate for the desired level of social contribution?
5. Will the strategy increase employment?	5. Will the strategy provide a clear stimulus to the organization?

Despite efforts to develop formal systematic processes for evaluating and selecting alternative strategies, the process does not lend itself to routine thinking. The somewhat diverse nature of strategic planning of goals and strategies represents an important distinction between this process and the management control process on which this book focuses. Not only is strategic planning flexible but also the broad strate-

[7] Adapted from W. H. Newman and I. P. Logan, *Strategy, Policy, and Central Management,* 7th ed., (Cincinnati, Ohio: South-Western Publishing, 1976), p. 77.

[8] Adapted from C. Roland Christensen et al., *Business Policy: Text and Cases,* 4th ed. (Homewood, Ill.: Richard D. Irwin, 1978), pp. 136–139.

gies that result often are not written down in a document corresponding to the formal budget documents associated with the management control process. An individual decision, such as to enter a new market, does generate documents to implement that particular decision; but in few companies can one find a book that brings together all the past decisions that collectively define the organization's strategies, though many companies do have a written statement of policies.

To complete this brief discussion of goals and strategies, we need to consider how they relate to management control systems and how management control systems may influence the selection of strategies. This requires an understanding of the way management control systems are designed.

MANAGEMENT CONTROL DESIGN—KEY VARIABLES

A management control system should be designed to facilitate planning for the implementation of strategies, to motivate managers to achieve organization goals, and to develop information for the evaluation of performance in achieving goals. It relies heavily on measurements to do this; and to measure effectively, the strategy must lend itself to measurement of performance, and the management control system must be designed to provide suitable measures. If either does not exist, the management control system can be of little help in implementing the strategies. Alternative strategies may be more practical.

Since profitability is a dominant goal in most companies, most management control systems are designed to measure profitability. In addition to measuring profitability, the system may help implement strategies by developing measures of the performance of certain key activities of the organization that normally lead or indicate the future profitability of the organization. These variables are called *key variables*. They are also called "strategic factors," "key success factors," "key result factors," and "pulse points." In most situations, there will be key variables for the organization as a whole, and other, perhaps different, key variables for division or other segments within the organization.

The development of means of identifying and measuring key variables to implement strategies represented a signal improvement in the technology of management control systems. Some of the developments in organization behavior (previously reviewed) suggest that additional improvements in the ability to develop management control systems may be possible.

Let's examine the idea of key variables and attempt to gain further insights into means of implementing strategies through management control systems.

Nature of Key Variables

The identification of key variables requires a thorough understanding of the economics of the organization. Some help in identifying key variables can be found by developing a model of an organization and examining it to discover the sensitivity of profits to various factors. Usually, however, the key variables used for measuring the success of an organization are uncovered by discussions with persons who have acquired a deep understanding of the organization through long experience with it. These persons know intuitively the important things to watch—and these are the key variables. A key variable seems to have the following characteristics:

1. It is *important* in explaining the success or failure of the organization.
2. It is *volatile* and can change quickly, often for reasons not controllable by the manager.
3. It is significant enough that *prompt action* is required when a change occurs.
4. It is not easy to *predict changes* in the key variable.
5. The variable can be *measured,* either directly or via a surrogate. For example, customers *satisfaction* cannot be measured directly, but its surrogate, *number of sales returns,* can be a key variable.

One way to isolate and identify key variables is to look at the raison d'être of the industry and of the particular organization within that industry. A useful question is: "Why should our company be able to operate at a satisfactory profit?" Thinking about this fundamental question should lead to a careful spelling out of the functions that the company is performing and why its customers are willing to pay for them. Further thought should then be devoted to the question of why the company, rather than its competitors, should be able to attract profitable volume. Finally, it may be possible to pinpoint those activities that need to be done particularly well if the organization is to enjoy greater success.

Another approach to the identification of key variables is to examine the way decisions are made. What decisions does management regard as major ones? What are the factors that management is concerned about in making these decisions? For many types of discretionary expenditures, what will be the source of revenue from which the company will recover this cost and earn a profit? Questions such as these should lead eventually to the identification of the elements that are critical to the success of a company in a competitive environment. Not all of these elements are key variables. From the long list of answers to the questions, such as those listed above, the designer of the management control system must select those few which have the characteristics of volatility, importance, need for prompt action, difficulty of prediction, and measurability. These are the key variables. Measuring and reporting their performance will enable the management control system to implement organization strategies by motivating control of the key variables that govern strategy success.

Exception variables. In addition to the key variables, the management control system provides information on a large number of other variables that do not need management attention unless they behave in an exceptional manner. These are the *exception variables*. They are identified in the same manner as the key variables. Some cost elements in a factory, such as direct material and direct labor costs and certain elements of overhead cost, are examples. Normally, exception variables can be expected to behave as planned, and need to be subject to management scrutiny only when they do not perform as expected. The management control system should be designed to identify and call attention to exception variables only when there is a significant deviation from plan—*the exception principle*. By contrast, the current behavior of key variables is always reported and is carefully scrutinized by management.

Measures of profitability, key variable, and exception variables, and similar performance measures are used in the management control system to assure that strategies are being carried out and that goals are being attained. Should the management control system indicate that strategies were being implemented and goals were not being attained, senior management would want to review the strategies.

While key variables normally refer to organization-wide activities, more precise key variables for environmental, production, marketing, finance, logistics, and asset activities may be used to assure precise implementation of strategies and plans. These require different types of key variables.

Types of Key Variables

Each company must determine its own key variables for its management control system. Nevertheless, some key variables are common to all companies generally and many are common to companies in a given industry. These universal type of key variables may be classified as environmental, functional, (primarily marketing and production), or asset variables. These three categories will be examined to illustrate further use of the concept of a key variable in management control systems. While the list of key variables is divided into the three categories for illustrative purposes, there is obviously overlap among them. Also, there should be no implication that a company's management control system should select one or two key variables in each category. Conceivably, all the relevant key variables for a given company could be marketing variables, or some other functional variables.

Environmental variables. There are four environments in which key variables may be found: general economic conditions, policies of government, developments in the industry, and actions of competitors. The state of the economy, as measured by gross national product, leading indicators, or narrower measures that reflect conditions in the particular company's market, is obviously a significant environment key variable. Some companies do not treat measures of performance in the four environments areas as distinctive key variables. Instead, they consider them as they are reflected in organization or functional key variables. For example, they may be absorbed in the marketing function variables listed in the next section.

Marketing key variables. Some aspects of the marketing effort are key variables in most businesses, not only because of the need to take prompt action in the marketing area if results are not satisfactory but also because of the need to make prompt adjustments in production and other plans if a significant change in the volume of business seems to be on the horizon. In addition to sales and other specific marketing items reported in the income statement, other marketing key variables are:

1. Bookings, sales, orders, or back orders. In companies that manufacture for future delivery, the nature and volume of sales orders booked is sometimes more important than current sales volume as an indicator of marketing strategy success or as an indication that other plans may require adjustment.

2. Market share. Unless the key variable of market share is watched closely, a deterioration in the company's competitive position can be obscured by reported increases in sales volume that results from generally favorable business conditions. To indicate the extent of the need for management control of this variable, it is common practice for automobile dealers to report their sales to automobile manufacturers every 10 days, and detailed information on market share is published for their use a few days later.

3. Gross margin percentage. A change in the average gross margin percentage of a product line is a key variable because it may signal a change in the sales mix of products or in the proportion of sales that cannot be made at regular prices.

4. Key account orders. In companies that sell to retailers, the orders received from certain important accounts—large department stores, discount chains, supermarkets, mail-order houses—may provide an early indication of the success of the entire marketing strategy.

5. Promotional indicators. The renewal date on magazine subscriptions, the direct-mail response rate for companies that rely on direct mail as a marketing tool, the coupon returns for companies that use advertisements with coupons, are all key indicators of the success of marketing strategies.

Production and logistics key variables. In an ideal world, products would flow through a factory as smoothly and uneventfully as a river normally flows between its banks. But just as a flood causes havoc in a watershed, so unexpected events can cause havoc in the factory—or in the distribution network that leads from factory to consumer. Strategies must be developed to sense and to deal with unexpected developments. Some illustrative key or exception production variables that may warrant special attention of the management control system and prompt management action if unsatisfactory situations develops are listed below:

1. *Cost control exception variable.* In typical companies, managements assume that actual costs are in line with standard costs unless a red flag is raised in accordance with the management by exception principle. In other companies, particularly when the profit margin as a percentage of sales is small, costs must be monitored all the time because a small change in costs can have a major impact on profits.

2. *Capacity utilization variable.* Because some costs are fixed, unit costs and profits are significantly influenced by fluctuations in production volume. Volume fluctuations reflect, in part, the ability of production people to schedule and adjust capacity utilization to current production requirements. Similarly, in a professional organization, the percentage of the total available professional hours that is billed to clients, *sold time,* is a key measure of fixed-resource utilization. In a hotel, *occupancy rate,* the percentage of rooms occupied each day, is the capacity utilization measure. For most organizations, a measure of capacity utilization is a key variable.

3. *Quality control.* In many companies, acceptable quality can be taken for granted. For them, quality control is an exception variable. In others, a departure from the highest quality standards can be catastrophic. For such companies, some measurement of the quality of output is a key variable.

4. *Raw material costs.* If the costs of raw materials tend to fluctuate widely, price movements need to be watched closely so management can change inventory levels and product prices or adopt alternative product formulations. In such companies, raw material prices are a key variable all the time. Under unusual economic conditions, they may become a key variable in most companies.

5. *On-time delivery.* In companies in which fulfillment of delivery promises are important and in which delivery on time is difficult, the percentage of late shipments is a variable that may warrant special management attention.

Asset variables. Profitability is a function both of income and of the assets employed in generating that income. In some companies, the management control system must pay special attention to the behavior of assets, particularly current assets, if asset control strategies are to be implemented. Typical asset key variables include:

1. Inventory turnover. A change in inventory turnover (sales divided by average inventory) is a key variable not only because it may signal that the return on investment is decreasing but also because it may indicate the need for special management actions, such as developing new methods of financing. Also, it could be a symptom that something is wrong with either the production process, with the communication between the sales and production departments, or with inventory control procedures. In some companies, inventory write-offs is another type of key variable.

2. Accounts receivable outstanding. The amount of accounts receivable, measured by number of days of uncollected sales, is a key variable in many companies, because an unfavorable change will have an impact on cash flow and financing requirements, and may be a symptom of poor credit policies, financial difficulties of customers, or other problems.

3. Investment return. In banks, insurance companies, and other companies whose profitability is heavily dependent on their ability to make good investments, income earned on investments is a key variable. In banks, the spread between interest income earned and the cost of money is important. The measurement of investment return is complicated because of the necessity of combining both interest and dividend yield with the effect of market price fluctuations.

The above list of key variables is only indicative. Managers have other "pet" key variables that they have developed on the basis of years of experience. In some cases, they are not able to explain the reason why they believe these variables to be important; but if the key variable does the job of signaling the need for prompt management action, the management control system should accept it as satisfactory and use it to implement activities at all levels—from strategic planning to policies, programs, and division control.

Recapitulation

We have examined the nature of management control systems and found them to be the means by which managements implement their strategies to achieve organization goals. Because management controls rely on the response of people to management control system information, we examined the nature of people behavior in organizations and have found that, to motivate people to achieve organization goals, the management control system must be structured in such a way that individuals will realize their personal goals while achieving organization goals. To understand the functioning of organizations, to which management control systems must relate, we have examined organization goals and strategies and have found that management control system measures have to relate to key variable in organization activities if strategies are to be developed and implemented in a timely manner.

In the foregoing process, we have noted that information is the central element in management control systems. This suggests we should examine the notion of information before discussing aspects of management control systems in greater depth. In the next chapter we consider the concept of information, the full scope of it, and then relate it to the management control systems task.

SUGGESTED ADDITIONAL READINGS

Ackoff, Russell L. *Creating the Corporate Future.* New York: John Wiley & Sons, 1981.

Aguilar, Frances J. *Scanning the Business Environment.* New York: Macmillan, 1967.

Andrews, Kenneth R. *The Concept of Corporate Strategy.* Homewood, Ill.: Dow Jones-Irwin, 1971.

Ansoff, H. Igor, et al., eds. *From Strategic Planning to Strategic Management.* New York: Wiley Interscience, 1976.

Cordiner, Ralph J. *New Frontiers for Professional Managers.* New York: McGraw-Hill, 1956.

Hofer, Charles W., and **Schendel, Dan,** eds. *Strategic Management: A New View on Business Policy and Planning.* Boston: Little, Brown, 1978.

Hosmer, L. T. *Strategic Management.* Englewood Cliff, N.J.: Prentice-Hall, 1982.

Lorange, P. *Implementation of Strategic Planning.* Englewood Ciffs, N.J.: Prentice-Hall, 1982.

Lorange, Peter, and **Vancil, 'Richard F.** *Strategic Planning Systems.* Englewood Cliffs, N.J.: Prentice-Hall, 1977.

Pritchard, R. E. *Strategic Planning and Control Techniques for Profit: A Handbook for Small Business Owners.* Englewood Cliffs, N.J.: Prentice-Hall, 1981.

Radford, K. J. *Strategic Planning.* Reston, Va.: Reston Publishing, 1980.

Salamon, G., and **Thompson, K.** *Control and Ideology in Organizations.* Cambridge, Mass.: MIT Press, 1980.

Sloan, Alfred O., Jr. *My Years with General Motors.* Garden City, N.Y.: Doubleday, 1964.

Steiner, George A., and **Miner, John B.** *Management Policy and Strategy.* New York: Macmillan, 1977.

Stonich, P. J., ed. *Implementing Strategy: Making Strategy Happen.* Cambridge, Mass.: Ballinger Publishing, 1982.

Summer, Charles E. *Strategic Behavior in Business and Government.* Boston: Little, Brown, 1980.

Taylor, Bernard, and **Sparkes, John R.,** eds. *Corporate Strategy and Planning.* New York: John Wiley & Sons, 1977.

Vancil, Richard F. *Decentralization: Managerial Ambiguity by Design.* Homewood, Ill.: Dow Jones-Irwin, 1979.

CASE 3–1
General Motors Corporation*

In an article in the *NACA Bulletin,* January 1, 1927, Albert Bradley described the pricing policy of General Motors Corporation. At that time, Mr. Bradley was general assistant treasurer; subsequently, he became vice president, executive vice president, and chairman of the board. There is reason to believe that current policy is substantially the same as that described in the 1927 statement. The following description consists principally of excerpts from Mr. Bradley's article.

GENERAL POLICY

Return on investment is the basis of the General Motors policy in regard to the pricing of product. The fundamental consideration is the average return over a protracted period of time, not the specific rate of return over any particular year or short period of time. This long-term rate of return on investment represents the official viewpoint as to the highest average rate of return that can be expected consistent with a healthy growth of the business, and may be referred to as the economic return attainable. The adjudged necessary rate of return on capital will vary as between separate lines of industry as a result of differences in their economic situations; and within each industry there will be important differences in return on capital resulting primarily from the relatively greater efficiency of certain producers.

The fundamental policy in regard to pricing product and expansion of the business also necessitates an official viewpoint as to the normal average rate of plant operation. This relationship between assumed normal average rate of operation and practical annual capacity is known as standard volume.

The fundamental price policy is completely expressed in the conception of standard volume and economic return attainable. For example, if it is the accepted policy that standard volume represents 80 percent of practical annual capacity, and that an average of 20 percent per annum must be earned on the operating capital, it becomes possible to determine the standard price of a product—that is, that price which with plants operating at 80 percent of capacity will produce an annual return of 20 percent on the investment.

* This case was prepared by R. N. Anthony, Harvard Business School.

STANDARD VOLUME

Costs of production and distribution per unit of product vary with fluctuation in volume because of the fixed or nonvariable nature of some of the expense items. Productive materials and productive labor may be considered costs which are 100 percent variable, since within reasonable limits the aggregate varies directly with volume, and the cost per unit of product therefore remains uniform.

Among the items classified as manufacturing expense or burden there exist varying degrees of fluctuation with volume, owing to their greater or lesser degree of variability. Among the absolutely fixed items are such expenses as depreciation and taxes, which may be referred to as 100 percent fixed since within the limits of plant capacity the aggregate will not change, but the amount per unit of product will vary in inverse ratio to the input.

Another group of items may be classified as 100 percent variable, such as inspection and material handling; the amount per unit of product is unaffected by volume. Between the classes of 100 percent fixed and 100 percent variable is a large group of expense items that are partially variable, such as light, heat, power, and salaries.

In General Motors Corporation, standard burden rates are developed for each burden center, so that there will be included in costs a reasonable average allowance for manufacturing expense. In order to establish this rate, it is first necessary to obtain an expression of the estimated normal average rate of plant operation.

Rate of plant operation is affected by such factors as general business conditions, extent of seasonal fluctuation in sales likely within years of large volume, policy with respect to seasonal accumulation of finished and/or semifinished product for the purpose of leveling the production curve, necessity or desirability of maintaining excess plant capacity for emergency use, and many others. Each of these factors should be carefully considered by a manufacturer in the determination of size of a new plant to be constructed, and before making additions to existing plants, in order that there may be a logical relationship between assumed normal average rate of plant operation and practical annual capacity. The percentage accepted by General Motors Corporation as its policy in regard to the relationship between assumed normal rate of plant operation and practical annual capacity is referred to as standard volume.

Having determined the degree of variability of manufacturing expense, the established total expense at the standard volume rate of operations can be estimated. A *standard burden rate* is then developed which represents the proper absorption of burden in costs at standard volume. In periods of low volume, the unabsorbed manufacturing expense is charged directly against profits as unabsorbed burden, while in periods of high volume, the overabsorbed manufacturing expense is credited to profits, as overabsorbed burden.

RETURN ON INVESTMENT

Factory costs and commercial expenses for the most part represent outlays by the manufacturer during the accounting period. An exception is depreciation of capital assets which have a greater length of life than the accounting period. To allow for this element of cost, there is included an allowance for depreciation in the burden rates used in compiling costs. Before an enterprise can be considered successful and worthy of continuation or expansion, however, still another element of cost must be reckoned with. This is the cost of capital, including an allowance for profit.

Thus, the calculation of standard prices of products necessitates the establishment of standards of capital requirement as well as expense factors, representative of the normal average operating condition. The standard for capital employed in fixed assets is expressed as a percentage of factory cost, and the standards for working capital are expressed in part as a percentage of sales, and in part as a percentage of factory cost.

The calculation of the standard allowance for fixed investment is illustrated by the following example:

Investment in plant and other fixed assets	$15,000,000
Practical annual capacity	50,000 units
Standard volume, percent of practical annual capacity	80%
Standard volume equivalent (50,000 × 80%)	40,000 units
Factory cost per unit at standard volume	$1,000
Annual factory cost of production at standard volume (40,000 × $1,000)	$40,000,000
Standard factor for fixed investment (ratio of investment to annual factory cost of production; $15,000,000 ÷ $40,000,000)	0.375

The amount tied up in working capital items should be directly proportional to the volume of business. For example, raw materials on hand should be in direct proportion to the manufacturing requirements—so many days' supply of this material, so many days' supply of that material, and so on—depending on the condition and location of sources of supply, transportation conditions, etc. Work in process should be in direct proportion to the requirements of finished production, since it is dependent on the length of time required for the material to pass from the raw to the finished state, and the amount of labor and other charges to be absorbed in the process. Finished product should be in direct proportion to sales requirements. Accounts receivable should be in direct proportion to sales, being dependent on terms of payment and efficiency of collections.

THE STANDARD PRICE

These elements are combined to construct the standard price as shown in Exhibit 1. Note that the economic return attainable (20 percent in the illustration) and the standard volume (80 percent in the illustration) are long-run figures and are rarely changed;[1] the other elements of the price are based on current estimates.

EXHIBIT 1 Illustration of Method of Determination of Standard Price

	In relation to	*Turnover per year*	*Ratio to sales annual basis*	*Ratio to factory cost annual basis*
Cash	Sales	20 times	0.050	—
Drafts and accounts receivable	Sales	10 times	0.100	—
Raw material and work-in-process	Factory cost	6 times	—	0.16⅔
Finished product	Factory cost	12 times	—	0.08⅓
Gross working capital			0.150	0.250
Fixed investment			—	0.375
Total investment			0.150	0.625
Economic return attainable, 20%			—	—
Multiplying the investment ratio by this, the necessary net profit margin is arrived at			0.030	0.125
Standard allowance for commercial expenses, 7%			0.070	—
Gross margin over factory cost			0.100 *a*	0.125 *b*

$$\text{Selling price, as a ratio to factory cost} = \frac{1+b}{1-a} = \frac{1+0.125}{1-0.100} = 1.250$$

If standard cost = \$1,000

Then standard price = \$1,000 × 1.250 = \$1,250

DIFFERENCES AMONG PRODUCTS

Responsibility for investment must be considered in calculating the standard price of each product as well as in calculating the overall price for all products, since products with identical accounting costs may be responsible for investments that vary greatly. In Exhibit 1, a uniform standard selling price of $1,250 was determined. Let us now suppose that this organization makes and sells two products, A and B, with

[1] A Brookings Institution survey reported that the principal pricing goal of General Motors Corporation in the 1950s was 20 percent on investment after taxes. See Robert F. Lanzillotti, "Pricing Objectives in Large Companies," *American Economic Review*, December 1958.

EXHIBIT 2 Variances in Standard Price Due to Variances in Rate of Capital Turnover

	Product A		Product B		Total product (A plus B)	
	Ratio to sales annual basis	*Ratio to factory cost annual basis*	*Ratio to sales annual basis*	*Ratio to factory cost annual basis*	*Ratio to sales annual basis*	*Ratio to factory cost annual basis*
Gross working capital	0.150	0.250	0.150	0.250	0.150	0.250
Fixed investment	—	0.500	—	0.250	—	0.375
Total investment	0.150	0.750	0.150	0.500	0.150	0.625
Economic return attainable, 20%	—	—	—	—	—	—
Multiplying the investment ratio by this, the necessary net profit margin is arrived at	0.030	0.150	0.030	0.100	0.030	0.125
Standard allowance for commercial expenses, 7%	0.070	—	0.070	—	0.070	—
Gross margin over factory cost	0.100	0.150	0.100	0.100	0.100	0.125
	a	*b*	*a*	*b*	*a*	*b*
Selling price, as a ratio to Factory cost $= \frac{1+b}{1-a}$	$\frac{1. + 0.150}{1. - 0.100} = 1.278$		$\frac{1. + 0.100}{1. - 0.100} = 1.222$		$\frac{1. + 0.125}{1. - 0.100} = 1.250$	
If standard cost equals	$1,000		$1,000		$1,000	
Then standard price equals	$1,278		$1,222		$1,250	

equal manufacturing costs of $1,000 per unit and equal working capital requirements, and that 20,000 units of each product are produced. However, an analysis of fixed investment indicates that $10 million is applicable to product A, while only $5 million of fixed investment is applicable to product B. Each product must earn 20 percent on its investment in order to satisfy the standard condition. Exhibit 2 illustrates the determination of the standard price for product A and product B.

From this analysis of investment, it becomes apparent that product A, which has the heavier fixed investment, should sell for $1,278, while product B should sell for only $1,222, in order to produce a return of 20 percent on the investment. Were both products sold for the composite average standard price of $1,250, then product A would not be bearing its share of the investment burden, while product B would be correspondingly overpriced.

Differences in working capital requirements as between different products may also be important due to differences in manufacturing methods, sales terms, merchandising policies, etc. The inventory turnover rate of one line of products sold by a division of General Motors Corporation may be six times a year, while inventory applicable to another line of products is turned over 30 times a year. In the second case, the inventory investment required per dollar cost of sales is only one fifth of that required in the case of the product with the slower turnover. Just as there are differences in capital requirements as between different classes of product, so may the standard requirements for the same class of product require modification from time to time due to permanent changes in manufacturing processes, in location of sources of supply, more efficient scheduling and handling of materials, etc.

The importance of this improvement to the buyer of General Motors products may be appreciated from the following example. The total inventory investment for the 12 months ended September 30, 1926, would have averaged $182,490,000 if the turnover rate of 1923 (the best performance prior to 1925) had not been bettered, or an excess of $74,367,000 over the actual average investment. In other words, General Motors would have been compelled to charge $14,873,000 more for its product during this 12-month period than was actually charged if prices had been established to yield, say, 20 percent on the operating capital required.

CONCLUSION

The analysis as to the degree of variability of manufacturing and commercial expenses with increases or decreases in volume of output, and the establishment of "standards" for the various investment items, makes it possible not only to develop "Standard Prices," but also to forecast, with much greater accuracy than otherwise would be possible, the capital requirements, profits, and return on capital at the different rates of operation, which may result from seasonal conditions or from changes in the general business situation. Moreover, whenever it is necessary to calculate in advance the final effect on net profits of proposed increases or decreases in price, with their resulting changes in volume of output, consideration of the real economics of the situation is facilitated by the availability of reliable basic data.

It should be emphasized that the basic pricing policy stated in terms of the economic return attainable is a policy, and it does not absolutely dictate the specific price. At times, the actual price may be above, and at other times below, the standard price. The standard price calculation affords a means not only of interpreting actual or proposed prices in relation to the established policy, but at the same time affords a practical demonstration as to whether the policy itself is sound. If the prevailing price of product is found to be at variance with the standard price other than to the extent due to temporary causes, it follows that prices should be adjusted; or else, in the event of conditions being such that prices cannot be brought into line with the standard price, the conclusion is necessarily drawn that the terms of the expressed policy must be modified.[2]

Questions

1. An article in *The Wall Street Journal,* December 10, 1957, gave estimates of cost figures in "an imaginary car-making division in the Ford–Chevrolet–Plymouth field." Most of the data given below are derived from that article. Using these data, compute the standard price. Working capital ratios are not given; assume that they are the same as those in Exhibit 1.

Investment in plant and other fixed assets	$600,000,000
Required return on investment	30% before income taxes
Practical annual capacity	1,250,000
Standard volume—assume	80%
Factory cost per unit:	
Outside purchases of parts	$ 500*
Parts manufactured inside	600*
Assembly labor	75
Burden	125
Total	$1,300

* Each of these items includes $50 of labor costs.

"Commercial cost," corresponding to the 7 percent in Exhibit 1, is added as a dollar amount, and includes the following:

[2] This paragraph is taken from an article by Donaldson Brown, then vice president, finance, General Motors Corporation, in *Management and Administration,* March 1924.

Inbound and outbound freight	$ 85
Tooling and engineering	50
Sales and advertising	50
Administrative and miscellaneous	50
Warranty (repairs within guarantee)	15
Total	$250

Therefore, the 7 percent commercial allowance in Exhibit 1 should be eliminated, and in its place $250 should be added to the price as computed from the formula.

2. What would happen to profits and return on investment before taxes in a year in which volume was only 60 percent of capacity? What would happen in a year in which volume was 100 percent of capacity? Assume that nonvariable costs included in the $1,550 unit cost above are $350 million; i.e., variable costs are $1,550 − $350 = $1,200. In both situations, assume that cars were sold at the standard price established in Question 1, since the standard price is not changed to reflect annual changes in volume.

3. In the 1975 model year, General Motors gave cash rebates of as high as $300 per car off the list price. In 1972 and 1973 prices had been restricted by price control legislation, which required that selling prices could be increased only if costs had increased. Selling prices thereafter were not controlled, although there was always the possibility that price controls could be reimposed. In 1975, demand for automobiles was sharply lower than in 1974, partly because of a general recession and partly because of concerns about high gasoline prices. Does the cash rebate indicate that General Motors adopted a new pricing policy in 1975, or is it consistent with the policy described in the case?

4. Is this policy good for General Motors? Is it good for America?

CASE 3–2
General Electric Company *(A)**

The General Electric Company is a large multilocation corporation engaged in the manufacture and marketing of a wide variety of electrical and allied products. In 1964, there were almost 400 separate product lines and over three million catalog items. Sales volume in that year

* Note: With the exception of the statistical information and publicly known facts presented in the introduction of this case, the sources for the facts making up the body of this case are William T. Jerome, III, *Executive Control—The Catalyst* (New York: John Wiley & Sons, 1961), pp. 217–37; and Robert W. Lewis, "Measuring, Reporting and Appraising Results of Operations with Reference to Goals, Plans and Budgets," *Planning, Managing and Measuring the Business,* A Case Study of Management Planning and Control at General Electric Company (New York: Controllership Foundation, 1955). This case was prepared by R. N. Anthony, Harvard Business School.

totaled $4,941 million, and net income was $237 million. Total employment was about 262,000.

Early in the 1950s, General Electric initiated an extensive decentralization of authority and responsibility for the operations of the company. The basic unit of organization became the product department. As of 1964, there were over 100 of these departments.

The company recognized that if this decentralization was to be fully effective it would need an improved system of management control. It also recognized that any improved system of control would require better measures of performance. To meet this need, the company established a measurements project and created a special organizational unit to carry out this project. This case summarizes the main features of this project, with particular emphasis on measuring performance of the operating (i.e., product) departments.

THE MEASUREMENTS PROJECT

The measurements project was established in 1952. Responsibility for the project was assigned to accounting services, one of the corporate functional services divisions. A permanent organizational unit, initially called measurement service, was set up to carry out this project.

An early step in the measurements project was the development of a set of principles by which the project was to be governed. Five such principles were formulated:

1. Measurements were to be designed to measure the performance of *organizational components,* rather than of *managers.*
2. Measurements were to involve common *indexes* of performance, but not common *standards* of performance. (For example, rate of return on investment might be the index of performance common to all product departments, but the standard in terms of this index might be 12 percent for one department and 25 percent for another.)
3. Measurements were to be designed as aids to judgment in appraisal of performance, and not to supplant judgment.
4. Measurements were to give proper weight to future performance as well as current performance, in order to facilitate the maintenance of a balance between the long run and the near term.
5. Measurements were to be selected so as to facilitate constructive action, not to restrict such action.

The overall measurements project was divided into three major subprojects:

1. Operational measurements of the results of a product department.

2. Functional measurements of the work of engineering, manufacturing, marketing finance, employee and plant community relations, and legal components of the organization.

3. Measurements of the work of managing as such—planning, organizing, integrating, and measuring itself.

The first step in the subproject on operational measurements was to develop an answer to the following question:

> What are the specific areas for which measurements should be designed, bearing in mind that sound measurements of overall performance require a proper balance among the various functions and among the aspects (planning, organizing, for example) of managing?[1]

In seeking an answer to this question, the organization made a careful analysis of the nature and purposes of the basic kinds of work performed by each functional unit with the purpose of singling out those functional objectives that were of sufficient importance to the welfare of the business[2] as a whole, to be termed "key result areas."

THE KEY RESULT AREAS

In order to determine whether an area tentatively identified according to the preceding analytical framework was sufficiently basic to qualify as a key result area, the organization established a criterion in the form of the following test question:

> Will continued failure in this area prevent the attainment of management's responsibility for advancing General Electric as a leader in a strong, competitive economy, even though results in all other key areas are good?[3]

As an outcome of analysis and application of this test, eight key result areas were decided on. These were as follows:

1. Profitability.
2. Market position.
3. Productivity.
4. Product leadership.
5. Personnel development.
6. Employee attitudes.
7. Public responsibility.
8. Balance between short-range and long-range goals.

Each of these key result areas is described below.

[1] Lewis, "Measuring, Reporting and Appraising Results of Operations," p. 30.

[2] The word "business" is used here to refer to a product department, not to the whole company.

[3] Ibid., p. 30.

Profitability

The key index used by General Electric to measure profitability was "dollars of residual income." Residual income was defined as net profit after taxes, less a capital charge. The capital charge was a certain percentage (say, 6 percent) of the net assets assigned to the department; it corresponded to an imputed interest charge. The criteria formulated to guide the development of a satisfactory measure of profitability were expressed as follows:

1. An index that recognized the contribution of capital investment to profits.
2. An index that recognized what human work and effort contribute to profits.
3. An index that recognized the "corporate facts of life" (e.g., one consistent with General Electric's needs and organizational objectives).
4. An index that served to make the operating decisions of individual managers in the company's best interests.

In the process of selecting and developing a measure of profitability, the measurements organization considered several more conventional indices, including rate of return on investment, ratio of profit to sales, and ratio of profit to value added. A weakness of these ratios or indices was stated in this way:

> . . . the acid test of an index should be its effectiveness in guiding decentralized management to make decisions in the best interests of the company overall, since operating managers' efforts naturally will be to improve the performance of their businesses in terms of the index used for evaluation. This test points up the particular weakness of rate of return and of other ratio indexes, such as per cent profit to sales. This weakness is the tendency to encourage concentration on improvement of the *ratios* rather than on improvement in *dollar* profits. Specifically, the business with the better results in terms of the ratios will tend to make decisions based on the effect the decisions will have on the particular business's current *ratio* without consideration of the *dollar* profits involved. This tends to retard incentive to growth and expansion because it dampens the incentive of the more profitable businesses to grow.[4]

Market Position

Performance in this key result area was measured in terms of the share of the market obtained during a given measurement period. The measurement was expressed as a percentage of available business in

[4] Ibid., p. 32.

the market. Market, as used in this sense, was expressed in dollars or units, kilowatt-ampere, or other meaningful terms.

> The first major consideration in designing market position measurements is a determination of what constitutes a product line and what constitutes the market for each product line of a business. A product line may be defined as a grouping of products in accordance with the purposes they serve or the essential wants they satisfy. The definition is somewhat misleading in that a product line may be a broad classification, such as clocks, or it may be a narrow classification, such as alarm clocks, kitchen clocks, or mantel clocks. In addition, product lines may overlap so that a particular product could be included in several product lines. Hence, the actual grouping of products by product lines must be accurately identified.
>
> There may be wide variations in the interpretation of what constitutes the market for a given product line. Therefore, it is important that for each of their lines, our product departments identify such things as:
>
> 1. Whether the market includes not only directly competing products but also indirectly competing products (electric ranges versus electric ranges; electric ranges versus all types of ranges—electric, gas, oil, and others).
> 2. Whether the market includes sales by all domestic competitors or only those reporting to trade associations.
> 3. Whether the market includes imports, if foreign sellers are competing in the domestic market.
> 4. Whether the market includes export sales.
> 5. Whether the market includes captive sales.
> 6. Whether the market is considered to be represented by sales to distributors, or to retailers, or to ultimate users.
>
> In other words, in establishing measurements of market position there should be a clear understanding of precisely what comprises the product line and what comprises the market. The purpose of having sharp definitions of these two items is, of course, to avoid being misled into thinking we are doing better than we actually are simply because of failure to identify the nature and extent of our competition.[5]

Productivity

Although the concept of productivity is a relatively simple one—a relationship of output of goods and services to the resources consumed in their production—this concept proved a difficult one to make operational as a measure of performance. For the national economy as a whole, it has been the practice to look at productivity simply in terms of the amount of output per unit of labor input. In any given firm, however, labor is only one of the factors contributing to output. There-

[5] Ibid., p. 33.

fore, the company sought to develop an index that would accomplish two things: (1) broaden the input base so as to recognize that capital as well as labor contributed to improvements in productivity, and (2) eliminate from the measure those improvements contributed by suppliers of materials.

On the output side of the productivity ratio, the company considered several refinements of sales billed. One such refinement was the use of value added (e.g., sales billed less the cost of goods or services acquired outside the company). On the input side, the company considered payroll dollars plus depreciation dollars. Payroll dollars were included in the variable, rather than labor hours, so as to give effect to differences in the labor skills employed. The inclusion of depreciation charges constituted an attempt to include the consumption of capital resources. All factors were to be readjusted for changes in the price level, so that changes in the resulting ratio would more nearly reflect real changes in productivity.

Product Leadership

Product leadership was defined as "the ability of a business to lead its industry in originating or applying the most advanced scientific and technical knowledge in the engineering, manufacturing and marketing fields to the development of new products and to improvements in the quality or value of existing products."[6] To make this definition operational, procedures were established for appraising periodically the products of each department. These appraisals were directed at providing answers to the following questions:

1. How did each product compare with competition and with company standards?
2. Where within the company was the research conducted upon which the product was based?
3. Who first introduced the basic product and subsequent improvements, General Electric or a competitor?

The appraisal procedures were based largely on qualitative rather that quantitative considerations. Appraisals were made by appropriate experts from the areas of engineering, marketing, accounting, and manufacturing. In general, these experts were located within the product department for which the appraisal was to be made. Standard forms were employed so as to facilitate as high a degree of consistency as possible. The trends revealed by these appraisals over a period of time were considered to be as significant as the specific information revealed by an appraisal for a particular period.

[6] Ibid., pp. 35–36.

Personnel Development

For the purposes of measurement, personnel development was defined as "the systematic training of managers and specialists to fill present and future needs of the company, to provide for further individual growth and retirements and to facilitate corporate growth and expansion."[7] Management of General Electric defined personnel development as including "programs in each field of functional endeavor, such as engineering, manufacturing, marketing and finance, and broad programs aimed at developing an understanding of the principles of managing. Such programs must be designed to provide a continuous flow of potentially promotable employees in sufficient numbers to permit proper selection and development of individuals for each position. And, at the same time, these programs must encourage competition and initiative for further individual growth."[8]

Three steps were involved in the measurement of performance in this key result area. (1) The basic soundness of the various programs or techniques being sponsored by a product department for the development of its employees was appraised. (2) An inventory was taken of the available supply of trained men, as well as their qualifications, for the key positions that must eventually be filled within the department. (3) The effectiveness with which the department executed its personnel development programs was evaluated.

The first step consisted of judgments regarding the adequacy of the following elements in the development process:

Recruitment. How good a job was being done in the selection of candidates for the development process?

On-the-job training. What programs were available for training candidates, for providing information and knowledge about both general company matters and job particulars, and for advanced training for those who had been on the job for a while?

Review and counsel. Was there any provision for periodically reviewing the performance of the men, for discussing with an individual the caliber of his work, for providing help and consultation, and for identifying especially promising talent?

Placement. What was being done to see that recruits were placed in jobs commensurate with their interests and abilities, that the more promising were rotated, and that promotions came to those who merited them?

The second step was accomplished with the aid of manning tables and related inventorying procedures. These procedures were directed primarily at determining the training background of each employee in the inventory; that is, graduates of company-sponsored programs,

---

[7] Ibid., p. 37.

[8] Ibid.

those hired from outside the company, and those who attained their positions without the benefit of a company-sponsored program.

The investigating group used two statistical measures in carrying out the third step. The first of these was the ratio of the number of employees promoted (both within department and through transfer to another department) in a given period (usually a year) to the total number of employees regarded as "promotable" during the same period. The second measure was tied in with the personnel rating procedure employed throughout the company. At the conclusion of each performance review cycle, the rating forms for a particular department were analyzed to determine the proportions of employees whose performance was considered to be *(a)* improving, *(b)* unchanged, and *(c)* deteriorating.

Employee Attitudes

For purposes of developing measurements of performance in this key area, the group defined an attitude as "a generalized point of view towards objects, events or persons which might serve to influence future behavior." It used two basic approaches to the measurement of attitudes. The first involved the use of statistical indicators, such as turnover rate, absenteeism, number of grievances, lateness, and accident experience. The second approach involved a periodic survey of employees through questionnaires.

Several shortcomings were recognized in the first approach. (1) The statistical indicators provided little or no information about underlying causes. (2) In general, the indicators told of trouble only after the harm had been done. (3) Because these indicators were traditionally associated with the personnel functions, managers tended to minimize their importance or else place responsibility for improvement on the personnel function. (4) Unfavorable trends in certain of these indicators might be due to external factors (e.g., short labor supply) rather than to some shortcomings of management.

The attitude survey made use of a standardized questionnaire designed to reveal the attitudes of employees in a number of broad areas. The survey was administered at intervals of about 18 months. Results for each attitude area were tabulated in terms of proportion of responses that were favorable. Tabulations were made by work groups and not by individual employees; this practice helped protect the anonymity of responses, and thus the validity of the surveys.

Public Responsibility

This key result area evolved from General Electric's recognition of its obligation to conduct itself as a good citizen within society, complying faithfully with the laws and ethics governing business conduct. The company believed its progress required not only an active recognition of the broad public interest, but also a responsiveness to certain special publics who had a stake in the success of the business—namely, shareowners, customers, employees, vendors, dealers and distributors, the plant community, educational institutions, and government.

While the responsibility to certain publics such as shareowners, educational institutions, and the federal government could best be measured from an overall company viewpoint rather than departmentally, nevertheless, the actions taken by a product department (including the individual acts of employees of that department) could have an important impact on the whole company's reputation as a good corporate citizen. Accordingly, the company attempted to assure wholehearted observance of the legal and ethical standards of business by insisting that all managerial and professional employees at least once a year conduct periodical surveys of the activities of those who reported to them with respect to antitrust compliance, conflict of interest, and other areas of business practice. These matters were discussed with each individual, who then signed a statement affirming his understanding and compliance.

Other measurements related to the effectiveness of department action in strengthening the company's reputation and business relationships. With respect to fulfilling obligations to customers, it was determined that the previously mentioned product leadership and market position areas were the best indicators. For the remaining publics, the following measures were recommended.

Shareowners. The total shares of General Electric Company stock were to be "allocated" to the various operating components that were assigned responsibility for preserving and enhancing "their portion" of the shareowners' investment in the company.

Vendors, dealers, and distributors. Suppliers of raw materials and parts were to be surveyed periodically to determine their appraisal of the department's practices in conducting its business as compared with the practices of others who bought from them. Dealers and distributors were likewise to be interviewed from time to time to measure whether these important relationships were being responsibly maintained.

Plant community. Again, comprehensive reaction surveys were to be used, aimed at identifying the impact of the actions of a product department on the individuals who made up the community. These reactions disclosed by the opinion surveys were to be supplemented by use of trends developed from various types of data such as community wage rates, number of employment applications received, volume of purchases made locally, contributions to local charities, and participation in civic, church, and business organizations.

Balance between Short-range and Long-range Goals

This factor was set out separately as a key result area in order to emphasize the importance of the long-term survival and growth of the company. Short-range goals and performance had to be balanced against the need for satisfactory performance 5, 10, 15 years in the future, since undue pressure for current profits could, in effect, borrow from the future.

Various means were employed to experiment with suggested measures in this key result area. However, it is important to note that when the eight key result areas were established, each of the first seven had both short-range and long-range dimensions. The eighth area, balance between short-range and long-range goals, had been specifically identified to make sure that the long-range health of the company would not be sacrificed for short-term gains. The plans, goals, and actions in each of the other areas were, therefore, to be appraised in terms of both their short-term and their long-term implications.

INITIAL IMPLEMENTATION

During the period after the measurements project was established in 1952, deep research work was carried on to establish the specific measurements in each of the eight key result areas. Before communicating these measures to the product departments, the investigators reviewed the recommendations in each area with operating personnel and with officers, for their comments, suggestions, and final approval.

The company's business planning, budgeting, and forecasting program incorporated the use of selected key result areas in (1) reviewing the recent history and current status, (2) setting standards for each department, (3) planning to achieve the standards, and (4) periodic reporting and measurement of accomplishment. Since the first four key result areas lent themselves readily to numerical evaluations, they were a part of the planning, budgeting, forecasting, reporting, and measuring system. Building on this experience in using the key result areas to plan and measure performance, management at the General Electric Company made the search for effective business measurements a continuing, evolutionary process.

Questions

1. For the purpose described, how should profitability be defined? The definition should be specific enough so that a quantitative measure can be constructed from it.

2. What, if anything, do the factors other than profitability add to the proposed measurement system? Isn't the impact of the other factors reflected in the profitability measure if it is properly constructed?

CASE 3–3*
Microflex, Inc.

In February 1960, Mr. Donald Sears, the recently elected president of Microflex, Inc., decided to seek outside aid in solving the company's problem of rapidly declining profits. After making some inquiries among his friends in the business community, Mr. Sears decided to contact Mr. S. T. Glickman, a professor of business administration at a nearby campus of the University of California. Mr. Sears' letter to Mr. Glickman is quoted in part below.

> We are, with increasing frequency, being asked to submit price breakdowns with our quotations. I assume that this practice will increase. [As a taxpayer, I applaud it.] We have for some years successfully competed, using what the trade calls "ball park" estimates. This method is now losing us orders in highly competitive situations. It also does not satisfy my banker's background as a proper basis on which to do our business. Finally, I am sure that as the profit margins of the large companies continue to be squeezed in this area, we will be losing more and more business on very fine margins.

Mr. Glickman responded to Mr. Sears' inquiry, and agreed to visit the Beverly Hills plant in order to learn more about the problems.

HISTORY OF MICROFLEX, INC.

Microflex, Inc., was founded in 1947 by Mr. K. T. Duncan, an engineer and an inventor who had recognized a need for high-quality flexible tubing components in aircraft manufacturing. Although the flexible metal tube (FMT) developed by Mr. Duncan was not a new product, it did incorporate certain technical improvements which he thought made his product superior to those offered by competitors. Essentially, the product was an inner core of convoluted stainless steel tubing which looked something like a cylindrical accordion. The convolutions in the inner core permitted the tubing to be expanded, compressed, or curved in any direction. In a completed assembly the inner core was covered with a metallic braid and supplied with the appropriate kind of end fitting to adapt the assembly to the ultimate use planned by the purchaser. The FMT product line manufactured by Microflex included assemblies with an inside diameter ranging from 3/16 of an inch up to 2 inches. All assemblies were produced to customers' specifications concerning the length of the assembly (up to 20 feet) and the type of end fittings to be attached.

---

* This case was prepared by Richard F. Vancil, Harvard Business School.

The Korean conflict and the accompanying increase in aircraft construction caused a rapid growth in business for Microflex during the early 1950s. Sales increased more slowly after 1955, but the high point was actually reached in 1957 when the sales volume was slightly in excess of $1,400,000. Income statements for the years 1958 and 1959 are presented in Exhibit 1. Mr. Sears thought that the recent decline in sales volume was the joint effect of a decline in the government's procurement of aircraft and the development of a new type of flexible

EXHIBIT 1

MICROFLEX, INC.
Statement of Income
For 1958 and 1959

	1959	*1958*
Net sales	$1,279,810	$1,321,056
Cost of goods sold:		
Raw materials used	$ 432,706	$ 423,742
Factory labor	285,833	282,718
Experimental materials and supplies	21,614	17,902
Outside labor	14,432	24,842
Factory expense	40,985	38,263
Heat, light, and power	8,080	7,084
Insurance	6,701	6,214
Depreciation	39,334	34,166
Freight	9,038	13,508
Repairs	2,774	5,278
Rent	8,381	4,130
Truck expense	784	1,384
Cost of goods sold	870,662	859,231
Gross profit	409,148	461,825
Administrative, selling, and other expenses:		
Executive salaries	54,347	49,502
Office and sales salaries	99,900	82,415
Sales commissions	81,704	73,120
Telephone and telegraph	16,515	13,363
Travel and entertainment	24,651	29,018
London office	23,115	—
Taxes: Property	3,738	3,232
Payroll	19,496	17,813
Office supplies	8,692	11,960
Postage, dues, subscriptions, etc.	2,910	2,128
Legal and audit services	12,583	8,773
Advertising	15,488	4,632
Employee's Blue Cross	2,861	46
Total expenses	366,000	296,002
Operating profit	43,148	165,823
Other income and expense (net)	1,927	(3,033)
Profit before taxes	41,221	168,856
State and federal income taxes	16,400	86,203
Net income	$ 24,821	$ 82,643

assembly, with a plastic inner core, by several of Microflex's competitors. The profit decline in 1959 was, in Mr. Sears' opinion due primarily to poor control of factory labor costs. One of his first actions as president had been to conduct a thorough review of the problem. "Over the last three months," he told Mr. Glickman, "we've increased productivity enormously. Our current factory force is down 40 percent from the 1959 levels, and only a fraction of that is due to the lower volume."

Early in 1959, Mr. Duncan, then in his early 60s, decided to retire from active management of the business and live abroad. He was able to persuade Mr. Donald J. Sears, then a vice president of a large Los Angeles bank, to accept the position as president. Mr. Sears assumed his duties in October 1959. Mr. Duncan retained 100 percent stock ownership of the corporation, but Mr. Sears was granted certain stock options which were designed to permit him to acquire a significant percentage of the company's equity if he so desired. Mr. Duncan assumed the title of director of foreign operations, and from his London office he planned to promote the sale of Microflex's products in Europe and to search for new products for the company. A final executive change in the fall of 1959 was the election of Mr. Lesley Curry to the newly created position of controller.

FACILITIES

As a starting point for his investigation, Mr. Glickman decided to examine in greater detail the previous pricing policies of the company. First, he made a tour of the company's production facilities. All the company's administrative and manufacturing departments were housed in one steel building, consisting of four bays of about 3,000 square feet each. One of these bays was used for offices, and the other three were the factory, with usage as follows:

	Square feet
Machining	2,800
Welding	800
Assembly and final inspection	1,600
Parts inspection	600
Storeroom	1,500
Shipping	300
Carpenter shop	500
Lavatories and miscellaneous	900
Total	9,000

In addition to this space, which the company owned, approximately 5,000 square feet of space was rented at another location. Of this, 4,500 square feet was used for various production operations, and 500 feet was used as an office.

PRODUCTION

An FMT assembly was not inherently complex in a technical sense, but because of the end use of the product, the assembly had to be produced to meet rigid "aircraft" specifications. As a result, a significant number of the factory employees were engaged in inspection and quality control activities rather than in direct manufacturing. All inner core (hose) and outer covering (braid) were purchased from outside vendors. Because of satisfactory quality control by these vendors, the company did not inspect hose and braid (except for a quick visual inspection) until the final assembly was pressure tested for leaks or other defects just prior to shipping. End fittings were either purchased outside or manufactured in the company's machining department. Parts purchased outside were subjected to a rigid inspection of all critical dimensions before each lot was accepted. Parts manufactured by Microflex from aluminum or stainless steel bar stock were carefully inspected as they came off the machines. Only parts which passed inspection were allowed to enter the storeroom, where they were housed until issued for use on a specific production order. In the assembly department, the hose and braid were cut to appropriate lengths according to customers' specifications, and the end fittings were attached either mechanically or by welding or brazing.

At Mr. Glickman's request, the accounting department prepared an analysis by function of the factory employees on the payroll during 1959.

Analysis of factor labor, 1959	*Payroll*
Machining	$ 69,380
Welding and brazing department	34,339
Assembly department	60,853
Experimental work on new products	46,819
Parts inspection	14,483
Assembly inspection	18,999
Storeroom	9,968
Shipping	6,074
General maintenance	20,401
Truck drivers	4,517
Total	$285,833

PRICING POLICIES

Mr. Glickman asked the sales manager, Mr. C. F. Wheaton, to describe the company's pricing procedures and any other background information pertinent to the current problem. Mr. Wheaton explained that Microflex employed no field salesmen, and that all orders were received through a firm of manufacturer's representatives called Technical Products Distributors, Inc., (TPD).

Mr. Wheaton felt that for a company the size of Microflex, the use of a manufacturer's representative was not only more economical than using salesmen, but also permitted the company to get a broader and more intensive coverage of its market. Microflex paid TPD a 7 percent commission on all orders (including repeat orders) received from customers serviced by TPD. Mr. Wheaton personally dealt with one nearby customer, and orders received from this customer were the only source of business to Microflex which were not subject to the 7 percent commission.

The primary function of the TPD salesmen was to convince the purchaser that Microflex might be the best supplier for the part desired and to secure the purchaser's permission for Microflex to submit a quote on the part. Almost all Microflex's orders resulted from such bids. If the customer agreed to solicit a bid from Microflex, detailed specifications for the required assembly were forwarded to Microflex, either directly by the customer or through the TPD salesman. Typically, purchasing agents in the aircraft industry would request quotes from two or more suppliers. For small components such as those manufactured by Microflex, however, the purchasing agent would rarely bother to solicit more than three price quotations.

All price quotations were prepared by Mr. Wheaton and his staff, using cost information provided by the production manager. Mr. Wheaton said that, depending on the level of business activity, his department prepared from 200 to 400 price quotations each month, and usually received between 100 to 200 orders per month. It was a rare order that exceeded 50 assemblies, and the usual order quantity was from 3 to 30 units.

Mr. Wheaton explained that during the early 1950s, when the company was growing very rapidly, the method of determining price quotations had been quite informal. As an example of the way that he determined a price, he found in his files the worksheet that he had prepared for a part quoted in the summer of 1959.

	Quoted July 10,1959
Part No. 6794:	
Material cost	$ 8.16
Multiplier	2.50
Total cost	20.40
Percent commission	1.60
Total selling price	22.00

To arrive at the price of $22 per unit, Mr. Wheaton had first asked the production manager for an estimate of the material cost in the assembly. The estimated cost of $8.16 represented the actual cost of purchased materials such as hose, braid, and certain end fittings, plus the production manager's estimate of the cost to Microflex for producing in its own machine shop the remaining end fittings which were not purchased outside. Mr. Wheaton then multiplied this material cost by a "factor" of 2.5. This factor varied, he said, depending upon his feel for the market and the reasonableness of the final price he arrived at. A 7 percent commission for TPD was then added to total cost to arrive at the total selling price. On this quotation for part No. 6794, Microflex received the order.

For Part No. 4791, Mr. Wheaton produced his worksheet for a very large FMT assembly which had been quoted on in February 1959.

	Quoted February 18, 1959	
Part No. 4791:		
End fittings cost	$ 45.00	
Multiplier	2	
Total for end fitting		$ 90.00
Hose and braid cost	172.00	
Multiplier	1.5	
Total for hose and braid		258.00
Total cost		348.00
Commission		26.00
Total selling price		374.00

The pricing procedure for this part was essentially the same as for part No. 6794, except that in this case different multipliers were used for the cost of hose and braid. Mr. Wheaton explained that to use a large multiplier on this assembly, where the cost of materials was very great, would result in a price which was too high to be successful. Microflex was successful in this price quotation and received an order for six units at a price of $374 each.

In the summer of 1959, the volume of new orders received by Microflex began to decline sharply. Mr. Wheaton knew that this decline, in part, was due to the fact that the volume of business in the aircraft industry was declining. According to the TPD salesman with whom Mr. Wheaton was in frequent contact, however, Microflex was suffering more from the decline than were its competitors. Apparently this was due to the fact that, as the volume of available business shrank, some suppliers were lowering their price quotations in an effort to achieve a greater percentage of the available business. In the face of this increasing competition, Mr. Wheaton had begun to feel less and less satisfied with his pricing procedures. He said that he had never been really "comfortable" with the method of pricing that he had been using, because it relied to a great extent on his personal judgment and his feel for the market. He pointed out that since he had very little direct contact with his customers, he did not think that his feel for the market was sensitive enough to measure the need for a small reduction in prices. Furthermore, he was uncertain as to the extent to which Microflex could reduce its prices and still operate profitably. Mr. Wheaton did not know how much prices needed to be cut in order to meet his competition, because the purchasing agents usually would not divulge to the unsuccessful bidder the price that had been quoted by the successful supplier.

Another fault with the old method of determining prices was that when Mr. Wheaton was out of the office, price quotations would be prepared by his assistant or other members of his staff, and these people might use a multiplier different from the one Mr. Wheaton might have used.

Finally, Mr. Wheaton pointed out, the aircraft companies had recently been taking greater interest in their suppliers' costs, and Microflex had received several requests from its customers to provide detailed cost information. As an example of these requests, Mr. Wheaton showed Mr. Glickman forms received from a major aircraft manufacturer. (Exhibit 2.) Mr. Glickman knew that, under federal procurement regulations, these companies had a right to demand submission of these data.

Mr. Wheaton was concerned about the reasons why these manufacturers wanted the cost information. He had discussed the matter with several TPD salesmen, and their impression was that the purchasing departments of the aircraft manufacturers examined the cost breakdowns to make sure that the suppliers costs were approximately in line with what was considered reasonable in the industry. For example, factory overhead rates usually exceeded 200 percent of direct labor costs, but an overhead rate in excess of 300 percent was considered unacceptable unless supported by a detailed explanation of the allowable costs included in the overhead. Similarly, the administrative overhead rate usually ran from 20 to 30 percent of factory cost. Sales commissions, identified as such, were not chargeable on government contracts, and the government was reluctant to allow a profit margin in excess of 10 percent of the total price.

Mr. Wheaton knew that Microflex was not bound by these industry practices in quoting prices to aircraft companies and, in fact, cost breakdowns were usually not requested with the original price quotation. The problem was that, after Microflex was notified that it had received an order, the customer might then request the company to supply a cost breakdown to support the quoted price. In response to these requests, Mr. Wheaton prepared a set of figures that arrived at the required total amount, based on estimates of labor and material costs which allowed an overhead percentage that did not appear too

EXHIBIT 2

VENDOR COST BREAKDOWN (PRODUCTION)

VENDOR PART NUMBER ________

COMPANY ____________________ BOEING PART NUMBER ________ Date ______

Cost Breakdown for ______ Units – We have previously manufactured ______ Units
(Qty.) (Qty.)

A separate Cost Breakdown should be made for each quantity quoted

Direct Labor:		Rate/Hour	Total	Overhead %	Overhead Dollars	$ PER UNIT
Fabrication	____	____	____	____	____	
Processing	____	____	____	____	____	
Subassembly	____	____	____	____	____	
Final Assembly	____	____	____	____	____	
Testing	____	____	____	____	____	
If classified as Direct Labor:						
Planning	____	____	____	____	____	
Inspection	____	____	____	____	____	
Tool Maintenance	____	____	____	____	____	
Packaging & Shipping	____	____	____	____	____	
Other (explain)	____	____	____	____	____	
Total Direct Labor plus Overhead on Direct Labor						

Material	Dollars	$ Scrap	Total	Overhead %	Overhead Dollars	$ PER UNIT
Raw Material	____	____	____	____	____	
Purchased Parts	____	____	____	____	____	
Subcontracted						
Material	____	____	____	____	____	
Labor	____	____	____	____	____	
Total Direct Material plus Overhead on Direct Material						

Engineering: (sustaining) ______ % of ____________________

Other: ______ % (explain) ____________________

Total Manufacturing Cost ....

General & Administrative: ______ %

Other: ______ % (explain) ____________________

Profit: ______ % ....

TOTAL ....

Nonrecurring Cost	Dollars
Engineering ______ Hours @ $ ______ per Hour	
Tooling ______ Hours @ $ ______ per Hour	
Tooling Material Cost	
Qualification ______ Hours @ $ ______ per Hour	
Other Nonrecurring Cost (explain) ____________________	
____________________	
____________________	
Total Nonrecurring Cost	

Nonrecurring Cost Amortized ______ Units ....
(Qty.)

TOTAL UNIT SELLING PRICE TO BOEING ....

____

By (Signature) – Title

high and a total cost breakdown that conformed to industry standards. He had never received any requests for further information about his cost breakdowns. He was not sure how he would respond if an auditor from one of his customers showed up to verify the cost information he had supplied.

NEW PRICING METHODS

Mr. Wheaton's first recommendation to the new president, Mr. Sears, was that a new method of pricing be devised. Mr. Sears, Mr. Curry, and Mr. Wheaton then worked together exploring alternative pricing mechanisms. In November 1959, a large aircraft manufacturer asked Microflex to submit separate price quotations for 19 different types of FMT assemblies. Microflex's management group decided to use this series of price quotations as a test of several different pricing formulas. The result of the experience was that Microflex received orders for only 3 of the 19 components. TPD salesmen were normally unable to receive competitive price data, but because of the experimental nature of these price quotations, the salesman was able to obtain the lowest bid on each component. In 16 instances, the successful bid was from 5 percent to 50 percent lower than Microflex's price, with the average successful bid from 10 to 20 percent lower than Microflex. Mr. Wheaton showed Mr. Glickman the worksheets for several quotations used in this experiment.

The quotation for part No. 5797 was one of the three successful ones in the experiment. Mr. Wheaton pointed out that the only significant difference between the two parts was that No. 5797 had a lower direct labor cost in relation to direct material cost than No. 7243 had.

The method used to quote on part No. 6792 was quite different from any procedure the company had ever used before, and represented the results of Mr. Curry's analysis of available cost information. Under this new procedure, material cost was the estimated purchase cost to Microflex and was not multiplied by any factor. Machining and assembly labor were costed at $2 per hour, factory overhead was then added at the rate of $5.08 for each labor hour, and general and administrative overhead was added at a rate of $5.69 for each labor hour. A profit equal to 12.5 percent of the total cost was then added to arrive at the total selling price. Microflex was the successful bidder on part No. 6792, but this same method of price determination was used on 10 other parts in the experiment and, in each case, a competitor quoted a lower price than Microflex. In spite of this low success ratio using the new method, Mr. Wheaton thought it was an improvement over the old method because it added overhead based on direct labor costs, a procedure which was more in line with the normal costing formulas in the industry. He was still concerned, however, because Microflex's overhead rates, particularly the administrative overhead rate, was much higher than the industry "norm."

	Quoted November 17, 1959
Part No. 5797:	
Material cost $33.62 × 1.5*	$ 50.43
Machining and assembly labor:	
0.5 hours at $3.00 × 3*	4.50
Total cost	54.93
Commission	4.15
Total selling price	59.08
Part No. 7243:	
Material cost $33.62 × 1.5*	50.43
Machining and assembly labor:	
1.5 hours at $3.00 × 3*	13.50
Total cost	63.93
Commission	4.80
Total selling price	68.73
Part No. 6792:	
Material cost	68.58
Machining and assembly labor:	
3.5 hours at $2.00	7.00
Factory overhead 3.5 hours at $5.08	17.78
General and administrative overhead	
3.5 hours at $5.69	19.92
Total cost	113.28
Profit 12.5% of cost	14.16
Total selling price	127.43

* Multiplier.

Since the November experiment, Mr. Wheaton told Mr. Glickman that he had continued to use a variety of pricing formulas, none of which had appeared to be more successful than any other. His enthusiasm for the new pricing formula had waned because of the results it had produced on several occasions.

	Quoted December 4, 1959
Part No. 3472:	
Material cost	$ 6.21
Assembly labor .71 hours at $2.00	1.42
Overhead .71 hours at $10.77	7.65
	15.28
Profit 12.5% of cost	1.91
Total selling price	17.19

Microflex had produced part No. 3472 for the same customer early in 1958 at price of $18.10 per unit. As was usually the case when a customer reordered after a lapse of several months, the customer had requested a new price quotation before placing a new order. Mr. Wheaton finally decided not to lower the price to that indicated by the pricing formula. The customer had placed an order for 15 units when Mr. Wheaton informed him that the previous price of $18.10 was still effective.

	Quoted January 11, 1960
Part No. 5726:	
Material cost	$ 9.84
Assembly labor, .72 hours at $10.17	7.32
Total cost	17.16
Profit 12.5% of cost	2.15
Total selling price	19.31

The request for a price quotation on part No. 5726 was also a reorder. The original price on this component had been $27. In this instance, Mr. Wheaton decided to lower the price for the reorder to $23.10 per unit, and the customer had accepted the new price.

Near the end of their conversation, Mr. Wheaton showed Mr. Glickman a request for a price quotation received that morning. The customer wished to reorder part No. 2764. The original order on this part had been placed in early May 1959 at a price of $27.38.

In deciding whether or not to change the original price, Mr. Wheaton had figured what the price on this part should be, using the new pricing formula.

Since the price using the new method was nearly twice that computed by the old method, Mr. Wheaton examined the two calculations carefully. He pointed out that the cost of materials to Microflex had not changed significantly during the period. The $8.50 cost for end fittings used in the original price quotation had represented the production manager's estimate of the cost of nuts, which were purchased outside, plus the cost of other end fittings which were manufactured by Microflex, using $0.94 worth of bar stock and 2.3 hours of machining labor. When these costs were set out separately and the new pricing formula applied to them, the result was to increase the indicated price on the part to $51.85. Mr. Wheaton thought that the new pricing formula was more accurate than the old one, and it was obvious to him that the company had lost money on the part when it was produced at a price of $27.38. Nevertheless, he was sure that, if he quoted the price of $51.85 to the customer, his bid would be rejected. Mr. Wheaton asked Mr. Glickman what price should be charged for this article, and Mr. Glickman said that he would like to look at the cost records more carefully before attempting to answer the question.

	Quoted May 1959
Part No. 2764:	
End fittings cost—\$8.50 × 2*	\$17.00
Hose and braid cost—\$5.09 × 1.5*	7.64
Total cost	24.64
Commission 7.5%	1.85
Total selling price	26.49

* Multiplier.

		New quote requested in February 1960
Part No. 2764:		
Material cost:		
Hose and braid		\$ 5.09
Nuts (purchased)		1.12
Bar stock		0.94
Labor:		
Machining	2.30 hours	
Assembly	.75 hours	
	3.05 hours at \$2.00	6.10
Factory overhead	3.05 hours at \$5.08	15.49
General and administrative overhead	3.05 hours at \$5.69	17.35
Total cost		46.09
Profit 12.5% of cost		5.76
Total selling price		51.85

ADDITIONAL COST INFORMATION

At Mr. Glickman's request, Mr. Curry described the accounting system used by Microflex. Mr. Curry said that his system was quite simple to operate because the company used only one income account for all sales, and maintained 25 expense accounts, as shown in Exhibit 1. The depreciation expense account included depreciation on both the building and equipment and, Mr. Curry said, roughly 50 percent of the total was for the building alone. The Outside Labor Expense account received a variety of charges for miscellaneous services performed by outside contractors. For 1959 the detail was as follows:

Outside Labor—1959	
Special services requested by customers:	
Packing and crating	\$ 3,462.33
Rust proofing	2,278.95
X-ray and other special testing	3,998.50
Plating	606.51
Parking lot repairs	990.49
Pumping septic tank	982.49
Unclassified	2,113.49
Total	\$14,432.27

The Factory Expense account received an even greater variety of charges. Mr. Curry explained that it would be almost impossible to analyze all the transactions in this account during 1959, because the goods and services received had been purchased from more than 100 vendors. Mr. Glickman asked that an effort be made to pull out the most significant items included in the expense account, and the following analysis was prepared after several hours of work by a clerk in the accounting department.

Factory Expense—1959	
Manufacturing supplies and small tools	$13,488.17
Welding and brazing materials	4,487.01
Inspection gauges and supplies	2,253.50
Packing and shipping supplies	2,993.21
Drafting supplies and equipment	1,414.35
Building maintenance supplies and services	1,333.82
Unclassified invoices	15,015.32
Total	$40,985.38

The Freight account was primarily the expense incurred by Microflex on incoming shipments of supplies and materials purchased by Microflex. On most shipments of finished goods, freight was paid by the customer, but in some cases where freight cost was absorbed by Microflex, the expense was charged into the Freight account.

Mr. Glickman also asked Mr. Curry for the following analysis of the office and sales salaries during 1959.

Analysis of office and sales salaries, 1959	*Payroll*
Shop foreman	$ 5,760
Production and manager and staff	21,000
Purchasing agent and clerk	7,800
Drafting department	14,100
Controller and clerk	11,280
Office manager, receptionist, and secretaries	16,560
Sales manager and staff	23,400
Total	$99,900

Mr. Curry said that he would be happy to provide Mr. Glickman with any additional information he desired, if this information could be obtained from the available accounting records.

Questions

1. Do you think the list of 25 expense accounts (Exhibit 1) provides adequate detail for management purposes? What new accounts, if any, would you establish?

2. Using the account structure you recommend in Question 1, classify the accounts according to whether you consider the expense to represent

(*a*) direct labor, (*b*) direct material, or (*c*) overhead. What subdivisions within the overhead group (factory overhead, selling overhead, and so forth) would you recommend?

3. Using the expense classification you prepared in Question 2, devise a pricing formula for Microflex which you believe Mr. Wheaton and his staff should use for pricing new business and reorders. What price should be quoted for part No. 2764 in February 1960?

CHAPTER 4

Information

It has always been with us and it is now the base of management control systems. At first unnamed, ages and ages ago, it was merely the perceived experiences each human being sensed and stored in his or her brain for use at some future time in deciding what to do or not to do in a particular situation. Then several ancestors of ours, of an unusual bent, started making gestures to describe to one another their experiences and the product, known as information, came into being. Gradually, the gestures gave way to verbal ejaculations and these, over time, assumed uniform meanings until a verbal language emerged for the identification of things and actions. This development enabled people, in deciding what or what not to do, to access not only information about their personal experiences but also information about the experiences and thoughts of others.

But these early developments in information and communication were inadequate to overcome the limited ability of the human mind to recall past experiences and the limits of the ill-structured verbal communication process. Then one happy day one human being, possibly a descendent of those with the unusual bent, developed a symbol to represent a verbal word and these symbols multiplied and grew until the written word became a means of storing information for future recall and for communicating information from one person to another. Soon the written word expanded to include the written number and the measurement dimension of information development came into being. These developments were followed by the printing press and telecommunication, and man's ability to control the environment and improve the human lot increased.

But as the amount of information available to every human being increased, the total cost of developing it (collecting, printing, and delivering) increased as well, though the unit cost per bit of information has likely decreased. Then information, in the form of books, reports, or telephone messages, became an economic product to be bought and sold like any other commodity.

Consistently and increasingly the production and sale of information has increased until today the technology devoted to the production and delivery of reliable and relevant information represents one of the world's greatest assets.

Before going further in our systematic drift to the realization that the management control system is to a large degree an information system and that ways of developing information are constantly improving, we need to understand something about the notion of information as a product developed, among others, in management control systems. Let us examine the nature of information, its costs, and the amount and value of it.

NATURE OF INFORMATION

In our society, and in most of the world, information pervades every nook and cranny of our lives. Information is a stimulus that motivates us to take one action, rather than another, or even to act at all. While man has several organs (eye, ear, tongue, skin, nose) to receive direct stimuli that lead to action, in this complex interrelated world we use information, more than all else, to guide and direct us to the satisfaction of our wants and needs. We continuously develop new information by new processes and communicate it with new methods. Those who develop and use management control systems need to have more than cursory knowledge of the product and the processes, because, as Norbert Weiner has suggested, organizations are held together by "the possession of means for the acquisition, use, retention and transmission of information."[1]

What then is the nature of this wonderful product that influences our lives so extensively and in so many ways? Some years ago, C. West Churchman defined information as "recorded experience which is useful for decision-making."[2] In organizations, information comes in so many shapes and forms, both quantitative and qualitative, that it is frequently difficult to determine which recorded experience is decision useful and can be included as part of management control systems. Consideration of three overlapping dominant basic characteristics, listed below, will help us in developing management control systems.

1. From a management control system perspective, the most useful definition of information is that it is a product that *reduces uncertainty* about which act to perform or *reassures* a decision maker

---

[1] Norbert Weiner, *Cybernetics: Control and Communications in the Animal and the Machine* (Cambridge, Mass.: MIT Press, 1965), p. 161.

[2] C. West Churchman, *Prediction and Optimal Decision* (Englewood Cliffs, N.J.: Prentice-Hall), 1961, p. 100.

about a prior action. The businessman with the options of buying either product A or product B is given information when the management control system reveals that product A will contribute more to organization strategy.

2. A second characteristic of information is that it may perform an *awareness function.* When management control systems have a responsibility for contributing to the development of organization strategies, in addition to the primary responsibility of assuring that strategies are carried out, a definition of information as a product that reveals possible opportunities for organization action is a useful guide. This definition complements the first role of information by assuring that more alternative courses of actions are considered by the decision maker.
3. A third characteristic of information is that it serves the *evaluation function.* It is relevant to the aspect of management control systems that discloses the extent that planned actions and expected outcomes are realized.

The characteristics are not directly useful in developing management control systems, but they are background concepts useful in identifying the type of information to be used in management control systems. To illustrate the process involved, a teacher given the task of implementing the strategy of educating students to use management control systems must tell the students what is expected of them (reduce their uncertainty about what action to take), must present the material in such a way that students perceive additional areas they need to study (make them aware of additional opportunities), and must give them grades on their performance (evaluate the extent that planned accomplishments were realized). The management control system might provide some information useful to the teacher in developing the strategy, but it is in developing information to see that the strategy is carried out that the three characteristics of information guide the selection of appropriate measures of performance.

Clearly, there is no way of knowing how well the teacher's instructions reduced the uncertainty of students about what action to take. Surrogate measures of the desired information are used, and we ask the students what action they are taking and use those responses to measure the teacher's effectiveness. Similarly, in giving grades to students for their performance, the teacher uses the results of an examination to estimate student performance.

The surrogate measures and the development of improved surrogates of things in management control systems provide the information product we shall examine in detail later; but the criterion used to identify good surrogates is the extent to which it possesses one or more of the three characteristics of information. For example, a comparison of a measure of actual performance in a month or year with budgeted performance is a common management control system measure used to help implement a long-term strategy. The comparison measure is a surrogate measure and may not reflect actual performance well, particularly if a manager were motivated to beat the budget rather than implement the strategy.

So just as it does not make much sense for a management control system to develop behavioral measures to motivate a manager by providing a reward of prestige when the manager wants more money, it does not make much sense for a management control system to develop short-term performance measures (monthly budget/actual comparisons) when the manager is pursuing a long-term strategy not reflected in the financial budget. The manager will not pay any attention to such measures. They do not possess any of the characteristics of information and have no information content.

Years of experience, however, indicate that most management control system measures do help carry out organization strategies, but we should not accept them blindly—and improvement is always possible. One concept helpful in developing measures that provide information is the value of information.

Value of Information

Suppose an oil company can buy drilling rights to some property for \$10 million, and it is convinced that the \$10 million investment would be worthwhile if the property contained at least 5 million barrels of crude oil. It is uncertain as to how much oil the property does contain. It can reduce this uncertainty by obtaining additional information. For example it can conduct additional seismic shots, or it can ask the opinion of a petroleum geologist. In order to obtain this information, it must incur additional costs. Information theory describes a technique for deciding how much the company can afford to pay for this additional information. Since the technique is usually described in the context of problems involving sampling, the amount that the company can afford to pay is called the *expected value of sample information.*

More generally, the approach can be used to describe the nature of an optimum information system in a company. In an optimum system, the difference between the expected value of sample information furnished by the system and the cost of obtaining this information is at a maximum.

There are severe limitations to the use of information theory in the real world, however. A fundamental problem is that the expected value of information depends on the decision maker's judgment. If the petroleum company, on the basis of information now available, is already pretty well convinced that the property does contain at least 5 million barrels of crude oil, additional information is much less valuable to it than would be the case if it were more uncertain about the true state of nature; that is, the actual quantity of crude oil. Information theory provides a technique for probing the decision maker's own judgment as to how valuable such additional information would be, but the technique requires the identification of the decision maker's *subjective probabilities* (i.e., his current belief as to the likelihood that various quantities of crude oil exist on the property) and his *utiles* (i.e., how strongly he feels about the necessity for making the right decision). In order to identify these amounts, a lengthy dialogue between the decision maker and the analyst is required, and its outcome is tentative at best. Thus, although the approach has the appearance of being objective, the values used in the technique actually are highly subjective.

Furthermore, the theory requires that there be a clear specification of the problem under consideration and of the nature and cost of the additional information that might be purchased as an aid in making the decision. Most business problems are not that clear-cut. In the usual case, the problem is not sharply defined and there are several alternative solutions. Moreover, information in an information system is used for several purposes, and it is usually not feasible to associate a specific piece of information with a specific problem and hence compare its value with its cost.

Finally, many decision makers draw on the information that flows through an information system. The problem of quantifying the judgments of each of them as to the expected value of additional information can be insuperable.

Thus, the practical application of information theory is limited to problems like the oil well drilling rights situation described above; that is, problems in which the decision is both important enough to warrant the expenditure of much management time in quantifying the value of additional information and also specific enough so that the nature of additional information that might be obtained, the extent to which it will reduce the decision maker's uncertainty, and its cost, can all be stated.[3]

For our purposes, this aspect of information theory provides only some useful general notions (which could perhaps be derived equally well by common sense): The purpose of information is to reduce a decision maker's uncertainty about the "state of nature," that is, about what is the actual situation in the real world; and the value of additional information should exceed its cost.

These general notions are helpful in analyzing information systems even though the value of the information cannot be measured.

One application is that if no one uses a given piece of information, it follows that the information has no value, and the cost of collecting and

[3] For a thorough explanation of the technique and how to apply it to such problems, see Howard Raiffa, *Decision Analysis: Introductory Lectures on Choices under Uncertainty* (Reading, Mass.: Addison-Wesley Publishing Co., Inc., 1968).

disseminating the information is therefore wasted. Useless information exists more often than is commonly supposed. It is collected because at one time there was a need for it, but it continues to be collected even though the need has vanished. For example, during the early 1970s, when selling prices were controlled, many companies set up elaborate systems that were used to justify proposed price increases to the federal authorities. Some companies continued these systems long after price controls were discontinued.

Reporting information in more detail than is useful is another example of costs that exceed the value of the information; in fact, too much detail may actually detract from its value. For example, consider the following report:

	Sales, Current Week		
Territory	*Actual*	*Budget*	*Variance*
A	$103,537.82	$102,600.000	$ 937.82
B	58,026.28	51,300.00	6,726.28
C	86,273.99	76,660.00	9,673.99
D	75,337.20	80,300.00	(4,962.80)
E	146,482.31	152,400.00	(5,917.69)
F	107,386.47	110,400.00	(3,013.53)
etc.			

Readers could learn all they need to know about the sales volume in each territory, relative to that in other territories and relative to the budget, if these numbers were reported in rounded off form:

	Sales, Current Week (000 omitted)		
Territory	*Actual*	*Budget*	*Variance*
A	$103.5	$102.6	$ 0.9
B	58.0	51.3	6.7
C	86.3	76.7	9.7
D	75.3	80.3	(5.0)
E	146.5	152.4	(5.9)
F	107.4	110.4	(3.0)

MANAGEMENT CONTROL INFORMATION

In management control, information is used for planning, coordinating, and evaluating. Different types of information are needed for each activity and, within each, the relevant information depends on the situation, environment, behavior desired, and cost and value of the information. We shall discuss the specifics of the use of information later, and consider now some general comments on the nature of information that is used for the management control system.

Information for Planning

Investigating what to do and how to do it is referred to as "planning." Information helpful for this function is future-oriented, and a significant part of it is obtained from external sources, though past experience is obviously the starting base in planning future activities.

Planning information frequently contains information about a previously unknown uncertainty. Whether new opportunities for actions arise from research within the organization or from changes in the environment, good planning needs information about new possible courses of actions.

The management control system should be so designed that it monitors well the environment and solicits ideas from everyone in the organization for new opportunities. Essentially, the management control system should collect information from sources such as the following:

1. The internal diary of organization activities (accounting, marketing, and production).
2. Actions of competitors (advertising, cost statistics).
3. Developments in the industry (product improvements, new products and services).
4. Government actions (policies, treaties, court decisions, regulations).
5. General economic conditions (price level, economic activity, demand shifts).

Information for Coordinating

The best laid plans of mice and men often go astray, so the poet wrote, and we all know that the other person caused it. How, then, should the organization develop cooperation among all the people associated with the organization; and what kind of information is needed to help coordinate the activities of each so the organization will function as a unified whole? Telling people is not enough. Information for coordination is largely the uncertainty-reduction type of information. To reduce the uncertainty of workers about what to do and when to do it, and how to do it efficiently and effectively, the coordinating information needs to be as precise as possible and unambiguous, except by design. Possibly for that reason, coordinating information uses numbers for budgets, standards, and even objectives. Communication research suggests that redundancy (saying the same thing several times in the information transmission) should be used to reduce uncertainty. Coordinating information includes such items as detailed budgets and standards, job procedure manuals, statement of organization goals and subunit objectives, authority and responsibilities, policy guidelines, and detailed plans of various types. It aims to assure that everyone in the organization is sufficiently informed to be able to perform well for the total organization. It leaves to other aspects of control the task of motivating people to do what they should do and evaluating their performance.

The management control system is designed to provide, to appropriate people, information for coordination in the most suitable form to assure realization of organization goals.

Information for Evaluation

Exhibit 4–1 is a diagram of the essentials of the entire management control process. It provides a basis for making comments about the type of information that is useful in management control, generally, and in the management control system, in particular.

EXHIBIT 4–1 Information Flow in the Control Process

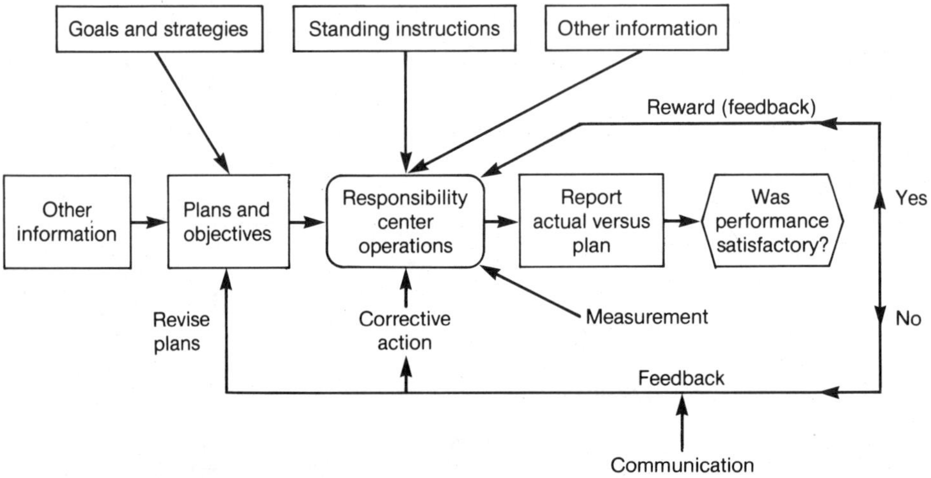

Note: Lines indicate flow of information (i.e., messages).

The management control process starts with the preparation of plans that, if completed, will help realize the goals and objectives of the organization. These plans are made within the context of the strategies decided on in the strategic planning process. They are expressed as programs, budgets, objectives, and in other terms.

Each responsibility center manager uses the organization plans as a guide to its operations, including task planning. The comprehensive organization plans are not a complete guide, because operations also are influenced by current information from both external and internal sources. Such information may suggest that operations should not proceed in exact conformance with the plan. If the production budget was based on a sales estimate of $1 million and the current estimate is that sales will be $1.5 million, the actual operating production schedule should take account of this new information.

Standing instructions. In addition to information about plans for a specified time period or a specified project, managers are provided information about the types of action they are expected to take, or to refrain from taking, under various circumstances. These may be called "standing instructions." They may be informal (in the sense of an understanding that "this is the way we do things in this company"), or they may be formal and written in procedures manuals or similar documents. They seldom refer to a specific time period and remain in effect until they are changed.

The nature of these standing instructions varies among companies. For some organizations, they may not be extensive. On the other hand, the larger and more complex the company, the greater the number and degree of detail of the formal standing instructions. This is necessary to assure that employees throughout the company handle similar problems in a consistent manner. For example, a large chain of retail stores usually has detailed instructions, including report forms, for handling customer complaints of various types; whereas in a small, independent store, the manager probably would use his or her personal judgment in handling customer complaints, without formal rules. Standing instructions are often characterized as red tape, and organizations having a number of them are called "bureaucracies," with both terms intended to be derogatory; however, large and complex organizations could not operate efficiently without them.

Standing instructions also vary, depending on the level of organization. At lower levels, they tend to be stated in considerable detail, with relatively little latitude permitted in their application. At higher levels, they are stated in more general terms and allow considerable room for judgment. Some, such as instructions forbidding the acceptance of bribes or discrimination in the treatment of minority employees, apply equally at all levels. These are usually set forth separately from other standing instructions and are likely to be called "policy statements."

Performance information. Performance measures are the obvious types of information for control. Data on actual performance are gathered during the conduct of operations. Periodically, information on these measurements is communicated to the manager supervising the responsibility center manager, where it is used to evaluate performance. The evaluation process starts with an analysis of information comparing actual performance with planned performance. Based on this analysis, and on other information that may explain why actual performance differed from planned performance, the manager makes a judgment on whether performance was good, and, if not, the causes of poor operating performances.

Performance measurements vary with the level of the organization. At lower levels, measurements tend to be detailed, specific, and quantitative, and attention is focused on specific deviations from stated standards. At higher levels, the standards tend to be more general, and attention is focused on performance of the unit as a whole, on key results variables, and on exception variables.

Management judgments about performance give rise to other types of information feedback. If performance is judged to be satisfactory, information on this judgment is communicated to the responsibility center manager with appropriate commendation. The intent is to motivate the responsibility center manager to continue performing in a way that is consistent with the goals of the organization. If the performance is judged to be unsatisfactory, either or both of two types of feedback signals are communicated: (1) the manager of the responsibility center may be instructed to take corrective action, or (2) the plans may be revised.[4]

Good performance does not necessarily mean that actual performance conforms to the plans. New information, available after the plan was made, may indicate that departure from the plan is desirable. Good performance is performance that is consistent with organization's goals, and the plans may not reflect the actions that, under current conditions, are those most likely to achieve these goals.

Nature of control information. While Exhibit 4–1 indicates that feedback occurs after the performance evaluation judgment, the fact of the matter is that informal feedback occurs within the responsibility center all during the conduct of operations. The responsibility center manager reacts to new information and adjusts operations accordingly. If this new information indicates that a significant change in operations should be made, the manager is responsible for acting on this information as soon as it is perceived, without waiting for it to be communicated through the formal control reports.

It has been said that in a good operating system the management control system reports "should contain no surprises." This means that the competent manager should become aware of conditions that require a change in plans, should take the necessary corrective action, and should informally inform higher management of the situation before the superior receives the formal control report. In that context the function of the management control system is to motivate the local manager to spot problems early. If the formal management control report does communicate previously unknown news of unsatisfactory performance, the reason is likely to be that the manager is not doing a good job or has not kept the superior advised of what actually is going on.

Evaluation of performance always involves a comparison of actual performance with something. The report of actual performance is meaningful only when it is compared with a standard. Presumably, the budget and accompanying statement of objectives provides the best first approximation to such a standard; but performance can also be judged against other standards, including the person's intuitive judg-

[4] Technically, in engineering there are two types of feedback. *Positive feedback* occurs when information increases the positive deviation of performance from a steady state. *Negative feedback* occurs when information brings performance closer to a steady state. The type of feedback that occurs in control systems is, therefore, *negative* feedback. Customarily, however, the word "negative" is not used; it simply confuses those who are not well versed in systems theory.

ment of what is an appropriate amount of cost, revenue, or profit under the circumstances.

The full management control process involves action. The communication of information is part of the process; but control is obviously ineffective if nothing happens after the information has been communicated. Although control reports are feedback devices, they are only one part of the feedback loop. Unlike the thermostat, which acts automatically in response to information about temperature, a control report does not by itself cause a change in performance. A change results only when managers take actions that lead to change. Thus, in management control, the feedback loop requires the evaluation report plus management action.

Finally, although the process may, and often does, lead to a revision of plans, it seldom leads to a change in goals or strategies. A heating system is in control when the system keeps the temperature at the standard set in the thermostat. The corresponding standard in a management control system is the goal of the organization, which is not necessarily expressed in the budget or other control device.

Motivational Reports and Economic Reports

Evaluation reports are of two general types. One is intended to report on personal performance, and the other to report on unit economic performance. Since the first type is intended to motivate managers, it is often termed a *motivational report*. A motivational report compares actual performance of a responsibility center with what the manager should have had the responsibility center do under the prevailing circumstances. Presumably, the budget states the responsible manager's commitment to a certain level of performance, and motivational evaluation reports show how well he or she carried out this commitment. Behavioral considerations are important in using motivational reports.

An *economic report* on an organization unit, such as a division, is designed to show how well the responsibility center has performed as an economic entity. An economic report would ordinarily include all the costs of the responsibility center, including allocated costs, whereas a motivational report may show only those elements of cost that the manager can influence.

The motivational report may show that the responsibility manager is doing an excellent job, considering the circumstances; but if the economic analysis shows that the responsibility center is not making an adequate contribution to company goals, corrective action may nevertheless be necessary. For example, the manager of a downtown department store may be doing the best job possible; but if the economic report indicates the store is operating at a loss (because of the movement of business out of the downtown area and into suburban shopping centers), the store may be closed. This action does not reflect unfavorably on the manager's performance.

Critics of a management control system sometimes overlook the fact that it includes the two types of reports and criticize a motivational report based on controllable costs as being an inadequate economic report, or vice versa. It must be appreciated that each type of control report has its place in a management control system.

Appropriate Standards

Formal standards used in evaluation reports are of three types: (1) predetermined standards or budgets, (2) historical standards, or (3) external standards.

Predetermined standards or budgets, if carefully prepared, are excellent standards. They are the basis against which actual performance is compared in many well-managed companies. But if the budget numbers were collected in a haphazard manner, they obviously will not provide a reliable basis for comparison. Moreover, if the environmental uncertainties affecting responsibility center performance are great, predetermined standards may be so unreliable that they are not worth the trouble of preparing them.

Historical standards are records of past actual performance. Results for the current month may be compared with results for last month, or with results for the same month a year ago. This type of standard has two serious weaknesses: (1) conditions may have changed between the two periods in a way that invalidates the comparison, and (2) the prior period's performance may not have been acceptable. A supervisor whose spoilage cost is $500 a month, month after month, is consistent; but we do not know, without other evidence, whether the performance was consistently good or consistently poor. Despite these inherent weaknesses, historical standards are used in many companies, often because valid predetermined standards are not available.

External standards are standards derived from the performance of other responsibility centers or of other companies. The performance of one branch sales office may be compared with the performance of other branch sales offices. If conditions in these responsibility centers are similar, such a comparison may provide an acceptable basis for evaluating performance.

Limitations on standards. A variance between actual and standard performance is meaningful only if it is derived from a valid standard. Although it is convenient to refer to "favorable" and "unfavorable" variances, these words imply that the standard is a reliable measure of what performance should have been. Even a standard cost may not be an accurate estimate of what costs should have been under the circumstances. This situation can arise for either or both of two reasons: (1) the standard was not set properly; or (2) although set properly in the light of conditions existing at the time, changed conditions have made the standard obsolete. An essential first step in the analysis of a variance is an examination of the validity of the standard.

Engineered and discretionary costs. Engineered costs are items of cost for which the proper amount of costs that should be incurred can be estimated reliably, such as the direct material cost and the direct labor cost of a pair of shoes. Discretionary costs are items of costs whose amount can be varied at the discretion of the manager of the responsibility center; and there is no reliable way of deciding what the "right" amount of cost should be. In evaluating responsibility center performance, engineered costs are viewed as essentially different from discretionary costs. With respect to engineered costs, the general rule is the lower, the better. The objective is to spend as little as possible, consistent with quality and safety standards. The supervisor who reduces engineered costs below the standard amounts usually should be congratulated.

Concerning discretionary costs, the situation is more complicated. Often good performance is spending the budgeted amount agreed on, because spending too little may be as bad as, or worse than, spending too much. A factory manager can easily reduce current costs in the short run by skimping on maintenance or on training; a marketing manager can reduce advertising or sales promotion expenditures; senior management may eliminate a research department. None of these actions may be in the overall best interest of the company, although all of them result in lower costs on the current performance report.

These distinctions are the basis for distinguishing between two types of responsibility centers, namely, an *engineered expense center,* in which engineered costs predominate, and a *discretionary expense center,* in which discretionary costs predominate.

CONTROL OF INFORMATION

We have focused on management control systems information, and have limited our discussion to the cost, amount, value, and quality of the information used. Techniques are obviously essential in applying these concepts, and we need to keep them in mind in developing management control systems; but they are best discussed as a specialized area. Conceptually, the distinction between the information processing area, where the parameters of the desired information are taken as given, and the management control area is that the latter sets the parameters for the former. Obviously, in practice there is overlap between the two areas, because one cannot understand techniques for processing information efficiently without an understanding or appreciation of the purpose for which the information will be used.

SUGGESTED ADDITIONAL READINGS

Anderson, D. L., and **Raun, D. L.,** eds. *Information Analysis in Management.* New York: John Wiley & Sons, 1978.

Boulding, Kenneth E. "The Economics of Knowledge and the Knowledge of Economics." *American Economic Review,* vol. 56, no. 2, 1966.

Churchman, C. West. *The Design of Inquiring Systems.* New York: Basic Books, 1971.

Davis, Gordon B. *Management Information Systems: Conceptual Foundations, Structure and Development.* New York: McGraw-Hill, 1974.

Demsetz, H. "Information and Efficiency: Another Viewpoint." *Journal of Law and Economics,* vol. 12, 1969.

Driver, M. J., and **Mock, T. J.** "Human Information Processing, Decision Style Theory and Accounting Information Systems." *The Accounting Review,* July 1975.

Geldschmidt, Y. *Information for Management Decisions.* Ithaca, N.Y.: Cornell University Press, 1970.

Lawler, Edward E., III, and **Rhode, John Grant.** *Information and Control in Organizations.* Santa Monica, Calif.: Goodyear Publishing, 1976.

Libby, Robert, and **Lewis, Barry.** "Human Information Processing Research in Accounting: The State of the Art." *Accounting Organizations and Society,* 2(1977):245–68.

Marschak, J. "Economics of Inquiring, Communicating, Deciding." *American Economic Review,* vol. 58, no. 2, 1968.

Morris, Charles. *Signification and Significance.* Cambridge, Mass.: MIT Press, 1964.

Murdick, Robert G., and **Ross, Joel E.** *Information Systems for Modern Management.* Englewood Cliffs, N.J.: Prentice-Hall, 1971.

Newell, Allen, and **Simon, Herbert.** *Human Problem Solving.* Englewood Cliffs, N.J.: Prentice-Hall, 1972.

Prince, Thomas R. *Information Systems for Management Planning and Control.* 3d ed. Homewood, Ill.: Richard D. Irwin, 1975.

Raiffa, Howard. *Decision Analysis: Introductory Lectures on Choices under Uncertainty.* Reading, Mass.: Addison-Wesley Publishing, 1968.

Shubik, M. "Information, Rationality and Free Choice in a Future Democratic Society." *Daedalus,* vol. 96, 1967.

Schultz, George P., and **Whisler, Thomas L.,** eds. *Management Organization and the Computer.* New York: Free Press, 1960.

Whisler, Thomas L. *Information Technology and Organization Change.* Belmont, Calif.: Wadsworth, 1970.

CASE 4–1
Empire Glass Company (*A*)*

ORGANIZATION

Empire Glass Company was a diversified company organized into several major product divisions, one of which was the Glass Products Division. This division was responsible for manufacturing and selling glass food and beverage bottles. Each division was headed by a divisional vice president who reported directly to the company's executive vice president, Landon McGregor.

Mr. McGregor's corporate staff included three men in the financial area—the controller, the chief accountant, and the treasurer. The controller's department consisted of only two men—Mr. Walker and the assistant controller, Allen Newell. The market research and labor relations departments also reported in a staff capacity to Mr. McGregor.

All the product divisions were organized along similar lines. Reporting to each product division vice president were several staff members in the customer service and product research areas. Reporting in a line capacity to each individual vice president were also a general manager of manufacturing and a general manager of marketing. The general manager of manufacturing was responsible for all the division's manufacturing activities. Similarly, the general manager of marketing was responsible for all the division's marketing activities. Both of these executives were assisted by a small staff of specialists. There was also a controller and supporting staff in each division. Exhibit 1 presents an organization chart of the Glass Product Division's top management group. All the corporate and divisional management group were located in British City, Canada. Exhibit 2 shows the typical organization structure of a plant within the Glass Products Division.

PRODUCTS AND TECHNOLOGY

The Glass Products Division operated a number of plants in Canada producing glass food and beverage bottles. Of these products, food jars constituted the largest group, including jars for products like tomato catsup, mayonnaise, jams and jellies, honey, and soluble coffee. Milk bottles and beer and soft drink bottles were also produced in large quantities. A great variety of shapes and sizes of containers for wines, liquors, drugs, cosmetics, and chemicals were produced in smaller quantities.

---

* This case was prepared by David Hawkins, Harvard Business School.

EXHIBIT 1 Glass Products Division Top Management and Staff

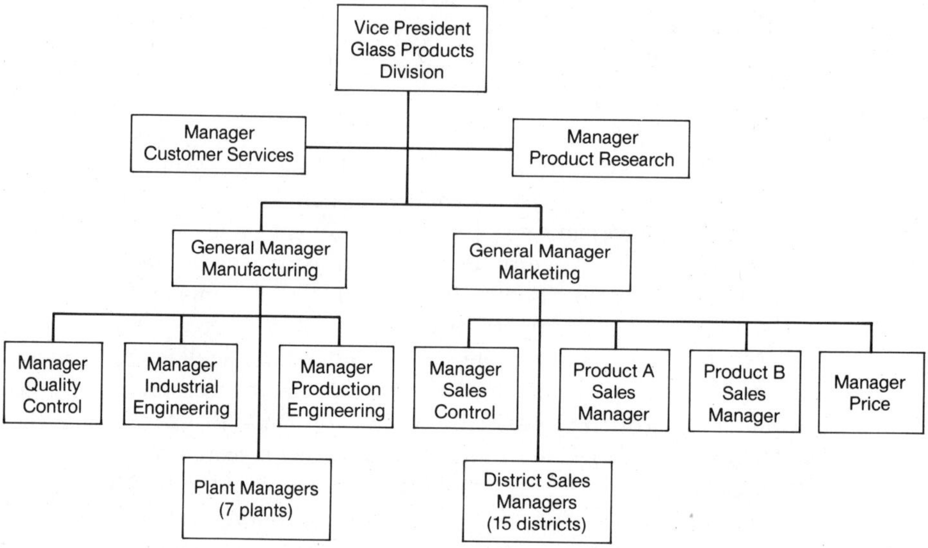

EXHIBIT 2 Typical Plant Organization—Glass Products Division

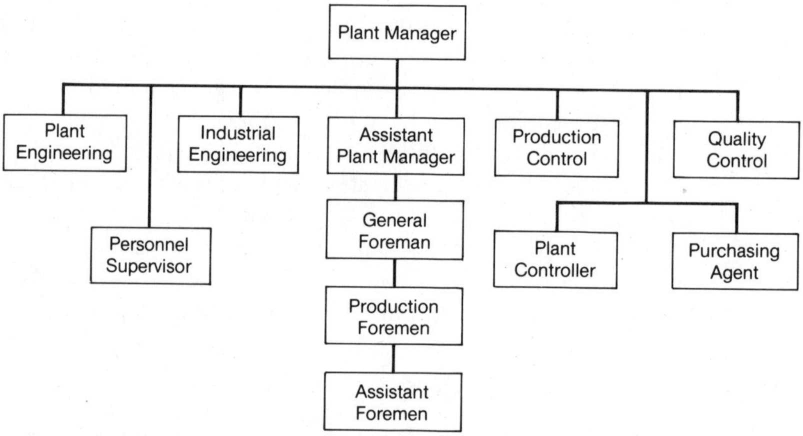

Most of the thousands of different products, varying in size, shape, color, and decoration were produced to order. According to British City executives, during 1963 the typical lead time between the customer's order and shipment from the plant was between two and three weeks.

The principal raw materials for container glass were sand, soda ash, and lime. The first step in the manufacturing process was to melt batches of these materials in furnaces of "tanks." The molten mass was then passed into automatic or semiautomatic machines, which filled molds with the molten glass and blew the glass into the desired shape. The ware then went through an automatic annealing oven or lehr, where it was cooled slowly under carefully controlled conditions. If the glass was to be coated on the exterior to increase its resistance to abrasion and scratches, this coating—often a silicone film—was applied at the lehr. Any decorating (such as a trademark or other design) was then added, the product inspected again, and the finished goods packed in corrugated containers (or wooden cases for some bottles).

Quality inspection was critical in the manufacturing process. If the melt in the furnace was not completely free from bubbles and stones (unmelted ingredients or pieces of refinery material), or if the fabricating machinery was slightly out of adjustment, or molds were worn, the rejection rate was very high. Although a number of machines were used in the inspection process, including electric eyes, much of the inspection was still visual.

Although glassmaking was one of the oldest arts, and bottles and jars had been machine molded at relatively high speed for over half a century, the Glass Products Division had spent substantial sums each year to modernize its equipment. These improvements had greatly increased the speed of operations and had substantially reduced the visual inspection and manual holding of glassware.

Most of the jobs were relatively unskilled, highly repetitive, and gave the worker little control over work methods or pace. The moldmakers who made and repaired the molds, the machine repairmen, and those who made the equipment setup changes between different products were considered to be the highest classes of skilled workers. Wages were relatively high in the glass industry. Production employees belonged to two national unions, and for many years bargaining had been conducted on a national basis. Output standards were established for all jobs, but no bonus was paid to hourly plant workers for exceeding standard.

MARKETING

Over the years, the sales of the Glass Products Division had grown at a slightly faster rate than had the total market for glass containers. Until the late 1950s, the division had charged a premium for most of its products, primarily because they were of better quality than competitive products. In recent years, however, the quality of the competitive products had improved to the point where they now matched the division's quality level. In the meantime, the division's competitors had retained their former price structure. Consequently, the Glass Products Division had been forced to lower its prices to meet its competitor's lower market prices. According to one division executive:

> Currently, price competition is not severe, particularly among the two or three larger companies that dominate the glass bottle industry. Most of our competition is with respect to product quality and customer service. . . . In fact, our biggest competitive threat is from containers other than glass. . . .

Each of the division's various plants shipped their products throughout Canada to some extent, although transportation costs limited each plant's market primarily to its immediate vicinity. While some of the customers were large and bought in huge quantities, many were relatively small.

BUDGETARY CONTROL SYSTEM

In the fall of 1963, James Walker, Empire Glass Company, controller, described the company's budgetary control system to a casewriter. Mr. Walker had been controller for some 15 years. Excerpts from that interview are reproduced below.

Mr. Walker's Interview

> To understand the role of the budgetary control system, you must first understand our management philosophy. Fundamentally, we have a divisional organization based on broad product categories. These divisional activities are coordinated by the company's executive vice president, while the head office group provides a policy and review function for him. Within the broad policy limits, we operate on a decentralized basis; each of the decentralized divisions performs the full management job that normally would be inherent in any independent company. The only exceptions to this philosophy are the head office group's sole responsibilities for sources of funds and labor relations with those bargaining units that cross division lines.
>
> Given this form of organization, the budget is the principal management tool used by head office to direct the efforts of the various segments of the company toward a common goal. Certainly, in our case, the budget is much more than a narrow statistical accounting device.

Sales Budget

> As early as May 15 of the year preceding the budget year, top management of the company asks the various product division vice presidents to submit preliminary reports stating what they think their division's capital requirements and outlook in terms of sales and income will be during the next budget year. In addition, corporate top management also wants an expression of the division vice president's general feelings toward the trends in these particular items over the two years following the upcoming budget year. At this stage, head office is not interested in too much detail. Since all divisions plan their capital

requirements five years in advance and had made predictions of the forthcoming budget year's market when the budget estimates were prepared last year, these rough estimates of next year's conditions and requirements are far from wild guesses.

After the opinions of the divisional vice presidents are in, the market research staff goes to work. They develop a formal statement of the marketing climate in detail for the forthcoming budget year and in general terms for the subsequent two years. Once these general factors have been assessed, a sales forecast is constructed for the company and for each division. Consideration is given to the relationship of the general economic climate to our customers' needs and Empire's share of each market. Explicitly stated are basic assumptions as to price, weather conditions, introduction of new products, gains or losses in particular accounts, forward buying, new manufacturing plants, industry growth trends, packaging trends, inventory carry-overs, and the development of alternative packages to or from glass. This review of all the relevant factors is followed for each of our product lines, regardless of its size and importance. The completed forecasts of the market research group are then forwarded to the appropriate divisions for review, criticism, and adjustments.

The primary goal of the head office group in developing these sales forecasts is to assure uniformity among the divisions with respect to the basic assumptions on business conditions, pricing, and the treatment of possible emergencies. Also, we provide a yardstick so as to assure us that the company's overall sales forecast will be reasonable and obtainable.

The product division top management then asks each district manager what he expects to do in the way of sales during the budget year. Head office and the divisional staffs will give the district sales managers as much guidance as they request, but it is the sole responsibility of each district sales manager to come up with his particular forecast.

After the district sales managers' forecasts are received by the divisional top management, the forecasts are consolidated and reviewed by the division's general manager of marketing. Let me emphasize, however, that nothing is changed in the district sales manager's budget unless the district manager agrees. Then, once the budget is approved, nobody is relieved of his responsibility without top management approval. Also, no arbitrary changes are made in the approved budgets without the concurrence of all the people responsible for the budget.

Next, we go through the same process at the division and headquarters levels. We continue to repeat the process until everyone agrees that the sales budgets are sound. Then, each level of management takes responsibility for its particular portion of the budget. These sales budgets then become fixed objectives.

I would say we have four general objectives in mind in reviewing the sales forecast:

1. A review of the division's competitive position, including plans for improving that position.

2. An evaluation of its efforts to gain either a larger share of the market or offset competitors' activities.
3. A consideration of the need to expand facilities to improve the division's products or introduce new products.
4. A review and development of plans to improve product quality, delivery methods and service.

Manufacturing Budgets

Once the vice presidents, executive vice president, and company president have given final approval to the sales budgets, we make a sales budget for each plant by breaking down the division sales budgets according to the plants from which the finished goods will be shipped. These plant sales budgets are then further broken down on a monthly basis by price, volume, and end use. With this information available, the plants then budget their gross profit, fixed expenses, and income before taxes. Gross profit is the difference between gross sales, less discounts, and variable manufacturing costs—such as direct labor, direct material and variable manufacturing overheads. Income is the difference between the gross profit and the fixed costs.

The plant manager's primary responsibility extends to profits. The budgeted plant profit is the difference between the fixed sales dollar budget and the sum of the budgeted variable costs at standard and the fixed overhead budget. It is the plant manager's responsibility to meet this budget profit figure, even if actual dollar sales drop below the budgeted level.

Given his sales budget, it is up to the plant manager to determine the fixed overhead and variable costs—at standard—that he will need to incur so as to meet the demands of the sales budget. In my opinion, requiring the plant managers to make their own plans is one of the most valuable things associated with the budget system. Each plant manager divides the preparation of the overall plant budget among his plant's various departments. First, the departments spell out the program in terms of the physical requirements, such as tons of raw material, and then the plans are priced at standard cost.

The plant industrial engineering department is assigned responsibility for developing engineered cost standards and reduced costs. Consequently, the phase of budget preparation covered by the industrial engineers includes budget standards of performance for each operation, cost center, and department within the plant. This phase of the budget also includes budgeted cost reductions, budgeted unfavorable variances from standards, and certain budgeted programmed fixed costs in the manufacturing area, such as service labor. The industrial engineer prepares this phase of the budget in conjunction with departmental line supervision.

Before each plant sends its budget into British City, a group of us from head office goes out to visit each plant. For example, in the case of the Glass Products Division, Allen Newell, assistant controller, and I, along with representatives of the Glass Products Division manufacturing staffs visit each of the division's plants. Let me stress this point:

We do not go on these trips to pass judgment on the plant's proposed budget. Rather, we go with two purposes in mind. First, we wish to acquaint ourselves with the thinking behind the figures that each plant manager will send in to British City. This is helpful, because when we come to review these budgets with the top management—that is, management above our level—we will have to answer questions about the budgets, and we will know the answers. Second, the review is a way of giving guidance to the plant managers in determining whether or not they are in line with what the company needs to make in the way of profits.

Of course, when we make our field reviews we do not know what each of the other plants is doing. Therefore, we explain to the plant managers that while their budget may look good now, when we put all the plants together in a consolidated budget the plant managers may have to make some changes because the projected profit is not high enough. When this happens, we must tell the plant managers that it is not their programs that are unsound. The problem is that the company cannot afford the programs. I think it is very important that each plant manager has a chance to tell his story. Also, it gives them the feeling that we at headquarters are not living in an ivory tower.

These plant visits are spread over a three-week period, and we spend an average of half a day at each plant. The plant manager is free to bring to these meetings any of his supervisors he wishes. We ask him not to bring in anybody below the supervisory level. Then, of course, you get into organized labor. During the half day we spend at each plant we discuss the budget primarily. However, if I have time I like to wander through the plant and see how things are going. Also, I go over in great detail the property replacement and maintenance budget with the plant manager.

About September 1, the plant budgets come into British City, and the accounting department consolidates them. Then, the product division vice presidents review their respective divisional budgets to see if the division budget is reasonable in terms of what the vice president thinks the corporate management wants. If he is not satisfied with the consolidated plant budgets, he will ask the various plants within the division to trim their budget figures.

When the division vice presidents and the executive vice president are happy, they will send their budgets to the company president. He may accept the division budgets at this point. If he doesn't, he will specify the areas to be reexamined by division and, if necessary, by plant management. The final budget is approved at our December board of directors' meeting.

Comparison of Actual and Standard Performance

At the end of the sixth business day after the close of the month, each plant wires to the head office certain operating variances, which we put together on what we call the variance analysis sheet. Within a half-hour after the last plant report comes through, variance analysis sheets for the divisions and plants are compiled. On the morning of the seventh business day after the end of the month, these reports are usually on the desks of the interested top management. The variance analysis sheet highlights the variances in what we consider to be critical areas. Receiving this report as soon as we do helps us at head office to take timely action. Let me emphasize, however, we do not accept the excuse that the plant manager has to go to the end of the month to know

EXHIBIT 3 Profit-Planning and Control Report

MONTH					YEAR TO DATE		
Income Gain (+) or Loss (-) From		Actual	Ref.		Actual	Income Gain (+) or Loss (−) From	
Prev. Year	Budget					Budget	Prev. Year
			1	Gross Sales to Customers			
			2	Discounts & Allowances			
			3	Net Sales to Customers			
%	%		4	% Gain (+)/Loss (-)		%	%
				DOLLAR VOLUME GAIN (+)/ LOSS (-) DUE TO:			
			5	Sales Price			
			6	Sales Volume			
			6(a)	Trade Mix			
			7	Variable Cost of Sales			
			8	Profit Margin			
				PROFIT MARGIN GAIN (+)/ LOSS (-) DUE TO:			
			9	Profit Volume Ratio (P/V)*			
			10	Dollar Volume			
%	%	%	11	Profit Volume Ratio (P/V)*	%	%	%
	Income Addition (+)				Income Addition (+)		
			12	Total Fixed Manufacturing Cost			
			13	Fixed Manufacturing Cost-Transfers			
			14	Plant Income (Standard)			
%	%	%	15	% of Net Sales	%	%	%
	Income Addition (+) Income Reduction (−)				Income Addition (+) Income Reduction (−)		
%	%	%	16	% Performance	%	%	%
			17	Manufacturing Efficiency			
	Income Addition (+)				Income Addition (+)		
			18	Methods Improvements			
			19	Other Revisions of Standards			
			20	Material Price Changes			
			21	Division Special Projects			
			22	Company Special Projects			
			23	New Plant Expense			
			24	Other Plant Expenses			
			25	Income on Seconds			
			26				
			27				
			28	Plant Income (Actual)			
%	%		29	% Gain (+)/Loss (−)		%	%
%	%	%	30	% of Net Sales	%	%	%
			36A				
Increase (+) or Decrease (-)				EMPLOYED CAPITAL	Increase (+) or Decrease (-)		
			37	Total Employed Capital			
%	%	%	38	% Return	%	%	%
			39	Turnover Rate			

Plant ______ Division ______ Month ______ 19___

what happened during the month. He has to be on top of these particular items daily.

When the actual results come into the head office, we go over them on the basis of exception; that is, we only look at those figures that are in excess of the budgeted amounts. We believe this has a good effect on morale. The plant managers don't have to explain everything they do. They have to explain only where they go off base. In particular, we pay close attention to the net sales, gross margin, and the plant's ability to meet its standard manufacturing cost. Incidentally, when analyzing the gross sales, we look closely at the price and mix changes.

All this information is summarized on a form known as the Profit Planning and Control Report No. 1 (see Exhibit 3). This document is backed up by a number of supporting documents (see Exhibit 4). The plant PPCR No. 1 and the month-end trial balance showing both actual

EXHIBIT 4 Brief Description of PPCR No. 2—PPCR No. 11

Individual plant reports

Report	*Description*
PPCR No. 2	Manufacturing expense: Plant materials, labor, and variable overhead consumed. Detail of actual figures compared with budget and previous year's figures for year to date and current month.
PPCR No. 3	Plant expense: Plant fixed expenses incurred. Details of actual figures compared with budget and previous year's figures for year to date and current month.
PPCR No. 4	Analysis of sales and income: Plant operating gains and losses due to changes in sales revenue, profit margins and other sources of income. Details of actual figures compared with budget and previous year's figures for year to date and current month.
PPCR No. 5	Plant control statement: Analysis of plant raw material gains and losses, spoilage costs, and cost reductions programs. Actual figures compared with budget figures for current month and year to date.
PPCR No. 6	Comparison of sales by principal and product groups: Plant sales dollars, profit margin and P/V ratios broken down by end product use (i.e., soft drinks, beer). Compares actual figures for year to date and current month.

Division summary reports

Report	*Description*
PPCR No. 7	Comparative plant performance, sales and income: Gross sales and income figures by plants. Actual figures compared with budget figures for year to date and current month.
PPCR No. 8	Comparative plant performance, total plant expenses: Profit margin, total fixed costs, manufacturing efficiency, other plant expenses and P/V ratios by plants. Actual figures compared with budgeted and previous year's figures for current month and year to date.
PPCR No. 9	Manufacturing efficiency: Analysis of gains and losses by plant in areas of materials, spoilage, supplies and labor. Current month and year to date actuals reported in total dollars and as a percentage of budget.
PPCR No. 10	Inventory: Comparison of actual and budget inventory figures by major inventory accounts and plants.
PPCR No. 11	Status of capital expenditures: Analysis of the status of capital expenditures by plants, months and relative to budget.

and budget figures are received in British City at the close of the eighth business day after the end of the month. These two very important reports, along with the supporting reports (PPCR No. 2, PPCR No. 11) are then consolidated by the accounting department on PPCR-type forms to show the results of operations by division and company. The consolidated reports are distributed the next day.

In connection with the fixed cost items, we want to know whether or not the plants carried out the programs they said they would carry out. If they have not, we want to know why they have not. Here, we are looking for sound reasons. Also, we want to know if they have carried out their projected programs at the cost they said they would.

In addition to these reports, at the beginning of each month the plant managers prepare current estimates for the upcoming month and quarter on forms similar to the variance analysis sheets. Since our budget is based on known programs, the value of this current estimate is that it gets the plant people to look at their programs. Hopefully, they will realize that they cannot run their plants on a day-to-day basis.

If we see a sore spot coming up, or if the plant manager draws our attention to a potential trouble area, we may ask that daily reports concerning this item be sent to the particular division top management involved. In addition, the division top management may send a division staff specialist—say, a quality control expert if it is a quality problem—to the plant concerned. The division staff members can make recommendations, but it is up to the plant manager to accept or reject these recommendations. Of course, it is well known throughout the company that we expect the plant managers to accept gracefully the help of the head office and division staffs.

Sales-manufacturing Relations

If a sales decline occurs during the early part of the year, and if the plant managers can convince us that the change is permanent, we may revise the plant budgets to reflect these new circumstances. However, if toward the end of the year the actual sales volume suddenly drops below the predicted sales volume, we don't have much time to change the budget plans. What we do is ask the plant managers to go back over their budgets with their staffs and see where reduction of expense programs will do the least harm. Specifically, we ask them to consider what they may be able to eliminate this year or delay until next year.

I believe it was Confucius who said: "We make plans so we have plans to discard." Nevertheless, I think it is wise to make plans, even if you have to discard them. Having plans makes it a lot easier to figure out what to do when sales fall off from the budget level. The understanding of operations that comes from preparing the budget removes a lot of the potential chaos and confusion that might arise if we were under pressure to meet a stated profit goal and sales declined quickly and unexpectedly at year-end, just as they did last year. In these circumstances, we don't try to ram anything down the plant managers' throats. We ask them to tell us where they can reasonably expect to cut costs below the budgeted level.

Whenever a problem arises at a plant between sales and production, the local people are supposed to solve the problem themselves. For example, a customer's purchasing agent may insist he wants an immediate delivery, and this delivery will disrupt the production department's plans. The production group can make recommendations as to alternative ways to take care of the problem, but it's the sales manager's responsibility to get the product to the customer. The salesmen are supposed to know their customers well enough to judge whether or not the customer really needs the product. If the sales manager says the customer needs the product, that ends the matter. As far as we are concerned, the customer's wants are primary; our company is a case where sales wags the rest of the dog.

Of course, if the change in the sales program involves a major plant expense which is out of line with the budget, then the matter is passed up to division for decision.

As I said earlier, the sales department has the sole responsibility for the product price, sales mix, and delivery schedules. They do not have direct responsibility for plant operations or profit. That's the plant management's responsibility. However, it is understood that sales group will cooperate with the plant people wherever possible.

Motivation

There are various ways in which we motivate the plant managers to meet their profit goals. First of all, we only promote capable people. Also, a monetary incentive program has been established that stimulates their efforts to achieve their profit goals. In addition, each month we put together a bar chart which shows, by division and plant, the ranking of the various manufacturing units with respect to manufacturing efficiency.[1] We feel the plant managers are 100 percent responsible for variable manufacturing costs. I believe this is true, since all manufacturing standards have to be approved by plant managers. Most of the plant managers give wide publicity to these bar charts. The efficiency bar chart and efficiency measure itself is perhaps a little unfair in some respects when you are comparing one plant with another. Different kinds of products are run through different plants. These require different setups, etc., which have an important impact on a position of the plant. However, in general, the efficiency rating is a good indication of the quality of the plant manager and his supervisory staff.

Also, a number of plants run competitions within the plants which reward department heads, or foreman, based on their relative standing with respect to a certain cost item. The plant managers, their staffs, and employees have great pride in their plants.

---

[1] Manufacturing efficiency $= \frac{\text{Total actual variable manufacturing costs}}{\text{Total standard variable manufacturing costs}} \times 100\%$

The number one item now stressed at the plant level is *quality*. The market situation is such that in order to make sales you have to meet the market price and exceed the market quality. By quality I mean not only the physical characteristics of the product but also such things as delivery schedules. As I read the company employee publications, their message is that if the company is to be profitable it must produce high-quality items at a reasonable cost. This is necessary so that the plants can meet their obligation to produce the maximum profits for the company in the prevailing circumstances.

The Future

An essential part of the budgetary control system is planning. We have developed a philosophy that we must begin our plans where the work is done—in the line organization and out in the field. Perhaps, in the future, we can avoid or cut back some of the budget preparation steps and start putting together our sales budget later than May 15. However, I doubt if we will change the basic philosophy.

Frankly, I doubt if the line operators would want any major change in the system; they are very jealous of the management prerogatives the system gives to them.

It is very important that we manage the budget. We have to be continually on guard against its managing us. Sometimes, the plants lose sight of this fact. We have to be made conscious daily of the necessity of having the sales volume to make a profit. And when sales fall off and their plant programs are reduced, they do not always appear to see the justification for budget cuts. Although I do suspect that they see more of the justification for these cuts than they will admit. It is this human side of the budget to which we have to pay more attention in the future.

Question

Comment on the strong points and the weak points in the management control system of Empire Glass Company. What changes, if any, would you suggest?

CASE 4–2
National Tractor and Equipment Company*

National Tractor and Equipment Company, Inc., was a manufacturer of a number of products, including a wide line of farm tractors. Trac-

* This case was prepared by R. N. Anthony, Harvard Business School.

tors were divided into several fairly well-defined types, according to their capacity, and National manufactured tractors of each type. This case deals with one of these types, here referred to as a type X.

Fixed costs represented a relatively large share of total costs at National, and, therefore, achieving a strong sales position was an important means of reducing unit costs and improving profits. Consequently, a major objective of the company was to be the sales leader in each of the several types. If National was not the leader during a particular year, its goal was to surpass whoever was the leader. If National was the leader, its goal was to maintain the size of its lead.

The company had experienced a rather erratic showing in sales of type X tractors over the previous several years. Though National had been the sales leader in four of the previous six years (1970–75) its lead in 1973 and 1974 had been slim, and in 1975 its chief competitor took over first place. Meanwhile, profits of this division of its business had fluctuated widely. Accordingly, early in 1976 the controller's department made a sales analysis of the type X tractor division.

William Lawrence, who was given the job of making the analysis, decided to use the approach the controller had used for other analyses. Usually, these analyses started with a comparison of actual costs or actual profit with some bench mark, such as the budget or the figures for some prior year when performance was satisfactory. The analyst then sought to isolate and quantify the various causes of the difference between actual and the standard applied in that particular case.

In the case of tractors, since management's objective was to surpass the sales leader, unit sales of the leading competitor—here called competitor A—seemed to be the most logical standard. Competitor A had sold 13,449 type X tractors in 1975 compared with 10,356 for National—a deficiency of 3,093. (A copy of Mr. Lawrence's analysis as presented to management appears as an appendix to this case.)

Mr. Lawrence began his analysis by looking at the profits and return on assets of the type X tractor division (see Exhibit 1). Both had improved significantly over the 1973 and 1974 levels. However, in 1975 National dropped from the first-place sales position it had held during 1973 and 1974 and this was of grave concern to management. Furthermore, its market share had decreased from 25.0 percent to 23.5 percent (see Exhibit 2). Both of its major competitors had increased their market shares, and competitor A had outsold National for the first time in five years.

Mr. Lawrence next prepared the sales portion of the table that appears as Exhibit 3 in the appendix. This exhibit compares sales of type X tractors by National and competitor A for the preceding three years, 1973–75. The major task, then—and this was the crux of the analysis—was to identify and analyze those factors that accounted for the volume difference in each of the three years.

After he had completed this initial analysis, Mr. Lawrence, representing the controller's department, met with representatives of the sales department and the product development department. Together, they discussed the various factors that might have accounted for the volume differences in each of the three years under review. Using their collective judgments and estimates, they broke down the volume difference into as many specific factors as they could agree on. All the remaining factors, they decided, must have accounted for the remaining difference, although they could not agree on the proportions; so they gave the total under other factors.

The first matter that Mr. Lawrence called to the attention of this group was that a major fire in one of competitor A's plants in the latter part of 1974 had severely limited production. He had compiled monthly production estimates for competitor A for 1974 and the two prior years. He then had gathered estimates of industry sales during those years and developed certain relationships that seemed to him to hold among estimated monthly sales, actual monthly sales, and actual monthly production for 1972 and 1973 by competitor A. When he applied these relationships to 1974, it seemed evident to him that competitor A had produced significantly fewer type X tractors than it normally would have during the months when its plant was shut down.

Mr. Lawrence then had looked at sales patterns during 1972 and 1973 so that he could make an estimate of how much this lost production had resulted in a shifting of demand from 1974 to 1975; he tried to estimate how many competitor A customers for type X tractors delayed purchase of a new type X tractor from 1974 to 1975 because of the fire. In addition to research with the data available in his office, Mr. Lawrence traveled around the country and talked to distributors and dealers. He became convinced that a large number of potential purchasers of tractors annually had deferred their purchases of new type X tractors. Some of competitor A's dealers had had no type X tractors in stock in the latter part of 1974 because of the fire, and others had had only a limited supply.

On the basis of Mr. Lawrence's analysis and the collective judgments of the other members, the group agreed that the fire caused a shift of 1,500 of competitor A's tractor sales from 1974 to 1975. This shift was recorded as a minus factor in 1975 and a plus factor in 1974.

Sales of type X tractors to government agencies was another factor studied by this group. Since government sales figures were published, the group ascertained that National outsold competitor A by 138 units. Government sales depended almost entirely on price; therefore, this was the type of business a tractor manufacturer could "buy" depending on how badly he wanted it.

Mr. Lawrence had done a considerable amount of research into the advantage that competitor A enjoyed because of its larger owner body.[1] National's owner body had always been smaller than competitor A's, but National had made sizable gains since 1967. There was a tendency for the owner of a tractor to buy the same make when he purchased a new tractor; thus, competitor A enjoyed an advantage. Mr. Lawrence wanted to know *how much* this advantage was. An annual survey made by the trade association of the industry indicated the behavior of a representative sample of buyers of new type X tractors. This survey indicated that owners of competitor A's tractors were more loyal than were National tractor owners (see Table 1). Using these survey results, Mr. Lawrence was able to calculate the advantage to competitor A of its larger owner body. Although only the calculations for 1975 are shown, he applied the same methodology to 1973 and 1974. Members of the group were impressed with this analysis and agreed to accept Mr. Lawrence's figures—a net advantage of 700 units for competitor A in 1975.

The next factor he analyzed was product differences. National did not have so varied a product line as did competitor A. Because of this, National dealers were at a competitive disadvantage for certain models of type X tractors. The group was able to agree on the approximate extent of this disadvantage.

The last main heading for variances listed in Exhibit 3 was other factors, which the group thought accounted for the remaining difference between National's sales and competitor A's sales. Mr. Lawrence had prepared a thorough analysis of these factors, too. For example, he had heard that competitor A built a more efficient and more durable type X tractor. He tried to quantify the effect of these variables by use of the data shown in Tables 3 and 4. He also requisitioned five National type X tractors and five competitor A type X tractors, and arranged to have these tractors tested at National's experimental farm to determine their operating characteristics, including power, performance, durability, reliability, and economy. Mr. Lawrence himself actually drove some of these tractors. He also inspected each tractor and its performance at the end of the testing period.

The group could not agree, however, on the quantitative effect on sales volume of these factors or of the remaining factors listed under other. Therefore, they were represented by one figure. The total variance of all the factors affecting market penetration, of course, equaled the difference in sales between National and competitor A.

Questions

1. Are analyses of this type within the proper scope of a controller's function?
2. Can you suggest a better way of making the analysis?
3. What action, if any, should be taken on the basis of this study?

---

[1] Owner body is the number of tractors in the hands of owners.

APPENDIX
An Analysis of Type X Tractors*

PROFITS, ASSETS, AND AFTERTAX RETURNS

Exhibit 1 depicts National's profits, assets, and return on assets for the years 1970–75. Profits have ranged from a high of $2.7 million in 1972 to a loss of $200,000 in 1974 and a profit of $2.5 million in 1975. Return on assets employed in 1975 was 20.5 percent after taxes.

EXHIBIT 1 Profits, Assets, and Aftertax Returns

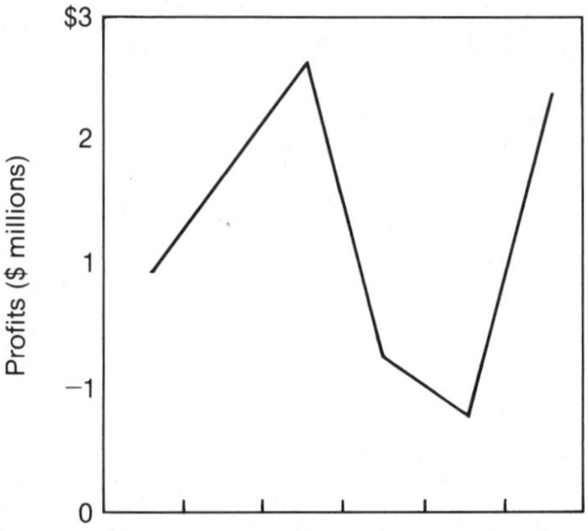

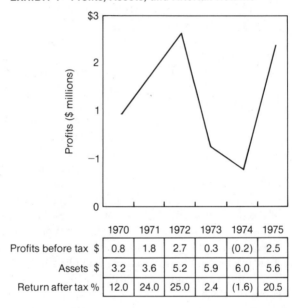

	1970	1971	1972	1973	1974	1975
Profits before tax $	0.8	1.8	2.7	0.3	(0.2)	2.5
Assets $	3.2	3.6	5.2	5.9	6.0	5.6
Return after tax %	12.0	24.0	25.0	2.4	(1.6)	20.5

MARKET PENETRATION VERSUS COMPETITION

Exhibit 2 shows National's penetration of the domestic market for type X tractors for 1970–75, compared with its two major competitors.

National's penetration rose from 24.3 percent in 1970 to a peak of 35.5 percent in 1971. In 1975, National's penetration was 23.5 percent. Competitor A's penetration, which was 27.9 percent in 1970, fell to a low of 21.8 percent in 1971 and then increased to 30.5 percent in 1975. In four out of the last six years, National outsold competitor A in the

* Prepared by the Controller's department.

EXHIBIT 2 Market Penetration versus Competition

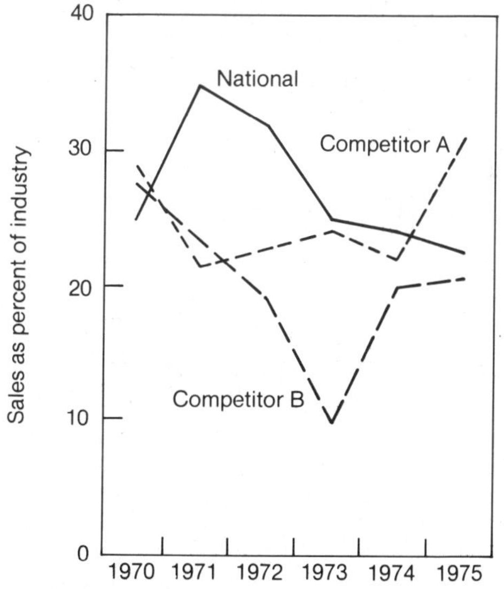

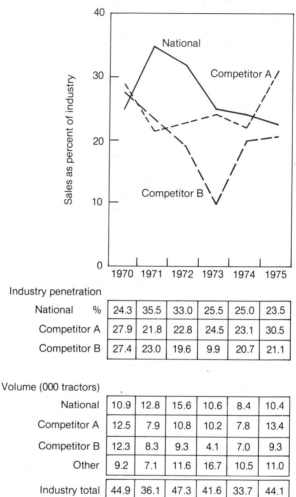

Industry penetration						
National %	24.3	35.5	33.0	25.5	25.0	23.5
Competitor A	27.9	21.8	22.8	24.5	23.1	30.5
Competitor B	27.4	23.0	19.6	9.9	20.7	21.1

Volume (000 tractors)						
National	10.9	12.8	15.6	10.6	8.4	10.4
Competitor A	12.5	7.9	10.8	10.2	7.8	13.4
Competitor B	12.3	8.3	9.3	4.1	7.0	9.3
Other	9.2	7.1	11.6	16.7	10.5	11.0
Industry total	44.9	36.1	47.3	41.6	33.7	44.1

type X tractor market. Competitor B's penetration moved from 27.4 percent in 1970 to 23.0 percent in 1971 but declined to 9.9 percent in 1973 rising to 21.1 percent in 1975.

Exhibit 3 sets forth those factors that account for differences in market penetration between National and competitor A—its chief competitor in the type X tractor market. The upper portion of the table compares National's and competitor A's sales during the years 1973–75. The lower portion of the table shows the various factors that account for the differences between National's and competitor A's share of the market in each of these years. National's volume was 10,611 units in 1973 compared to competitor A's 10,246. In 1975 National's

EXHIBIT 3 Sales of Type X Tractors and Factors Affecting Market Penetration (National versus Competitor A, 1973 to 1975)

	Jan.–Dec. 1973		Jan.–Dec. 1974		Jan.–Dec. 1975	
	Units	*Percent of market**	*Units*	*Percent of market**	*Units*	*Percent of market**
Sales:						
National	10,611	25.5%	8,431	25.0%	10,356	23.5%
Competitor A	10,246	24.5	7,828	23.1	13,449	30.5
National over/(under) A	365	1.0%	603	1.9%	(3,093)	(7.0%)
Factors affecting market penetration:						
Effect of major fire at one of competitor A's plants	—	—	1,500	4.5	(1,500)	(3.4)
Sales to government agencies	(3)	—	321	1.0	138	0.3
Competitor A's advantage in size of owner body	(850)	(2.0)	(660)	(1.9)	(700)	(1.6)
Product differences	(269)	(0.6)	(1,071)	(3.2)	(1,986)	(4.5)
Other factors: Customer attitudes toward National; Operating cost; Durability and quality; National's price position; National's distribution system; Sales administration; Other factors	1,487	3.6	513	1.5	955	2.2
Total variance	365	1.0%	603	1.9%	(3,093)	(7.0%)

* These percentages were calculated from the rounded numbers given on the preceding page; if calculated from the exact number of units, they would be somewhat different.

volume was 10,356 units, representing a market penetration of 23.5 percent, compared with A's volume of 13,449 units and 30.5 percent of the market. In 1975 National was outsold by 3,093 units.

Turning to the specific factors that account for this volume difference, we have estimated that the effect of a major fire at one of competitor A's plants in the last half of 1974, which halted production for nearly five months, resulted in a deferral of demand for 1,500 of its type X tractors from 1974 to 1975. This estimate is based on our knowledge of competitor A's output in 1974 compared with other years, and represents our best estimate as to what sales might have been without the fire. In 1975 these 1,500 units represented 3.4 percent of market penetration. In 1975 National sold 138 more units to government agencies, equivalent to 0.3 percent of market penetration. We shall examine the effect on our market penetration of differences in the size of our respective owner bodies in subsequent tables.

The product differences result from gaps in our product line that prevent National from entering certain segments of the type X tractor market, thereby providing competitor A with a clear product advantage. For example, competitor A offers a larger variety of attachments and related equipment which increase the number of different jobs its tractor can perform. We have estimated, for each year, the net market advantage accruing to competitor A because of its broader product line.

Other factors, whose effects cannot be measured quantitatively, are summarized at the bottom of the table, including customer attitudes toward National with respect to operating cost, durability, quality, and similar factors. In 1975 these other factors, in total, represented a net advantage to National of 955 units, or 2.2 percent of market penetration.

BASIS FOR ESTIMATED ADVANTAGE TO COMPETITOR A OF OWNER BODY

Exhibit 4 shows the estimated number of National and competitor A type X tractors in operation for the years 1967–75.

In 1967, it is estimated that competitor A had approximately 88,000 type X tractors in operation, while National had approximately 27,000 units in use. By 1975, National units in operation had more than quadrupled to a level of approximately 127,000 units. Competitor A units, on the other hand, had increased by almost 100 percent to a level of 158,000 units. During this period, National units as a percent of competitor A increased from 31 percent in 1967 to 80 percent in 1975. At the same time, our variance, in terms of units, decreased from 60,700 in 1967 to 31,200 in 1975.

EXHIBIT 4 Units in Operation

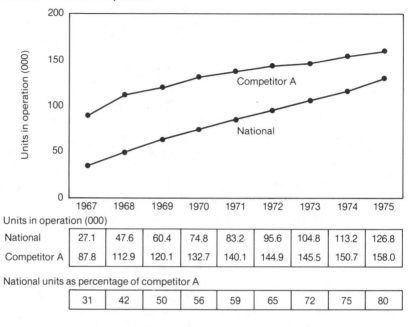

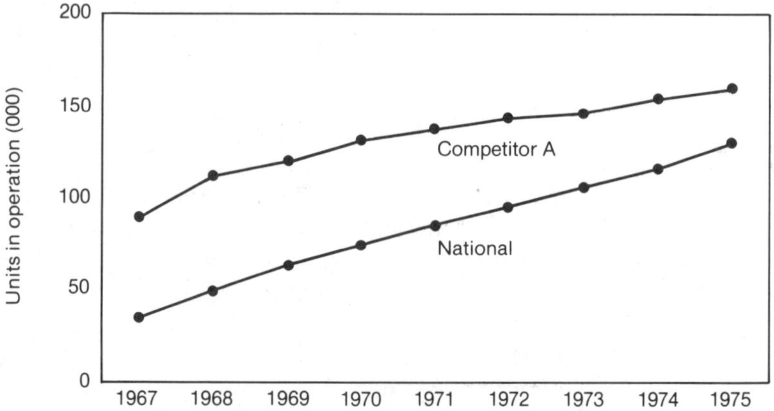

Units in operation (000)

	1967	1968	1969	1970	1971	1972	1973	1974	1975
National	27.1	47.6	60.4	74.8	83.2	95.6	104.8	113.2	126.8
Competitor A	87.8	112.9	120.1	132.7	140.1	144.9	145.5	150.7	158.0

National units as percentage of competitor A

31	42	50	56	59	65	72	75	80

National units over/(under) competitor A (000)

(60.7)	(65.3)	(59.7)	(57.9)	(56.9)	(49.3)	(40.7)	(37.5)	(31.2)

Because of the importance of owner loyalty, competitor A's advantage in owner body represents an automatic advantage in market penetration, as indicated in the succeeding pages.

1975 Type X Replacement Patterns

Table 1 indicates the relative loyalty in 1975 of National and competitor A type X tractor owners. In this sample, 48 percent of the National owners who replaced a tractor bought a new National, 27 percent bought an A model, and 25 percent bought some other type X

TABLE 1*

	Make purchased			
Make replaced	*National*	*A*	*Other*	*Total*
National	48%	27%	25%	100%
Competitor A	13	73	14	100
Other	17	20	63	100

* Source: Replacement analysis published annually by trade association.

tractor. In contrast, 73 percent of A owners bought a new A, 14 percent bought some type X tractor other than National, and 13 percent of A owners purchased a National tractor when they reentered the market.

EFFECT ON DIFFERENCES IN OWNER BODY ON 1975 TRACTOR PURCHASES

In Table 2, we have calculated the effect of owner bodies on type X tractor purchases in 1975. We have used actual figures for the size of National and competitor A owner bodies but have assumed that all

TABLE 2

	Make replaced (thousands of units)			
Make replaced	*National*	*A*	*Other*	*Total purchased*
National	5.0	2.8	2.6	10.4
Competitor A	3.6	6.4	3.4	13.4
Other	3.7	3.8	12.8	20.3
Total	12.3	13.0	18.8	44.1
Penetration	27.9%	29.5%	42.6%	100.0%
National (under) competitor A:				
Percentage points (1.6)				
Units (0.7)				

other factors, including owner loyalty rates, are equal. In this calculation, we have applied National loyalty to both National and competitor A owner bodies. Based on these premises, one would expect National to have a deficiency in market penetration relative to competitor A of 1.6 percent solely as a result of the differences in the size of the two owner bodies, with National market penetration at 27.9 percent and competitor A penetration at 29.5 percent.

TYPE X TRACTOR WARRANTY EXPENSE[2]

Some indication of National's type X tractor quality and durability problem is found in the level of our warranty expense as shown in Table 3. From 1970 to 1973 our warranty expense on the average type X tractor increased from $21.48 to $55.06, an increase of $33.58 per unit. Since 1973 warranty costs have declined to $31.38, a reduction of $23.68. Expense on all components, with the exception of the hydraulic system, has increased over 1970 levels. It seems clear that warranty

[2] Warranty expense is the amount spent by National for replacements and repairs to tractors in use for which it had accepted responsibility. The company kept detailed records of such costs, broken down not only in the main classifications indicated in Table 4, but also for individual parts within each classification.

TABLE 3

	Model year						1975 (over)/under 1970	
	1970	*1971*	*1972*	*1973*	*1974*	*1975*	*Per unit*	*Percent*
Engine	$11.30	$ 7.56	$28.05	$28.40	$22.58	$12.76	$(1.46)	(13%)
Transmission	3.70	3.09	3.90	6.60	6.00	7.19	(3.49)	(94)
Hydraulic system	.80	.46	.74	5.21	1.35	.57	.23	29
Electrical	.65	1.14	1.93	3.88	4.40	3.27	(2.62)	(403)
Other	5.03	4.20	5.20	10.97	8.90	7.59	(2.56)	(51)
Total	21.48	16.45	39.82	55.06	43.23	31.38	(9.90)	(46%)

costs of over $31 per unit are too high and represent an unsatisfactory level of quality as far as the user is concerned.

NATIONAL N–50 TYPE X TRACTOR—WARRANTY AND DESIGN[3] COST

Table 4 indicates changes in warranty expense and design costs per unit on the N–50 tractor in the 1973, 1974, and 1975 models. In total, during this period, warranty expense has been reduced approximately $33, while design costs have increased $36. Engine warranty expense on this model had declined $40 per unit, while design costs have increased $24. In the case of the transmission, warranty expense has increased $3.30 per unit, despite an increase of $1.77 per unit in design costs.

TABLE 4 Changes by Year

	1973 (over)/under 1972		1974 (over)/under 1973		1975 (over)/under 1974		1975 (over)/under 1972	
	Warranty	*design*	*Warranty*	*design*	*Warranty*	*design*	*Warranty*	*design*
Engine	$ 9.80	$(3.74)	$24.00	$(12.99)	$6.48	$ (7.62)	$40.28	$(24.35)
Transmission	(2.69)	(1.31)	.59	—	(1.20)	(.46)	(3.30)	(1.77)
Hydraulic system	(4.48)	(8.90)	3.87	.94	.77	(2.97)	.16	(10.93)
Electrical	(1.93)	—	(.53)	(1.09)	1.13	.32	(1.33)	(.77)
Other	(5.70)	4.17	2.00	(.50)	1.33	(1.73)	(2.37)	1.94
Total	(5.00)	(9.78)	29.93	(13.64)	8.51	(12.46)	33.44	(35.88)

[3] Design cost refers to the costs of the tractor itself. These costs are a function of the way in which the tractor is designed. For example, the total standard cost of the 1973 model was $9.78 more than the total standard cost of the 1972 model; the designers had devised a more expensive tractor in 1973. In making the comparisons, wage rates and material costs are held constant.

CASE 4–3
Pierce-Irwin Corporation

In early November 1964, Mr. Frank Wood, manager of the Eastern Service Depot (ESD) of the Pierce-Irwin Corporation (PICOR) telephoned one of his former professors at a prominent graduate school of business. Mr. Wood indicated that he had a "measurement problem" and would like a second-year M.B.A. candidate to join his staff during the Christmas holidays to assist him in analyzing and resolving his problem.

Asked to outline the problem, Wood responded: "As you know, one of PICOR's basic objectives is to provide its customers with service second to none. The ESD, as an arm of the marketing function, has the responsibility of satisfying Eastern customer demand for replacement parts for PICOR equipments. We think that it is on the basis of our performance as a service depot that most of our customers evaluate the company's ability to minimize down-time on PICOR equipment and that outstanding service from ESD is crucial to attaining the corporate objective of unequaled service. Our problem, then, is to measure our performance against a stated objective; it's a basic problem in accounting (auditing)."

On December 14, 1964, Mr. Michael B. Allen, the M.B.A. candidate selected to work with PICOR's ESD, met with several members of Mr. Wood's staff. The first days of Allen's association with PICOR were devoted to gaining a thorough understanding of the objectives, functions, and procedures of the ESD. Time for investigation and analysis was limited, since Allen was expected to work to produce fruitful recommendations on the information and analysis required to measure ESD performance against PICOR's stated objective.

PICOR HISTORY

PICOR was founded as a partnership in 1939 in Lowell, Massachusetts. The company's founders, Randolph Pierce and Oscar Irwin, had been impressed by the opportunities that seemed to exist in the field of electronics while they were taking their degrees at M.I.T. After forming the partnership, with assets of $312, Pierce and Irwin designed and built several basic test instruments on a part-time basis. A switchover to full-time production followed the introduction and demonstration of these instruments to several industries in the states of Massachusetts, Rhode Island, Connecticut, and New Hampshire.

The firm was incorporated in 1947, when sales reached $850,000; by 1950, sales reached $1,370,000; and, by 1961, sales totaled $49,600,000. During these first two decades of the company's life, expansion of the product line was Pierce's major interest. In 1964, PICOR had over 200 basic test instruments, principal among which were oscilloscopes, audio-oscillators, vacuum tube voltmeters, noise and distortion analyzers, signal generators, power meters, electronic counters, and waveguide and coaxial instrumentation for microwave work. A continuing objective of the firm was "to provide the market with instruments of the most advanced design and the finest craftmanship for the accurate measurement of electrical phenomena and to support its products with the utmost in customer service and technical service."

Manufacturing facilities were continually expanded to keep pace with the steady growth in volume. In the early 1960s, PICOR operated seven manufacturing facilities, which provided a total of almost 15 acres of floor space. Production facilities were located in Lowell and Holyoke, Massachusetts; Fullerton, California; Denver, Colorado; Dayton, Ohio; Renton, Washington; and Rotterdam, Netherlands. Marketing operations were carried out throughout the United States and in most of the industrialized countries of the free world.

CORPORATE ORGANIZATION

PICOR's operations were managed through the executive department, with headquarters in Lowell, Massachusetts. Two operating groups were responsible for Manufacturing and Marketing. Manufacturing was responsible for the operation of PICOR's seven plants. Marketing was split into two subdivisions: Sales and Service. The service division include the ESD (in Lowell, Massachusetts), the newly established Western Service Depot (WSD) in San Mateo, California, and the Technical Service Department. The ESD originally served as a centralized warehouse for all replacement parts and components, but, in August of 1964, the WSD was established. The service depots were then organized to satisfy demand for replacement parts and components for customers in their assigned regions. The field sales organization was broken into six regional divisions (see Exhibit 1 for a schematic diagram of the firm's functional organization): Western, Northeastern, Central, Southern, European, and Asia. Each of these six regional sales divisions had two or more sales offices located in key marketing centers. There were 18 sales offices in the United States and 6 sales offices in Europe and Asia. The ESD filled replacement orders of customers served by the northeastern, central, southern, and European regional sales divisions; WSD served the western and Asia regional sales divisions.

EXHIBIT 1 Schematic Organization Chart

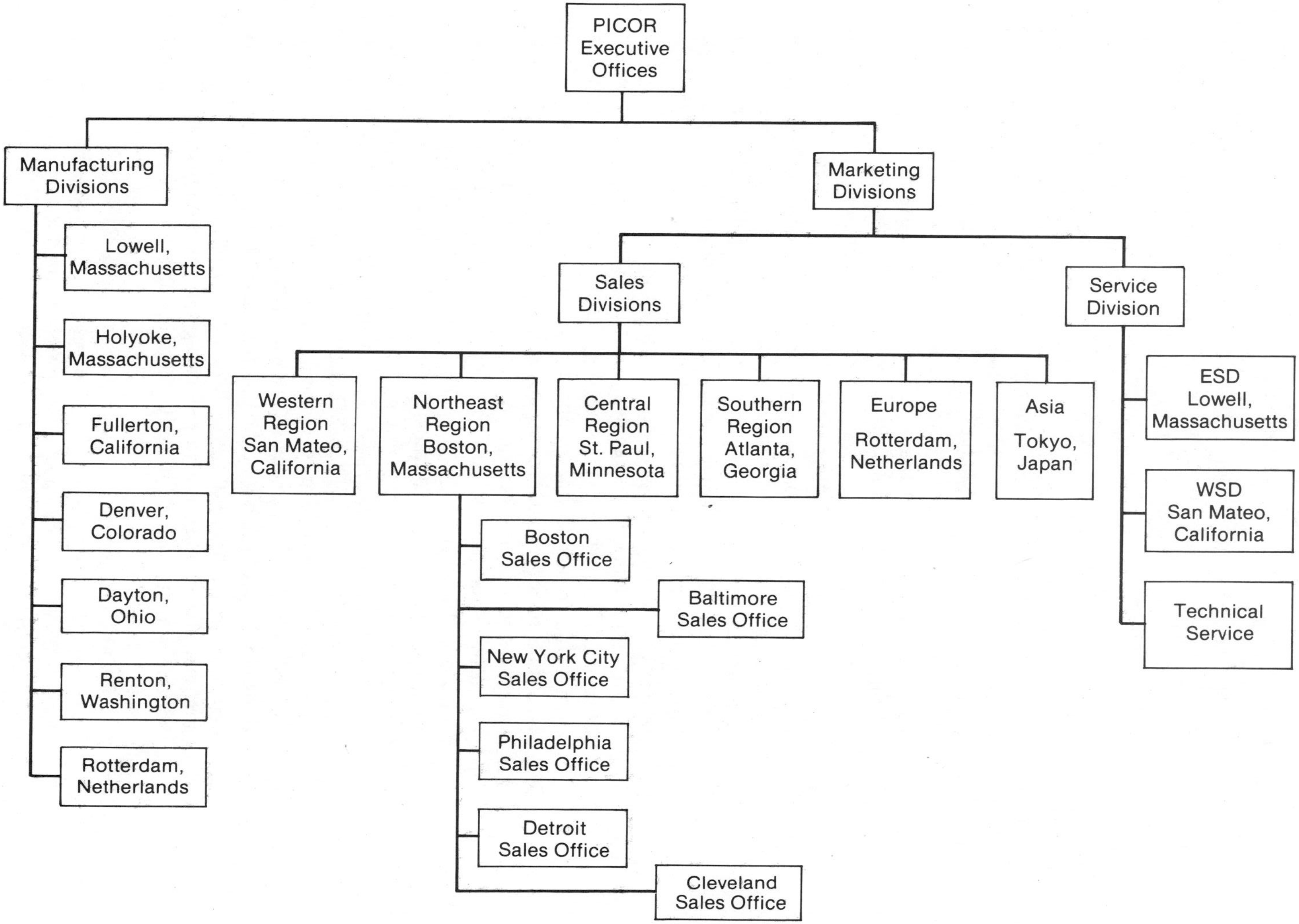

During an average month, ESD would ship approximately $300,000 worth of parts in response to some 6,000 orders. The median order was for less than $40 and over 50 percent of the incoming orders requested only one line-item.

ESD OPERATIONS

Mr. Wood noted that though the ESD was considered a profit center and was partially evaluated by PICOR executives on the basis of its profitability, its prime function was to minimize the time lag between the point at which the customer recognized a need for a replacement part and the delivery of the replacement to the customer's plant. Expanding on this objective, Wood explained that "as long as the customer feels his down-time was at a reasonable minimum and less than would have been experienced in dealing with PICOR's competition, we have fulfilled our function as a service depot. In other words, when we say our objective is to minimize the time lag, we really mean 'provide the minimum available time lag.' Now, in translating the corporate objective of service second to none into time minimization, we're making one crucial assumption about our customers: namely, that they order replacement parts on the basis of an immediate need."

Allen questioned the significance of this assumption: "Even if the bulk of ESD activity is occasioned by stocking orders, aren't we providing outstanding service by minimizing lead times, providing a stable lead-time history, and proving to our customers that they need not invest heavily in replacement parts for PICOR equipment?"

Asked about the trade-off between functioning as a profit center and satisfying the service objective, Wood remarked: "We're prepared to lose money on individual transactions. Otherwise, we wouldn't bother filling the 35 cent orders. But we feel that overall, ESD can show a contribution to corporate profit and overhead and still provide the best service in the industry. The ESD is not, of course, a profit-maximizing division; our role is to provide the marketing function with a convincing, crucial sales argument in favor of PICOR instruments so as to improve the profitability of the company as a whole. When we budget our operation, there's no pressure to sacrifice service for divisional margins: the exercise is always based on the assumption that we are a service activity which, happily enough, more than covers its direct costs."

PICOR encouraged its customers to deal solely with their local sales offices. Orders for replacement parts were usually placed with the local sales office. The sales office prepared the PICOR documentation (see Exhibit 2, a flowchart of the order processing). The sales office handled all customer contact with almost no exceptions: (1) parts were shipped directly from the service depot to the customer's specified

EXHIBIT 2 Simplified Order-Processing Flowchart

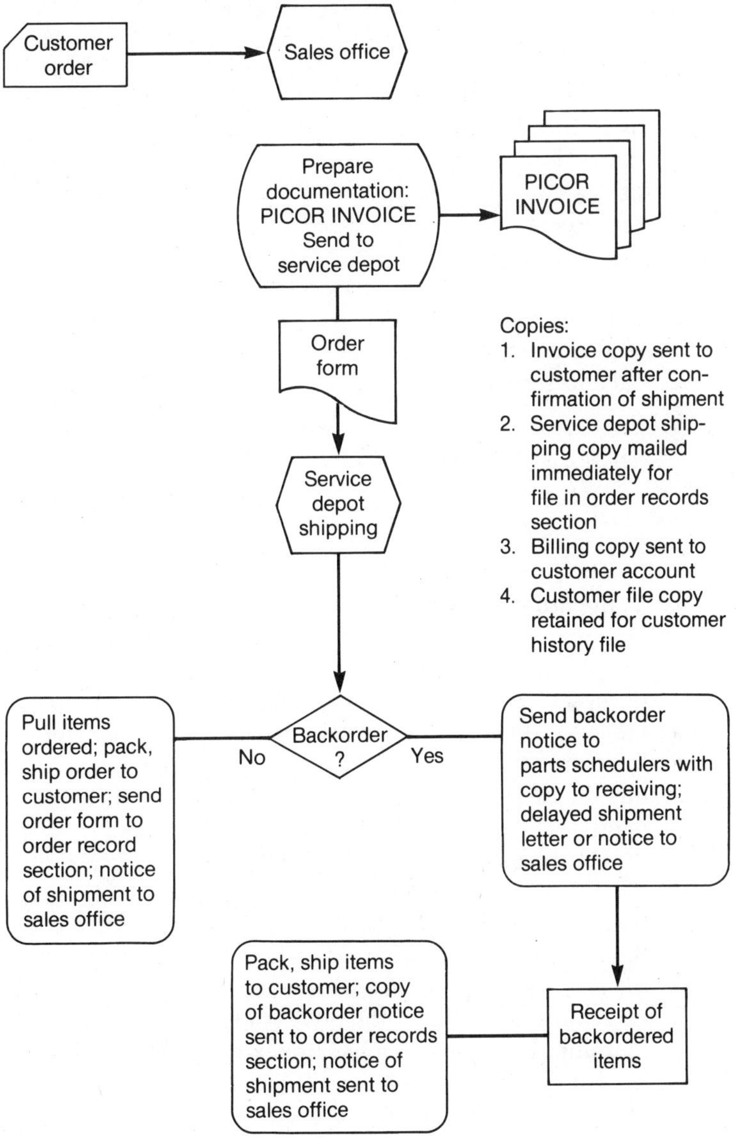

receiving location; (2) if an item were back ordered at the service depot, a note indicating delayed shipment would be sent directly from the service depot to the sales office; and (3) when back-ordered items were shipped, a shipping notice would be sent to the sales office. The service depot executed virtually all its actions on a PICOR invoice prepared at the sales office. In the event of a stock-out condition at the service depot, a back-order notice would be prepared in order to insure expediting of the restocking and shipment of the parts.

The service depot specified the mode of shipment in virtually all cases (the only exception was in the rare event the customer did specify mode of shipment) and bore all transportation charges. The decision as to mode of shipment was based on a standing policy of least-time delivery to the customer's specified receiving station. ESD and WSD used air freight in all instances in which other modes of shipment from their location were less rapid, except when the customer specified a delivery date that permitted use of low-cost shipping.

Stocking decisions at the service depots were based on analysis of demand history, demand forecasts, and EOQ calculations (which included estimated stock-out costs based on an ABC analysis of historical and forecast demand).

ESD PERFORMANCE SAMPLING

In attempting to measure the service level achieved by ESD, Wood had initiated the "Friday Sample" in 1962. The Friday Sample attempted to measure the percentage of orders shipped on the same day as the order was received. At the close of business each Friday, Wood assembled copies of the order forms received at ESD during the week. The number shipped same day was divided by total number received during the week to develop a "Same Day" performance index. Wood indicated that the index varied between 90 percent and 95 percent, indicating that ESD was shipping that percentage of orders on the same day the order was received. This ESD Performance Rating was prominently displayed throughout the ESD building.

On the first Friday with PICOR, Allen remained after normal closing hours, chatting with the manager of the shipping section. The full work force remained to work overtime for nearly an hour. Allen asked the shipping section manager about the overtime work, and received the following reply: "We work about an hour overtime every Friday to make sure that we don't have a backlog of leftover orders on Monday morning. If we had a big backlog, we'd have to clean that up before we started filling Monday's orders, and then the performance index would drop way down. Mr. Wood wants each week's work load to be 'normal,' whatever that means."

On Wednesday, December 16, Allen and Wood met to discuss Allen's project. In response to Allen's first question, Wood ruled out the possibility of directly contacting customers or PICOR competitors in any survey work. Wood indicated that he was interested in measuring (1) ESD's efficiency in processing orders that could be filled from stock (this was the purpose of the Friday Sample); (2) the impact of each link in the order-processing chain (customer to sales office to ESD to customer) on the speed with which customer orders were filled; and (3) the significance of back-ordered items to PICOR customers and to PICOR. Wood indicated that he recognized the impact of nonrandom selection of the day for the ESD weekly performance survey.

Wood and Allen focused their attention on the different kinds of measures that might be used. Wood's performance rating had dealt with orders. Allen suggested alternative measures of efficiency, remarking that "counting the number of times separate line-items are requested gives us one measure of customer demand. Dollar value, or inventory cost, or number of units, or number of customers submitting an order may be equally significant measures of our activity. We may fill 90 percent of the orders received; but analyzing the 10 percent we back order, we may find 10 percent of the customers who submitted orders that day, or we might find the back-order delays running two weeks. These other indicators may provide a more meaningful measure of customer satisfaction. The percentage of requests filled the same day provides a good measure of ESD efficiency, but when I took this job, you indicated an interest in measuring the extent to which ESD met the objective of providing good service. Have we changed our minds? Or, have we made a simplifying assumption that internal efficiency is identical with providing good service as measured by customer satisfaction?"

"If we can't go to the customer and if we can't find out what kind of service the competition is providing, we at least ought to be able to develop some measure of the level of service—as opposed to the efficiency of the ESD."

Wood responded by saying, "Mike, you've got a good point. We want to operate efficiently, but our major objective is providing service. Perhaps it would be well if we both put our feet on our desk this afternoon and tried to figure out just what we can measure in order to evaluate our service level. Take back orders, for instance: the customer is interested in how long he has to wait; if price has anything to do with value, service might be measured by the dollar value of back-ordered items; or, if we assume price and time are both relevant, we'd want a measure of the dollar-days back ordered, wouldn't we? Or, perhaps the percentage of customers who placed orders that receive back-order notices each day would be a good indicator, suggesting revision of our stocking policy if that number shows an uptrend. Now, that's useful because it not only tells us about our ability to fill orders for customers but it also gives us a place to look if we feel our performance is either below par or deteriorating."

Allen commented: "Are we agreed, then, that we want to evaluate both efficiency and service level? and that in measuring efficiency we can define an 'optimum' system and measure our through-put time against the optimum? and . . ."

Wood interrupted: "Wait a minute, Mike. I thought we were going to use some variation of the ESD Performance Rating to measure efficiency. Through-put is tough to define because we only operate on a one-shift basis."

Allen responded: "I guess that's right, Mr. Wood. But now, in evaluating our service level, we want to define service in such a way that it's measurable on the basis of internally available data. We've got a number of variables: days, customers, orders, dollars, units, line-items. And these can be put together in almost any variation or combination. I'm going to have to bat those combinations and variations around for awhile; but I'll see if I can't come up with some way to measure service, using those variables, against historical levels of service, measured the same way."

Wood concluded the discussion by commending Allen on the amount of insight he had gained and by offering one word of warning: "Watch out for the fallacy of looking at dollars too hard. The price of the part may be no measure of its value to the customer—remember the old arguments about 'for the want of a nail, a shoe was lost; for the want of a man, the battle was lost;' and so on. If our customers' electronic counter is out of commission, the opportunity cost may be many times the price of parts to repair it; and it's really the customer's opportunity cost we want to minimize."

Question

As Allen, prepare the procedure(s) you will recommend to Mr. Wood to achieve his objectives.

PART TWO

The Management Control Structure

In Chapter 1, management control was defined as "the process by which management assures that the organization carries out its strategies effectively and efficiently." Depending on the situation in a given organization, this process may relate to either or both of two structures: (1) the organization structure, (2) projects. The discussion of management control as related to projects (e.g., research/development projects, construction projects, production of motion pictures) is deferred to Chapter 16. In Part Two we have limited the discussion to the type of management control that focuses on organization units.

A key concept in this discussion is that of the responsibility center. A responsibility center is any organization unit headed by a manager who is responsible for its activities.

Characteristics of a responsibility center that are relevant to the management control process are discussed in Chapter 5. All responsibility centers produce outputs (that is, they do something), and all have inputs (that is, they use resources). They can be classified on the basis of the measurement of inputs and outputs into one of four types: revenue centers, expense centers, profit centers, and investment centers.

In a ***revenue center,*** *outputs are measured in monetary terms, but inputs are not measured in monetary terms. These responsibility centers usually are part of the marketing organization. They are discussed briefly in Chapter 5.*

In an ***expense center,*** *the management control system measures inputs in monetary terms, but does not measure outputs in monetary terms. Various types of expense centers are discussed in Chapter 5.*

In a ***profit center,*** *the management control system measures both inputs and outputs in monetary terms; that is, inputs are measured in terms of cost and outputs in terms of revenues. Profit is the difference between costs and revenues. Profit centers are discussed in Chapter 6. Many profit centers transfer products (either goods or services) to other profit centers within the company. The price used in measuring the amount of products transferred is called a "transfer price." Chapter 7 is devoted to a discussion of transfer pricing.*

In an ***investment center,*** *the control system measures not only the inputs and outputs in monetary terms but also measures the investment that is employed in the responsibility center. Investment centers are discussed in Chapter 8. Chapter 8 also discusses some of the organizational considerations that are involved in deciding whether a responsibility center should, or should not, be treated as an investment center.*

CHAPTER 5

Responsibility Centers: Revenue and Expense Centers

In the first part of this chapter, we discuss the nature of responsibility centers in general. In the second part, we discuss revenue centers and expense centers, which are two types of responsibility centers.

RESPONSIBILITY CENTERS

We have used the term *responsibility center* to denote any organization unit that is headed by a responsible manager. In a sense, a company is a collection of responsibility centers, each of which is represented by a box on the organization chart. These responsibility centers form a hierarchy. At the lowest level in the organization there are responsibility centers for sections, work shifts, or other small organization units. At a higher level there are departments or divisions that consist of several of these smaller units plus overall departmental or divisional staff and management people; these larger units are also responsibility centers. And from the standpoint of top management and the board of directors, the whole company is a responsibility center. Although even these large units fit the definition of responsibility center, the term is used to refer primarily to the smaller, lower-level units within the organization.

Nature of Responsibility Centers

A responsibility center exists to accomplish one or more purposes; these purposes are its *objectives*. Presumably, the objectives of an individual responsibility center are intended to help achieve the overall goals of the whole organization. These overall goals are decided upon in the strategic planning process, and are here assumed to have been established prior to the beginning of the management control process.

Exhibit 5–1 is a schematic diagram that shows the essence of any responsibility center. A responsibility center uses inputs, which are

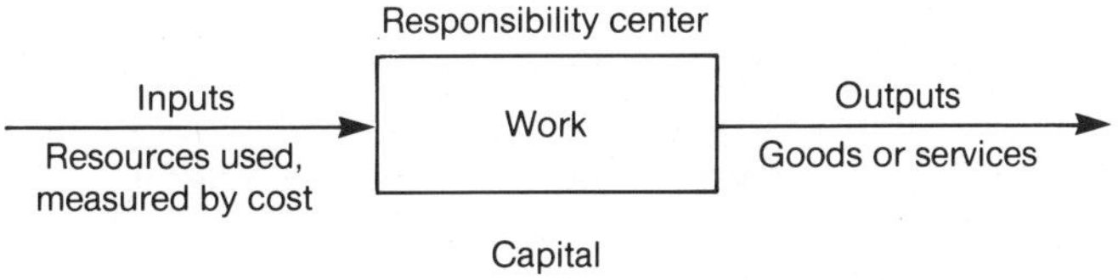

physical quantities of material, hours of various types of labor, and a variety of services. It works with these resources, and it usually requires working capital, equipment, and other assets to do this work. As a result of this work, the responsibility center produces outputs, which are classified either as goods, if they are tangible, or as services, if they are intangible. Presumably, these outputs are consistent with the responsibility center's objectives, but this is not necessarily so. For example, a manufacturing center may produce more goods than the marketing department can sell, or it may provide goods of inferior quality. These are outputs even though they are not consistent with the company's overall objectives. Whatever a responsibility center produces, whether good or bad, desired or unwanted, constitute its outputs.

The goods and services produced by a responsibility center may be furnished either to another responsibility center or to the outside world. In the former case, they are inputs to the other responsibility center; in the latter case, they are outputs of the whole organization. Revenues are the amounts earned from selling these outputs.

Measurement of Inputs and Outputs

The amount of labor, material, and services used in a responsibility center are physical quantities: hours of labor, quarts of oil, reams of paper, and kilowatt-hours hours of electricity. In a management control system it is convenient to translate these amounts into monetary terms. Money provides a common denominator that permits the amounts of individual resources to be combined. The monetary amount is ordinarily obtained by multiplying the physical quantity by a price per unit of quantity (e.g., hours of labor times a rate per hour). This amount is called "cost." Thus the inputs of a responsibility center are ordinarily expressed as costs. Cost is a monetary measure of the amount of resources used by a responsibility center.

Note that inputs are resources *used* by the responsibility center. The patients in a hospital or the students in a school are *not* inputs. Rather, it is the resources that are used in accomplishing the objectives of *treating* the patients or *educating* the students that are the inputs.

Although inputs almost always can be measured in terms of cost, outputs are much more difficult to measure. In a profit-oriented organization, revenue is often an important measure of output, but such a measure is rarely a complete expression of outputs; it does not encompass everything that the organization does. In many responsibility centers, outputs cannot be measured satisfactorily. How can one measure the value of the work done by a public relations department, a quality control department, or a legal staff?

In many nonprofit organizations, no good quantitative measure of output exists. A school can easily measure the number of students graduated, but it cannot measure how much education each of them acquired. Although outputs may not be measured, or may not even be measurable, it is a fact that every organization unit *has* outputs; that is, it does something.

Efficiency and Effectiveness

The concepts stated above can be used to explain the meaning of efficiency and effectiveness, which are the two criteria for judging the performance of a responsibility center. The terms *efficiency* and *effectiveness* are almost always used in a comparative, rather than in an absolute, sense; that is, we do not ordinarily say that Responsibility Center A is 80 percent efficient, but rather that it is more (or less) efficient than Responsibility Center B, or more (or less) efficient currently than it was in the past.

Efficiency is the ratio of outputs to inputs, or the amount of output per unit of input. Responsibility Center A is more efficient than Responsibility Center B either (1) if it uses less resources than Responsibility Center B, but has the same output, or (2) if it uses the same amount of resources as Responsibility Center B and has a greater output than Responsibility Center B. Note that the first type of measure does not require that output be quantified; it is only necessary to judge that the outputs of the two units are approximately the same. If management is satisfied that Responsibility Centers A and B are both doing a satisfactory job, and if it is a job of comparable magnitude, then the unit with the lower inputs (i.e., the lower costs) is the more efficient. The second type of measure does require some quantitative measure of output; it is, therefore, a more difficult type of measurement in many situations.

In many responsibility centers, a measure of efficiency can be developed that relates actual costs to some standard—that is, to a number that expresses what costs should be incurred for the amount of measured output. Such a measure can be a useful indication of efficiency; but it is never a perfect measure for at least two reasons: (1) recorded costs are not a precisely accurate measure of resources consumed, and (2) standards are, at best, only approximate measures of what resource consumption ideally should have been in the circumstances prevailing.

Effectiveness is the relationship between a responsibility center's outputs and its objectives. The more these outputs contribute to the objectives, the more effective the unit is. Since both objectives and outputs are often difficult to quantify, measures of effectiveness are difficult to come by. Effectiveness, therefore, is often expressed in nonquantitative, judgmental terms, such as "College A is doing a first-rate job, but College B has slipped somewhat in recent years."

An organization unit should be *both* efficient and also effective; it is not a case of choosing one or the other. Efficient responsibility centers are those that do whatever they do with the lowest consumption of resources; but if what they do (i.e., their output) is an inadequate contribution to the accomplishment of the organization's goals, they are ineffective. If a credit department handles the paperwork connected with delinquent accounts at a low cost per unit, it is efficient; but if it is unsuccessful in making collections, or if in the process of collecting accounts it needlessly antagonizes customers, it is ineffective. Drucker states that "there is a sharp clash today between stress on the efficiency of administration (as represented, above all, by the governmental administrator and the accountant) and stress on effectiveness (which emphasizes results)."[1] There should not in fact be a "sharp clash" between efficiency and effectiveness, nor is there substantial evidence that such a clash exists. Management's emphasis should be on both these criteria.

The role of profits. One important objective in a profit-oriented organization is to earn profits, and the amount of profits is therefore an important measure of effectiveness. Since profit is the difference between revenue, which is a measure of output, and expense, which is a measure of input, profit also is a measure of efficiency. Thus, profit measures both effectiveness and efficiency. When such an overall measure exists, it is unnecessary to determine the relative importance of effectiveness versus efficiency. When such an overall measure does not exist, it is feasible and useful to classify performance measures as relating either to effectiveness or to efficiency. In these situations, there is the problem of balancing the two types of measurements. For example, how do we compare the profligate perfectionist with the frugal manager who obtains less than the optimum output?

Although profit is an important joint measure of effectiveness and efficiency, it is a less than perfect measure for several reasons: (1) monetary measures do not exactly measure either all aspects of output or all inputs; (2) standards against which profits are judged may not be accurate; and (3) at best, profit is a measure of what has happened in the short run, whereas we are presumably also interested in the long-

[1] Peter F. Drucker, *The Age of Discontinuity* (New York: Harper & Row, 1969), p. 197.

run consequences of management actions. These points are discussed in more depth in Chapter 12.

As stated in the introduction to Part Two, there are four types of responsibility centers based on the nature of the monetary inputs or outputs, or both, that are measured: revenue centers, expense centers, profit centers, and investment centers. In revenue centers, only outputs are measured; in expense centers, only expenses are measured; in profit centers, both revenues and expenses are measured; and in investment centers, the relationship between profits and investment is measured. We discuss revenue centers and expense centers in the next part of the chapter.

REVENUE CENTERS

In a revenue center, outputs are measured in monetary terms, but no formal attempt is made to relate inputs or expense to outputs (if expense were matched against revenues the unit would be a profit center). Revenue centers are found primarily in marketing organizations. Budgets, or sales quotas, are prepared for sales made, or orders booked, for the revenue center as a whole, and for the individual salespersons who work in it; and records of actual sales or orders are compared with these budgets. In this book, we do not discuss revenue centers as such. We shall discuss the measurement of revenue as part of our discussion of profit centers.

Each revenue center is also an expense center. The primary measurement, however, is revenue. The cost includes only those controlled directly by the revenue center management. Consequently, these are not profit centers because the expenses are incomplete. The control of expenses in these units is discussed in the section on expense centers.

EXPENSE CENTERS

Expense centers are responsibility centers for which inputs, or expenses, are measured in monetary terms, but in which outputs are not measured in monetary terms. There are two general types: engineered expense centers and discretionary expense centers. They correspond to two types of costs. Engineered costs are elements of cost for which the "right" or "proper" amount of costs that should be incurred can be estimated with a reasonable degree of reliability. The direct labor and direct material costs incurred in a factory are examples. Discretionary costs are those for which no such engineered estimate is feasible; the amount of costs incurred depends on management's judgment as to the amount that is appropriate under the circumstances.

Engineered Expense Centers

Engineered costs are usually expressed as standard costs. If one can establish standard costs for an expense center, a measure of output can be determined by multiplying the physical quantity of the output by the unit standard costs for each of the units produced and summing the results. The total actual cost is compared to the total standard cost of the output and variances are analyzed. The manager of the expense center is evaluated on how well he or she keeps actual costs at or below these standard costs.

It should be emphasized that in engineered expense centers there are other important tasks that are not measured by costs alone. It is necessary to control the effectiveness of these aspects of performance. For example, expense center supervisors are responsible for the quality of the products and for the volume of production, in addition to their responsibility for cost efficiency. It is necessary, therefore, to prescribe the type and amount of production and to set specific quality standards; otherwise, manufacturing costs could be minimized at the expense of quality or volume.

There are few, if any, responsibility centers in which all items of cost are engineered. Even in highly automated production departments, the amount of indirect labor and of various services used can vary with management's discretion. Thus, the term *engineered expense center* refers to responsibility centers in which engineered costs predominate, but does not imply that valid engineering estimates can be made for each and every cost item.

Control systems for engineered expense centers are described in cost accounting texts and, therefore, are not discussed in detail in this book.

Discretionary Expense Centers

Some organization units have outputs that are not measured in monetary terms. These are principally administrative staff units (e.g., accounting, legal, industrial relations), research and product development organizations, and some types of marketing activities.[2]

By definition, the efficiency or effectiveness of these organization units cannot be measured in monetary terms. Monetary control is expressed in terms of expenses only. Consequently, we call these organization units "discretionary expense centers." Usually, the control pro-

[2] There are activities within each of these categories for which financial standards may be set; for example, the handling of accounts receivable within the accounting department. These activities tend to be those with repetitive operations where the variables of performance can be controlled. Where this type of activity constitutes an important proportion of the total staff cost, it should be controlled by comparing actual costs against performance standards.

cess in a discretionary expense center starts with an annual budget or plan that management approves. Subsequently, actual expenses are compared to budget. These comparisons compare *budget input* to *actual input*. Since they do not measure output in monetary terms, they do not provide a complete measure of performance and, therefore, cannot be used as a basis for overall evaluation of the manager. Such a system will motivate the manager only to keep his or her expenses equal to the amount of the budget. Even though this motivation is incomplete, this is about as much as can be expected from the system.

General Control Characteristics

Budget formulation. The decision that management must make with respect to a discretionary expense budget is different from the decision that it must make with respect to the budget for an engineered expense center. For the latter, management must decide whether the proposed operating budget represents a reasonable and efficient task for the coming period. Management is not so much concerned with the magnitude of the task, because this is largely determined by the sales and production budgets. In formulating the budget for a discretionary expense center, however, management's principal task is to decide on the magnitude of the job that should be done.

In preparing a budget proposal for consideration by management, one should be careful not to include irrelevant data that might obscure the important information needed for this decision. Some budget proposals include a breakdown of the number of people by classification, the expense by each account, and a history of these costs for several years, all in great detail; but there may be little or no information about the tasks to be accomplished. If the proposal is of this nature, management must either rubber-stamp the budget, try to question individual expense items, or make arbitrary reductions. Questioning individual items is unlikely to be fruitful, for if a proposal has been prepared carefully, a reasonable rationale can be given for any individual expense (whether or not it is really justifiable). If management reduces a budget arbitrarily, it can expect to receive a budget proposal the following year that contains sufficient "water" so a reduction creates no hardship. The following questions should be asked with respect to a discretionary expense budget proposal:

1. What are the precise decisions that management should make?
2. Does the proposal include all the available information pertinent to making these decisions?
3. Does the proposal include irrelevant information which, at best, will tend to obscure the real issues?

As we stated above, it is important in any budget proposal to describe the tasks to be accomplished. These tasks can be generally divided into two types—*continuing* and *special*. *Continuing* tasks are those that continue from year to year; for example, financial statement preparation by the controller's office. *Special* tasks are projects that have a finite completion time; for example, developing and installing a standard cost system in a specified factory.

The technique called "management by objectives" is often used in describing specific tasks. Management by objectives is a formal process whereby a budgetee proposes to accomplish specific tasks and provides a means for measuring whether these tasks have been accomplished. Management by objectives is discussed in Chapters 12 and 15.

Type of control. The financial control exercised in a discretionary expense center is quite different from the financial control exercised through an operating expense budget for a manufacturing department. The latter attempts to minimize operating costs by setting a standard and reporting actual costs against this standard. Costs are minimized by motivating line managers to maintain maximum efficiency, and by giving higher management a means of evaluating the efficiency of departmental management. The main purpose of a discretionary expense budget, on the other hand, is to allow management to control costs by *participating in the planning*. Costs are controlled primarily by deciding what tasks should be undertaken and what level of effort is appropriate for each.[3]

Some authorities state that a tight budget is a good budget because a tight budget will result in more pressure to reduce costs than one that is easily attainable. While this philosophy may have merit for a standard cost budget, it is of questionable validity for a discretionary expense budget. The head of a discretionary expense center can easily cut costs by reducing the magnitude of the job that is done. However, when this happens, the individual responsible for spending the money is making the decision about the job to be done. Such decisions should properly be made by higher management.

The general rule, then, is that discretionary expense budgets should reflect as closely as possible the *actual costs* of doing the tasks that should be done. A deviation from this rule should be backed by adequate reasons, and this condition should be known to management when the budget is presented for approval.

Measurement of performance. In discretionary expense centers, the performance report is used to ensure that the budget commitment will not be exceeded without management's knowledge. It is not a means for evaluating the efficiency of the manager. This is in contrast

[3] Management, of course, may set certain kinds of standards to be used companywide; for example, the ratio of secretaries to professionals or the relative amounts to be spent on dues to professional societies, and so forth.

to the report in an engineered expense center, which helps higher management evaluate the efficiency of manufacturing management. If these two types of responsibility centers are not carefully distinguished, management may treat the report for a discretionary expense center as if it were an indication of efficiency. If this is done, the people responsible for spending may be motivated to spend less than budgeted. This pressure toward lower costs may possibly result in the task being done for less money, but it is more likely that the lower spending will be accomplished by less output. In any event, there is little point in trying to increase the efficiency by such indirect methods as rewarding executives who spend less than budget.

Control over spending can be exercised by requiring that management approval be obtained before the budget can be overrun. Sometimes, a certain percentage of overrun (say, 5 percent) is allowed without additional approval. If the budget really sets forth the best estimate of actual costs, there is a 50 percent probability that it will be overrun, and this is the reason that some latitude is often permitted.

In the following paragraphs, we discuss three of the most common types of discretionary expense centers: administrative centers, research/development centers, and marketing centers.

ADMINISTRATIVE CENTERS

Administrative centers include the top management, divisional management, and managers who are responsible for staff units.

Control Problems

The control of administrative staff expense is particularly difficult because of (1) the near impossibility of measuring output, and (2) the frequent lack of congruence between the goals of the staff department and the goals of the company.

Difficulty in measuring output. Some staff activities, such as payroll accounting, are so routinized that they can be regarded as engineered expense centers. For others, however, the principal output is advice and service; and there are no valid means of measuring the value, or even the amount, of this output. If output cannot be measured, it is not possible to set cost standards and measure financial performance against these standards. A budget variance, therefore, cannot be interpreted as representing either efficient or inefficient performance. Even where the budget is subdivided into tasks, the results cannot be interpreted in terms of efficiency or inefficiency. For instance, if the finance staff were given a budget allowance to "develop a standard cost system," a comparison of actual cost to budgeted cost would in no way tell management how effectively or efficiently the job had been done. The job of development and installation might have been poor, regardless of the amount spent.

Lack of goal congruence. In most administrative staff offices, it is to the benefit of the manager to have as excellent a department as he or she possibly can have. Superficially, it may appear that an excellent department is best for the company. Actually, a great deal depends on how one defines an "excellent department." For example, an excellent controller's department can answer immediately any question involving accounting data. The cost of the system required to do this, however, might far exceed the benefits it provides. Similarly, an excellent legal staff never would permit the slightest flaws in any contract that it approves. However, the cost of making reviews that are thorough enough to detect all flaws is high. The potential loss from minor undetected flaws may be much less than the cost of ensuring perfection. As another example, it is to the benefit of the manager of training to have the most complete and up-to-date visual aid devices; yet, the benefits received may not be worth the cost.

Thus, although the manager of a staff office may want to develop the "ideal" operation, such an ideal can cost more than its benefits to the company. There also can be a tendency to "empire build" or to "safeguard one's position," without regard for its value to the company.

The severity of these two problems—the difficulty of measuring output and the lack of goal congruence—is fairly directly related to the size and prosperity of the company. In small and medium-sized businesses, senior management is in close personal contact with the staff units and can determine from personal observation what they are doing and whether a unit is worth the expense. Also, in a business with low earnings, discretionary expenses are often kept under tight control. In a large business, senior management cannot possibly know about, much less evaluate, all the staff activities; and in a profitable company, there is a temptation to approve staff requests for constantly increasing budgets.

The severity of these two problems is also related directly to the organizational level of the staff activity. For example, at the plant level, the administrative staff tends to be carefully controlled by the plant manager who has personal knowledge of what is happening. Furthermore, there is less discretion in the tasks to be performed. At the divisional level, the staff has more discretion in the tasks to be performed by the staff than at the plant level. However, there is less discretion at the divisional level than at the corporate level. In general, the type of staff activity that is performed at the plant and divisional level is closely related to organizational objectives. Most of the highly discretionary cost centers (e.g., public relations) are located at the corporate level.

Budget Formulation

The budget proposal for an administrative center often consists of the following components:

1. A section covering the basic costs of the department. This includes the costs of "being in business" plus the costs of all activities which *must* be undertaken and for which no general management decisions are required.
2. A section covering the discretionary activities of the department. This includes a description of the objectives and the estimated costs of each such activity. The purpose of this part of the budget presentation is to provide information to allow management to make cost-effective decisions. For example, management may decide that some of the activities are not worth the cost. Senior management, therefore, is able to decide the magnitude of the tasks to be done.

Some companies include a section explaining the activities that would be curtailed or canceled if the budget were reduced 5 or 10 percent, and a section explaining the activities that would be increased or started if the budget were increased 5 or 10 percent. Most companies, however, do not require such estimates; they prefer that departmental managers concentrate their efforts on preparing the best possible budget for the activities that they believe should be undertaken.

Measurement of Performance

A monthly report comparing actual expenses with budget is usually prepared. As indicated earlier, this report is not designed to measure efficiency but rather to keep management informed about possible cost under- or overruns. There are few accounting problems associated with such reports. Actual costs are usually recorded in at least the same detail as that required for reporting purposes. Detailed reports are designed for the most part to help the manager of the administrative unit control costs. Top management usually needs only summaries by department.

Management Considerations

The problem for management is that, even under the best circumstances, the management control system is of limited help in determining the optimum level of expenses. Consequently, the decisions on how much to spend must be based largely on executive judgment. These decisions become more difficult as staff offices become more numerous and specialized. It is not unusual to have a dozen staff groups in corporate headquarters. They include, among others, legal, treasury, controller, systems and operations research, industrial relations, community relations, government relations, personnel, and planning staffs. The president often has neither the time nor the specialized knowledge to exercise more than cursory control over these activities. Consequently, many of the larger companies have an administrative vice president, to whom all or most of these staff functions report. This assures adequate attention by an executive with the time and expertise required to plan and exercise the necessary control over these staff activities.

RESEARCH/DEVELOPMENT CENTERS

Control Problems

The control of research/development expense is difficult for the following reasons:

1. Results are difficult to measure quantitatively. As contrasted with administrative activities, research/development usually has at least a semitangible output in terms of patents, new products, or new processes. Nevertheless, these outputs and their relation to inputs are difficult to measure and appraise. A complete "product" of a research/development group may require several years of effort; consequently, inputs as stated in an annual budget may be unrelated to outputs. Even if an output can be identified, a reliable estimate of its value often cannot be made. Even if the value of the output can be calculated, it is usually not possible for management to evaluate the efficiency of the research/development effort because of its technical nature. The causal connection between the input and the output often cannot be established. A brilliant effort may come up against an insuperable obstacle; whereas a mediocre effort may, by luck, result in a bonanza.

2. The goal congruence problem in research/development centers is similar to that in administrative centers. The research manager typically wants to build the best research organization that money can buy, even though this might be more expensive than the company can afford. A further problem is that research people often may not have sufficient knowledge of (or interest in) the business to determine the optimum direction of the research efforts.

3. Research/development can seldom be controlled effectively on an annual basis. A research project may take years to reach fruition, and the organization must be built up slowly over a long time period. The principal cost is for the work force. The right scientific talent is often difficult to obtain, and a person working on a given project often cannot be easily replaced because only that person has knowledge of the project. Consequently, it is inefficient to have short-term fluctua-

tions in the work force. It is not reasonable, therefore, to reduce research/development costs in years when profits are low and increase them in years when profits are high. Research/development must be looked at as a long-term investment, not an activity that varies with short-run corporate profitability.

Approach to Control

Management makes essentially three decisions concerning research/development activities. It must:

1. Decide the amount and timing of financial commitment to research/development.
2. Decide the direction of the research/development effort.
3. Evaluate the effectiveness of the research/development group.

Only the first of these decisions is related to the calendar year and then only when the annual program is viewed as part of a longer program; the annual budget is not governing in making any of these decisions.

Financial Commitment

A decision must be made by senior management as to the amount of funds that will be made available for research/development over a period of years. This program, of course, should be reviewed periodically and changed if change is desirable. The advantage of a long-range program is that the change will be made in the *entire plan* and the total effect of these changes can be evaluated. When a research/development budget is approved on an annual basis, it is difficult to make intelligent changes because the impact of any change is not restricted to a single year.

This long-range plan or program can be used for two purposes:

1. As a guide to approving specific projects.[4]
2. As a guide to approving the annual budget.

Specific Projects

Except in the most unusual circumstances, top management must decide the type of research to be undertaken. This is usually done by a research committee that reviews and approves individual projects (or groups of projects) before they are undertaken by the research staff.

[4] A project is a specific research task with a definite end or accomplishment. There can be wide variances in the size and type of task. For our purposes, think of a project as a specific job to be done.

The research committee is usually composed of the president or executive vice president, the director of research, the director of marketing, plus other executives who are likely to use the research results. The research committee does not concern itself with the availability of funds each time that it approves a specific project. Its concern is whether the amount of money requested should be spent on the particular research proposed, rather than in some other way. If the number of worthwhile projects increases to the point where the long-range plan will not provide enough funds, the plan should be reconsidered.

The management control of specific projects is discussed in more detail in Chapter 17.

Annual Budgets

If a company has developed a long-range research/development expenditure program and has implemented this program with a system of project approval, preparation of the annual research/development budget is a fairly simple matter. The annual budget is the calendarization of the expected expenses for the budget period. If the annual budget is in line with the long-range plan and the approved projects (as it should be), the budget approval is routine, and its main function is to assist in cash and other planning. Preparation of the budget does give management an opportunity for another look at the research/development program. Management can ask the question: "Is this the best way to use our resources next year?" Also, the annual budget ensures that actual costs will not exceed budget without management knowing about it. Significant variances from budget should be approved by management *before they are incurred.*

Measurement of Performance

Each month or each quarter, actual expenses are compared to budgeted expenses for all responsibility centers and also for projects. These are summarized progressively for managers at higher levels. The purpose of these reports is to assist the managers of responsibility centers to plan their expenses and to assure their superiors that expenses are within approved plans.

In many companies, two types of reports are provided to management. The first type compares the latest forecast of total cost with the approved project, for each active project. This is prepared periodically and given to the executive or group of executives that approves the research projects. The main purpose of this report is to help determine whether changes should be made in approved projects. The second type is a report of actual expenses compared with the budget. Its main purpose is to help the research executives in expense planning and to make sure expense commitments are being met. Neither report informs management about the efficiency or effectiveness of the research effort.

In addition to the financial information, the executive or group of executives responsible for approving and modifying projects is provided with other information; for example, the problems or successes in technical developments, the outlook for successful completion of particular projects, and the results of the latest field testing.

One method for evaluating the research/development staff is to have a formal review made periodically of completed research results over the past several years. This can be particularly valuable when these results are compared with the research accomplishments of competitors. Another technique for measuring efficiency and effectiveness is to employ a firm of consultants to make an evaluation. Some indication of efficiency might be obtained by comparing the expenses and work force employed with industry averages, where this information is available. These techniques, however, only assist management's subjective evaluation. In the final analysis, top management must be assured that the research/development effort receives the time and expertise necessary for adequate evaluation.

Management Considerations

1. If a company depends upon research for its future products (and most large companies do), it is vital that the right amount of money be spent, that it be spent for the right things, and that the research effort be staffed by highly competent people. Information on planned and actual expenses can be of only limited help in assuring that the correct decisions on these matters are made.

2. Research/development expenses are similar to capital investments. Consequently, the annual budget is an unsatisfactory vehicle for making basic decisions with respect to research/development. Instead, these decisions should be made without the time constraints inherent in an annual budget. Subsequently, the impact of these decisions on the timing of expenses can be incorporated into the annual budget.

3. Research/development expenses are controlled in terms of projects. The accounting organization is responsible for maintaining a record of actual costs by project and presenting these results. The projection of the cost of completion of each project in process should be made by the research staff.

4. The impact of an error in judgment concerning either the amount or direction of spending can be much greater in research than in administration. It may take a much longer time to correct the effects of an error in research effort. Moreover, the impact on profits can be much greater, even if the error can be corrected quickly.

The problems described in this section apply more to research than to development. The closer a development project is to the production stage, the more practical it is to use, at least to some degree, industrial engineering measures of efficiency.

MARKETING CENTERS

In many companies, the activities that are grouped under the heading of marketing consist of two quite different types; and the control that is appropriate for one type is quite different from the control that is appropriate for the other. One set of activities relates to filling orders, and they are called "order-filling" or *logistics* activities. The other type relates to efforts to obtain orders. These are the true marketing activities, and are sometimes labeled as such. Alternatively, they may be called "order-getting" activities. Thus, one set of activities takes place *after* an order has been received, and the other set takes place *before* an order has been received. In both types of activities, there are administrative functions that have the same characteristics as those discussed in a previous section, so no further mention of them will be made here.

Logistics Activities

Logistics activities are those involved in getting the goods from the company to its customers and collecting the amounts due from customers. The responsibility centers that perform these functions are fundamentally similar to expense centers in manufacturing plants. They are not discussed separately here.

Marketing Activities

True marketing activities—that is, those directed at obtaining orders—have two important characteristics that affect the management control problem.

1. The output of a marketing organization can be measured; however, it is difficult to evaluate the effectiveness of the marketing effort because the environment in which it operates cannot be controlled. For example, economic conditions or competitive actions, over which the marketing department has no control, may be different from that expected when the sales quotas were established.

2. Meeting the budgetary commitment for selling expense will normally be a minor part of the evaluation of marketing performance. If a marketing group sells twice as much as its quota, it is unlikely that management will worry too much if it exceeded its budget by 10 percent. The impact of sales volume on profits is so great that it tends to overshadow the cost performance. Few companies evaluate a market-

ing organization primarily on its ability to meet its cost targets. The sales target is the critical factor in evaluation.

The control techniques that are applicable to logistics activities are generally not applicable to marketing activities. Failure to appreciate this fact can lead to wrong decisions. For example, a manager, realizing that fixed budgets result in inequitable situations when the sales volume is high with a consequent high amount of sales commissions, may attempt to cure the problem by adjusting the sales budgets for changes in volume. Indeed, a reasonably good correlation may often be found between volume of sales and the level of sales promotion and advertising (and even the cost of sales staff). This may be taken to mean that sales expenses are variable with sales volume; however, budgets adjusted for changes in sales volume cannot be used to control selling expenses that are incurred *before* the time of sale. Advertising or sales promotion expense, for example, should not be adjusted upward or downward as sales volume changes, unless, of course, management wishes to base its advertising expenses on the volume of sales, on the theory that the higher the sales volumes, the more the company can afford to spend on advertising.

Summary. To summarize, a marketing responsibility center has three types of activities and, consequently, three types of activity measures.

First, there is the amount of revenue that the activity generates. This is usually measured by comparing actual revenue to budgeted revenues. Physical quantities sold compared to quotas may also be measured.

Second, there is the order-filling or logistic activity. In many respects, these related costs are engineered expenses. Order-filling costs are *not* discretionary expenses. If orders are to be delivered and accounts collected, these expenses must be incurred.

Third, there are order-getting costs. Order-getting costs *are* discretionary. Also, if a responsibility center is responsible for revenues, but not for profits, someone with profit responsibility must decide on the amount to be spent on these expenses. A revenue center is not a profit center because the cost of the goods that itmarkets is not charged to this activity. A manager of a revenue center, therefore, is not in a position to make a tradeoff between order-getting expenses and the resulting profit that these costs will generate. As we explain in Chapter 6, a revenue center can be converted to a profit center by charging the center with the costs of the goods that it sells.

CASE 5–1
New Jersey Insurance Company*

On July 16, 1984, John W. Montgomery, a member of the budget committee of the New Jersey Insurance Company, was reading over the current budget report for the law division in preparation for a conference scheduled for the next day with the head of that division. He held such conferences quarterly with each division head. Mr. Montgomery's practice was to think out in advance the questions he wished to ask and the points he thought he should make about each division's performance.

The law division of the New Jersey Insurance Company (NJIC) was responsible for all legal matters relating to the company's operations. Among other things, it advised company management on current and prospective developments in tax and other legislation and on recent court decisions affecting the company. It represented the company in litigation, counseled the departments concerned on the legal implications of policies, such as employee benefit plans, and it examined all major contracts to which the company was a party. It also rendered various legal services with respect to the company's proposed and existing investments.

As shown in Exhibit 1, the head of the law division, William Somersby, reported directly to top management. This relationship ensured that Mr. Somersby would be free to comment on the legal implications of management decisions, much the same as would an outside counsel. The law division was divided into five sections. This case is concerned with only two of these sections, the individual loan section and the corporate loan section. It does not attempt to describe completely the work of these two sections or the professional service rendered by the lawyers.

INDIVIDUAL LOAN SECTION

The individual loan section was responsible for the legal processing of loans made to individuals and secured by mortgages on real property. The loan instruments were submitted by independent companies situated throughout the country. The company made no loans directly to individual borrowers, although at one time it had made direct loans in the New Jersey area. Most common among the loans submitted by the independent companies were FHA, VA, and conventional loans on homes, ranging in amounts from $80,000 to $200,000. These loans usu-

* This case was prepared by Robert N. Anthony, Harvard Business School.

EXHIBIT 1 Partial Organization Chart

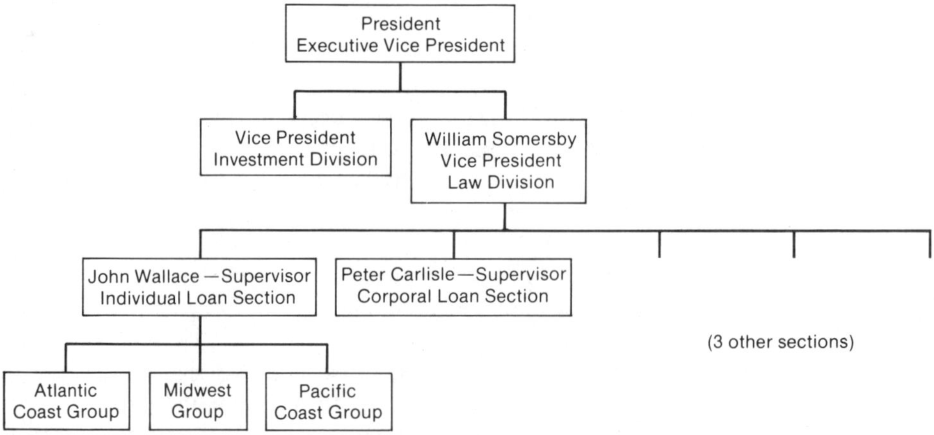

ally were made directly by banks or similar financial institutions organized for the purpose. They would batch together a number of loans and sell them to NJIC in a package. The insurance company purchased many thousands of such loans each year.

The investment division of the company was responsible for establishing the terms of these loans, including their amount, interest rate, and maturity. An independent company would submit to the investment division an offer to sell a mortgage loan. It was the function of this division to determine whether or not the property to be mortgaged and the mortgagor were acceptable to NJIC for a mortgage loan. After the proposed loan was approved and its terms worked out, the investment division would forward to the law division the note, mortgage, and related papers which it received from the seller.

The major function of the individual loan section was to perform the legal work necessary on all new loans purchased and on all existing loans. Among other things, it had to check all the loan instruments to make sure they did, in fact, protect the interests of NJIC as required by law and by the investment division. Organizationally, the section was divided into three groups, each headed by an attorney and each responsible for a geographical section of the country—Atlantic Coast, Midwest, and Pacific Coast. In addition to the three attorneys who headed regional groups, there were two other attorneys—one who helped out in busy spots and took over a group in case of sickness or vacation, and another who was in a training status.

Other than these five attorneys and a supporting secretarial staff, the section was comprised of 26 so-called mortgage examiners. These were persons who had had no formal legal training, but who had been carefully selected and company trained to check over and approve certain of the loan transactions that came into the section. Because of the repetitive nature of the routine loan transactions, management believed that properly selected and trained laymen could, under the supervision of lawyers, perform this task, which at one time had been performed only by lawyers. Problem cases were referred by the mortgage examiners to the attorneys. John Wallace, head of the individual loan section, estimated that it took about three months initially to train a person to do this type of work. It then took about a year and a half of on-the-job training and experience before the examiner achieved a satisfactory rate of output, and two to three years before the average examiner reached optimum performance.

Since the work performed by the mortgage examiners was repetitive, management felt that it could exercise considerable control over a substantial part of this section. Based on a time study, a work standard of 12 loan transactions per examiner per day had been established some years previously, and this standard later was raised to 15. Records were maintained within the section of the number of loan transactions received each day, the number processed by each examiner, and the backlog.

In evaluating the work of individual examiners, some judgment had to be exercised in applying this standard. For example, in the Atlantic Coast group, an examiner sometimes received a batch of loan transactions in which the mortgaged properties were in a single, large housing subdivision. The legal issues in these transactions tended to be the same. In other parts of the country, however, loans tended to come from scattered localities and thus would be quite different from one another in many respects. A supervisor, therefore, in applying the standard would have to be familiar with the type of work an examiner was doing.

BUDGET PROCESS

Although considerable control could be achieved over the output of individual examiners, control over the entire section was a more difficult problem. Each September, the budget committee of the company issued a memorandum to all division heads, asking them to prepare a budget for the operation of their division during the following year.

The basic intent of the budget process was to get division heads to plan and report in advance the scope of their operations for the following year. Usually, the budgets were prepared by anticipating first the changes in activity levels from the current year and then the cost implications of these changes. Management checked each individual budget for reasonableness, and also checked the total expected cost and revenue to ensure that the overall anticipated profit was satisfactory. The budget was viewed as a device for informing management of the plans a division head had for the coming year so that management could appraise these plans in relation to what other divisional heads had planned and in relation to company policy. The budget was also considered to be a measure of a division head's ability to plan the division's operations and then to operate in accordance with that plan.

On receipt of the budget committee's memorandum in September, division heads began forecasting operations within their divisions for the following year. First, each section head made plans for the section. For example, the individual loan section obtained an estimate of the amount of money that the investment division would have available for individual loans in the following year. Based partially on this estimate and partially on its estimated needs for other activities, the individual loan section developed a budget. This estimate, along with the estimated budgets for the other sections of the law division, was reviewed by Mr. Somersby. The law division then sent its budget to the budget committee for review. Usually, the law division's figures were accepted. Each quarter during the year, actual performance to date was compared with budgeted performance. Heads of divisions were required to explain large deviations from projected estimates.

Although management within the law division could, in theory, vary the size of the staff in the individual loan section, in fact, there was great reluctance to increase or decrease the work force unless a definite trend in volume was apparent. One reason for this was company policy. The company felt a great responsibility toward its employees, and as a matter of policy would lay off or discharge employees only for serious offenses. This same policy made management reluctant to hire new employees unless there was assurance that the need for them was permanent. Therefore, the law division tended to maintain a staff sufficient to handle a minimum work load, and it supplemented this with overtime.

Another reason for the tendency to maintain a level work force of mortgage examiners was the cost of selecting and training them. Management went to great pains to select outstanding clerks for these jobs. This was followed by a thorough course of study and on-the-job training. Because of this large investment, management wanted to be sure that anyone trained for this job would be needed permanently in the section.

Management within the individual loan section, in attempting to achieve control over the section as a whole and yet in keeping with company policy, had devised several controls. Occasionally, when the work load lessened, supervisors would call the investment division to see if they could get some work that, although perhaps not quite ready to be sent over as a complete batch, could, nevertheless, be sent in parts. Also, since in periods when loan applications were low foreclosures tended to increase, the mortgage examiners were trained to handle some aspects of foreclosures, and this provided a degree of dovetailing in the work flow. Other than these measures, however, the division preferred to rely on overtime work. The use of outside law firms was out of the question for this type of work because of the far greater cost, even in comparison with overtime wages.

CORPORATE LOAN SECTION

The corporate loan section was a much different kind of operation. A corporate loan, generally for a much larger amount than an individual loan, was one made directly by NJIC to a borrower, such as an industrial or commercial enterprise or a public utility. The loan might be either secured or unsecured. An important advantage to a borrower of this type of loan, compared with a loan evidenced by a bond issue sold to the general public, was that the borrower was not required to furnish a formal prospectus or file a registration statement with the SEC.

In this type of loan, financial determinations, such as the amount of the loan, interest rate, timing of repayments, restrictive covenants, and so forth were made by the investment division, as was the case with individual loans, but by a different section in that division. Because of the size and complexity of corporate loans, the corporate loan section worked closely with the investment division people, who made these financial determinations. This involved sitting in on the negotiations and rendering advice on all the terms of the transaction. It was the responsibility of the corporate loan section to ensure that the final loan instruments protected the interests of NJIC in the manner intended by the financial people.

On this type of loan, for various reasons, the corporate loan section almost without exception retained well-known outside counsel. One important reason was that an opinion from such an independent law firm contributed to the marketability of the investment in the event of a sale at a later date. Further, in many of these transactions, a number of other investors were involved, and NJIC's law division could not appropriately represent these other investors. If NJIC was the leading investor, it did, however, select the outside counsel to be retained. In addition, it was not possible, without greatly increasing the size of the present staff, for company attorneys to handle all the legal work connected with this type of loan, especially at the time of peak loads. Under this system, any one lawyer had a large number of loan negotiations in process at all times with various outside counsel, and this was beneficial both to the individual and to the company in providing lawyers with a broad base of experience in a variety of situations. The background and experience of company attorneys assured the company of consistency of policy in the negotiation of direct placements.

A substantial part of the work in corporate loans consisted of drafting legal documents. The extent to which company attorneys relied on outside counsel to perform parts of this work depended on the complexity of the transaction (company attorneys tended to do more of the work on more complex transactions) and on how busy company attorneys were. In general, company attorneys handled as a minimum enough of the work to be thoroughly familiar with all aspects of the transaction. In many cases, they prepared the first drafts of all legal papers. But in the event that first drafts were left to outside counsel, company attorneys reviewed the work and redrafted it as necessary.

Borrowers were required to pay all expenses incurred in employing outside counsel. However, NJIC made clear to both prospective borrowers and to outside counsel that the counsel were representing NJIC and that their loyalty belonged to NJIC, much the same as for a company attorney. Even though the borrower paid the fee for outside counsel, the head of the corporate loan section, Peter Carlisle, checked closely on the fees charged by outside counsel. Over the years, a thorough tabulation of fees charged for different types of legal work throughout the country had been built up. Mr. Carlisle, simply by referring to this tabulation, could readily determine whether a particular fee was apparently out of line. If there was any substantial deviation, he looked into the case more closely to determine if there was some reasonable explanation; if not, he discussed the matter with the outside counsel and adjusted the fee. Over the years, NJIC had established excellent working relationships with many law firms throughout the country.

The control procedure in this section was substantially different from that in the individual loan section. At the initiation of each transaction, Mr. Carlisle was consulted by the attorney to whom it was referred. Reassignments to equalize the work load of the various attorneys were made as necessary. A degree of control also was achieved through weekly staff conferences with Mr. Carlisle. At this conference, lawyers raised individual problems they had encountered. In addition to keeping Mr. Carlisle informed in detail on what was going on, the conference provided an opportunity for each staff member to draw on the experience of other lawyers, and it served as a vehicle for developing a consistent policy on various matters. Also, the discussion of current negotiations made it more likely that in case of illness another lawyer would be prepared to take over the work.

Another control device was the current work assignment report which each attorney in the section submitted to Mr. Carlisle. Because corporate loan transactions took varying amounts of time to complete, ranging from several weeks to many months, it was found that daily and, in some cases, weekly reports were not feasible. Accordingly, each attorney submitted a report when his work situation suggested to him that a new one was desirable. Each report covered all the time elapsed since the preceding report.

At the top of this report the lawyer briefly indicated his current work status, such as "fully occupied" or "available." Although a detailed format was not prescribed, in general the report described briefly how the lawyer's present jobs were going, what kinds of problems were involved, and what he had completed since his previous report. These reports, in addition to supplementing Mr. Carlisle's knowledge of what was being done in this section, helped tell who was available for more work.

The amount of time a lawyer had to spend on a particular job was not predictable. Major variables were the number and complexity of restrictive covenants in an unsecured note, for example, and the terms and provisions of the security instruments in a secured transaction. The number and complexity of the various covenants in these security instruments did not necessarily vary with the size of the loan, but depended, rather, on the nature, size, and credit standing of the corporate borrower. Many times, a relatively small loan was more complicated than a larger one.

Also, even though the details of a loan had been worked out initially to the satisfaction of the borrower and NJIC, and, even though the loan had been in effect for a considerable period of time, borrowers frequently came back to NJIC to ask for waivers or modifications; that is, they requested changes in the restrictive covenants, the terms, or other conditions or agreements. Such events increased the difficulty of planning in advance how a lawyer was to spend his time.

Unusually heavy work loads in the section were met not only by overtime but also by increasing to the extent feasible the amount of work given to outside counsel. Within limitations, the lawyer responsible for a particular job generally decided how much work would be assigned to outside counsel.

Although the corporate loan section followed the same budget procedure as the individual loan section, one of the variable factors—that is, the extent to which work was delegated to outside counsel—did not affect the budget, since the borrower paid for these services.

BUDGET REPORTS

Mr. Montgomery was thoroughly familiar with the background information given above as he began his review of the law division's budget performance for the first half of 1984. The report he had before him consisted of a summary page for the law division (Exhibit 2) and a page for each of the five sections, two of which are shown in Exhibits 3 and 4. The budget figures on the report were one half the budget for the year.

EXHIBIT 2 Budget Report, Law Division—First Six Months, 1984

Sections	*Budget*	*Actual*	*Over budget*	*Under budget*
Individual loans	$1,698,893	$1,753,154	$54,261	
Corporate loans	1,641,302	1,598,073		$43,229
(Three other sections omitted)	—	—	—	—
Total	$5,082,448	$5,107,822	$25,374	
Number of full-time employees	166	160		6

EXHIBIT 3 Budget Report, Individual Loan Section—First Six Months, 1984

Costs	*Budget*	*Actual*	*Over budget*	*Under budget*
Employee costs:				
Salaries, full-time	$824,092	$ 832,201	$ 8,109	
Salaries, part-time	—	—	—	
Salaries, overtime	4,500	33,610	29,110	
Borrowed labor	—	5,905	5,905	
Employee lunches	17,055	19,180	2,125	
Insurance retirement, etc.	84,819	86,441	1,622	
Social Security	21,205	21,610	405	
Total	951,671	998,947	47,276	
Direct service costs:				
Photography	9,205	10,667	1,462	
Tracing	370	690	320	
Mimeograph	407	587	180	
Reproduction	237	515	278	
Total	10,219	12,459	2,240	
Other costs:				
Rent	100,230	100,230		
Office supplies	2,267	3,067	800	
Equipment depreciation and maintenance	11,940	11,940		
Printed forms	3,842	5,367	1,525	
Travel	2,835	3,155	320	
Telephone	7,577	8,690	1,113	
Postage	3,057	3,227	170	
Prorated company services	36,810	37,405	595	
Professional dues	50	100	50	
Miscellaneous	395	567	172	
Total	169,003	173,748	4,745	
Grand total	$1,130,893	$1,185,154	$54,261	
Number of full-time employees	46	46		

EXHIBIT 4 Budget Report, Corporate Loan Section—First Six Months, 1984

Costs	*Budget*	*Actual*	*Over budget*	*Under budget*
Employee costs:				
Salaries, full-time	$738,720	$707,488		$31,232
Salaries, part-time	3,000	—		3,000
Salaries, overtime	3,000	—		3,000
Borrowed labor				
Employee lunches	10,325	9,355		970
Insurance retirement, etc.	87,745	81,497		6,248
Social Security	31,936	30,375		1,561
Total	874,726	828,715		46,011
Direct service costs:				
Photography	3,637	3,353		284
Tracing	730	265		465
Mimeograph	—	67	67	
Reproduction	—	35	35	
Total	4,367	3,720		647
Other costs:				
Rent	61,953	61,953		
Office supplies	1,850	2,955	1,105	
Equipment depreciation and maintenance	7,740	7,740		
Printed forms	445	915	470	
Travel	1,930	1,880		50
Telephone	2,275	2,835	560	
Postage	420	390		30
Prorated company services	20,213	18,357		1,856
Professional dues	200	200		
Miscellaneous	183	413	230	
Total	$ 97,209	$ 97,638	$ 429	
Grand total	$976,302	$930,073		$46,229
Number of full-time employees	26	24		2

Questions

1. In what ways does Mr. Somersby control the operations of the sections of his division? In what ways does top management control the operation of the law division?

2. What possibilities for improving control, if any, do you think should be explored?

3. As Mr. Montgomery, what comments would you make and what questions would you ask Mr. Somersby about the performance of the two sections of the law division for the first six months of 1984?

CASE 5–2 Moulding Motors, Inc.

Mr. Richard Todd, the chief purchasing agent for the Mercobile Division of Moulding Motors, called in one of his buyers, Mr. Tom Roswald, to discuss Mr. Roswald's purchasing performance. Mr. Todd had just received the January report of buyer's performances, which indicated that Mr. Roswald had incurred a $500,000 loss on a seat-spring-assembly contract. This report was prepared by the estimators of the parts cost control department, who measured a buyer's performance by differences between negotiated prices and the so-called price objectives for purchased parts.

Organization of the Company

Moulding Motors, Inc., was a large, decentralized, multiplant manufacturer of automobiles and trucks. Each division manager was considered to be operating an autonomous unit and was responsible to an executive vice president for his division's profitability.

Sales of the Mercobile Division, which assembled and sold the medium-priced line of Mercobiles, had been approximately $1.8 billion the previous year. The division operated several assembly plants located throughout the country. Parts and subassemblies, amounting to about $1.2 billion, were purchased either from other divisions of Moulding Motors or from outside vendors. The division had no facilities for manufacturing these parts and subassemblies.

Parts Cost Control System

The highly competitive automobile market required that Mercobile maintain close control over costs. Annually, Moulding's top management established total price objectives for the new Mercobile models based on the price bracket in which they were to be sold and on anticipated market conditions. Mercobile Division management then broke down the total price objective for each model into percentages for material, assembly, distribution and other costs, and profit.

To control material costs, a system had evolved of continual cost and price estimates through the annual cycle of planning new models and engineering, developing, and procuring the parts for these models. Mr. Todd's parts cost control department was responsible for this task. Of the 97 employees in the department, 80 were estimators or supervisors, each of whom had several years of machine shop or time-study experience. These men maintained their familiarity with production processes, material market information, price trends, labor rates, and other pertinent data through reading a number of current periodicals in these fields. The estimators were responsible for providing cost estimates for important body and chassis parts, which, although they comprised only 21 percent of the total number of such parts, amounted to 94 percent of the cost of the body and chassis. They were also responsible for cost estimates for the tooling. Virtually all the tooling necessary for the fabrication of body and chassis parts was designed and purchased by the Mercobile Division. This tooling was provided the division's suppliers once contracts were signed. Cost control of engine parts was not the Mercobile Division's responsibility. This work was performed by an engine engineering division.

Each year the estimators provided tentative cost estimates of future models based upon clay models. Working only with what they could see of the interior and exterior body mock-ups and their knowledge of current costs, they developed detailed estimates of the cost *differences* between the proposed model's parts and the same parts for the current model. These "variance estimates" were based on operational changes that the estimators thought would be necessary, that is, changes in either the type, quantity, or cost of the material or labor required, and changes in labor times, labor rates, and overhead rates.

After the clay model had been approved, parts-cost estimates of the variances were refined, based first on broad structural drawings and, later, on detailed engineering drawings. During these development and engineering phases, variances for one item were typically estimated from five to seven times.

In the final phase, that of actual procurement, the estimators provided the buyers with individual part price objectives, which were the actual costs of the part on the current model plus or minus the estimated variances based upon the final engineering drawings.

The Buyer's Use of Estimates

Once a buyer received notification to purchase specific parts, he initiated requests for bids for the parts from suppliers, stating the specifications and anticipated monthly demand; at the same time he requested a price estimate from the parts cost control department.

The parts cost control department then completed and sent back to the buyer a price estimate sheet showing the part number, the actual price currently being paid for the same part, and the price that the estimating department thought should be paid in the coming year. The price estimate sheet did not show a detailed cost breakdown but indicated the extent to which the estimated price varied from the actual price as a result of either a design change or a change in the anticipated price level. Thus, if the current actual price for a particular part was

$0.75 per unit and the estimated price was $0.72 per unit, the price estimate sheet would show whether a design change and/or price level change caused the difference. In this case, the estimate sheet might show that a design change was expected to decrease the unit price by $0.04 and that an increase in price levels was expected to increase the unit price by $0.01, resulting in a net unit cost decrease of $0.03.

In negotiations with vendors, the buyer used the estimate as his target price, although he attempted to negotiate a lower price. The estimates were particularly useful to the buyers when only one or two vendors supplied particular parts and components. In these cases, the buyers were handicapped by not being able to undertake comparative price analyses. Since the Mercobile Division bought parts or components from the manufacturing divisions of Moulding Motors, and since in some cases these divisions were the only possible suppliers, the Mercobile buyers found the estimates of particular help in negotiating the price at which to procure parts from these divisions.

When the buyer completed a transaction, he recorded the price he paid for the part or component on the price estimate sheet. The estimate sheet was then returned to the parts-cost control department, where a record was kept, showing for each buyer the past month's negotiated savings or losses compared with the estimated price objectives. Once a month a report of each buyer's performance was sent to Mr. Todd, the Mercobile Division's chief purchasing agent.

Special Pricing Studies

Whenever a buyer or a member of the parts cost control department thought that an estimated price was out of line, as occurred when over a period of three or four years the accumulated variances for annual changes did not accurately reflect the current manufacturing costs, a special estimate was made that resulted in a new cost figure and price objective. Such studies differed from the typical estimates of variances in that the latter merely considered the cost variances attributable to design or price level changes.

In making a special pricing study, the estimator studies the engineering prints and then carefully defined each operation required for the fabrication. When possible, the estimator visited the manufacturer of the part or component. During these visits the estimators gathered as much information as possible about the operations performed, the type of equipment used, the operating time, and so on. However, even the manufacturing divisions of Moulding Motors refused to permit estimators to time operations or to obtain cost information; the manufacturing divisions, being autonomous, were in the same position as that of other vendors in selling their products to the Mercobile Division.

After he had picked up as much information as he could from the plant visit, the estimator proceeded to fill out a work sheet, entering the type, quantity, and price of material; the labor time, allowances, and rate; and the overhead charges. After he had estimated the costs for each part, he estimated the costs for any assembly operations. Finally, the cost of the individual parts and the cost of any assembly operations were totaled. To this total were added freight costs, general and administrative expenses, and profit, to give a final price.

The prices developed from these special studies were then sent to the buyer as his price objective.

The Seat-Spring Study

In the previous December, when the procurement of parts for the next year's Mercobiles was being initiated, Mr. Tom Roswald, a buyer of special assemblies, received a price objective from the parts cost control department of $14 a set for front- and back-seat-spring assemblies, one of the many items that he procured. Mr. Roswald decided that, since no new estimates of this assembly had been made for several years, the price might possibly be out of date. He, therefore, requested the parts cost control department to study the seat-spring-assembly manufacturing processes and determine a new price objective.

After a careful study of engineering drawings for the seat-spring assembly, the section supervisor of the body-cost estimating section and two of his estimators spent a day at the plants of each of the two suppliers of these assemblies. The three men were particularly interested in the vendors' facilities, their method of fabricating and assembling the seat springs, the manpower required, and the time of the production cycle. After they had concluded these plant visits, the two estimators, with some assistance from their supervisor, spent three weeks in developing a new price objective. Worksheets were made out detailing each fabrication operation for the several side members of the frames, for the springs, and for the assembly of side members and springs into a completed unit. The estimators used as a basis the same production processes and equipment the two vendors were using. (Only in exceptional instances when the vendor was grossly inefficient would an estimator suggest changes in production methods.)

Once the detailed work sheets had been completed, they were summarized on a final worksheet to which was added freight, general administrative expenses, and profit, to arrive at the purchase price objective. The revised purchase price objective for the seat-spring assemblies indicated that each set should cost $11.50, in contrast to the prior estimated cost of $14 a set.

When Mr. Roswald received the new purchase price objective, he contracted the two vendors and explained that the price his division was willing to pay for the seat springs in the coming year would be substantially less than the price paid in the past year. The larger vendor of the two, the Bornley Company, agreed to review its past year's price. In mid-January, the buyer and four estimators visited the Bornley Company and spent two days comparing their material, labor, and overhead cost data with data of the Bornley Company. On the basis of this review, the Bornley Company representatives agreed that they could reduce the price of seat-spring assemblies to $13.35 a set. At the same time, the purchase price objective developed by the Mercobile estimators was adjusted upward to $11.60 a set on the basis of the additional information they had received during the talks.

Because of the still existing spread in price, further negotiations were conducted the following week at the Mercobile Division's buying offices. After two days of negotiations, the Bornley Company finally reached an agreement with Mr. Roswald to supply the seat-spring assemblies for $12.50 a set. In the meantime, the Mercobile Division estimators had increased their purchase price objective to $11.75 a set.

Once the Bornley Company had agreed to the $12.50 figure, Mr. Roswald reached a quick settlement with the second vendor to supply seat-spring assemblies at the same price.

Meeting with Mr. Todd

In February, after he had received the January report showing the performance of his buyers, Mr. Todd, the Mercobile Division's chief purchasing agent, called in Mr. Roswald. Mr. Todd explained to Mr. Roswald that his purchasing performance for the month of January had been fine except for the seat-spring-assembly procurement. "According to my monthly report on buyers' performance," Mr. Todd said, "on the seat-spring assembly you lost over $500,000 compared with your purchase price objective. What I want to know is how this happened? Was it a poor job of estimating or was it a poor job of buying?"

Questions

1. Appraise the parts cost control system at the Mercobile Division of Moulding Motors.
2. How effective is the system of reporting negotiated gains or losses in procurement as a means of appraising buyers' performance?
3. Is Mercobile's system of providing price objectives to buyers applicable to other industries?
4. Did Mr. Roswald do a poor job of procuring the seat-spring assemblies, or was there a poor job in estimating the price?

CASE 5–3
Westport Electric Corporation

On a day in the late autumn of 1983, Peter Ensign, the controller of Westport Electric; Michael Kelly, the manager of the budgeting department (reporting to Ensign); and James King, the supervisor of the administrative staff budget section (reporting to Kelly) were discussing a problem raised by King. In reviewing the proposed 1984 budgets of the various administrative staff offices, King was disturbed by the increases in expenditure that were being proposed. He believed that, in particular, the proposed increases in two offices were not justified. King's main concern, however, was with the entire process of reviewing and approving the administrative staff budgets. The purpose of the meeting was to discuss what should be done about the two budgets in question and to consider what revisions should be made in the approval procedure for administrative staff budgets.

ORGANIZATION OF WESTPORT

Westport Electric is one of the giant U.S. corporations that manufactures and sells electric and electronic products. Sales in 1983 were in excess of $5 billion, and profits after taxes were over $400 million. The operating activities of the corporation are divided into four groups, each headed by a group vice president. These groups are: the Electrical Generating and Transmission Group; the Home Appliance Group; the Military and Space Group; and the Electronics Group. Each of these groups is comprised of a number of relatively independent divisions, each headed by a divisional manager. The division is the basic operating unit of the corporation and each is a profit center. The divisional manager is responsible for earning an adequate profit on his investment. There are 25 divisions in the corporation.

At the corporate level there is a research and development staff and six administrative staff offices, each headed by a vice president, as follows: finance; industrial relations; legal; marketing; manufacturing; and public relations. The responsibilities of the administrative staff offices, although they vary depending upon their nature, can be divided into the following categories:

1. *Top management advice.* Each of the staff offices is responsible for providing advice to the top management of the corporation in the area of its specialty. Also, all of the staff vice presidents are members of the Policy Committee, the top decision-making body of the corporation.

2. *Advice to operating divisions and other staff offices.* Each staff office gives advice to operating divisions and, in some instances, to other staff offices. (An example of the latter is the advice the legal staff might give to the finance staff with respect to a contract.) In theory, at least, the operating divisions can accept or reject the advice, as they see fit. In most cases, there is no formal requirement that the operating divisions even seek advice from the central staff. In fact, however, the advice of the staff office usually carries considerable weight and divisional managers rarely ignore it.
3. *Co-ordination among the divisions.* The staff offices have the responsibility for coordinating their areas of activities among the divisions. The extent of this coordination varies considerably, depending upon the nature of the activity. For example, the finance staff has the greatest amount of this coordination to do, because it is necessary to establish and maintain a consistent accounting and budgetary control system. On the other hand, the legal and public relations staffs have no direct representation in the activities of the divisions.

Exhibit 1 is an organization chart of the Westport Electric Corporation.

EXHIBIT 1 Organization Chart—January 1, 1984

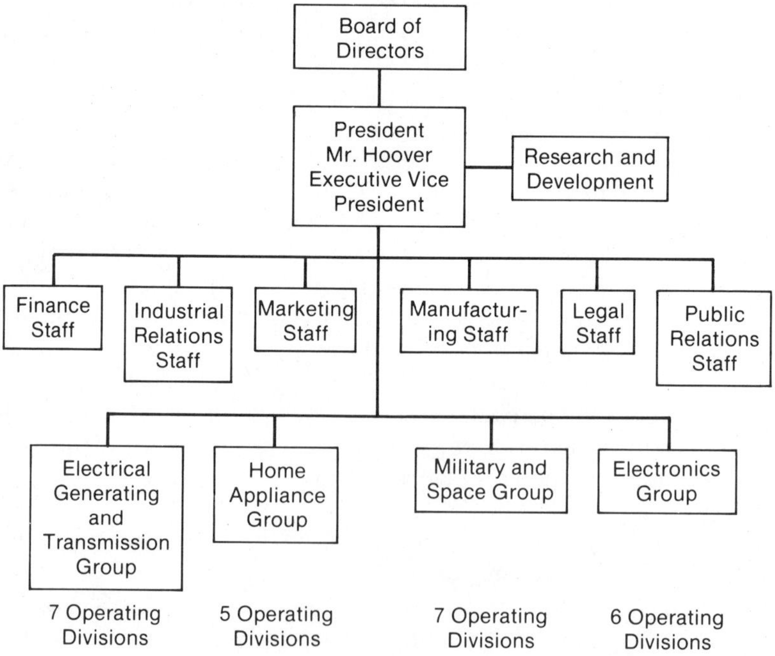

THE BUDGETING ORGANIZATION

Exhibit 2 provides a partial organization chart of the finance staff. As you can see from the chart, Ensign, the controller, reports to the

EXHIBIT 2 Finance Staff—January 1984

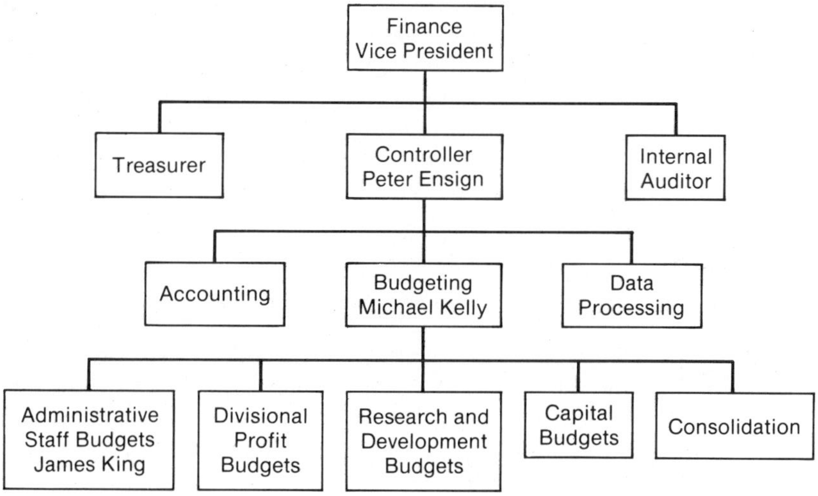

finance vice president. Reporting to him is Kelly, who is in charge of the budgeting department. Reporting to Kelly is King, who is in charge of the administrative staff budget section.

Approval Procedure

Information submitted. In the early autumn of each year, the budgeting department issues instructions and timetables for the preparation, submission, and approval of the budgets for the coming year. Since we are concerned in this case with the administrative staff budgets, we will limit our description to the nature of the information submitted by each administrative staff office.

Each staff office completes the following schedule:

Budget by expense classification. This schedule shows the proposed budget, last year's budget, and the current year's expected actual costs, by expense classification (professional salaries, clerical salaries, supplies, consulting services, utilities, and so forth). The purpose of this schedule is to compare the new budget with the current year's budget and the current year's expected actual costs by expense categories.

Budget by activity. This schedule shows the same information as the previous schedule except that the information is classified by organizational component. The purpose of this schedule is to show which activities are being increased, which decreased, and which new activities are being proposed.

Explanation of changes. This schedule is really a letter that accompanies the budget proposal and explains the reasons for the proposed budget. Explanations are divided into the following categories: economic changes (i.e., changes in the general level of wages and materials); increases or decreases in existing activities; new activities added and old activities dropped.

These reports are submitted by each administrative staff office to the budgeting department two weeks before the office is to present its proposed budget.

Presentation of Budget Proposal

Each administrative staff office budget was approved by the president and the executive vice president in a budget review meeting. The finance vice president sat in on all the budget presentations but had no official power to approve or disapprove.

On the day scheduled for presentation, the vice president of the administrative staff office whose budget was to be approved would make a presentation to the president and executive vice president. The presentation would be based on the budget schedules previously submitted, but the explanations justifying the proposals might go into much greater detail. For example, last year the marketing vice president used three-dimensional colored slides to describe a new activity that he was proposing to organize.

Attending these meetings were the president, the executive vice president, the administrative staff office vice president and his principal executives, the finance vice president, the controller, the budgeting manager, and the particular budget supervisor involved.

Typically, a budget meeting would proceed as follows: The presentation would be made by the administrative staff vice president. During the presentation, questions would be raised by the president and the executive vice president. These would be answered by the administrative staff vice president or one of his executives. At the one end of the presentation, the president and executive vice president would decide whether to approve the budget or whether to curtail some of the proposed activities. Before the final decision, the finance vice president would be asked to comment. In almost every case, he would agree with the decision of the president and executive vice president.

Once approved, the budget became authorization to undertake the budgeted activity for the coming year.

Function of the Budgeting Department

The functions of the budgeting department with respect to administrative staff budgets has been to prescribe the schedules to be submitted and timetable for their submission and to "keep the presentations honest." In fulfilling the last function, the budgeting department analyzed the proposed budgets and made sure that the facts were correctly stated. For instance, they checked to make sure that the increase due to economic changes were accurate; or, in some present activity were to be dropped, they made sure that the cost of this activity was shown as a reduction, so that the cost savings could not be used to hide an increase in another activity. The details of the presentation were worked out beforehand between James King and the administrative assistant to the administrative staff vice president involved. When the presentation was made, the budgeting department would be asked to concur with the financial information being presented. The budgeting department, however, took no position on the appropriateness of the proposed budget or the efficiency of the activity. It was this situation that bothered James King.

BUDGET EVALUATION

This was James King's second year as supervisor of the administrative staff budget section. Prior to that, he had been the budget manager in the Electric Stove Division. At the divisional level, the budget analysts exercised considerable influence over the level of efficiency represented in the operating budgets. For example, in the Electric Stove Division, the divisional controller attended every divisional budget meeting and argued long and hard for rejecting any budget that he believed was not sufficiently "tight." Because he had had a considerable amount of experience in the operations of that division, he was usually successful. King found it hard to reconcile the attitude of the finance vice president (who never seemed to raise any objections to the proposed budgets) with his former boss, the controller of the Electric Stove Division. Consequently, he asked to meet with Ensign and Kelly to see if something could not be done to improve the evaluation techniques for administrative staff budgets. Below is an edited version of the meeting between Ensign, Kelly, and King on this problem:

King: All we do about these budgets is to make sure that the accounting figures are correct. We don't do anything about the efficiency represented by the figures and I know for a fact that it is lousy in at least two cases and I have my suspicion about some of the others.

Kelly: Tell Peter about Legal.

King: Earlier this year, you remember, we hired a consultant to work with our Data Processing Group. We gave the contract to the legal staff to look over and it took them three months before they approved it. They had all kinds of nitpicking changes that didn't amount to a hill of beans, but which took up everybody's time.

Shortly after the contract was approved, I had a college friend of mine visiting who's a lawyer in one of the biggest New York firms. We discussed the matter and he looked over the original contract and the revised one and was astounded at the time that it had taken to get it approved. He said that a simple contract like that would be handled in a day or two by an outside lawyer. Since then, I find that everyone in the organization seems to feel the same way about Legal. They take forever to do a five-minute job and they never stick their necks out in the slightest.

To add insult to injury, this year the Legal staff is asking for a 30 percent increase in their budget to take care of the added cost resulting from the expansion of their work load. The trouble is that unless we do something, they will get this increase.

Ensign: If everyone feels that the Legal staff is so inefficient, why should Mr. Hoover [the president] approve their budget?

King: I think that Mr. Hoover has neither the time nor the knowledge to evaluate the Legal staff. Any time Mr. Hoover asks for anything from them, he gets superdeluxe treatment. Since none of us are lawyers we have a hard time proving inefficiency, but we know it is there.

Ensign: What is the other budget that you think is out of line?

King: Industrial relations—especially management training: We are spending more money on senseless training than you can shake a stick at. It's not only costing us money, but it is wasting management's time. For instance, last month we all had to take a course in quality control. It was the most simple-minded course I have ever seen. They gave us a test at the end to see how much progress we have made. I gave a copy of the test to my secretary and she got a 100 percent, without taking the course, or really even knowing what quality control is. Out in the division, the training was even worse. At one time they had a slide film that was supposed to teach us economics in three lessons! The film consisted of "Doc Dollar" explaining to "Jim Foreman" about money markets, capitalism, and so forth. We all felt that it was an insult to our intelligence. In their new budget, industrial relations is proposing to increase training by nearly 50 percent and, because the general profit picture is so good, it will probably be approved.

Ensign: If the training program is so bad, why don't we hear more complaints?

King: I will have to admit that I feel more strongly than most of the other people, a lot of managers and supervisors just go along with these programs because to be against management training is like being against motherhood. Also, the personnel evaluation forms that industrial relations prescribes have a section on the performance of the individual in these courses. I guess people are afraid to rebel against them because it might hurt their chances of promotion. The point is, at best, they are not worth the money that they cost. No one seems to get much out of them as far as I can see, so we certainly don't want to *increase* the training budget.

The conversation continued for some time. Although he did not express it in exactly these terms, King's other concern was a lack of goal congruence between the activities of the administrative staff office and the earnings for the corporation. It seemed to him that each administrative staff officer, at best wanted to have the "best" operation in the country and, at worst, was simply interested in building an empire. Even the best operation, however, might cost much more than it was worth in terms of increasing profits. He was also concerned about the ability of the president and the executive vice president to evaluate the efficiency and the effectiveness of the staff offices, or even to decide whether additional activities were really worthwhile. King, therefore, believed it was necessary for someone to evaluate the budget proposals critically, as they did at the divisional level.

The meeting closed with Ensign asking Kelly and King to prepare a proposal that would solve the issue raised in the meeting.

Question

What should Westport Electric do about the evaluation problem raised in the case?

CHAPTER 6

Profit Centers

When financial performance in a responsibility center is measured in terms of profit, which is the difference between the revenues and expenses, the responsibility center is called a "profit center." In this chapter, we first discuss considerations involved in deciding whether profit centers should be created. The first part of the discussion focuses on major organization units, which are called "divisions," and then other types of profit centers are discussed. We also discuss alternative ways of measuring the profitability of a profit center.

DIVISIONALIZATION

A functional organization is one in which each of the principal functions of manufacturing and marketing are performed by separate organization units. When such an organization is converted to one in which each of the major organization units is responsible for both the manufacturing and the marketing of a product or a family of products, the process is called "divisionalization." In general, a company divisionalizes because it wishes to delegate more authority to operating managers. If a manager has profit responsibility, it is practical to delegate decisions involving trade-offs between costs and revenues further down the line. For example, a manager who is responsible only for marketing activities will be motivated to make sales promotion expenditures that maximize sales, whereas a manager who is responsible for profits will be motivated to make sales promotion expenditures that optimize profits. A manager who is responsible only for costs (e.g., a plant manager) might be motivated to minimize cost even at a sacrifice in quality or the volume of sales. When the manager is made responsible for profits, the motivation is to balance increased costs against increased contribution from a higher volume of sales. The ability to measure performance in terms of profitability makes the delegation of responsibility more feasible. The comprehensiveness of the profit measure makes detailed decision making by headquarters management less necessary.

Some generalizations to keep in mind about organizations are:

1. All companies are organized functionally at some level.
2. The difference between a functional organization and a divisional organization is a continuum. Between the extremes of the entirely functional organization and the entirely divisionalized organization are all types of combinations of functional and divisional organizations.
3. Complete authority for generating profits is never delegated to a segment of the business. The degree of delegation differs among businesses.

Delegation of Authority

As a general rule, responsibility should be delegated down to the lowest point in an organization where all of the relevant information is available.[1] There are several advantages in doing so. First, a decision may be made more quickly by the person close to the activity than by a higher-level manager who is not directly involved. Second, much information about a particular situation is known only to the person close to the activity. It often is difficult to communicate adequately such things as environmental or cultural conditions to higher level managers. A third advantage is that most decisions are not made on the basis of a precise analysis of data. Precise data are usually not available. Often only the person near the activity has a sufficient intuitive "feel" for a situation. The last two advantages can be very important in a business segment that operates in a different culture (e.g., a foreign subsidiary).

Conditions for delegating profit responsibility. Many management decisions involve making an optimum trade-off between costs and revenues; for example, advertising expenses generate sales, and quality control costs result in satisfied customers, which, in turn, increase revenues. Before such a trade-off decision can be delegated safely to a lower-level manager, two conditions must exist:

1. The manager must have all of the available *relevant information.*
2. There must be some way to measure how effectively he or she is making decisions.

These two conditions limit the delegation of authority for profit responsibility. To the extent that these conditions cannot be met, profit re-

[1] There are many exceptions to this generalization. For example, some decisions may be so important that they should be checked by a higher-level manager. Or, it may be felt that a higher-level manager is more able, even though that manager has no additional information.

sponsibility cannot be safely delegated. Since cost/revenue trade-off decisions are so prevalent, the inability to delegate this type of decision results in a higher degree of centralized decision making. The problem, then, is to determine the lowest point in an organization where these two conditions prevail.

Advantages of Divisionalization

1. The *speed* of operating decisions may be increased because many decisions do not have to be referred to corporate headquarters.
2. The *quality* of many decisions may be improved because they can be made by the person most familiar with the situation.
3. Headquarters management may be *relieved of day-to-day decisions* and can, therefore, concentrate on higher-level activities.
4. *Profit consciousness* may be enhanced. Line managers, being responsible for profits, should be looking constantly for ways to improve them.
5. *Measurement of performance is broadened.* Profitability is a more comprehensive measure of performance than the measurement of either revenues or expenses separately. It measures the effects of management actions that affect *both* revenues and expenses.
6. Line managers, with fewer corporate restraints, should be freer to use their *imagination and initiative.*
7. A division provides an excellent *training ground* for management. Because a division is similar to an independent company, the divisional manager is trained in managing all of the functional areas. At the same time, it provides an excellent means for evaluating divisional management's potential for higher management jobs.
8. If a company is pursuing a strategy of diversification, divisionalization facilitates use of different talents and expertise in different types of situations. For example, people best trained in managing a given type of business can be assigned to work exclusively in that business if it is in a separate division.
9. Divisionalization provides top management with information on the *profitability of components* of the company.

Difficulties with Divisionalization

1. To the extent that decisions are decentralized, top management may *lose some control.* A series of control reports is not as effective as an intimate knowledge of an operation. With divisionalization, top management must change its approach to control. Instead of personal direction, senior management must rely to a considerable extent on management control reports.

2. Competent *divisional managers* are needed and they may not be available in a functional organization because there may not have

been sufficient opportunities for them to develop general management competency.

3. Organization units that were once cooperating as functional units may have to compete with one another. An increase in one divisional manager's profits may decrease that of another's. As a consequence, cooperation among divisions may be adversely affected. This decrease in cooperation may manifest itself in a manager's unwillingness to refer sales leads to another division, even though that division is better qualified to follow up on the lead, to production decisions that have undesirable cost consequences on other divisions, or to the hoarding of personnel or equipment, which, from the overall company standpoint, would be better off assigned to, or used in, another division.

4. *Friction* can increase. There may be arguments over the appropriate transfer price, the assignment of common costs, and the credit for revenues that were generated jointly by the efforts of two or more divisions.

5. There may be too much emphasis on *short-run profitability* at the expense of long-run profitability. In the desire to report high current profits, the divisional manager may skimp on research/development, training programs, or maintenance. This tendency is particularly prevalent when the turnover of divisional managers is relatively high. In these circumstances, managers may have good reason to believe that their actions may not come home to roost until after they have moved to other jobs.

6. There is no completely satisfactory system for insuring that each division, by optimizing its own profits, will *optimize company profits*. (This point is discussed in Chapters 7 and 8.)

7. If headquarters management is more capable or has more comprehensive information than the average divisional manager, the *quality* of some of the decisions may be reduced.

8. Divisionalization may cause *additional costs* because it may require additional management and staff personnel.

Constraints on Divisional Authority

A divisional manager must be able to exercise a significant amount of control over the factors that affect the profitability of the division. To realize fully the advantages listed above, the divisional manager would have to be as autonomous as the president of an independent company. As a practical matter, however, such autonomy is not feasible. If a company were divided into completely independent units, the organization would be giving up the advantages of size or synergism. Also, top management would be abdicating its responsibility if it delegated to divisional management all the authority that the board of directors gives to the chief executive. Consequently, divisionalized organizations represent trade-offs between divisional autonomy and corporate constraints. The effectiveness of a divisionalized organization is largely dependent upon how well these trade-offs are made.

Constraints from other divisions. One of the main problems associated with divisionalization occurs when divisions must deal with one another. It is useful to think of managing a profit center in terms of control over three types of decisions: (1) the product decision (what goods or services to make and sell); (2) the procurement or sourcing decision (how to obtain or manufacture the goods or services); and (3) the marketing decision (how, where, and for how much are these goods or services to be sold). If a divisional manager makes all three of these decisions, there is usually no difficulty in assigning profit responsibility and measuring performance. In general, the greater the degree of integration within a company, the more difficult it becomes to assign complete responsibility to a single profit center for these three activities. If, for example, the product, procurement, and marketing decisions for a single product line are split among two or more divisions, it can be difficult to separate the contribution of each division to the overall success of the product line.

If the responsibility for decisions about a product line is divided among two or more divisions, it is necessary to establish some system to assign fairly the profits to the divisions that have contributed to its design, manufacturing, and marketing. This is a function of the transfer price, and, as is discussed in Chapter 7, transfer price problems may be difficult.

Constraints from corporate management. The constraints imposed by corporate management can be grouped into three types: (1) those resulting from strategic considerations, particularly financing decisions; (2) those resulting because uniformity is required; and (3) those resulting from the economies of centralization.

Most companies restrict certain decisions, such as the acquiring of capital, to the corporate level, at least for domestic activities. Consequently, one of the major constraints on divisions results from corporate control over investment in new assets. Divisions must compete with one another for a share of the available funds. Thus, a division could find its expansion plans thwarted because another division has convinced senior management that it has a more attractive program. In addition to financial constraints, corporate management exercises other strategic constraints. For example, restrictions on markets and products are often imposed. Also, the maintenance of the proper corporate image may require constraints on the quality and engineering of products or the development of public relations activities.

Companies impose some constraints on divisions because of the necessity for conformity. One constraint that exists almost universally is that divisions must conform to corporate accounting and management control systems. Some companies require large amounts of planning and reporting information from each profit center. Another example of a major uniformity constraint is personnel and industrial relations policies.

Certain services are centralized at corporate headquarters because it is more economical to have a central unit provide a particular service to all divisions (e.g., the legal staff) or because a central service is required (e.g., internal auditing). To some extent, all staff offices provide service to divisions, and divisions are generally required to use some of these services. Other examples of staff services are public relations, data processing and systems, and training.

In general, these corporate constraints do not cause severe problems in decentralization so long as they are dealt with explicitly. Divisional management should understand the necessity for most of them, and should accept them with good grace. The major problems seem to revolve around the optional service activities. Often divisions believe (sometimes rightly) that they can obtain a particular service more cheaply from an outside source. The problems of charging divisions for corporate services is discussed in Chapter 7.

The Movement to Divisionalize

Although E. I. du Pont de Nemours & Co. and the General Motors Corporation divisionalized in the early 1920s,[2] most companies in the United States remained functionally organized until after the end of World War II. Since that time a great many of the major U.S. corporations have divisionalized.

A study by Richard F. Vancil shows the extent that manufacturing companies have divisionalized in the past three decades.[3] Questionnaires were sent to 684 manufacturing companies whose financial officers were members of the Financial Executives Institute. Forty-six percent of these firms responded. Only 17 of them reported that they did not have two or more profit centers. Vancil states: "It would be an overstatement to conclude that 95 percent of U.S. manufacturing firms have profit centers; many people who received the questionnaire may have failed to return it *because* they had no profit centers. . . . On balance, it seems safe to conclude that a substantial majority of large manufacturing firms have profit centers."

---

[2] See Alfred D. Chandler, Jr., *Strategy and Structure* (Cambridge, Mass.: MIT Press, 1962), chaps. 2 and 3; and Alfred P. Sloan, Jr., *My Years with General Motors* (Garden City, N.Y.: Doubleday, 1964).

[3] Richard F. Vancil, *Decentralization: Management Ambiguity by Design* (Homewood, Ill.: Dow Jones-Irwin, 1979), pp. 144–45.

A similar result was obtained by James S. Reece and William A. Cool in a survey of the *Fortune "1,000"* industrial companies.[4] Of the 620 companies responding, 95.8 percent had profit centers.

Divisionalized corporations can be classified into three general categories:

First, there are the diversified companies (conglomerates), such as International Telephone and Telegraph Corporation, Litton Industries, and Textron. For this type of company, divisionalization is ideal; it is difficult to see how they could operate in another way.

Second, there is the single industry, multiproduct company, such as General Electric Company, Westinghouse Electric Corporation, E. I. du Pont de Nemours & Co., and Union Carbide Corporation. In this type of company, also, divisionalization is generally the most effective way of organizing, although the decision is not always as clear-cut as with the diversified company.

Third, there is the large integrated company with one principal product line, such as the steel companies, the automobile companies, and the petroleum companies. In this type of company, the decision to divisionalize is even less clear-cut. Many major decisions are made centrally. Furthermore, this type of company tends to have large amounts of intracompany transfers because of its integrated nature; and many of the transferred goods have no outside market source, which makes it difficult to arrive at valid transfer prices. However, the very size of some of these companies made divisionalization almost necessary. Also, most of them have products not related to their principal product lines.

When a company in the third category is divisionalized, the delegation of authority tends to be more restricted than in the case with the other two types. For example, in the automobile business, vehicle product and pricing decisions are made at the very top of the organization. Furthermore, many of the manufacturing divisions sell exclusively to other divisions; and the buying divisions are restricted either by the nature of the product or company rule to purchasing from inside sources.

There are, of course, many firms that do not fit precisely into one of these three categories that use profit centers successfully. For example, Warnaco is a single industry, integrated company, which has several profit centers, each of which manufactures and sells apparel.

Some Considerations in Divisionalization

Personnel matters. In considering the relative importance of the advantages and difficulties listed above, a company would do well to

[4] James S. Reece and William A. Cool "Measuring Investment Center Performance" *Harvard Business Review*, May–June 1978.

give special attention to the personnel problems involved in the establishment of profit centers. A divisionalized company requires talent that may not be found in an organization in which profit responsibility has been centralized. If this talent is not available within the organization, it must be acquired either through training or employment from the outside. If management is unable or unwilling to do this, then the company should approach divisionalization with caution.

There are three personnel requirements:

1. Senior management must know how to use management control reports in planning, controlling, and coordinating profit center operations.
2. A divisionalized company requires capable divisional managers. A functionally organized company may have few executives who are broad enough in their outlook to take on the responsibility for a division.
3. A divisionalized company requires capable financial and budget analysts at both the central staff and the divisional levels. Such talent may be scarce.

One major activity. If a company has a single activity on which its success hinges, it is doubtful whether responsibility for this activity can be delegated to a divisional manager. In this circumstance, an attempt to decentralize profit responsibility may result merely in a more expensive and cumbersome control and communications system. For example, a medium-sized company, with one major product line and several smaller and relatively unrelated products, divided its activities into profit centers. Top management, however, continued to spend most of its time and energy on the major product line, making most of the decisions that normally would be made by a divisional manager. This company was, in fact, only decentralizing the responsibility for the smaller product lines, and this situation should have been recognized in the organization plan.

Similar major activities. Decentralized profit responsibility seems best adapted to companies that are composed of several *dis*similar businesses. In these companies, management is unable to be intimately acquainted with the relevant details of all of the businesses; therefore, it delegates the day-to-day decisions to different people in each activity who are familiar with the various problems. If, on the other hand, the activities of a company are similar, it may be desirable for one group to make many of the day-to-day decisions for *all* of the activities. For example, a central marketing group might make all of the advertising, sales promotion, and new product decisions for the entire company. When a central group does this, a divisional manager cannot, of course, be held responsible for that aspect of profit performance. Hence, there may be no real decentralization of profit responsibility.

Any company whose major activities are related closely to one another should carefully consider alternative methods of control before decentralizing profit responsibility. Not only is it more expensive to have each division make its own decisions, but the quality of these decisions might be inferior to those that would be made centrally. Furthermore, coordination among the activities is very important when they are related; this coordination tends to be more difficult to accomplish properly with a decentralized profit center system.

Indivisible responsibility. As stated earlier, to be able to decentralize profit responsibility successfully, a company must divide its operations into logical profit-determining units. The existence of serious transfer pricing problems is sometimes indicative of the fact that profit responsibility is not clearly segregated. To the extent that divisions buy from and sell to each other, two or more divisions are sharing in marketing, production, and product planning decisions. Transfer pricing problems also indicate sometimes that profit centers are not really independent. These problems occur principally when outside competitive prices are unavailable, which implies there is no effective outside competition and that the concept of the division as an independent company is fictional because, if there is no effective outside competition, the profit centers *must* deal with each other.

Alternatives to Divisionalization

Even large and complex companies need not necessarily divisionalize. There may be less drastic and less expensive methods of minimizing their problems. Here are four of them.

1. Split executive responsibility. One way to relieve the pressure on senior management is to divide executive responsibilities among the top executives. For example, if long-range planning is a problem, then planning may be separated from administering; that is, the chief executive officer may be responsible for planning and the chief operating officer for day-to-day management.

2. Decentralize functional responsibility. Delegation of certain functional responsibilities may be an excellent way to relieve pressures on top management's time. For such delegation, management can select functional activities that have the most capable staff, or ones to which top management can make the least contribution, or ones that are less vital to the success of the company. For example, in a company that was largely marketing-oriented, the president delegated the responsibility for manufacturing to a vice president. The president was then able to devote most of his time to marketing and product decisions. Decentralization on this basis can be done with little additional cost and with no disruption to the current organization.

3. Strengthen the staff. In some situations, the real problem is lack of adequate staff assistance, and this will not be solved by divisionalization. Some operating executives regard staff people as a type of parasite, and they keep the staff small. Divisionalization can be a very expensive substitute for an adequate central staff.

4. Decentralize minor activities. If a company has several more-or-less minor activities, which are unrelated to its main products, these activities might be set up as profit centers under the control of a headquarters' executive. Such an arrangement does not require the sophisticated control system that full decentralization would require. The responsible executive controls by personal observation, by direct communication with general managers, and by the usual accounting reports. In this way, top management is in a position to devote most of its time to its main business.

OTHER PROFIT CENTERS

So far in this chapter we have been considering the problem of divisionalization, which is the process of reorganizing a functional organization into profit centers. Divisionalization involves major changes in any company. It often involves different ways of doing business, and it can involve considerable additional expense. As a consequence, the decision to divisionalize is one of the major decisions that any company makes.

There are, in addition to major divisions, other profit centers. Often these can be created without difficulty. Some examples are described below.

Functionally Organized Businesses

A divisionalized company is divided into segments that are treated as far as practical as independent profit-generating units. Within these divisions, subunits may be functionally organized. In such divisions, as well as in companies that are functionally organized, it is sometimes desirable that one or more of the functional units be treated as profit centers. The purpose of this part of the chapter is to describe examples of this type of profit center.

Marketing. Any marketing activity can be made into a profit center by charging the cost of the products sold[5] to the responsible marketing manager. The transfer of costs provides the marketing manager

[5] Note that this charge may be made outside of the books of account. A profit report that shows the revenues generated and the costs of these products could be prepared and used for control. There need be no transfer of costs (in the form of prices) between organization units as there is in divisionalized profit centers.

with the relevant information to make the optimum revenue/cost trade-offs. Since the manager is measured on profitability, there is a check on how well these decisions are being made. Also, since the managers are being evaluated on profitability, they will be motivated to maximize profits. Note that the marketing manager should be charged with a *standard* cost, not an actual cost. This separates manufacturing cost performance from the marketing performance. The former is affected by changes in the levels of efficiency that are outside of the control of the marketing manager.

When should a marketing activity be given profit responsibility? This is when the marketing activity is in the best position to make the principal cost/revenue trade-offs. This often occurs where different conditions exist in different geographical areas, for example, a *foreign marketing activity*. In such an activity, it may be difficult to control centrally such decisions as: How to market a product? How much to spend on sales promotion, when to spend it, and on which media? How to train salesmen or dealers? Where and when to establish new dealers?

To summarize, it is relatively easy to treat a marketing activity as a profit center. All that is necessary is to charge the activity with the relevant costs. The decision whether to do this is determined by the point in the organization where the relevant marketing information is available. Delegation of profit responsibility can be made only to this point.

Manufacturing. The manufacturing activity is usually a cost center, and the management of such activities is judged on the basis of performance against standard costs and overhead budgets. Problems can occur because standard cost performance does not measure how well all of the responsibilities of the manufacturing manager are being performed. For example:

1. Quality control may be inadequate. Products of inferior quality may be shipped to obtain standard cost credit.
2. Manufacturing managers may be reluctant to interrupt production schedules in order to produce an emergency order to accommodate a customer.
3. When a manager is measured against standards, there may be no incentive to manufacture products that are difficult to produce nor even to expand production.
4. There may be little incentive to improve standards.

As a consequence, where the performance of the manufacturing activities are measured against standards, it is necessary that quality control, production scheduling, make-or-buy decisions, and the setting of standards be controlled by someone outside of the manufacturing organization. Where this is not practical, some companies measure manufacturing activities on profitability.

A common way of measuring a manufacturing activity on profitability is to give this activity credit for the selling price of the products minus the estimated cost of sales and distribution. Note that there are many factors influencing the volume of sales that are outside the control of the manufacturing manager. The purpose of measuring him or her on profitability is to provide an incentive to maximize profits, rather than to minimize costs. Although such an arrangement is far from perfect, it seems to work better in some cases than the alternative of holding the manufacturing operation responsible only for costs. Profit centers of this type are often designated as "pseudo" profit centers to indicate that they have limited direct control over profits.

Service organizations. Many service organizations are well suited to the profit center form of organization. Thus, consulting firms, public accounting firms, architectural firms, and engineering firms can be divided into profit centers by so arranging the accounting system that each unit is credited for the revenue it generates and is charged for the costs that it incurs. In some instances (e.g., an engineering firm), a project manager may use specialized internal services which, in turn, also may be profit centers. Such units have considerable control over the product (the type of service), the revenues, and the costs of their operations. Consequently, profitability can be an effective way of measuring performance. Top management must be careful, however, not to generate such pressure for profitability that the quality of the service declines.

Other organizations. A company that has branch operations, responsible for marketing the company's products in a particular geographical area, is often a natural for a profit center type of organization. Even though the branch managers have no manufacturing or procurement responsibilities, profitability is often the best single measure of their performance. Furthermore, the profit measurement is frequently an excellent motivating device. Thus, the individual stores of most retail chains are organized as profit centers, and the branches of many commercial banks are profit centers.

Some companies organize their customer service units as profit centers. Such units are responsible for product installation, for servicing equipment upon request of the user and for making repairs required by warranty agreements, or for other reasons. In such units, however, the profit center approach may be dysfunctional. It may lead the unit to skimp on its work in order to reduce costs, and thereby damage the company's reputation.

MEASURING PROFITABILITY

There are two types of profitability measurements in a profit center, just as there are for the organization as a whole. There is, first, a measure of *management performance,* in which the focus is on how well the manager is doing. This measure is used for planning, coordinating, and controlling the day-to-day activities of the profit center, and as a device for providing the proper motivation to the manager. Second, there is a measure of *economic performance,* in which the focus is on how well the profit center is doing as an economic entity. The messages given by these two measures may be quite different.

In almost every instance, the necessary information for both purposes can be obtained from a single underlying set of data. Since the management measure is used frequently, but the economic measure only on those occasions when economic decisions must be made, considerations relating to personal performance measurement have first priority in systems design; that is, the system is designed to measure personal performance routinely, and economic measures are derived from them.

Problems in Profit Measurement

Because a profit center is part of a company, and its transactions with other parts of the company are not always at arm's length, problems in measuring profits arise that are not present in organizations that are independent entities. There are three types of such problems: (1) transfer prices, (2) common revenues, and (3) common costs. Transfer pricing is deferred to Chapter 7, and the other two problems are discussed below.

Common revenues. Although, in most circumstances, the measurement of the revenues earned by a profit center is straightforward, there are some situations in which two or more profit centers participated in the work that gave rise to the sale, and ideally each should be given appropriate credit for its part in the transaction. For example, the principal contact between the company and a certain customer may be a salesperson from Division A, but on occasion the customer may place orders with the Division A salesperson for products carried by Division B. Although the Division A salesperson should be motivated to seek such orders, he or she is unlikely to do so if all the revenue resulting from them is credited to Division B. Similarly, a customer of a bank may carry an account in Branch C, which is credited for the revenue generated by this account, but the customer may prefer to do some banking business with Branch D because it is more conveniently located or for other reasons; Branch D is unlikely to be eager to provide services to such a customer if all the revenue is credited to Branch C.

Many companies have not given much attention to the solution of these common revenue problems. They take the position that the identification of precise responsibility for revenue generation is too complicated to be practical, and that sales personnel must recognize that they are working not only for their own profit center but also for the overall good of the company. Some companies do attempt to untangle the responsibility for common sales. They may, for example, credit the division that takes an order for a product handled by another division (Division A in the above example) with the equivalent of a brokerage commission or finder's fee. In the case of a bank, the branch performing a service may be given explicit credit for that service, even though the customer's account is kept in another branch.

Common costs. Goods or services that are furnished to one profit center by another profit center are valued at a transfer price as discussed in Chapter 7. Services that are furnished by staff units and other common costs, if charged at all, should be charged to profit centers on a basis that reflects the actual consumption of the service and on the basis of specific requests made by the responsibility center that wants the service, to the extent that this is feasible. In these circumstances, the services are controllable costs, and the profit center can be held responsible for incurring them.

When such direct charging is not feasible, common costs can be allocated to profit centers on some reasonable basis. Such an allocation is necessary for the measurement of the economic performance of the profit center. Opinions differ on whether allocated costs are useful in management performance measurement, as will be discussed in the next section.

Types of Profitability Measures

The profitability of a profit center can be measured in essentially five different ways: (1) as the contribution margin, (2) as direct divisional profit, (3) as controllable divisional profit, (4) as income before income taxes, or (5) as net income. The nature of these measures is indicated by Exhibit 6–1, and each is discussed below.

EXHIBIT 6–1 Income Statement

			Measure
Revenue		$1,000	
Cost of sales		600	
Gross margin		400	
Variable expenses		180	
Contribution margin		220	← (1)
Other divisional expenses	$60		
Charges from other divisions	30	90	
Direct divisional profit		130	← (2)
Controllable corporate allocations		10	
Controllable divisional profit		120	← (3)
Other corporate allocations		20	
Income before taxes		100	← (4)
Taxes		50	
Net income		$ 50	← (5)

1. Contribution margin. The principal argument for measuring profit center performance on the basis of contribution margin is that the fixed expenses are noncontrollable by the profit center manager, and that the manager should therefore focus his or her attention on maximizing the spread between revenue and variable expenses. The problem with this method is that some fixed expenses are entirely controllable and that almost all fixed expenses are partially controllable. As discussed in Chapter 5, many items of expenses, although not varying with the level of activity, can be changed at the discretion of the profit center manager. Presumably, top management wants the profit center to be concerned with these discretionary expenses and to keep them in line with amounts agreed on in the budget formulation process. A focus on the contribution margin tends to direct attention away from this responsibility.

This problem could be corrected by defining contribution margin as revenues minus all controllable divisional expenses. There can, however, be differences of opinion with respect to the controllability of expenses. In fact, there are probably very few divisional expenses that cannot in some way be influenced by the divisional manager. Insurance and property taxes, for example, are in some cases noncontrollable by the profit center manager because the insurance coverage is set by corporate policy and the property taxes by the municipality; however, the profit center manager may be able to reduce insurance expenses by reducing the amount of insured property (such as inventory and fixed assets), or by reducing fire or safety hazards. Consequently, many companies measure the performance of the divisional manager as profits after deducting all expenses for which the divisional manager is directly responsible.

2. Direct divisional profit. This measure shows the amount that the division contributes to the general overhead and profit of the corporation. It incorporates all expenses incurred in or directly traced to the division, regardless of whether or not these items are entirely controllable by the divisional manager. With the use of this measure, it is not necessary to allocate corporate expenses to divisions.

The principal weakness of this measure is that it cannot be used as a reliable economic measure of performance because it excludes some headquarters expenses that have been incurred on behalf of the division.

3. Controllable divisional profit. Headquarters expenses should be divided into two categories: controllable and noncontrollable. The former includes headquarters expenses that are controllable, at least to a degree, by the divisional manager. Consequently, if these costs are included in the measurement system, the profit will be after the deduction of all expenses that may be influenced by the divisional manager. Controllable divisional profits, however, cannot be compared directly with published data, or with trade association data that report the profits of other companies in the industry because it excludes general headquarters expenses. Consequently, the next measurement would be divisional profits after subtracting the division's share of *all* headquarters expenses. This is income before taxes.

4. Income before taxes. In this measure, all pretax expenses are allocated to some division. The basis of allocation reflects the relative amount of expense that is incurred for each division or, alternatively, the amount of benefit received by each division.

The sum of the profits of all the divisions equals the pretax profit of the company. Division managers are given the message that the division has not earned a profit unless all expenses are covered; and they may be motivated to raise questions about the amount of corporate overhead, which can lead to desirable actions. (One company sold its corporate airplane because of complaints about its costs from profit center managers.) This measure can be used as a basis for comparison with published data and for other economic analyses of the inherent profit potential of the division.

5. Net income. Not many companies measure performance of domestic divisions at the bottom line, the amount of net income after income tax. There are two principal reasons for this: *(a)* In many situations, the income after tax is a constant percentage of the pretax income, so there is no advantage in incorporating income taxes; and *(b)* decisions that have an impact on income taxes, are made at headquarters, and it is believed that divisional profitability should not affect, or be affected by, these decisions.

In some companies, however, the effective income tax rate *does* vary among divisions. For example, a division with large equipment purchases may have a larger investment tax credit than other divisions. Also, foreign subsidiaries or divisions with foreign operations may have different effective income tax rates. In these situations, it may be desirable to allocate income tax expenses, not only to measure the economic profitability of the division but also to motivate the divisional manager to minimize taxes.

Business Practice

A study by James S. Reece and William R. Cool surveyed business practice with respect to divisional profit measurement.[6] Some of the results of this study are shown on Exhibit 6–2.

[6] James S. Reece and William R. Cool, "Measuring Investment Center Performance," *Harvard Business Review*, May–June 1978, p. 36.

EXHIBIT 6–2 Methods of Measuring Profit

Survey question:

Is profit center or investment center "profit" calculated in a manner consistent with the way net income is calculated for your shareholder reports?

	Number	*Percentage*
Yes	239	40%
No	351	59
No answer	4	1
Total	594	100%

If your answer was no, in which of the following ways does the profit center's calculation differ from net income calculation? (Check as many as apply.)

	*Number**	*Percentage of 351 companies**
No taxes are assessed to profit centers	249	71%
No depreciation charge is deducted	11	3
The depreciation calculation differs	25	7
No corporate administrative expenses are allocated to the center	173	49
No interest charges on corporate debt are allocated to the center	225	64
Profit center reports use direct (variable) costing rather than full (absorption) costing	19	5
Other differences exist	51	15

* Includes multiple responses.

Other Performance Measures

The foregoing discussion has been limited to measurements of a division's performance as measured by financial data. As pointed out in Chapter 4, financial data provides an incomplete measurement at best, and at worst it is seriously misleading. Nonfinancial measures of performance, therefore, are important in the management of profit centers, just as they are in the management of independent companies. This topic is discussed in subsequent chapters.

CASE 6–1
Bultman Automobiles, Inc.*

William Bultman, the part owner and manager of an automobile dealership, felt the problems associated with the rapid growth of his business

* This case was prepared by David Hawkins and John Yeager, Harvard Business School.

EXHIBIT 1

BULTMAN AUTOMOBILES, INC.
Income Statement
For the Year Ended December 31, 1983

Sales of new cars			$3,821,875
Cost of new sales		$3,156,405	
Sales remuneration		162,370	
			3,318,775
			503,100
Allowances on trade*			116,115
			386,985
Sales of used cars		2,395,690	
Appraised value of used cars	$1,907,275		
Sales remuneration	91,560		
		1,998,835	
		396,855	
Allowances on trade*		61,115	
			335,740
			722,725
Service sales to customers		347,510	
Cost of work		256,985	
		90,525	
Service work on reconditioning:			
Charge	236,580		
Cost	244,310	(7,730)	82,795
			805,520
General and administrative expenses			491,710
Profit before taxes			$ 313,810

* Allowances on trade represent the excess of amounts allowed on cars taken in trade over their appraised value.

were becoming too great for him to handle alone. (See Exhibit 1 for current financial statements.) The reputation he had established in the community led him to believe that the recent growth in his business would continue. His long-standing policy of emphasizing new car sales as the principal business of the dealership had paid off, in Mr. Bultman's opinion. This, combined with close attention to customer relations so that a substantial amount of repeat business was available, had increased the company's sales to a new high level. Therefore, he wanted to make organizational changes to cope with the new situation. Mr. Bultman's three "silent partners" agreed to this decision.

Accordingly, Mr. Bultman divided up the business into three departments: a new car sales department, a used car sales department, and the service department. He then appointed three of his most trusted employees managers of the new departments: John Ward was named manager of new car sales, Marty Ziegel was appointed manager of used car sales, and Charlie Lassen placed in charge of the service department. All of these men had been with the dealership for several years.

Each of the managers was told to run his department as if it were an independent business. In order to give the new managers an incentive, their remuneration was calculated as a straight percentage of their department's gross profit.

Soon after taking over as the manager of the new car sales department, John Ward had to settle upon the amount to offer a particular customer who wanted to trade his old car as part of the purchase price of a new one with a list price of $14,400. Before closing the sale, Mr. Ward had to decide the amount of discount from list he would offer the customer and the trade-in value of the old car. He knew he could deduct 15 percent from the list price of the new car without seriously hurting his profit margin. However, he also wanted to make sure that he did not lose out on the trade-in.

During his conversations with the customer, it had become apparent that the customer had an inflated view of the worth of his old car, a far from uncommon event. In this case, it probably meant that Mr. Ward had to be prepared to make some sacrifices to close the sale. The new car had been in stock for some time, and the model was not selling very well, so he was rather anxious to make the sale if this could be done profitably.

In order to establish the trade-in value of the car, the manager of the used car department, Mr. Ziegel, accompanied Mr. Ward and the customer out to the parking lot to examine the car. In the course of his appraisal, Mr. Ziegel estimated the car would require reconditioning work costing about $800, after which the car would retail for about $4,200. On a wholesale basis, he could either buy or sell such a car, after reconditioning, for about $3,600. The wholesale price of a car was subject to much greater fluctuation than the retail price, depending on color, trim, model, etc. Fortunately, the car being traded in was a very popular shade. The retail automobile dealers handbook of used car prices, the "Blue Book," gave a cash buying price range of $3,100 to $3,300 for the trade-in model in good condition. This range represented the distribution of cash prices paid by automobile dealers for that model of car in the area in the past week. Mr. Ziegel estimated that he could get about $2,500 for the car "as-is," (i.e., without any work being done to it) at next week's auction.

The new car department manager had the right to buy any trade-in at any price he thought appropriate, but then it was his responsibility to dispose of the car. He had the alternative of either trying to persuade the used car manager to take over the car and accepting the used car manager's appraisal price, or he himself could sell the car through wholesale channels. Whatever course Mr. Ward adopted, it was his primary responsibility to make a profit for the dealership on the new cars he sold, without affecting his performance through excessive allowances on trade-ins. This primary goal, Mr. Ward said, had to be "balanced against the need to satisfy the customers and move the new cars out of inventory—and there was only a narrow line between allowing enough on the used car and allowing too much."

After weighing all these factors, with particular emphasis on the personality of the customer, Mr. Ward decided he would allow $4,800 for the used car, provided the customer agreed to pay the list price for the new car. After a certain amount of haggling, during which the customer came down from a higher figure and Ward came up from a lower one, the $4,800 allowance was agreed upon. The necessary papers were signed, and the customer drove off.

Mr. Ward returned to the office and explained the situation to Ronald Bradley, who had recently joined the dealership as accountant. After listening with interest to Mr. Ward's explanation of the sale, Mr. Bradley set about recording the sale in the accounting records of the business. As soon as he saw the new car had been purchased from the manufacturer for $10,000, he was uncertain as to the value he should place on the trade-in vehicle. Since the new car's list price was $14,400 and it had cost $10,000, Mr. Bradley reasoned the gross margin on the new car sale was $4,400. Yet Mr. Ward had allowed $4,800 for the old car, which needed $800 repairs and could be sold retail for $4,200 or wholesale for $3,600. Did this mean that the new car sale involved a loss? Mr. Bradley was not at all sure he knew the answer to this question. Also, he was uncertain about the value he should place on the used car for inventory valuation purposes.

Bradley decided that he would put down a valuation of $4,800, and then await instructions from his superiors.

When Marty Ziegel, manager of the used car department, found out what Mr. Bradley had done, he went to the office and stated forcefully that he would not accept $4,800 as the valuation of the used car. His comment was as follows:

"My used car department has to get rid of that used car, unless John [new car department manager] agrees to take it over himself. I would certainly never have allowed the customer $4,800 for that old tub. I would never have given any more than $2,800, which is the wholesale price less the cost of repairs. My department has to make a profit too, you know. My own income is dependent on the gross profit I show on the sale of used cars, and I will not stand for having my income hurt because John is too generous toward his customers."

Mr. Bradley replied that he had not meant to cause trouble, but had simply recorded the car at what seemed to be its cost of acquisition, because he had been taught that this was the best practice. Whatever response Mr. Ziegel was about to make to this comment was cut off by the arrival of William Bultman, the general manager, and Charlie Lassen, the service department manager. Mr. Bultman picked up the phone and called John Ward, the new car sales manager, asking him to come over right away.

"All right, Charlie," said Mr. Bultman, "now that we are all here, would you tell them what you just told me."

Mr. Lassen, who was obviously very worried, said: "Thanks Bill. The trouble is with this trade-in. John and Marty were right in thinking that the repairs they thought necessary would cost about $800. Unfortunately, they failed to notice that the rear axle is cracked, which will have to be replaced before we can sell the car. This will use up parts and labor costing about $600.

"Besides this," Lassen continued, "there is another thing which is bothering me a good deal more. Under the accounting system we've been using, my labor cost for internal jobs is calculated by taking the standard Blue Book[1] price for the labor required for a job and deducting 25 percent. Normally, the Blue Book price is about equal to the estimated time required to do the work, multiplied by twice the mechanic's hourly rate. On parts, an outside customer pays list price, which has about a 40 percent gross margin; but on internal work the parts are charged at cost plus 20 percent, which is less than half the margin. As you can see from my department statement, calculating the cost of parts and labor for internal work this way didn't even cover a pro rata share of my department's overhead and supplies. I lost over $7,000 on internal work last year.

"So," Lassen went on, "on a reconditioning job like this which costs out at $1,400, I don't even break even. If I did work costing $1,400 for an outside customer, I would be able to charge him about $1,900 for the job. The Blue Book gives a range of $1,840 to $1,960 for the work this car needs, and I have always aimed for the middle of the Blue Book range. That would give my department a gross profit. Since it looks as if a high proportion of the work of my department is going to be the reconditioning of trade-ins for resale, I figure that I should be able to make the same charge for repairing a trade-in as I would get for an outside repair job.

Messrs. Ziegel and Ward both started to talk at once at this point. Mr. Ziegel, the more forceful of the two, managed to edge Mr. Ward out: "This axle business is unfortunate, all right, but it is very hard to spot a cracked axle. Charlie is likely to be just as lucky the other way next time. He has to take the rough with the smooth. It is up to him to get the cars ready for me to sell."

Mr. Ward, after agreeing that the failure to spot the axle was unfor-

---

[1] In addition to the Blue Book for used car prices, there is a Blue Book which gives the range of charges for various classes to repair work. Like the used car book, it is a weekly, and is based on the actual charges made and reported by motor repair shops in the area.

tunate, added: "This error is hardly my fault, however. Anyway, it is ridiculous that the service department should make a profit out of jobs it does for the rest of the dealership. The company can't make money when its left hand sells to its right."

William Bultman, the general manager, was getting a little confused about the situation. He thought there was a little truth in everything that had been said, but he was not sure how much. It was evident to him that some action was called for, both to sort out the present problem and to prevent its recurrence. He instructed Mr. Bradley, the accountant, to "work out how much we are really going to make on this whole deal," and then retired to his office to consider how best to get his managers to make a profit for the company.

A week after the events described above, William Bultman was still far from sure what action to take to motivate his managers to make a profit for the business. During the week, Charlie Lassen, the service manager, had reported to him that the repairs to the used car had cost $1,540, of which $720 represented the cost of those repairs which had been spotted at the time of purchase, and the remaining $828 was the cost of supplying and fitting a replacement for the cracked axle. To support his own case for a higher allowance on reconditioning jobs, Lassen had looked up the duplicate invoices over the last few months, and had found other examples of the same work that had been done on the trade-in car. The amount of these invoices totaled $1,812, which the customers had paid without question, and the time and materials that had gone into the jobs had been costed at $1,340. As described by Lassen earlier, the cost figures mentioned above included an allocation of departmental overhead, but no allowance for general overhead or profit. In addition, Lassen had obtained from Mr. Bradley, the accountant, the cost analysis shown in Exhibit 2. Lassen told Bultman

EXHIBIT 2 Analysis of Service Department Expenses for Three Months Ended December 31, 1983

	Customer jobs	*Reconditioning jobs*	*Total*
Number of jobs	61	55	116
Direct labor	$21,386	$19,764	$ 41,150
Supplies	7,412	6,551	13,963
Department overhead (fixed)	6,312	5,213	11,525
	35,110	31,528	66,638
Parts	16,287	17,334	33,621
	51,397	48,862	100,259
Charges made for jobs to customers or other departments	69,502	47,316	116,818
Profit (loss)	18,105	(1,546)	16,559
General overhead proportion			11,416
Departmental profit			$ 5,143

that this was a fairly typical distribution of the service department expense.

CASE 6–2
Vereinigte Deutsche Wagen, A.G.*

In October 1980, Rolf Ernst, financial director of Vereinigte Deutsche Wagon, A.G. (VDW), was considering what, if any, changes should be made to that part of the accounting system used to measure the financial performance of the company's sales subsidiaries. The system had operated without significant change for many years; however, the events of 1980 brought out in a rather dramatic fashion some of the problems with measuring the profitability of the sales subsidiaries. The immediate impetus for considering a change was a letter describing the 1980 situation of VDW, Suisse, from Hans Weber, the financial director of that sales subsidiary (Appendix A). Consequently, Mr. Ernst believed that this would be an appropriate time to review the entire accounting and control system for the sales subsidiaries.

THE ORGANIZATION

VDW was a multinational manufacturer of passenger automobiles with 1980 revenues in excess of DM (Deutsche Marks) 15 billion. Headquarters were located in Munich, Germany, and manufacturing and sales were conducted throughout Europe and parts of Africa.

Staffs

Exhibit 1 is an organization chart of VDW as of January 1, 1981. The headquarters staff, although reporting to the managing director, was also responsible for providing the operating director with the appropriate staff services.

Most of the functions of headquarters personnel were duplicated at all operating levels down to the manufacturing plants and the sales subsidiaries. For example, there was a finance function in product development, manufacturing, and marketing. There was a finance director for stampings, engine and power train, and assembly. Each of

* This case was prepared by John Dearden, Harvard Business School.

the manufacturing plants had financial directors. Each of the sales subsidiaries had finance directors. With the exception of product development, staff members reported directly to the operating manager and functionally to a headquarters staff counterpart. All product-planning personnel were responsible directly to the director of product development, regardless of their geographical location.

Operations

Operations were divided into three functional areas: product development, manufacturing, and marketing.

Product development. This area was responsible for the styling and engineering of all new products lines and the improvement of all existing product lines. Both the marketing and manufacturing operations had product-planning personnel assigned to them. These people reported directly to the director of product development.

Manufacturing. Its operations were divided into three groups: stampings, engine and power train, and assembly. There were several plants in each group.

Manufacturing operations were located in three countries: Germany, France, and Italy. All three countries had stamping plants, engine and power train plants, and assembly plants. For the most part, the stamping plants located in each country provided stamped parts for the assembly plants within the same country; however, all stamping plants provided some parts for assembly plants in the other two countries. For the most part, the engine and power train plants were rationalized to obtain the maximum economies of scale. Consequently, all engine and power train plants produced parts for all assembly plants. Some assembly plants assembled only one product line, some assembled several. Some product lines were assembled exclusively in one assembly plant. Other product lines were assembled at two assembly plants.

The total manufacturing capacity by country was Germany 50 percent, France 30 percent, and Italy 20 percent.

Marketing. Operations were composed of 24 sales subsidiaries, one for each country within which the company sold vehicles. Most of these subsidiaries were in Europe, although some were located in Africa. All sales subsidiaries sold the full range of product lines.

ACCOUNTING AND CONTROL

VDW employed a dual accounting system. First, there was an accounting system for fiscal and tax purposes. Second, there was a system for management control.

The Fiscal Accounting System

An accounting system was maintained in each country for fiscal and tax purposes. Under this system, each country was a profit center, and products were bought and sold among units of the company at transfer prices. Transfer prices were negotiated by the financial directors of the units involved. The objective of these negotiations was to develop prices that distributed the profits or losses among the participating units as fairly as possible, so as to avoid conflict with fiscal authorities. The fiscal accounting system was *not* used to measure the financial performance of either the operations within a country or the financial performance of the managers of those operations.

The Management Control System

For control purposes, the top management of VDW looked only at company-wide revenues, costs, and profits. Each quarter, total company profits were assigned first to product line, and then reassigned to market area. *All* costs and revenues were assigned to some product and to some market area. Thus, the sum of the profits before taxes of all product lines equalled the sum of the profits of all market areas, which in turn equalled the total company profit shown on the external financial statement. The performance of managers in manufacturing and product development was measured on the basis of cost targets and a number of nonfinancial objectives; for example, quality, meeting time commitments, and so forth. Since the issue in this case concerns the measurement of market area financial performance, the specific methods for measuring product development or manufacturing performance are not described.

MEASURING MARKET PERFORMANCE

Market area profitability analysis was based on two underlying principles:

1. Only company-wide revenues, costs, and returns were considered. All accounting transactions involving transfer prices for the sales and purchases of vehicles and components were eliminated.
2. *All* companywide costs, revenues, and assets were assigned to some market area profitability.

Revenues

Revenues were the actual revenues received in each market area converted to Deutsche marks.

Variable Costs

Variable manufacturing costs included direct material, direct labor, and variable overhead. The latter included the variable portion of indirect labor, utilities, supplies, maintenance, and fringe benefits. The variable costs of the components produced by the engine and power train plants, the stamping plants, and the assembly plant were calculated each quarter for each product line and each model within the product line. Each marketing area was charged with the specific variable cost for each product and model sold. Where two products were produced at different assembly plants, the variable costs incurred by the assembly plant that produced the specific vehicle were charged to the marketing area receiving the vehicle. Then companywide manufacturing costs were calculated for each type of vehicle.

Fixed Costs

Manufacturing. An average unit-fixed manufacturing cost was calculated for each component based on the relative standard direct labor content. Then a total unit-fixed manufacturing cost was assigned to each product line and model, representing the sum of the unit-fixed manufacturing costs for all manufactured components included in the vehicle, plus the unit-fixed cost of assembly.

Special tools, launching costs, and product development. The amortization of special tools, launching costs, and product development was assigned directly to product line and model where possible. Common costs were assigned to applicable product lines on the basis of relative unit sales volume. Unit costs were calculated by dividing the total costs by the unit sales volume for each product line and for each model within product line.

Marketing. Marketing costs were assigned directly to sales subsidiaries where this was possible. Common marketing costs were allocated to market area on the basis of the relative volume of sales revenues.

Administration. Administration costs were assigned directly to market area where possible. Common administrative costs were allocated to market area on the basis of relative volume of sales revenues.

Summary. A unit-fixed manufacturing cost, special tool cost, launching cost, and product development cost were calculated for each model. These unit costs were multiplied by the number of the appropriate models sold by each sales subsidiary. In addition to the above, each sales district was assigned unique marketing and administrative costs, plus a share of the common costs based on the relative sales revenue in each market area.

Assets were also assigned to product and marketing area so a "return on assets" could be calculated.

An Example of Profitability Analysis

The following tabular example provides a hypothetical and somewhat simplified picture of how the profitability of the sales subsidiaries was calculated. This example assumes that there are two product lines and two models within each product line. Product line 1 has model A and model B. Product line 2 has model C and model D. There are four sales subsidiaries: W, X, Y, and Z.

Product Line Statistics—First Quarter, 1981

	Product line 1		*Product line 2*	
	Model A	*Model B*	*Model C*	*Model D*
Unit volume	1,000	2,000	3,000	4,000
Price per unit	DM10,000	DM12,000	DM20,000	DM25,000
Cost per unit				
Variable cost:				
Italy		6,000[a]		13,000[b]
Germany	4,000	5,000[c]		11,000[d]
Fixed mfg. costs	2,000	3,000	4,000	5,000
Other fixed costs[e]	1,000	1,000	1,500	2,000

a. Vehicles delivered to subsidiaries W and X.
b. Vehicles delivered to subsidiaries W and Y.
c. Vehicles delivered to subsidiaries Y and Z.
d. Vehicles delivered to subsidiaries X and Z.
e. Other fixed costs include special tools, launching, and product development.

Subsidiary Statistics—First Quarter, 1981

	Unit sales volumes				
Model	*Subsidiary W*	*Subsidiary X*	*Subsidiary Y*	*Subsidiary Z*	*Total*
A	250	200	300	250	1,000
B	1,000	500	300	200	2,000
C	1,000	500	500	1,000	3,000
D	1,000	1,000	1,500	500	4,000
Total	3,250	2,200	2,600	1,950	10,000

Marketing and Administrative Costs (DM 000)

	Sub. W	*Sub. X*	*Sub. Y*	*Sub. Z*	*Total*
Marketing:					
Unique	3,000	5,500	5,000	4,000	17,500
Common					15,000
Administration:					
Unique	100	300	600	500	1,500
Common					16,000

Market Area Profitability—First Quarter 1981 (DM 000)

	Sub. W	*Sub. X*	*Sub. Y*	*Sub. Z*	*Total*
Revenues:					
Model A	2,500	2,000	3,000	2,500	10,000
Model B	12,000	6,000	3,600	2,400	24,000
Model C	20,000	10,000	10,000	20,000	60,000
Model D	25,000	25,000	37,500	12,500	100,000
Total	59,500	43,000	54,100	37,400	194,000
Variable costs:					
Model A	1,000	800	1,200	1,000	4,000
Model B[a]	6,000	3,000	1,500	1,000	11,500
Model C	4,000	2,000	2,000	4,000	12,000
Model D[a]	13,000	11,000	19,500	5,500	49,000
Total	24,000	16,800	24,200	11,500	76,500
Contribution	35,500	26,200	29,900	25,900	117,500
Fixed costs:[b]					
Model A	750	600	900	750	3,000
Model B	4,000	2,000	1,200	800	8,000
Model C	5,500	2,750	2,750	5,500	16,500
Model D	7,000	7,000	10,550	3,500	28,000
Total	17,250	12,350	15,350	10,550	55,500
	18,250	13,850	14,550	15,350	62,000
Mkt. & adm.[c]	12,586	12,682	14,249	10,483	50,000
Net profit	5,664	1,168	301	4,867	12,000

a. Calculation of variable costs for models B and D:

Model B:					
Volume	1,000	500	300	200	
Unit var. cost	6,000	6,000	5,000	5,000	
Total var. cost (DM 000)	6,000	3,000	1,500	1,000	11,500
Model D:					
Volume	1,000	1,000	1,500	500	
Unit var. cost	13,000	11,000	13,000	11,000	
Total var. cost (DM 000)	13,000	11,000	19,500	5,500	49,000

b. Includes manufacturing fixed costs, special tool amortization, launching costs, and product development costs.

c. Allocation of marketing and administrative costs. (See table below.)

Allocation of Marketing and Administrative Costs (DM 000)

	Sub. W	*Sub. X*	*Sub. Y*	*Sub. Z*	*Total*
Unique costs	3,100	5,800	5,600	4,500	19,000
Common costs*	9,486	6,882	8,649	5,983	31,000
Total	12,586	12,682	14,249	10,483	50,000

* Common costs were allocated on the basis of the subsidiaries' sales volume.

MEASURING THE PERFORMANCE OF SALES SUBSIDIARY MANAGERS

Responsibilities of Sales Subsidiary Managers

Pricing. Vehicle price recommendations were submitted to the headquarters marketing staff for review. Differences of opinion between the subsidiary manager and the staff were negotiated; disputes that could not be resolved readily were reviewed with the top operating management for decision.

Sales volume and mix. The subsidiary manager was entirely responsible for all of the sales within the country, although headquarters staff units often provided guidance. The subsidiary manager was responsible for dealer recruitment, development, and control. He or she was also responsible for all local advertising and sales promotion, including special incentives. In short, all sales activities within the country were the direct responsibility of the subsidiary manager.

Costs. The subsidiary manager was responsible for all costs incurred within the country. This included all subsidiary administration and selling costs, as well as all warranty costs incurred by the dealers.

The Bases for Measuring Actual Performance

How well sales subsidiary managers met their responsibilities was measured in financial and nonfinancial terms.

Financial. Financial performance was evaluated by comparing actual performance with the profit budget prepared by the subsidiary manager and approved by headquarters management. In order to arrive at the figures for the profit budget, each year each subsidiary manager prepared: (1) a revenue budget based on budgeted prices, unit volumes, and accessory installations; (2) a cost budget based on the expected expenditures incurred directly by the subsidiary. These budgets, calculated in Deutsche marks, were submitted to headquarters for review and approval. Budgets were approved after negotiating changes, where such changes were deemed appropriate by the top operating management.

Subsequently, each subsidiary manager was provided with the following costs based on company-wide budgets:

Unit-variable cost by model.

Unit-fixed manufacturing cost by model.

Unit-special tool amortization, launching costs, and product development costs by model.

Total allocated sales costs.

Total allocated administrative costs.

Total allocated assets.

On the basis of these figures, the managers prepared a profit budget for the subsidiary, stressing profits and returns on sales and assets.

Each quarter the actual costs and revenues were calculated, and the remainder of the year projected. Thus, each quarter there was an updated estimate of the profitability for the year. This estimate was compared to the original budget, and variances analyzed and explained. Each subsequent quarter was composed more of actual costs and revenues and less of projections. The final quarter compared the actual costs and revenues for the year with the original budget. Note that each quarter all items of costs and revenues were completely recalculated to reflect the latest figures for the year.

Nonfinancial measures. The performance of subsidiary managers was also evaluated on the basis of three nonfinancial measures, as follows:

1. Market penetration.
2. Percentage recovery of price-level and exchange-rate changes. This was the relationship between sales-price increases and price-level increases plus changes in the exchange rate of the local currency relative to the Deutsche mark.
3. Mix and option rates. This measured the improvement in the profits per car.

EVENTS IN 1980

In 1980, two events occurred that were not anticipated in the 1980 budget. First, the sale of vehicles fell significantly below budget as a result of the recession in Europe. Second, fixed manufacturing costs and launching costs seriously exceeded budget. As a result, beginning in the first quarter of 1980, major changes were made to all of the budgeted allocations. These shifts reduced the profitability of all marketing areas, with many areas even showing losses.

One of the subsidiaries that was most severely affected was VDW, Suisse. This situation led to a day-long discussion in April between Hans Weber, the financial director of VDW, Suisse, and Rolf Ernst, the finance director of VDW, A.G. The principal topic discussed in the meeting was the drop in profits and returns by VDW, Suisse, in spite of improvements in sales, volume and mix, and locally incurred costs. At the end of the discussion, Rolf Ernst asked Hans Weber to prepare a letter describing his objections to the accounting system and his reasons for these objections. This letter is reproduced as Appendix A.

On receipt of Weber's letter, Ernst assigned members of his staff to review two of the issues raised by Weber. Memoranda covering these issues are reproduced in Appendixes B and C.

APPENDIX A
Vereinigte Deutsche Wagen, A.G.

Mr. Rolf Ernst
Financial Director
Vereinigte Deutsche Wagen, A.G.
Munich, Germany

Subject: Profit decline in VDW, Suisse

August 21, 1981

Dear Mr. Ernst:

Our discussion of July 17 isolated three reasons for the decline in profitability of VDW, Suisse, from a budgeted 1980 profit of DM 13.9 million to a loss of DM 2.1 million. These were:

1. The variable costs increased because the sourcing of some models was changed from an assembly plant in Germany to an assembly plant in Italy. Not only are the variable costs considerably higher in Italy, but the plant utilization is much lower. This also increased fixed costs.
2. The world-wide sales of vehicles was 25% less than was anticipated in the budget. Because the vehicle sales of VDW, Suisse, was higher than budget, the subsidiary was assigned a much higher amount of allocated fixed costs.
3. Fixed costs were and are expected to be considerably higher than budget. In particular, development and launching costs of Model X, which had just been introduced, were considerably in excess of budget. This model is selling well in Switzerland and, consequently, VDW, Suisse, was assigned a relatively large proportion of these costs.

PROBLEMS

This situation distorts managerial performance and misrepresents the contribution made by this subsidiary, particularly in period-to-period comparisons.

Managerial Performance

So far in 1980, VDW, Suisse has equalled or exceeded its budgeted goals on the items that it controls. Sales volume is somewhat above budgeted levels, the product mix and option rates are at budget, price recovery is only slightly below budget, and local selling and administrative costs are approximately at budget. (The only costs above budget are warranty expenses. This resulted from unanticipated quality problems with Model X.) Yet the profit performance of VDW, Suisse, is DM 16.0 million worse than budget. The entire decline has been caused by factors completely beyond the control of management.

In our discussion, you assured me that management was measured on performance factors other than profit. This, however, creates a dilemma for management. Nonfinancial goals can often be met by taking action that may be contrary to the overall interests of the company. For example, we could increase the sale of Model X by offering special incentives, minimizing option installation, and increasing sales and promotional effort. In fact, we really should do this because it is our best defense against the threat of increasing Japanese imports. Yet if we were to do this, we would lower all the nonfinancial ratios except market penetration. Also, we would exceed our budgeted marketing costs. Not only would we change all of our ratios, but our profits would actually decrease! This occurs because the fixed cost per unit on Model X is so high that, if we lowered our price, we would sustain a loss on each unit sold. Yet, it would seem to me that any increase in volume would be desirable this year in view of the current amount of excess manufacturing capacity.

Subsidiary Performance

As I indicated, this year VDW, Suisse, will show a loss, down from a DM 12.6 profit in 1979. This would seem to indicate that we are experiencing a profit slump. Yet, this is completely untrue. We are having our best year yet. The reason for the profit decrease is entirely due to causes outside of Switzerland, in particular the lower sales volumes in the rest of Europe. Does top management understand this? I find this situation very difficult to explain to our operating managers.

We agree that the problem is not an easy one and is largely compounded by lower overall business activity at source locations. It would seem to us, however, that because of these major fluctuations in accounted profit results, we need to review alternatives that more appropriately identify the true worth of profit center contributions. We realize, in the end analysis, that all fixed costs must be recovered, and satisfactory returns earned on all assets. For the present, however, it would appear that incremental profits are the appropriate decision profits. The presentation of data based on the present fully accounted conventions is totally accepted, and we recognize that it is not practical to calculate incremental profits for every market every month. Your present measurement, however, does not properly identify our true contribution and my operating management is very heavily criticized for actions that we believe were in the best interests of the company. We realize that the problem is not new but because of the magnitude of the aberration we suggest a coordinated corporate review be made on how best to reflect data to management.

Best regards,

Hans Weber
Director of Finance

APPENDIX B
Vereinigte Deutsche Wagen, A.G.

MARKET PROFITABILITY REVIEW—FIXED-MARKET CONCEPT

Market profitability is presently projected using the latest economic profits* less an allocation of fixed costs based on ratios calculated using the latest volume and cost estimates. Only fixed costs directly related to a market are allocated specifically. These represent about 20 percent of total fixed costs. The use of estimated actual volume to allocate fixed costs is termed the "variable market concept." Alternative methods would be the "fixed market concept," where allocations are based on budgeted ratios that remain fixed throughout the year, and the "unit fixed cost concept," in which the budgeted amount of fixed costs is allocated regardless of volume or cost level changes.

The basic advantage of the fixed market concept is that performance in one market is not affected by sales performance in another market. *The major disadvantage is that movements from budget are amplified—because volume changes are translated directly into economic profits*. This can lead to substantial distortion in year-to-year comparisons within markets and intra-year distortions among markets as returns in individual years differ from a fully accounted approach.

The variable market concept tends to have the opposite advantages and disadvantages of the fixed-market concept. It results in the perfor-

* Editor's note: Economic profit is revenue minus variable costs.

mance of one market affecting others, but year-to-year comparisons at equal volume are not distorted.

The unit-cost concept would avoid the problems of the above but could result in major differences between total corporate profits and operational profits if volume was substantially off budget. Such a large consolidation item would be unacceptable.

The use of a fixed or variable market allocation basis for fixed costs becomes a trade-off between the incentive advantages to managing directors under the fixed concept and the more representative trend profits that occur with the variable concept. A potential plan to reduce the financial disadvantages of the present methodology would be to change the primary measurement to a variable system, while maintaining the fixed system for performance measurement of general managers. Finance staff recommends implementation of the latter change for the 1981 budget, with all historical years restated. This could lead to situations where management presentations would show performance different from how the managing directors would be measured. If sales group prefers, performance measurement also can use the variable concept.

September 19, 1980.

EXHIBIT 1 Organization as of January 1, 1981

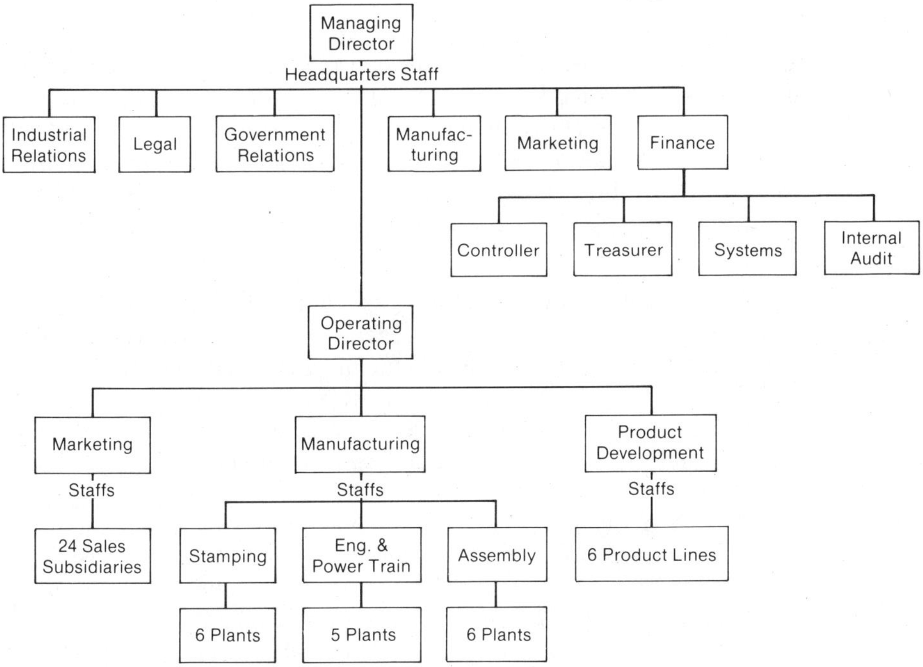

Source: Company organization manual.

APPENDIX C
Vereinigte Deutsche Wagen, A.G.

MARKET PROFITABILITY REVIEW—AVERAGE SOURCING

At present, the product profit system details the cost of each vehicle in each market. The revenue and cost assumptions are provided by the relevant sales and manufacturing areas and reflect the actual vehicle sourcing pattern. As a result, the costs of identical vehicles assembled in different plants will vary because of differences in labor and material costs, in freight patterns, in plant capacity utilization, and in other factors. This system provides an accurate estimate of the actual cost incurred in producing a specific vehicle in a specific plant, and offers the following advantages:

1. It provides an excellent base for financial analysis—all costs and revenues can be tracked from sales/manufacturing input.
2. It highlights problems—a comparison of variable cost data between sources can lead to the identification of cost-saving opportunities.
3. Proposals for product or capacity changes must be based on actual costs to evaluate the correct corporate profit effect.

An alternative to use of specific sourcing would be to provide cost data on an "average-source basis." The major advantage of such a policy would be to eliminate potential profit distortions that result from sourcing decisions that are not within the control of managing directors. Although this change has advantages for financial incentives, this value appears to be outweighed by the following weaknesses:

1. Elimination of sourcing variances from market profits would require average-source material, labor, overhead, and freight costs. This would require the development of theoretical costs. The development of these data would necessarily lead to cost increases.
2. The product system is fully computerized and does not have the capability to derive average-source costs without a major change to existing computer systems.
3. The use of average-source costs would mask specific pricing problems, such as tax and duty in Scandinavian markets. In these markets, the tax and duty implications are a function of the transfer price charged by the national company owning the final assembly source. It is essential that specific tax and duty levels are reflected in pricing decisions to ensure full recovery of costs.

4. Even if average sourcing were used, intermarket comparisons would still include substantial factors outside the direct control of managing directors, such as exchange rates. Use of average sourcing could lessen attention to real issues, such as source/sales exchange rate changes that require positive action.

Continued use of specific sourcing is recommended.

September 30, 1980

CHAPTER 7

Transfer Pricing

One of the principal problems in operating a profit center system is to devise a satisfactory method of accounting for the transfer of goods and services from one profit center to another, in those companies having significant amounts of these transactions. A survey by Richard Vancil[1] of 291 divisionalized manufacturing companies found that about 85 percent of the profit centers transfer goods, and that transfers of services and joint use of common facilities existed in 55 percent and 71 percent of companies, respectively.

In this chapter we discuss various approaches to arriving at transfer prices for transactions between profit centers and the system of negotiation and arbitration that is essential when transfer prices are used. We also discuss the pricing of services that corporate staff units furnish to profit centers.

OBJECTIVES OF TRANSFER PRICES

If two or more profit centers are jointly responsible for product development, manufacturing, and marketing, each share in the revenue that is generated when the product is finally sold. The transfer price system is the mechanism for distributing this revenue. In distributing revenue, the system should do so in such a way that it accomplishes three things:

1. It should provide each segment with the relevant information required to determine the optimum trade-off between *company* costs and revenues.
2. Profits should reflect how well the cost/revenue trade-offs have been made. Each segment of the business should be able to maximize company profits by maximizing divisional profits.

[1] Richard F. Vancil, *Decentralization: Management Ambiguity by Design* (Homewood, Ill.: Dow Jones-Irwin, 1979), p. 169.

3. The profits shown by each profit center should reflect the contribution of that profit center to the total company profits.

The transfer price is extremely important because it affects the ability of a profit center manager to make optimum decisions. Also, the measurement of the financial performance of the profit center manager, as well as the profit center itself, is affected by the transfer price system. Incorrect transfer prices create incorrect measurements which, in turn, result in incorrect decisions.

TRANSFER PRICING METHODS

Some writers use "transfer price" to refer to the amount used in accounting for *any* transfer of goods and services between responsibility centers. We use a somewhat narrower definition and limit the term *transfer price* to the value placed on a transfer of goods or services among two or more *profit centers*. Such a price would normally include a profit element because an independent company would not normally transfer goods or services to another independent company at cost or less. The term *price,* as used here, has the same meaning as it has when it is used in connection with transactions between independent companies.

When profit centers of a company buy and sell from each other, there are two decisions that must be made periodically for each product that is being produced (or that may be produced) by one division and sold to another. First, it must be decided *where* the product is to be produced; that is, whether it is to be produced inside the company or purchased from an outside vendor. This is the *sourcing* decision. Second, if produced inside, it is necessary to determine a *transfer price.*

Transfer price systems can range from the very simple to the extremely complex, depending on the nature of the business. We start with the simple situations and describe increasingly complex situations.

Available Markets

The simplest transfer price situation occurs where there are outside markets to which the inside producer can sell its products and where there are outside sources from which the inside user can buy the products it requires. In this instance, the only transfer price policy necessary is to give the manager of each profit center the right to deal with either insiders or outsiders at his or her discretion. The market, thus, establishes the transfer price. The decision to deal inside or outside is also made by the marketplace. If a buyer cannot get a satisfactory price from the inside source, he or she is free to buy from the outside.

As long as the selling profit center can sell all of its products, either to insiders or outsiders, and as long as the buying profit center can obtain all of its requirements from either outsiders or insiders, this method is optimum. The market price represents the opportunity cost to the seller of selling the product inside. This is so because, if the product were not sold inside, it would be sold outside. From a company point of view, therefore, the relevant cost of the product is the market price, because that is the amount of cash that has been foregone by selling inside. The transfer, therefore, price represents the opportunity cost to the company.

This is the only situation where a transfer price system fulfills all of the three requirements stated above and yet needs no central administration.

Excess or shortage of industry capacity. Suppose the selling profit center cannot sell to the outside market all it can produce. This situation occurs when there is excess capacity in the industry. The company may not optimize profits to the extent that the buying profit center purchases from the outside while capacity is available on the inside.

On the other hand, suppose the buying profit center cannot obtain all of the product it requires from the outside, while the selling profit center is selling to the outside. This situation occurs when there is a shortage of capacity in the industry. In this case, the output of the buying profit center is constrained and, again, company profits may not be maximized.

If the amount of intracompany transfers is small or the situation temporary, most companies let the buyers and sellers work out their own relationships without central intervention. Even if the amount of intracompany transfers is significant, some companies still do not intervene, on the theory that the benefits of keeping the profit centers independent offsets the loss from suboptimizing company profits.

Some companies allow either the buying or the selling profit center to appeal a sourcing decision to a central person or committee. For example, a selling profit center could appeal a buying profit center's decision to buy a product from outside when capacity was available inside. In the same way, a buying profit center could appeal a selling profit center's decision to sell outside. The person or group (hereafter called an "arbitration" committee) would, then, make the sourcing decision on the basis of the company's best interests. In every case, the transfer price would be the competitive price. In other words, the appealing profit center is appealing only the sourcing decision. It must accept the product at the competitive price. In some instances, however, the competitive price may be adjusted downward to reflect savings by the selling division from dealing inside the company. For example, there would be no bad debt expense and smaller selling costs.

A word of caution is in order at this point. In some companies, given the option, the buying profit centers prefer to deal with an outside source. Some of this is based on service. Outside sources are perceived to provide better service. Some of it may also be based on the internal rivalry often experienced in divisionalized companies. For whatever reason, management should be aware of the strong political overtones that sometimes occur in transfer price negotiations. It is by no means assured that a profit center will voluntarily buy from the inside source when excess capacity exists.

Integrated costs. A second problem can occur when products are transferred at a competitive price and internal capacity is available. There will always be "upstream" fixed costs and profits that may *not* be considered by the profit center ultimately selling to the outside.

To illustrate this problem, assume that Division C manufactures and sells cardboard boxes in an integrated paper company. It buys the paperboard from Division B which, in turn, buys the pulp to make the paperboard from Division A. The prices and costs for a ton of boxes is as follows:

	A	*B*	*C*	*Consolidated*
Price	$75	$150	$350	$350
Costs:				
Material	20	75	150	20
Other variable costs	25	25	200	250
Total	45	100	350	270
Contribution	$30	$ 50	0	$ 80

Note that the variable cost to Division A was $45 to produce enough pulp to make a ton of boxes. This was sold to Division B for $75, so Division A earned a contribution of $30. Division B, in turn, added $25 in variable cost and sold the paper board to Division C for $150. Division C, however, can sell the boxes in the outside market for only $350. Because it would earn no contribution on the sale, Division C would have litle incentive to pursue such a sale aggressively. The company, however, would earn a contribution of $80. Although this example is exaggerated, a somewhat similar situation exists on all sales in an integrated company.

It is always possible for representatives of Division C to meet with representatives of Divisions A and B to decide on an outside selling price and to negotiate a distribution of the contribution that would be earned. If this were done, there would be no problem, because the optimum action for the three divisions would be the optimum action for the company. In many cases, however, there may be hundreds of transactions taking place monthly, so there would have to be some formal mechanisms for the three divisions to consult together on bids or, given a market price, whether to sell at that price. Such mechanisms seem to be used rarely in business. In fact, divisions often guard their cost structure so jealously that Division C may not even know what the costs of the upstream divisions are.

It certainly can be argued that what is best for the company also will be best for the divisions involved. This must be so because all of the contribution will go to participating divisions. The greater the total contributions, therefore, the more would be earned by the participating divisions. The problem is that mechanisms for communications and negotiations among divisions may not be available. Consequently, the division that sells to an outside customer will tend to make decisions based on its own cost structure.

This is the most serious problem in transfer pricing because (1) it exists almost universally, and will occur to some extent any time there is unused capacity in the upstream profit centers; and (2) rarely is anything done about this problem, except in highly integrated companies (and not always then).

Methods for handling this problem are described later in this chapter.

Limited Markets

In many integrated companies, markets for the buying or selling profit centers may be limited. There are several reasons for this.

First, the existence of internal capacity might limit the development of external capacity. If most of the large companies in an industry are highly integrated, as in the pulp and paper industry, there tends to be little independent production capacity for the intermediate products. Thus, these producers can handle only a limited amount of demand. When internal capacity becomes tight, the market is quickly flooded with demands for the intermediate products. Even though outside capacity exists, it may not be available to the integrated company unless this capacity is used on a regular basis. If the integrated company does not purchase a product on a regular basis, it might have trouble obtaining it from the outside when capacity is short.

Second, if a company is the sole producer of a differentiated product, no outside capacity exists.

Third, if a company has made significant investment in facilities, it is unlikely to use outside sources even though outside capacity exists, unless the outside selling price approaches the company's variable cost, which is not usual. For practical purposes, the products produced are captive.

Even in the case of limited markets, the transfer price that best satisfies the requirements of a profit center system is still the *competitive* price. Consider the following:

1. Competitive prices will measure the contribution of each profit center to the total company profits. If internal capacity were not available, the company would buy outside at the competitive price. The difference between the competitive price and inside cost is the money saved by making instead of buying.
2. A competitive price measures how well a profit center may be performing against competition.
3. A competitive price is independent of internal conditions.

The problem is: How does a company obtain a competitive price if it does not buy or sell the product in an outside market? Here are some ways:

1. If *published market prices* are available, they can be used to establish transfer prices. However,
   a. These should be prices actually paid in the market.
   b. The conditions that exist in the outside market should be consistent with those existing within the company. For example, market prices that are applicable to relatively small purchases (e.g., a "spot" market), would not be competitive for what is essentially a long term commitment.
2. Market prices may be set by *bids*. This can generally be done only if the bidder has a reasonable chance of obtaining the business by being the low bidder. For example, one company accomplishes this by buying about one half of a particular group of products outside the company and one half inside the company. The company puts *all* of the products out to bid, but selects one half to stay inside. The company obtains valid bids because the bidders can expect to get some of the business. Note that a company requesting bids solely to obtain a competitive price will soon find that either no one bids or the bids are of questionable value.
3. If the *manufacturing profit center* sells other products in *outside markets,* it is often possible to replicate a competitive price on the basis of the outside price. For example, a manufacturing profit center earns 10 percent over standard cost on the products that it sells to outside markets. It can, then, replicate a competitive price by adding 10 percent to the standard cost of the proprietary products. Of course, the manufacturing processes for both the competitive and proprietary products must be similar.
4. If the *buying profit center* purchases similar products from the *outside* market, it may be possible to replicate competitive prices

for proprietary products. This can be done by calculating the cost of the difference in design and other conditions of sale between the competitive products and the proprietary products.

If there are no ways to approximate valid competitive prices, the remaining option is to develop *cost-based* transfer prices. This is discussed in the next part of the chapter.

Cost-based Transfer Prices

If competitive prices are not available, transfer prices may be set on the basis of cost plus a profit, even though such transfer prices may be complex to calculate and the results less satisfactory. There are two decisions that must be made in a cost-based transfer price system:

1. How to define cost.
2. How to calculate the profit markup.

The cost basis. The usual basis is standard cost. Actual costs should not be used because manufacturing inefficiencies will then be passed on to the buying profit center. If standard costs are used, there is a need to develop an incentive to set tight standards or to improve standards by adding new facilities.

Some companies have tried using "efficient producer" costs, but someone has to decide what these costs will be.

This brings up a second problem: Are prices to be negotiated? If they are to be negotiated, the negotiating parties need detailed instructions because the divisions are negotiating a satisfactory cost level. Also, the company needs an arbitration committee to interpret these rules and settle disputes.

If prices are set by the central staff, then the profits of both profit centers are dependent upon the central staff. In which case, the manager often feels that he or she does not control profitability.

The profit markup. It is necessary to decide how to calculate the profit markup. In this case, also, there are two decisions:

1. On what is the profit markup to be based?
2. What is the level of profit allowed?

The simplest base is a *percent of costs*. If this is done, however, no account is taken of capital required. A better base is the amount of *investment,* but there is a major problem in calculating this investment. If the historical cost of the fixed assets is used, new facilities designed to reduce prices could actually increase costs because old assets are undervalued. Thus, when the old assets are replaced by new assets, the price could increase.

A second problem with the profit allowance is the amount of the profit. Top management's perception of financial performance of a profit center will be affected by the profit it shows. Consequently, to the extent possible, the profit allowance should be the best approximation of the rate of return that would be earned if the division were an independent company.

One solution is to base the profit allowance on the investment required to meet the volume needed by the buying profit centers. This investment would be calculated at a "standard" level, with fixed assets and inventories at current replacement costs.

Management considerations. As indicated, there are a number of serious problems with cost-based transfer price. The principal things to be considered are:

1. Transfer prices should not encourage the manufacturing profit center to fail to maintain tight standards or fail to improve productivity by making appropriate investments. Manufacturing profit centers should have the same motivation to reduce costs that they would have if their prices were based on outside competition.
2. The performance factors should always be segregated by responsibility. For example, manufacturing inefficiencies should not be passed on to the buying profit center.
3. In general, a fairly elaborate administrative procedure is required if the profit centers are to negotiate their own prices (a procedure that we recommend). When the marketplace is removed as a basis for pricing, the parties must negotiate on internal conditions, specifically allowable levels of costs and profits.

If competitive prices are unavailable or cannot be replicated, the manufacturing operation is usually captive and manufactures differentiated products entirely within the company. Under these circumstances, serious consideration should be given to making this operation a cost center, or at least a "pseudo" profit center as described in Chapter 6.

UPSTREAM FIXED COSTS AND PROFITS

We explained earlier that most integrated companies face problems because the profit centers that finally sell to the outside customer may not be even aware of the amount of upstream fixed costs and profits included in their internal purchase prices. Even if they were aware of it, they might have to reduce their own profits to optimize company profits. Clearly, this is an unsatisfactory situation. Yet, it exists in almost all transfer price situations. In this part of the chapter, we explain some methods companies used to reduce this problem.

Agreement among Divisions

A company could establish a formal mechanism whereby representatives from the contributing divisions meet periodically to decide on outside selling prices and on the distribution of the profit for products having significant amounts of upstream fixed costs and profits in the purchase price to the division that ultimately sells to the outside. To make this mechanism workable, the review process should be limited to decisions that involve a high level of activity. As we stated earlier, actions that maximize the profits of the company will also maximize the profits of the profit centers affected.

Two-Step Pricing

Another way to handle the problem of upstream fixed costs and profits is to establish a transfer price that includes two charges. First, a charge is made for each unit sold that is equal to the standard variable cost of production. Second, a periodic (usually monthly) charge is made that is equal to the fixed costs associated with the facilities reserved for the buying division, plus a profit based on a return on the resources reserved for the buying division. For example, assume the following conditions:

Division X (Manufacturer)

	Product A	*Product B*
Expected sales to Division Y	$ 100,000	$ 100,000
Variable cost per unit	5.00	10.00
Total annual fixed costs assigned to product	480,000	480,000
Investment in working capital and facilities to produce products	1,200,000	1,500,000
Competitive return on investment	10%	10%

The transfer price for product A would be $5 for each unit that Division Y purchases plus $40,000 per month (480,000 ÷ 12) for fixed cost, plus $10,000 per month $\left(\frac{1,200,000}{12} \times .10\right)$ for profit.

The transfer price for product B would be $10 for each unit that Division Y purchases, plus $40,000 per month for fixed costs plus $12,500 $\left(\frac{1,500,000}{12} \times .10\right)$ for profit.

The fixed-cost calculation is based on the capacity that is reserved for the production of each of the products that is sold to Division Y. The investment represented by this capacity then is allocated to each of these products. The return on investment that Division Y earns at standard cost on competitive (and, if possible, comparable) products is calculated and multiplied by the investment assigned to the product.

In the example just given, we have calculated the profit allowance as a fixed amount. It would be appropriate under some circumstances to divide the investment into variable (e.g., receivables and inventory) and fixed (physical assets) components. Then, a profit allowance based on a return on the variable assets would be added to the standard variable cost for each unit sold.

Following are some points to consider about this method of pricing:

1. The monthly charge for fixed costs and profits would be negotiated periodically and would depend on the capacity reserved for the buying division.

2. Some questions may be raised about the accuracy of the cost and investment allocation. Actually, in most situations there is no great difficulty in assigning costs and assets to individual products. In any event, approximate accuracy is all that is needed. The principal problem is usually not the allocation technique; rather, it is the decision about how much capacity is to be reserved for the various products. Moreover, if capacity is reserved for a group of products sold to the same division, there is no need to allocate fixed costs and investments to individual products in the group.

3. Standard variable costs are not always the same as marginal costs. Where there is a real possibility that marginal costs might vary significantly from standard variable costs, some system should be developed for monitoring the costs and communicating to management when such differences develop.

4. Under this pricing system, the manufacturing division's profit performance is not affected by sales volume, which solves the problem that arises when other division's marketing efforts affect the profit performance of a purely manufacturing division.

5. There could be some conflict between the interests of the manufacturing division and the interests of the company. If capacity is limited, the manufacturing division can increase its profit by selling outside, because the outside selling price will be higher than the standard variable cost. Consequently, if divisional managers have the choice of using their capacity to produce parts for outside sale, it will be to their advantage to do so. (This weakness is mitigated by stipulating that the selling divisions have first claim on the capacity they have contracted for.)

6. This method is similar to the "take or pay" pricing that is sometimes used in public utilities, coal companies, and other long-term contractors.

Profit Sharing

Where the two-step pricing system just described does not appear to be appropriate, a profit-sharing system might be used to ensure congruence of division interest with company interest. This system operates somewhat as follows:

1. The product is transferred to the marketing division at standard variable cost.
2. After the product is sold, the divisions share the contribution earned, which is the selling price minus the variable manufacturing and marketing costs.

This method of pricing is often appropriate when the demand for the manufactured product is not steady enough to warrant the permanent assignment of facilities, as in the two-step method. In general, this method accomplishes the purpose of making the marketing division's interest congruent with the company's. There can be, however, practical problems in calculating the contribution, finding an equitable method to divide it, and in administering the system.

Two Sets of Prices

A third possible solution to the problem of the manufacturing division that sells only to a marketing division is to have two sets of transfer prices. The manufacturing division's revenue is credited at the outside sales price, minus a percentage to cover marketing costs. The buying division is charged the variable standard costs (or, sometimes,

EXHIBIT 7–1 Transfer Pricing Policies for Goods

	Respondents specifying the method used			
Method used	*Number*	*Number total*	*Percentage*	*Percentage total*
Variable cost:				
Variable standard	7	11	2.9	4.6
Variable actual	4		1.7	
Full cost:				
Full standard	30	61	12.5	25.5
Full actual	31		13.0	
Cost, plus or negotiated:				
Profit on sales	7	93	2.9	38.9
Profit on investment	7		2.9	
Negotiation	53		22.2	
Full cost + markup	26		10.9	
Market price:				
Competitor's price	28	74	11.7	31.0
Market price—list	41		17.2	
Market price—bid	5		2.1	
Total	239*	239*	100.0	100.0

* Of the 249 companies reporting that they transfer goods between profit centers, 239 specified the transfer pricing policies.

the total standard cost). The difference is charged to a headquarters account and eliminated when the divisional statements are consolidated.

This method gives the manufacturing division an incentive to help maximize profits, rather than simply minimizing costs. The marketing division is motivated to make correct short-term product and pricing decisions. The method has the disadvantage, however, of making divisional profits greater than company profits. Consequently, top management must be aware of this situation in evaluating divisional profitability.

Exhibit 7–1 summarizes the results of a survey made by Richard F. Vancil of the transfer pricing practices of 239 divisionalized manufacturing companies.[2]

ADMINISTRATION OF TRANSFER PRICES

Most transfer price systems require formal procedures to operate successfully. They are described in this section.

Negotiation among Divisions

In most companies, divisions negotiate transfer prices with each other; that is, transfer prices are not set by a central staff group. Perhaps the most important reason for this is the belief that one of the primary functions of line management is to establish selling prices and to arrive at satisfactory purchase prices. If control of pricing is left to the headquarters staff, line management's ability to affect profitability is reduced. Also, many transfer prices require a degree of subjective judgment. Consequently, a negotiated transfer price often is the result of compromises made by both buyer and seller. A headquarters group, however, must try to rationalize transfer prices that may have to be set in a somewhat arbitrary manner. When headquarters establishes the transfer prices, it is always possible for division managers to argue that their low profits are due to the arbitrariness of the transfer prices. A third reason for having the divisions negotiate their prices is that they usually have the most information on markets and costs and, consequently, are best able to arrive at reasonable prices.

If the divisions are to negotiate prices, they must know the ground rules within which these negotiations are to be conducted. In a few companies, headquarters inform divisions that they are free to deal with each other or with outsiders as they see fit. Where this is done and there are outside sources and outside markets, no further administra-

---

[2] Ibid.

tive procedures are required, assuming senior management really means that the divisions are free to deal outside the company. The price is set in the outside marketplace and, if divisions cannot agree on a price, they simply buy from or sell to outsiders. In most companies, however, some administrative procedures are desirable. If divisions are required to deal with one another, they do not have the threat of doing business with competitors as a bargaining point in the negotiation process. Consequently, the headquarters staff must develop a set of rules that govern both pricing and sourcing of intracompany products.

Sourcing and transfer pricing rules. The extent and formality of the sourcing and transfer pricing rules will depend to a great extent on the amount of intracompany transfers and the availability of markets and market prices. The greater the amount of intracompany transfers, and the less the availability of market prices, the more formal and specific the rules must be. In some instances, all that is required is to tell the divisions that goods will be transferred at prevailing market prices. If such prices are readily available, there are few problems. Sourcing can be controlled by having headquarters review make-or-buy decisions that affect revenues in excess of a specified amount.

If there are significant amounts of intracompany transfers and if competitive prices are not available for all products, guidelines similar to the following have been found to be useful:

1. Divide products into two main classes:

   Class I includes all products for which top management wishes to control the sourcing. These would normally be the large-volume products, products where no outside sources exist, and products where for quality or secrecy reasons the company wishes to maintain control over manufacturing.

   Class II are all other products. In general, these are products that can be produced outside the company without any significant disruption to present operations. These are products of relatively small volume, produced with general purpose equipment. Class II products are transferred at market prices.
2. The sourcing of Class I products can be changed only with permission of central management.
3. The sourcing of Class II products is determined by the divisions involved. Both the buying and selling divisions are free to deal either inside or outside the company.

Under this arrangement it is possible to concentrate on the sourcing and pricing of a relatively small number of high-volume products. A list of products by classification should be provided, as well as specific instruction about how the prices of each product should be established. There should be rules for establishing market-based prices and rules for establishing cost-based prices. It is not unlikely that all of the different methods described in the preceding section would be used. If divisions are to negotiate, they must know how each product is to be priced, and this is the purpose of the set of rules.

It is important that line managers do not spend an undue amount of time on transfer price negotiations. Guidelines for these negotiations, therefore, should be specific enough so skill in negotiations is not a significant factor in the determination of the transfer price. Without such rules, the most stubborn manager will negotiate the most favorable prices.

Arbitration

No matter how specific the pricing rules are, there may be instances where divisions will not be able to agree on a price. For this reason, there should be some procedure for arbitrating transfer price disputes.

There can be widely different degrees of formality in transfer price arbitration. At one extreme the responsibility for arbitrating disputes is assigned to a single executive; for example, the financial vice president or the executive vice president, who talks to the division managers involved and then announces the price orally.

The other extreme is to set up a committee. Usually such a committee will have three responsibilities:

1. To settle transfer price disputes.
2. To review sourcing changes.
3. To change the transfer price rules where appropriate.

The degree of formality employed depends on the extent and type of potential transfer price disputes. In any case, transfer price arbitration should be the responsibility of a high-level headquarters executive or group, since arbitration decisions can have an important effect on divisional profits.

Arbitration can be conducted in a number of ways. With a formal system, both parties submit a written case to the arbitrator. The arbitrator reviews both positions and decides on the price. In establishing a price, the assistance of other staff offices may be obtained. For example, the purchasing department might review the validity of a proposed competitive price quotation, or the industrial engineering department might review the appropriateness of a disputed standard labor cost. As indicated above, in less formal systems, the presentations may be largely oral.

It is important that relatively few disputes should be submitted to arbitration. If a large number of disputes are arbitrated, this indicates that the rules are not specific enough, the rules are difficult to apply, the divisional organization is illogical, or divisionalization should not have been adopted. In short, it is a symptom that something is wrong.

Not only is arbitration time-consuming to both line managers and headquarters executives, but also arbitrated prices often satisfy neither the buyer nor the seller.

In some companies, there is such an onus involved in submitting a price dispute to arbitration that very few are ever submitted. If, as a consequence, legitimate grievances do not surface, the results are undesirable. Preventing disputes from being submitted to arbitration will tend to hide the fact that there are problems with the transfer price system.

TRANSFER PRICING AND COST-TYPE CONTRACTS

In some instances, a division that is working on a cost-type government contract may purchase material or parts from another division of the company. The question then arises as to whether the cost allowed under the contract is the selling division's cost or a transfer price that includes a profit margin. Clearly, in most instances, it will be to the company's benefit to use the transfer price.

Government regulations state that transfers from other divisions, subsidiaries, or affiliates will be at cost, except under the following conditions:

1. The transfer price is based on an established catalog or market price of commercial items sold in substantial quantities to the general public.
2. It is the result of adequate price competition and is the price at which an award was made to an affiliated organization after obtaining quotations on an equal basis from such organizations and from one or more outside sources that normally produce the item or its equivalent in significant quantities.[3]

The price calculated above must not be in excess of the selling division's current price to its most favored customer. Also, the transfer price should be adjusted, when appropriate, to reflect the quantities being procured and may be adjusted for the actual costs of any modifications required by the contract.

Cost Accounting Standard 414 requires a capital charge on fixed assets as an element of cost. Consequently, even where the transfer is at cost, an element of profit is included.

Even where all of the requirements above are met, contracting officers may determine that a particular transfer price is unreasonable. If they so determine, however, they must support this position with appropriate facts.

---

[3] Armed Services Defense Acquisition Regulations. (These regulations are used by many government agencies.)

The implication of these transfer price regulations for managers is that special care should be taken in establishing transfer prices for divisions working on government contracts. Otherwise, the company may suffer a real economic loss.

PRICING CORPORATE SERVICES

In this section we describe some of the problems associated with charging divisions for services furnished by corporate staff units.

It is useful to classify central services in the following three types:

1. Those central services over which the division has no control.
2. Those central services that the division must accept, but for which the amount of the service is at least partially controllable by the division.
3. Those central services over which the division has the discretion of using or not using.

No Control by the Division

Divisions ordinarily cannot control the services rendered by such staff offices as accounting, public relations, industrial relations, and legal. The divisions must accept these services and have little, if anything, to say about the amount that is spent on them.

The principal problem with these services is whether to allocate the costs to the operating divisions. As indicated in Chapter 6, the main reasons given for allocating them are:

1. If operating managers pay for a service whether they use it or not, they will be more likely to use it.
2. Operating managers will be more likely to exert pressure to keep down those costs (by complaining) if they must pay for them.
3. Divisional profits will be more realistic and comparable to outside firms because, presumably, the outside firm would have to pay for comparable services.

The main argument against allocation is that it is not controllable by the operating managers and, therefore, may only annoy them.

If top management does decide to allocate these costs, the usual cost accounting techniques for estimating the fair share applicable to each profit center are satisfactory. When the divisional managers prepare their profit budgets, they should be provided with an amount to include for these services. Subsequently, one twelfth of this amount should be charged each month to the division. In this way, the allocation will not affect the comparison between budgeted and actual divisional profit performance, and variances will appear in the reports of the responsibility center that incurred the costs. An exception to this generalization might occur if personnel costs or prices for purchased services increase significantly during the budget period; it would seem appropriate to pass on these increased costs to the users.

Control over Amount of Service

In some cases, divisions must accept a central service; but the amount of the service that it accepts may be controllable. Management Information Systems (MIS) and research/development are two examples. There are three schools of thought about such services.

One school holds that a division should pay the variable *costs* of the discretionary services. If it pays less than this, it will be motivated to use more of the service than is economically justified. For example, if divisional managers did not have to pay for their reports, they might request reports from the MIS department, even though these were of little value to them. On the other hand, if divisional managers pay more for a service than the variable cost to the company, they might elect not to use certain services because their value was not equal to the cost. If the value of the service were more than the variable cost to the company, however, it might be a mistake for the operating manager to reject this service.

A second school advocates a price equal to the variable cost plus a fair share of the fixed costs. It is argued that, if the divisions do not believe the services are worth at least this amount, then there is something wrong with either the quality or the efficiency of the service unit. Furthermore, divisions may be permitted to obtain services from an outside source if they can do so at a price that is lower than the company's full cost. If services are procured from an outside source, this is another signal that something may be wrong with the company's service unit. It also is argued that full costs represent the company's long-run costs and this is the amount that should be paid. If full costs are used, however, they should be *budgeted* costs, with the exception stated above.

A third school of thought advocates a price that is equivalent to the market price, or to full cost plus a profit margin. The market price would be used if available (e.g., the costs charged by a computer service bureau); if not, the price would be full cost plus a return on investment. The rationale for this position is that the capital employed by the service unit should earn a return just as much as the capital employed by manufacturing divisions. Said another way, the divisions would incur the investment if they provided their own services. Xerox Corporation uses this approach, as indicated by the following:

> Each application was subjected to an industrial engineering study to establish its standard cost. The standard costs used market based

> prices for computer resources. The company then charges users the standard cost for processing their applications throughout the year and actual costs are also tracked and available to users on request. Where several users share the benefits of a computer application the processing costs are allocated between them. Users decide upon a "fair" appropriation of the costs. If one user decides to eliminate his report, the other users must pick up the added costs. The intent is to provide accountability to those that benefit from computer resources, and to provide feedback information so those that benefit can more effectively behave as responsible users.[4]

The decision on pricing depends to a considerable extent on the wishes of management. If management wants to encourage divisions to use a central service (e.g., operations research or computer systems), it might provide them at variable cost, or even less, at least for a time period. On the other hand, if management believes that the profit centers should pay a price that approximates the cost of an outside service, it might charge full cost or even more.

Discretionary Use of Services

In some cases, management may decide that divisional use of a central service unit is optional to the operating divisions. The divisions may use an outside service, develop internal capability, or simply not use the service at all. This type of arrangement is most often found in such activities as information processing or internal consulting groups. These service units are independent; they must stand on their own feet. If the services are not used by the divisions, the scope of their activity will be contracted or they may even be eliminated entirely. In effect, management is delegating the responsibility for supporting these particular central services to the users.

In some instances, service groups of this type are made into profit centers. To the extent that they are treated as profit centers, the transfer price is set according to the considerations described earlier.

Simplicity of the Pricing Mechanism

The prices charged for corporate services will not accomplish their intended result unless they are sufficiently straightforward that division managers understand their significance. Computer experts are accustomed to dealing with complex equations, and the computer itself provides information on the use made of it on a second-by-second basis

[4] Session chairman Richard L. Nolan, "A Panel Session—Charge-out System for Management Acceptance and Control of the Computer Resource," *Proceedings, National Computer Conference, 1974,* pp. 1013.

and at low cost. There is sometimes a tendency, therefore, to charge computer users on the basis of rules that are so complicated that the user cannot understand them. Often the user cannot understand what the effect on costs would be if he or she decided to use the computer for a given application, or alternatively, to discontinue a current application. Such rules tend to be self-defeating.

APPENDIX
Some Theoretical Considerations

There is a considerable body of literature on theoretical transfer pricing models. Few, if any, of these models are used in actual business situations, however, and, for reasons explained below, it is unlikely that they ever will be widely used. Consequently, reference to these models has been omitted in the body of this chapter. Although these models are not directly applicable to real business situations, they are useful in conceptualizing transfer price systems. The purpose of this appendix is to give a brief description of some of these models and to provide references for the interested student.

Transfer pricing models may be divided into three types: (1) models based on classical economic theory, (2) models based on mathematical models such as linear programming, and (3) models based on game theory.

Economic Models

The classic economic model was first described by Jack Hirschleifer in a 1956 article. Professor Hirschleifer developed a series of marginal revenue, marginal cost, and demand curves for the transfer of an intermediate product from the transferor (the selling division) to the transferee (the final processing division). He used these curves to establish transfer prices, under various sets of economic assumptions, that would optimize the total profit of the two divisions. Using the transfer prices thus developed, the two divisions would produce the maximum total profit by optimizing their divisional profits. The two-step pricing system described in the chapter is an adaptation of this type of model.

The difficulty with the Hirschleifer model is that it can be used only when a specified set of conditions exist: It must be possible to estimate the demand curve for the intermediate product; the assumed conditions must remain stable; there can be no alternative uses for the facilities used to make the intermediate product; and the model is applicable only to the situation in which the selling division makes a single intermediate product, which it transfers to a single buying division, which uses that intermediate product in a single final product. Such conditions exist rarely, if at all, in the real world.

Mathematical Programming Models

In contrast with the marginal cost approach of the economic models, the mathematical programming models are based on an opportunity cost approach. These models also incorporate capacity constraints. They may develop a linear program that calculates an optimum company-wide production pattern; and, using this pattern, they calculate a set of values that impute the profit contribution of the scarce resources. These are termed *shadow prices*, and one process of calculating them is called "obtaining the dual solution" to the linear program. If the variable costs of the intermediate products are added to their shadow prices, a set of transfer prices results that should motivate divisions to produce according to the optimum production pattern for the entire company. This is so because, if these transfer prices are used, each division will optimize its profits only by producing in accordance with the patterns developed through the linear program.

If reliable shadow prices could be calculated, they would be useful in arriving at transfer prices. However, to make the programming model manageable, even on a computer, many simplifying assumptions must be incorporated in it. It is assumed that the demand curve is known, that it is static, that the cost function is linear, and that alternative uses of production facilities and their profitability can be estimated in advance. As is the case with the economic model, these conditions rarely exist in the real world.

Shapley Value

The theoretical literature has a number of articles advocating the use of a number termed the *Shapley value* as the transfer price.[5] The Shapley value was developed in 1953 by L. S. Shapley, as a method of dividing the profits of a coalition of companies or individuals among its individual members in proportion to the contribution that each of them made. This is a problem that arises in the theory of games, and the Shapley value is generally considered to provide an equitable solution to that problem.

Whether or not the same technique is applicable to the transfer price problem is a highly debatable issue. Although the method has

[5] For a description and bibliography, see Daniel L. Jensen, "A Class of Mutually Satisfactory Allocations," *The Accounting Review*, October 1977, pp. 842–56.

been described in the literature for a number of years, there is only one practical application reported. This is the calculation of telephone charges to various telephone users at Cornell University. In part, the reason for its lack of acceptance is that the computation is lengthy unless there are only a few products involved in the transfer. In part, the reason is that many of those who have studied the Shapley method do not believe that its underlying assumptions are valid for the transfer pricing problem.

Practical Problems with Models

The theoretical models have three limitations that prevent their use in real-world situations:

1. As already noted, the models are based on simplifying assumptions that do not exist in the real world.
2. The models assume the availability of information that usually cannot be obtained.
3. In general, the models assume that transfer prices will be imposed by the central staff, and denies the importance of negotiation among divisions. As indicated in the body of the chapter, division managers usually have better information than is available to the central staff. Indeed, if the central staff could determine the optimum production pattern, the question arises as to why this pattern is not imposed directly, rather than attempting to arrive at it indirectly via the transfer price mechanism.

SUGGESTED ADDITIONAL READINGS

Abdel-Khaiik, Rashad, A.; and **Lusk, Edward J.** "Transfer Pricing—A Synthesis." *The Accounting Review,* January 1974.

Benke, Ralph L., and **James Don Edwards.** "Transfer Pricing: Techniques and Uses." *Management Accounting,* June 1980.

———. *Transfer Pricing Technique and Uses.* New York: National Association of Accountants, 1980.

Hirschleifer, Jack. "On the Economics of Transfer Pricing." *Journal of Business,* July 1956.

Horngren, Charles T. *Cost Accounting, A Managerial Emphasis.* Englewood Cliffs, N.J.: Prentice-Hall, 1962. Chapter 19.

Kaplan, Robert S. *Advanced Management Accounting.* Englewood Cliffs, N.J.: Prentice-Hall, 1982. Chapter 14.

Madison, Roland L. "Responsibility Accounting and Transfer Pricing: Approach with Caution." *Management Accounting,* January 1979.

Mailahdt, Peter. "An Alternative to Transfer Pricing." *Business Horizons,* October 1975.

Onsi, Mohamed. "A Transfer Price System Based on Opportunity Cost." *The Accounting Review,* July 1970.

Ronen, J., and **McKinney, G., III.** "Transfer Pricing for Divisional Autonomy." *Journal of Accounting Research,* Spring 1970.
Shillinglaw, Gordon. *Managerial Cost Accounting.* 5th ed. Homewood, Ill.: Richard D. Irwin, 1982. Chapter 26.
Solomons, David. *Divisional Performance: Measurement and Control.* Homewood, Ill.: Richard D. Irwin, 1968, chap. VI.
Watson, David J. H., and **Baumler, John L.** "Transfer Pricing: A Behavioral Context." *Accounting Review,* July 1975.

CASE 7–1
Birch Paper Company*

"If I were to price these boxes any lower than $480 a thousand," said James Brunner, manager of Birch Paper Company's Thompson Division, "I'd be countermanding my order of last month for our salesmen to stop shaving their bids and to bid full-cost quotations. I've been trying for weeks to improve the quality of our business, and if I turn around now and accept this job at $430 or $450 or something less than $480, I'll be tearing down this program I've been working so hard to build up. The division can't very well show a profit by putting in bids that don't even cover a fair share of overhead costs, let alone give us a profit."

Birch Paper Company was a medium-sized, partly integrated paper company, producing white and kraft papers and paperboard. A portion of its paperboard output was converted into corrugated boxes by the Thompson Division, which also printed and colored the outside surface of the boxes. Including Thompson, the company had four producing divisions and a timberland division, which supplied part of the company's pulp requirements.

For several years, each division had been judged independently on the basis of its profit and return on investment. Top management had been working to gain effective results from a policy of decentralizing responsibility and authority for all decisions except those relating to overall company policy. The company's top officials believed that in the past few years the concept of decentralization had been successfully applied and that the company's profits and competitive position had definitely improved.

Early in 1957, the Northern Division designed a special display box for one of its papers in conjunction with the Thompson Division, which

* This case was prepared by Neil E. Harlan, Harvard Business School.

was equipped to make the box. Thompson's staff for package design and development spent several months perfecting the design, production methods, and materials to be used. Because of the unusual color and shape, these were far from standard. According to an agreement between the two divisions, the Thompson Division was reimbursed by the Northern Division for the cost of its design and development work.

When all the specifications were prepared, the Northern Division asked for bids on the box from the Thompson Division and from two outside companies. Each division manager was normally free to buy from whatever supplier he wished; and even on sales within the company, divisions were expected to meet the going market price if they wanted the business.

In 1957, the profit margins of converters such as the Thompson Division were being squeezed. Thompson, as did many other similar converters, bought its paperboard, and its function was to print, cut, and shape it into boxes. Though it bought most of its materials from other Birch divisions, most of Thompson's sales were made to outside customers. If Thompson got the order from Northern, it probably would buy its linerboard and corrugating medium from the Southern Division of Birch. The walls of a corrugated box consist of outside and inside sheets of linerboard sandwiching the fluted corrugating medium. About 70 percent of Thompson's out-of-pocket cost of $400 for the order represented the cost of linerboard and corrugating medium. Though Southern had been running below capacity and had excess inventory, it quoted the market price, which had not noticeably weakened as a result of the oversupply. Its out-of-pocket costs on both liner and corrugating medium were about 60 percent of the selling price.

The Northern Division received bids on the boxes of $480 a thousand from the Thompson Division, $430 a thousand from West Paper Company, and $432 a thousand from Eire Papers, Ltd. Eire Papers offered to buy from Birch the outside linerboard with the special printing already on it, but would supply its own inside liner and corrugating medium. The outside liner would be supplied by the Southern Division at a price equivalent of $90 a thousand boxes, and it would be printed for $30 a thousand by the Thompson Division. Of the $30, about $25 would be out-of-pocket costs.

Since this situation appeared to be a little unusual, William Kenton, manager of the Northern Division, discussed the wide discrepancy of bids with Birch's commercial vice president. He told the vice president: "We sell in a very competitive market, where higher costs cannot be passed on. How can we be expected to show a decent profit and return on investment if we have to buy our supplies at more than 10 percent over the going market?"

Knowing that Mr. Brunner had on occasion in the past few months been unable to operate the Thompson Division at capacity, it seemed odd to the vice president that Mr. Brunner would add the full 20 percent overhead and profit charge to his out-of-pocket costs. When asked about this, Mr. Brunner's answer was the statement that appears at the beginning of the case. He went on to say that having done the developmental work on the box, and having received no profit on that, he felt entitled to a good markup on the production of the box itself.

The vice president explored further the cost structures of the various divisions. He remembered a comment that the controller had made at a meeting the week before to the effect that costs which were variable for one division could be largely fixed for the company as a whole. He knew that in the absence of specific orders from top management Mr. Kenton would accept the lowest bid, which was that of the West Paper Company for $430. However, it would be possible for top management to order the acceptance of another bid if the situation warranted such action. And though the volume represented by the transactions in question was less than 5 percent of the volume of any of the divisions involved, other transactions could conceivably raise similar problems later.

Questions

1. In the controversy described, how, if at all, is the transfer price system dysfunctional?
2. Describe other types of decisions in the Birch Paper Company in which the transfer price system would be dysfunctional.

CASE 7–2
Strider Chemical Company*

On December 9, 1982, the president of the Strider Chemical Company, which had sales of around $175 million, announced that on January 1, 1983, the company would be reorganized into separate divisions. Until that time, the company had been organized on a functional basis, with the manufacturing, sales, finance, and research departments each under one man's responsibility. Six divisions were to be set up—four by product group and two by geographical area. Each division was to have its own production, sales, and accounting staff, and a general manager who would be responsible for its operation. The division's operating performance was to be judged by the profit it produced in relation to the investment assigned to it. It was anticipated that the procedure for computing the investment base and the return thereon would have to

* This case was prepared by R. N. Anthony, Harvard Business School.

be carefully worked out if the resultant ratio was to be acceptable to the new division managers as a reasonable measure of their performance.

One of the biggest obstacles to the establishment of the desired monthly profit and loss statement for each division was the pricing of products for transfer from one to another of the various divisions. At the time the divisions were established, the company's president issued a policy statement upon which a pricing procedure was to be based. The president's statement follows.

STATEMENT OF POLICY

The *maximum,* and usual, price for transfers between profit units is that price which enables the producing unit to earn a return on the investment required, consistent with what it can earn doing business with the *average* of its customers for the product group concerned.

Established prices will be reviewed each six months or when a general change in market prices occurs.

DISCUSSION

Pricing policy between operating units is particularly important, because to the extent that the price is wrong, the return on one segment of the business is understated, and the return on another is overstated. This not only gives a false measure of how well individuals are performing, but also may make for bad decisions on the business as a whole, which will affect everyone.

Certain elements of expense that may not be found in intracompany relations are:

1. Deductions for cash discounts, freight, royalties, sales taxes, customer allowances, etc.
2. Usual selling expenses and, in many cases, order and billing services.
3. Certain customer services by the research laboratories, such as sales services where this applies.

The producing division that acts as a supplier will establish a price by discounting its *regular price* structure for the elements listed above which apply.

In case the buying division disagrees with the price as computed above, it will explain the basis of its disagreement to the president, who will decide what is to be done.

We are hopeful that this policy will work out equitably, giving each division a fair basis for the business they do. If, in practice, it is found that the policy is not working properly, is complicated in its application or calculation, or is working a hardship, the policy will have to be changed.

The largest of the newly formed divisions, the Williams Division, was strongly affected by the problem of transfer prices, since about 23 percent of its sales would be to other divisions.

With only three weeks before the separation into divisions, it was important that a schedule of prices be quickly established for the transfer of products between divisions. The Williams Division's task was complicated by its large number of products. There were several hundred different compounds and materials for which a price had to be fixed. It was, therefore, partly for the sake of expediency that the Williams Division chose to set the prices on the basis of direct manufacturing cost. The figures used in this method were more readily available than those used in setting a price based on the current market price.

A week after the president's policy statement on transfer pricing had been distributed, the Williams Division issued an interpretation of the policy which stated its proposed method for setting prices for the sale of products by the Williams Division to other divisions. The key paragraphs from this statement were as follows:

> The Williams Division will charge the same price to another division as it charges to the average of its existing customers, less an allowance for those expenses incurred with average customers but not with interdivisional customers. These noncomparable expenses to be deducted include Sales Deductions and a part of Selling Expenses. The prices will be calculated in terms of a markup or multiplier factor on Direct Manufacturing Cost. A markup will be recalculated each six months, based on the prior twelve months' experience with regular customers.

The markup for the first six months of 1983 will be 1.41 times Direct Manufacturing Cost as shown by the following computation which uses actual data for the 12-month period ended October 31, 1982:

		Dollars	Percent
Gross sales to outside customers		$5,126,328	
Less: Amounts not applicable to internal sales:			
a. Freight, royalties, sales taxes	$ 58,625		
b. Selling expenses	260,123		
Total deductions		318,748	
Adjusted sales		4,807,580	100%
Direct manufacturing cost		3,404,923	71
Margin		1,402,657	29%
Computation: 100 ÷ 71 = 1.41 times			

By the end of March 1983, the president had received a number of letters from division managers, raising questions about transfer prices. Three of these are summarized on the next page.

1. The Williams division questioned the price which the Johnson Division had established for compound A, a raw material for the Williams Division. The Johnson Division had initially calculated a markup of 1.33, computed in the same way the Williams Division computed its markup of 1.41. At a markup of 1.33, however, the Johnson Division would show a net loss, since the division had not operated at a profit in the preceding 12 months. It therefore raised its markup to 1.41, the same as that used by the Williams Division. At this markup, it would show about the same profit as that of the Williams Division. The Williams Division argued that this markup violated company policy.

2. The International Division questioned the transfer price of several products it purchased from the Williams Division for sale abroad. It said that at these prices the International Division could not meet competitive prices in European markets and still make a profit.

3. The Western Division purchased chemical B from the Williams Division for resale to its own customers. It submitted data to show that at the computed transfer price the Western Division would be better off to manufacture chemical B in one of its own plants. Rather than do this, it proposed that the transfer price be cut by 15 percent, which would still leave a margin over direct manufacturing cost for the Williams Division.

As of the end of March, the president had not acted on any of these letters, other than to reply that existing relationships between divisions should be continued until further notice, and that after the questions had been decided, adjustments in transfer prices would be made retroactive to January 1.

In view of the numerous questions that had already arisen about the markup, the president was considering the possibility of transferring all products at cost, without any markup.

Question

What changes, if any, should be made in the transfer price practices of Strider Chemical Company?

CASE 7–3
Zemblan Electronics Corporation*

In April 1983, S. C. Halloway, corporate controller of the Zemblan Electronics Corporation, received the following memorandum from J. D. Walcott, controller of the Circuits Division:

* This case was prepared by R. N. Anthony, Harvard Business School.

INTEROFFICE MEMORANDUM

April 5, 1983

TO: *S. C. Halloway*

FROM: *J. D. Walcott*

SUBJECT: *Recommendation on the method of determining the divisional share of cost-based government contract fees*

When one of our equipment or systems divisions that has a cost-reimbursable government contract engages a sister components division to produce necessary components for the contract, it is only fair that the components division be given a fair share of the total fee receivable from the government.

At present, fees are shared among the divisions through after-production negotiations without regard to the initial estimate of the fee. I propose, with our division managers' approval, that, regardless of whether the actual production cost is over or under the estimated cost, the components divisions should be given the fee credit as originally estimated. The following two examples illustrate the present and suggested methods.

Example 1. A year ago, the Santa Ana systems division asked from us a "bid" for 7,000 units of a certain type of ceramic part. We estimated the total production cost of $294,000 and added a 10 percent profit of $29,400 for the part, and on this basis obtained the order from the systems division. When the job was completed and the parts delivered, we billed the systems division for the amount of $256,900, as calculated below:

Actual total production cost	$227,500
Originally estimated profit	29,400
Total price	256,900

But the systems division has written back to us that we would be allowed a credit of only $245,700, as calculated below:

Actual total production cost		$227,500
Allowable profit		18,200
Total cost	$227,500	
Actual profit percent earned on the contract	8%	
	18,200	
Total price allowable		245,700

The systems division and we are still negotiating as to what fee we are entitled to. The systems division argues that it cannot allow any more profit than 8 percent, instead of 10 percent as originally agreed on, because actual costs on the overall contract exceeded the initial cost estimate on which the overall fee on the contract was based. We feel, however, that we are entitled to 10 percent profit, because decrease in total profit on the contract was caused by the systems division itself or other subcontracted divisions, not by our division. If anything, we should be rewarded for being efficient enough to show a cost underrun. If my proposal is adopted, we shall automatically receive the originally estimated profit of $29,400 without going through meaningless after-production negotiations.

Example 2. We have recently finished producing 1,000 units of KTN 21 circuit for the La Jolla equipment division. Our original bid was based on the following estimate:

Estimated total production cost	$1,250,000
Estimated profit ($1,250,000 × 7%)	87,500
Estimated total price	1,337,500

Unfortunately, however, our actual cost has turned out to be $350,000 above our estimate, that is, $1,600,000. We have billed the equipment division as follows:

Actual production cost	$1,600,000
Originally estimated profit (see above)	87,500
Total price	1,687,500

Despite a cost overrun of $350,000, we have asked as our share of the fee only $87,500 as originally estimated by us and accepted by the equipment division.

The proposed method of fee determination would eliminate uncertainty and unnecessary after-production negotiations.

It had been Mr. Halloway's practice to answer as soon as possible all inquiries, recommendations, and memoranda from any individuals in the company, and he wanted in this instance, too, to express his opinion promptly on Mr. Walcott's memorandum. Before a final ruling on the specific recommendation, however, he wanted to be sure that his decision would be consistent with Zemblan's management philosophy of decentralization, policies governing interdivisional relationships, and other aspects of interdivisional pricing.

Zemblan, a fast growing, large electronics company with sales of $400 million in 1982, consisted of six highly decentralized divisions—three equipment divisions and three components divisions. The equipment divisions were the Santa Ana Systems Division, the La Jolla Equipment Division (mostly for government contracts), and the Commercial (nongovernmental) Apparatus and Equipment Division. The Circuits Division, of which Mr. Walcott was the controller, was one of the three components divisions. Approximately 70 percent of the total outside sales of the company were made by the equipment divisions, and 30 percent from the components divisions. Although policy with respect to operating components divisions was nowhere written or otherwise made explicit, at least one executive thought the divisions were indispensable for the long-run survival and continued growth of the company, because technological advances in the equipment divisions—the basis of the company's success—were made possible largely through inventions and breakthroughs originating in the components divisions.

The divisions were allowed or encouraged to lead their own lives, with minimum interference from the top management. A major criterion in the evaluation of the divisional performance was the return on investment. The elements in the return-on-investment calculation were materially controllable by the division management.

A list of products made by each division was drawn up and approved by top management; a division could not make the products listed by other divisions. Otherwise, the divisions could manufacture and sell almost any products within their capabilities. The equipment divisions were free to purchase their component needs either internally or externally; that is, either from their sister components divisions or from outside suppliers. The components divisions were also free, in general, to sell their products internally or externally, except for a few classified items. The volumes of internal and external purchases were significant for all equipment divisions; the volumes of internal and external sales were significant for all components divisions.

Prices for the interdivisional transactions not covered by government contracts were determined through arm's-length negotiations between the divisions concerned. Therefore, all transfers from the components divisions to the commercial apparatus and equipment division were so priced. For the transactions covered by government contracts—that is, transactions between the government equipment divisions and the components divisions—the determination of transfer prices was more complex. If the contract held by the buying division was noncost-recoverable—that is, of the fixed-price type—the procedure was the same as that involving nongovernment contracts.

If the contract was of cost-recoverable type—e.g., cost plus a fixed fee (CPFF)[1]—the process was as follows: First, the buying division would ask the selling division to submit a bid. Second, the selling division would estimate its recoverable production cost (the cost elements included in the government's definition of cost), and the profit or

[1] In a CPFF contract, the company is reimbursed for its actual cost (in accordance with a detailed definition of cost) plus a fixed dollar amount of fee. The dollar amount of the fee is determined when the contract is signed, and is based on a percentage (from 3 percent to 12 percent, depending on the risks involved) of the *estimated* cost. The CPFF contract is used only when the uncertainties involved in contract performance are of such magnitude that it is not possible to establish a firm price or an incentive arrangement at any time during the life of the contract.

fee percentage anticipated by the buying division on the overall contract, and submit the price thus determined to the buying division. Sometimes, the buying division adjusted downward the fee percentage allowable to the selling division according to the additional risk it was taking as the "prime contractor." Third, if this bid was acceptable, the buying division would award an order to the selling division. Fourth, the selling division would produce and deliver the parts and invoice the buying division. Fifth, the buying division would either accept the amount in the invoice, or would protest and begin negotiations with the buying division.

If a dispute arose, it might be over the fee or profit element alone, as in Example 1 of the above memorandum. In other cases, it might be over the cost element, also, if the actual cost substantially exceeded the estimated cost of the original bid. If the actual cost was below the estimate, Mr. Halloway said, "the buying division had to be charged at the actual cost (plus profit element), because the government agency would not allow any more than the actual cost." Thus a dispute over the cost element arose only when the actual was above the estimate. The divisions, according to Mr. Halloway, were encouraged to resolve disputes between themselves; the corporate management intervened rarely and only with reluctance.

"Of course, if the buying division could recover the actual cost from the government," Mr. Halloway said, "it was for the good of the company that the buying division should be charged at the actual cost and try to recover it." But when a cost overrun could not be wholly recovered because a maximum price ceiling was specified in the contract, "the dispute was real"; according to Mr. Halloway, "neither the selling nor the buying division likes to absorb the loss." The cause of cost overrun could be inefficiency, carelessness, wrong forecast, unforeseen technical difficulties, error in the buying divisions' specifications, or any combination of these.

Mr. Halloway felt that he had been greatly restricted by government procurement regulations in choosing the best method of transfer pricing. He preferred, he said, negotiated prices based on market as transfer prices; but the government tended to prefer the cost-based transfer prices.

If an equipment division first asked for bids both from its sister division and from an outside supplier, but finally decided to award the subcontract to the sister division, government auditors would require "costs" as transfer prices, although an objective outside market price was available in the bid made by the outside supplier. Likewise, if a components division was asked to make a bid by its sister equipment division and by an outside equipment manufacturer (the last two competing for the same government contract), and if the sister equipment division was awarded the contract and gave the components division the job, the transfer price had to be based on cost. On the other hand, if the outside equipment division obtained the contract and subcontracted with the Zemblan components division, the price would be a negotiated market price. Mr. Halloway had been asking government auditors to broaden their interpretation of the clause and to allow transfer pricing based on the negotiated market price.

Mr. Walcott made the following comments in relation to his memorandum:

> My proposal is fair to everyone concerned. Under the recommended method, we are not always the winner: We will be rewarded if we are efficient; we will be penalized if we are inefficient.
>
> We are willing to go further than the proposal. We would be happy if we were held responsible for the estimates of both cost and profit—not just the estimate of profit, as suggested in the present proposal. Penalize us if we couldn't meet the bid price, including both cost and profit element; reward us if we economize on our costs.
>
> In connection with Example 2 in my memorandum, I don't know exactly how the La Jolla equipment division made the decision to give us the KTN 21 job, but it is possible that it had asked a couple of outside suppliers to make a bid, and the suppliers' bid price might have been higher than ours. If the suppliers' bid had been lower than $1,600,000 it would have been unfair for the La Jolla division to be charged $1,600,000 by us. The best way would be to make the initial bid price final, no matter what the actual cost is.

Question

What should the transfer price policy be?

CASE 7–4
Medoc Company*

The Milling Division of the Medoc Company milled flour and manufactured a variety of consumer products from it. It's output was distributed as follows:

1. Approximately 70 percent (by weight) was transferred to the Consumer Products Division and marketed by this division through retail stores. The Consumer Products Division was responsible for these items from the time of packaging; that is, it handled warehousing, shipping, billing, and collections as well as advertising and other sales promotion efforts.

* This case was prepared by R. N. Anthony, Harvard Business School.

2. Approximately 20 percent was sold by the Milling Division as flour to large industrial users.

3. Approximately 10 percent was flour transferred to the Consumer Products Division and sold by that division to industrial users, but in different industries than those serviced directly by the Milling Division.

Counting each size and pack as one unit, there were several hundred products in the line marketed by the Consumer Products Division. The gross margin percentage on these products was considerably higher than that on flour sold to industrial users.

Wheat was purchased by the grain department, which was separate from the Milling Division. The price of wheat fluctuated widely and frequently. Other ingredients and supplies were purchased by the Milling Division.

The Milling Division and Consumer Products Division were two of 15 investment centers in the Medoc Company.

Products were transferred from the Milling Division to the Consumer Products Division at a unit price that corresponded to actual cost. There was a variation among products, but on the average, this cost included elements in the following approximate proportions:

Flour	30%
Other ingredients and packaging material	25
Labor and variable overhead	20
Nonvariable overhead	25
	100%

Also, 75 percent of the Milling Division's investment was charged to the Consumer Products Division in computing the latter's return on investment. This investment consisted of property, plant, equipment, and inventory, all of which was "owned and operated" by the Milling Division.

This transfer price resulted in friction between the Milling Division and the Consumer Products Division, primarily for three reasons:

1. As in many process industries, unit costs were significantly lower when the plant operated at capacity. Indeed, the principal reason for accepting the low-margin industrial business was to permit capacity operations. There was general agreement that acceptance of such business at a low margin, or even at something less than full cost, was preferable to operating at less than capacity. In recent years, the Milling Division had operated at at least 98 percent of capacity.

The Milling Division alleged that the Consumer Products Division was not aggressive enough in seeking this capacity-filling volume. The Milling Division believed that the Consumer Products division could increase the volume of consumer sales by increasing its marketing efforts and by offering more attractive special deals, and that it could do more to obtain industrial business at a price which, although not profitable, nevertheless would result in a smaller loss than what the Milling Division incurred from sales made to the industry it served. This additional volume would benefit the company, even though it reduced the average profit margin of the Consumer Products Division. The Consumer Products Division admitted that there was some validity in this argument, but pointed out that it had little incentive to seek such business when it was charged full cost for every unit it sold.

2. The Consumer Products Division complained that, although it was charged for 75 percent of the investment in the Milling Division, it did not participate in any of the decisions regarding the acquisition of new equipment, inventory levels, etc. It admitted, however, that the people in the Milling Division were technically more competent to make these decisions.

3. The Consumer Products Division complained that, since products were charged to it at actual cost, it must automatically pay for production inefficiencies that were the responsibility of the Milling Division.

A careful study had been made of the possibility of relating the transfer price either to a market price or to the price charged by the Milling Division to its industrial customers. Because of differences in product composition, however, this possibility had been definitely ruled out.

The Consumer Products Division currently earned about 20 percent pretax return on investment, and the Milling Division earned about 6 percent.

Top management of the Medoc Company was convinced that, some way or other, the profit performance of the Milling Division and the Consumer Products Division should be measured separately; that is, ruled out the simple solution of combining the two divisions for profit-reporting purposes.

One proposal for solving the problem was that the transfer price should consist of two elements: *(a)* a standard monthly charge representing the Consumer Products Division's fair share of the nonvariable overhead, plus *(b)* a per-unit charge equivalent to the actual material, labor, and variable overhead costs applied to each unit billed. Investment would no longer be allocated to the Consumer Products Division. Instead, a standard profit would be included in computing the fixed monthly charge.

The monthly nonvariable overhead charge would be set annually. It would consist of two parts:

1. A fraction of the budgeted nonvariable overhead cost of the Milling Division, corresponding to the fraction of products that was estimated would be transferred to the Consumer Products Division (about 80 percent). This amount would be changed only if there were

changes in wage rates or other significant noncontrollable items during the year.

2. A return of 10 percent on the same fraction of the Milling Division's investment. This was higher than the return that the Milling Division earned on sales to industrial users. The selection of 10 percent was arbitrary because there was no way of determining a "true" return on products sold by the Consumer Products Division.

Questions

1. Is the general approach to transfer pricing proposed here—namely, a nonvariable dollar amount per month, plus a variable amount per unit—better than the present method in this situation? Why?

2. Suggest improvements in the details of the proposed method.

CASE 7–5
General Appliance Corporation*

ORGANIZATION

The General Appliance Corporation was an integrated manufacturer of all types of home appliances. As shown in Exhibit 1, the company had a decentralized, divisional organization consisting of four product divisions, four manufacturing divisions, and six staff offices. Each division and staff office was headed by a vice president. The staff offices had

EXHIBIT 1 Organization Chart

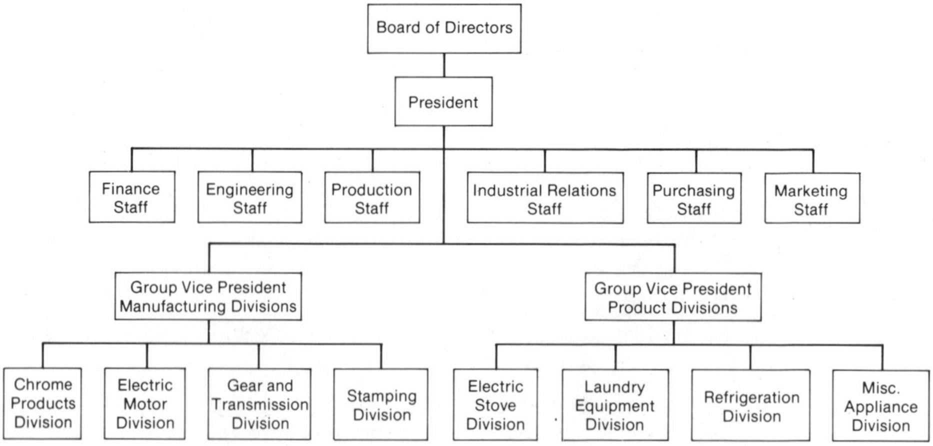

* This case was prepared by John Dearden, Harvard Business School.

functional authority over their counterparts in the divisions, but they had no direct line authority over the divisional general managers. The company's organization manual stated: "All divisional personnel are responsible to the division manager. Except in functional areas specifically delegated, staff personnel have no line authority in a division."

The product divisions designed, engineered, assembled, and sold various home appliances. They manufactured very few component parts; rather, they assembled the appliances from parts purchased either from the manufacturing divisions or from outside vendors. The manufacturing divisions made approximately 75 percent of their sales to the product divisions. Parts made by the manufacturing divisions were generally designed by the product divisions; the manufacturing divisions merely produced the parts to specifications provided to them. Although all the manufacturing divisions had engineering departments, these departments did only about 20 percent of the total company engineering.

TRANSFER PRICES

The divisions were expected to deal with one another as though they were independent companies. Parts were to be transferred at prices arrived at by negotiation between the divisions. These prices generally were based on the actual prices paid to outside suppliers for the same or comparable parts. These outside prices were adjusted to reflect differences in design of the outside part from that of the inside part. Also, if the outside price was based on purchases made at an earlier date, it was adjusted for changes in the general price level since that date. In general, the divisions established prices by negotiation among themselves; but if the divisions could not agree on a price, they could submit the dispute to the finance staff for arbitration.

SOURCE DETERMINATION

Although the divisions were instructed to deal with one another as independent companies, in practice this was not always feasible, because a product division did not have the power to decide whether to buy from within the company or from outside. Once a manufacturing division began to produce a part, the only way the product division buying this part could change to an outside supplier was to obtain permission of the manufacturing division or, in case of disagreement, appeal to the purchasing staff. The purchasing staff had the authority to settle disputes between the product and manufacturing divisions with respect to whether a manufacturing division should continue to produce a part or whether the product division could buy outside. In nearly every case of dispute, the purchasing staff had decided that the part would continue to be manufactured within the company. When the manufacturing divisions were instructed to continue producing a part, they had to hold the price of the part at the level at which the product division could purchase it from the outside vendor.

In the case of new parts, a product division had the authority to decide on the source of supply. Even for new parts, however, a manufacturing division could appeal to the purchasing staff to reverse the decision if a product division planned to purchase a part from an outside vendor.

STOVE TOP PROBLEM

The Chrome Products Division sold to the Electric Stove Division a chrome-plated unit that fitted on the top of the stove; the unit had to be resistant to corrosion and stain from spilled food. It was also essential that the unit remain bright and new-looking. The Chrome Products Division had been producing this unit since January 1, 1982; prior to that time, it had been produced by an outside vendor.

The unit in question was produced from a steel stamping. Until June 1983, the stamping was processed as follows:

Operations	*Processes*
1.	Machine buffing
2.	Nickel plating
3.	Machine buffing
4.	Chrome plating
5.	Machine buffing

About the middle of 1982, the president of General Appliance Corporation became concerned over complaints from customers and dealers about the quality of the company's products. A customer survey appeared to indicate quite definitely that in the previous year the company's reputation as a producer of quality products had deteriorated. Although this deterioration was believed to have been caused principally by the poor performance of a new electric motor, which was soon corrected, the president had come to the conclusion that the overall quality of the company's products had been decreasing for the past several years. Furthermore, he believed that it was essential for the company to reestablish itself as a leader in the production of quality products. Accordingly, early in 1983 he called in the manufacturing vice president (i.e., the director of the manufacturing staff office) and told him that for the next six months his most important job was to bring the quality of all products up to a satisfactory level.

In the course of carrying out this assignment, the manufacturing vice president decided that the appearance of the chrome-plated stove top was unsatisfactory. Until now, the bases for rejection or acceptance of this part by the quality control section of the Chrome Products Division were a corrosion test and an appearance test; appearance was largely subjective and, in the final analysis, dependent on the judgment of the quality control person. In order to make the test more objective, three tops were selected and set up as standards for the minimum acceptable quality. Because better than average units were selected, rejects increased to over 80 percent. Personnel from the Chrome Products Division and the manufacturing staff jointly studied the manufacturing process to find a way of making the stove tops conform to the new quality standards. They added copper plating and buffing operations at the beginning of the process, and a hand-buffing operation at the end of the manufacturing cycle. The total cost of these added operations was 40 cents a unit. As soon as the new operations were put into effect in June 1983, the rejection rate for poor quality declined to less than 1 percent.

In July 1983, the Chrome Products Division proposed to increase the price of the stove top by 45 cents; 40 cents represented the cost of the added operations, and 5 cents was the profit markup on the added costs. The current price, before the proposed increase, was $5 a unit. This price had been developed as follows:

Price charged by an outside producer (12/31/81)	$4.50
Design changes since 12/31/81	0.25
Changes in raw materials and labor prices since 12/31/81	0.25
Price as of June 30, 1983	5.00

The Electric Stove Division objected to the proposed price increase, and after three weeks of fruitless negotiations it was decided that the dispute should be submitted to the finance staff for arbitration. The positions of the parties to the dispute are summarized below.

Chrome Products Division

In a letter to the vice president for finance, the general manager of the Chrome Products Division stated that he believed he was entitled to the increased price because:

1. He had been required by the manufacturing staff to add operations at a cost of 40 cents a unit.
2. These operations resulted in improved quality that could benefit only the Electric Stove Division.
3. The present price of $5.00 was based on old quality standards. Had the outside supplier been required to meet these new standards, the price would have been 45 cents higher.

Electric Stove Division

The general manager of the Electric Stove Division, in appealing the price increase, based his position on the following arguments:

1. There had been no change in engineering specifications. The only change that had taken place was in what was purported to be "acceptable appearance." This was a subjective matter that could not be measured with any degree of precision. Further, both the particular case and the possible effects of establishing a precedent were objectionable. "If we were to pay for any change in quality standards, not accompanied by a change in engineering specification, we would be opening up a Pandora's box. Every division would request higher prices based on giving us better quality based on some subjective standard. Every request by this division to a manufacturing division to improve quality would be accompanied by a price increase, even though we were requesting only that the quality be brought up to competitive levels."
2. The Electric Stove Division had not requested that quality be improved. In fact, the division had not even been consulted on the change. Thus, the division should not be responsible for paying for a so-called improvement that it neither requested nor approved.
3. Whether there was any improvement in quality from the customer's viewpoint was doubtful, although to the highly trained eye of the quality control personnel there may have been an improvement. The customer would not notice a significant difference between the appearance of the part before and after the change in quality standards.
4. Even if there were an improvement in quality perceptible to the consumer, it was not worth 45 cents. By adding 45 cents to the cost of the stove, features could be added that would be far more marketable than the quality improvement.
5. Any improvement in quality only brought the part up to the quality level that the former outside producer had provided. The cost of the improved quality, therefore, was included in the $5.00 price.

Finance Staff Review

The finance staff reviewed the dispute. In the course of this review, the engineering department of the manufacturing staff was asked to review the added operations and comment on the acceptability of the proposed cost increases. The quality control department of the manufacturing staff was asked to verify whether quality was actually better as the result of the added operations and whether the new units were of higher quality than the units purchased from the outside vendor 18 months ago. The engineering department stated that the proposed costs were reasonable and represented efficient processing. The quality control department stated that the quality was improved and that the new parts were of superior quality to the parts previously purchased from outside sources.

THERMOSTATIC CONTROL PROBLEM

One of the plants of the Electric Motor Division produced thermostatic control units. The Laundry Equipment Division bought all its requirements for thermostatic control units (about 100,000 a year) from the Electric Motor Division. The Refrigeration Division used a similar unit, and until 1981 it had purchased all its requirements (20,000 a year) from an outside supplier, the Monson Controls Corporation. In 1981, at the request of the Electric Motor Division, the Refrigeration Division purchased 25 percent of its requirements from the Electric Motor Division. In 1982, this percentage was increased to 50 percent, and in 1983 to 75 percent. In July 1983, the Refrigeration Division informed the Monson Controls Corporation that beginning January 1, 1984, it would buy all its thermostatic control units from the Electric Motor Division. The Refrigeration Division made these source changes as a result of Electric Motor Division requests, which were, it said, "in the best interests of the company." The units made outside and inside were comparable in quality, and the price paid to the Electric Motor Division was the same as the price paid to the Monson Controls Corporation. The Laundry Division also paid this same price to the Electric Motor Division.

In 1980, the demand for this kind of thermostatic control unit was high in relation to the industry's production capacity. Between 1981 and 1983, several appliance companies, including the General Appliance Corporation, built or expanded their own facilities to produce this unit, so that by the middle of 1983 the production capacity of the independent companies considerably exceeded the demand. One of the results of this situation was a declining price level. Prices of the Monson Controls Corporation had been as follows:

1980	$3.00
1981	2.70
1982	2.50
1983 (January–June)	2.40

As a result of these price reductions, which the Electric Motor Division had met, the profits of the Electric Motor Division on this product had dropped from a before-tax profit of 15 percent on its investment in 1980 to nearly zero in 1983.

In August 1983, after being told it could no longer supply the Refrigeration Division, the Monson Controls Corporation reduced its price to the Refrigeration Division by 25 cents, retroactive to July 1. The price reduction was not reflected immediately in the intracompany price, because the three divisions involved had agreed to use $2.40 for the entire year.

In October 1983, the Electric Motor Division and the Refrigeration Division were negotiating 1984 prices. The Refrigeration Division proposed a price of $2.15, the price paid to the Monson Controls Corporation. The Electric Motor Division, however, refused to reduce its prices below $2.40 to either the Refrigeration Division or the Laundry Equipment Division. After several weeks of negotiations, the disagreement was submitted to the finance staff for settlement.

Electric Motor Division

The Electric Motor Division based its refusal to accept the last price reduction of the Monson Controls Corporation on the premise that it was made as a last, desperate effort to continue supplying General Appliance Corporation with this part. (Monson Controls Corporation continued to supply General Appliance Corporation with other products, although this control unit had been a major item.) As support for this premise, the Electric Motor Division indicated that at the lower price it would lose money. Since it was as efficient as the Monson Controls Corporation, it concluded that Monson must also be losing money. The price was, therefore, a distress price and not a valid basis for determining an internal price. To support its case further, the Electric Motor Division pointed out the downward trend in the price of this part as evidence of distressed pricing practices growing out of the excess capacity in the industry.

The general manager of Electric Motor Division stated that it was going to take all his ability and ingenuity to make a profit even at the $2.40 price. At $2.15, he could never be in a profit position; and if forced to accept a price of $2.15, he would immediately make plans to close the plant and let outside suppliers furnish all the thermostatic control units.

Laundry Equipment Division

The Laundry Equipment Division based its case for a $2.15 price on the intracompany pricing rules that required products to be transferred between divisions at competitive prices. The general manager pointed out that his annual volume was 100,000 units a year, compared to a total of only 20,000 for the Refrigeration Division. He believed that with his higher volume he could probably obtain an even more favorable price if he were to procure his requirements from outside the corporation.

Refrigeration Division

The Refrigeration Division based its case on the fact that the division not only could, but did, buy the thermostatic control unit from a reliable outside supplier for $2.15. The division was sure that the Monson Controls Corporation had capacity to produce all its requirements and would be happy to do so for $2.15 a unit. Since patronage had been transferred to the Electric Motor Division only as a favor and to benefit the company as a whole, the Refrigeration Division believed it was unjust to make it pay a higher price than it would have paid if the division had never allowed the business to be taken inside the company.

As further evidence to support its case, the Refrigeration Division pointed to an agreement made with the Electric Motor Division at the time it had agreed to purchase all its requirements of the thermostatic control unit from that division. This agreement read, in part: "In the event of a major pricing disparity, it is agreed that further model requirements will be competitively sourced [i.e., sourced to the lowest bidder]."

The Refrigeration Division stated that in the light of the major pricing disparity it should be allowed to request quotations from outside suppliers and place the business outside should such a supplier bid lower than the Electric Motor Division.

Finance Staff Review

In the course of arbitrating this transfer price dispute, the finance staff asked the purchasing staff to review the outside market situation for the thermostatic control unit. The purchasing staff replied that there was excess capacity and that, as a result of this, prices were very soft. Eventually, the prices would rise either when the demand for comparable units increased or when some of the suppliers went out of business. The purchasing staff had no doubt that the Refrigeration Division could purchase all its requirements for the next year or two for $2.15 a unit, or even less. The purchasing staff believed, however, that if all the corporation's requirements for this unit were placed with outside suppliers, the price would rise to at least $2.40 because this action would dry up the excess capacity.

TRANSMISSION PROBLEM

The Laundry Equipment Division began production of automatic washers shortly after the end of World War II. Initially, it had purchased its transmissions from two sources—the Gear and Transmission Division and the Thorndike Machining Corporation. The transmission had been developed and engineered by the Thorndike Machining Corporation. In consideration of an agreement to buy one half of its transmissions from the Thorndike Machining Corporation, the General Appliance Corporation had been licensed to produce the transmission. The agreement ran from 1973 to 1983; at the expiration of the 10 years,

General Appliance would have the right to use the design without restrictions.

In early 1981, nearly two years before the end of the agreement, the management of the General Appliance Corporation decided that it would not extend the agreement when it expired, but that it would expand the facilities of the Gear and Transmission Division enough to produce all the company's requirements. Accordingly, in March 1981, the Thorndike Machining Corporation was notified that beginning January 1, 1983, the General Appliance Corporation would manufacture all its own transmissions and, consequently, would not renew the current agreement.

This notification came as a surprise to the Thorndike Machining Corporation; furthermore, its implications were very unpleasant, because the General Appliance Corporation took a major share of the output of an entire plant, and there was little likelihood that the lost business could be replaced. The Thorndike Machining Corporation consequently faced the prospect of an idle plant and a permanent reduction in the level of profits.

In April 1981, the president of the Thorndike Machining Corporation wrote to the president of the General Appliance Corporation, asking that the decision not to extend the current agreement be reconsidered. He submitted a proposed schedule of price reductions that would be made if the current agreement was extended. He stated that these reductions would be possible because *(a)* Thorndike would be better off to obtain a lower price than to abandon the special-purpose machinery used for transmissions, and *(b)* it expected increases in productivity. These proposed reductions were as follows:

Present price	$14.00
Price effective 7/1/81	13.50
Price effective 7/1/82	13.00
Price effective 7/1/83	12.50
Price effective 7/1/84	12.00

The letter further stated that the corporation had developed a low-cost transmission suitable for economy washers; this transmission was designed to cost $2 less than the present models, and could be made available by January 1, 1984.

On receiving a copy of the letter, the general manager of the Laundry Equipment Division reopened the issue of continuing to buy from the Thorndike Machining Corporation. He had been interested in adding to the line a low-cost automatic washer, and the possibility of a $10 transmission appealed to him. The general manager of the Gear and Transmission Division, however, was interested in expanding his production of transmissions; and to satisfy the Laundry Equipment Division he offered to develop a unit that would be comparable in price and performance to the proposed Thorndike Machining Corporation's economy unit. The offer was set forth in a letter signed by the general manager of the Gear and Transmission Division, dated April 22, 1981. The general manager of the Laundry Equipment Division accepted this offer, and no further question was raised about continuing to buy from the Thorndike Machining Corporation.

During the next two months, the engineering departments of the Gear and Transmission and the Laundry Equipment divisions jointly determined the exact performance features needed for the economy transmission; some of these features were different from those of the proposed Thorndike transmission. In June 1981, the general manager of the Gear and Transmission Division wrote a letter to the general manager of the Laundry Equipment Division, outlining the agreed-on engineering features and including the following price proposal:

Proposed selling price of Thorndike model		$10.00
Probable cost (assuming 11% profit)		9.00
Add:		
Cost of added design features	$0.85	
Increased cost of material and labor since date of quotation	0.75	1.60
Total cost		10.60
Profit		1.06
Adjusted price of G & T Unit		$11.66

The letter went on to say: "Because a price of $11.66 will not give us our objective profit, we proposed to sell you this unit for $12. We believe that this is a fair and equitable price, and decidedly to your benefit."

This letter was never acknowledged by the Laundry and Equipment Division.

In October 1981, the Gear and Transmission Division submitted a project proposal to the top management of the corporation, requesting money to build facilities to produce the new economy transmission. The project proposal included a profit projection based on a $12 price. The Laundry Equipment Division was quoted in the project proposal as agreeing to the price. There was no objection to this statement from the Laundry Equipment Division personnel who were asked to comment on the proposed project. The project was approved, and the Gear and Transmission Division proceeded to buy and install the equipment to produce the new transmission.

In the latter part of 1981, the Gear and Transmission Division opened negotiations with the Laundry Equipment Division on the price of the new transmission, proposing $12 plus some minor adjustments for changes in cost levels since the previous year. The Laundry Equipment Division refused to accept the proposed price and countered with an offer of $11.21, developed as follows:

Proposed selling price of Thorndike model		$10.00
Adjustments:		
Cost of added design features	$ .85	
Cost of eliminated design features	(.50)	
Increased cost of material and labor since date of quotation	.75	
Net cost change	1.10	
Profit on added cost	.11	
Total price increase		1.21
Proposed price		$11.21

The Gear and Transmission Division refused even to consider this proposal, and after several days of acrimonious debate both divisions decided to submit the dispute to the finance staff for arbitration.

Laundry Equipment Division

The Laundry Equipment Division based its case on the following argument:

1. The division could have purchased a transmission, comparable in performance characteristics to the Gear and Transmission Division's unit, from the Thorndike Machining Corporation for $11.21.
2. The Gear and Transmission Division had agreed to this price in consideration of being allowed to produce all the transmissions.
3. The intracompany pricing policy was that the supplying divisions should sell at competitive prices.

The general manager of the Laundry Equipment Division stated that it would be unfair to penalize him for keeping the transmission business inside the corporation as a benefit to the Gear and Transmission Division, particularly in the light of the promise made by the general manager of the Gear and Transmission Division.

The general manager also stated that he had not protested the price proposal included in the May 1981, letter, because he believed that it was then too early to open negotiations. His cost analysis had not evaluated the proposal, but he assumed that the Gear and Transmission Division was approximately correct in its evaluation of the cost differences from the Thorndike unit. His position was that the difference of 34 cents between the adjusted Thorndike price and the quoted gear and transmission price was not worth negotiating until nearer the production date. The Laundry Equipment Division had naturally assumed that the Gear and Transmission Division would live up to its agreement, and therefore regarded the request for $12 as just a negotiating gimmick.

Gear and Transmission Division

The Gear and Transmission Division based its case on two arguments:

1. The $10 quotation of the Thorndike Machining Corporation was invalid because it represented a final desperate effort to keep a share of the transmission business. A price of this nature should not form a long-term intracompany pricing base. If the Thorndike Machining Corporation had received the business, it would have eventually raised its price.

2. The Laundry Equipment Division did not object to the Gear and Transmission Division's price proposal until after the facilities to build the transmission were already in place. The $12 price was used in the calculations that showed the profitability of the project, and on which the project approval was based. If the Laundry Equipment Division wished to object, it should have done so when the project was presented to top management. Because facilities were purchased on the assumption of a $12 price, the Laundry Equipment Division should not be allowed to object after the money has been spent.

Finance Staff Review

A review by the finance staff disclosed the following:

1. If the Thorndike Machining quotation of $10 were adjusted for the cost effect of changes in performance characteristics and the increase in general cost levels since the original quotation, the price would be $11.25, or approximately the same as that proposed by the Laundry Equipment Division. The price of $11.66 developed by the Gear and Transmission Division was in error because it failed to allow for a design elimination that would reduce the cost of the Thorndike unit by 50 cents.

2. At $12, the Gear and Transmission Division could expect to earn an aftertax profit of 15 percent on its investment; this was equal to its profit objective. At the $11.25 price, the division would earn about 6 percent after taxes.

3. The purchasing staff stated that in its opinion the transmission could be obtained from the Thorndike Machining Corporation at the quoted price level for the foreseeable future.

Questions

1. As a member of the finance staff, how would you settle these intracompany disputes?

2. Should the company's intracompany price policy and its procedure for negotiating differences be changed?

CASE 7–6
Warren Corporation*

Warren Corporation was a large conglomerate. A significant portion of its business was in electronics. In this area, there were 15 profit centers, and most of these profit centers dealt with one another. More than 50 percent of the sales in some of these profit centers were to other Warren units. The central finance staff had developed a manual that prescribed company policy with respect to intracompany relationships, particularly how transfer prices were to be established. This manual was changed when decisions of the Price Arbitration Committee made it evident that it was incomplete or that policy had changed. In some respects, these revisions were like the codification of common law, in that decisions of the Price Arbitration Committee were incorporated into the transfer pricing rules in the same way that court decisions affect legal principles.

The Price Arbitration Committee (called hereafter PAC), had been set up to arbitrate intracompany pricing disputes. It consisted of three staff vice presidents—finance, manufacturing, and purchasing. The secretary of this committee was the manager of the price analysis department of the finance staff. This department was responsible for providing staff service to the PAC.

This case presents three disputes that were submitted to the PAC by divisional managers of the Warren Corporation.

PRODUCT DEVELOPMENT

Division X produced a low-volume, high-grade line of electronic products. Its engineering group had spent $300,000 developing a new type of unit to be attached to one of its major products. When the development was completed, a marketing survey showed that the number of units that was likely to be sold would not warrant the expenditure required for the tooling and facilities to produce the new unit. The total number of units likely to be sold by Division X was only 2,500 annually. Consequently, the project was shelved.

Division Y sold an electronic product, with a much higher sales volume, that could use the new unit. Six months after the project was shelved, at a company-wide meeting of certain research personnel, a research manager of Division Y learned of this new unit and requested a copy of the blueprints. This was provided to him.

* This case was prepared by John Dearden, Harvard Business School.

Within the next nine months, Division Y decided to produce the new unit and proceeded to purchase the necessary tools and facilities. About three months later (a year and a half after Division X had shelved the project) the general manager of Division X heard that Division Y was going to produce the unit that had been developed by his division. He immediately called in his controller and told him to send Division Y a bill for $300,000. He was particularly interested in receiving payment because the Division X's profits were less than budget. Since the costs of development had been written off in the previous year, the $300,000 would be a direct increase in profitability.

Division Y refused to pay and Division X brought the matter to the PAC. *The Intracompany Pricing Manual* said nothing about the transfer of research and development costs.

Division X based its case on a statement in the manual that said: "In general, divisions will deal with each other in the same way that they deal with outside companies." Division X's position was that, if it was independent, it could have sold the blueprint for at least $300,000 to an outside company. (Company rules forbade the sale of research findings to outside companies, however.)

The position of Division Y was that the product was marginal. If Division Y had to pay $300,000 for the blueprints, it would not have gone ahead with the project.

SPLIT SOURCING

Division A bought a complex electronic component. Of the total quantity, 50 percent was purchased from an outside source, and 50 percent was purchased from Division B. The outside source had developed the component and had licensed Division B to produce it in consideration of a five-year contract to provide half of Warren's requirements. The contract with the outside source established an initial price, with provision for annual negotiations. These negotiations were to determine the amount that the price would be reduced as manufacturing efficiency increased. Division A requested detailed information from Division B on the manufacturing processes to be able to negotiate with the outside source more effectively. If the engineers of Division A knew precisely in what ways and the extent to which Division B was increasing its efficiency, they could pinpoint the amount of the price reduction that should be obtained. Division B refused to provide this information. Division A submitted the dispute to the PAC.

The Intracompany Pricing Manual stated that split-sourced products should be transferred within the company at the same price as that charged by the outside source. Nothing else was said about split-source pricing.

Division B based its refusal on the statement that "Divisions deal with each other in the same way that they deal with outside companies." Under no conditions, it stated, would it provide customers with details of its production process. Furthermore, Division B pointed out that it would be "cutting their own throats." The greater the price reduction that Division A negotiated, the lower would be the profits of Division B.

Division A based its case on company welfare. Company profits would be maximized if Division B cooperated with Division A.

RESERVED CAPACITY

Division S was essentially a marketing division. It purchased most of its products from Division M. The transfer price agreement was that products were transferred at the standard variable cost per unit, plus a monthly charge equal to the fixed costs assigned to the products produced for Division S, including a 10 percent return on the investment associated with these products. By agreement, half of the capacity of Plant M–1 was reserved for Division S. The other half of the capacity of that plant was used by Division M to produce products that were sold to outside customers. Plant M–1 could produce either Division S products or Division M products on all of its facilities.

During the current year the demand for Division S products declined, while the demand for Division M products increased. As a result, about 75 percent of the capacity for Plant M–1 was used to produce products for Division M and only 25 percent was used for products of Division S. Division S objected to paying for 50 percent of the capacity of Plant M–1. Division M refused to reduce the price and the case was submitted to the PAC.

The Intracompany Pricing Manual stated that products of the type produced by Division M for Division S should be priced at "the standard variable cost per unit plus a monthly charge equal to the fixed costs and 10 percent of the book value of the assets assigned to the capacity reserved for the products of the buying division."

Division M argued that it had reserved 50 percent of the capacity of Plant M–1 for Division S. Division S, however, was not using this capacity currently. Because the demand was sufficiently strong for Division M products, Division M utilized this excess capacity. It would be foolish to leave it idle. If, however, Division S had needed the capacity, Division M would have been able and willing to provide it.

Division S felt that, to pay Division M for capacity that Division M was using, was unfair to Division S. Division S felt that it should pay just for the capacity that it was using, or, at a maximum, for the capacity it used plus the cost of any idle capacity up to a total of 50 percent of Plant M–1's capacity.

Questions

1. How would you settle each of these disputes?
2. In each case, how, if at all, would you change the manual?

CASE 7–7
Universal National Company*

The Universal National Company was a large aircraft and missile manufacturer with a concentration of plants on the West Coast and a number of divisions in other parts of the country as well as overseas. (The basic organization of the company is indicated by the simplified organization chart, included as Exhibit 1.) Its Aircraft Division, the unit from

EXHIBIT 1 Partial Organization Chart

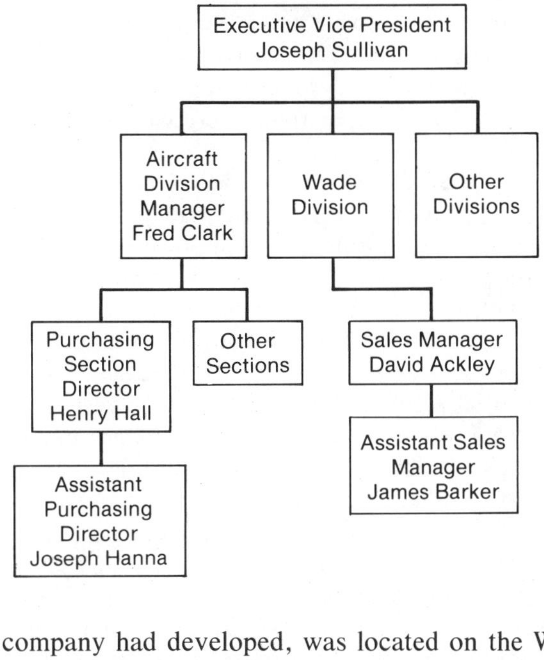

which the company had developed, was located on the West Coast. Recently, it was awarded a contract for the production and delivery of 100 Sky Haul troop carriers. The contract was placed on a cost-plus incentive fee basis, which means that there was a negotiated target price with an incentive formula under which Universal and the govern-

* This case was prepared by Robert N. Anthony, Harvard Business School.

ment would share 50/50 any saving below this target. The Aircraft Division in the two previous years had been just breaking even. Management expected that the award of the Sky Haul contract would restore the division to its position as one of the major profit contributors in the company.

In fact, the company's executive vice president, Joseph Sullivan, was determined that the Aircraft Division would achieve its former profit position; and, to this end, he called in major management personnel from the division and lectured them in rather blunt terms about the need for a dramatic profit improvement. He told them that if they did not do it with the Sky Haul contract, they would never do it.

Fred Clark, the Aircraft Division manager, had recently developed a Profit Improvement Program (PIP). The idea behind it was to get people excited over profits: to get them to concentrate on profit improvement. The initials PIP were written over the walls in the plants and corridors. Each department was given a PIP mandate in terms of cost reduction goals, seminars were held throughout the division, and special PIP announcements were made over the plant loudspeakers.

Henry Hall, divisional director of purchasing, made a comprehensive analysis of the material requirements for the Sky Haul contract. He recognized that, along with several other items, the automatic direction finder was extremely critical to the success of the program. Whereas the Sky Haul contract was let as a straight production contract, the model actually was an advanced one, calling for a number of basic improvements. In particular, the automatic direction finder had to meet requirements that, while within the state of the art, called for considerable improvement over previous production.

Hall determined there were three logical sources for this radio direction finder: the Bolster Company located in New York, the Acme Radio Electronics Company of Chicago, and the Wade Division of Universal National located in the Midwest. On the basis of previous experience, Hall thought that the Bolster Company probably would be the best source. However, he was fairly sure that all three sources would be able to pass the facility survey. He was willing to make the award to whichever company made the best cost proposal, although he did not want the Wade Division to obtain the order.

Hall discussed the problem with Joseph Hanna, his assistant. Hanna felt that the Wade Division looked upon the Aircraft Division as a captive customer. On past jobs it had shown an unwillingness to respond quickly to changes to keep the Aircraft Division informed of progress, and objectively to evaluate and adopt suggestions. There were times when the Wade Division sales manager, David Ackley, did not even return a critical call for several days. Hall agreed with this opinion. In fact, he wondered if Wade really could be considered a qualified supplier. Two years previously, when he was head of quality control, the Aircraft Division had found unsatisfactory a radio transmitter that Wade had produced. Other sources that previously had produced similar radio transmitters had had serious difficulty also; but as Hall said: "The difference was that they did something about it. They didn't sit on their duff or submit long, cumbersome memos blaming everything on the Aircraft Division's specifications and inspection practices."

Hall thought Wade really did not belong in the electronic business. It had been a small radio manufacturer that branched into electronics in a big way in World War II. Since the mid-1940s, it had gained an increasingly large part of the market for electronics equipment for commercial aircraft. Hall believed that its chief trouble was that it was trying to cut cost and did not worry enough about quality.

Hall said:

> The automatic direction finder should cost somewhere around $150,000; but I am sure Wade, with its five and dime tactics, will bid considerably below that.

Hanna said:

> If you let them bid, we're sunk. They'll come in with a low price and nobody will be able to get them out of here; but their people will never go out of their way to be helpful to us. We'll have to beg for the equipment. Also, it's nothing for them to make a change without even telling us about it. I have to admit some of the changes they have made in past products were pretty ingenious, with regard to getting the cost down, but they raised havoc with the rest of the job. No interface at all.

Hall and Hanna spent a few hours reviewing their experience with the only prior order that they had placed with Wade for automatic direction finders. They concluded that there was no doubt about it—Wade's prices were low, but the rejection rate was high and the delivery rate was only fair. They admitted that there had been a number of specification changes on that job, and that their own incoming inspection department had been going through a major crisis at that time. Thus, it might be unfair to blame Wade; but both Hall and Hanna still were convinced Wade was wrong for the direction finder job.

Also, they vividly remembered some of the clashes they had had with Mr. Ackley. Ackley refused to respond to urgent calls and refused to incorporate changes immediately. At one point he had refused to take back sets that had to be repaired because of damage during transit. He wanted a memo listing the exact nature of the damage—and a written admission that the Aircraft Division was responsible for filing any necessary claims.

Hall gave much thought to the Wade problem and finally decided that, if Wade had not been a division of Universal National, he would not consider it for the bid listed. He mentioned the problem briefly to Clark, the division manager, who said:

> Henry, if there is any way you can get rid of Wade, get rid of them. It's more difficult to do business inside than it is outside. They are a bunch of prima donnas; but just one thing, Henry, they are always running in to see Sullivan, so make sure you're right.

A month later the Aircraft Division released the request for bids to the two outside vendors. Both had been qualified previously on the basis of investigations including plant surveys.

Hall was not surprised that when the bids came in Bolster was low; but he was surprised that the bids ranged from $185,000 each to $220,000. As a result of fairly intensive negotiations with Bolster, Hall was able to negotiate the price down to $180,000 each. A patent problem proved to be more knotty than expected, and all in all it took a month to negotiate the proposed subcontract with Bolster.

Hall had just sent the subcontract to the company's contracting officer for the latter's approval in accordance with the terms of the prime contract, with a request for urgent action because of contract lead time, when he received a call from Clark, the division manager, who said:

> Henry, I just came out of Sullivan's office. Sullivan is hopping mad and I am, too. I thought I told you to see that Wade was taken care of on this finder. Ackley and some other clowns were there. They really burned us.

In summary, this is what the Wade people had told Sullivan during a two-hour meeting: They were not even asked to bid on the automatic direction finder, even though in the previous year the division had put something like $1 million of independent research and development money into this product area. They said that troop carriers were going to be one of the biggest markets for the future. They claimed that they had now matched their reputation for low cost with technical proficiency and they were now the leader in the field. They said that they needed this job to start exploiting the independent research and development money the company had spent. They also said they badly needed it to absorb fixed overhead until the radio receiver market recovered—probably the following year. They also claimed that their reputation in the marketplace had suffered a staggering blow. Bolster was going all over the industry telling Wade's customers that Universal National would not even deal with Wade, and that, on the Sky Haul contract, they were not even asked to bid. In fact, Ackley said he did not even know about this procurement until one of his customers asked him if there was any truth to the story that Wade was going out of the finder business. Sullivan was particularly incensed about what he called the waste of independent research and development money and the unabsorbed overhead. "Henry," Clark continued, "I want to talk to you later about how you made this mistake; but right now do one thing first—get a bid quotation from Wade."

Hall tried to remind Clark about their previous conversation. He wanted to give Clark reasons why he felt it was the wrong thing to go to Wade. He also wanted to tell Clark that it was too late. Although the subcontract with Bolster had not yet been executed, it had been written in final form and submitted to the contracting officer.

Hall called Bolster Company and told it that it would have to hold up on the direction finder order. He then put a call through to Sullivan's office for Ackley, who he thought was there, but was unable to get through to Ackley. He left a message for Ackley to stop by. Not having heard from Ackley in two hours, he called Sullivan's office again and was told that Ackley had just left for Wade. He called Wade and talked to Ackley's assistant, James Barker. He explained the situation and said that the important thing was for Wade to get its estimate in right away. Barker pointed out that he needed the prints before he could make an estimate. He said it might take two or three weeks to evaluate the prints and to price the job. Hall replied, "That's not good enough. You make sure Ackley calls me as soon as his plane gets in." Hall then sent an expediter by plane to Wade with the prints.

Hall called again the next day; but he could not reach Ackley, nor could he reach Barker. However, the secretary to both men said that Ackley had left a message for him, as follows:

> Would you please touch base with Wade's regional representative on the West Coast?

This man would receive a commission for the sale and, Ackley thought, he should earn it. Ackley said they wanted Hall to make sure the company got its money's worth from this sales representative.

About this time, Hall received a call from David Ford, the sales manager of Bolster Company. Ford wanted to know what to do with the $250,000 in anticipatory costs they had spent in order to meet the short delivery dates on the order. There ensued a long argument between the two men about who was responsible for incurring this expense. Ford said that all he wanted was the $250,000 the company had incurred in trying to help Hall—money that was spent with Hall's full knowledge and agreement.

At this point, Hall had a recurrence of an old ulcer attack and was hospitalized for a week. He had to stay in bed at home for an additional week. When he returned to his office he found that the quote had been received from Wade Division. The price was $250,000 and the quoted delivery was four weeks behind that required. And, if this were not enough, Wade had conditioned its bid on a number of waivers being made in the specification.

Hall went into Clark's office with the quotes from Wade. At this point Clark decided that he should take over the problem until it was finally resolved and a subcontractor was selected and a final price determined. He called Ackley and told him that, if Wade received the order, he wanted to send a team of Aircraft Division personnel to the Wade plant to help expedite the order to meet the prime contractor's delivery requirements. Included in this team would be men from the Aircraft Division's engineering, production, purchasing, quality control, and inspection departments. Their assignment would be to help iron out problems on the spot with Wade personnel.

Ackley's reply to Clark was:

> These panic visits never solve anything. They create more problems than they resolve. There is only one way of doing business and that is in an orderly fashion. As far as I am concerned, I am going to do business the right way. That means that we will perform in accordance with our quotation. If you want to make a change, you should issue a change order in accordance with the changes clause and I will process it like any other change and submit my quotation for an increase in price and delivery time as equitable under the circumstances. The one thing I do not want is a lot of oral communications that no one will remember later on. That's the trouble with doing business inside. People depart from proven business practices and the whole deal gets fouled up.

One week later, Clark got Ackley to agree on a new set of specifications and a compromise delivery date. Ackley also agreed to drop his price $532 to reflect the deletion of a fastener from the equipment.

About this time, Clark got a call from the resident Air Force contracting officer wanting to know why his purchasing agent was considering a subcontract with Wade at $250,000, when he could get it from Bolster for $180,000.

Clark believed that he had negotiated as hard as he could to get the Wade Division to reduce its price. He felt that $249,468 was its rock bottom offer, and he believed that this represented an out-of-pocket expense to Wade of about $150,000 per unit for each of the 100 units he was ordering. He wanted to keep peace in the organization. He knew that Sullivan had his eyes on the Aircraft Division's profit figure for this contract. He also knew that he was in trouble for not calling in Wade earlier and that, if he did not give it the order, Ackley would take the dispute back to Sullivan. He wondered whether he should present all the facts to Sullivan or let Wade have the contract and absorb part of the difference in his own profit and loss statement—or let the Bolster Company go ahead with the order and just wait to see what happened.

He wondered, further, what the decision and the consequences for him personally would be if he took the dispute to Sullivan.

CASE 7–8
Quality Metal Service Center *(A)*

The following conversation took place between Edward Brown, president and chief executive officer of Quality Metal Service Center, and Robert Sheldon, vice president and regional manager of the midwestern region of the company, during a quarterly performance review meeting in early July 1982:

Brown: Bob, we at head office are spending excessive time refereeing the complaints of district and regional managers regarding transfer prices. What is your analysis of our present transfer pricing system?

Sheldon: The system seems designed to leave everyone with the feeling of being cheated! District managers complain about lost or unprofitable sales resulting from unfilled transfer requests, even though I supply half of my sales volume to the districts at cost. Furthermore, district managers believe that the inventory allocation, plus the proposed fixed-asset allocation, are unfair because they have to earn a return on assets they don't control. But if allocations are eliminated, my region must implicitly earn a return on assets which are used to support the districts' transfer business. As it stands, I think the system treats the regions unfairly; but, naturally, I would have a biased viewpoint.

Brown: I'll tell you what. Let's schedule an 8:30 meeting this Thursday morning. Call up Jack Horvath [manager, Detroit District] and get him to attend. I'll contact our controller; he ought to shed some light on this problem. Let's see if we can generate some good ideas to mitigate this internal grief.

Background

Quality Metal Service Center was established a century ago as a local metals distributor. It grew into a firm with national distribution, with sales in 1981 of over $300 million. Quality bought metals from many of the mills in the United States in large lots, in various locations, and sold them to small and medium-sized companies that could not afford to purchase and inventory sizeable mill quantities.

The product line offered by Quality Metal Service included stainless steel, nickel alloys, aluminum, brass, copper, carbon alloys, and carbon steel. The company had 30 broad product groups and over 20,000 different product items. These items were shipped to customers in variable lots, sizes, usually in a short lead-time. Quality Metal Service also did three preproduction processings, consisting of minor product modifications to meet customer requirements, examples of which include torch-cutting, sawing, flattening, shearing, bending, grinding, and polishing.

Currently, Quality Metal Service Center operated in 27 locations, in markets representing about 75 percent of metal consumption in the United States. There were four regions, each of which had 4 to 7 districts, for a total of 23 districts. Corporate staff support included departments in finance, marketing, operations, and human resources.

Performance Evaluation and Incentives

Each region and district was an investment center, with its performance measured by return on assets (ROA). Managers had an incentive bonus—meeting and exceeding targeted levels of ROA. The incentive bonus for a district manager was based 75 percent on the district's performance and 25 percent on the performance of the region to which the district belonged. Similarly, the bonus for a regional manager was based 75 percent on region performance, and 25 percent upon corporate results.

The bonus for a district manager's staff, however, was based solely on the performance of that district, and the bonus of a regional manager's staff was based solely on the performance of that region.

Distribution Policy

Each of the four geographic regions had a central warehouse; smaller "feeder" warehouses were located in each district. Since districts and regions were evaluated separately by measurement of ROA, corporate policy allowed each location to buy from and sell to internal centers or external firms, thus allowing unrestricted decision making by district and regional managers.

Each region also had its own sales and credit staff, who were responsible for customer transactions in the immediate area. Of the total sales revenue within a region, the regional office generated about one third; about two thirds were generated in the districts.

The company established Economic Order Quantity guidelines for the purchase of inventory. Metals were stored in district warehouses only if local demand was sufficient to justify this. Otherwise, inventory was kept in the regional warehouses and distributed to the districts as needed. Transfer of inventory generally occurred between a region and its districts. However, in some cases, orders were filled by transfers between districts within a region, or by districts across regions.

Although a region based its purchases, in part, on projected sales demand in its districts, there was *no* obligation for the districts to acquire that inventory from the regional warehouse. In other words, a region acquired inventory at its own risk.

Two types of transfers occurred in the network. The first, known as a "stock transfer," was executed when a district replenished its inventory of a given item by ordering it, in advance, from the designated internal supplier of that item, usually its region. Lead times for stock transfers were sufficient to allow supplying centers to plan and smooth anticipated workloads. The second, which was called a "customer transfer," resulted when an order was placed by a customer for an item not normally stocked by the district, or for an item that was out of stock in the district. The district purchased the required material from another district or region, wherever the inventory was available. If the material was not available within the company, it was often purchased from a competitor, sometimes at a loss. A loss was worthwhile if it prevented the customer from shifting all its business to a competitor.

There were at least three differences between stock and customer transfers: (1) stock transfers typically gave the supplying center long lead times, whereas customer transfers typically involved short lead times; (2) customer transfers were made when there was a specific order from a customer, whereas the receiving center requested stock transfers based on projected sales demand; and (3) many customer transfers involved products which were not normally stocked by the receiving center.

Transfer Pricing Policy

Currently, the same transfer price policy applied to both stock and customer transfers. Transfer prices were based on cost and was the sum of three components:

1. The replacement cost of the transferred inventory.

2. A predetermined amount for the handling costs incurred by the supplying center.

Labor costs were based upon time-and-motion studies done for each major product line. These studies were conducted about three years ago in one of the regional warehouses and had not been updated. However, annual inflation adjustments were made to the labor rates. At one time, the company had used separate handling costs for stock transfers and customer transfers; the justification was that a supplying district incurred higher variable expenses for handling customer transfers, because of the short lead times involved. This practice, however, was discontinued—because of the practical difficulties involved in clearly distinguishing stock transfers from customer transfers.

3. Transportation costs. If the receiving district used its own trucks to transport the inventory, no expense was charged. If the region's trucks were used, the expense was charged at an average cost

per mile. Also, the receiving district was charged for any rail freight incurred in the transfer.

In addition to the charge for each transaction, each district was charged a quarterly amount for its share of the region's fixed costs. This amount was calculated by measuring the percentage of the region's capacity that was used by the district in the previous quarter. If, for example, a district's cost of sales from internal transfers in the previous quarter was 10 percent of the region's cost of sales, then 10 percent of regional fixed expenses for the current quarter was charged to that region.

In addition to these transferred costs, the region's inventory assets were also allocated to districts monthly. This calculation involved the calculation of a turnover rate and the division of net inventory transferred by the turnover rate. The resulting number represented the level of inventory necessary to support the transfers. The following equations summarize these calculations:

$$\frac{\text{Cost of sales (including transfers) of the region}}{\text{Average inventory of the region}} = \text{Turnover rate}$$

$$\frac{\text{Cost of the inventory transferred}}{\text{Turnover rate}} = \text{Inventory necessary to support internal transfers}$$

The inventory figure arrived at by the above calculations was then transferred to the asset base of the district, and that of the region was reduced correspondingly.

There was no provision for a similar allocation of fixed assets. The company was, however, considering the following proposal for allocating fixed assets:

Land and Buildings would be allocated to receiving districts on the basis of the ratio of the total transfers to its total usage from stock. This method would allocate assets according to the percentage of capacity used by other districts. To summarize this method:

$$\frac{\text{Cost of materials transferred}}{\text{Total cost of sales and transfers}} = \text{Percentage of Buildings and Land allocated to receiving districts}$$

Machinery and Equipment would be allocated to receiving districts on the basis of the ratio of the supplier's processing revenue to its total processing revenue. To summarize this method:

$$\frac{\text{Processing revenue related to transferred materials}}{\text{Total processing revenue}} = \text{Percentage of Machinery and Equipment allocated to other districts}$$

The preceding description relates to transfers from regions to districts. The same rules applied to transfers between districts.

Excerpts from Transfer Pricing Committee Meeting—July 15, 1982

Brown: [C.E.O.] Good morning, gentlemen. As you know, we're meeting to discuss possible problems with our present transfer pricing system. Jack, I'm interested in your perspective. How would you evaluate the status quo?

Horvath: [district manager] I would like to discuss two topics at this point. First, asset allocations affect districts unfairly. We can't earn an adequate return on allocated inventory assets; in fact, districts have no control over regional inventory assets. Since regions allocate much of their inventory assets to districts, regions don't have much incentive to operate efficiently. In addition, we are now considering fixed-asset allocations, which will magnify the inequities!

Sheldon: [V.P. & R.M.] Jack, asset allocations are necessary in a cost-based transfer pricing system. As it stands, you enjoy free use of my region's fixed assets.

I know the nature of your second complaint. You're not satisfied with my region's delivery performance on the inventory transfers to your district.

Horvath: Correct. We've lost sales and profits because we can't obtain needed inventory from the regional warehouse.

Sheldon: Keep in mind that half of my sales volume goes to districts such as yours. I think you are in an enviable position—being able to take full markup on items you don't stock. And what's to prevent you from buying metals from outside companies?

Horvath: Our district does so. But you supply the inventory at cost.

Sheldon: That's right. Look at my choices: I can transfer such materials to you and break even, or my salesmen can sell it and we improve our ROA.

Horvath: Now that your motives are clear, I can see why my district is losing sales.

Sheldon: Jack, my point is simply that you shouldn't acquire my inventory at cost. There should be a profit in it for both of us.

Horvath: I do not concede that point at all, Bob. If it weren't for us, you couldn't afford to have the large facility and inventories which help you capture a greater share of your own markets. You would only be half this size if it weren't for us.

Sheldon: That is not correct, Jack. Half of my inventory, half of my facility and equipment, and about one third of my human resources are devoted to servicing, at best, break-even business. I am not sure that districts such as yours, which are heavily dependent on the inventory of others, would be profitable if measured by a more equitable accounting system.

Horvath: Bob, that's sour grapes! With the kind of inventory you have at your disposal, your sales to your customers should be twice what they are. If that happened, only a third of your volume would be transfers and you would far exceed your ROA objective. Furthermore, "equity" is a matter of perspective! As an example, district profits are reduced when regions sell inventory to outside customers instead of filling district transfer requests. When districts are forced to purchase from outside firms, we're the ones who only break even.

Brown: You're both making good points, but let's move on. Jack, do you have any more to add?

Horvath: Yes. The variable and fixed-cost allocations are not accurate. The variable handling expenses are based on an outdated cost structure of one of our regional offices. I can certainly handle the materials a lot cheaper than that!

Next, fixed-cost allocation, in my opinion, should be based on the current quarter's capacity utilization and not on the previous quarter's usage, as we do at present.

The result of all this is that my transfer costs are much higher than what they should be and, in addition, I do not get accurate cost data on which to base my short-term marketing decisions.

Brown: What's your input, Bradley?

Morton: [controller] While setting transfer prices, we're really taking money out of one pocket and putting it in the other; the bottom line for the company doesn't change. Still, devising a good transfer pricing system is problematic. We've just heard an exchange between a D.M. and a R.M. and I sympathize with both. If we adjust the mechanism, any positive effect upon one center will be offset by an equally negative effect upon another.

Brown: That's true to a point, but if all levels make better decisions, it might be possible that everyone benefits. What about your analysis of the present system?

Morton: Well, I share the concerns of both Bob and Jack. But from my point of view, I find our method very laborious. The bookkeeping aspects of this system are nontrivial, to say the least. We have to calculate quarterly fixed-expense allocations. Further, the handling charges have to be adjusted order by order. Of course, the biggest headache involves the inventory asset allocations, which are calculated for each center in the company.

Brown: Anything else?

Morton: Yes. The ROA calculations are a bit inaccurate. Right now, there is no provision for fixed-asset allocation. No doubt, this would add to my bookkeeping. But since we are currently allocating inventory assets, it is logical we ought to make a similar fixed-asset allocation. This would help to "round out" our present allocation system and give accurate ROAs.

Brown: This is all very informative, gentlemen. I used to believe that supplying districts had sufficient incentive in the current system. For example, transfers help the supplying districts to improve their inventory turnover, to stock slow-moving items, and to buy in large quantities. However, no one here has really defended our cost-based approach. And I can see problems with record-keeping, too. So, let's do the following. Brad, get your staff to list each reasonable transfer pricing alternative, and distribute the report to us and to all of the vice presidents. We'll meet again in two weeks.

The report referred to above is Exhibit 1.

EXHIBIT 1

TO: Transfer Pricing Committee

FROM: B. W. Morton, Controller

SUBJECT: Transfer Pricing Proposals

I have discussed below four alternative transfer pricing proposals.

OPTION 1: MARKET PRICE

The supplying district is given credit for the market price less a predetermined percentage for selling expense on all sales made internally. This method is based on the following factors:

(1) The supplying district incurs all of the plant expense involved in receiving, storing, and shipping the inventory.
(2) The supplying district carries (and is charged for) the inventory.
(3) The supplying district has (and is charged for) all of the plant and equipment necessary to house the large inventory.

Since the receiving district makes the sales effort, the receiver's profit approximates the "commissions" that are received on mill direct shipments, i.e., the receiver is compensated only for marketing efforts, at the predetermined rate. Under this arrangement, no allocations are made between centers either for inventory assets or for fixed assets.

Variation

Stock transfers could be assessed differently from customer transfers. For example, stock transfers could be made at cost, whereas customer transfers could be made at market price.

OPTION 2: COST PLUS MARKUP

Supplying district is compensated on internal transfers in the same amount as the overall gross profit percentage attained on its outside sales. The mechanics of this method are as follows:

A. Determine the overall gross profit percentage on outside sales for the supplying district during the preceding quarter. Gross profit is computed as follows:

Sales to outside customers.
Less: Cost of inventory sold to outside customers.
Related variable expenses.

B. Determine the total cost of inventory transferred internally plus a predetermined amount for variable expenses for the current month for the supplying district.

C. Multiply the figure (from step B) by the gross profit percentage (from step A).

D. The cost of the inventory including predetermined variable expenses (from step B) plus the gross profit (from step C) is credited to the supplying district and charged to the receiving district.

E. No allocations are made between centers either for inventory assets or for fixed assets.

Variations

(1) Gross profit percentages could be calculated for each individual product, instead of using a district total.
(2) Stock transfers and customer transfers could be handled differently (as explained in Option 1).

OPTION 3: PROFIT SHARING

Gross profit on all internal transfers is split 50/50 between supplying and receiving districts. The mechanics of this method are as follows:

A. The cost of the inventory plus related variable expenses are credited to the supplying district and charged to the receiving district.

B. After the inventory is sold, the supplying and receiving centers share the gross profit earned equally. The gross profit is calculated as follows:

Sales Revenues.
Less: Cost of the inventory.
Variable expenses at the supplying center.
Sales commission and other variable selling expenses.

C. No allocations are made between centers either for inventory assets or for fixed assets.

Variations

(1) The percentage of profits to be shared between supplying and receiving centers could be varied.

(2) Stock transfers could be treated differently as compared to customer transfers (as explained in Option 1).

OPTION 4: INTERCOMPANY ELIMINATION

The supplying center is compensated on internal transfers in the same amount as the overall gross profit percentage attained on its outside sales (the mechanics here are identical to Option 2). The receiving center is charged for the cost of the inventory plus related variable costs. The difference is charged to Head Office. Under this arrangement, there are no allocations for inventory and fixed assets.

Variations

(1) Gross profit percentages could be established for each individual product, instead of using a district total.
(2) Stock transfers and customer transfers could be treated differently (as explained in Option 1).

These are background materials for the Committee meeting on Thursday, July 29 at 10:00 A.M. in the Board Room. The agenda for this meeting would be to evaluate each of the four alternatives and make suitable changes in our transfer pricing system.

If you have any questions, please call me.

Questions

Note: While answering assignment questions 1 through 5 below, stay within two constraints: accept the present organization structure of QMSC; and accept the investment center approach to evaluating the performance of the regions and the districts. These constraints are relaxed in question 6.

1. Critically evaluate the strengths and weaknesses of Quality's current transfer pricing system. Currently, do district and regional managers make decisions which are consistent with overall corporate interests?
2. Consider the firm's policy of allocating inventory assets for ROA measurement. Should the fixed assets of supplying centers be allocated as well? Should asset allocations be eliminated completely? How would these decisions affect the measured performance of districts and regions?
3. A number of customers of the Detroit District have ordered a total of 10,000 cwt of carbon steel sheet. The district's inventory of that item is exhausted. Answer the following:
   a. Assume that the district acquires the metal from the Midwest Region. Using the information supplied below, calculate the contribution made by QMSC by selling the 10,000 cwt of carbon steel sheet. Also, calculate the contribution earned by the Detroit District and the Midwest

Region under the present transfer pricing system as well as under each of the four alternative transfer pricing proposals listed in the Controller's memo.

Midwest region		*Detroit district*	
Acquisition price	$10/cwt	Selling expenses (actual)	$35,000
Variable expenses (predetermined)	$0.45/cwt	Selling expenses (predetermined)	20% of market price
Variable expenses (actual)	$0.50/cwt	Market price	$15.50/cwt
Overall gross profit Percentage for the previous quarter	15%		

Note: Ignore fixed expenses and asset allocations.

b. One of the district's competitors has offered to sell the Detroit District carbon steel sheet in a quantity of 10,000 cwt for $117,500 (Note: the Detroit District would not be able to buy 10,000 cwt at the same price of $10/cwt paid by the Midwest Region since manufacturers, such as United States Steel, sell in lots much larger than 10,000 cwt.) Under each one of the transfer pricing alternatives, where should the manager of the Detroit District acquire the metal from? What is in the overall interest of the company?

4. Critically evaluate the four transfer pricing proposals outlined in the Controller's memo. Should the company adopt one of these alternatives? Why? Should the company adopt an alternative not listed in the Controller's memo? If so, develop a system which would promote goal congruence among managers and which would also be administratively feasible.
5. How should the company go about implementing a new transfer pricing system, given the views expressed by the Regional Manager and the District Manager?
6. Do you agree with the current organization structure of QMSC? Also, do you agree that each one of the regions and the districts should be evaluated as an investment center? If you feel that the present organization structure and the responsibility structure are inappropriate, propose a better alternative. Be sure to indicate which managers would be cost centers, which managers would be profit centers, and which ones would be investment centers in your proposed structure. Be prepared to provide the rationale regarding the financial responsibilities.

CASE 7–9
Ballwin Oil Corporation

It was October 14, 1981. Decisions concerning the 1982 operating budget for Ballwin Oil Corporation (BOC) were to be made the following week. Jim Blakely, senior vice president of BOC and president of the Petroleum Products Company, was very concerned with two transfer price arrangements which existed within his realm of responsibilities. These two issues would need to be resolved as part of the budget-setting process. The two arrangements had caused much debate and consternation during the previous year. He hoped to prevent a repeat of that series of events.

One controversy had arisen between Ballwin Gas Products (BGP) and Ballwin Petrochemical Company (BPC) in respect to the transfer price for internally sourced ethane. The other problem had arisen between BGP and Ballwin Products Trading Company (BPT). It involved the transfer price for non-ethane products processed at BGP's largest plant complex located in Beaumont, Texas.

Reflecting on these two specific problems had served to make Mr. Blakely aware of a general transfer pricing issue which existed within BOC. This issue revolved around the question of whether there should be a policy which favored the consistent use of either cost-based or market-based transfer prices.

Company Background

Ballwin Oil Corporation was an integrated oil company engaged primarily in the exploration for and production, transportation, and marketing of crude oil and natural gas, and in the refining, transportation, and marketing of petroleum products. Sales and other operating revenues during 1980 totaled $9.8 billion. Net income for the same year was $432 million.

The corporation was divided into four operating companies (see Exhibit 1). The president of each company reported to one of the two executive vice presidents at the corporate headquarters in Houston, Texas. In addition, four senior vice presidents headed the four primary staff groups and reported to Ballwin's third executive vice president. BGP, BPT, and BPC were the three major divisions organized under Ballwin Petroleum Products.

This organizational structure was officially put into place on January 1, 1981. It was the second major reorganization which BOC had undergone in six years. The first reorganization took place in 1975 in an attempt to gain some of the many alleged advantages of decentralization by splitting the company into many operating units. The 1981 reorganization was an attempt to correct a structure which had become perceived as being "top-heavy."

Natural Gas Liquids

There are basically two types of petroleum wells—oil wells and gas wells (see Exhibit 2). Oil wells are those that are completed for the

EXHIBIT 1 Organizational Chart

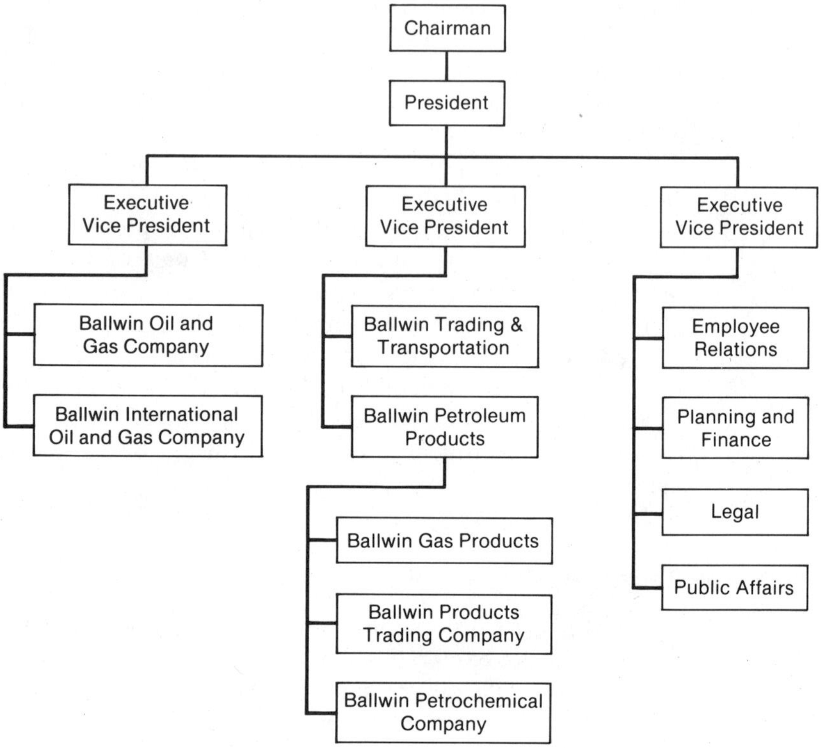

production of crude oil. Any gas which is present in the crude oil stream is referred to as associated gas. The hydrocarbons from an oil well are put through a field separator at the wellhead, or close to it, which removes the associated gas. Similarly, gas wells are those that are completed for the production of natural gas. Any oil which is present in the natural gas stream is referred to as condensate. The natural gas stream is put through a field separator, which removes the condensate.

Natural gas (both associated gas and gas emanating from a gas well) is sent through a series of gathering lines to a processing plant. Despite the fact that the natural gas has gone through field separators, some heavier hydrocarbons may still exist in the gas stream. In addition, cooler temperatures, which may exist in the pipeline, cause a fraction of the gas stream to become liquids. Thus, the gas stream is further processed at extraction plants to remove the additional gas liquids. If the price of gas liquids are greater than the price of natural gas, the stream will be further cooled in order to remove the maximum amount of natural gas liquids (technologically and/or legally).

EXHIBIT 2 Gas Liquids Product Flow

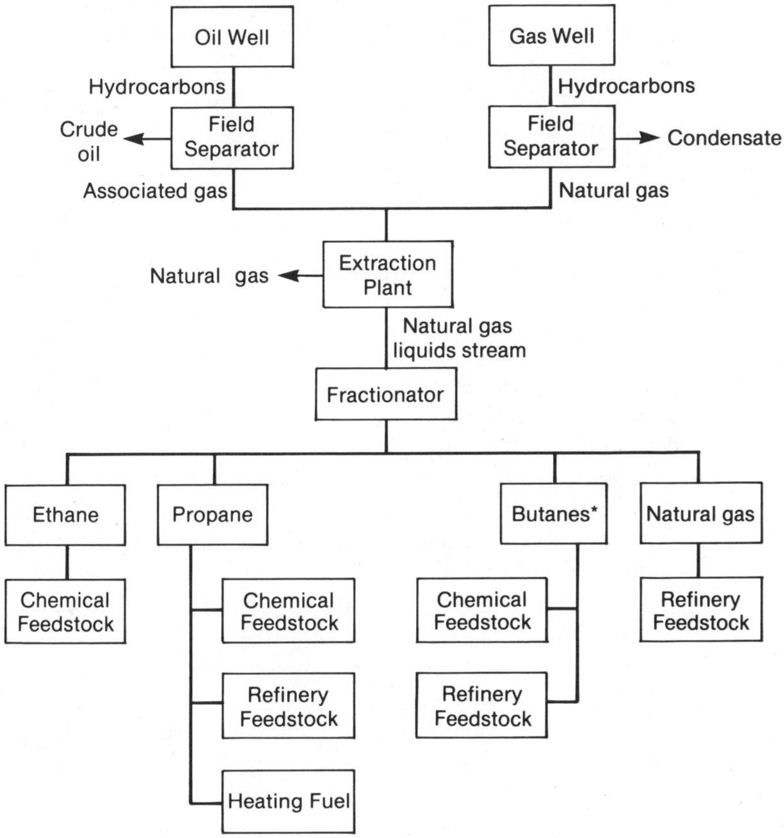

* This category includes iso-butane and normal butane.

Legal constraints exist concerning the minimum BTU level which the remaining gas stream may contain. Since gas liquids possess a greater BTU content than the other portions of the natural gas stream, the removal of the gas liquids reduces the overall BTU content of the remaining gas stream. In order to increase the BTU content of this remaining gas stream, a portion of the stream—commonly called "inerts"—are often removed. These inerts consist of a portion of the gas stream which contains no BTU value. Obviously, the greater the amount of inerts which can be removed, the greater the amount of gas liquids which can be removed.

Fractionators. After processing at the extraction plant, the gas liquids stream is sent to a fractionator, where the stream is separated into individual gas liquids. They are ethane, propane, butane, and natural gasoline. Four basic methods are used to recover these natural gas liquids. Each method is designed in such a way as to make it possible to extract the maximum amount of a certain gas liquid.

The only natural gas liquid to be considered an end product is propane. (All the others are raw materials and must be blended.) The largest demand sector for propane is the residential/commercial heating market. Ethane, butane, and propane are all used as petrochemical feedstocks. Butane, propane, and natural gasoline are used as feedstocks in the refining industry.

Product Flow within Ballwin Petroleum Products

Ballwin Gas Products. BGP owned and operated 12 field plants, which were located primarily in Texas, Louisiana, and Oklahoma, and one major plant in Beaumont, Texas. Most of the field plants were located in areas where BOC had significant concentrations of oil and gas wells. A few such plants were designed, however, to serve independent oil and gas firms. For the most part, the field plants contained extraction units, which removed the gas liquids from the natural gas stream, and fractionators, which separated the gas liquid stream into individual gas liquids.

Seventy-five percent of BGP's input during 1980 was sourced from a natural gas transmission subsidiary of Ballwin Oil and Gas Company, BOGC. The remaining 25 percent was from external sources. All of BGP's volume was sold through BPT.

Ballwin Products Trading Company. BPT was largely a marketing and transportation company for gas liquids. In order to economically and efficiently serve their markets, the company also bought from and sold to third parties. BPT occasionally handled crude oil, condensate, and refined products. However, for the most part, the trading of these items was handled through Ballwin Trading and Transportation Company (see Exhibit 1).

BPT had made substantial capital investments during the past decade for storage and other facilities. As a result, the company was able to handle greater quantities of products and, thus, expand and better serve their markets. Inventories during their traditional peak season of September and October and accounts receivable during their peak season of January and February both reached almost $400 million during 1980.

In the same year, BPT sourced 35 percent of its product from external sources and 65 percent from internal sources. Sixty percent of BPT's internal sourcing (or 39 percent of its total volume) was from BGP. BPT had the responsibility for procuring BGP's external feedstock and for selling its entire output. The other 40 percent of BPT's internal input was sourced from divisions of BOGC.

BPT sold 70 percent of its volume to third parties during 1980. Of the 30 percent which was sold internally, the primary customer was BPC.

Ballwin Petrochemical Company. BPC operated a variety of plants throughout the Southwest and Southeast. Among these was an ethylene plant located on the Gulf Coast about 50 miles from Beaumont. Its primary source of raw materials was shipped, via pipeline, from BGP's Beaumont facilities.

BPC bought butane and ethane from BPT. The company provided approximately 80 percent of BPC's total butane and ethane needs. Ethane and propane, which were often available in the outside market in a comingled state, also were sourced by BPC from third parties. BPC paid a fee to BGP to have the comingled stream processed at fractionators, which were owned and operated by BGP.

Transfer Prices within Ballwin Oil Corporation

Many different transfer pricing arrangements existed between the various divisions and subsidiaries of BOC. The different arrangements developed as a result of a multiplicity of factors, which included, among others: tradition, regulation, third-party business, and visibility to the outside world.

Tradition dictated many of the transfer pricing arrangements between the divisions. Many of these arrangements had been established years before under much different circumstances. However, once a division had become a party to a certain transfer price arrangement, its management was often quite unwilling to give up their share of the pie.

One of the more interesting variables was whether a division was regulated. It was common within BOC, as was the case within many firms in the oil and gas industry, to have a group of managers who wanted to push as much profit as possible into nonregulated divisions. because profits were often limited in the regulated sectors.

As one might expect: the greater the amount of third-party business, the less impact a transfer price had on the division involved. Often, divisions which sourced and sold very little of their product lines internally used a market-based transfer price for their internal transactions. Because of these divisions' large percentage of outside dealings, a market price was not difficult to establish. In addition, whatever the transfer price, it had little impact on the total reported profit of such a division.

The amount of visibility to the outside world which a division had might also affect the transfer pricing arrangement. For instance, BPC was closely watched by certain members of the financial community. This was due to its relative newness; the fact that many other inte-

EXHIBIT 3 Product Flows within Ballwin Petroleum Products: A Partial Description

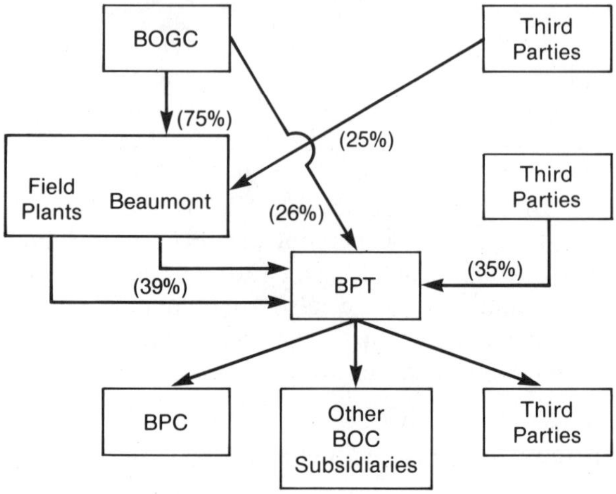

grated oil companies had established similar operations, with less than satisfactory results; and because it provided an example of how well BOC's management and management style might fare in a reasonably open, competitive market. As a result, certain members of BOC's management were anxious to report reasonably healthy profits in this division.

Exhibit 4 contains a partial list of transfer price arrangements within Ballwin Petroleum Products.

EXHIBIT 4 Price Flows

Source	*Use*	*Product*	*Pricing arrangement*
BOGC	BGP	Gas liquids	Market price
Third party	BGP	Gas liquids	Market price
BGP (field plants)	BPT	Gas liquid products	Commission*
BGP (Beaumont)	BPT	Gas liquid products	Negotiated
BGP (Beaumont)	BPC	Ethane	Negotiated
Third party	BPC	Ethane	Market price
Third party	BPT	Gas liquid products	Market price
BPT	Third party	Gas liquid products	Market price

* BPT was paid a commission for selling BGP products to third-party customers.

Intracompany Price for Ethane

The product flow for the ethane, which was produced at Beaumont, involved BOGC, BGP, BPT and BPC. The gas stream was primarily purchased from BOGC and was processed by BGP. The ethane then flowed through BPT (with no profit accruing to BPT) to BPC.

The transfer price for ethane (which was produced at BGP's Beaumont complex) between BGP and BPC was based on a rather complex formula. It was the sum of the following components: (1) the cost paid to a subsidiary of BOGC for raw materials; (2) allocated charges for operating costs at the extraction unit and fractionator, allocated charges based on the overhead at the Beaumont plant complex, and an allocation of the corporate overhead, which had been allocated to the Beaumont complex; and (3) an allocation designed to help yield a 14–18 percent return on the net book value of the Beaumont facilities.

For example, during August 1981, the average price for raw materials was equivalent to 22¢ per gallon of ethane produced.[1] In addition, the allocations, based on operating costs at both the extraction unit and the fractionator, and the plant and corporate overhead charges summed to 3¢ per gallon. The charge needed to attain the prespecified return on investment added another 4¢ per gallon. Thus, the transfer price was 29¢ per gallon.

A problem had developed because BGP's management thought that they should be receiving market value for the product. During August 1981, the average market price was 35¢ per gallon. Thus, management believed that the transfer price should be 35¢ per gallon, resulting in a 10¢ per gallon "profit" to BGP. They argued that the profit was necessary in order to convince upper management of their need for additional capital expenditures.

On the other hand, BPC's management argued that the ethane extraction unit and fractionator at the Beaumont complex had been built primarily for BPC. They pointed out that they were, by far, the single biggest consumer of the facility's output and that their ethylene plant had been built to use the BGP output. They, therefore, reasoned that they should pay "bare knuckles" cost. "Bare knuckles" cost in the example just cited would have resulted in a transfer price of 25¢ per gallon.

Transfer Price from BGP to BPT

The transfer price BPT paid BGP for products which were produced at the Beaumont facilities was negotiated by the general manager of the two entities. It was based upon the difference between (1) the cost of the natural gas liquid stream, plus the full cost of production; and (2) the composite third-party selling price for all gas liquids.[2]

[1] A BOGC gas pipeline subsidiary was paid for the gas liquid stream that was removed from its natural gas stream. Payment was made on the basis of BTUs removed, using the market price.

[2] The full cost included all items of cost, direct or allocated, except for a "return on capital invested."

Both the production costs and the selling prices were based on a weighted average of the various gas liquids products changing hands. The third-party selling price numbers were estimated in advance by the marketing research and planning department, a staff group which served Ballwin Petroleum Products.

Every year, the heads of the two entities negotiated a split of the difference. For example, for 1981, the staff group estimated that total costs would be 25¢ per gallon and the average market price would be 48¢ per gallon. The two groups agreed on a 60/40 split. Thus, the transfer price between BGP and BPT was 38.8¢ per gallon.[3]

If the predicted market price and costs for a particular month differed from the actual numbers, the transfer price was adjusted one month in arrears. For example, the actual, average market price was 52¢ per gallon during August 1981 and the total full costs of production were 26¢ per gallon. Therefore, in September, BPT paid BGP 2.8¢ per gallon for all products sold in August.[4]

BPT's management was not at all satisfied with this arrangement. They believed that they should receive 70 percent of the profit and that the 1981 transfer price should have been 31.9¢ per gallon [(0.48 − 0.25)(30 percent) + 0.25 = $0.319]. Management argued that they bore virtually all of the risk in this particular arrangement. In the cases when BGP took the risk (as was the situation in the field plants), BPT paid a transfer price which resulted in their earning an 8 percent commission on the sales price of the products actually sold. Put in the earlier context, this was comparable to an 83/17 split.[5]

Other Areas of Concern

Jim Blakely pondered the problems which had arisen concerning the two transfer price arrangements. His mind wandered to the upcoming meetings he had scheduled with the managers who were involved. He knew that each manager would argue very convincingly for his or her position. In addition, he was well aware of the fact that the discussion could become reasonably emotional. This assumption was due to the fact that the MBO (management by objectives) evaluation system, which was in place at Ballwin, resulted in bonus payments that normally provided between 20 and 40 percent of a manager's income.

As the financial objectives included in the MBO system were often a function of the individual divisions' reported profits, he knew that the

---

[3] ($0.48 − 0.25)(60 percent) + 0.25 = $0.388.

[4] ($0.52 − 0.26)(60 percent) + 0.26 = $0.416;
$0.416 − 0.388 = 0.028

[5] ($0.48 × 0.08 = 0.0384); (0.48 − .0384 = 0.4416);
((0.48 − 0.25)(83.3%) + 0.25 = $0.4416)

transfer price arrangements had to be considered when setting the MBO objectives. The firm's announced, explicit policy was to alter all MBO objectives whenever the transfer price arrangements were changed. Thus, he felt that the MBO reward system was immune from influencing any one manager's bonus payments. However, he could not say that his managers were convinced of this fact.

The 1982 operating budget was to be finalized within one month. At that time, it was "set in concrete." One year earlier, the budget had been approved as scheduled. However, the two transfer price arrangements that are currently in question had not been settled until December. Thus, the revised bonus targets for MBO evaluation purposes did not tie neatly to the original budget targets.

His final major concern was the notion among some executives that the unregulated and the highly visible segments should be made to look good to the outside world. The regulated versus unregulated argument had once had a substantial amount of influence on decision making in Ballwin Petroleum Products. However, since January 1981, when controls on the price of gas liquids were completely lifted, the argument had lost most of its claim to validity. Still, he knew that he would receive pressure to make BPC, an externally visible segment, look profitable.

Decisions to Be Made

Jim Blakely was determined to settle the two transfer price disputes within the next few days. However, he knew agreements would not come easily. Furthermore, he knew that the agreements might serve only as short-term solutions.

In respect to the more broadly based question of whether he should invoke a policy which favored the consistent use of either cost-based or market-based transfer prices, he was still quite uncertain. He knew that he had the authority to make such a policy decision—at least for the Ballwin Petroleum Products operations—but he wasn't entirely convinced that it was a sound idea.

CHAPTER 8

Investment Centers

In a profit center, the focus is on profit as measured by the difference between revenues and expenses. In an investment center, this profit is compared with the assets employed in earning it. Many people consider an investment center as a special type of profit center, and use the term *profit center* for both. Our reason for treating them separately is primarily pedagogical; that is, there are so many problems involved in measuring the assets employed in a profit center that the topic warrants a separate chapter.

In this chapter we first discuss each of the principal types of assets that may be employed in an investment center. The sum of these assets is termed the *investment base*. We then discuss the two methods of relating profit to the investment base: (1) the percentage return on investment (ROI), and (2) residual income. Finally, in view of the problems involved in measuring assets employed, we discuss the question of whether a division should or should not be set up as an investment center; and, if not, the alternative methods that can be used to control assets employed.

STRUCTURE OF THE ANALYSIS

The purposes of measuring assets employed are analogous to those discussed for profit centers in Chapter 6, namely:

1. To provide information that is useful in making decisions about assets employed and to motivate managers to make sound decisions; that is, decisions that are in the best interests of the company.
2. To measure the performance of the division as an economic entity.

In examining the several alternative treatments of assets and in comparing ROI and residual income—the two ways of relating profit to assets employed—we are primarily interested in how well the alternatives serve these two purposes.

It should be recognized at the outset that a focus on profits without consideration of the assets employed to generate those profits is an inadequate basis for control. Except in certain types of service organizations in which the amount of capital is insignificant, an important objective of a profit-oriented company is to earn a satisfactory return on the capital which its investors have supplied. A profit of $1 million in a company that has $10 million of capital does not represent as good a performance as a profit of $1 million in a company that has only $5 million of capital.

Unless assets employed are taken into account it is difficult for senior management to compare the profit performance of one division with that of another division or with that of similar outside companies. Comparisons of absolute differences in profits are not meaningful if the divisions use different amounts of resources; clearly, the greater the resources used, the greater should be the profits. Such comparisons are used both to judge how well divisional managers are performing and also as a basis for deciding how resources should be allocated.

In general, divisional managers have two performance objectives. First, they should generate adequate profits from the resources at their disposal (subject of course to legal and social constraints). Second, they should invest in additional resources only when such investment will produce an adequate return. Conversely, they should disinvest if the expected annual profits of any resource divided by its selling price is less than the company's cost of capital. The purpose of relating profits and investments is to motivate the divisional manager to accomplish these objectives. As we shall see, however, there are significant practical difficulties involved in creating a system that focuses on both profits and assets employed.

Exhibit 8–1 is a hypothetical, simplified set of divisional financial statements that will be used throughout this analysis. (In the interest of simplicity, income taxes have been omitted from this exhibit and will generally be omitted in the discussion of this chapter. Inclusion of income taxes would change the magnitudes in the calculations that follow, but would not change the conclusions.) The exhibit shows the two ways of relating profits to assets employed; namely, return on investment and residual income.

Return on investment is a *ratio*. The numerator is income, as reported on the income statement. The denominator is assets employed. In Exhibit 8–1, the denominator is taken as the corporate equity in the division. This amount would correspond to the sum of noncurrent liabilities plus shareholders' equity in the balance sheet of a separate company. It is mathematically equivalent to total assets less current liabilities, and also to noncurrent assets plus working capital. (This statement can be easily checked against the numbers in Exhibit 8–1.)

EXHIBIT 8–1 Divisional Financial Statements

Balance Sheet
($000)

Current Assets:			Current Liabilities:	
Cash		$ 50	Accounts payable	$ 90
Receivables		150	Other current	110
Inventory		200		
Total current assets		400	Total current liabilities	200
Fixed Assets:				
Cost	$600		Corporate equity	500
Depreciation	−300			
Book value		300		
Total assets		700	Total equities	700

Income Statement

Revenue		$1,000
Expenses, except depreciation	$850	
Depreciation	50	900
Income before taxes		100
Capital charge ($500 × 10%)		50
Residual income		50

Return on investment $\frac{\$100}{\$500} = 20\%$

Residual income (RI) is a dollar amount, rather than a ratio. It is found by subtracting a capital charge from the reported income. This capital charge is found by multiplying the amount of assets employed by a rate, which in Exhibit 8–1 is 10 percent. We shall discuss the derivation of this rate in a later section.

In the study by James S. Reece and William R. Cool[1] 620 companies out of the *Fortune "1,000"* companies answered a questionnaire. Of those responding 96 percent or 594 companies had either profit centers or investment centers. Profit centers were used by 185 (23 percent) and investment centers by 459 (77 percent). Of the companies using investment centers, 65 percent evaluated them on the basis of ROI alone and 28 percent used both ROI and RI. Only 2 percent used RI alone. This contrasts with an earlier study that showed 52 percent of the companies surveyed used ROI only, 41 percent used both, and 6 percent used RI only.[2] (This would appear to indicate that ROI is increasing in popularity while RI is decreasing.) With a sample size of 459, and considering the latitude with which different companies use ROI (see page 343), it is doubtful if these differences are significant.

[1] James S. Reece and William R. Cool, "Measuring Investment Center Performance," *Harvard Business Review*, May–June, 1978.

[2] John S. Mauriel and Robert N. Anthony, "Misevaluation of Investment Center Performance," *Harvard Business Review*, March–April 1966.

For reasons to be explained later, residual income is conceptually superior to return on investment; and we shall therefore generally use residual income in our examples. Nevertheless, it is clear from the survey that return on investment is more widely used in business than residual income.

MEASUREMENT OF ASSETS EMPLOYED

In this section, we discuss alternative ways of measuring the principal items that constitute the investment base in a division and evaluate these alternatives.

Cash

Most companies control cash centrally because central control permits the use of a smaller cash balance than would be the case if each division held cash balances sufficient to provide the necessary buffer for the unevenness of cash inflows and cash outflows. Divisional cash balances may well be only the "float" between daily receipts and daily disbursements. Consequently, the actual cash balances at the division level tend to be much smaller than would be required if the division were an independent company. Many companies, therefore, calculate the cash to be included in the investment base by means of a formula. For example, General Motors is reported to use 4.5 percent of annual sales; Du Pont uses two months' costs of sales minus depreciation. The formula is designed to approximate the amount of cash the division would have if it were an independent company.

There are two reasons for including cash at a higher amount than the nominal balance normally carried by divisions. First, the higher amount is necessary to permit comparability among divisions or with outside companies. Second, if only the actual cash were shown, the return shown by internal divisions would be abnormally high and might be misleading to top management.

Some companies omit cash from the investment base on the theory that the investment base consists of working capital plus fixed assets. These companies reason that the amount of cash approximates the current liabilities; if this is so, the sum of the accounts receivable and the inventories will approximate the amount of working capital.

Receivables

Division management may be able to influence the level of receivables, not only indirectly by its ability to generate sales but also directly by establishing credit terms, by approving individual credit accounts and credit limits, and by its vigor in collecting overdue amounts. In the interest of simplicity, receivables often are included at the actual end-of-period balances, although the average of intraperiod balances is conceptually a better measure of the amount that should be related to profits. If the division does not control credits and collections, receivables may be calculated on a formula basis. This formula should be consistent with the normal payment period; for example, 30 days' sales where payment is normally made 30 days after the shipment of goods.

Inventories

Inventories are ordinarily treated in a manner similar to receivables; that is, they are often recorded at end-of-period amounts even though intraperiod averages would be conceptually preferable. If the company uses LIFO for financial accounting purposes, a different valuation method is ordinarily used for divisional profit reporting because, in periods of inflation, the LIFO inventory balances tend to be unrealistically low. In these circumstances, inventories should be valued at standard or average costs, and these same costs should be used to measure cost of sales on the divisional income statement.

If work-in-process inventory is financed by *advance payments* or by *progress payments* from the customer, as is typically the case with goods that require a long manufacturing period, these payments are usually subtracted from the gross inventory amounts.

Some companies subtract *accounts payable* from inventory on the grounds that the amount of accounts payable represents financing of part of the inventory by vendors, at zero cost to the division; the corporate capital required for inventories is only the difference between the gross inventory amount and accounts payable. If the division can influence the payment period allowed by vendors, the inclusion of accounts payable in the calculation encourages the manager to seek the most favorable terms. In times of high-interest rates or credit stringency, the manager might be encouraged to consider the possibility of foregoing the cash discount in order, in effect, to have additional financing provided by vendors. On the other hand, delaying payments unduly to reduce net current assets may not be in the company's best interest since it may hurt its credit rating.

Working Capital in General

As can be seen from the above, there is considerable variation in how working capital items are treated. At one extreme, companies include all current assets in the investment base, with no offset for any current liabilities. This is sound from a motivational standpoint if the divisions have no influence over accounts payable or other current liabilities. It overstates the amount of corporate capital required to finance the division, however, because the current liabilities are a source of capital, often at zero interest cost. At the other extreme, all current liabilities (except current obligations to the corporation) may be deducted from current assets, as was done in calculating the investment base in Exhibit 8–1. This provides a good measure of the capital provided by the corporation, on which it expects the division to earn a return. It may, however, imply that the division manager is responsible for certain current liabilities over which he or she has no control.

Property, Plant, and Equipment

In financial accounting, fixed assets are initially recorded at their acquisition cost, and this cost is written off over the asset's useful life by the depreciation mechanism. Most companies use a similar approach in measuring divisional profitability in the division's asset base. This causes some serious problems in using the system for its intended purposes. In this part of the chapter, we shall examine these problems.

Acquisition of new equipment. Suppose a division has an opportunity to acquire a new machine at a cost of $100,000. This machine is estimated to produce cash savings of $27,000 a year for five years. If the company has a required return of 10 percent, such an investment is attractive, as shown by the calculations in section A of Exhibit 8–2. The proposed investment has a net present value of $2,400, and therefore should be undertaken. However, if the machine is acquired, and if the division measures its asset base as shown in Exhibit 8–1, the reported residual income of the division in the first year will decrease, rather than increase. The income statement without the machine and the income statement if the machine is acquired are shown in section B of Exhibit 8–2. It should be noted that with the acquisition of the machine, income before taxes has increased, but this increase is more than offset by the increase in the capital charge. Thus, the residual income calculation signals that profitability has decreased, whereas the economic facts are that profitability has increased. Under these circumstances, the division manager may not be motivated to purchase this machine.

Note that in Exhibit 8–2 depreciation was calculated on the straight-line basis. If it had been calculated on an accelerated basis, which is not uncommon, the discrepancy between the economic facts and the reported results would have been even greater.

In later years, the amount of residual income will increase, as the book value of the machine declines, as shown in Exhibit 8–3, going from −$3,000 in year 1 to $5,000 in year 5. The increases in residual income each year do not represent real economic changes. They ap-

EXHIBIT 8–2 Incorrect Motivation for Asset Acquisition ($000)

A. *Economic calculation:*

Investment in machine	$100
Life, 5 years	
Cash inflow, $27,000 per year	
Present value of cash inflow ($27,000 × 3.791*)	102.4
Net present value	2.4
Decision: acquire the machine	

B. *As reflected on divisional income statement:*

	As in Exhibit 8–1		*First year with machine*	
Revenue		$1,000		$1,000
Expenses, except depreciation	$850		$823	
Depreciation	50	900	70	893
Income before taxes		100		107
Less capital charge at 10%†		50		60
Residual income		50		47

Note: Income taxes are not shown separately for simplicity. Assume they are included in the calculation of the cash flow and expense.

* 3.791 is the present value of $1 per year for five years at 10 percent.

† Interest on the new machine is calculated at its beginning book value, which for the first year, is $100 × 10% = 10. We have used the beginning-of-the-year book value for simplicity. Many companies use the average book value $\left(\frac{100 + 80}{2} = 90\right)$. The results will be similar.

pear to show constantly improving profitability, whereas, the facts are that there has been no real change in profitability subsequent to the time the machine was acquired. Generalizing from this example, it is evident that divisions that have old, almost fully depreciated assets will tend to report larger residual income than divisions that have newer assets.

EXHIBIT 8–3 Effect of Acquisition on Reported Annual Profits ($000)

Year	*Book value at beginning of year (a)*	*Income* (b)*	*Capital charge† (c)*	*Residual income (b − c)*	*ROI (b ÷ c)*
1	100	7	10	−3	7%
2	80	7	8	−1	9
3	60	7	6	1	12
4	40	7	4	3	18
5	20	7	2	5	35

Note: True return = approximately 11 percent.

* $27,000 cash inflow − $20,000 depreciation = $7,000.

† 10 percent of beginning book value.

If profitability is measured by return on investment, the same inconsistency exists, as shown in the last column of Exhibit 8–3. Although we know from the present value calculation that the true return is about 11 percent, the divisional financial statement reports that it is less than 10 percent in the first year, and that it increases from year to year. Furthermore, the average of the five annual percentages shown is 16 percent, which far exceeds what we know to be the true annual return.

It is evident that if depreciable assets are included in the investment base at net book value, divisional profitability is misstated, and division managers may not be motivated to make correct acquisition decisions.

Gross book value. The fluctuations in residual income and return on investment from year to year in the above example can be avoided by including depreciable assets in the investment base at gross book value, rather than net book value. Some companies do this. If this were done, the investment each year would be the $100,000 original cost, and the additional income would be $7,000 ($27,000 cash inflow − $20,000 depreciation). The residual income, however, would be decreased by $3,000 (= $7,000 − $10,000 interest), and the return on investment would be 7 percent (= $7,000 ÷ $100,000). Both of these numbers indicate that the division's profitability has decreased, which is not in fact the case. Return on investment calculated on gross book value always understates the true return.

Equipment replacement. If a new machine is being considered as a replacement for an existing machine that has some undepreciated book value, we know that the undepreciated book value is irrelevant in the economic analysis of the proposed purchase (except indirectly as it may affect income taxes). Nevertheless, in the calculation of divisional profitability, the removal of the book value of the old machine can have a substantial effect. Gross book value will increase only by the difference between the cost of the new machine and the cost of the old. Net book value will increase only by the difference between the net book value after year 1 of the new machine and the net book value of the old. In either case, the relevant amount of additional investment is understated, and the residual income is correspondingly overstated. Managers, therefore, are encouraged to replace old equipment with new equipment, even in situations in which such replacement is not economically justified. Furthermore, divisions that are able to make the most replacements will show the greatest improvement in profitability.

Disposition of assets. If assets are included in the investment base at their original cost, then the division manager is motivated to get rid of them, even if they have some usefulness, because the division's investment base is reduced by the full cost of the asset.[3]

Annuity depreciation. If, instead of straight-line depreciation, depreciation is calculated by the annuity basis, the divisional profitability calculation will show the correct residual income and return on investment, as demonstrated in Exhibits 8–4 and 8–5. This is because the

---

[3] For a complete analysis of this and other problems of accounting for depreciable assets, see John Dearden, "Problem in Decentralized Profit Responsibility," *Harvard Business Review*, May–June 1960.

EXHIBIT 8–4 Profitability Using Annuity Depreciation—Smoothing Residual Income ($000)

Year	Beginning book value	Cash inflow	Residual income*	Capital charge†	Depreciation‡
1	$100.0	$ 27.0	$0.6	$10.0	$ 16.4
2	83.6	27.0	0.6	8.4	18.0
3	65.6	27.0	0.6	6.6	19.8
4	45.8	27.0	0.6	4.6	21.8
5	24.0	27.0	0.6	2.4	24.0
		135.0	3.0	32.0	100.0

* The reason for using annuity depreciation is to make the residual income the same each year by changing the amount of depreciation charged. Consequently, we must estimate the total residual income earned over the five years. A 10 percent return on $100,000 would require five annual cash inflows of $26,378. The actual cash inflows are $27,000. Therefore, the residual income (the amount in excess of $26,378) is $622 per year.

† This is 10 percent of the balance at the beginning of the year.

‡ Depreciation is the amount required to make the residual income (profits after the capital charge and depreciation) equals $622 per year (rounded here to $600). This is calculated as follows:

$$\$27.0 - \text{Capital charge} - \text{Depreciation} = \$0.6$$

therefore

$$\text{Depreciation} = \$26.4 - \text{Capital charge}$$

EXHIBIT 8–5 Profitability Using Annuity Depreciation—Smoothing Return on Investment ($000)

Year	Beginning book balance	Cash inflow	Net profit*	Depreciation†	Return on beginning investment
1	$100.0	$ 27.0	$11.0	$ 16.0	11%
2	84.0	27.0	9.2	17.8	11
3	66.2	27.0	7.3	19.7	11
4	46.5	27.0	5.1	21.9	11
5	24.6	27.0	2.4	24.6	10‡
		135.0	35.0	100.0	10

* A return on $27,000 a year for five years on an investment of $100,000 provides a return of approximately 11 percent on the beginning of the year investment. Consequently, in order to have a constant 11 percent return each year, the net profit must equal 11 percent of the beginning of the year investment.

† Depreciation is the difference between the cash flow and the net profit.

‡ Difference results because the return is not exactly 11 percent.

annuity depreciation method exactly matches the recovery of investment that is implicit in the present value calculation. Annuity depreciation is the opposite of accelerated depreciation, in that the annual amount of depreciation is low in the early years when the investment values are high and increases each year as the investments decrease; the rate of return remains constant.

The examples in Exhibits 8–4 and 8–5 show the calculations when the cash inflows are level in each year. Equations are available that derive the depreciation for other cash flow patterns, such as a decreasing cash flow as repair costs increase, or an increasing cash flow as a new product gains market acceptance.[4]

Very few managers accept the idea of a depreciation allowance that increases as the asset ages, however. They visualize accounting depreciation as representing physical deterioration or loss in economic value. Therefore, they believe that accelerated or straight-line depreciation is a valid representation of what is taking place, while annuity depreciation is not. Consequently, it is difficult to convince management to use the annuity method for divisional profit measurement.

Annuity depreciation also presents some practical problems. For example, a depreciation schedule is developed on the basis of an estimated cash flow pattern. If the actual cash flow pattern differs from that assumed, even though the total cash flow might result in the same rate of return, some years would show higher than expected profits and others would show lower. Should the depreciation schedule be changed each year to conform with the actual pattern of cash flow? This would not seem to be practical. Annuity depreciation would not be desirable for income tax purposes, of course; and although, as a "systematic and rational" method, it clearly is acceptable for financial accounting purposes, companies do not use it in their financial reporting. Indeed, surveys of company practice in measuring divisional profitability show practically no use of the annuity method.[5]

Other valuation methods. A few companies depart from the use of either gross book value or net book value in calculating the investment base. Some use net book value but set a lower limit, usually 50 percent, as the amount of original cost that can be written off; this lessens the distortions that occur in divisions with relatively old assets. A difficulty with this method is that a division with fixed assets that have a net book value of less than 50 percent of gross book value can decrease its investment base by scrapping perfectly good assets. Other companies depart entirely from the accounting records, and use an approximation of the current value of the asset. They arrive at this amount by a periodic appraisal of assets (say, every five years or when a new division manager takes over), by adjusting original cost by an index of changes in equipment prices, or by using insurance values.

A major problem with using nonaccounting values is that they tend to be subjective, as contrasted with accounting values which appear to be objective and generally not subject to argument. Consequently, accounting data have an aura of reality for operating management. Although the intensity of this sentiment will vary with different managers, the further one departs from accounting numbers in measuring

[4] See Harold Bierman, Jr., "ROI as a Measure of Managerial Performance," *Financial Executive,* March 1973.

[5] John J. Mauriel and Robert N. Anthony, "Misevaluation of Investment Center Performance," *Harvard Business Review,* March–April 1966. Also Reece and Cool, "Measuring Investment Center Performance."

financial performance, the more the system seems like playing a game of numbers to many divisional managers and, often, to higher levels of management also.

A related problem with using nonaccounting amounts in internal management control systems is that divisional profitability will be inconsistent with the corporate profitability reported to the shareholders. Although the management control system need not necessarily be consistent with the external financial reporting, as a practical matter some managements regard net income, as reported on the financial statements, as constituting the "name of the game." Consequently, they do not favor an internal system that uses a different method of "keeping score," regardless of its theoretical merits. Another problem with the economic value approach is deciding how the economic values are to be determined. Conceptually, the economic value of a group of assets is equal to the present value of the flow of funds that these assets will generate in the future. As a practical matter, it is not possible to determine this amount. For plant and equipment, it is possible to use published indexes of replacement costs. This, however, solves only the easiest part of the problem, because this method provides no means for valuing the intangible assets. Also, most price indexes are not entirely relevant because they usually make no allowance for the impact of changes in technology.

In any case, the inclusion in the investment base of fixed asset at other than the amounts derived from the accounting records appears to be so little used that it is of little more than academic interest (see Exhibit 8–6).

Two studies of industry practices in calculating the investment base in investment centers are summarized in Exhibits 8–7 and 8–8.

EXHIBIT 8–6 Valuation of Plant and Equipment

	Percent of respondents using method	
	*Vancil Survey**	*Reece & Cool Survey†*
Gross book value (original cost)	15%	14%
Net book value (cost less accumulated depreciation)	85	85
Replacement cost		2
	100%	101%‡

* Richard F. Vancil, *Decentralization: Management Ambiguity by Design* (Homewood, Ill.: Dow Jones-Irwin, 1979), p. 351.

† James S. Reece and William R. Cool, "Measuring Investment Center Performance," *Harvard Business Review*, May–June 1978, p. 42.

‡ Includes multiple responses.

EXHIBIT 8–7 Assets Included in Investment Base

	Percent of respondents including the asset in the investment base	
	*Vancil Survey** *239 respondents*	*Reece & Cool Survey†* *459 respondents*
Current assets:		
Cash	64%	63%
External Receivables	98	94
Intracompany Receivables	46	
Inventories	98	95
Other current assets	78	76
Fixed assets:		
Used solely by profit centers:		
Land and buildings	96	94
Equipment	98	83
Used two or more profit centers:		
Land and buildings	56	45
Equipment	46	41
Assets of headquarters, central research, or similar units	25	16
Other assets:		
Investments	49	N.A.
Goodwill	40	N.A.
Capitalized rent charges	92	N.A.

N.A. = not available.

* Richard F. Vancil, *Decentralization: Management Ambiguity by Design* (Homewood, Ill.: Dow Jones-Irwin, 1979), p. 349.

† James S. Reece and William R. Cool, "Measuring Investment Center Performance," *Harvard Business Review,* May–June 1978, p. 36.

EXHIBIT 8–8 Liabilities Deducted in Measuring Investment Base

	Percent of respondents deducting the liability from the investment base	
	*Vancil Survey**	*Reece & Cool Survey†*
Current external payables	49%	51%
Current intracompany payables	29	30
Other current liabilities	42	45
Deferred taxes	19	N.A.
Other noncurrent liabilities	77	20

N.A. = not available.

* Richard F. Vancil, *Decentralization: Management Ambiguity by Design* (Homewood, Ill.: Dow Jones-Irwin, 1979), p. 351.

† James S. Reece and William R. Cool, "Measuring Investment Center Performance," *Harvard Business Review,* May–June 1978, p. 40.

Leased Assets

Suppose the division whose financial statements are shown in Exhibit 8–1 sold its $300,000 of fixed assets, returned the proceeds of the sale of corporate headquarters, and then leased back the assets at a rental rate of $60,000 per year. As shown in Exhibit 8–9, the division's income before taxes would be reduced because the new rental expense would be higher than the depreciation charge that has been eliminated. Nevertheless, residual income would be increased because the higher cost would be more than offset by the decrease in capital charge. Because of this tendency, division managers will be induced to lease assets, rather than own them, under any circumstances in which the interest charge that is built into the rental cost is less than the capital charge that is applied to the division's investment base. (Here, as elsewhere, this generalization is an oversimplification, because in the real world the impact of income taxes must also be taken into account.)

EXHIBIT 8–9 Effect of Leasing Assets—Income Statement ($000)

	As in Exhibit 8–1		*If assets are leased*	
Revenue		$1,000		$1,000
Expenses other than below	$850		$850	
Depreciation	50	900		
Rental expense			60	910
Income before taxes		100		90
Capital charge $500 × 10%		50		
$200 × 10%				20
Residual income		50		70

Many leases are financing arrangements; that is, they provide an alternative way of obtaining the use of assets that otherwise would be acquired by funds obtained from debt and equity financing. Financial leases are usually viewed as being similar to debt. Financing decisions are usually made by corporate headquarters. For these reasons, restrictions are usually placed on the division manager's freedom to lease assets.

If a company acquired assets by means of a financial lease, *Statement of Financial Accounting Standard* No. 13 requires that these be shown on the financial statements at their capitalized amount. As a consequence, divisional assets acquired through financial leases will be consistent with assets acquired from direct investment.

Idle Assets

If a division has idle assets that can be used by other divisions, often the division is permitted to exclude them from the investment base if it classifies them as available. The purpose of this is to encourage division managers to release underutilized assets to divisions that may have better use for them. However, if the fixed assets cannot be used by other divisions, permitting the divisional manager to remove them from the investment base could result in dysfunctional actions. For example, it could encourage the division manager to idle partially utilized assets that are not earning a return equal to the division's profit objective. If there is no alternative use for the equipment, *any* contribution from this equipment will improve company profits.

Noncurrent Liabilities

Ordinarily, a division receives its permanent capital from the corporate pool of funds. The corporation obtained these funds from debt securities, from equity investors, and from retained earnings. To the division, the total amount of these funds is relevant; but the sources from which they were obtained are irrelevant. In unusual situations, however, a division's financing may be peculiar to its own situation. For example, a division that builds or operates residential housing uses a much larger proportion of debt capital than is the case with typical manufacturing and marketing divisions. Since this capital is obtained through mortgage loans on the division's assets, it may be appropriate to account for the borrowed funds separately and to compute a residual income based on the assets that were obtained from general corporate sources, rather than on total assets.

The Capital Charge

The rate used to calculate the capital charge is set by corporate headquarters. It should be higher than the corporation's rate for debt financing because the funds involved are a mixture of debt and higher cost equity. Usually, the rate is set somewhat below the company's estimated cost of capital (assuming that a company can calculate its cost of capital, which rarely is the case) so that the residual income of an average division will be above zero.

Although conceptually a good argument could be made for using different rates for divisions with different risk characteristics, in practice this is rarely done; that is, the same rate is used for all divisions. Some companies do use a lower rate for working capital than for fixed assets. This may represent a judgment that working capital is less risky than fixed assets because the funds are committed for a shorter time period. In other cases, the lower rate is a way of compensating for the fact that the company included inventory and receivables in the investment base at their gross amount (i.e., without a deduction for accounts payable); the lower rate is an implicit recognition of the fact that funds obtained from accounts payable have no interest.

Industry Practice

The great majority of companies include fixed assets in their investment base at their net book value. They do this because this is the amount at which the assets are carried in the financial accounts and therefore represents, according to the accounts, the amount of capital that the corporation has employed in the division. Managements recognize the fact that this method gives misleading signals; but they believe it is the responsibility of users of the divisional profit reports to make allowances for these errors in interpreting the reports, and that alternative methods of calculating the investment base are so subjective that they are not to be trusted. They reject the annuity depreciation approach on the grounds that it is inconsistent with the way in which depreciation is calculated for financial statement purposes.

The foregoing description indicates a large number of alternatives exist for calculating the investment base. Some are better than others for the purposes for which divisional residual income or return on investment are used. No practical method provides a perfect measure of the profitability of the division. Considerable thought is warranted in deciding on the best set of rules for a given situation.

RESIDUAL INCOME VERSUS ROI

Most companies employing investment centers evaluate divisions on the basis of the return on investment percentage. They do this because the meaning of ROI is well understood, and ROI data are available for other companies or industries that can be used as a basis of comparison. The dollar amount of residual income does not provide such a basis for comparison. Nevertheless, the residual income approach has some inherent advantages over ROI.

The most important advantage of residual income over ROI is that all divisions will have the same profit objectives for comparable investments, while the ROI approach provides a different incentive for investments.

An ROI objective may be a constant objective set by top management that is meant to represent the long-run potential of the division, or it may be an annual objective based, for example, on the profit budget. If a division is expected to meet a constant ROI objective, a division manager will not be likely to propose a capital investment unless it is expected to earn a return at least as high as this objective. Thus, a division with an objective of 20 percent ROI would not invest at less than this rate, while a division with an objective of 5 percent ROI would benefit from anything over this rate. Since the profit objectives of some divisions are higher than the company's overall rate of return for capital expenditures, and the profit objectives of other divisions are lower, this situation can cause seriously dysfunctional capital investment actions. For similar reasons, inventories in one division will have a different implicit carrying charge from identical types of inventories in another division that has a different profit objective.

It can be argued, of course, that, if the ROI objective is based on the annual profit budget, the ROI objective will be reduced to take into account the planned investment for the coming year when it is more than the planned investment for the current year. Thus, a manager with a 1982 ROI objective of 25 percent would still be motivated to make an investment in 1983 that earned only 15 percent, because the 1983 ROI objective would be reduced to take into account the new investment. In some cases, this might be a valid argument. Much depends on how divisional managers are evaluated, however. If they are evaluated on the basis of *both* budgeted profits and budgeted investment, separately, then the argument is valid. However, in this instance, the managers are being evaluated on the basis of two separate measures and, thus, it is not on their ROI objective. If they are evaluated on the basis of meeting their ROI objective, then they could well be motivated to take action contrary to the company's interest. For example, if the ROI objective is 24 percent, they will decrease their ability to meet this objective if they use less than this rate in the inventory carrying charges when calculating optimum inventory levels. Also, they could improve their chances of meeting their profit objective by deferring investments that are expected to earn less than 24 percent, even though such investments had been included in their profit budget.

A second advantage of residual income is that different interest rates may be used for different types of assets. For example, a relatively low rate can be used for inventories, while a higher rate can be used for investments in fixed assets. Furthermore, different rates can be used for different types of fixed assets to take into account different degrees of risk. In short, the measurement system can be made consistent with the decision rules that affect the acquisition of the assets. It follows that the same type of asset can be required to earn the same return throughout the company, regardless of the profitability of the particular division. Thus, divisions should act consistently in decisions involving investments in new assets.

The difference between ROI and residual income is shown in Exhibit 8–10. Assume that the company's required rate of return for investing in fixed assets is 10 percent after taxes, and that the companywide cost of money tied up in inventories and receivables is 4 percent after taxes. The top section of Exhibit 8–10 shows the ROI calculation. Columns 1 through 5 show the amount of investment in assets that has been budgeted by each division for the coming year. Column 6 is the amount of budgeted profit. Column 7 is the budgeted profit divided by the budgeted investment. Column 7 shows, therefore, the ROI objectives for the coming year for each of the divisions.

EXHIBIT 8–10 Difference between ROI and RI ($000)

ROI Method:

Division	(1) Cash	(2) Receivables	(3) Inventories	(4) Fixed assets	(5) Total investment	(6) Budgeted profit	(7) ROI objective
A.	$10	$20	$30	$60	$120	$24.0	20%
B.	20	20	30	50	120	14.4	12
C	15	40	40	10	105	10.5	10
D	5	10	20	40	75	3.8	5
E.	10	5	10	10	35	(1.8)	(5)

Residual Income Method:

		Current assets			Fixed assets			
Division	(1) Profit potential	(2) Amount	(3) Rate	(4) Required earnings	(5) Amount	(6) Rate	(7) Required earnings	Budgeted residual income (1) − [(4) + (7)]
A.	24.0	$60	4%	$2.4	$60	10%	$6.0	$15.6
B.	14.4	70	4	2.8	50	10	5.0	6.6
C.	10.5	95	4	3.8	10	10	1.0	5.7
D.	3.8	35	4	1.4	40	10	4.0	(1.6)
E	(1.8)	25	4	1.0	10	10	1.0	(3.8)

In only one division (C) is the ROI objective consistent with the company-wide cutoff rate, and in no division is the objective consistent with the company-wide 4% cost of carrying current assets.

Division A would decrease its chances of meeting its profit objective, if it did not earn at least 20 percent on added investments in either current or fixed assets; whereas divisions D and E would benefit from investments with a much lower return.

The residual income method corrects these inconsistencies in the following manner: The profit budget of each division is calculated. The investments, multiplied by the appropriate rates (representing the companywide rules), are subtracted from the budgeted profit. The resulting amount is the budgeted residual income. Periodically, the actual residual income is calculated by subtracting from the actual profits the actual investment multiplied by the appropriate rates. The lower section of Exhibit 8–10 shows how the budgeted residual income would be calculated.

For example, if Division A earned $28,000 and employed average current assets of $65,000 and average fixed assets of $65,000, its actual residual income would be calculated as follows:

$$\begin{aligned} RI &= 28{,}000 - .04(65{,}000) - .10(65{,}000) \\ &= 28{,}000 - 2{,}600 - 6{,}500 \\ &= 18{,}900 \end{aligned}$$

This is $3,300 = ($18,900 − $15,600) better than its objective. Note that if any division earns more than 10 percent on added fixed assets, it will increase its residual income. (In the case of C and D, the additional profit will decrease the amount of negative residual income, which amounts to the same thing.) A similar result occurs for current assets. Inventory decision rules will be based on a cost of 4 percent for financial carrying charges. (There will be, of course, additional costs for physically storing the inventory.) In this way, the financial decision rules of the divisions will be consistent with those of the company.

The residual income method solves the problem of differing profit objectives for the same asset in different divisions and the same profit objective for different assets in the same division. Residual income makes it possible to incorporate in the measurement system the same decision rules that are used in the planning process. The more sophisticated the planning process, the more complex can be the residual income calculation. For example, assume that the capital investment decision rules called for a 10 percent return on general-purpose assets and 15 percent return on special-purpose assets. Divisional fixed assets could be classified accordingly, and different rates applied when measuring performance. (Managers may be reluctant to make new nonprofitable investments that improve working conditions, reduce pollution, or meet other social goals. Investments of this type would be much more acceptable to divisional managers if they are expected to earn a reduced return on them.)

It should be noted that many companies use a capital charge that is less than the required earnings rate. That is, the capital charge is frequently closer to the company's borrowing rate than to its cost of capital. To the extent that this inconsistency exists, residual income will not achieve perfectly the results described above.

Analysis of Economic Performance

Although ROI has severe limitations as a measure of management performance, it is useful as a measure of economic performance. Areas of profit deficiency can be diagnosed and, thus, management's attention may be directed to potential areas of improvement. Areas for analysis could include divisions, product lines, geographical areas, and so forth. The analyst should start with the accounting results adjusted if accounting conventions resulted in unrealistic amounts. Fixed assets might be adjusted to economic values, LIFO inventories increased to current market value, and depreciation adjusted to reflect a realistic amount based on the economic value of the assets. The life of the asset could be adjusted to the best estimate of its actual life, if this is different from the average life used in the accounting records. Profits could be adjusted for unusual or nonrecurring items. After these adjustments, the return on investment can be calculated for all meaningful activities. Those showing less than a satisfactory return are candidates for further study—to find out how profits can be improved or to decide whether the activity should be discontinued. Note, however, that this analysis would be merely for diagnosis. Any action must be based on an evaluation of future cash flows for alternative courses of action.

Using ROI as a diagnostic technique does not result in the problems created by using ROI to measure managerial performance because:

1. Analysts can make such adjustments to the accounting data as they believe are necessary to make them meaningful. Consequently, it is not necessary to convince a divisional manager of the appropriateness of the adjustments, because they are not held accountable for them.
2. The results of the analysis are used to pinpoint areas that need attention. The action taken would depend on the circumstances; however, this action would not be aimed at improving ROI, but rather at improving cash flow.

ALTERNATIVES TO INVESTMENT CENTERS

The residual income method does not solve all the problems of measuring profitability in an investment center. In particular, it does not solve the problem of accounting for fixed assets discussed above unless annuity depreciation is also used, and this is rarely done in practice. If gross book value is used, a division can increase its residual income by taking action contrary to the interest of the company, as shown in Exhibit 8–2. If net book value is used, residual income will increase simply from the passage of time. Furthermore, residual income will be temporarily depressed by new investments because of the high net book value in the early years. Residual income does solve the problem created by differing profit potential. All divisions, regardless of profitability, will be motivated to increase investments if the rate of return from a potential investment exceeds the required rate prescribed by the measurement system.

Another problem of measuring the investment base is that some assets tend to be undervalued when they are capitalized, and others are omitted altogether. Many elements of investment are expensed, rather than capitalized. Although the purchase cost of fixed assets is ordinarily capitalized, an equal amount of investment in start-up costs, new product development, dealer organization, and so forth may be written off as expenses and, therefore, not appear in the investment base. This situation applies especially in marketing divisions. Often in these divisions the accounted investment is limited to inventories, receivables, and office furniture and equipment. In a purely marketing division, the understatement of true investment is usually clear; consequently, residual income is often ignored. However, when a group of divisions with varying degrees of marketing responsibility are ranked, the division with the relatively smaller manufacturing operations will tend to have the highest residual income.

In view of all these problems, some companies have decided not to create investment centers. The alternative is to make an interest charge for controllable assets only, and to control fixed assets by separate devices.

Controllable assets are, essentially, receivables and inventory. Divisional management can make day-to-day decisions that affect the level of these assets. If these decisions are wrong, serious consequences can occur—quickly. For example, if inventories are too high, unnecessary capital is tied up in them and the risk of obsolescence is increased; whereas, if inventories are too low, production interruptions or lost customer business can result from the stockouts. To focus attention on these important, controllable items, some companies include a capital charge for them as an element of cost in the divisional income statement. This acts both to motivate divisional management properly and also to measure the real cost of resources committed to these items.

Investments in fixed assets are controlled by the capital budgeting process before the fact and by postcompletion audits to determine whether the anticipated cash flows, in fact, materialized. This is far from completely satisfactory, of course, because often it is not possible to measure precisely how actual results compare with those predicted in the original projects. In most cases, however, serious deviations can be ascertained.

The argument for evaluating profits and investments separately is that this often is consistent with what senior management wishes the divisional manager to accomplish; namely, to obtain the maximum long-run cash flow from the investments the manager controls, and to add investments only when they will provide a net return in excess of the company's cost of providing that investment.

Investment decisions are controlled at the point where these decisions are made. Consequently, the capital investment analysis procedure is of primary importance in investment control. Once the investment has been made, it is largely a sunk cost and should not influence future decisions. Nevertheless, management wants to know when capital investment decisions have been made incorrectly, both because some action may be appropriate with respect to the person responsible for the mistakes, and also because some safeguard to prevent a recurrence may be appropriate.

At best, residual income will not provide accurate information on the effectiveness of new investment decisions, because divisional profits are affected by many factors other than the consequences of new investments. Companies that use ROI or residual income, therefore, must also use some form of postcompletion audit if they are to control capital investments adequately.

Students of management control systems disagree on whether it is better to use residual income or whether it is better to evaluate profit performance and investment performance separately. Most seem to favor residual income. The main reason is the belief that it is important to have a single measurement of financial performance. For example, if the actual profit was better than the budgeted profit and the investment performance was worse, how does management measure the overall financial performance? Residual income weighs the impact of the poorer investment performance against the improved profit performance and provides this single measure. Another reason for using residual income is that it might motivate managers to be more careful about adding investments that may not be profitable. A third reason is that only major capital expenditures can be examined carefully by corporate headquarters. Many minors acquisitions (e.g., routine replacements) are for practical purposes almost solely decided by the divisional manager and, in total, these can be significant.

In view of the disadvantages of ROI, it seems surprising that it is so widely used in the United States. Reece and Cool conclude that the disadvantages of ROI are exaggerated, and that designers of control systems are aware of the conceptual flaws of the ROI approach but do not believe that these flaws are more than hypothetical. We know from personal experience that the conceptual flaws of ROI for performance evaluation are real and do result in dysfunctional conduct on the part of divisional managers. We are unable to determine the extent of this dysfunctional conduct, however, because few managers are likely to admit its existence and many are unaware of it when it *does* exist. The likelihood of dysfunctional conduct seems related to the importance attached to meeting the ROI objective. Some companies calculate the divisional ROI but place primary importance on some other financial objective for evaluating performance (e.g., meeting the budgeted profit goal). Other companies, however, *do* place primary emphasis on meeting the ROI objective and this latter group is in greater danger of inducing dysfunctional actions on the part of divisional managers.

CORPORATE RECOVERY RATE

Yuji Ijiri has proposed a method of measuring financial performance, which he called the "Corporate Recovery Rate," or CRR.[6]

---

[6] Yuji Ijiri, "Recovery Rate and Cash Flow Accounting," *The Financial Executive*, March 1980.

CRR is a ratio. The numerator is the algebraic sum of the cash flow from operations, interest expense, changes in working capital, and proceeds from the sale of fixed assets. The denominator is the sum of all assets in operation, with fixed assets included at their gross book value.

It is proposed that the CRR should replace ROI in measuring the financial performance of businesses or segments of businesses. First, cash flow is *not* subject to the more-or-less arbitrary accounting rules. Second, this is the same technique that is used to calculate the return on investment in capital budgeting analysis. If the cash flows are equal and the life of the investment can be estimated within reasonable limits, the reciprocal of the CRR will be the basis for calculating the internal rate of return. For example, if the cash flows were $150 per year and the investment $1,000 and the life 10 years, the CRR would be 150/1,000 or 15 percent. The reciprocal then is 1,000/150 = 6.67, which is, of course, the payback. From a present value table, the internal rate of return of this project is 8.1 percent.

Ijiri was concerned primarily with using CRR as a measure of past financial performance. Kaplan,[7] however, suggests that it might be used as a method for measuring investment center performance. He suggests that "a residual cash flow measure, analogous to the RI measure, might provide a better base for maximizing behavior of divisional managers."[8] It is true that, for an expansion project, the RI would be increased if the actual internal rate of return exceeded the RI return, assuming that (1) the cash flows were equal each year and (2) the time period of each project was the same as the average time used to determine the IR percentage. However, in real life, annual cash flows are almost never equal, and the length of the life of projects will vary considerably. Also, although the technique could work with new projects, considerable distortion would result in replacement projects. Since fixed assets are included in the investment base at gross book value, the increase in assets in a replacement investment will be equal to the difference between the cost of the new asset and the cost of the old asset. Normally, this will be considerably less than the actual cash invested. The rate of return on a replacement investment, therefore, could be considerably higher for the division than the true rate earned by the company. Consequently, this technique will not solve the problems described earlier in this chapter.

---

[7] Kaplan, Robert S., *Advanced Management Accounting* (Englewood Cliffs, N.J.: Prentice-Hall, 1982), pp. 546–48.

[8] Ibid, p. 548.

CASE 8–1
Investment Center Problems*

1. The ABC Company has three divisions—A, B, and C. Division A is exclusively a marketing division; Division B is exclusively a manufacturing division; and Division C is both a manufacturing and marketing division. Listed below are some financial facts for each of these divisions:

	Division A	*Division B*	*Division C*
Current assets	$100,000	$ 100,000	$100,000
Fixed assets	—	1,000,000	500,000
Total assets	$100,000	$1,100,000	$600,000
Profits before depreciation and market development costs	$200,000	$200,000	$200,000

Required:

Assume that the ABC Company depreciates fixed assets on a straight-line basis over 10 years. To maintain its markets and productive facilities, it has to invest $100,000 per year in market development in Division A and $50,000 per year in Division C. This is written off as an expense. It also has to replace 10 percent of its productive facilities each year. Under these equilibrium conditions, what are the annual rates of return earned by each of the divisions?

2. The D Division of the DEF Corporation has budgeted aftertax profits of $1 million for 1983. It has budgeted assets as of January 1, 1983, of $10 million, consisting of $4 million in current assets and $6 million in fixed assets. Fixed assets are included in the asset base at gross book value. The net book value of these fixed assets is $3 million. All fixed assets are depreciated over a 10-year period on a straight-line basis.

   The manager of the D Division has submitted a capital investment project to replace a major group of machines. The financial details of this project are as follows:

New equipment:	
Estimated cost	$2,000,000
Estimated aftertax annual savings*	300,000
Estimated life	10 years

* Note: In solving these problems, ignore income taxes. Most of the problems state that savings or earnings are "after taxes." Assume that the amount of income taxes will not be affected by alternative accounting treatment.

Old equipment to be replaced:	
Original cost	$1,500,000
Original estimate of life	10 years
Present age	7 years
Present book value ($1,500,000 − $1,050,000)	$450,000
Salvage value	0

*These are cash inflows, disregarding depreciation and capital gains or losses (except for their tax impact).

Required:

The capital investment project was approved and the new machinery was installed on January 1, 1983. Calculate the rate of return that is earned on the new investment, using the divisional accounting rules, and calculate the revised 1983 and 1984 budgeted rate of return:

a. Assuming that the investment and savings are exactly as stated in the project.

b. Assuming that the investment is overrun by $500,000 and the annual savings are only $200,000.

3. Assume that everything is as stated in problem 2, except that the fixed assets are included in the divisional assets base at their net book value at the end of the year. Answer the questions in problem 2 for 1983 and 1984.

4. The G Division of the GHI Corporation proposes the following investment in a new product line.

Investment in fixed assets	$100,000
Annual profits before depreciation but after taxes (i.e., annual cash flow)	25,000
Life	5 years

The GHI Corporation uses the time-adjusted rate of return, with a cutoff rate of 8 percent in evaluating its capital investment proposals. A $25,000 cash inflow for five years on an investment of $100,000 has a time-adjusted return of 8 percent. Consequently, the proposed investment is acceptable under the company's criterion. Assume that the project is approved and that the investment and profit were the same as estimated. Assets are included in the divisional investment base at the average of the beginning of the year's net book value.

Required:

a. Calculate the rate of return that is earned by the G Division on the new investment for each year and the average rate for the five years, using straight-line depreciation.

b. Calculate the rate of return that is earned by the G Division on the new investment for each year, and the average for the five years using the sum-of-the-years'-digits depreciation.

5. A proposed investment of $100,000 in fixed assets is expected to yield aftertax cash flows of $16,275 a year for 10 years. Calculate a depreciation schedule, based on annuity-type depreciation, that provides an equal rate of return each year on the investment at the beginning of the year, assuming that the investment and earnings are the same as estimated.

6. The JKL Company uses the residual income method for measuring divisional profit performance. The company charges each division a 5 percent return on its average current assets and a 10 percent return on its average fixed assets. Listed below are some financial statistics for three divisions of the JKL Company.

	Division		
	J	*K*	*L*
Budget data ($000s):			
1983 budgeted profit	$ 90	$ 55	$ 50
1983 budgeted current assets	100	200	300
1983 budgeted fixed assets	400	400	500
Actual data ($000s):			
1983 profits	80	60	50
1983 current assets	90	190	350
1983 fixed assets	400	450	550

Required:

a. Calculate the ROI objective and actual ROI for each division for 1983.
b. Calculate the RI objective for each division for 1983.
c. Calculate the actual RI for each division for 1983 and calculate the extent that it is above or below objective.

7. Refer to the budgeted profits and assets of the three divisions of the JKL Company provided in problem 6. Listed below are four management actions, together with the financial impact of these actions. For each of these situations, calculate the impact on the budgeted ROI and RI for each division. (Another way of looking at this problem is to calculate the extent to which these actions help or hurt the divisional managers in attaining their profit goals.)

Situation 1. An investment in fixed assets is made. This action increases the average fixed assets by $100,000 and profits by $10,000.

Situation 2. An investment in fixed assets is made. This action increases the average assets by $100,000 and profits by $7000.

Situation 3. A program to reduce inventories is instituted. As a result inventories are reduced by $50,000. Increased costs and reduced sales resulting from the lower inventory levels reduce profits by $5000.

Situation 4. A plant is closed down and sold. Fixed assets are reduced by $75,000 and profits from reduced sales are decreased by $7500.

CASE 8–2
Marden Company

A typical division of Marden Company had financial statements as shown in Exhibit 1. Accounts receivable were billed by the division, but customers make payment to bank accounts (i.e., lockboxes) maintained in the name of Marden Company and located throughout the country. The debt item on the balance sheet is a proportionate part of the corporate 9 percent bond issue. Interest on this debt was not charged to the division.

EXHIBIT 1

MARDEN COMPANY
Typical Division Financial Statements
Balance Sheet,
End of Year (condensed; $000)

Assets		*Equities*	
Cash	$ 100	Accounts payable	$ 400
Accounts receivable	800		
Inventory	900		
Total current assets	1,800	Total current liabilities	400
Plant and equipment, cost	1,000	Debt	700
Depreciation (straight line)	400	Equity	1,300
Plant and equipment, net	600		2,000
Total assets	$2,400	Total equities	$2,400

Divisional Income Statement

Sales	$4,000
Costs, other than those listed below	3,200
Depreciation	100
Allocated share of corporate expenses	100
Income before income tax	600

Question

Recommend the best way of measuring the performance of the division manager. If you need additional information, make the assumption you believe to be most reasonable.

CASE 8–3
Diversified Products Corporation*

The Diversified Products Corporation manufactured consumer and industrial products in more than a dozen divisions. Plants were located throughout the country, one or more to a division, and company headquarters was in a large eastern city. Each division was run by a division manager and had its own balance sheet and income statement. The company made extensive use of long- and short-run planning programs, which included budgets for sales, costs, expenditures, and rate of return on investment. Monthly reports on operating results were sent in by each division and were reviewed by headquarters executives.

The Able Division of the Diversified Products Corporation manufactured and assembled large industrial pumps, most of which sold for more than $1,000. A great variety of models were made to order from the standard parts that the division either bought or manufactured for stock. In addition, components were individually designed and fabricated when pumps were made for special applications. A variety of metalworking machines were used, some large and heavy, and a few designed especially for the division's kind of business.

The division operated three plants, two of which were much smaller than the third and were located in distant parts of the country. Headquarters offices were located in the main plant, where more than 1,000 people were employed. They performed design and manufacturing operations as well as the usual staff and clerical work. Marketing activities were carried out by sales engineers in the field, who worked closely with customers on design and installation. Reporting to Mr. Allen, the division manager, were men in charge of design, sales, manufacturing, purchasing, and budgets.

The division's product line had been broken down into five product groups, so that the profitability of each could be studied separately. Evaluation was based on the margin above factory cost as a percentage of sales. No attempt had been made to allocate investment to the product lines. The budget director said this not only would be difficult in view of the common facilities, but also such a mathematical computation would not provide any new information, since the products had approximately the same turnover of assets. Furthermore, he said it was difficult enough to allocate common factory costs between products, and even margin on sales was a disputable figure. "If we were larger,"

---

* Although not previously copyrighted, this case was written by Professor William Rotch, University of Virginia, published by Intercollegiate Case Clearing House (ICH4C53R), Soldiers Field, Boston, and reproduced here with the permission of the author.

he said, "and had separate facilities for each product line, we might be able to do it. But it wouldn't mean much in this division right now."

Only half a dozen men ever looked at the division's rate of return, for other measures were used in the division's internal control system. The division manager used shipments per week and certain cost areas, such as overtime payments, to check on divisional operations.

THE DIVISION MANAGER'S CONTROL OF ASSETS

During 1983, the total assets of the Able Division were turned over approximately 1.7 times, and late that year they were made up as follows:

Cash	12%
Accounts receivable	21
Inventory:	
Raw material	7
About 3% metal stock	
About 4% purchased parts	
Work-in-process	11
About 7% manufactured parts	
About 4% floor stocks	
Finished goods	2
Machinery (original cost)	29
Land and buildings (original cost)	18
	100%

Cash (12 Percent of Total Assets)

The Able Division, like all divisions in the Diversified Products Corporation, maintained a petty cash account in a local bank to which company headquarters transferred funds as they were needed. This local working account was used primarily for making up the plant payroll and for payment of other local bills. Payment of suppliers' invoices as well as collection of accounts receivable was handled by headquarters for Able as well as for most of the other divisions.

The division's cash account at headquarters was shown on the division's balance sheet as cash and marketable securities. The amount shown as cash had been established by agreement between top management and the division manager, and was considered by both to be about the minimum amount necessary to operate the division. The excess above this amount was shown on the division's balance sheet as marketable securities, and earned interest from headquarters at the rate of 6 percent a year. It was this account which varied with receipts and disbursements, leaving the cash account fixed as long as there was a balance in the securities account. It was possible for the securities account to be wiped out and for cash to decline below the minimum agreed on; but if this continued for more than a month or two, corrective action was taken. For Able Division, the minimum level was equal to about one month's sales, and in recent years cash had seldom gone below this amount.

Whether or not the company as a whole actually owned cash and marketable securities equal to the sum of all the respective divisions' cash and security accounts was strictly a headquarters matter. It probably was not necessary to hold this amount of cash and securities, since the division accounts had to cover division peak needs and, from headquarters' point of view, not all the peak needs necessarily occurred at the same time.

The size of a division's combined cash and marketable securities accounts was directly affected by all phases of the division's operations that used or produced cash. It also was affected in three other ways. One was the automatic deduction of 48 percent of income for tax purposes. Another was the payment of "dividends" by the division to headquarters. All earnings that the division manager did not wish to keep for future use were transferred to the corporation's cash account by payment of a dividend. Since a division was expected to retain a sufficient balance to provide for capital expenditures, dividends were paid generally only by the profitable divisions that were not expanding rapidly.

The third action affecting the cash account occurred if cash declined below the minimum, of if extensive capital expenditures had been approved. A division might then "borrow" from headquarters, paying interest as if it were a separate company. At the end of 1983, the Able Division had no loan and had been able to operate since about 1976 without borrowing from headquarters. Borrowing was not, in fact, currently being considered by the Able Division.

Except for its part in the establishment of a minimum cash level, top management was not involved in the determination of the division's investment in cash and marketable securities. Mr. Allen could control the level of this investment by deciding how much was to be paid in dividends. Since only a 6 percent return was received on the marketable securities and since the division earned more than that on its total investment, it was to its advantage to pay out as much as possible in dividends. When asked how he determined the size of the dividends, Mr. Allen said that he simply kept what he thought he would need to cover peak demands, capital expenditures, and contingencies. Improving the division's rate of return may have been part of the decision, but he did not mention it.

Accounts Receivable (21 Percent of Total Assets)

All accounts receivable for the Able Division were collected at company headquarters. Around the 20th of each month, the accounts were run off and the report was forwarded to the division. Though, in theory, Mr. Allen was allowed to set his own terms for divisional sales, in practice it would have been difficult to change the company's usual terms. Since Able Division sold to important customers of other divisions, any change from the net-30-days terms would disturb a large segment of the corporation's business. Furthermore, industry practice was well established, and the division would hardly try to change it.

The possibility of cash sales in situations in which credit was poor was virtually nonexistent. Credit was investigated for all customers by the headquarters credit department, and no sales were made without a prior credit check. For the Able Division, this policy presented no problem, for it sold primarily to well-established customers.

Inventory, Raw Material Metal Stock (about 3 Percent of Total Investment)

In late 1983, inventory as a whole made up 20 percent of Able Division's total assets. A subdivision of the various kinds of inventory showed that raw material accounted for 7 percent; work-in-process, 11 percent; and finished goods and miscellaneous supplies, 2 percent. Since the Able Division produced to order, finished goods inventory was normally small, leaving raw material and work-in-process as the most significant classes of inventory.

The raw material inventory could be further subdivided to separate the raw material inventory from a variety of purchased parts. The strictly raw material inventory was composed primarily of metals and shapes, such as steel sheets or copper tubes. Most of the steel was bought according to a schedule arranged with the steel companies several months ahead of the delivery date. About a month before the steel company was to ship the order, Able Division would send the rolling instructions by shapes and weights. If the weight on any particular shape was below a minimum set by the steel company, Able Division would pay an extra charge for processing. Although this method of purchasing accounted for the bulk of steel purchases, smaller amounts were also bought as needed from warehouse stocks and specialty producers.

Copper was bought by headquarters and processed by the company's own mill. The divisions could buy the quantities they needed, but the price paid depended on corporate buying practices and processing costs. The price paid by Able Division had generally been competitive with outside sources, though it often lagged behind the market both in increases and in reductions in price.

The amounts of copper and steel bought were usually determined by the purchasing agent without recourse to any formal calculations of an economic ordering quantity. The reason for this was that, since such a large number of uncertain factors continually had to be estimated, a formal computation would not improve the process of determining how much to buy. Purchases depended on the amounts on hand, expected consumption, and current delivery time and price expectations. If delivery was fast, smaller amounts were usually bought. If a price increase was anticipated, somewhat larger orders often were placed at the current price. Larger amounts of steel were bought, for example, just before an anticipated steel strike, when steel negotiations were expected to result in a price increase, and perhaps also in a delay in deliveries.

The level of investment in raw material varied with the rates of purchase and use. Mr. Allen could control this class of asset within a fairly wide range, and there were no top management directives governing the size of his raw material inventory.

Inventory, Purchased Parts and Manufactured Parts (about 11 Percent of Total Assets—4 Percent from Raw Material, 7 Percent from Work-in-process)

The Able Division purchased and manufactured parts for stock to be used later in the assembly of pumps. The method used to determine the purchase quantity was the same as that used to determine the length of production run on parts made for work-in-process stocks. The number of parts bought or manufactured was based on a series of calculations of an economical ordering quantity (EOQ).

Inventory, Floor Stocks (about 4 Percent of Total Investment)

Floor stock inventory consisted of parts and components being worked on and assembled. Items became part of the floor stock inventory when they were requisitioned from the storage areas, or when delivered directly to the production floor. Pumps were worked on individually, so that lot size was not a factor to be considered. Mr. Allen could do little to control the level of floor stock inventory, except to see that there was no excess of parts piled around the production area.

Inventory, Finished Goods (2 Percent of Total Investment)

As a rule, pumps were made to order and for immediate shipment. Finished goods inventory consisted of those few pumps on which shipment was delayed. Control of this investment was a matter of keeping it low by shipping the pumps as fast as possible.

Land, Buildings, and Machinery (47 Percent of Total Investment)

Since the Able Division's fixed assets, stated at gross cost, comprised 47 percent of total assets at the end of 1983, the control of this particular group of assets was extremely important. Changes in the level of these investments depended on retirements and additions, the additions being entirely covered by the capital budgeting program.

Diversified Products Corporation's capital budgeting procedures were described in a planning manual. The planning sequence was as follows:

1. Headquarters forecasts economic conditions. (March)
2. The divisions plan long-term objectives. (June)
3. Supporting programs are submitted. (September) These are plans for specific actions, such as sales plans, advertising programs, and cost-reduction programs, and include the facilities program which is the capital expenditure request. The planning manual states under the heading, "General Approach in the Development of a Coordinated Supporting Program," this advice:

> Formulation and evaluation of a supporting program for each product line can generally be improved if projects are classified by purpose. The key objective of all planning is return on assets, a function of margin and turnover. These ratios are, in turn determined by the three factors in the business equation—volume, costs, and assets. All projects, therefore, should be directed primarily at one of the following:
>
> To increase volume.
> To reduce costs and expenses.
> To minimize assets.

4. Annual objective is submitted. (November 11, by 8:00 A.M.) The annual objective states projected sales, costs, expenses, profits, and cash expenditures and receipts, and shows pro forma balance sheets and income statements.

Mr. Allen was "responsible for the division's assets and for provision for the growth and expansion of the division." Growth referred to the internal refinements of product design and production methods as well as to the cost-reduction programs. Expansion involved a 5- or 10-year program, including about 2 years for construction.

In the actual capital expenditure request there were four kinds of facilities proposals:

1. Cost-reduction projects, which were self-liquidating investments. Reduction in labor costs was usually the largest source of the savings, which were stated in terms of the liquidation period and the rate of return.
2. Necessity projects. These included replacement of worn-out machinery, technical changes to meet competition, and facilities for the safety and comfort of the workers.
3. Product-improvement projects.
4. Expansion projects.

Justification of the cost-reduction proposals was based on a comparison of the estimated rate of return (estimated return before taxes divided by gross investment) with the 20 percent standard, as specified by headquarters. If the project was considered desirable and yet showed a return of less than 20 percent, it had to be justified on other grounds and was included in the necessities category. Cost-reduction proposals made up about 60 percent of the 1984 capital expenditure budget, and in earlier years these proposals had accounted for at least 50 percent. Very little of Able Division's 1984 capital budget had been allocated specifically for product improvement and none for expansion, so that most of the remaining 40 percent was to be used for necessity projects. Thus, a little over half of Able Division's capital expenditure was justified primarily on the estimated rate of return on the investment. The remainder, having advantages that could not be stated in terms of the rate of return, was justified on other grounds.

Mr. Allen was free to include what he wanted in his capital budget request, and for the three years that he had been division manager his requests had always been granted. However, no large expansion projects had been included in the capital budget requests of the last three years. Most of the capital expenditures had been for cost-reduction projects, and the remainder were for necessities. Annual additions had approximately equaled annual retirements.

Since Mr. Allen could authorize expenditures of up to $100,000 per project for purposes approved by the board, there was, in fact, some flexibility in his choice of projects after the budget had been approved by higher management. Not only could he schedule the order of expenditure but, in some circumstances, he could substitute unforeseen projects of a similar nature. If top management approved $50,000 for miscellaneous cost-reduction projects, Mr. Allen could spend this on the projects he considered most important, whether or not they were specifically described in his original budget request.

For the corporation as a whole, about one quarter of the capital expenditure was for projects of under $100,000, which could be authorized for expenditure by the division managers. This portion was considered by top management to be about right; if, however, it rose much above this fraction, the $100,000 dividing line would probably be lowered.

Questions

1. For each asset category, discuss whether the basis of measurement used by the company is the best for the purpose of measuring divisional return on investment. If, in your opinion, it is not the best, suggest an improvement.
2. Comment on the general usefulness of the return-on-investment measure. Could it be made a more effective device?

CASE 8–4
Cheetah Division*

The Cheetah Division of the Multi-National Motors Corporation designed and sold Cheetah automobiles and parts to dealers throughout the United States and Europe. The division was responsible for designing, engineering, and marketing its products; but the Assembly Division manufactured Cheetah products.

Each division of Multi-National Motors was responsible for earning a return on its investment. Investment in Multi-National was calculated as follows:

Cash: 10 percent of the costs of sales.
Receivables } Average end-of-month actual balances.
Inventories }
Fixed assets: Average actual gross book value at end of the month.

Profits were calculated in accordance with the company's accounting system. Because of its relatively low asset base (few fixed assets) and its high profit potential, the Cheetah Division had a profit objective of 45 percent after taxes.

INVENTORY CONTROL PROBLEM

In addition to marketing automobiles, the Cheetah Division was responsible for supplying repair and replacement parts and accessories to its dealers throughout the country. This required an extensive warehouse system since parts were supplied for automobiles as much as 15 years old. The system handled over 20,000 different parts, with annual sales in excess of $100 million.

In 1983, the corporation established an operations research group, with responsibility for reviewing inventory control procedures throughout the company. In carrying out this assignment, members of this group visited the Cheetah Division.

An important inventory control problem was one involving buying current model parts at the end of the model year. At the end of each model year, any parts to be discontinued with the new model became past model service parts. A past model service part was usually much more expensive to produce (and consequently buy) than a current model part because of setup time and the short length of the run. For example, at the end of the 1983 model year, front fenders were to be changed. During regular production, fenders were run continuously over an automated line. There was no setup cost, and production was

* This case was prepared by John Dearden, Harvard Business School.

very efficient. Consequently, the manufacturing cost of a 1983 fender was low during the 1983 model year. Once the part had been discontinued, however, the costs of production became quite high. It was necessary to pull the dies out of storage, clean them, place them in presses, try them out (usually involving spoiling a certain amount of material) and then run off the required number of parts without any automation. Thus, the cost of a past model service part was typically several times higher than what it was as a current model part.

Because of this cost differential, it was usual to order at the end of a model year a relatively large supply of those parts that were to be discontinued. A formula had been developed that provided the economic order quantity. This formula determined the point where the added cost of carrying the inventory was equal to the cost savings from buying at current model prices. The formula was quite complex and need not be described here. An important feature of the formula, however, was that the cost of carrying inventory included a return on the capital tied up in the inventory. The operation research group reviewed the formula and agreed that it was a reasonable method for calculating the economic order quantity. The group, however, was surprised to find that the Cheetah Division used a 45 percent capital cost for carrying inventory. Other divisions used between 10 and 15 percent in their inventory decision formulas. Currently, the corporation had over $500 million invested in government securities that were earning over 10 percent before taxes.

The operations research group raised two questions concerning the economic order quantity formula:

1. They questioned whether 45 percent was not much too high a percentage for the capital charge of carrying inventories. Their estimate was that it should be no more than 12 percent.
2. They questioned the fact that the Cheetah Division used the purchase price (charged by the Assembly Division) to calculate the investment in the inventory. The company's out-of-pocket cost of most parts was between 50 percent and 60 percent of the purchase price.

The controller of the Cheetah Division met with the operations research group and told them bluntly that he had no intention of changing the formula. This formula optimized his rate of return, he believed. If he followed the group's suggestions he would be lowering the rate of return that his division earned. He stated that if it was really to the benefit of the company for him to use a 12 percent cost of investment on 60 percent of his purchase price, he would be glad to comply provided that the Cheetah Division were given the benefit of the increased profit that the company would earn. Otherwise, he would continue to do as he was instructed—and that was to maximize the division's return on investment.

THE PARTS WAREHOUSE PROBLEM

In 1982 the Cheetah Division was in the process of building two new parts warehouses on the West Coast. At that time, the Sparrow Division of Multi-National requested that Cheetah provide some space in those warehouses for Sparrow parts. Sparrow was a much smaller division than Cheetah and could not justify economically a new warehouse. However, the location on the West Coast of two new supply points would improve the effectiveness of Sparrow's distribution system. Sparrow asked for space equal to about 10 percent of the total.

After the warehouses had been completed and both the Cheetah and Sparrow parts systems were placed in operation, the question of charging for the service came up. Cheetah proposed that Sparrow pay a proportionate share of the cost of running the warehouses plus a return on their proportionate share of the investment. The calculation was made as follows:

10% of cost of operating warehouses	$ 200,000
10% of the investment in warehouses:	
$2,000,000	
90% of $2,000,000.	1,800,000
Total annual charges	2,000,000

The Sparrow Division was astounded with the charge, which was several times higher than the going rate for available leased warehouse space. Sparrow agreed with the $200,000 but disagreed violently with paying $1,800,000 for the return on investment. The Cheetah Division pointed out that it had invested $2,000,000 at the request of Sparrow and that it had to earn $1,000,000 before taxes on this investment in order to earn 45 percent after taxes. The Sparrow Division said that it could lease space anywhere on the West Coast for a fraction of Cheetah's charge and that was what it proposed to do. Sparrow stated that Cheetah may have a 45 percent return but Sparrow was lucky to break even *without the exorbitant rental.*

Question

How should each of these problems be resolved?

CASE 8–5
Lemfert Company*

Lemfert Company was a large manufacturing company organized into divisions, each with responsibility for earning a satisfactory return on its investment. Division managers had considerable autonomy in carrying out this responsibility. Some divisions fabricated parts; others—here called "end-item divisions"—assembled these parts, together with purchased parts, into finished products and marketed the finished products. Transfer prices were used in connection with the transfer of parts among the various fabricating divisions and from the fabricating divisions to the end-item divisions. Wherever possible, these transfer prices were the lowest prices charged by outside manufacturers for the same or comparable items, with appropriate adjustments for inbound freight, volume, and similar factors.

Parts that were not similar to those manufactured by outside companies were called "type K items." In most fabricating divisions, these items constituted only 5 to 10 percent of total volume. In Division F, however, approximately 75 percent of total volume was accounted for by type K items. Division F manufactured 10 such items for various end-item divisions; they were less than 5 percent of the total cost of any one of these end-item divisions. The procedure for arriving at the transfer price for type K items is described below.

First, a tentative transfer price was calculated by the value analysis staff of the corporate purchasing department and was submitted to the two divisions involved for their consideration. This price was supposed to be based on the estimated costs of an efficient producer plus a profit margin. An "efficient producer" was considered to be one conducting its purchasing and using modern equipment in a manner that could reasonably be expected of the company's principal competitors.

The material cost portion of the total cost was based on current competitive price levels. Direct labor cost was supposed to reflect efficient processing on modern equipment. Overhead cost represented an amount that could be expected of an efficient producer using modern equipment. Depreciation expense, expenditures on special tooling, and a standard allowance for administrative expense were included in the overhead figure.

The profit margin was equal to the divisional profit objective applied to the cost of the assets employed to produce the product in question. Assets employed was the sum of the following items:

Cash and receivables—18 percent of the total manufacturing cost.

* This case was prepared by R. N. Anthony, Harvard Business School.

Inventories—the value of the optimum inventory size required at standard volume.

Fixed assets—the depreciated book value (but not less than one-half original cost) of assets used to fabricate the part, including a fair share of buildings and other general assets, but excluding standby and obsolete facilities.

The percentage used for cash and receivables was based on studies of the cash and receivable balances of the principal outside manufacturers of parts similar to those manufactured in the fabricating divisions. The standard volume was an estimate of the volume that the plants should *normally* be expected to produce, which was not necessarily the same as current volume or projected volume for the next year.

For an average division, the budgeted profit objective was 20 percent of assets employed; but there were variations among divisions. The divisional budget profit objective multiplied by the assets employed, as calculated above, gave the profit margin for the item. This profit was added to the cost to arrive at the suggested transfer price, which then was submitted to the two divisions. If either the buying or the selling division believed that the price thus determined was unfair, it first attempted to negotiate a mutually satisfactory price. If the parties were unable to agree, they submitted the dispute to the controller for arbitration. Either party might appeal the results of this arbitration to the executive vice president.

Questions

1. Are these the best transfer price practices for the Lemfert Company? If not, how should they be revised?
2. For what types of companies would the revised policy not be best? Why?
3. Do you think the attempt to measure profitability in Division F is worthwhile? If not, how would you measure performance in this division?

CASE 8–6
Schoppert Company

Mr. P. A. Franken, controller of Schoppert, was considering the appropriateness of available means for appraising the annual operating results for each of the company's product lines. Schoppert Gereedschapfabrieken, N.V., located near Leiden in the Netherlands, manufactured a variety of hand tools, such as wrenches, screwdrivers, chisels, and so forth. The company produced several hundred different products, but from the point of view of sales and production these could be grouped into five quite different product lines or groups.

Mr. Franken was interested in applying the concept of return on investment to the evaluation of the company's individual product lines. He stated his reasons for this as follows:

> When a company sells a number of different product groups there is a danger that the relative position of each product group in the total is judged by the profit made on the turnover of each separate group. There is a tendency to judge the yield of each group by comparing these percentages. In doing so, one forgets that the first purpose of a business is to make a profit on its employed capital, and that making a profit on the turnover is only a means to that purpose. As some of our product groups for a given turnover need a much higher employed capital than others, I think it is necessary to take these differences into account, by showing the profit in each product group as a percentage of the employed capital.

PRODUCT-LINE PROFIT

The company regularly prepared product-line income statements based on what was known as a cost price calculation. The profit for each product line was obtained by deducting product costs from turnover (sales) for the product line. There were four elements of cost in the product-line income statements, as follows:

1. *Variable cost.* These included raw materials, direct labor, paint, solder, and the like. These were standard costs, which were based on time studies, product specifications, and so forth, and could be traced directly to individual products. They tended to vary more or less proportionately with volume of production. These variable costs accounted for about 74 percent of total costs at normal volume levels.
2. *Direct fixed costs.* These included costs of operating and maintaining factory buildings (allocated on a square meter basis), costs of maintenance of machinery, machine depreciation, interest, cleaning, and so forth. All of these except the building costs could be readily traced to small groups of products. They were allocated to individual products on the basis of machine hours. These costs accounted for about 12 percent of total costs at normal volume levels.
3. *Plant costs.* These included such things as maintenance, operation, and depreciation of forklift trucks, salaries and wages of supervisory and clerical staffs, and maintenance of office buildings. These costs were allocated to product lines on a value-added basis; that is, the total of the costs included in groups 1 and 2 above, less

the costs of raw material. At usual operating levels they amounted to about 8 percent of total costs.

4. *Head office expenses.* These included wages and salaries of head office personnel and of management, maintenance and depreciation of head office buildings and equipment, and laboratory expense. They were allocated to products on the basis of the ratio of these costs to the total of costs in groups 1, 2, and 3, including raw material. They usually amounted to about 6 percent of all other costs.

These cost calculations provided a basis for overall evaluation of product lines and for selling price calculations. For control purposes the company had a system of manufacturing expense budgets and standards for the variable and traceable costs in each department.

PRODUCT-LINE INVESTMENT

Evaluation and appraisal of the results of each of the product lines was traditionally made by comparing this profit with sales. Mr. Franken, for reasons given earlier, felt that this product-line profit should be compared with the investment necessary to support production and sale of the product line.

EXHIBIT 1 Analysis of Product-line Profits*

	Product line					
	A	*B*	*C*	*D*	*E*	*Total*
Investment	fl. 56.0	fl. 11.8	fl. 1.6	fl. 1.0	fl. 0.6	fl. 71.0
Sales	118.0	18.5	3.3	1.2	1.0	142.0
Profits	4.5	.6	.4	.2	.2	5.5
Profit as percent of investment	8.0%	5.1%	25.0%	20.0%	33.3%	7.7%
Profits as percent of sales	3.8%	3.2%	12.1%	16.7%	20.0%	3.9%

* Monetary amounts are in millions of Dutch guilders.

To do this it was necessary to determine what the investment in each product line actually was. Mr. Franken made an analysis of product-line investments, which he regarded only as a preliminary step. His procedures are described below and the results, for the five product groups, are shown in Exhibit 1.

Current Assets

In the case of current assets, it was possible to trace the investment in stocks (inventories) directly to the product groups. Accounts receivable could also be traced to the product groups that gave rise to them.

Mr. Franken deducted accounts payable (also traceable to product lines) from accounts receivable in determining product-line investments.

Mr. Franken felt that it was not possible to relate cash to individual product groups: that the amount of cash required by any particular product group could not be determined accurately. Consequently, he excluded cash from his calculations of product-line investments.

Fixed Assets

In dealing with fixed assets, Mr. Franken used replacement value less accumulated depreciation, rather than net book value based on historical cost. He felt that the use of historical cost would make it impossible to compare departments with each other, if some utilized older machinery purchased when price levels were lower while others worked with machinery that had a much higher cost as a result of price inflation.

Mr. Franken initially used insured values as an estimate of replacement value, but he expected to develop a system of price indexes that would permit a more precise determination of replacement value. From insured value an allowance of 40 percent (of insured value) was deducted to give an approximation of replacement value less accumulated depreciation. In the case of depreciation, as in the case of replacement value, Mr. Franken looked forward to the development of more refined procedures for determining the amounts involved.

Most buildings, machinery, and equipment could be traced directly to individual product groups. In a great many cases, the machinery used by Schoppert was quite highly specialized and was used only for manufacturing certain specific products.

In the case of buildings and other facilities utilized by more than one product group, and in the case of such things as the company's head office and its research laboratory, the problem was considerably more complex. Mr. Franken simply allocated these costs to product lines on the basis of the costs that were traceable to the product lines.

The value of current assets (less accounts payable) and of machinery and equipment traced directly to product lines amounted to about 90 percent of total assets (not including cash and less accounts payable and depreciation). Thus, the allocated portion of product-line investment represented about 10 percent of the total.

Questions

1. What were Mr. Franken's objectives in designing the new product-line income statements?

2. Are the statements likely to meet these objectives in their present form, or would you suggest some improvements?

CASE 8–7
Quality Metal Service Center *(B)*

In early March 1982, Edward Brown, president and chief executive officer of Quality Metal Service Center, made the following comments to a case writer who was studying the company's management control system:

> Recently I read an article[1] where the authors argued that the short-term focus of corporate control systems is a possible factor leading to reduced productivity in the United States. Although I am satisfied with our past performance, I must admit that we are capable of achieving even higher levels of sales and profits. Considering the market expansion and the state of competition, I feel we might have missed out on some growth opportunities. Perhaps our controls have inhibited managers from pursuing our goals of aggressive growth and above-average Return On Assets, as compared to the industry.

Quality distributed 20,000 metal products from our regional warehouses and 23 district warehouses, each with its own sales and support organizations. Each district manager reported to a regional manager. Further information about the company and its control system is given in the *(A)* case.

District Organization

Typically, a district manager had under him a warehouse superintendent, a sales manager, a credit manager, a purchasing manager, and an administration manager. The duties of these managers are described below.

The *warehouse superintendent* oversaw transportation, loading and unloading, storage, and preproduction processing.

The *sales manager* coordinated a staff that included "inside" salespersons, who established contracts and took orders over the phone, and an "outside" team, who made direct customer contacts and closed large deals. Sales price and discount terms were generally established by the *district manager;* freight adjustments were also made at the district level. This department also attempted to implement one of the corporate objectives, which stressed special orders and high-margin sales.

The *purchasing manager* acquired inventory from the regional warehouse, other districts, and outside companies. Within overall con-

[1] Hayes and Abernathy, "Managing Our Way to Economic Decline," *Harvard Business Review,* July–August 1980.

straints described in the *(A)* case, the purchasing manager had authority to choose suppliers and negotiate credit terms. Payments to suppliers were handled centrally at the home office.

Capital expenditures in excess of $5,000 and all leasing decisions required corporate approval.

Transfer Pricing Policy[2]

Districts receiving inventory from the regional warehouse or other districts were charged for the sum of (1) the replacement cost of the transferred inventory, (2) variable handling costs incurred in the supplying center, and (3) transportation costs. In addition, a fraction of the supplying center's fixed expenses was transferred to the receiving district as a lump sum. This fraction was calculated by measuring the percentage of the supplier's capacity used by the receiving district in the previous quarter.

Transfers of the centers' inventory assets were made at the end of each month so as to provide more accurate ROA figures for performance evaluation. This calculation involved the division of net inventory transferred by the turnover rate. The resulting number represented the level of inventory necessary to support the transfers. The following equations summarize these calculations:

$$\frac{\text{Cost of sales (including transfers) of the supplying district}}{\text{Average inventory of the supplying district}} = \text{Turnover rate}$$

$$\frac{\text{Cost of the inventory transferred}}{\text{Turnover rate}} = \text{Inventory necessary to support internal transfers}$$

The inventory figure arrived at by the above equations was then transferred to the asset base of the receiving center, while that of the supplying center was reduced correspondingly.

Responsibility Allocation and Measurement

Districts managers were responsible for attaining predetermined ROA levels, which were agreed to at the beginning of the year. This control was used, in conjunction with Quality's incentive system, to motivate district managers to increase profits while ensuring efficient asset utilization.

The following items were included in the asset base for ROA calculations:

[2] For a more detailed discussion, refer to Quality Metal Service Center *(A)*.

1. Land, warehouse buildings, and equipment—base at gross book value.
2. Leased buildings and equipment (excepting for leased trucks)—at the capitalized lease value. (Expenses on leased trucks were deducted from the center's income statement.)
3. Inventory. Average inventory, in units, was calculated for the period. The replacement costs, based on current mill price schedules, was determined for these units.
4. The average accounts receivable balance for the period.

Cash was excluded from districts' assets because the amounts were trivial. As a general rule, accounts payable was not deducted from the asset base. However, an adjustment was made if the negotiated credit period was greater than the company standard of 30 days. If this occured, "deferred inventory," a contra-asset account, was deducted from the amount of the inventory value, for the time period in excess of the 30-day standard. This was equivalent to a reduction of inventory assets corresponding to the excess credit period. For example, if a district negotiated a credit period of 50 days, then the inventory expenditure of 20 days was removed from the asset base. A penalty was not assessed if the negotiated credit period was less than the 30-day company standard.

Income before taxes, for each district, was calculated in accordance with generally accepted accounting principles (GAAP), except for cost of sales, which was calculated as based on current inventory replacement values. Expenses were separated into controllable and noncontrollable categories. Controllable expenses included such items as warehouse labor and sales commissions. Rent, utilities, and property taxes were examples of noncontrollable expenses.

No corporate overhead expenses were allocated to the districts. A few years ago, the company had considered a proposal to allocate corporate overheads to the districts. However, the proposal had been rejected on the grounds that the "allocation bases" were arbitrary and that such expenses could not be controlled at the district level.

Performance Evaluation and Incentives

ROA was the sole performance criterion for evaluation of district managers. The incentive bonus for district managers was based on a formula which tied the bonus to the ROA target. Bonus payments started at 90 percent of the target. No qualitative factors were considered in deciding on the bonus amount.

At the beginning of each year, top management defined an overall ROA objective. The ROA for 1982 for the company was 18 percent (after tax). The corporate office then advised the regional managers of their specific profit and asset targets consistent with the firm's overall goals. The regional managers, in turn, apportioned their targets to their district managers. Once these targets were established, they were considered fixed for the purpose of incentive compensation. Thus, the *original* budget, setting forth profit and asset targets, was the basis on which incentive compensation decisions were made, though this budget was revised each quarter. Exhibit 1 contains the detailed procedure used to calculate the incentive bonus. The calculations determined an applicable payout rate, which was multiplied by the district manager's base salary to give the amount of bonus. The size of the bonus depended upon the amount of the manager's base salary and upon how far 90 percent of the ROA target was exceeded, subject to a maximum.

EXHIBIT 1 Incentive Calculation Procedure

Step 1: Measure actual profit and compare it with targeted profit.

Step 2: Multiply the difference between actual profit and targeted profit by 1.5.

Step 3: If actual profit is greater than targeted profit, add the amount calculated in step 2 to the targeted asset base.

If actual profit is less than transferred profit, subtract the amount calculated in step 2 from the targeted asset base.

Step 4: Measure actual asset base, and compare it with adjusted asset base from step 3.

Step 5: If actual assets exceed the adjusted asset base, multiply excess by the targeted ROA for the district, and charge this amount to profits.

$$\text{Assets overemployed} \times \text{District ROA target} = \text{Charge to profits}$$

If actual assets are less than the adjusted asset base, multiply difference by the district's ROA target, and credit this to profits.

$$\text{Assets underemployed} \times \text{District ROA target} = \text{Credit to profits}$$

Step 6: Adjusted profits are compared with 90% of the original profit objective.

$$\text{Adjusted profits} - (90\% \text{ of objective}) = \text{Incentive profits}$$

Step 7:

$$\frac{\text{Incentive profit}}{90\% \text{ of objective}} = \text{Payout rate}$$

Step 8: Payout rate × Manager's base salary = Bonus payable

Step 9: Bonuses are awarded on the basis of incentive profits. If incentive profits are less than zero, no bonus is awarded. The bonus increases in proportion to incentive profit, with a maximum bonus of 75 percent of manager's base salary.

The bonus of a district manager was also affected by his region's performance. Currently, 75 percent of a district manager's bonus was based on district performance, and 25 percent was based on his region's performance. The bonus of the district manager's staff was based solely on the performance of that district.

Meeting with the Columbus District Manager

A few days after speaking with Ed Brown, the case writer visited Ken Richards, the district manager for the Columbus Service Center. Ed recommended him as one of the company's brightest and most successful district managers.

Ken said that he was satisfied with the performance of his district, except for the problem of obtaining inventory from other districts and regions. The district had consistently earned a ROA well above 30 percent.

For 1982, his targeted figure for operating profit was $3,800,000; targeted assets were set at $10,000,000. He felt that an ROA of 38 percent (before taxes) was reachable, considering historical performance and market opportunities.

As of March 1982, Ken was reviewing a capital investment proposal (for the purchase of new processing equipment), which he had received from his sales manager (Exhibit 2). Before submitting the proposal to corporate headquarters for approval, Ken wanted to make sure that the new investment would have a favorable effect on his incentive bonus for 1982. Using 1982 profit and asset targets as the bench mark, he compared his incentive bonus for 1982 with or without the new investment. These calculations are shown in Exhibit 3.

EXHIBIT 2

TO: Kenneth Richards, District Manager.

FROM: Elizabeth Barret, Sales Manager

SUBJECT: Purchase of Processing Equipment

This district, at present, sells no inventory that has been altered through preproduction processing. Such alterations can be made at other districts with processing capabilities; but many customers in this area complain that, because of transportation time, the lead times are too great to satisfy their needs in acquiring such inventory.

Market research has established that a reasonable demand for processed inventory exists within this district. Therefore, our district should consider obtaining the processing equipment necessary to satisfy this demand.

EXHIBIT 2 ***(continued)***

The economics of this project is summarized in the attached sheet. Let me provide some information as background for these calculations.

We can acquire the equipment for $600,000; since its expected life is 10 years (negligible salvage value), Quality would benefit from a 10 percent Investment Tax Credit, making the net investment equal to $540,000.

Sales projections were made by the district's sales department, and costs were based upon the experiences of districts with processing capabilities. Growth in sales and costs include a 7 percent inflation factor and projected increases in production.

Annual cash flows are calculated by adjusting Earnings After Taxes to account for depreciation, which is expensed by the sum-of-the-years'-digits method; and growth in Working Capital investment, which is calculated using our standard 20 percent of sales on incremental growth. The resultant end-of-year cash flows, discounted at the cost of capital of 15 percent (which is the rate head office requires on projects in similar risk class such as this one), yield a positive net present value of $286,000. The payback period for this project is 4.5 years, which is well within the company's criteria of 10 years.

This investment is worth your careful consideration, Ken. This district has the opportunity to expand into a new market, and to benefit from favorable earnings and positive sales growth.

I hope you will submit this proposal to the home office for consideration. Please let me know if you have any questions.

Sd/-

Elizabeth Barret

EXHIBIT 2 (*concluded*) Processing Equipment Proposal

	1982	1983	1984	1985	1986	1987	1988	1989	1990	1991
I. Cash flows (000s):										
Sales[1]	$ 600	$ 1,375	$ 1,510	$ 1,665	$ 1,830	$ 2,010	$ 2,215	$ 2,435	$ 2,680	$ 2,945
Cost of sales	[560]	[1,145]	(1,236)	(1,355)	(1,490)	(1,660)	(1,845)	(2,051)	(2,290)	(2,545)
Earnings before taxes	40	230	274	310	340	350	370	384	390	400
Tax at 50 percent	(20)	(115)	(137)	(155)	(170)	(175)	(185)	(192)	(195)	(200)
Earnings after taxes	20	115	137	155	170	175	185	192	195	200
Depreciation	110	100	85	75	65	55	45	35	20	10
Investment in working capital[2]	(120)	(155)	(25)	(35)	(30)	(35)	(45)	(40)	(50)	535
Cash flow	10	60	197	195	205	195	185	187	165	745
A. Investment in working capital:										
20% of sales	120	275	300	335	365	400	445	485	535	590
Old level	0	120	275	300	335	365	400	445	485	535
Increase in working capital	(120)	(155)	(25)	(35)	(30)	(35)	(45)	(40)	(50)	(55)
Recovery of working capital										590
Net incremental investment in working capital	(120)	(155)	(25)	(35)	(30)	(35)	(45)	(40)	(50)	535

II. Project evaluation:
- A. Payback period: 4.5 years
- B. Internal rate of return: 24 percent
- C. Net present value (at 15% cost of capital)

Present value of cash inflows	= $826,000
Present value of cash outflows	= 540,000
Net present value	= $286,000

[1] Revenue for 1982 reflects three-month start-up period.
[2] Investment in working capital, shown in I.A. below.

EXHIBIT 3 Incentive Bonus for Columbus District Manager for 1982

A. Incentive bonus for 1982 without the new project

	Target for 1982	*Projected actual for 1982**
Profit.	$ 3,800,000	$ 3,800,000
Asset.	10,000,000	10,000,000

Incentive profit = Actual profit − (90% of targeted profit)
$3,800,000 − $3,420,000 = $380,000

$$\text{Payout rate} = \frac{\text{Incentive profit}}{\text{90\% of targeted profit}}$$

$$= \frac{\$380{,}000}{\$3{,}420{,}000} = 11.1 \text{ percent}$$

Therefore, incentive bonus without the new project = 11.1% of base salary.

* Assumes that actual results exactly meet the targets in 1982.

B. Incentive bonus for 1982 with the new project

	Target for 1982	*Projected actual for 1982**
Profit	$ 3,800,000	$ 3,840,000
Asset	10,000,000	10,720,000

Step 1: Actual profit − Targeted profit = Difference.

$3,840,00 − $3,800,000 = $40,000

Step 2: Difference × 1.5 = Asset adjustment.

$40,000 × 1.5 = $60,000

Step 3: Targeted asset + Asset adjustment = Adjusted assets.

$10,000,000 + $60,000 = $10,060,000

Step 4: Actual asset − Adjusted asset = Asset overemployed.

$10,720,000 − $10,060,000 = $660,000

Step 5: Asset overemployed × District ROA target = Charge to profits.

$660,000 × 38% = $250,800

Actual profits − Charge to profits = Adjusted profits.

$3,840,000 − $250,800 = $3,589,200

Step 6: Adjusted profits − 90% of targeted profit = Incentive profit.

$3,589,200 − $3,420,000 = $169,200

Step 7:
$$\frac{\text{Incentive profit}}{\text{90\% of targeted profit}} = \text{Payout rate.}$$

$$\frac{\$169{,}200}{\$3{,}420{,}000} = 4.95\%$$

Therefore, incentive bonus with the new project = 4.95% of base salary.

* Reflects marginal effect of project implementation *only* (i.e, an addition of earnings before taxes of $40,000 and an addition to assets of $720,000 ((equipment $600,000 plus working capital $120,000)). Otherwise, assumes that other district operations meet targets exactly in 1982.

Questions

1. Is the capital investment proposal described in Exhibit 3 an attractive one for Quality Metal Service Center?

2. Should Ken Richards, the Columbus district manager, send that proposal to home office for approval?

3. Comment on the general usefulness of ROA as the basis of evaluating a district manager's performance. Could this performance measure be made more effective?

4. In deciding the investment base for evaluating managers of investment centers, the general question is: What practices will motivate the district managers to use their assets most efficiently, and to acquire the proper amount and kind of new assets? Presumably, when his return on assets is being measured, the district manager will try to increase his ROA, and we desire that the action he takes towards this end be actions that are in the best interest of the whole corporation. Given this general line of reasoning, evaluate the way Quality computes the "investment base" for its districts. For each asset category, discuss whether the basis of measurement used by the company is the best for the purpose of measuring district's return on assets. What are the likely motivational problems that could arise in such a system? What can you recommend to overcome such dysfunctional effects?

5. While computing district profits for performance evaluation purposes, should there be a charge for income taxes? Should corporate overheads be allocated to districts? Should profits be computed on the basis of historical costs or on the basis of replacement costs? Evaluate these issues from the standpoint of their motivational impact on the district managers.

6. Evaluate Quality's incentive compensation procedure. Does the present system motivate district managers to make decisions which are consistent with the interests of the firm? If not, make specific recommendations to improve the system.

PART THREE

The Management Control Process

A management control system, like any system, consists of both a structure and a process. In Part Two, we focused on the main elements of the control structure, *that is, on the various types of responsibility centers and on the techniques that were appropriate for planning and controlling performance in each of them. In Part Three, we focus on the main steps in the management control* process. *Because one cannot discuss structure without mentioning how the structure works, there is some overlap between Parts Two and Three.*

The principal steps in the control process are, in chronological order: programming, budget preparation, and the analysis and appraisal of performance. These steps are discussed in Chapters 9 through 12. Chapter 13 describes the use of executive compensation plans in the management control process.

CHAPTER 9

Programming

Programming is the process of deciding on the nature and size of the several programs that are to be undertaken in implementing an organization's strategies. In an industrial company, the programs are structured essentially by products or product lines.

The process of programming involves three related, but separable, activities. The first activity involves the preparation and analysis of proposals for new programs, and making decisions on these proposals. The second is the analysis of ongoing programs, with the objective of improving the profitability of these programs. The third is the system for coordinating the separate programs so as to optimize the functioning of the company as a whole. An organization should perform all three of these activities competently, but many organizations do not. Some organizations are effective at formulating and analyzing individual program proposals, but they have no formal programming system; other organizations have a well-developed programming system, but they do an inadequate job of analyzing the individual proposals for new programs that flow through the system, or they are overly complacent about the status of existing programs. Each of these three aspects of programming is discussed in this chapter.

RELATION TO OTHER PROCESSES

Programming is to be distinguished from strategic planning, which precedes it in time, and from budget preparation, which follows it.

Relation to Strategic Planning

In Chapter 1 we drew a line between two management processes, strategic planning and management control. Programming, although part of management control, is close to the line dividing these two processes, and it is therefore of some importance to distinguish between them. The distinction is not crucial, however, and, as is the case in most matters relating to organizations, the line is not a sharp one. In fact, some authors use the term *long-range planning* to encompass both strategic planning and programming, and others use *strategic planning* for the process that we define as "programming."

In the strategic planning process, management decides on the goals of the organization and the main strategies for achieving these goals. Conceptually, the programming process takes these goals and strategies as given and seeks to identify programs that will implement the strategies effectively. The decision by an industrial goods manufacturer to diversify into consumer goods is a strategic decision. Having made this basic decision, a number of programming decisions then must be made: whether to implement the strategy by acquisition or by building a new organization, what product lines to emphasize, whether to make or to buy, what marketing channels to use, and so on.

In practice, there is a considerable amount of overlap between strategic planning and programming. Studies made during the programming process may indicate the desirability of changing goals or strategies. Conversely, strategic planning usually includes a preliminary consideration of the programs that will be adopted as means of achieving goals.

An important reason for making a separation in practice between programming and strategic planning is that the programming process tends to become institutionalized, and this tends to put a damper on purely creative activities. Segregating strategic planning as a separate activity, either organizationally or at least in the thinking of top management, can provide an offset to this tendency. Strategic planning should be an activity in which creative, innovative thinking is strongly encouraged.

In many companies, goals and strategies are not stated explicitly or communicated clearly to the managers who need to use them as a framework within which program decisions are made. Thus, in a formal programming process an important first step often is to write descriptions of these goals and strategies. This may be a difficult task, for, although top management presumably has an intuitive feel for what they are, the goals and strategies may not have been verbalized with the specificity that is necessary if they are to be used in making program decisions. This topic was discussed in more detail in Chapter 3.

Relation to Budget Preparation

Both programming and budget preparation involve planning, but the types of planning activities are different in the two processes. The budgeting process focuses on a single year, whereas programming focuses on activities that extend over a period of several years. A budget is, in a sense, a one-year slice of the organization's programs although, for reasons discussed in Chapter 10, this is not a complete description of a budget; the budgeting process involves more than simply carving out such a slice.

Programming precedes budgeting, and in the budget process the approved program is essentially taken as a given. Thus, having decided on its consumer product lines and on the arrangements for manufacturing and marketing these products, the company mentioned in the preceding section would prepare a budget showing planned revenues and expenses for the forthcoming year.

Another difference between a program and a budget is that the former is essentially structured by product lines or other programs, while the latter is structured by responsibility centers. This rearrangement of the program—so it corresponds to the responsibility centers charged with executing it—is necessary because the budget will be used to motivate performance before the fact and to appraise performance after the fact, and motivation and appraisal are activities that must be related to organizational responsibilities.

ANALYSIS OF PROPOSED PROGRAMS

Ideas for new programs can arise anywhere in the organization. They can originate with the chief executive, with a headquarters planning staff, or in various parts of the operating organization. Some units are a more likely source than others, for fairly obvious reasons. The research/development organization is expected to generate ideas for new products or processes, the marketing organization for marketing innovations, and the production engineering organization for new equipment and manufacturing methods. Proposals for programs are essentially either *reactive* or *proactive;* that is, they arise either as the reaction to a perceived threat to the company, such as rumors of the introduction of a new product by a competitor, or they represent an initiative designed to capitalize on a newly perceived opportunity.

Because a company's success depends in part on its ability to find and implement new programs, and because ideas for these can come from a wide variety of sources, it is important that the atmosphere be such that these ideas do come to light and that they receive appropriate management attention. A highly structured, formal system may create the wrong atmosphere for this purpose, and it is therefore important that the system be flexible enough and receptive enough so that good new ideas do not get killed off before they come to the attention of the proper decision maker.

It is also important that, wherever possible, the adoption of a new program be viewed not as a single all-or-nothing decision but rather as a series of decisions, each one involving one relatively small step in testing and developing the proposed program, with full implementation and its consequent significant investment being decided upon if, but only if, the tests indicate that the proposal has a good chance of success. Most new programs are not like the Edsel automobile, which involved the commitment of several hundred million dollars in a single decision; rather, they involve many successive decisions: agreement that the initial idea for a product is worth pursuing, then examining its technical feasibility in a laboratory, then examining production problems and cost characteristics in a pilot plant, then testing consumer acceptance in test markets, and only then making a major commitment to full production and marketing. The system must provide for these successive steps, and for a thorough evaluation of the results of each step as a basis for making the decision on the next step.

Capital Investment Analysis

Most proposals require significant amounts of new capital. Techniques for analyzing such proposals are described in many sources and are not repeated here.[1] In general, the techniques attempt either to find *(a)* the net present value of the project, that is, the excess of the present value of the estimated cash inflows over the amount of investment required, with present value being determined by discounting the flows at a rate that the company believes to be a satisfactory return on investment; or, *(b)* the internal rate of return implicit in the relationship between inflows and outflows. An important point is that these techniques are not in fact used in a great many situations in which, conceptually, they are applicable.[2] There are at least four reasons for not using present value techniques in analyzing certain types of proposals:

1. The proposal may be so obviously attractive that a calculation of its net present value is unnecessary. A newly developed machine that reduces costs so substantially that it will pay for itself in a year is an example.
2. The estimates involved in the proposal are so uncertain that making present value calculations is believed to be not worth the effort—one can't draw a reliable conclusion from unreliable data.

---

[1] See Robert N. Anthony and James S. Reece, *Accounting Principles,* 5th ed. (Homewood, Ill.: Richard D. Irwin, 1983), chap. 22; and John Dearden, *Cost Accounting and Financial Control Systems* (Reading, Mass.: Addison-Wesley Publishing, 1973), chap. 13.

[2] See the following surveys for information on the prevalence of various techniques in practice: James S. Fremgen, "Capital Budgeting Practices: A Survey," *Management Accounting,* May 1973, pp. 19–25; Lawrence J. Gitman and John R. Forester, Jr., "A Survey of Capital Budgeting Techniques Used by Major U.S. Firms," *Financial Management,* Fall 1977, pp. 66–71; Lawrence J. Gitman and Vincent A. Mercurio, "Cost of Capital Techniques Used by Major U.S. Firms," *Financial Management,* Winter 1982, pp. 21–29; and Lawrence D. Schall et al., "Survey and Analysis of Capital Budgeting Methods," *Journal of Finance,* March 1978, pp. 281–92.

This situation is especially common when the results are heavily dependent on estimates of sales volume of new products for which no good market data exist.[3]

3. The rationale for the proposal is something other than increased profitability. The present value approach assumes that the "objective function" is to increase profits in some sense; but many proposed investments are justified on the grounds that they improve employee morale, improve the company's image, or are needed for safety reasons.
4. There is no feasible alternative to adoption of the proposal. An investment that is required to comply with antipollution legislation is an example.

The management control system must provide an orderly way of reaching a decision on proposals that cannot be analyzed by quantitative techniques; these proposals may amount to half the funds that the company commits to capital projects. In particular, the fact that these proposals do exist means that systems that attempt to rank projects in order of profitability are likely not to be practical because many projects do not fit into a mechanical ranking scheme.

Analytical Techniques

Instead of, or as a part of, the conventional approach to capital investment analysis, several analytical techniques have been proposed as an aid to decision making. Some of these are discussed briefly in this section.[4]

Probabilistic estimates. The idea of expressing estimates of future events in stochastic terms, rather than as single numbers, is not new. "Optimistic/best guess/pessimistic" budgets were described in textbooks in the 1950s and probably earlier. The largest effort involving probabilities was the PERT system, which is a control system that was at one time required to be used on all major Defense Department contracts. Conditions favored the adoption of the PERT system: A genuine need for a better system existed, large amounts of money were at stake, top management in the Department of Defense backed the system vigorously, and an elaborate education program was set up. Nevertheless, although a type of PERT system continues in wide-

[3] For an excellent discussion of this point, see Bela Gold, "The Shaky Foundations of Capital Budgeting," *California Management Review,* Winter 1976, pp. 51–59.

[4] For an excellent collection of articles describing new approaches, see Alfred Rappaport, ed., *Information for Decision Making,* 2d ed. (Englewood Cliffs, N.J.: Prentice-Hall, 1975). See also, Arnoldo C. Hax, and Karl M. Wig, "The Use of Decision Analysis in Capital Investment Problems," *Sloan Management Review,* Winter 1976, pp. 19–48; this article also has an excellent bibliography.

spread use, the probabilistic feature has largely been abandoned. The essential reason for its failure was that people did not trust the validity and/or the weighting of the probabilistic estimates. Thus, widespread use of these techniques depends on whether confidence in the validity of the estimates is warranted and on whether, even if warranted, decision makers will have enough confidence in the data to use them.

Risk analysis. If probabilistic estimates of even rough validity can be made, they can be used not only as an improved estimate of a variable (by means of the calculation of its *expected value*) but also as raw material for a new type of information, the amount of risk inherent in a project. If the estimate involves only one variable, such as sales volume, the easily computed *standard deviation* provides a good measure of the amount of risk—or more accurately, of uncertainty—in the estimate. If, as is usually the case, several variables are involved in the problem and some of these are interdependent, the problem is more complicated. The risk or uncertainty in such a situation can be measured by what is called the "Monte Carlo" method. In this method, the estimated profitability of a project is computed by using one set of revenue or cost estimates, with each number in this set being selected at random from the probability distribution of each variable. This process is repeated many times, sometimes a thousand times, by a computer. A frequency distribution of the results of these separate trials is computed, and the standard deviation, or other measure of dispersion, of this frequency distribution indicates the uncertainty of the project.[5]

Sensitivity analysis. Another approach to measuring the riskiness of a proposed project is called "sensitivity analysis." It does not require that a probability distribution be estimated and, thus, can be used in situations in which such estimates are not feasible. It simply involves varying the estimates of one of the variables by a stated amount, say 5 percent or 10 percent, and calculating what this does to the profitability of the project. Doing this calculation for each variable in succession shows which of them have the most influence on the overall profitability of the project and, therefore, which need to be considered most carefully when the decision on the project is being made.

Decision Tree Analysis

For some problems a single decision has to be made, and as a consequence of that decision estimated revenues will be earned and estimated costs will be incurred. There is another class of problems in which a series of decisions has to be made, at various time intervals, with each decision influenced by the information that is available at the

[5] This technique is described by David B. Hertz, "Risk Analysis in Capital Investment," *Harvard Business Review*, January–February 1964, pp. 95–106.

time it is made. An analytical tool that is useful for such problems is the *decision tree.*

In its simplest form, a decision tree is a diagram that shows the several decisions or *acts* and the possible consequences of each act; these consequences are called "events." In a more elaborate form, the probabilities and the revenues or costs of each event's outcomes are estimated, and these are combined to give an *expected value* for the event.

Since a decision tree is particularly useful in depicting a complicated series of decisions, any brief illustration is somewhat artificial. Nevertheless, the decision tree shown in Exhibit 9–1 will suffice to show how the technique works.

EXHIBIT 9–1 Decision Tree Analysis

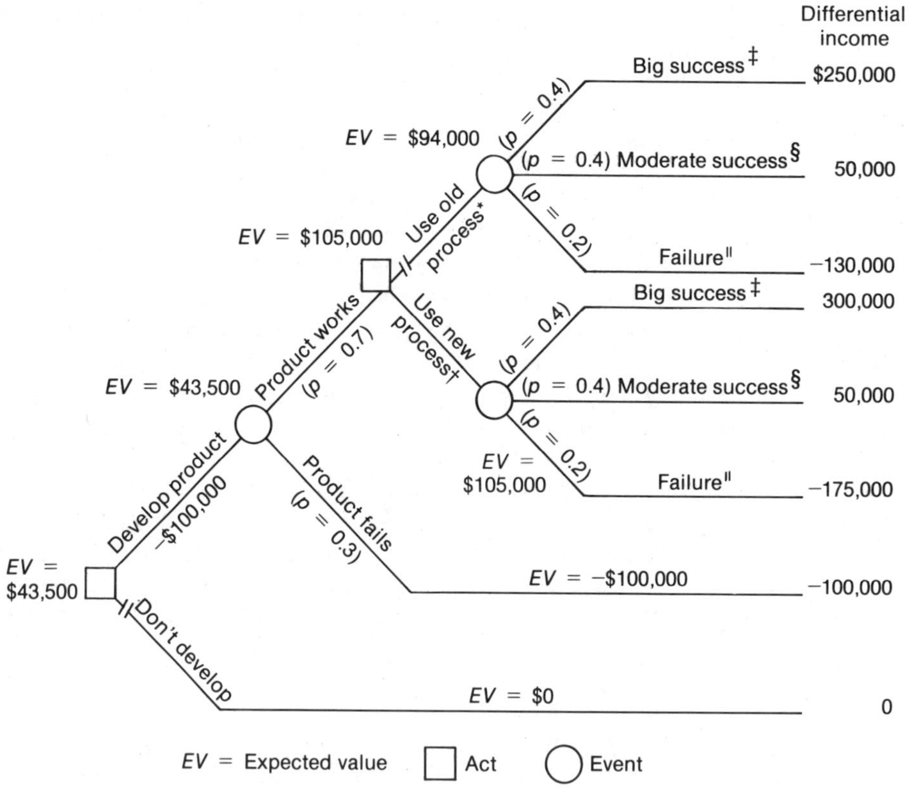

The assumed situation is this. A company is considering whether to develop and market a new product. Development costs are estimated to be $100,000, and there is a 0.7 probability that the development effort will be successful; that is, that the product developed will work (perform its intended function). If the product works, it will be produced and marketed. There are two production processes available. An old process costs $50,000 differential fixed costs plus $2 variable cost per unit. A new process, employing more equipment and less labor, costs $100,000 differential fixed costs and $1 per unit. The process must be chosen *before* any sales results are known. It is estimated that—

a. If the product is a big success (probability 0.4) 100,000 units will be sold at $6 each. Production costs using the old process will be $250,000 ($50,000 + 100,000 × $2), giving income (after subtracting the $100,000 development cost) of $250,000. If the new process is used, production costs will be $200,000 ($100,000 + 100,000 × $1), and income will be $300,000.

b. If the product is a moderate success (probability 0.4), 50,000 units will be sold at the $6 price. Either old or new process production costs will be $150,000, giving income (net of development costs) of $50,000.

c. If the product is a failure (probability 0.2), only 5,000 units will be sold at $6 each. Production will cost $60,000 using the old process, or $105,000 using the new process, giving losses of $130,000 and $175,000, respectively.

To decide *(a)* whether or not to develop the product, and *(b) if* the product works, whether to use the old or new process, the decision tree must be "collapsed" or "folded back," using these rules:

1. Replace each *event* "node" with the expected value of that event's outcomes.
2. At each *act* "node," choose the act with the highest expected value.

These expected values (EVs) are shown in Exhibit 9–1. For example, *if* the product is developed, *if* it works, and *if* management chooses to use the old process, then the EV of the three possible sales outcomes is $94,000 (=0.4 × $250,000 + 0.4 × $50,000 + 0.2 × $−130,000). Similarly, if the developed product works, using the new process has an EV of $105,000. Therefore, *if* the product is successfully developed, management should use the new process; this is shown by "chopping off" (with the double "hash mark") the branch labeled "Use Old Process." Now, if the development is undertaken, either the product will work, with an EV of $105,000, or it will fail, with a loss of $100,000. (Following a product failure, the probability of this loss is 1.0, so the EV is $−100,000.) Thus, the expected value of the decision to undertake development is $43,500 (0.7 × $105,000 + 0.3 × $−100,000); but the EV of not developing the product (which is the base case), is $0. Therefore the development effort should be undertaken, as indicated by "chopping off" the "Don't Develop" branch. In sum, the *optimal strategy*—that is, the sequence of decisions having the highest EV—is to develop the product and, if development succeeds, to use the new production process. That strategy has an EV of $43,500.

This does not mean, however, that the ultimate outcome is "guaranteed" to be differential income of $43,500; in fact, *none* of the possible outcomes results in $43,500 income, as can be seen by looking at the decision tree endpoint values. Rather, it means that, based on the estimates made in considering this decision, management should "gamble" and go ahead with the development because the *expected* payoff from this gamble is positive, whereas if the gamble is not taken there will be zero payoff.

This approach to decision making is a powerful one if, *but only if,* the probabilities can be estimated. As stated above, there are relatively few situations in the real world where such estimates can be made with sufficient reliability that the decision maker will trust them.

Preference analysis. The techniques described in the preceding paragraphs focused on an analysis of the project itself. It is conceptually possible to go one step further and take into account the personal preferences of the decision maker. In general, people vary as to their *risk aversion;* that is, their willingness to accept projects with a high degree of risk if they promise a correspondingly high payoff. Techniques developed as a part of the *theory of games* provide a way of quantifying a given decision maker's risk aversion and incorporating this into the analysis of a project.

Limitations on analytical techniques. Although there are many theoretical articles and books on the techniques mentioned above, they are not widely used in practice. The reasons for this discrepancy between theory and practice are those given earlier, particularly the second reason, namely, that the analysis necessarily involves estimates, and these estimates are often so "shaky" that it is not worthwhile to apply sophisticated techniques to them. Nevertheless, analysts should be aware of the existence of these techniques because, if reliable data are available, they are powerful tools.

Benefit/Cost Analysis

To use the capital budgeting techniques, the analyst must make monetary estimates of both the outlays and the savings or additional profits involved in the proposed investment. The techniques then make it possible to judge whether the benefits exceed the outlays (i.e., the cost of the project). In many situations, reliable estimates of both these sets of factors is not possible. In such situations, the analyst may use a less rigorous, but nevertheless valuable, technique called "benefit/cost analysis."

If the benefits from the proposed project are either the savings resulting from, for example, the introduction of more efficient equipment, or the additional profit resulting from new products or from increased volume of existing products, then they can be expressed as monetary amounts. For some proposed projects, however, the benefits are more nebulous; the projects are proposed to improve working conditions, to create a more favorable "image" of the company in the eyes of the public, to increase product quality, to decrease pollution of the environment, or for other reasons whose magnitude cannot be expressed as dollar amounts. In other proposals, the dollar magnitude of some of the benefits can be estimated; but there are other benefits whose magnitude cannot be measured. Therefore, in estimating the total benefits, both the measured and the unmeasured elements must be taken into account.

Benefit/cost analysis incorporates these unmeasured factors. In its most general form, the analyst merely attempts to identify the unmeasured benefits and to judge, subjectively, whether, all things considered, the benefits probably exceed the cost. In more sophisticated versions, point values and weights are assigned to the unmeasured benefits, and these are aggregated and compared with the costs.

In most capital budgeting problems, the cost component is much easier to estimate than the "benefit" component. Benefit/cost techniques provide a way of getting some handle on the merits of the project, even when monetary estimates of benefits cannot be made. In all cases, of course, the project should not be approved unless the benefits, however estimated, are expected to exceed the costs.

Overall Corporate Models

If the behavior of each important variable in a company can be estimated, and if the relationships among the variables can be expressed as mathematical equations, the decision maker can have a powerful tool for analyzing proposed projects. The important factors about the costs and benefits of a proposed alternative can be fed into this overall corporate model, and the effect on profitability can be calculated.

With the advent of computers, the use of such models has become widespread. With a microcomputer costing a few thousand dollars, and a software spreadsheet program costing a few hundred dollars, as many as 80 variables can be stated—and the computer will calculate the overall effect of a proposal in a few seconds.[6] With larger com-

---

[6] The most widely used computer program is Visicalc; similar programs are available from other vendors. Computer models designed specifically for colleges and universities, hospitals, banks, and several types of manufacturing companies are available from commercial sources.

puters, hundreds or thousands of variables can be incorporated into the model. Once a company undertakes the construction of such a model, the model can be so expanded and refined thereafter that it becomes an increasingly valid reflection of the interactions within the company.

Companies are experimenting with two approaches to an overall corporate model: the optimization approach and the heuristic approach.

In the *optimization* approach, the objective is to make a single model that encompasses all variables and that explains the profitability of the company under a given set of circumstances. This approach requires the use of *linear programming,* which is a device for finding the optimum combination of variables when there are constraints (such as production capacity limitations) on the amount of resources available. Estimating the behavior of variables and of the interaction among them is complicated, and to date very few companies have been able to make estimates that are reliable enough to produce a model in which managers have confidence. Nevertheless, many companies are working to develop such a model.

The *heuristic* approach is less ambitious and, therefore, more practical. Instead of attempting to model all variables in the company at once, the mathematical expressions are developed only for certain segments of the company for which reliable estimates can be made. These are termed *blocks*. The results of the analysis of these blocks are then fitted into a conventional income statement and balance sheet, the other items on which are developed by simple extrapolation. These financial statements constitute the overall model. In the Sun Oil Company model, for example, one block estimates the investment required for new service stations to achieve a specified market share for the coming year. Another block estimates the amount of crude oil and other raw materials that will be produced in the coming year on the basis of the number of wells available and the estimated output of each. The outputs of each of these blocks are combined with those of other blocks to provide an estimate of net income and of balance sheet amounts.[7]

Program Analysis Systems

Whether or not a formal analysis is made, there must be some systematic way of considering individual program proposals. The system is usually referred to as a capital budgeting system since the proposals require the commitment of capital funds. A capital budgeting system has these seven main elements:

---

[7] George W. Gershefski, "Building a Corporate Financial Model," *Harvard Business Review,* July 1969.

1. The originator of a proposal prepares a description of it and a justification for it, or such a justification is prepared on behalf of the originator by an appropriate staff unit. If the proposal is amenable to formal analysis, the justification includes a summary of this analysis.

2. A high-level staff unit analyzes the proposal (unless this unit originated the proposal) and submits its recommendations to the decision maker. Most program proposals are decided on by top management of the company, or by top management of a division for proposals relating to only one division. For important projects, this stage of the process may require a long time—sometimes a year or more—during which questions are raised and answered, alternatives are explored, and every possible effort is made to examine the soundness of the proposal. Much discussion and persuasion and much staff work on details of the proposal occur during this stage.

3. A capital budget is prepared, usually once a year. The capital budget is usually prepared separately from the operating budget, and in many companies it is prepared at a different time and cleared through a capital appropriations committee that is separate from the budget committee. In the capital budget, projects often are classified under headings such as the following:

a. Cost reduction and replacement.
b. Expansion of existing product lines.
c. New product lines.
d. Health and safety.
e. Other.

Within these classifications, individual projects are often listed in what is believed to be the order of their desirability; and the estimated expenditures are broken down by years, or by quarters, so that the funds required for each time period are shown. A blanket amount is included for the total of smaller projects that are not listed individually.

4. The budget is considered, revised if necessary, and approved. Usually, final approval is made at the board of director level. In preparing the capital budget, management must appraise not only the individual projects but also the total amount of funds requested. It may happen that the funds required for desirable projects total more than the amount of money that management thinks should be spent. In this event, a worthwhile project might not be approved simply because the funds are not available.

5. Approval of the capital budget usually means approval of the projects *in principle,* but does not constitute final authority to proceed with them. For this authority, a specific authorization request is prepared for the project, spelling out the proposal in more detail, perhaps with firm bids or price quotations on the new assets. These authoriza-

tion requests are approved at higher or lower levels in the organization depending on their magnitude.

6. Work to accomplish the project is begun. The control system used in this connection is discussed in Chapter 17.

7. In some companies, there is a procedure designed to follow up on capital projects once they have gone into operation. Its purpose is to find out whether the original estimates of costs and earnings in fact work out in practice. In many situations, however, it is not feasible to identify earnings with specific projects, so such a follow-up cannot be made.

ANALYZING ONGOING PROGRAMS

There is a natural human tendency to assume that the future is going to resemble the past. Consequently, long-range plans are often prepared simply by extrapolating from the current situation. In the dynamic environment within which most businesses operate, such extrapolations are likely to be unrealistic, and reliance on them is dangerous. A preferable approach is to make a thorough analysis of each major segment of the company and to adopt programs that are consistent with the opportunities that exist for that segment.

Product Line Analysis

A natural focus for such an analysis is an individual product or product line. Some companies are organized by divisions, each of which is responsible for a product line, and in these companies the analysis of product lines can be made by divisions. An approach to such an analysis, suggested by Robert V. L. Wright of Arthur D. Little, Inc., is described briefly in the following paragraphs.[8]

A product line is classified in terms of the maturity of its industry and the company's competitive position within the industry. Four stages of maturity are identified as indicated in Exhibit 9–2.

> An *embryonic* industry (for example, laser measuring devices) is normally characterized by rapid growth, changes in technology, great pursuit of new customers, and fragmented and changing shares of market; a *growth* industry is one that is still growing rapidly, but customers, market shares, and technology are better known and entry into the industry is more difficult (as illustrated by RCA's attempt to enter the computer business); a *mature* industry (like automobiles or paper in this country) is characterized by stability in known customers, technology, and in shares of market, although the industries may still be mar-

[8] Adapted from Robert V. L. Wright, *A System for Managing Diversity* (Cambridge, Mass.: Arthur D. Little, Inc., 1974).

EXHIBIT 9–2 Product Life Cycle

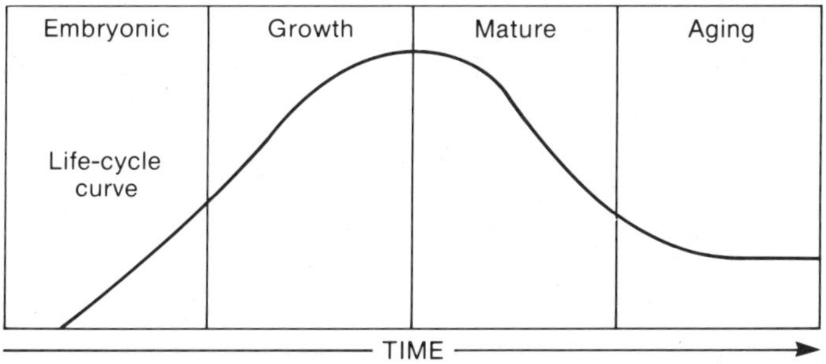

Source: Robert V. L. Wright, *A System for Managing Diversity* (Cambridge, Mass.: Arthur D. Little, Inc., 1974), p. 10.

ket-competitive; and *aging* industries (such as men's hats) are best described by falling demand, a declining number of competitors, and, in many such industries, a narrowing of the product line.[9]

The product line is also classified according to its competitive position into five categories: dominant, strong, favorable, tenable, or weak. As a basis for these classifications, and for thinking about desirable courses of action, the staff assembles data on the size, strengths, and weaknesses of each major competitor, the size and composition of the market and expected changes in it, and company data on the product line.

This two-way classification suggests a 4 × 5 matrix, and different practices are appropriate for product lines that are in each cell in such a matrix. The characteristics for each stage of maturity are listed in Exhibit 9–3. Management's task is then to examine the division's activities and, if necessary, plan changes in these activities so they are consistent with those appropriate for the stage of maturity and competitive position. If a formal programming system, as described in the next section, is used, these plants provide the starting point in formulating the program for the product line.

The completed analysis and the resulting program should be the subject of a thorough discussion between divisional management and top management, because it should set forth a course of action that will govern the operations of the division for some time to come. Even if the program is judged to be optimum from the standpoint of the division, it nevertheless is subject to change if it does not fit into the overall corporate program. For example, a division may contemplate an expansion of its product lines into markets that are better served by some other division; decisions on divisional ''charters''—that is, the boundaries within which each division is supposed to operate—are clearly

[9] Ibid., p. 7.

EXHIBIT 9–3 Management Characteristics by Stage of Industry Maturity

Management activity or function	*Embryonic industry*	*Growth industry*	*Mature industry*	*Aging industry*
Managerial role	Entrepreneur	Sophisticated market manager	Critical administrator	"Opportunistic milker"
Planning time frame	Long enough to draw tentative life cycle (10)	Long-range investment payout (7)	Intermediate (3)	Short-range (1)
Planning content	By product/customer	By product and program	By product/market/function	By plant
Planning style	Flexible	Less flexible	Fixed	Fixed
Organization structure	Free-form or task force	Semipermanent task force, product or market division	Business division plus task force for renewal	Pared-down division
Managerial compensation	High variable/low fixed, fluctuating with performance	Balanced variable and fixed, individual and group rewards	Low-variable/high-fixed group rewards	Fixed only
Policies	Few	More	Many	Many
Procedures	None	Few	Many	Many
Communication system	Informal/tailor-made	Formal/tailor-made	Formal/uniform	Little or none, by direction
Managerial style	Participation	Leadership	Guidance/loyalty	Loyalty
Content of reporting system	Qualitative, marketing, unwritten	Qualitative and quantitative, early warning system, all functions	Quantitative, written, production-oriented	Numerical, oriented to written balance sheet
Measures used	Few fixed	Multiple/adjustable	Multiple/adjustable	Few/fixed
Frequency of measuring	Often	Relatively often	Traditionally periodic	Less often
Detail of measurement	Less	More	Great	Less
Corporate departmental emphasis	Market research; new product development	Operations research; organization development	Value analysis Data processing Taxes and insurance	Purchasing

Source: Robert V. L. Wright, *A System for Managing Diversity* (Cambridge, Mass.: Arthur D. Little, Inc., 1974), p. 12.

the province of top management. Also, the divisional estimates of its need for additional capital may be inconsistent with the overall corporate financial plan. A mature product line is usually treated as a "cash cow"; that is, it is milked to the maximum feasible extent so as to provide the funds needed by the growth divisions. The manager of a cash cow division may not be happy about such a policy, based on the belief that at least a certain percentage of the funds generated "belongs" to the division. Corporate management may well decide otherwise. One company, for example, specifically outlined its policy as follows, in guidelines furnished to divisions:

> The primary role of profit centers in mature industries will be to provide funds to the corporation. While we are prepared in special circumstances to invest in these units for a limited period of time for specific purposes, these profit centers should be taking steps to improve their cash flow through the rationalization of their marketing, distribution, product line and/or production methods.
>
> Any investment in profit centers in mature industries will be expected to produce a significantly improved ROI over the unit's previous performance.
>
> If we feel that a profit center does not have a high probability of meeting stated objectives, we will not hesitate to sell or liquidate it.
>
> For those profit centers where the risk of not achieving planned performance is high, we will be looking for a commensurately higher rate of return.
>
> We will only invest in those aging businesses where there is an immediate prospect of additional high cash flow.

Zero-base Review

The type of analysis described above is focused on a product line. Different approaches are necessary for staff units and other activities whose profitability cannot be measured directly. Some companies have a systematic plan for reviewing all these aspects of their operations over a period of years. This approach has come to be called a "zero-base review." According to a regular schedule, each ongoing activity is studied intensively, perhaps once every five years. In contrast with the usual budget review, which takes the current level of spending as the starting point, this more intensive review attempts to build up, de novo, the resources that actually are needed by the activity. It may even challenge the need for having the activity at all. These studies are especially important when discretionary costs predominate. Basic questions are raised, such as: (1) Should the function be performed at all? (2) What should the quality level be? Are we doing too much? (3) Should it be performed in this way? (4) How much should it cost?

As a part of this approach, it is desirable to compare costs and, if feasible, output measures for similar operations. Comparisons may identify activities that appear to be out of line, and thus lead to a more thorough examination of these activities. Such comparisons can be useful even though there are problems in achieving comparability, finding a "correct" relationship between cost and output in a discretionary cost situation, and danger in taking an outside average as a standard. They often lead to the following interesting question: If other organizations get the job done for $X, why can't we?

Although sometimes called "zero-base budgeting," such a review actually is not part of the annual budgeting process, for there isn't enough time to conduct it during that process. A zero-base review is time consuming, and it is also likely to be a traumatic experience for the managers whose operations are being reviewed. This is one reason why such reviews are scheduled once every four or five years, rather than annually. This review establishes a new base for the budget, and the annual budget review attempts to keep costs reasonably in line with this base for the intervening period until the next review is made.

Zero-base review is difficult. Managers under scrutiny will not only do their best to justify their current level of spending but they may also do their best to thwart the entire effort. They consider the annual budget review as a necessary evil, but zero-base review as something to be put off indefinitely in favor of "more pressing business." If all else fails, they sometimes create enough doubts that the findings are inconclusive and the status quo prevails.

FORMAL PROGRAMMING SYSTEMS

Although most large organizations have a system for analyzing and deciding on individual program proposals along the lines described in the preceding sections, fewer companies have a formal method of bringing together all programs into an overall plan for the company. The development of such formal long-range plans has been rapid in the last decade, however. A formal long-range plan provides senior management with a better basis for making judgments about the overall balance among the different parts of the company. By showing the future implications of decisions that have already been made, it provides a starting point in the analysis of proposed new programs. It provides a frame of reference for the preparation of the annual budget. And it encourages managers at all levels to think more deeply and more systematically about the future, thus offsetting the natural tendency to focus on immediate, fire-fighting problems. Offsetting these advantages is the fact that the process is expensive, especially in its use of management time, since it is successful only if managers, including senior management, devote a considerable amount of time to it.

Time Period

The long-range plan typically covers a period of five future years, of which the first year is the year for which the next budget will be prepared. Its end products are a set of financial statements for this period, together with clarifying information on the actions that are implied by the accounting numbers. These statements are not necessarily prepared for each of the five years. To save paperwork, some companies prepare statements only for the budget year, the following year, and the fifth year, omitting the third and fourth years. Even though complete plans are prepared for only a 5-year period, some aspects of the program may be extended for a longer interval, such as 10 or even 20 years. For example, electrical generating and distribution companies customarily make plans for new generating facilities and for revisions in their power distribution networks for 20 years or more into the future; and timber companies make plans for the full cycle of the growth of trees, which may be 40 years.

Steps in the Process

The principal steps in a formal programming process are as follows:

1. Preparation of assumptions and guidelines.
2. Preparation of the divisional plans.
3. Review and approval of plans.

The process requires several months. If it is to be completed in time to serve as the starting point in the preparation of an annual budget for a year beginning January 1, it must be completed by some time in October, and perhaps earlier. To meet this deadline, it must be started in the spring of the year. The timetable is particularly long if provision is made for recycling the plans—that is, for a sequence that involves the submission of one plan, discussion of it with senior management, and a revision of this plan based on the senior management discussion. Such recycling is especially desirable in the first few years of a formal programming system, because of the unfamiliarity of managers and their staffs with the process.

Assumptions and Guidelines

The process starts with the preparation of guidelines and assumptions that are to govern the preparation of the program. The analytical work leading to these guidelines is done by a headquarters staff, which either is a separate planning staff reporting to senior management or is a part of the controller organization. The decisions, however, are made by senior management.

The guidelines issued by corporate management include a statement of goals, assumptions about the external environment, and a statement of policies that are to be followed in preparing the program.

The statement of goals includes:

1. Financial goals, expressed as earnings per share, return on investment, or similar numbers, specified year by year if feasible.
2. Inventory goals, expressed as turnover rates, and receivables goals, expressed as days' sales or comparable ratios.
3. Growth goals, usually expressed in terms of sales revenue.

Environmental assumptions include:

1. The trend of growth in gross national product, and an assumption about cyclical movements in GNP in the next year or two.
2. The rate of inflation in general, and the changes in labor rates, prices of important raw materials, and selling prices in particular.
3. Interest rates and, if relevant, currency exchange rates.
4. Market conditions, including the growth in principal markets the company serves, changes in the relative importance of distribution channels, anticipated government legislation or other action affecting the product, competitive influences, and profit margins.
5. Production factors, including probable new technology and other factors affecting production.

Statements regarding corporate policy include:

1. The amount of new capital likely to be available either from retained earnings or from new financing.
2. Divisional charters, including the products that each division can make, the products it can sell, the markets it can serve, the extent to which one division is expected to use the production facilities of other divisions for products it sells but does not make, and the marketing facilities of other divisions for products it makes but does not sell.
3. Policy on acquisitions and divestments.
4. Personnel policies, compensation policies, and policies on training, promotion, and rotation of managers.

These guidelines and assumptions, together with instructions on the format and content of the planning document itself, are sent to the divisions. In some companies, the first statement is regarded as tentative, and divisional managers are asked to comment on it and to suggest revisions. After discussion between division managers and senior management, a revised set of assumptions and guidelines is disseminated.

The preliminary discussion may take the form of a summit conference, in which corporate management and divisional managers meet, usually for several days and usually at a location which isolates participants from day-to-day pressures. The summit conference may lead to a rethinking of the goals and strategies of the company and, thus, to a revision of the guidelines. Discussions at this stage may also lead to changes in divisional charters.

Preparation of the Plan

Based on the guidelines and assumptions, the divisions and other operating units then prepare their five-year plan. As a starting point, they have the plan that was prepared the previous year, but changes in the environment often require considerable revision in these plans. Many decisions that will affect the division during the next five years have already been made in the capital budgeting process; and the implications of these decisions, both on capital outlays and the consequent impact on operations, are incorporated in the plan. (If there is no five-year plan, there is a tendency to overlook the fact that previously approved cost-saving investments are supposed to result in lower costs when they come on stream; costs should be adjusted downward at this time.)

As is the case with the preparation of guidelines, much of the analytical work in the preparation of the plan is done by the divisional staff, but the final judgments are made by divisional management. Members of the headquarters staff often visit the divisions during this process, for the purpose of clarifying the guidelines, assumptions, and instructions, and in general to assist in the planning process.

The end product of this process may be a fairly bulky document. It typically has the following parts:

1. A *summary,* written personally by the division manager, giving an overview of the plan.
2. A *marketing plan,* describing for each product line and market: the planned penetration, the tactics to be used in achieving this share of market, pricing policies, anticipated actions of competitors and how they will be dealt with, technological developments and their implementation, advertising and other promotional efforts, and the size and nature of the marketing organization.
3. A *production plan,* including changes in plant capacity, inventory levels, warehousing and other logistics activities, and staffing levels, wage and salary schedules, and other aspects of the personnel program.
4. A *staff plan,* describing the nature and size of the several staff units, with reasons for changes in them.
5. A *research/development plan,* identifying major research/development projects individually as well as the total size of the research/development effort.

6. A *capital expenditure plan,* in which capital expenditures that have already been approved are identified separately from those that will subsequently be submitted for approval.

7. *Financial statements,* including balance sheets, income statements, and funds flow statements. These usually are accompanied by historical data in order to show trends.

Review and Approval of Plans

When the divisional plan reaches headquarters, the staff makes a preliminary examination of it to insure that it conforms to instructions, that the division has not strayed outside the boundaries set by its charter, that the assumptions have been incorporated properly, and that the document is internally consistent. Problems uncovered during this examination are discussed with the divisional staff and are resolved. This discussion does not directly address the question of the adequacy of the plan in achieving the corporate goals; such matters are discussed at the management level, not at the staff level. As a basis for this discussion, headquarters staff notes matters that corporate management should discuss with division managers.

The discussion between corporate management and division managers is the heart of the formal programming process. If the plan submitted by the division is judged to be either overly optimistic or an inadequate contribution to corporate goals, corporate management raises questions about it. Such discussions usually require several hours, and often go on for a day or more for each division.

As a part of the headquarters review, the staff combines the plans for the several divisions into an overall plan for the company as a whole. The "first cut" of such an overall plan may reveal that the sum of divisional plans does not equal the corporate goals; for example, that earnings per share may be inadequate. This situation is termed a *planning gap*. There are only three ways to close a planning gap: (1) Find opportunities for improvements in the divisional plans, (2) plan on making acquisitions, or (3) revise the corporate goals. The easiest alternative is often viewed as that of making acquisitions, but this possibility may be unrealistic. Opportunities to boost sales revenues by acquiring other companies always exist, but finding acquisitions that will improve earnings per share is a much more difficult matter. In any event, the company's general policy on searching for acquisition opportunities is often governed by the need for additional earnings, as revealed by the planning gap.

The approved program that emerges from this discussion is the starting point in the preparation of the budget, but it is not by itself a budget. The budget is a fairly detailed statement of operations, is structured by responsibility centers, and is a bilateral commitment between the responsibility center managers and their superiors. The program is much less detailed, is structured by product lines or other programs, and cannot have the force of a commitment because of the uncertainties that are inherent in predicting events that are to occur at some considerable distance in the future.

Organization Relationships

In the foregoing description, we have referred to corporate management and division managers as if these were the only two managerial levels involved in the programming process. If the company has a large number of divisions, the chief executive officer does not have the time to carry on these discussions with each of them. In this case, the divisions are usually organized into groups, and a group vice president is responsible for leading the discussions with the managers of the division in his or her group and for then discussing the group's plans with the chief executive officer. The division managers usually participate in these discussions.

Furthermore, in highly decentralized companies the programming process may occur largely in divisions or groups within general guidelines established by corporate management. Corporate management would then review the completed programs, but would not participate actively in their formulation.

If the company is organized functionally, rather than by divisions, the preparation of a program is more complicated. In such a company, it is not possible to prepare the plan for each division without considering the activities of other divisions. Instead, the relationships among the functional units must be taken into account. For example, the staffing and material procurement plans of the production organization must be consistent with the sales program of the marketing organization. To assure that the various parts of the plan mesh with one another, the headquarters staff necessarily has a more important role in the preparation of the plan than is the case with a divisional organization. Since a division in a divisional organization consists of manufacturing, marketing, and other functional subunits, the divisional staff has a similar role in the preparation of divisional plans.

As emphasized above, programming is a line-management activity. A primary purpose is to improve the communication between corporate and divisional executives by providing a sequence of scheduled activities through which they can arrive at a mutually agreeable set of objectives and plans. Staff planners can greatly facilitate this process, but will usually be frustrated if they attempt to intervene in it too strongly. The staff planner's role in a divisionalized corporation is best conceived of as that of a catalyst. The staff's responsibility is to help corporate management do a better job of resource allocation among the divisions, and one way to do this is to assist division managers in doing a better job of developing plans for their businesses. If the division managers view staff planners as being influential in the corporate decision-making process, they will be reluctant to use the staff as a source of assistance in developing their own plans.

Designing a formal planning system for a divisionalized corporation is still a relatively mystical activity. Most corporations have had only a few years' experience in formal planning, and thus far the only safe generalization about such systems is that they tend to change fairly rapidly over time. The first year or two of a formal planning effort tends to be confusing and frustrating for both corporate and divisional managers. Many companies have worked the bugs out of the system, however, and find it valuable. Formal planning can help division managers to become more creative in identifying environmental opportunities and more explicitly rational in their analysis of strategic alternatives. Corporate management gains increasing confidence in the allocation of resources among the divisions. And both groups of managers benefit from the groundwork developed in the programming process as they engage in the next process, which is the preparation of the budget.

On the other hand, some companies have abandoned formal programming systems. The chief executive of a large company, who tried a formal programming system for several years and then gave it up, said:

> As long as there is a choice, as long as size or complexity or circumstances do not preclude it, we really ought to leave the planning of business to the people we ask to run it; that is, to our division managers.

Top Management Style

Programming is a management process; and the way in which it is conducted, if at all, in a given company is heavily dependent on the style of the chief executive officer of that company. Some chief executives prefer to make decisions without the benefit of a formal programming apparatus. If the controller of such a company attempts to introduce a formal system, he or she is likely to be wasting his time—and that of the line managers. No system will function effectively unless the chief executive actually uses it; and if other managers perceive that the system is not a vital part of the management process, they will give only lip service to it.

In some companies, the chief executive wants some overall programming apparatus for the reasons given earlier, but by temperament has an aversion to paperwork. In such companies, the system should contain all the elements described in earlier sections, but with a minimum amount of detail in the written documents, and relatively greater emphasis on informal discussion. In other companies, senior management prefers extensive analysis and documentation of plans, and in these companies the formal part of the system should be relatively elaborate.

In designing the system, it is important that the style of top management be correctly diagnosed and that the system be appropriate for that style. This is a difficult task, for formal programming has become somewhat of a fad, and some managers think they may be viewed as being old fashioned if they do not embrace all its trappings. Thus, they may instruct the staff to install an elaborate system, or permit one to be installed, even though they later are uncomfortable with it.

SUGGESTED ADDITIONAL READINGS

Gold, Bela. "The Shaky Foundations of Capital Budgeting." *California Management Review,* Winter 1976, pp. 51–59.

Hammond, J. S., III. "Better Decisions with Preference Theory." *Harvard Business Review,* November–December 1967, pp. 123–41.

Hax, Arnoldo C., and **Wig, Karl M.** "The Use of Decision Analysis in Capital Investment Problems." *Sloan Management Review,* Winter 1976, pp. 19–48.

Hertz, David B. "Risk Analysis in Capital Investment." *Harvard Business Review,* January–February 1964, pp. 95–106.

Livingstone, John L. *Management Planning and Control: Mathematical Models.* New York: McGraw-Hill, 1970.

Lorange, Peter, and **Vancil, Richard F.** *Strategic Planning Systems.* Englewood Cliffs, N.J.: Prentice-Hall, 1977.

Maciariello, Joseph A. *Program-Management Control Systems.* New York: John Wiley, 1978.

Raiffa, Howard. *Decision Analysis: Introductory Lectures on Choices under Uncertainty.* Reading, Mass.: Addison-Wesley Publishing, 1968.

Rappaport, Alfred, ed. *Information for Decision Making.* 2d ed. Englewood Cliffs, N.J.: Prentice-Hall, 1975.

Schlaifer, Robert O. *Analysis of Decisions under Uncertainty.* New York: McGraw-Hill, 1959.

Steiner, George A. *Top Management Planning.* New York: Macmillan, 1969.

———. *Strategic Planning.* New York: Free Press, 1979.

Weingartner, H. M. *Mathematical Programming and the Analysis of the Capital Budgeting Problems.* Englewood Cliffs, N.J.: Prentice-Hall, 1964.

CASE 9–1
The Quaker Oats Company*

Harry T. Ambrose had recently been appointed The Quaker Oats Company's director—long-range planning. An M.B.A. with nine years of managerial experience (but no previous exposure to the management of formal planning systems), in early 1971 Mr. Ambrose had the task of guiding the company through what was essentially the initiation of formal, long-range planning.

THE COMPANY

During the five-year period ended June 1970, Quaker Oats' per share earnings grew at an average annual rate of 11 percent. That performance was in striking contrast to the company's record in the five previous years, when earnings were almost on a plateau, and represented one of the best records achieved in the packaged food industry in the second half of the 1960s. Exhibit 1 presents a five-year review of Quaker Oats' financial performance.

A highly successful product-development program was the principal contributor to the improved earnings record of the company. Out of fiscal 1970's revenues of $598 million, the company spent $7.4 million on research and development, 21 percent higher than in fiscal 1969 and almost twice the amount spent five years earlier. Management felt that those expenditures were fully justified by the success achieved in the introduction of such new products as Aunt Jemima Complete Pancake Mix, Aunt Jemima Frozen French Toast, Quaker Instant Oats, King Vitamin (a nutritional cereal for children), and Ken-L Ration Burgers.

Also contributing to the company's improved earnings record was management's decision to minimize commodity operations and emphasize consumer-product areas in order to take greater advantage of the company's marketing capabilities. The decision to reduce commodity operations resulted in the divestiture of a line of country elevators in 1967 and a sizable feed operation early in 1969 and the acquisition of Fisher-Price toys, a manufacture of toys for preschool children, later that year. In addition, Quaker made several acquisitions outside the United States, including pet food companies in England and Canada and a leading manufacturer of chocolate in Mexico.

In recognition of the change in the company's product line and the broadening scope of its operations, Robert D. Stuart, Jr., the president and chief architect of Quaker Oats' growth since 1962, announced in

* This case was prepared by Richard F. Vancil, Harvard Business School.

EXHIBIT 1

THE QUAKER OATS COMPANY AND SUBSIDIARIES
Statement of Consolidated Income and Reinvested Earnings

	Year ended June 30				
	1970	*1969*	*1968 ($000)*	*1967*	*1966*
Revenues:					
Net sales	$597,652	$553,879	$547,194	$555,133	$498,358
Other income—net	2,745	2,738	956	881	432
	600,397	556,617	548,150	556,014	498,790
Cost and expenses:					
Cost of goods sold	399,426	375,661	382,419	403,010	358,178
Selling, general, and administrative expenses	142,572	129,675	122,693	115,132	103,750
Interest expense	4,433	2,083	2,315	2,417	1,950
	546,431	507,419	507,427	520,559	463,878
Income before federal and foreign income taxes	53,966	49,198	40,723	35,455	34,912
Federal and foreign income taxes	25,823	23,492	19,400	16,673	17,340
Income before extraordinary items	28,143	25,706	21,323	18,782	17,572
Extraordinary (charges) credits (net of income taxes)	—	(1,092)	—	898	—
Net income	28,143	24,614	21,323	19,680	17,572
Reinvested earnings:					
Dividends: Preferred stock	490	495	507	528	568
Common stock	11,737	10,704	9,710	8,868	8,864
Earnings reinvested during the year	15,916	13,415	11,106	10,284	8,140
Balance at beginning of year	139,567	129,996	118,890	108,606	100,466
Transfer to common stock re stock split	(3,731)	—	—	—	—
Excess of cost over par value of treasury preferred stock retired (95,489 shares)	—	(3,844)	—	—	—
Balance at end of year	$151,752	$139,567	$129,996	$118,890	$108,606
Per common share*:					
Income before extraordinary items	$ 2.21	$ 2.04	$ 1.72	$ 1.51	$ 1.41
Extraordinary (charges) credits	—	(0.09)	—	(0.07)	—
Net income	$ 2.21	$ 1.95	$ 1.72	$ 1.58	$ 1.41
Dividends declared	$ 0.94	$ 0.87	$ 0.80	$ 0.73	$ 0.73

* Adjusted for stock splits.

September 1970 a reorganization of the company's management structure. In the current management structure the following officers reported to the president and chief executive officer:

1. Group vice president, administration, who was responsible for corporate staff activities.
2. Group vice president, corporate development, who was responsible for research and development, for corporate planning, and for certain divisions formed to market new products.

3. Executive vice president, international.
4. Executive vice president, operations, who was responsible for manufacturing, engineering, purchasing, distribution, and employee relations.
5. Group vice president, grocery products, who was responsible for marketing activities.

The reorganization decentralized all operations into four major profit centers called "groups": grocery products (United States and Canada), international grocery products, industrial and institutional products, and toys and recreational products. Mr. Stuart stated that the toy and recreational group would be expanded considerably by means of internal growth and acquisitions. The decentralized corporate structure was expected to facilitate the implementation of top management's plans to continue to expand and diversify the enterprise. Exhibit 2 presents Quaker Oats' management structure after the 1970 reorganization.

PLANNING HISTORY

Quaker began long-range planning in fiscal 1965. The plans created that year, and annually thereafter, were primarily numbers-oriented estimates of income and requirements of capital. Emphasis was placed on the first year of the annual, three-year plans; the last two years were more or less extrapolations of the first year. Concentration was on existing businesses, which were treated in great financial detail.

Initially, responsibility for supervision of both long- and short-range plans reposed with a director of corporate planning. However, the corporate planner's heavy involvement in acquisition studies and negotiations, coupled with his limited staff capability, forced him to rely upon the controller's office for staff support in supervising, reviewing, and consolidating the company's plans. By mid-1968 responsibility for short-range planning (annual two-year plans) had been shifted to the corporate controller's office, which created a department entitled profit planning and analysis (PP&A) to handle the task. Responsibilities for long-range planning and acquisitions were split. When the director of long-range planning left the company in early 1969, the long-range planning position was left vacant.

Robert A. Bowen, vice president and controller since the mid-1960s, stated that while he had been in a position to influence the company's planning he had endeavored to gain a more explicit grasp of what made the business tick. He had collected, through the planning process, detailed quantitative indicators of product group performance over the previous three to four years. The "back data," as he termed this information, included historical comparisons of product expenses

EXHIBIT 2 Executive Reporting Relationships

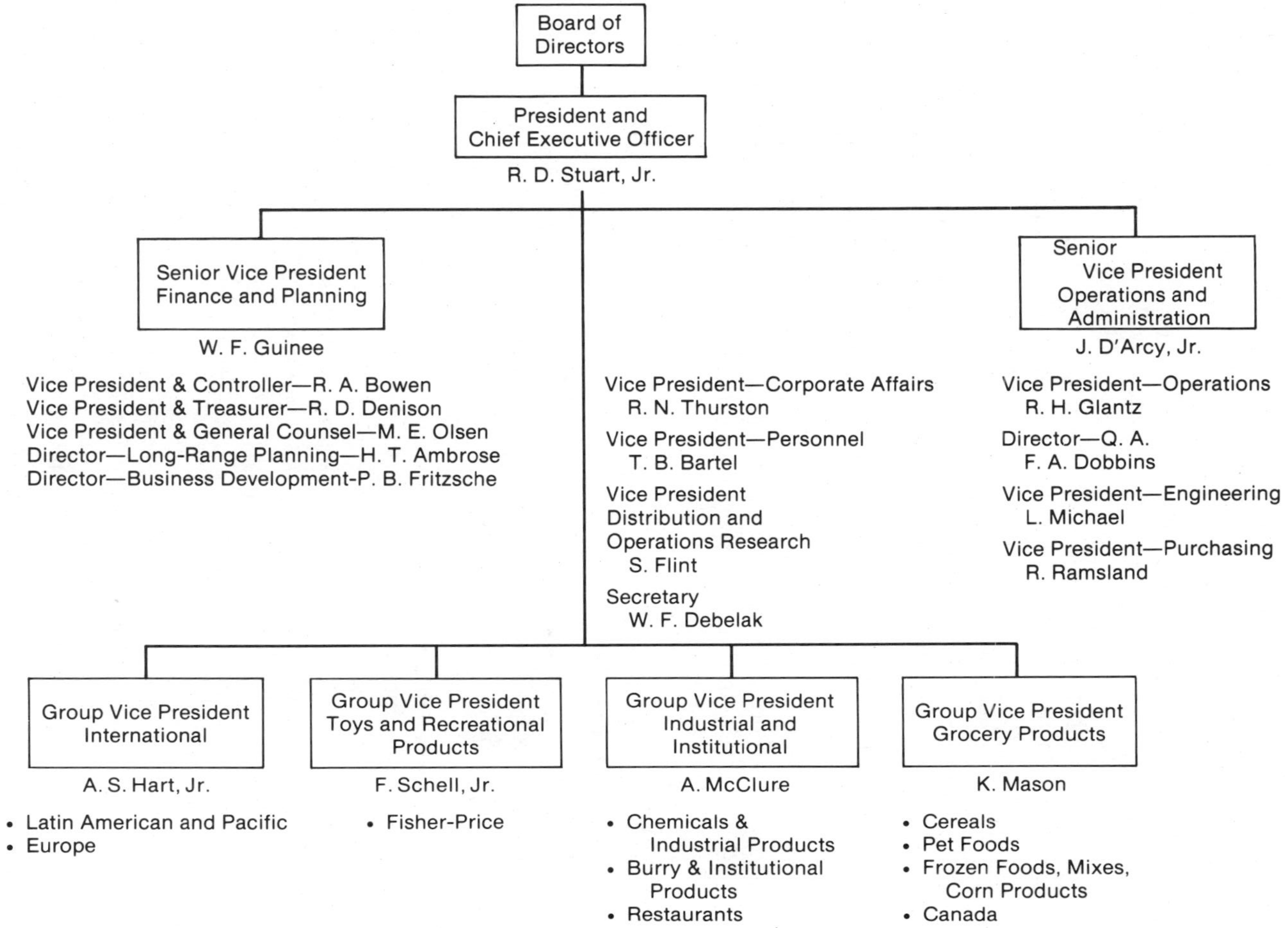

and asset utilization. In addition, Mr. Bowen had accumulated comparative information on ten of Quaker Oats' chief competitors. He had distributed relevant portions of the back data to Quaker's managers annually as a part of the planning process. Mr. Bowen intended to continue this practice, which he believed aided operating managers in formulating realistic operating plans.

However, in 1969 overall responsibility for Quaker's long-range planning processes was assumed by W. Fenton Guinee. Previously, the vice president of marketing services, Mr. Guinee had recently been appointed to the position of group vice president of corporate development. (In September 1970 his title was again changed to senior vice president, finance and planning.) After, in his words, "taking awhile to figure out what long-range planning was . . . through reading and discussion with the president and business school contacts," Mr. Guinee decided that Quaker needed more strategic thinking and fewer numbers in its plans. He characterized the company as evolving from a rather homogeneous business to a montage of partial profit centers and functional organizations in substantially different businesses and having different needs. Mr. Guinee thought that the information flows represented by plans should be altered to fit the changing management structure. In particular, plans should reflect the rationale behind operating management's decisions and performance.

Harry Ambrose's Job

Following extensive discussions with the president, in September 1970 Mr. Guinee appointed Harry T. Ambrose to the position of director of long-range planning. Mr. Ambrose was to aid Mr. Guinee in designing and overseeing a formal planning system which recognized the changing management needs of the company. Mr. Ambrose was instructed to work closely with the head of the profit-planning and analysis department in coordinating a formal planning system which accounted for both short-term and long-term planning needs.

To guide Mr. Ambrose in his work, Mr. Guinee gave him copies of memorandums exchanged by Messrs. Stuart and Guinee, which laid out their expectations regarding the formal planning system. Following is a summary of their position:

A. The purpose of long-range planning was to be:
   1. Develop agreement among divisional, group, and corporate management on written goals and strategies based on projections of long-term needs.
   2. Identify future resource needs of skills, personnel, organization, finances, and new businesses to allow for their development in an orderly manner.

B. No substantive changes in the concept, content, and administration of the two-year planning effort were to be contemplated.

C. The long-range plan was to cover five fiscal years beginning after the current fiscal year. (Quaker's fiscal year ran from July 1 to June 30.) The content of the long-range plan was to include:

   1. Description of current state of the business and of each of its major functional areas.
   2. Assumptions about future economy, social and political environment, technological developments, and competition.
   3. Recommended objectives.
   4. Recommended strategies.
   5. Identification of risks.

   The plans were to include statements describing a selected strategy supported by numbers defining the magnitude of growth, investments, and risks. The alternative strategies considered were to be described along with the reason for the one recommended. Compared with the two-year plan, in the five-year plan relatively greater emphasis was to be placed on the written statements and recommendations, with numbers being used to provide reasonably quantified approximations of the direction chosen, rather than as an instrument for controlling or for measuring managerial performance.

D. Responsibility for development of divisional plans was to rest with divisional vice presidents and/or general managers; for group plans, with group vice presidents; and for corporate plans, with the planning committee (identified as the president plus the two senior vice presidents).

E. Divisional management was to be responsible for securing approval of their plans from group management, who in turn was to be responsible for securing approval of group plans from the planning committee. The latter was to review group plans in detail, direct appropriate modifications and the development of a consolidated corporate plan for presentation to the executive committee of the board of directors.

F. Responsibility for the format and administration of both two-year and long-range plans was to be that of the senior vice president—finance and planning. Responsibilities of individual departments in finance and planning were to be as indicated in Exhibit 3.

G. For the first annual planning process, both the two-year and long-range planning efforts were to proceed concurrently, commencing in January 1971 and concluding in June of that year. Timing of future planning was to be reviewed after the completion of 1971's planning.

H. Review of the five-year plans was to be focused upon the quality of current and previous analyses and conclusions rather than the

EXHIBIT 3 Delineation of Responsibilities in Planning

	Two-year		*Five-year*	
	*Profit planning and analysis**	*Long-range planning*	*Profit planning and analysis**	*Long-range planning*
Develop manual	Primary	Collaborative	Collaborative	Primary
Develop financial format	Primary	None	Primary	Collaborative
Develop format for statement and recommendations	Primary	None	Collaborative	Primary
Provide financial back data	Primary	None	Primary	None
Coordinate planning	Primary	Primary	None	None
Consolidate into corporate figures	Primary	None	None	Primary
Critique plans	Primary	Collaborative	Collaborative	Primary
Identify deviations from plan	Primary	None	None	Primary

* Under direction of vice president–controller.

accuracy of numerical projections. Whereas responsibility for achievement of two-year plan goals was to rest primarily with the person responsible for operating a particular area, responsibility for the strategies selected in the five-year plan was to be shared between the person recommending the plan and the person approving it.

Remarks by Fenton Guinee

What we are trying to accomplish with our planning system must be considered in light of the corporate situation. Our determination to achieve profitable diversification as a basis for future growth has spurred some notable changes in the way the company is managed.

Operational responsibilities were restructured last September so that many of our managers now have overall responsibility for all four functions (marketing, finance, production, and personnel) instead of only one. We have found that this is a very difficult reorientation for some managers to make.

Even if we had not reorganized in 1970, we probably would reintroduce long-range planning now. Quaker needs to be looking beyond its immediate future and next year's profits to the issues which will determine its long-term viability.

But, also, we expect the introduction of a planning system at a time when the managers' tasks are changing to help them to define their new tasks. Sure, the work load is going to be enormous, but we are forcing them to look beyond their own previous functional expertises immediately. Therefore they are going to develop as general managers much quicker.

Harry's task is to work out a working balance between the amount and quality of effort managers put into short-term versus long-term planning. Right now we don't know what this balance should be. We do know, however, that each type of planning is important in its own right.

Short-term planning is well established at Quaker. We have fine budgeting and control systems. The managers use them and seem to believe in them. But the quality of the decisions made through these systems may begin to deteriorate if the decision makers lose pace with corporate objectives and strategies. Long-range planning should function to maintain this pace through the introduction of new information, analysis, and properly disseminated decisions.

Harry Ambrose's Comments

I suppose that I was selected for this job because my background was in line management [not staff] and because I am on good terms with most of the division managers. I was formerly director of materials purchasing under the old functional corporate setup, and I got to know most of the present division managers pretty well because my job took me all over the company.

Mr. Stuart and Mr. Guinee have pretty well thought out what they want planning to do and how Quaker ought to go about doing it. Nevertheless, there always remain a number of practical problems to be ironed out. This much I know from my own experience as a manager and from my investigations into how other companies plan.

I don't expect that we are going to leap right into an ideal planning system immediately. With the uncertainty arising from the new corporate structure and the two-year planning going on at the same time as long-range planning, I expect that long-range planning is not going to get as much attention as I would like.

Therefore, I think that I should try to achieve some limited objectives in planning this year. First, I would like to establish in the managers' minds that long-range planning is here to stay and is an important part of their jobs. Second, I would like to educate them in the rationale of long-range planning. In particular, I need to break them away from thinking that long-range planning is the extrapolation of short-term quantitative relationships. Quaker's managers must come to realize that different kinds of factors are at work in the long term and that because many of these factors are very intangible their handling requires the use of a disciplined, logical, technique.

There are a lot of factors which will determine the ultimate success or failure of the planning program. Certainly one of these factors will be the kind and quality of cooperation that I get from PP&A. It appears to me that the delineation of responsibilities in planning between PP&A and the long-range planning department was based primarily upon existing staff capabilities. In essence, any of the planning which dealt with financial statements was assigned to PP&A. Financial analysis is their specialty and they have a staff of about 12 skilled people. The long-range planning department consists of myself plus an assistant and a secretary.

Fortunately I have a good working relationship with the head of PP&A. We have managed to resolve amicably differences of opinion relating to the format and content of the long-range plans. In general, he tends to see more of a need in the plans for detailed, precise information than I do. For example, one of our arguments revolved around whether to round all financial data in the plans off to the nearest thousand dollars or the nearest million dollars. I finally managed to persuade him that the larger figure was adequate to indicate the direction and magnitude of financial results—which was all that was necessary for the long-range plans.

The head of PP&A also would like to see (as would I) the long-range plans precede the short-range plans so that the former could be used to provide direction for the latter. However, we differ on the question of how tight the linkage between long-range plans and short-range plans should be. His opinion (which is shared by Mr. Guinee) is that the forecast performance in the first two years of the five-year plan should be required to match precisely the forecast performance in the short-range plan. I believe that he feels that this requirement is necessary to gain commitment to, and inject reality in, the long-range plans. I feel that it would be more useful at this time to concentrate more upon developing the managers' ability to create alternative strategies than to tie them to a rigid planning program.

Questions

1. Evaluate Quaker Oats' planning system.
2. Do the various aspects of Quaker Oats' planning and control system tie together?
3. What advice would you give to Harry Ambrose concerning activities that will achieve his objectives?

CASE 9–2
Copley Manufacturing Company*

Copley Manufacturing Company had begun formal, corporate-wide planning in 1966. Its planning system was modified in 1967 and modified again in 1968. Company executives reviewed the experiences of these three years to see what lessons could be learned that would lead to an improved planning system.

Copley had grown fairly steadily in size and profitability since its founding in 1902; its growth was particularly rapid in the late 1950s and the 1960s. For most of its history, it was primarily a manufacturer of a wide line of cutting tools and related parts and supplies, and the cutting

* This case was prepared by Robert N. Anthony, Harvard Business School.

tool division in 1968 was the largest division. In 1968 there were eight other operating divisions, each making and selling a line of industrial products. Some of these divisions were the outgrowth of acquisitions; others had their origin in products developed by the corporate research department. Divisions had considerable autonomy. Sales volume in 1968 was $350 million, net income was $21 million, and there were 17,000 employees.

INTRODUCTION TO FORMAL PLANNING

The formal planning effort at the corporate level was an outgrowth of work initiated by Russell A. Wilde, in mid 1962. Mr. Wilde had been head of the Precipitator Division's commercial development department, and as such had been deeply involved in the division's efforts beginning early in 1962 to "plan ahead." Mr. Wilde's effort at the corporate level actually began as a search for companies to acquire, since Copley's top management saw the key question to be: "How should we diversify?" Within six months, Mr. Wilde was arguing that the crucial questions to be asked really were: "What are our objectives?" and "What is our potential?"

One result of the dialogue that followed was a request by Stanley Burton, president of Copley, for the divisions to look 10 years ahead and to predict sales, profit, cash flow, and return on investment. Mr. Wilde composed the actual questions asked of the divisions and coordinated collection of the data. The resulting consolidated growth projection was not ideal in the eyes of top management, but no imminent crisis was seen.

The 10-year look indicated that many of Copley's markets were mature, that its profits were indeed sensitive to cyclical swings, and that a large cash flow could be expected in the coming years. Before the end of 1963, Charles N. Sagan was appointed director of corporate development, reporting to Mr. Burton. Mr. Sagan was to be mainly concerned with growth through acquisition and merger.

Late in 1965, Mr. Sagan began reporting to Mr. Albert, executive vice president. The two easily agreed that regular formal planning should become part of management's way of life at Copley. They were encouraged to work toward this end when Samuel K. Savage, chairman of the board, suggested that Copley should do some five-year sales forecasting.

THE 1966 EFFORT

A Corporate Planning Committee was set up in February 1966 by Mr. Albert to guide the move toward a regular, formal planning process. The planning committee comprised the vice president for research, the controller, the corporate economist, Mr. Albert, and Mr. Sagan. The latter was named chief coordinator of the committee.

The planning committee met almost weekly for the next few months, and attacked two major questions:

1. By what process should formalized planning be ingrained into life at Copley?
2. What are appropriate corporate goals for Copley?

A year later, in early 1967, no answer had yet been given to the second question, but decisions were made concerning the first.

A March 21, 1966, memorandum from Mr. Albert to division general managers cited a need for regular formal planning and outlined a plan and schedule for starting such an effort. The basic idea was to survey divisional planning history and attitudes and, after discussions, to issue guidelines for the preparation of divisional "provisional plans."

VISITS BY CORPORATE GROUPS

The concept of formal planning activities was introduced to the organization through a series of visits to the divisions by corporate groups beginning June 6. The composition of the groups varied somewhat, but always included Mr. Albert and Mr. Sagan. In these introductory meetings, Mr. Albert explained the importance of the planning effort, and Mr. Sagan explained the details. Divisions were asked to produce a five-year plan by October 1, 1966. It was left to the divisions to decide exactly who would do what in the process and in what format the final plans would be presented. Corporate staff groups were also instructed to submit plans.

The controller described the financial data to be submitted in the five-year plan in a memorandum dated July 19, 1966, as follows:

> *Sales*—Please state past and future sales at 1966 prices and also in actual dollars, in total, by major product group, and by market group (e.g., domestic customers, export customers, intercompany).
>
> *Profit before Taxes*—Analyze projected dollars profit in terms of variance from projected 1966 dollars profit. The four significant areas of variance should be:
>
> *Price Realization*—The change in profit due to prices being higher or lower than 1966.
>
> *Volume and Product Mix*—The change in profit contribution due to changes in physical volume and product mix. This is calculated by applying 1966 contribution ratios to the change in physical volume, by product line.
>
> *Cost Variances*—Changes in unit variable costs or aggregate fixed costs should be stated. These aggregated changes should be sep-

arated into *price* (wage and material rates) variances and *efficiency* (all other) variances.

Profit after Taxes—Translate pretax to aftertax profit dollars for future years at the 1966 tax rate. Show income taxes and investment credit separately.

Cash Flow—The following should be shown by years in total and by product line where a determination can be made. *Full* product line data is not required, but some indication of cash flow, say inventories and capital expenditures, by product line will be helpful.

Profit after taxes.
Depreciation.
Accounts receivable.
Inventories.
Capital expenditures.
Other working capital items:
  Cash (working balance only).
  Prepaid expense.
  Accounts payable and accruals.
  Etc.
All other.
  Total Cash Flow

PLANNING REVIEW MEETINGS

Meetings to review divisional plans were held in November and December. As was expected, the format of the divisional plans and presentations varied widely. Attendance at the planning reviews varied, also. The planning committee always attended, as did the head of the division being reviewed. In addition, members of the Executive Committee attended on occasion. Divisions were free to bring whomever they wished to their planning review. Representatives of other divisions than the one being reviewed on a given day were not invited to attend.

PLANNING RESPONSE MEETINGS

A second series of meetings was started December 28, 1966. In these meetings, the planning committee commented on the divisional presentation to the division general managers. The divisions had been expecting some reaction by corporate management ever since the planning reviews, and these planning responses were designed to meet this expectation. Typical of these meetings was that of the Cutting Tool Division, whose general manager, Mr. Tyler, had recently become a member of the planning committee. The Cutting Tool Division discussion lasted three hours, with Mr. Tyler and the rest of the committee openly evaluating the Cutting Tool Division's plans and its planning review.

Mr. Albert sent a memorandum to the general manager of each division after its "planning response" meeting. Each memorandum summarized the major points agreed upon in the meeting, thanked the participants for their effort in 1966, and expressed the desire for continued progress in making planning a way of life for the Copley manager.

The results of the first planning cycle were judged as mixed by Mr. Sagan and by members of top management. It was generally felt that the divisions had made a good beginning, but that they had only begun to dent the planning task. Divisional plans were seen generally to be optimistic extrapolations of past operating trends. Some members of management criticized the effort as having been a numbers game. Others countered that these results were a necessary first step. Most agreed that the plans had been helpful in providing information that would aid top management in understanding better the various business activities of the corporation.

1967 ORGANIZATIONAL CHANGES

1967 witnessed a number of organizational changes that were to affect planning in major ways. Chief among these was the elevation of Mr. Albert to president in March. The corporate planning function moved up with Mr. Albert, continuing to report directly to him.

Several other important organizational changes followed shortly after. Two corporate staff functions were created, one for marketing and the other for research/development. Operating responsibility was further delegated: the International Division was to report to the new executive vice president, John A. Tyler, the former general manager of the Cutting Tool Division. The Cutting Tool Division was divided along product lines to become two separate divisions.

Two group vice presidents were named, each responsible for three divisions, with the remaining four divisions reporting directly to Mr. Tyler.

BEGINNING OF THE 1967 PLANNING ACTIVITIES

In contrast with the "numbers" orientation of the 1966 planning efforts, Mr. Sagan recommended an increased emphasis on strategic concepts in 1967. After some discussion, the planning committee decided to separate the formal planning cycle into three phases. The first phase, to be held in the spring, was termed the *Strategy Development* phase. The second, or *Quantitative,* phase would summarize, during the fall, the financial and manpower implications of the strategies selected in the first phase. The final, or *Action,* phase would aim to translate the results of planning into specific programs for action.

In mid-March, the new president, Mr. Albert, sent a letter to each division manager outlining the planning cycle for 1967 and the objectives for the planning efforts that had been agreed to by the planning committee.

The division's strategic plans were presented to corporate management by each division in a review meeting and subsequently evaluated in a response meeting. Unlike 1966, when they were held a month apart, these meetings in 1967 followed each other on the same day.

FURTHER DEVELOPMENTS IN 1967

Several developments were to impede progress of the planning efforts in 1967. As already mentioned, there was a new president, who introduced seven persons into new corporate executive positions. These changes in top management were temporarily disruptive to the planning effort.

Also, considerable management effort was required in assimilating a recently acquired large company and in working out the split-up of the old Cutting Tool Division into the two new divisions.

In 1966, the company had reported its highest sales and earnings ever. The annual report stated that prospects were for a strong 1967. But the machine tool industry was to suffer from depressed market conditions. Sales were down 1.6 percent from 1966; earnings per share declined 35.8 percent. Efforts to counter the unfavorable business conditions became a dominant preoccupation for key line executives.

On July 11, after completion of the strategy development phase of the planning cycle, the planning committee met to consider the planning efforts for the remainder of 1967. In view of the developments noted above, it decided against proceeding with the quantitative phase originally scheduled for the fall. It did, however, recommend that staff departments begin the planning process by analyzing past results and identifying resources, strengths, weaknesses, major problems, and major opportunities of their divisions. Mr. Albert approved the recommendations. The Corporate Goals Committee also lessened its efforts to prepare a statement of corporate goals.

In view of the disruption of formal planning at Copley, top management made special efforts to declare that long-range planning was there to stay. In a letter to division managers dated October 24, Mr. Albert explained the decision to curtail formal planning and emphasized that nothing would be allowed to stand in the way of doing the complete planning job in 1968. He reaffirmed his intention to emphasize planning at Copley in his president's statement in the 1967 annual report: "Long-range planning will become a way of life at our Company. By this medium we will set specific goals, allocate resources of talent and money, and measure our progress. There will be increased emphasis on the delegation of responsibility and in the measurement of performance against predetermined goals."

SITUATION IN 1968

The Copley Company recovered financially in 1968 with a 6.2 percent improvement in net sales and a 58 cent gain in earnings per share.

The Corporate Goals Committee held several informal dinner meetings during the first half of 1967 to discuss a framework developed by Mr. Sagan for arriving at corporate goals. Although a definite statement of corporate goals was not drawn up, the members generally felt that much progress had been made and that it had been a useful and educational experience for all who had participated. The committee as originally constituted was inactive in late 1967 and early 1968, but Mr. Sagan continued to work independently with Mr. Albert on the task. In line with these activities, Mr. Albert was quoted in the business press as stating corporate expectations to include a minimum annual profit growth of 10 percent and a return on equity of 12.5 percent.

In 1968, the planning process in large part came to be influenced and administered by Mr. Tyler, executive vice president. Mr. Tyler, who had moved up from head of the Cutting Tool Division when Mr. Albert assumed the presidency of Copley, enjoyed the reputation among his colleagues as a hard-driving, no-nonsense line manager who had little patience for elaborate staff support.

In Mr. Tyler's opinion, division managers had been planning in previous years largely to satisfy the requirements set by the planning staff and had failed to become committed to the plans. He saw voluminous documentation required in 1967 to present a divisional strategy and financial plan as one reason for this failure to identify with the planning output. Thus, in 1968, division managers were asked to present each product group strategy in a statement of two pages or less and the related financial five-year plan on only one page.

The divisional strategy statements were to cover information on such items as industry trends, market size, competition, and major opportunities or threats, as well as a description of the proposed strategic response. For the financial plan, divisions were required to submit figures for only the first, second, and fifth years of the five-year plan. The purpose of this abbreviation was to reduce the time spent on the numbers, thereby allowing divisional management more time for strategic considerations.

The management review process was also altered. Divisional presentations before the planning committee was replaced by two other meetings. The first of these was a one-hour "pre-meeting" attended by Mr. Albert, Mr. Tyler, the division general manager, and the responsible group vice president. In this pre-meeting Albert and Tyler explained Copley's strategy and acquisition policy, and reviewed the findings and conclusions of the Product Line Study. During the remainder of the hour, the division manager had to explain and to defend the division's strategy for the coming year. At the end of the one-hour meeting the president gave his decision on the division's plans. This review was immediately followed by a three-hour meeting in which the division manager and his staff presented their plans for the first time to the remaining members of the Executive Committee and to selected members of the corporate staff.

Mr. Sagan, director of corporate development, became visibly disturbed by the recent turn of events in planning. He felt himself increasingly limited to corporate merger and acquisition studies. He was fearful that the company would revert to a short-term orientation if it continued along the present path. In voicing these objections to Mr. Albert, he realized that the formal planning system that he had worked so hard to develop was at stake. As a result of these discussions, he felt that he still had the full confidence and support of the chief executive. At the same time, Mr. Albert publicly acknowledged the benefits of getting increased line involvement in planning.

RECENT DEVELOPMENTS

In an interview in late 1969, Mr. Tyler described recent developments:

> As was John Albert's desire, we believe planning is now a way of life at Copley. There just does not appear to be as much need today for a structured management of the process with a planning department per se at the corporate level. This is not to say that all line managers develop plans and strategies to the same degree of effectiveness. But the actual responsibility for planning has been placed directly on the line—that is, the executive vice president, the group vice presidents, and in turn, their various division managers.
>
> For various reasons, Charlie Sagan left the company earlier this year. Fred Fisher has been appointed director of corporate development, but his job description was rewritten to put the emphasis on the planning and execution of growth through acquisition.
>
> The planning process in 1968 followed pretty well the steps we had laid out.
>
> In January 1969 we changed the format for the divisional planning presentations. My letter of January 30 [Exhibit 1] describes our current system of informing all key managers within the company of each division's long-range plans and broad strategies.
>
> This technique of communicating divisional plans was preceded in December of 1968 by a two-day conference in Bermuda with essentially the same group in attendance. At that conference, we reviewed all of the divisional plans up until that point and announced the broad corporate goals and strategies.

EXHIBIT 1 Letter Announcing a Series of Executive Meetings (excerpts)

January 30, 1969

It is always difficult to draw lines across an organization, but those to whom this letter is addressed are either managing profit centers or are directing broad staff functions vital to Copley's operations and to its future growth.

We believe it is important to provide the means for keeping each person in this group better informed of the plans and progress of each division and each staff function as well as the total corporate programs.

The method selected to provide better communications will be tested over the next twelve months and will involve a series of nine meetings; the time and place of each are listed on the attached schedule. Each meeting will start at 1:30 P.M. on the first Monday of the month. They will end at 5:00 P.M. A different division will host each meeting on a rotating basis.

An agenda is planned as follows. From 1:30 to 2:00 P.M. five or six prepared talks of five minutes' duration will be given on subjects of current and general interest selected by the chairman in consultation with others. The following half hour (2:00–2:30) will be devoted to announcements from both the floor and the chairman.

At 2:30, the division manager serving as host will take charge of the meeting. He will have a total of two and one half hours during which he is asked to present his long-range plans, allow time for questions and comments, and complete a plant tour of some portion of his facilities.

The group of key executives in attendance does not make up a decision-making committee or a review board in the general sense. They are, however, encouraged to ask questions for interpretation and better understanding. The long-rang plans presented by the division manager will previously have been approved by the president, executive and group vice presidents. The division managers are asked to present their plans in simply written reports using an expanded outline technique. Copies will be reproduced by the division manager following the meeting on a request basis.

This test period will last through the February 1970 meeting. If it is felt these meetings cannot be made to serve their original intention, they will be discontinued.

/s/ John A. Tyler
Executive Vice President

In the same interview Mr. Tyler furnished a copy of a recent talk in which he stated his personal belief about management:

> I believe that corporate planning is *the* major responsibility of top management. It involves the direction of the whole company (not the parts) in deciding specifically what businesses the company wants to be in, in determining what rate of growth is desirable, in determining what method of growth is intended (research, acquisition, merger). I am a

believer in decentralization; in delegating a great deal of authority; giving people their head; permitting some experiments and some mistakes; but sink or swim is the theory.

I do not believe in too many specialized staff functions to clutter up an organization. I avoid "assistant to's" and "administrative assistants" except for short-term projects or as training spots in someone's career.

I believe a good manager by definition must put out the daily fires, improve the current quarter's earnings, and at the same time be a long-range planner. If a manager cannot do both, I do not believe the solution lies in shoring him up via a corporate planning department. I *do* believe it lies in using the talent of both line and specific staff personnel who surround him.

I believe in using the talents already present in marketing, finance, research, and manufacturing—and the head of each of these areas must be a planner himself or *he* will fail. I am opposed to separating the division managers from the top management by allowing any staff group to represent or speak for them—or to take their cues from them.

I believe that America's greatest companies succeeded because one man or group of individuals with strong convictions made things happen. They had vision and used intuition in varying degrees but they did their own planning and monitoring of results. I may be overgeneralizing, but normally a company has its best all-around talent in top line positions. They are there because they have a good balance of talents and experience. For that reason, their judgment should have the greatest influence in strategy formation as well as final decision making. By this, I do not mean to imply that line personnel think more strategically than staff personnel. The opposite may, in fact, be true. There are often individuals way down the organization in both line and staff who are thinking persons.

Finally, I strongly believe there is a great tendency in American business to overmanage, overplan, overstaff, and overorganize, which is contributing in a major way to our declining ability to compete in world markets. Our fixed costs in staff and management are often a larger factor than factory labor in making us noncompetitive.

Questions

1. How do you appraise for formal planning efforts at the Copley Company?
2. What do you predict will occur with respect to formal planning at Copley?
3. How would *you* handle formal planning at Copley?

CASE 9–3
Geebold Company *(A)*

Richard Monroe, controller of Geebold Company, sent the article which is abridged below to his assistant, Thomas Ritzman, with a memorandum in which he requested Ritzman to recommend whether the approach should be considered for adoption by the Geebold Company, either as presented or in some modified form.

Geebold Company was considerably larger than the company used as an illustration in the article. Its capital budgeting procedure required that all projects involving expenditures over $100,000 be approved by the president and board of directors. In the preceding year, there had been 15 such projects. A net present value was estimated for most of these projects, but in some cases the estimates were quite rough.

The article was entitled "Capital Budgeting: A Pragmatic Approach," and is reproduced in abridged form below.[1]

The utilization of theoretically optimal investment criterion, such as (1) accept any investment proposal which has a net present value greater than zero, or (2) accept those projects with the highest rate of return until the cutoff rate is reached, does not directly consider many practical constraints. Furthermore, a pragmatic approach, such as "accept those projects that appear desirable," is equally unpalatable. One possible method of treating both theoretical and practical considerations is to examine all possible combinations of investment alternatives to determine the effect of each combination on all of the corporate objectives. Although this method will certainly work, the computational task becomes huge when a large number of projects is considered. Thus, a more efficient and operational method is required.

A possible approach to this problem is to use the technique of linear programming to determine the optimal set of investment proposals. The objective of the approach would be to maximize the IRR (internal rate of return) or the NPV (net present value) of those investment alternatives under consideration subject to a set of constraints. The constraints, in addition to the supply of capital available, would be those factors, such as earnings per share, ROI (return on investment), dividends per share, R&D expenditures, and so forth, which management feels should be considered as operational or practical objectives of the firm.

It should be pointed out that ours is not the first attempt to apply linear programming techniques to the capital budgeting decision. In a doctoral dissertation published in 1963, H. Martin Weingartner at-

[1] By Alexander A. Robicheck, Donald G. Ogilvie, and John D. C. Roach. Abridged, by permission, from *Financial Executive,* April 1969.

tempted to utilize linear programming and integer programming in analyzing certain traditional problems of capital budgeting: namely, investment planning under capital rationing and under imperfect capital markets.

Other authors, such as Van Horne and Charnes, have also attempted to apply linear programming to capital budgeting problems. More recently, in a parallel study less broad in scope, Lerner and Rappaport describe an approach using linear programming and the net present values of projects. All of these authors have been influential in their attempt to introduce linear programming to the realm of capital budgeting decisions.

CAPITAL BUDGETING AS A LINEAR PROGRAMMING PROBLEM

Linear programming (LP) is a mathematical technique that provides optimal solutions to certain classes of problems. The problem must meet the following requirements: (1) the objective to be maximized must be stated in mathematical form; (2) the maximization of the objective must be subject to constraints or limits on certain resources or variables in the problem; (3) all relationships must be linear in character; and (4) there must be more than one way of solving the problem.

In a typical practical capital budgeting situation, the objective may be to maximize IRR or NPV, subject to constraints on the amount of cash available for investment, required earnings per share, limitations for particular projects, and so forth.

Perhaps the best way to illustrate how LP can be applied in practice is to present a simple case example. The example is intended merely to illustrate the methodology and is not necessarily representative of a real life situation.

CASE ILLUSTRATION

The company, its current status, and its objectives. The relevant information for this hypothetical company is shown in Exhibit 1. The company is relatively small, with aftertax earnings of $500,000 for the year just ended. Since there are 100,000 shares outstanding, the earnings per share (EPS) were $5. Management estimates earnings for the current year before any new investments to be $470,000 or $4.70 per share. Total cash currently available is $1.2 million, and estimated cash flow for the current year from existing projects without any new investment is $1.13 million.

Section B of Exhibit 1 summarizes the factors that the management feels reflect the company's operational goals. Desirous of a 6 percent growth in EPS, next year's goal is earnings of at least $5.30 per share, or $530,000 total. Management feels a 40 percent dividend payout ratio

EXHIBIT 1 Company Information

A. *Current data:*		
Actual earnings after taxes last year		$ 500,000
Number of shares outstanding		100,000
Earnings per share		$ 5.00
Cash available for investments and dividends		1,200,000
Estimated earnings for current year without new investment		470,000
Estimated cash flow for current year without new investment		1,130,000
B. *Goals and requirements for current year:*		
Earnings per share—minimum (6% increase)		5.30
Total earnings required		530,000
Less estimated earnings without new investment		470,000
Incremental earnings required from new investment		60,000
Cash flow required—minimum		1,300,000
Less estimated cash flow without new investment		1,130,000
Incremental cash flow required from new investments		170,000
Minimum R&D expenditures		300,000
Minimum "necessary" expenditures		60,000
Minimum dividends on last year's earnings (40 percent of earnings)		200,000
Cash available for new investments		1,200,000
Less: R&D expenditures	$300,000	
Necessary expenditures	60,000	
Dividends	200,000	560,000
Net cash available for new investments		$ 640,000

is appropriate. Therefore, a dividend of $2 per share ($200,000) is expected to be paid soon based on last year's earnings. Management estimates that $300,000 should be expended for R&D projects, and $60,000 is required for certain other necessary projects. Since the total capital available is $1.2 million, the amount available for new projects is $640,000. A minimum cash flow of $1.3 million is considered desirable for the current year.

Investment opportunities. With this company background information in mind, we can now analyze the investment opportunities open for consideration. Exhibit 2 summarizes five possible investment alternatives. The data for these projects are presented so that both the accounting income and the cash flow for each year are evident. The calculations in Exhibit 2 assume that the revenues and expenses estimated for determining the marginal accounting income are identical to the marginal revenues and marginal expenses necessary for calculating the cash flows. Under traditional accounting practices, this equality is not always maintained. Also for the sake of simplicity, straight-line depreciation is assumed for all projects for both tax and reporting purposes.

Exhibit 3 shows the initial investment required, the first year's accounting income, the first year's cash flow, and the computed internal rate of return for each of the five projects. In calculating the rate of

EXHIBIT 2 Investment Opportunities ($000)

(1) Period	(2) Investment	(3) Revenues	(4) Expenses	(5) Depreciation	(6) Operating income (3) − (4 + 5)	(7) Taxes (50%) .5(6)	(8) Accounting income (6) − (7)	(9) Cash flow (3) − (4) − (7)
				Project A				
1	100	140	85	25	30	15	15	40
2		175	100	25	50	25	25	50
3		175	100	25	50	25	25	50
4		175	100	25	50	25	25	50
				Project B				
1	300	100	80	60	(40)	(20)	(20)	40
2		400	200	60	140	70	70	130
3		1100	600	60	440	220	220	280
4		900	400	60	440	220	220	280
5		1500	800	60	640	320	320	380
				Project C				
1	200	300	140	100	60	30	30	130
2		200	80	100	20	10	10	110
				Project D				
1	300	230	105	75	50	25	25	100
2		300	125	75	100	50	50	125
3		350	145	75	130	65	65	140
4		400	165	75	160	80	80	155
				Project E				
1	200	200	110	40	50	25	25	65
2		200	110	40	50	25	25	65
3		220	120	40	60	30	30	70
4		240	130	40	70	35	35	75
5		270	140	40	90	45	45	85

EXHIBIT 3 Summary of Investment Opportunities

	Project				
	A	*B*	*C*	*D*	*E*
Initial investment ($000)	100	300	200	300	200
First year's accounting income ($000)	15	−20	30	25	25
First year's cash flow ($000)	40	40	130	100	65
Internal rate of return	30.4%	45.6%	13.5%	24.2%	22.2%

return, the investment cost was assumed to have been incurred on the first day of the first year, and all of the revenues and expenses were assumed to occur at the end of the respective periods.

Application of the LP procedure. For this particular example, the assumption will be made that management wishes to maximize the average IRR subject to the various constraints noted above. The formulation of the problem is as follows:

Maximize:

$$Z = .304X_1 + .456X_2 + .135X_3 + .242X_4 + .222X_5$$

where the X_js represent the amount of funds (in thousands of dollars) committed to project j and the coefficients preceding each X_j stand for the project IRRs shown in Exhibit 3. Average IRR is obtained by dividing Z by 640, the total funds available.

Subject to:

1. Budget constraint

$$X_1 + X_2 + X_3 + X_4 + X_5 \leqslant 640$$

The amount allocated to all projects cannot exceed $640,000, the total amount available.

2. Project constraints

$$\begin{aligned} 0 &\leqslant X_1 \leqslant 100 \\ 0 &\leqslant X_2 \leqslant 300 \\ 0 &\leqslant X_3 \leqslant 200 \\ 0 &\leqslant X_4 \leqslant 300 \\ 0 &\leqslant X_5 \leqslant 200 \end{aligned}$$

The commitment of funds to any one project cannot exceed the project's maximum required funds or be negative.

3. Earnings constraint

$$\frac{15}{100}X_1 - \frac{20}{300}X_2 + \frac{30}{200}X_3 + \frac{25}{300}X_4 + \frac{25}{200}X_5 \geqslant 60$$

The first year's earnings contributions from the accepted new project must be at least $60,000.

4. *Cash flow constraint*

$$\frac{40}{100}X_1 + \frac{40}{300}X_2 + \frac{130}{200}X_3 + \frac{100}{300}X_4 + \frac{65}{200}X_5 \geq 170$$

The first year's cash flow from the new projects must be at least $170,000.

The results of this capital budgeting model are given in Exhibit 4. As indicated in these results, the optimal solution is to accept all of Projects A and E, place $55,500 into Project B and $284,500 in Project D. No funds are committed to Project C. If this optimal allocation is made, the average IRR will be 26.4 percent. This is the highest obtainable average IRR, given the management constraints on the allocation process. (It should be noted that our formulation permitted acceptance of fractional projects. Should such fractional projects not be feasible, a technique called "integer programming" may have to be substituted for LP.)

EXHIBIT 4 Results of the Linear Programming Model

X_1 = Project A = 100.0
X_2 = Project B = 55.5
X_3 = Project C = 0
X_4 = Project D = 284.5
X_5 = Project E = 200.0
Z = Objective = 168.97

$$\text{Average IRR} = \frac{Z}{640} = \frac{168.97}{640} = 26.4\%$$

If the management of this company is convinced that no additional capital can be raised, and if they are unwilling to reduce any of their requirements for earnings, dividends, R&D, or necessary expenditures, then the usefulness of the LP model is exhausted. The optimal allocation has been determined. However, we seriously doubt that any management is so totally recalcitrant that they will not even question these requirements. This is where the additional information made available by LP becomes invaluable.

Dual variables. In addition to the data shown in Exhibit 4, the LP solution provides values for the so-called dual variables. These values are not reproduced here, but they provide the basis for testing the sensitivity of the solution to the changes in the various management-imposed restraints. For example, we can determine that the addition of $1,000 to cash available for new projects would increase Z by .360; that is, the IRR on the marginal $1,000 would be 36.0 percent. With this type of evidence confronting management, a decision may well be made either to raise additional capital from outside sources or to reduce the originally planned level of expenditures for R&D, necessary projects, or dividends.

Even more striking is the value of the dual variable for the earnings constraint—1.42. This means that if management were to reduce their earnings requirement by \$1,000 (from \$60,000 to \$59,000) the value of Z would increase by 1.42 and the average IRR would rise from 26.40 percent to 26.73 percent. This increase is accomplished by switching \$6,667 from Project D to Project B. In other words, the reduction in earnings requirements permits a shift of funds from a project with a relatively low IRR but an attractive first-year earnings to a project that offers a very high rate of return, but reports an accounting loss in the first year. Although ours is not the job to judge the validity or reasonableness of this earnings requirement, the LP solution points out the dramatic and severe opportunity cost associated with this policy.

On the other hand, analysis of the LP solution indicates that the minimum cash requirement presents no problems and that, for practical purposes, the minimum cash constraint has no effect on the allocation procedure.

This analysis in depth of the LP solution illustrates the value that can be obtained from utilizing a linear programming procedure to solve capital budgeting problems. It forces management to question the real worth of their various "practical" goals of constraints. Furthermore, it gives them a number, the value of the dual variable, against which they can compare, analyze, and question their own set of objectives.

CONCLUSION

The state of the art of capital budgeting has come a long way in the last 18 years. Corporate management has grown increasingly aware of the overwhelming importance of financial decisions on the future growth and profitability of the firm. A great deal of valuable theoretical work has been done in identifying and evaluating the critical variables in the firm's investment and financing decision, and some of this work has been adopted on a practical basis.

However, we are a long way from having the theory provide the answers to all the questions of the modern financial manager. The contemporary financial executive is painfully aware of the multiplicity of corporate goals and objectives which he must keep in a delicate balance. The model proposed in this article is designed to help bridge the gap between theory and practice. We do not propose it as the ultimate solution to these difficult problems, but we do believe it is a step in the right direction.

CHAPTER 10

Budget Preparation

This chapter presents an overview of the budgeting process, focusing on the preparation of budgets. The description of this process is continued in Chapters 11 and 12. In Chapter 11 we describe budget reporting techniques, with particular emphasis on analyzing profit budget variances. In Chapter 12, we describe the role of the profit budget in the evaluation of divisional management.

BUDGETS VERSUS FORECASTS

A budget differs in several respects from a forecast or a projection. A *budget* is a management plan, with the assumption that positive steps will be taken by the budgetee to make actual events correspond to the plan; whereas, a *forecast* is merely a prediction of what will most likely happen, carrying no implication that the forecaster will attempt to shape events so that the forecast will be realized. A projection is not a prediction, but an estimation of what will happen if various conditions and situations should exist. Typically, a projection is prepared using a computer to respond to "what if" types of questions.

A budget has the following characteristics:

1. It is stated in monetary terms, although the monetary amounts may be backed up by nonmonetary amounts (e.g., units sold or produced).
2. It generally covers a period of one year.[1]
3. It contains an element of management commitment, in that managers agree to accept the responsibility for attaining the budgeted objectives.
4. The budget proposal is reviewed and approved by an authority higher than the budgetee.

---

[1] In businesses that are strongly influenced by seasonal factors, there may be two budgets per year; for example, apparel companies typically have a fall budget and a spring budget.

5. Once approved, the budget can be changed only under specified conditions.
6. Periodically, actual financial performance is compared to budget and variances are analyzed and explained.

A *forecast* has the following characteristics:

1. It may or may not be stated in monetary terms.
2. It can be for any time period.
3. The forecaster does not accept responsibility for meeting the forecast results.
4. Forecasts are not usually approved by higher authority.
5. A forecast is updated as soon as new information indicates there is a change in conditions.
6. Variances from forecast are not analyzed formally or periodically. (The forecaster does some analysis, but this is to improve the ability to forecast.)

An example of a financial forecast is one that is made by the treasurer's office to help in cash planning. Such a forecast includes estimates of sales, expenses, capital expenditures, and so forth. The treasurer, however, has no responsibility for making the actual results conform to the forecast. It is not cleared with top management; it may change weekly or even daily, without approval from higher authority; and usually variances between actual and forecast are not systematically analyzed.

From management's point of view, a financial forecast is exclusively a planning tool; whereas a budget is both a planning tool and a control tool. All budgets include elements of financial forecasting, in the sense that the budgetee cannot be held responsible for certain events that affect his or her ability to meet budgeted objectives. If, however, a budgetee can change the so-called budget each quarter without formal approval (or, if the formal approval is perfunctory), such a budget is essentially a financial forecast rather than a true budget. It cannot be used for evaluation and control since by the end of the year, actual results will always equal the revised budget.

If one thinks of a spectrum with a pure budget system at one end and a pure financial forecasting system at the other, most budgetary control systems fall somewhere between these two extremes. The approximate location of a particular budgetary control system on this spectrum can be estimated by comparing the characteristics of the system with the characteristics just described. If a particular system happens to have more of the characteristics of a financial forecast than of a budget, this is not necessarily bad. It simply means that management must realize that it is more of a planning tool than a control tool.

TYPES OF BUDGETS

In this section, we describe some of the more common types of budgets. These budgets closely parallel the types of responsibility centers described in earlier chapters.

Expense Budgets

Expense budgets can be divided into two types:

A. Budgets involving engineered expenses in responsibility centers, in which output can be measured.
B. Budgets involving discretionary expenses in responsibility centers, in which output cannot be measured.

Engineered expense budgets. Manufacturing plants typically have engineered expense budgets, but they are also used in other organization units whose output is measurable. The basis for a manufacturing budget is the standard cost system. An annual production schedule is developed from the sales budget (to be described later), and the standard cost of material and direct labor for each element of cost is applied to each item of production. This is normally done by responsibility centers so that each department has a standard budgeted material amount (often by type of material) and a standard budgeted direct labor amount.

Next, overhead is estimated at the budgeted production volume and all overhead costs are charged directly or allocated to productive departments. Standard overhead rates are developed, usually by dividing the total overhead by a measure of activity, such as total standard direct labor dollars or hours.

Finally, overhead is divided into its variable and fixed elements, and budget equations are developed so that the budgeted overhead expense can be adjusted to the actual volume of production. These equations constitute the flexible budget. This provides the means for separating the spending variance, which is normally the responsibility of the operating manager, from the volume variance, which is normally not the responsibility of the operating manager. (Techniques for calculating spending and volume variance are described in Chapter 11.)

Engineered expense budgets have the following characteristics:

1. They are designed to measure efficiency. Normally, an unfavorable variance means that production costs are greater than they should have been (although this may not necessarily be the fault of the operating manager).
2. Operating managers accept almost complete responsibility for attaining budgeted goals, because most of the performance variables are under their control. The impact of the principal uncertainty,

variances in sales volume, is eliminated through the flexible budget.

Discretionary expense budgets. Techniques for budgeting discretionary centers were described in Chapter 5. To review, discretionary expense budgets have the following characteristics:

1. They are *not* designed to measure efficiency or inefficiency.
2. The budgetee is responsible for spending the amounts set forth, neither more nor less (with perhaps some leeway), unless a change is specifically approved.

Revenue Budgets

Revenue responsibility centers prepare two types of budgets. There is an expense budget, which was described in Chapter 5. There is a revenue budget, as described below.

A revenue budget consists of unit sales projections multiplied by expected selling prices. Of all of the elements of a profit budget, the revenue budget is the most critical, yet, at the same time, it is the element that is subject to the greatest uncertainty. The degree of uncertainty differs among companies, and within the same company the degree of uncertainty is different at different times. Companies with large back orders or companies where the sales volume is constrained by production capacity will have less uncertainty in sales projections than companies whose sales volume is subject to the uncertainties of the marketplace. The important management consideration of the revenue budget is that it usually contains forecasts of some conditions for which the sales manager cannot be held responsible. For example, the state of the economy or competitive pricing action are conditions which must be anticipated in preparing a revenue budget, yet the marketing manager has little control over them. Nevertheless, the manager does have a considerable degree of control over sales volume. Effective advertising, good service, good quality, and well-trained salespeople influence sales volume, and the manager does control these factors.

Revenue budgets have the following characteristics:

1. The budget is designed to measure effectiveness in marketing. Unfavorable variances from budget means that sales volume or prices are lower than top management believed was a reasonable goal.
2. The marketing manager cannot be held as completely responsible for meeting the budgeted objectives as is the case with expense budgets. Many of the uncertainties of the marketplace are beyond the manager's control, particularly in the short run. This limits the usefulness of a revenue budget in managerial evaluation.

In using actual performance compared with a revenue budget as a basis for evaluation, it is helpful if controllable variances can be separated from noncontrollable variances. Chapter 11 describes some techniques for doing this.

The Profit Budget

Where a manager has control over both revenues and expenses, the expense and revenue budgets can be combined into a profit budget. Because the profit budget includes the other budgets described above, and is the most important component of the annual comprehensive master operating budget, we will concentrate almost exclusively on profit budgets in the remainder of this chapter and in Chapters 11 and 12.

A profit budget is an annual profit plan. It consists of a set of projected financial statements for the coming year with appropriate supporting schedules. A profit budget has the following uses:

1. For a whole company, and for its individual profit centers, it is used:
   a. For resource allocation. An approved budget is the authority for the budgetee to use resources in attaining the budget objectives.
   b. For planning and coordinating the activities of the company or division. For instance, the profit budget can be the basis for assuring that production facilities are in line with sales forecasts and that cash availability is in line with expected disbursements.
   c. As a final check on the adequacy of the expense budgets. For example, even though top management has reviewed and tentatively approved all of the expense budgets, after the profit budget is prepared it may become evident that the expense budgets are too high and, as a result, budgeted profit is too low. A further review and revision of the expense budgets will then be made to bring them into line with projected revenues.
   d. For assigning to each manager the responsibility for his or her share of the financial performance of the company or division. For example, the marketing manager is assigned responsibility for the revenue budget. This budget can be further subdivided into regions and districts. The responsibility for meeting cost standards is assigned to the plants, and within plants, to departments. In this way, each manager knows what is expected. Subsequently the manager's actual financial performance can be compared to budgeted performance as stated in the overall plan.

2. Divisional profit budgets are used by top management:
   a. To review expected total company financial performance for the coming year and to take action where this performance is not satisfactory.
   b. To plan and coordinate the overall activities of the company.
   c. To participate in divisional planning.
   d. To exercise at least partial control over the divisions.

Two features of the profit budget should be noted:

1. The extent that it is used to measure managerial performance varies greatly among companies. It can be anywhere from a firm commitment of management to a "best estimate" of what will happen, with little responsibility for making it happen.
2. Closely associated with the above, is the degree of responsibility assigned to the profit center manager for attaining budgeted results. This can vary considerably among companies.

These two features are critical to the use of the profit budget in appraising divisional management. They are discussed in detail in Chapter 12.

REVIEW AND APPROVAL OF BUDGETS

The annual profit budget is initially prepared by the divisional managers using company-wide information provided by company staff and is reviewed and approved by senior management prior to the beginning of the year. There are several reasons for this review. First, each divisional plan must be consistent with the overall company plan, and plans among divisions must be consistent with each other. The review and approval procedure gives top management the capability of changing divisional budgets to obtain this consistency. Second, if the divisional profit budgets are to be used to any extent in evaluating divisional management, top management must be satisfied that each profit budget represents a reasonable task. In many situations the problem of ascertaining that each profit budget does represent a fair task is very difficult, and, in these instances the profit budget may have limited use in evaluation.

The amount of detail presented in a profit budget varies greatly from company to company. At one extreme, the budget proposal consists of summary financial forecasts with a few supporting financial schedules. At the other extreme, the proposed profit budget might run to hundreds of pages and include detailed marketing, production, and personnel plans. In general, the larger, more diversified and geographically dispersed the company, the more detail is required. Another important variable is the importance placed by management on the budgets and subsequent performance reports. The more reliance that management places on the profit budget as a control tool, the more detail is required.

BUDGET REVIEW PROCEDURES

In this part of the chapter we describe two commonly used procedures for reviewing and approving proposed profit budgets.

Comparison with Current Year

Ideally the budgeted profit of each division should be consistent with the profit potential of that division. Since divisional profit potential is likely to be limited by existing personnel, facilities, products, and markets, large changes between one year and another are usually unlikely. Consequently, the traditional budget review starts with the current year and describes the changes proposed for the coming year, together with the financial impact of those changes. (Because budget proposals are normally prepared before the end of the year, it may be necessary to forecast the last two or three months of the current year.)

When the budget review takes the form of an analysis of changes from the current year's performance, a budget proposal should normally include the following features:

First, the changes from the current year's actual profit performance should be described in terms that are meaningful to management. This may seem obvious. Nevertheless, it is surprising how frequently presentations are obscured by technical accounting details.

Second, changes in profit performance that are attributable to actions of operating management should be identified in such a way that top management will be able to see what actions the operating manager is proposing to take and the effect of these actions are expected to have on profits. Changes in profits resulting from events that can be only partially controlled by divisional management should be identified separately. For example, the effect of a change in wage rates as a result of a corporate union agreement should be separated from an improvement in the efficiency of direct labor costs resulting from better methods and equipment; and changes in sales volume as a result of general economic conditions should be separated from changes resulting from an increase in sales promotion.

Third, the proposal should take into consideration, as separate items, the impact of any major capital investment projects that affect the coming year's financial performance.

Presentation of budget proposal. There are, of course, many different methods for presenting a proposed budget to management for approval. In comparing the proposed budget with the current year's actual performance, an excellent way to attain the three features described above is to make this comparison in a manner that is consistent with the way actual variances from budget are analyzed. (These techniques are described in Chapter 11.) There are two reasons why this presentation for budget approval tends to be effective:

First, senior managers are familiar with variance analysis reports, so both the proposed format of the report and the information contained in it should be completely understood because they are used monthly, or at least quarterly.

Second, variance analyses techniques separate causes of changes into the elements involved and provide reasons for the changes. This is exactly the information management needs to know when approving a proposed budget.

Budget Based on a Program

This part of the chapter describes a technique used by several companies to supplement the review procedure described in the preceding section. The budget review is preceded by the preparation of a program, usually for a period of between two and five years. After the program has been reviewed and approved, the budget is developed from the first year of this program. The techniques for preparing a program were described in Chapter 9.

This procedure has several advantages over the traditional approach:

First, the planning occurs during most of the year instead of being concentrated in a month or two near the end of the year. This gives everyone more time to develop and review the plans.

Second, top management has a longer time horizon on which to base its approval, because the multi-year impact of any decision is given.

Third, the future programs are prepared in much less detail than the traditional budget. Consequently, revisions can be made more easily. Once the program is approved the operating division can prepare budgets in the detail required for complete variance analysis, without the likelihood that major revisions will be required subsequently.

Fourth, the second year of the program becomes a basis for comparing the following year's program. Where the first year of a new program differs from the second year of the last program (as it almost invariably will), operating management explains why. In this manner, senior management is informed about the way expectations have changed during the year. The two obvious disadvantages of this procedure are: first, it requires more time and effort; and, second, it is necessary to forecast at an earlier time and for a longer period.

BUDGET ADMINISTRATION

The Budget Department

The information flow of a budgetary control system is usually administered by the budget department. This department normally (but not always) reports to the corporate controller. It performs the following functions:

1. It publishes procedures and forms for the preparation of the budget.
2. It coordinates and publishes each year the basic corporatewide assumptions that are to be the basis for the budgets (e.g., assumptions about the economy).
3. It makes sure that information is properly communicated between interrelated organization units (e.g., sales and production).
4. It provides assistance to budgetees in the preparation of the budgets.
5. It analyzes the proposed budgets and makes recommendations first to the budgetee and subsequently to senior management.
6. It analyzes reported performance against budget, interprets the results, and prepares summary reports for top management.
7. It administers the process of making changes or adjustments to the budget during the year.
8. It coordinates and functionally controls the work of budget departments in lower echelons (e.g., divisional budget departments).

The Budget Committee

The budget committee may consist of the senior management: president, executive vice president and the financial vice president. (The latter may be a nonvoting member.) Sometimes the president, alone, performs the duty of the budget committee. Regardless of its composition, the budget committee performs a vital role. This committee meets to review and either approve or adjust each of the budgets. In a large, diversified company, the budget committee might meet only with the senior operating executives to review the budget for a division or group of divisions. In some companies, however, all profit center managers meet with the budget committee and present their budget proposals.

Usually, the budget committee must approve any budget changes made during the year.

Budget Revisions

One of the principal considerations in budget administration is the procedure for revising a budget after it has been approved. Clearly, if it can be revised at will by the budgetee, there would be no point in reviewing and approving the budget in the first instance. On the other hand, if the budget assumptions turn out to be so incorrect that the budget reports are meaningless, budget revisions would appear to be desirable.

There are two general types of procedures for budget revisions:

1. Procedures that provide for a systematic (say quarterly) updating of the budgets.
2. Procedures that allow revisions under special circumstances.

The first type of procedure is generally used where management uses the budgets essentially as a planning tool. If the budget is to be used for control and evaluation, a revision procedure that is as detailed and thorough as the original preparation process would be required. In most instances, this is impractical. Consequently, if a company frequently updates its budgets, it has more of a forecast system than a budget system.

If budget revisions are limited only to unusual circumstances, such revision should be adequately reviewed. In general, permission to make revisions should be difficult to obtain; that is, budget revisions should be limited to those circumstances where the approved budget is so unrealistic that it no longer provides a useful control device.

It should be noted that an up-to-date forecast is not a revised budget. As we shall describe in Chapter 11, good budget reporting systems include a current forecast of the expected annual results. Variance reports, however, analyze differences from the approved budget.

An important consideration in revising budgets is that managers should not be required to adhere to plans that subsequent events prove to be suboptimum. This can be a genuine problem in budgeting. Because of the time required for budget preparation and review, budgets may provide for actions that were planned months ahead of the time they take place. It is important that management actions be based on the latest information available. Consequently, managers should be allowed an opportunity to change their actions to reflect the latest information. This may not require a revised budget, because there should be a procedure that allows budget deviations to accommodate changed circumstances. That is, performance would be measured from the original budget, but explanations for reasonable variances would be acceptable. This has become increasingly important in the past few years in view of the much greater economic uncertainties today than existed 10 to 15 years ago.

BEHAVIORAL ASPECTS OF BUDGETS

One of the purposes of a management control system is to *motivate* the manager to be effective and efficient in attaining the goals of the organization. Although a detailed treatment of motivational considerations is outside of the scope of this book, some of these are mentioned briefly below.[2]

Degree of Difficulty

There appears to be general agreement that the ideal budget is one that is difficult to attain, but that the manager believes *is* attainable. If the budget is believed to be unattainable, the budgetee may be discouraged from trying. If it is too easy, and represents an inadequate challenge, it will not be a motivating force. An easy budget may even be dysfunctional; the budgetee may not perform up to maximum capability in order to avoid showing too large a favorable variance. This is particularly true if a large favorable variance results in a more difficult task for the following year.

Top-management Participation

Top-management participation is necessary for any budget system to be effective in motivating budgetees. Management must participate in the review and approval of the budgets, and the approval should not be a rubber stamp. Without this active participation in the approval process, there will be a great temptation for the budgetee to "play games" with the system; that is, some managers will submit easily attained budgets or budgets that contain excessive allowances for possible contingencies. In fact, even where there is adequate review and participation, there will always be "game playing" by some budgetees.

Management must also follow up on budget results. If there is no top-management feedback with respect to budget results, the budget system will probably not be effective in motivating the budgetee.

Fairness

For a budget to be effective, the budgetee must believe that the budget is a fair one. This means that the budget system will normally be a bottom up system with the budgetee preparing the initial budget proposal. This makes the review and approval process critical. If senior management change the budgeted amounts, it must convince the budgetee that such a change is reasonable. This is not always possible. Budgetees frequently express concern about the alleged arbitrariness of top-management changes. At the least, top management should listen to the budgetee's position and explain the reasons for its decisions.

---

[2] A very good description of the behavioral problems associated with budget systems can be found in G. H. Hofstede, *The Game of Budget Control* (New York: Barnes & Noble, 1968). Other references are listed at the end of this chapter.

Another important consideration in the budgetee's perception of fairness is the belief that the degree of difficulty in attaining the budget is consistent among the budgetees. Managers who were initially satisfied that they had reasonable budgets will change that opinion if other budgetees are perceived to have easier tasks. There is nothing more disruptive to an effective budgetary control system than substantial inequalities in the budgeted task. This is one reason why the top-management review is so important.

The Budget Department

The budget department has a particularly difficult behavioral problem. It must analyze the budgets in detail, and it must be certain that budgets are prepared properly and presented and that reports are accurate. To accomplish these tasks, the budget department sometimes must act in ways that line managers perceive as threatening or even hostile. For example, the budget department must try to ensure that the budget does not contain excessive allowances (or "water"). In doing so, it may find itself in direct opposition to the line manager. In other cases, the explanation of budget variances provided by the budgetee might hide or minimize a potentially serious situation. In such circumstances the budget department should "tell it the way it is," which may place the line manager in an uncomfortable position. As a consequence, the budget department often must walk a fine line between helping the line manager and insuring the integrity of the system.

In order to perform its function effectively, the members of the budget department must have a reputation for unquestionable integrity. If there is any question about their integrity, it becomes difficult, if not impossible, for them to perform the tasks necessary to maintain an effective budgetary control system. In addition to integrity, of course, the members of the budget department should have the personal skills required to deal effectively with people.

Organizational Structure

Two studies have thrown some interesting light on the relationship between organization structure and the budgeting process. The conclusions reached by the authors of these studies are given below.

W. J. Bruns and J. H. Waterhouse in a behavioral study, concluded that:[3]

> There are important interorganizational differences in budget-related behavior by managers. Those in highly structured organizations

[3] W. J. Bruns and J. H. Waterhouse, "Budgetary Control and Organization Structure," *Journal of Accounting Research,* Autumn 1975, p. 200.

tend to perceive themselves as having more influence, they participate more in budget planning, and they appear to be satisfied with budget-related activities. Managers in organizations where authority is concentrated are generally held accountable for fewer financial variables, they experience superior-initiated pressure, they see budgets as being less useful and limiting their flexibility, but they appear to be satisfied with the use of budgets by their superiors.

Based on a somewhat different situation, Vijay Sathe concluded that:[4]

The importance of budgeting as a tool for planning and resource allocation has long been recognized. Modern organization theory now permits a new understanding of the budgeting process. Since organizations in stable environments and operating with routine technologies can maintain effective control via procedure specification and centralized decision making, a top-down budgeting process can work well in these situations. In contrast, for organizations in uncertain environments and operating with nonroutine technologies, it is important that those at lower levels participate in the budgeting process since they have information relevant to the formulation of organizational plans. A bottom-up budgeting process appears best suited to these situations. In addition, budget flexibility (as represented by budget revisions during the year) is likely to be quite appropriate in these cases.

NONFINANCIAL OBJECTIVES

In this chapter, we have limited budgets to financial documents. Other nonfinancial objectives are usually also included in the annual review. Examples are market share, new product introduction, training programs, and so forth. These objectives should be specified in such a way that management can tell at the end of the year the extent they have been met. Most nonfinancial objectives should be included in the profit budget but not necessarily all of them. Nonfinancial objectives are commitments *in addition* to the financial commitment. For example, a manager may be expected to attain market share objective in addition to the profit objective. Nonfinancial objectives are considered further in Chapter 12.

QUANTITATIVE TECHNIQUES

In the past few years, there have been numerous articles on the use of mathematical techniques, often implemented by computers, in the budgetary control process. These articles fall into five general categories:

---

[4] Vijay Sathe, "The Relevance of Modern Organization Theory for Managerial Accounting," *Accounting Organizations and Society*, 3, no. 1 (1979):90.

1. The use of computer models that simulate the financial process.
2. The use of mathematical techniques to optimize costs or profits.
3. The use of probability estimates in the budgetary process.
4. Statistical forecasting.
5. Agency theory.

Although mathematical and computer techniques do improve the budgetary process, they do not solve the critical problems of budgetary control. The critical problems in budgeting tend to be in the behavioral area.

Simulation

Simulation is a method of approaching a problem by constructing a model of a real situation, and then manipulating this model in such a way as to draw some conclusions about the real situation. The preparation and review of a profit budget is a simulation process. One difficulty with a budget prepared manually is that it is time-consuming to manipulate it. Also, because of computation constraints, a great many simplifying assumptions must be made. Both of these constraints can be significantly reduced if the budget is converted into a computer model. Two activities that a computer model of the budget make practical are:

1. Management can ask what the effect of many different types of changes would be and receive almost instantaneous answers. This gives management a chance to participate more fully in the budgetary process.
2. A budget consists of many point estimates. A point estimate is the single "most likely" amount. For example, sales estimates are stated in terms of the specific number of units of each type of product to be sold. Point estimates are necessary for control purposes. For planning purposes, however, a range of probable outcomes is more helpful. After a budget has been tentatively approved, it may be possible with a computer model to substitute a probability distribution for each major point estimate. The model is then run a number of times and a probability distribution of the expected profits can be calculated and used for planning purposes.

Simulation is one of the most useful of the mathematical techniques used in the budgeting process.

Optimizing Techniques

Optimizing techniques are mathematical methods for finding a best solution where there are more than one independent variables. A number of optimizing techniques have been adapted to the budgetary process. For example, the budgetary process is used as a means for resource allocation. Techniques for combining linear programming with the budget preparation process make it possible to define a desirable end-of-the-year financial position and, then, determine the optimum way to reach this position.

Probability Estimates

We described earlier the use of probability estimates for planning purposes, after budget approval. It has been proposed (see Geebold Company *(B)* Case) that budgets be prepared using probability distributions instead of point estimates. That is, the budget committee would approve a number of probability distributions, rather than specific amounts. Subsequent variance analysis would be based on these probability distributions.

Forecasting

The budgeting process requires a considerable amount of forecasting. Although statistical forecasting preceded the computer by a great many years, the computer has made improved forecast techniques practical. Some of these techniques involve economic forecasting. Economic forecasts may be developed internally by large businesses or purchased from outside (e.g., from Data Resources, Inc.) by other businesses. Other techniques are used to predict conditions within a company. For example, multiple regression may be used to forecast cost-volume relationships.

Applications of statistical forecasting techniques are likely to improve the budgetary process. Even with the best of these techniques, however, there will always be considerable uncertainty in most business budgets.

Agency Theory

Agency theory attempts to formalize the relationships between a principal (e.g., a company president) and an agent (e.g., a divisional manager) as contracts. "This theory focuses on the design of performance measures and rewards so that subordinates are more likely to act in the interests of the whole organization."[5] This, of course, is one of the principal concerns of management control systems. Agency theory differs from the approach taken in this book in that "This analysis requires a formal specification of the economic agent's preferences and risk attitudes (as modeled by a utility function for wealth) and beliefs (as modeled by the agent's subjective probability distributions for random outcomes) as well as possible states of the world, actions and outcome functions."[6]

---

[5] Charles T. Horngren, *Cost Accounting: A Managerial Emphasis,* 5th ed. (Englewood Cliffs, N.J.: Prentice-Hall, 1982), page 688.

[6] Robert S. Kaplan, *Advanced Management Accounting* (Englewood Cliffs, N.J.: Prentice-Hall, 1982), page 607.

In spite of a great deal of published research, to date agency theory models have been so simplified that we do not see any practical use for them. However, some of the concepts may eventually lead to improvements in real world management control systems.

SUGGESTED ADDITIONAL READINGS

Quantitative Articles

Atkinson, Anthony A. "Standard Setting in Agency Theory." *Management Science,* September 1978, pp. 1351–61.

Buzby, Stephen L. "Extending the Applicability of Probabilistic Management Planning and Control Models." *The Accounting Review,* January 1974.

Demski, Joel S., and **Feltham, Gerald A.** "Economic Incentives in Budgeting Control Systems." *The Accounting Review,* April 1978.

Ferrara, William L., and **Hayya, Jack C.** "Towards Probabilistic Profit Budgets." *Management Accounting,* October 1970.

———. "Probabilistic Approaches to Return on Investment and Residual Income." *The Accounting Review,* July 1977.

Gershefski, George W. "Building a Corporate Model." *Harvard Business Review,* July–August 1969.

Ijiri, Y.; Kinard, J. C.; and **Putney, F. B.** "An Integrated Evaluation System for Budget Forecasting and Operating Performance with a Classified Budgeting Bibliography." *Journal of Accounting Research,* Spring 1968.

Larson, Steve, and **Mertz, C. Mike.** "Operations Research at Boise Cascade." *Management Accounting,* February 1978.

Lord, Robert J. "Budgeting." *Cost and Management,* May–June 1978.

Mock, Theodore J. "The Value of Budget Information." *The Accounting Review,* July 1977.

Onsi, Mohamed. "Factor Analysis of Behavior Variables Affecting Budgeting Slack." *The Accounting Review,* July 1977.

Raymond, R. C. "Use of Time-Sharing Computers in Business Planning and Budgeting." *Management Science,* April 1966.

Wheelwright, Steven C., and **Makridakis, Spyros.** *Forecasting Methods for Management.* 2d ed. New York: John Wiley & Sons, 1977.

Note: Also see Horngren, *Cost Accounting,* (chapter 20), and Kaplan, *Advanced Management Accounting,* (chapter 17) previously cited.

Behavioral Articles

Becker, Selwyn W., and **Green, David, Jr.** "Budgeting and Employee Behavior." *Journal of Business,* October 1962.

Bruns, W. J., and **Waterhouse, J. H.** "Budgetary Control and Organization Structure." *The Journal of Accounting Research,* Autumn 1975.

Collins, Frank. "The Interaction of Budget Characteristics and Personality Variables with Budget Response Attitudes." *The Accounting Review,* April 1978.

DeCoster, D. T., and **Fertakis, J. P.** "Budget Induced Pressure and Its Relationship to Supervisory Behavior." *Journal of Accounting Research,* Autumn 1968.

Hopwood, Anthony C. "Leadership Climate and the Use of Accounting Data in Performance Evaluation." *Accounting Review,* July 1974.

Otley, David T. "Budget Use and Managerial Performance." *The Journal of Accounting Research,* Spring 1978.

Ronen, J., and **Livingstone, J. L.** "An Expectancy Theory Approach to the Motivational Impacts of Budgets." *The Accounting Review,* October 1975.

Sathe, Vijay. "The Relevance of Modern Organization Theory for Management Accounting." *Accounting Organizations and Society,* 3, no. 1, 1979.

Schiff, Michael, and **Lewin, Avie Y.** "The Impact of People on Budgets," *Accounting Review*. July 1970.

Searfoss, D. G., and **Monczka, R. M.** "Perceived Participation in the Budget Process and Motivation to Achieve Budgets." *The Academy of Management Journal,* December 1973.

Swieringa, R. J., and **Moncur, R. H.** "The Relationship between Managers' Budget-Oriented Behavior and Selected Attitude, Position, Size, and Performance Measures." *Empirical Research in Accounting: Selected Studies 1972*. Chicago: University of Chicago Press, 1974.

Wallace, Michael E. "Behavioral Considerations in Budgeting," *Management Accounting*. August 1966.

CASE 10–1
National Motors, Inc.*

William Franklin, controller of the Panther Automobile Division of National Motors, a manufacturer of numerous products including a wide line of automobiles and trucks, was faced with a difficult decision in August 1983. Four months previously, the manufacturing office had submitted a supplemental budget in which it had requested additional funds for increased administrative costs in its operations control department. The controller's office had written a memorandum in reply, explaining why it thought this request was not justified, and the manufacturing office had now answered this memorandum.

Mr. Franklin now had three possible courses of action: (1) to concur with the manufacturing offices' position, in which case the request would undoubtedly receive the necessary approval of the general manager; (2) to continue his opposition, in which case his views and those of the manufacturing office would be placed before the general man-

* This case was prepared by R. N. Anthony, Harvard Business School.

ager, who would decide the issue; and (3) to reply with a further analysis, in the hope that the manufacturing office would become convinced of the soundness of his position.

During the last quarter of 1983 the Panther Automobile Division had absorbed the manufacturing activities of the Starling Automobile Division. Prior to this, the Starling Division had a mechanized system of parts control in its operations control department. The Panther Division, on the other hand, had been using a manual system in its corresponding department.

In December 1983, a study was made to determine which system would serve the division best. On the basis of an estimated reduction of 23 salaried people and of $276,000 in salary and other costs in the operations control department because of mechanization, the decision was made to completely mechanize the Panther Division's system of parts control. The results of this study were concurred in by the manufacturing office of the Panther Division.

MANUFACTURING OFFICE'S PROPOSED SUPPLEMENTAL BUDGET

In April 1983 the manufacturing office proposed in a supplemental budget that the Panther operations control department, now servicing both Starling and Panther automobiles, be allotted for 1983 a personnel ceiling of 109 people to handle the combined work load. Its proposal and reasoning are summarized in Exhibit 1 and in the following paragraphs.

EXHIBIT 1 Personnel Ceilings for Operations Control Department in 1983 (proposed by manufacturing office)

Positions	*Starling commitment 12/31/82*	*Starling savings*	*Proposed levels* Starling	Panther	Totals
Manager and secretary	2	2	—	2	2
Specifications control	20	12	8	17	25
Design parts control	31	12	19	48	67
Planning and control	7	3	4	11	15
Total	60	29	31	78	109

Exhibit 1 shows the Starling Division's personnel ceiling commitment as of December 31, 1982, the expected saving in numbers resulting from the consolidation, and the proposed ceiling for 1983. Since the manufacturing office believed that the new consolidated system of parts control in the operations control department was going to be about the same as the Starling Division's mechanized system, the standards that it used to develop the proposed personnel requirements were based on the Starling Division's work load and authorized personnel levels for 1982.

Specifications Control Section (25 People)

The work load determinant used in this activity was the number of specifications requests to be processed. In the previous year, 20 employees had been approved in the Starling Division's specifications control section: 5 were clerical and supervisory, 10 processed specifications requests, and 5 were involved in specifications follow-up. The specifications control procedure currently used in the Panther Division operations was generally the same as that used by Starling. But in the future, the specifications follow-up procedure would no longer be done in this section or, for that matter, in the operations control department.

In 1982, the 10 analysts in the Starling specifications control section had processed 2,964 specifications requests, or an average of 296 specifications each.

In the Panther Division, 3,680 specifications requests had been processed during 1982. The manufacturing office believed that a comparison of both Starling and Panther data, as shown in Exhibit 2, indicated that there was a definite relationship between the number of specifications requests processed and the number of unique, new model parts.

EXHIBIT 2 Relationship of Number of Parts to Specification Requests

Division	*Number of unique parts*	*Number of specifications requests*	*Specifications requests per unique part*
Panther	8,810	3,680	.42
Starling	6,584	2,964	.45
Total	15,394	6,644	.43

On the basis of the above calculations, the 1983 manufacturing office estimated the total number of specifications requests for 1983 for both Panther and Starling automobiles, and the personnel required to handle this work load as in Exhibit 3.

Design Parts Section (67 People)

The number of unique parts to be processed was used as the general work load determinant in this section. In 1982, for 6,584 parts there were 27 specifications coordinators in the Starling Division budget for

EXHIBIT 3 Estimates of Personnel Requirements for Specifications Control Section, 1983

A. Specifications requests and equivalent personnel:

Division	*Estimated number of unique parts**	×	*Specifications requests per unique part*	÷	*Actual output per man*	=	*Equivalent personnel*
Panther	11,600		.42		296		16.5
Starling	4,800		.45		296		7.3
Total	16,400						23.8

B. Salaried personnel requirements:

Division	*Equivalent personnel*	*Less planned efficiency (approx. 10%)†*	*Less planned overtime (approx. 5%)*	*Salaried ceiling required*
Panther	16.5	1.7	0.9	14
Starling	7.3	0.8	0.4	6
Total	23.8	2.5	1.3	20

C. Other personnel requirements:

Position	*Panther*	*Starling*	*Total*
Section supervisor and secretary	2	—	2
Unit supervisor	1	1	2
Clerk-typist	—	1	1
Total fixed	3	2	5‡
Total salaried and other			25

* The Panther Division had added a new car to its line, and the Starling Division had dropped one.

† "Planned efficiency" reduces the calculated personnel requirements to a level approximately consistent with the lowest work load level anticipated during the coming year. In order to handle periodic work load increases during a year, the department is forced to improve its efficiency and, if necessary, to utilize overtime or temporary clerical help from outside agencies.

‡ Same as Starling commitment of December 31, 1982.

EXHIBIT 4 Estimates of Personnel Requirements for Design Parts Section, 1983

A. Specifications coordinators requested:

Division	*1983 parts count*	*Estimated output per man*	*Equivalent personnel required*	*Less planned efficiency (approx. 10%)*	*Less planned overtime (approx. 5%)*	*Ceiling required*
Panther	11,600	242	48.0	4.7	2.3	41
Starling	4,800	242	19.8	1.9	.9	17
Total	16,400		67.8	6.6	3.2	58

B. Supervisory and clerical workers requested:

Position	*Panther*	*Starling*	*Total*
Section supervisor and secretary	2	—	2
Unit supervisors	2	1	3
Clerk-Typists	3	1	4
Total	7	2	9
Unit supervisors to coordinators	1:20	1:17	1:19
Clerk-typists to coordinators	1:13	1:17	1:15
Total for the section			67

an average of 242 parts per coordinator. According to Exhibit 4, which was drawn up in the manufacturing office, 58 specifications coordinators would be required to handle the combined work load in 1983 plus 9 supervisors and clerical workers.

Planning and Control Section (15 People)

The requirements for this section were determined by the manufacturing office as shown in Exhibit 5, based on an overall work load indicator of number of parts to be handled.

EXHIBIT 5 Estimate of Personnel Requirements for Planning and Control Section, 1983

Position	*Starling personnel*	*Number of unique parts for Starling, 1983*	*Parts per person*
Programming computer	3	6,584	2,195
Programming timing and coordination	2	6,584	3,292

	Number of unique parts, 1983		*Estimated output per person*	*Equivalent personnel*		*Personnel ceiling requested*		
	Panther	*Starling*		*Panther*	*Starling*	*Panther*	*Starling*	*Total*
Program timing and coordination	11,600	4,800	3,292	3.5	1.5	4	2	6
Programming	11,600	4,800	2,195	5.3	2.2	5	2	7
Total				8.8	3.7	9	4	13
Section supervisor and secretary							2	
Total for the section							15	

Manager's Office (2 People)

A personnel ceiling of two was requested: the manager and his secretary.

Estimated Dollar Requirements

The manufacturing office estimated that a total of $2,916,000 would be needed to operate the consolidated operations control department for 1983. This figure was broken down as follows:

Personnel	$2,320,000
Material and supplies	90,000
Computer services	490,000
Miscellaneous	16,000
Total	2,916,000

Personnel expenses. This estimate was based on the figure for actual salaries plus approved fringe benefits, in accordance with the level of requested salaried personnel ceilings.

Materials and supplies. This expense was about $20,000 higher than the 1982 Starling actual. According to the manufacturing office, the job to be accomplished now was about two-and-one-half times the job accomplished by the Starling Division in 1982 but the expense was only 30 percent greater. This was a result of efficiencies in programming and reporting, which, in turn, would result in savings in materials and supplies.

Computer services. Starling had spent $360,000 in 1982 to accomplish a job that was about 40 percent as great as the combined Starling-Panther job. Included in the proposed amount was $68,000 for start-up cost associated with the conversion of the manual Panther system to a mechanized system. Therefore, the real cost was $422,000 or only about 10 percent more than the 1982 Starling actual. The manufacturing office was proposing to do a job 150 percent greater than that done at Starling for only 10 percent more money. This was said to be the result of efficiencies in programming and reporting.

ANALYSIS BY THE CONTROLLER'S OFFICE

The controller's office did not concur with the manufacturing office's proposal. It summarized both the 1983 Panther Division's budget and the Starling Division's budget as approved prior to the consolidation, and compared these figures with those proposed by the manufacturing office. This summary is shown in Exhibit 6 and is explained in the following paragraphs.

Although the proposed combined Panther and Starling budgets for 1983 showed a decrease of 22 salaried personnel, there was an increase in cost of $136,000.

EXHIBIT 6 Budget Comparison for Salaried Personnel Prepared by Controller

	Panther Division		*Starling Division*		*Total*	
Budget status	Number	*Dollars (000)*	Number	*Dollars (000)*	Number	*Dollars (000)*
Approved	76	$1,444	55*	$1,336	131	$2,780
Proposed	78	1,948	31	968	109	2,916
Net change	(2)	(504)	24	368	22	(136)
Explanation of changes						
Savings from mechanization of Panther system	23†	276†	—	—	23	276
Savings from consolidation	—	—	24	368	24	368
Proposed increase to Panther budget	(25)	(780)	—	—	(25)	(780)
Net change	(2)	(504)	24	$ 368	22	(136)

( ) = Adverse effect on profit.
* Reflects the transfer of five specifications follow-up personnel out of the specifications control system.
† Based on study of December 1982, concurred in by manufacturing office.

The manufacturing office had referred to a saving of 24 people and $368,000 in the Starling Division. This reduction, according to the controller, was the result of (*a*) a reduction in the 1983 parts count and (*b*) a reduction of supervisory and clerical personnel. This saving of 24 people, therefore, had nothing to do with mechanization and would have occurred under either a mechanized or a manual system.

Although the main reason for mechanizing the Panther Division's system of parts control had been financial savings, the controller calculated what the combined budget would have been if, in fact, the Starling Division's system had been changed to a manual one comparable to the one in use by the Panther Division prior to the consolidation. The budget requirement for the Panther Division, of course, would not change. However, 35 people and $812,000 would be required for the Starling Division, on the basis of Panther Division's standards as developed in the manufacturing office's analysis. Thus, a comparison between the manual system and the mechanized system was as shown in Exhibit 7.

EXHIBIT 7 Controller's Revised Budget Comparison for Salaried Personnel, 1983

	Panther Division		*Starling Division*		*Total*	
System	*Number*	*Dollars (000)*	*Number*	*Dollars (000)*	*Number*	*Dollars (000)*
Combined manual systems	76	$1,444	35	$812	111	$2,256
Proposed mechanized systems	78	1,948	31	968	109	2,916
Difference between cost of mechanized system and manual system	(2)	(504)	4	(156)	2	(660)

According to Exhibit 7, the effect of the mechanization and the consolidation on the 1983 Panther budget, which was based on a manual system, was to increase the 1983 salaried personnel level by two people and to increase costs by $504,000. The controller was at a loss to know why these increases should result from mechanization. Moreover, the manufacturing office had committed itself to a saving of 23 people and $276,000 in the Panther Division, whereas the current proposal was 25 people and $780,000 *over* the levels committed.

The controller believed that budget figures under a *combined mechanized system,* instead, should be as shown in Exhibit 8.

EXHIBIT 8 Controller's Proposed Budget, 1983

Salaried personnel	*Panther*	*Starling*	*Total*
Number	53	31	84
Budget dollars (000)	$1,168	$968	$2,136

In this calculation, the Panther Division's number of salaried personnel was based on the premechanization figure (76) minus the saving agreed to by the manufacturing office as a result of mechanization (23). The Panther Division's budget dollars were based on the same sort of analysis—$1,444,000 minus $276,000. Starling Division's figures were those used in Exhibit 7, based on a reduced parts count, supervisory savings, and the functional transfer of personnel. The budget figures for the new division should be 84 people and $2,136,000.

On the basis of its analysis, the controller's office recommended that the manufacturing office at least not increase its 1983 costs for the operations control department over the level that would have occurred under a combined manual system. This meant a dollar budget of $2,256,000. Personnel reductions would be required to contain costs within recommended levels; these were set forth in Exhibit 9.

EXHIBIT 9 Detail of Controller's Recommended Budget, 1983

	Panther		*Starling*		*Total*	
Proposals	*Number*	*Dollars (000)*	*Number*	*Dollars (000)*	*Number*	*Dollars (000)*
Manufacturing office's request	78	$1,948	31	$968	109	$2,916
Controller's recommended reductions:						
Salary mix	—	170	—	—	—	170
Overtime	—	54	—	42	—	96
Required personnel (to meet financial objective)	25	394	—	—	25	394
Total recommended reductions	25	618	—	42	25	660
Total recommended level	53	1,330	31	926	84	2,256

PROTEST FROM THE MANUFACTURING OFFICE

The manufacturing office did not accept the controller's recommendation of a reduction of 25 salaried people and $660,000, though it agreed that, generally speaking, a mechanized operations control system should not be any more costly than the previously used manual system.

Work-load Content and Volume Adjustments

One of the arguments of the manufacturing office was that its proposed Starling–Panther budget included additional people to handle actual work load volume increases over the estimated levels used in developing the 1983 Panther budget for a manual system. The parts counts estimates used in developing the 1983 annual budget and the

EXHIBIT 10 Revised Estimates of Number of Unique Parts

Division	*1983 original budget estimates*	*Current known conditions*
Panther	10,200	11,600
Starling	—	4,800
Total	10,200	16,400

proposed consolidated mechanized budget were as shown in Exhibit 10.

According to the manufacturing office, in addition to increased work as a result of the added work load of the Starling Division there had been an increase of 1,400 parts in the Panther Division as a result of understated original estimates. This increased parts count would have resulted in a requirement for at least 10 more people under the manual system, at a cost of about $180,000, plus an estimated $8,000 for operating expenses.

Unavoidable Increases in Salary Mix

As a result of Starling–Panther consolidation and the consequent personnel changes, the average salary per employee retained in the operations control department had increased significantly. This resulted from the retention of employees on the basis of seniority. The approved budget provided for an average annual salary of $14,088. The Starling–Panther budget proposed by the manufacturing office for 1983 based on actual salaries, provided for an average annual salary in excess of $15,600. Therefore, if average salaries had remained unchanged after the consolidation, the manufacturing office's budget proposal would have been $183,120 less, as shown in Exhibit 11.

EXHIBIT 11 Budget Increase Due to Salary Mix

Salary base	*Proposed ceiling*	×	*Average annual salary*	=	*Total annual salaries*
At approved budget rates	109		$14,088		$1,535,592
At proposed budget rates	109		15,768		1,718,712
Difference					(183,120)

Association with Integrated Data Processing Plan

By implementing the mechanized operations control system, the manufacturing office contended that it had taken an inevitable step included in the company's integrated data processing plan, which provided for eventual establishment of a completely mechanized master parts control system. This step would make it possible to significantly reduce the original expense estimates associated with setting up this master system.

The original proposal, submitted prior to the consolidation of the two divisions, contained cost estimates of $189,774 during 1983 and $209,344 each year thereafter for providing a master parts control system to preproduction control. According to the manufacturing office, these cost estimates would have been increased to $223,744 and $318,482, respectively, as a result of the consolidation if a manual system were used. As a direct benefit of implementing a mechanized operations control system, however, the manufacturing office believed that it could show a saving of about $206,000 during 1983 and $196,000 for each year thereafter. See Exhibit 12.

EXHIBIT 12 Effective Cost Decrease Due to Mechanization

Revised cost factors	*1983*	*1984 going level*
Original cost estimates	$189,774	$209,344
Cost of consolidation and revised assumptions based on manual system	33,970	109,138
Total cost estimates to include effect of consolidation based on a manual system	223,744	318,482
Reduction in cost estimates to give effect to consolidation based on mechanized system	17,400	122,020
Savings directly associated with a mechanized versus manual system	206,344	196,462

Nonrecurring Cost Penalties

The manufacturing office's proposed budget included a nonrecurring cost penalty of $224,610, resulting from the change in organization and procedure. This was compromised of $144,610 in salaries and wages, and $80,000 in computer expense. If work volume remained at the same levels in future years, the manufacturing office felt that its budget could be revised as shown in Exhibit 13.

EXHIBIT 13 Future Savings of Nonrecurring Costs

Budget items	*1983*	*Future years*	*Reductions*
Average personnel ceiling	117	109	9
Personnel costs	$2,317,752	$2,173,142	$144,610
Computer expense	490,000	410,000	80,000
Other operating costs	108,272	108,272	—
Total	2,916,024	2,691,414	224,610

Functional Improvements and Advantages

The manufacturing office contended, furthermore, that a mechanized operations control system offered certain other advantages over a manual system.

1. It provided a single and better integrated program progress report that reflected the status of engineering, manufacturing, and purchasing actions against schedules on a more timely basis than did a manual system.
2. It provided a master file that, once stored in the computer, could be used to produce other useful information.
3. It was compatible with the objective to mechanize the issuance of specifications and would result in a more efficient method of handling this activity. The manufacturing office said that it could not put a dollar value on these advantages, but that it was reasonable to expect them to yield cost savings.

Summary

A cost comparison for a manual versus a mechanized operations control system, based on the above adjustments, was as shown in Exhibit 14.

EXHIBIT 14 Manufacturing Office's Summary of Adjusted Cost Estimates

	1983 Cost comparison (000)	
Costs	*Manual system*	*Mechanized system*
Unadjusted costs:		
Panther Division	$1,444	$1,948
Starling Division	812	968
	2,256*	2,916†
Increases:		
Parts count	(188)	—
Average salaries	(184)	—
Implementation of mechanized operations control system in accordance with company's integrated data processing plan	(224)	(18)
Total adjusted costs	2,852	2,934

* Estimated by controller's office.
† Proposed by manufacturing office.

The manufacturing office concluded its arguments by pointing out that the mechanized system cost only $82,000 a year more than a manual system, as shown in the preceding table, rather than $660,000 more, as stated by the controller.

Question

Take a position on the problem stated in the second paragraph of the case. In order to make a judgment on this problem, you should make a careful analysis of the arguments advanced by the controller's office and by the manufacturing office.

CASE 10–2
Midwest Ice Cream Company (*A*)*

Frank Roberts, marketing vice president of Midwest Ice Cream Company, was pleased when he saw the final earnings statement for the company for 1983. He knew that it had been a good year for Midwest, but he hadn't expected a large, favorable operating income variance. Only the year before, the company had installed a new financial planning and control system; 1983 was the first year for which figures comparing budgeted and actual results were available.

MIDWEST'S PLANNING AND CONTROL SYSTEM

The following description of the financial planning and control system installed at Midwest in 1983 is taken from an internal company operating manual:

The planning function

The starting point in making a profit plan is separating costs into fixed and variable categories. Some costs are purely variable and, as such, will require an additional amount with each increase in volume levels. The manager has little control over this type of cost, other than to avoid waste. The accountant can easily determine the variable manufacturing cost per unit for any given product or package by using current prices and yield records. Variable marketing cost per unit is based on the allowable rate, for example $0.06 per gallon for advertising. Costs that are not purely variable are classified as fixed, but they, too, will vary if significant changes in volume occur. There will be varying degrees of sensitivity to volume changes among these costs, ranging from a point just short of purely variable to an extremely fixed type of expense that has no relationship to volume.

The reason for differentiating between fixed and variable so emphatically is because a variable cost requires no decision as to when to

* This case was prepared by John Shank, Harvard Business School.

add or take off a unit of cost; it is dictated by volume. Fixed costs, on the other hand, require a management judgment on decisions to increase or decrease the cost. Sugar is an example of a purely variable cost. Each change in volume will automatically bring a change in the sugar cost; only the yield can be controlled. Route salesmen's salaries would be an example of a fixed cost that is fairly sensitive to volume, but not purely variable. As volume changes, pressure will be felt to increase or decrease this expense, but management must make the decision; the change in cost level is not automatic. Depreciation charges for plant would be an example of a relatively extreme fixed cost, in that large increases in volume can usually be realized before this type of cost is pressured to change. In both cases, the fixed cost requires a decision from management to increase or decrease the cost. It is this dilemma that management is constantly facing: to withstand the pressure to increase or be ready to decrease when the situation demands it.

The first step in planning is to develop a unit standard cost for each element of variable cost by product and package size. Examples of four different products and packages are shown in Exhibit 1. As already pointed out, the accountant can do this by using current prices and yield records for material costs and current allowance rates for marketing costs. Advertising is the only cost element not fitting the explanation of a variable cost given in the preceding paragraph. Advertising costs are set by management decision, rather than being an "automatic" cost item like sugar or packaging. In this sense, advertising is just like route salesmen's expense. For our company, however, management has decided that the allowance for advertising expense is equal to $0.06 per gallon for the actual number of gallons sold. This management decision, therefore, has transformed advertising into an expense that is treated as variable for profit planning.

After the total unit variable cost has been developed, this amount is subtracted from the selling price to arrive at a marginal contributon per unit, by product and package type. At any level of volume, it is easy to determine the contribution that should be generated to cover the fixed costs and provide profits. This will be illustrated in Exhibit 4.

Step 2 is perhaps the most critical of all the phases in making a profit plan, because all plans are built around the anticipated level of sales activity. Much thought should be given in forecasting a realistic sales level and product mix. Consideration should be given to the number of days in a given period, as well as to the number of Fridays and Mondays, as these are two of the heaviest days and will make a difference in the sales forecast.

Other factors that should be considered are (1) general economic condition of the marketing area, (2) weather, (3) anticipated promotions, and (4) competition.

Step 3 involves the setting of fixed-cost budgets based on management's judgment as to the need in light of the sales forecast. It is here that good planning makes for a profitable operation. The number of routes needed for both winter and summer volume is planned. The level of manufacturing payroll is set,[1] insurance and taxes are budgeted, and so on. After step 4 has been performed, it may be necessary to return to step 3 and make adjustments to some of the costs that are discretionary in nature.

Step 4 is the profit plan itself. By combining our marginal contribution developed in step 1 with our sales forecast, we arrive at a total marginal contribution by month. Subtracting the fixed cost budgeted in Step 3, we have an operating profit by months. As mentioned above, if this profit figure is not sufficient, then a new evaluation should be made of the fixed costs developed in step 3.

The following four tables (Exhibits 1–4) illustrate each of the four

EXHIBIT 1 Step 1: Establish Standards for Selling Price, Variable Expenses, and Marginal Contribution per Gallon (vanilla ice cream)

	Regular			
Item	*One-gallon paper container*	*One-gallon plastic container*	*Two-gallon paper container*	*Premium one-gallon plastic container*
Dairy ingredients	$0.53	$0.53	$0.53	$0.79
Sugar	0.15	0.15	0.15	0.15
Flavor	0.10	0.10	0.105	0.12
Production	0.10	0.16	0.125	0.16
Warehouse	0.06	0.08	0.07	0.08
Transportation	0.02	0.025	0.02	0.025
Total manufacturing	0.96	1.045	1.00	1.325
Advertising	0.06	0.06	0.06	0.06
Delivery	0.04	0.04	0.04	0.04
Total marketing	0.10	0.10	0.10	0.10
Total variable costs	1.06	1.145	1.10	1.425
Selling price	1.50	1.70	1.45	2.40
Marginal contribution/gallon before packaging	0.44	0.555	0.35	0.975
Packaging	0.10	0.25	0.085	0.25
Marginal contribution/gallon	0.34	0.305	0.265	0.725

EXHIBIT 2 Step 2: Vanilla Ice Cream Sales Forecast in Gallons

	January	*February*		*December*	*Total*
One gallon—paper	100,000	100,000	.....	100,000	1,200,000
One gallon—plastic	50,000	50,000	.....	50,000	600,000
Two gallon—paper	225,000	225,000	.....	225,000	2,700,000
One gallon—premium	120,000	120,000	.....	120,000	1,440,000
Total	495,000	495,000	.....	495,000	5,940,000

[1] Because this system is based on a one-year time frame, manufacturing labor is considered to be a fixed cost. The level of the manufacturing work force is not really variable until a time frame longer than one year is adopted.

EXHIBIT 3 Step 3: Budget Fixed Expenses

	January	*February*		*December*	*Total*
Manufacturing Expense:					
Labor	$ 7,333	$ 7,333	.....	$ 7,333	$ 88,000
Equipment repair	3,333	3,333	.....	3,333	40,000
Depreciation	6,667	6,667	.....	6,667	80,000
Taxes	3,333	3,333	.....	3,333	40,000
Total	20,667	20,667	.....	20,667	248,000
Delivery Expense:					
Salaries—General	10,000	10,000	.....	10,000	120,000
Salaries—Drivers	10,667	10,667	.....	10,667	128,000
Helpers	10,667	10,667	.....	10,667	128,000
Suppliers	667	667	.....	667	8,000
Total	32,000	32,000	.....	32,000	384,000
Administrative expense:					
Salaries	5,167	5,167	.....	5,167	62,000
Insurance	1,667	1,667	.....	1,667	20,000
Taxes	1,667	1,667	.....	1,667	20,000
Depreciation	833	833	.....	833	10,000
Total	9,333	9,333	.....	9,333	112,000
Selling expense:					
Repairs	2,667	2,667	.....	2,667	32,000
Gasoline	5,000	5,000	.....	5,000	60,000
Salaries	5,000	5,000	.....	5,000	60,000
Total	12,667	12,667	.....	12,667	152,000

planning steps for a hypothetical ice cream plant. (The numbers in the tables are not intended to be realistic.)

The control function

To illustrate the control system, we will take the month of January and assume the level of sales activity for the month to be 520,000 gallons, as shown in Exhibit 5. Looking back to our sales forecast (step 2) we see that 495,000 gallons had been forecasted. When we apply our marginal contribution per unit for each product and package, we find that the 520,000 gallons have produced $6,125 less standard contribution than the 495,000 gallons would have produced at the forecasted mix. So even though there has been a nice increase in sales volume, the mix has been unfavorable. The $6,125 represents the difference between standard profit contribution at forecasted volume and standard profit contribution at actual volume. It is thus due to differences in volume and to differences in average mix. The impact of each of these two factors is shown on the bottom of Exhibit 5.

Exhibit 6 shows a typical Departmental Budget Sheet comparing actual with budget. A sheet is issued for each department so the person responsible for a particular area of the business can see the items that are in line and those that need his attention. In our example, there is an unfavorable operating variance of about $22,700. You should note that the budget for variable cost items has been adjusted to reflect actual

EXHIBIT 4 Step 4: The Profit Plan

	Marginal contribution (see step 1)	*Gallons sold per month*	*Contribution*				
			January	*February*		*December*	*Total*
One gallon—paper	.34	100,000	$ 34,000	$ 34,000	.....	$ 34,000	$ 408,000
One gallon—plastic	.305	50,000	15,250	15,250	.....	15,250	183,000
Two gallon—paper	.265	225,000	59,625	59,625	.....	59,625	715,500
One gallon—premium	.725	120,000	87,000	87,000	.....	87,000	1,044,000
Total contribution			195,875	195,875	.....	195,875	2,350,500
Fixed costs (see step 3):							
Manufacturing costs			20,667	20,667	.....	20,667	248,000
Delivery expense			32,000	32,000	.....	32,000	384,000
Administrative expense			9,333	9,333	.....	9,333	112,000
Selling expense			12,667	12,667	.....	12,667	152,000
Total fixed			74,667	74,667	.....	74,667	896,000
Operating profit			121,208	121,208	.....	121,208	1,454,500
Income tax			60,604	60,604	.....	60,604	727,250
Net profit			$ 60,604	$ 60,604	.....	$ 60,604	$ 727,250

EXHIBIT 5 Contribution Analysis (January)

	Actual gallon sales	*Standard contribution per gallon*	*Total standard contribution*
One gallon—paper	90,000	0.340	$ 30,600
One gallon—plastic	95,000	0.305	28,975
Two gallon—paper	245,000	0.265	64,925
One gallon—premium	90,000	0.725	65,250
Total	520,000		189,750
Forecast (step 2): 495,000 gallons			
Forecasted marginal contribution (at 495,000 gallons)			195,875
Over (under) forecast			$ (6,125)

	Planned	*Actual*	*Variance due to volume:*		
Gallons	495,000	520,000	25,000 gallons × $0.3957	=	9.892F
Contribution	$195,875	$189,750	*Variance due to mix:*		
Avg. per gallon	$0.3957	$0.3649	$0.0308 × 520,000 gallons	=	16,017U
Difference	$0.0308		Total variance	=	6,125U

F = favorable; U = unfavorable.

EXHIBIT 6 Manufacturing Cost of Goods Sold (January)

	Month		*Year to date*	
	Actual	*Budget*	*Actual*	*Budget*
Dairy ingredients	$312,744	$299,000		
Sugar	82,304	78,000		
Flavorings	56,290	55,025		
Warehouse	38,770	37,350		
Production	70,300	69,225		
Transportation	11,514	11,325		
Subtotal, variable	571,922	549,925		
Labor	7,300	7,329		
Equipment repair	4,065	3,333		
Depreciation	6,667	6,667		
Taxes	3,333	3,333		
Subtotal, fixed	21,365	20,662		
Total	$593,287	$570,587		

volume, thereby eliminating wide cost variances due strictly to the difference between planned and actual volume.

Since the level of fixed costs is independent of volume anyway, it is not necessary to adjust the budget for these items for volume differences. The original budget for fixed cost items is still appropriate. The totals for each department are carried forward to an earnings statement, Exhibit 7. We have assumed all other departments' actual and budget are in line, so the only operating variance is the one for manu-

EXHIBIT 7 Earnings Statement (January)

	Month		*Year to date*	
	Actual	*Budget*	*Actual*	*Budget*
Total ice cream sales	$867,750	$867,750		
Mfg. cost of goods sold	$593,287	$570,592		
Delivery expense	52,804	52,800		
Advertising expense	31,200	31,200		
Packaging expense	76,075	76,075		
Selling expense	12,667	12,667		
Administrative expense	9,334	9,333		
Total expense	$775,367	$752,667		
Profit or loss	$ 92,383	$115,083		
Provision for income taxes	46,192	—		
Net profit or (loss)	46,191	—		

Actual profit before taxes	92,383		(1)	
Original profit forecast (step 4)	121,208		(2)	
Revised profit forecast based on actual volume	115,083		(3)	
	(2)	−	(3)	
Variance due to volume and mix (unfavorable)	= 121,208	−	115,083	= 6,125U
	(3)	−	(1)	
Variance due to operations (unfavorable	= 115,083	−	92,383	= 22,700U
	(2)		(1)	
Total variance	= (121,208	−	92,383)	= 28,825U

facturing. This variance added to the sales volume and mix variance of $6,125 results in an overall variance from the original plan of $28,825, as shown at the bottom of Exhibit 7.

The illustration here has been on a monthly basis, but there is no need to wait until the end of the month to see what is happening. Each week, sales can be multiplied by the contribution margins to see how much standard contribution has been generated. This can be compared to one fourth of the monthly forecasted contribution to see if volume and mix are in line with forecast. Neither is it necessary to wait until the end of the month to see if expenses are in line. Weekly reports of such items as production or sugar can be made, comparing budget with actual. By combining the variances as shown on weekly reports, and adjusting the forecasted profit figure, an approximate profit figure can be had long before the books are closed and monthly statements issued. More important, action can be taken to correct an undesirable situation much sooner.

Questions

1. Explain in as much detail as possible where *all* the numbers for Exhibits 1–4 would come from. (You will need to use your imagination; the case does not describe all details of the profit planning process.)
2. Explain the difference between a month's planned profit as shown in Exhibit 4 and a month's budgeted profit as shown in Exhibit 7. Why would Midwest want to have *two* target profit amounts for a given month? (Hint: Study the variance calculations at the bottom of Exhibit 7.)
3. Evaluate Midwest's planning and control processes.

CASE 10–3
Geebold Company *(B)*

Thomas Ritzman, assistant to the controller of Geebold Company, received from his boss an article, "Budgeting,"[1] to which was clipped this note: "Do you think we should seriously consider adopting the approach described in this article? If so, why? What additional information do we need in order to make up our minds? If not, why not? There is no urgency, but let's discuss this whenever you are ready to do so." Exerpts from the article follow.

Although it has been argued that the information contained in a probabilistic budget is essential for good management, there is practically no information available on its current use. It has not been shown that a probabilistic budget can be prepared within a firm, nor that the preparation of such a budget will change the actions or activities managers undertake. This paper relates one attempt, within a small firm, to establish both the feasibility and practical value of creating a probabilistic budget.

THE FIRM

Floral Transport is a small transport company specializing in the movement of perishable produce to Canada from the United States. The firm operates a fleet of modern highway tractors and temperature-controlled trailers between the grower's fields, the firm's southern consolidation terminal, and its customers in Canada.

Recently, in the face of growing volume, the firm substantially expanded its fleet. As a result of this expansion, Floral Transport has been seeking a more reliable process for estimating future operating results, for as the president declared: "I have to know if we're going to have problems meeting our payment commitments on our new equipment."

DEVELOPING THE PROBABILISTIC BUDGET

Answering this concern required forecasting what the year's operating results might be. To accomplish this objective, the president and his key personnel were asked to think about the uncertainties the business faced and to quantify their feelings about these uncertainties. These quantities and their interrelationships were combined by means of a Monte Carlo simulation to produce the probabilistic budget presented in Table 1.

[1] Robert J. Lord, "Budgeting," *Cost and Management,* May–June 1978. Used with permission.

TABLE 1 Fiscal 1977 Budget (based on 500 trials)

	Expected value	Cumulative probabilities (budget amounts in 000) .00	.25	.50	.75	1.00
Mileage	880,312	778	845	871	905	1058
Revenue per mile	$ 1.260	$1.098	$1.226	$ 1.27	$1.307	$1.375
Transport revenue	1,109,870	1,040	1,086	1,108	1,132	1,191
Manpower	199,139	161	189	197	207	253
Maintenance	77,450	55	71	77	83	102
Fuel	139,593	109	131	139	146	172
License and insurance	48,482	38	45	48	50	59
Hired vehicles	201,288	145	185	199	215	275
Redelivery	100,079	71	90	99	109	145
Total transport	776,031	666	734	761	794	925
Transport margin	343,839	223	317	347	374	446
Sales margin	28,267	21	26	27	30	38
Total margin	372,106	249	344	376	402	472
Utilities	7,997	7	7	7	8	8
Telephone	30,156	24	28	29	31	38
Facilities	7,982	7	7	7	8	8
Office wages	90,483	69	86	90	95	106
Office expenses	16,998	15	16	16	17	18
Running supplies	4,650	4	4	4	4	4
Warehouse expense	6,199	5	6	6	6	6
Property taxes	900	0	0	0	0	1
Total operating	165,365	144	160	165	170	183
Salaries	29,230	27	28	29	29	31
Professional fees	10,010	9	9	10	10	10
Interest	25,527	24	25	25	25	27
Travel	9,510	8	9	9	9	10
Advertising	2,002	1	1	2	2	2
Total administration	76,279	71	75	76	77	80
Depreciation	55,000	55	55	55	55	55
Total expenses	296,644	273	291	296	301	314
Profit	$ 75,462	−45	50	78	106	182
Cash flow (profit plus depreciation)	$ 130,462	10	105	133	161	237

Statistical descriptions of the uncertainties were elicited from the president and his key managers. These managers should have the best available information about the operations of the business, important competitive and operating trends, and the implication of these trends for the firm. More importantly, these key personnel will have to make policy and operating decisions based on what they believe the future will be.

Several techniques have been developed to obtain a manager's estimate of the uncertainties he faces. In developing the data for the Floral Transport model, we utilized a successive subdivision protocol incorporating the following questions:

1. What do you expect the value of *X* (the variable being elicited) to be? [(This answer is taken to be the respondent's .50 fractile on a cumulative density function.)]
2. You would be astonished (greatly surprised) if *X* was greater than what value? (This answer is taken to be the respondent's 1.00 fractile on a cumulative density function.)
3. You would be greatly surprised (astonished) if *X* was less than what value? (This answer was taken to be the respondent's .00 fractile on a cumulative density function.)
4. If I told you for certain *X* was between the .5 fractile (answer to Question 1) and the .00 fractile (answer to Question 3) would *X* be more or less than *Y* (a number chosen by the interviewer between .5 and the .00 fractiles)? This question was repeated with the value of *Y* changing until the interviewee became indifferent.
   (This answer is taken to be the respondent's .25 fractile on a cumulative density function), and finally
5. If I told you for certain *X* was between the .5 fractile (answer to Question 1) and the 1.00 fractile (answer to Question 2) would *X* be more or less than *Y*? (Again repeated until the indifference point.) (This answer was taken to be the .75 fractile of the cumulative density function.)

This protocol was utilized to generate the majority of uncertain inputs to the Floral Transport model (Table 2).

TABLE 2 Cumulative Density Functions Describing Major Uncertainties in the Floral Transport Model

	Points on cumulative density function				
	.00	*.25*	*.50*	*.75*	*1.00*
Growth (percent):					
Product line 1	0.0%	12.5%	20.0%	25.0%	30.0%
Product line 2	−10.0	−3.5	0.0	2.5	5.0
Product line 3	0.0	25.0	50.0	100.0	200.0
Product line 4	0.0	17.5	25.0	32.5	50.0
Product line 5	15.0	23.5	25.0	26.5	35.0
Product line 6	25.0	30.0	35.0	41.0	50.0
Product line 7	10.0	17.5	25.0	35.0	100.0
Margin:					
Product line 1	40.0	43.0	45.0	50.0	60.0
Product line 2	0.0	12.0	15.0	17.0	20.0
Product line 3	10.0	20.0	22.5	25.0	40.0
Transport revenue per mile	$0.80	$1.10	$1.15	$1.20	$1.25
Direct costs per mile (dollars):					
Manpower	0.18	0.21	0.225	0.24	0.30
Maintenance	0.05	0.075	0.09	0.10	0.125
Fuel	0.115	0.145	0.16	0.17	0.20
Licenses, permits, insurance	0.04	0.05	0.055	0.06	0.07
Hired vehicles	0.10	0.17	0.20	0.23	0.30
Redelivery	0.40	0.50	0.55	0.60	0.75
Communications	0.020	0.022	0.024	0.028	0.035

Generally, the elicitation process began with reference to current operating results. Then the manager reflected on changes in operating/external factors which might affect those results. For example, in considering the cost of fuel per mile, the president's thinking ran as follows:

> The records show that fuel is costing about 16 cents a mile, but I know we can expect a price increase of maybe as much as a nickel a gallon before the year is out. On the other hand, our new equipment is supposed to operate at 6 miles per gallon compared to the 4½ miles per gallon we're presently getting. Besides, by installing our own fuel supply tanks in the south we can reduce our highway purchases. Considering all these pieces I'd expect, in spite of the price increase, we'd maintain our fuel cost about where it is. If we don't see the price jump and the boys really baby the new tractors we might see 11 cents or 12 cents per mile; on the other hand if the price goes up more than a nickel and the drivers get "lead feet" it could jump as high as 20 cents.

It was decided that overhead costs were basically discretionary—that their amount would be decided upon by management. For this reason, the budget level of overhead costs was provided to the model. It was also decided that the only uncertainty associated with these overhead costs would be due to price changes. This uncertainty was built into the model by means of a spending variance distribution so that overheads would be within ±10 percent of budget two thirds of the time and within ±20 percent of budget 95 percent of the time.

Monte Carlo Simulation. All the data gathered was assembled and processed by means of a computer model written in SIMPAK. Briefly SIMPAK takes the data describing the uncertain inputs, generates detailed cumulative density functions for each of these elements,

TABLE 3 Other Input Data

	Quarter 1	*Quarter 2*	*Quarter 3*	*Quarter 4*
Overhead costs:				
Utilities	$ 2,000	$ 2,000	$ 2,000	$ 2,000
Facilities	2,000	2,000	2,000	2,000
Office wages*	29,000	22,000	20,000	20,000
Office expenses	5,000	4,000	4,000	4,000
Running supplies	1,600	1,250	1,000	800
Warehouse expenses	2,200	2,000	1,000	1,000
Property taxes	900	—	—	—
Salaries	7,000	7,200	7,500	7,500
Professional fees	3,500	2,500	2,000	2,000
Interest	6,000	6,500	6,500	6,500
Travel	2,500	2,500	2,500	2,500
Advertising	500	500	500	500
Depreciation†	10,000	15,000	15,000	15,000

* Management was in the process of reevaluating its clerical personnel requirements.
† Increase represents arrival of new highway equipment.

and makes the uncertainties available to the logic model provided by the analyst. The logic model describes the relationships between the various uncertainties, and the outputs to be generated by the model. As the model is executed, SIMPAK keeps track of the results of each of the up to 500 trials, generates average results and provides statistical profiles of the uncertainties associated with each element of the output report.

WHAT DOES IT ALL MEAN?

The Floral Transport probalistic budget provides information not available from the more traditional single figure, or point estimate budget. Additional information is available because, in effect, the results reported in Table 1 are based on a hypothetical world in which we get to operate the business many times for the same year. In some of these trials very unfavorable events take place, costs are high and revenues are low. During other trials very favorable events are met, efficiency and revenues are both high. Other times, various combinations of costs and revenues are experienced. The results of these many trials are recorded and, when analyzed, indicate the range of possible outcomes for each element of the budget, as well as indicating the likelihood or probability that various levels of revenue, expenses, and profitability will be achieved. For example, while the Floral budget indicates that a profit of $75,462 is expected for 1977, the probabilistic forecast indicates operating results could range anywhere from a loss of $45,000 to profits of $182,000. Based on the simulation results, we can make the following statements about this range of profits:

1. There is at least a 75 percent probability that the firm's profit will be at least $50,000.
2. There is only a 25 percent chance that the firm's profit will exceed $106,000.

For the management of Floral Transport, the probabilistic budget reinforces the president's concern about the volatility of his operations. While not probable, a loss as great as $45,000 could be generated this year.

Perhaps more significantly, there is only a 50 percent chance operations will generate a cash flow equal to the required $130,000 Floral must repay on its new equipment during the year.

Looking at the projections in more detail, the variability in Floral's profits can be attributed to the variability of transport expenses, to the variability of transport revenues, and to the variability in overhead costs (Table 4).

The challenge to Floral Transport's management is to determine what operational or policy changes the firm might undertake to reduce the variability in its results. Implicitly the challenge is to better control its operations—to both reduce costs and, perhaps more important, to reduce the variability within the firm's costs and revenues.

Establishing tighter control implies an understanding of the uncertainties Floral faces—their causes, and the extent to which they can be controlled. The greatest variability in Floral's transport expenses is in the "hired vehicles" expense account. The question facing the president is why is this expense so uncertain, and what can be done about it?

Floral rents equipment from other truckers, and from rental firms like Ryder when volume is greater than the firm's own capacity. If management could foresee extra demand, additional equipment could be added permanently to the fleet—capital investment could reduce the necessity to use hired vehicles and could reduce the likelihood of major breakdowns. To date, management has not had enough confidence in its ability to predict future volume to make this investment. Perhaps under probabilistic budgeting, where uncertainties can be more explicitly examined, this decision will be better addressed.

Fuel costs also vary. Management has already taken steps to reduce this variability and total fuel costs. The installation of fuel supplies at its depots means Floral's trucks will no longer be as susceptible to the vagaries of the retail highway fuel market, and the new "fuel-economy" tractors should reduce actual fuel consumption.

TABLE 4 Summary Budget ($000)

	Expected value	*Standard deviation*
Transport revenue	$1,110	$31.0
Expenses	766	45.8
Transport margin	344	42.6
Sales margin	28	3.0
Total margin	372	42.7
Operating	165	7.3
Administration	76	1.7
Depreciation	55	
Total expenses	296	7.5
Profit	$ 76	43.3

In summary, the information generated by the probabilistic budget, and the analysis of the results it projects raise serious questions about Floral's operations. If management responds appropriately to these questions, the variability (riskiness) of the firm's operations can be reduced. This appears a totally appropriate goal for the company. Probabilistic budgeting appears to be a potentially powerful tool for this firm—at least to the extent management can/will respond to the challenges it raises.

IMPLICATIONS FOR BUDGETING AND CONTROL

For planning, budgeting, and control in general, the advent of probabilistic budgeting also appears to raise important questions.

Inadequacies of Current Practices

Evaluating uncertainty. A common practice when planning is the use of sensitivity analysis to explore a project's riskiness. Typically, this means evaluating a project under various sets of assumptions—assuming the absolute worst future will prevail; and then, that the very best future will occur.

Unfortunately, this common practice tends to overstate the riskiness and variability of the project. In Table 5 a best/worst budget has been prepared for Floral Transport. Based on this analysis, Floral Transport looks extremely risky—profits could range anywhere from −$182,000 to +$293,000, which is a range substantially greater than the range described by Table 1 of −$45,000 to $182,000.

The worst/best analysis overstates the riskiness because it does not consider the co-variability of the elements of the budget. The variability of the Floral budget is reduced by the co-variability of the transport revenue and transport expenses. This relationship is not considered in the typical best/worst analysis—in fact, without a tool like probabilistic budgeting its effect would be almost impossible to even estimate.

TABLE 5 Doomsday/Most Optimistic Analysis* ($000)

	Worst case	*Best case*
Transport revenue	$1,040	$1,191
Transport expenses	925	666
Transport margin	115	525
Sales margin	21	38
Total	136	563
Operating expenses	183	144
Administration expenses	80	71
Depreciation	55	55
Total expenses	318	270
Profit (loss)	($182)	$ 293

* Based on the zero and 1.00 fractile values of Table 1.

Managing uncertainty. If we analyze the basic elements of most current management control system—a departmentalized or divisionalized structure, a process for setting long-range objectives and operating budgets coupled to routine reporting, evaluative, and reward systems—it is apparent that their form, their intent, and the activities associated with them remain basically suited to the management of stable situations.

Probabilistic budgets—or, more generally, the concept of recognizing uncertainty in our plans and our control practices—should alleviate these shortcomings. Recognizing the potential major uncertainties in operating plans should lead to more contingency planning. The recognition that operating results are highly volatile should lead managers to attempt to at least understand, and at best control that volatility. At least, this recognition should lead to a more thorough exploration of the underlying causes of the volatility. At best, managers should create plans to cope with these uncertainties.

But having contingency plans will not be enough. Management will have to know when and if its contingency plans should be undertaken. To make this decision, management will have to monitor, track, and report the actual behavior of the important uncertain factors in the plan/budget.

Behaviorally, the formal identification of the risks inherent in operating plans should have significant implications for the budget process. Since probabilistic budgets may indicate ranges of profits outside of management's expectations, it may be more difficult to set performance goals—is one's target the .5 fractile on the cumulative distribution, or should targets be stretch targets set at say the .6 fractile where there is only a 40 percent chance results could be better than the target?

In addition, since budgets will now be based on an explicit model of operations, it is likely that both the budget review process and the evaluation/reward processes will change. Rather than bargaining about "the point estimate" of next year's profit, divisional and corporate management may more usefully examine the operational model and uncertainties upon which forecast projections are based. Commitment will no longer be to a concrete dollar goal but to specific plans for identifying and coping with the uncertainties inherent in the budget.

Finally, the existence of the model may improve reporting and evaluation practices. For, after the fact, management will know what state of events, previously described as uncertain, actually occurred. By substituting these states into the model performance, targets congruent with the manager's original agreement will be available as the basis for judging actual performance.

Question

Discuss the questions given in the first paragraph of the case.

CHAPTER 11

Analyzing and Reporting Financial Performance

This chapter describes techniques for analyzing and reporting financial performance in companies that have a profit budget system. Since expense and revenue budgets are part of profit budgets, the discussion automatically includes these budgets as well.

CHARACTERISTICS OF A GOOD REPORTING SYSTEM

A good profit budget reporting system has the following characteristics:

1. It identifies the variances of actual performance from the budget according to the factors that caused them and the organization unit responsible.
2. It includes an annual forecast.
3. It includes an explanation of:
   a. The reason for variances.
   b. The action being taken to correct any unfavorable variances.
   c. The time required for any corrective action to be effective.

Each is discussed in this part of the chapter.

Variance by Causal Factor

A variance analysis is not meaningful unless the variances are reported separately in terms of the factors that caused them and the organization unit responsible. In particular, revenue variances should be separated from cost variances. Revenue variances, in turn, should be separated into price, mix, and volume variances, and cost variances should identify the causes of departures from budgeted standards.

Some companies simply place the actual results next to the profit budget for the period and show the difference between them, as illustrated in Exhibit 11–1.

EXHIBIT 11–1 Performance Report, January 1984 ($000)

	Actual	*Budget*	*Actual better (worse) than budget*
Sales	$875	$600	$275
Variable costs of sales	583	370	(213)
Contribution	292	230	62
Fixed overhead	75	75	—
Gross profit	217	155	62
Selling expense	55	50	(5)
Administration expense	30	25	(5)
Profit before taxes	$132	$ 80	$ 52

Such a statement shows that the profit is $52,000 higher than budgeted, principally because sales are higher than budgeted, but this is about all that it shows. The only other meaningful figures on the report are the fixed cost comparisons because these are not affected by the volume of sales. The reasons for the revenue increases are not shown. Further, the profit impact of the revenue variance is not shown, nor can the variable cost performance be evaluated. A report of this kind has little meaning; it may even be confusing. An effective report shows the causes for the variances and the impact of each of them on profits. Techniques for calculating profit budget variances are described later in this chapter.

Annual Forecast

Budget performance reports should, if feasible, show a current annual forecast for two principal reasons:

1. Management needs to know the significance of the variances. For example, management needs to know if a small variance in a current report is expected to develop into a large variance by the end of the year. Such a variance would be more important than a large variance that is expected to be reversed to zero by the end of the year. In short, top management can best judge the seriousness of a variance by its expected impact on profits for a period longer than the current month or quarter.
2. Management needs an up-to-date estimate of annual profits for planning purposes.

In some companies, particularly in times of great economic uncertainty, annual forecasts are so unreliable that management decides the effort required to make them is not worthwhile, but these circumstances are exceptional.

Reasons, Action, and Timing

If senior management is to use the budget performance report as a basis for controlling company activities, it must know the reasons for significant variances, the action being taken to correct unfavorable situations, and the expected timing of each corrective action. The annual forecast provides some information on the timing of corrective action. The annual forecast, however, is restricted to the budget year. Management also needs to know the total expected impact of variances when the correction time goes beyond the end of the current budget year.

The explanations of variances and the type and timing of the actions being taken must be obtained from the responsible operating manager. Much of this information is subjective and, consequently, there is the possibility of bias. Operating managers do not like to admit that variances were the result of their mistakes. The integrity of the budgetary system is dependent upon the impartiality of this part of the budget report, however. One of the most difficult problems in budgetary control is ensuring unbiased and unambiguous reporting. In some companies, both the divisional controller and the managers are held responsible for the accuracy of the entire budget report.

ANALYSIS OF VARIANCE—DIRECT COST SYSTEM

We discuss variance analysis using two systems of cost accounting; namely, (1) where a standard direct cost system is used, and (2) where a standard full cost system is used. Although the techniques differ, they lead to similar results. In this part of the chapter, we discuss variance analysis using a standard direct cost system. In the next section, we discuss variance analysis using a standard full cost system. A standard direct cost system is one that assigns only variable manufacturing cost to products. Fixed manufacturing costs are charged as expenses of the current period.

Exhibit 11–2 provides details of the budget shown in Exhibit 11–1.

Revenue Variances

In this section, we describe how to calculate the selling price, volume, and mix variances. The calculation is made for each product line separately, and the separate results are then added algebraically to give the total variance. A positive result is favorable (in the sense that it indicates that actual profit exceeded budgeted profit), and a negative result is unfavorable.

Actual sales for January 1984 were as shown in Exhibit 11–3.

EXHIBIT 11–2 Annual Profit Budget 1984 ($000)

	*Product A 1,200**		*Product B 1,200**		*Product C 1,200**		*Total profit budget*	
	Unit	*Total*	*Unit*	*Total*	*Unit*	*Total*	*Annual*	*Monthly*
Sales	$1.00	$1,200	$2.00	$2,400	$3.00	$3,600	$7,200	$600
Standard variable cost:								
Material	0.50	600	0.70	840	1.50	1,800	3,240	270
Labor	0.10	120	0.15	180	0.10	120	420	35
Variable overhead	0.20	240	0.25	300	0.20	240	780	65
Total variable cost	0.80	960	1.10	1,320	1.80	2,160	$4,440	370
Contribution	$0.20	240	$0.90	1,080	$1.20	1,440	$2,760	230
Fixed costs:								
Fixed overhead		300		300		300	900	75
Selling expense†		200		200		200	600	50
Administrative expense		100		100		100	300	25
Total fixed costs		600		600		600	1,800	150
Profit before taxes		$ (360)		$ 480		$ 840	$ 960	$ 80

* Standard volume (units).
† For this example, selling expenses are fixed; in most business situations, there usually is a variable element to be considered.

EXHIBIT 11–3 Actual Sales for January 1984
($000)

Product	Unit sales	Selling price	Dollar sales
A	100	$0.90	$ 90
B	200	2.05	410
C	150	2.50	375
Total	450		875

Price variance. The price variance is calculated by multiplying the difference between the actual price and the standard price by the actual volume. The calculation for the ABC Division is shown in Exhibit 11–4. It shows that the price variance is $75,000, unfavorable.

EXHIBIT 11–4 Calculation of Sales Price Variance, January 1984 ($000)

	Product			
	A	B	C	Total
Actual volume (units)	100	200	150	
Actual price	$ 0.90	$ 2.05	$ 2.50	
Budget price	1.00	2.00	3.00	
Actual over/(under) budget	(.10)	0.05	(0.50)	
Favorable/(unfavorable) price variance	(10)	10	(75)	(75)

Mix and volume variance. Often the mix and volume variances are not separated. The combined mix and volume variance is:

$$\text{Mix and volume variance} = (\text{Actual volume} - \text{Budgeted volume}) \times (\text{Budgeted unit contribution})$$

The calculation of mix and volume variance for the ABC Division is shown in Exhibit 11–5. It shows that the mix and volume variance combined is $150,000 favorable.

EXHIBIT 11–5 Sales Mix and Volume Variance, January 1984 ($000)

(1) Product	(2) Actual volume	(3) Budgeted volume	(4) Difference (2) − (3)	(5) Contribution	(6) Variance (4) × (5)
A	100	100	—	$ —	$ —
B	200	100	100	0.90	90
C	150	100	50	1.20	60
Total	450	300			$150

The volume variance results from selling more units than budgeted. The mix variance results from selling a different proportion of products from that contained in the budget. Because products earn different *contributions* per unit, the sale of different proportions of products from those budgeted will result in a variance. If the division has a "richer" mix, the actual profit is higher than budgeted; and if it has a "leaner" mix, the profit is lower. Since the volume and mix variances are interrelated, the techniques for separating them must be somewhat arbitrary. (Because of this, some companies do not separate mix and volume variances.) One such technique is described below. Other ways of making this calculation are equally acceptable.

Mix variance. The mix variance for each product is found from the following equation:

Mix variance

= [(Total actual volume of sales × Budgeted percentage) − (Actual volume of sales)][Budgeted unit contribution]

The total mix variance is the algebraic sum of these variances.

The calculation of the mix variance for the ABC Division is shown in Exhibit 11–6. It shows that a higher proportion of product B was sold and a lower proportion of product A. Since product B has a higher contribution than product A, the mix variance is favorable, by $35,000.

EXHIBIT 11–6 Calculation of Mix Variance, January 1984 ($000)

(1) Product	*(2)* Budgeted proportion	*(3)* Budgeted mix at actual volume	*(4)* Actual sales	*(5)* Difference (3) − (4)	*(6)* Unit contribution	Variance (5) × (6)
A	1/3	150*	100	(50)	$.20	$(10)
B	1/3	150	200	50	.90	45
C	1/3	150	150	—	—	
Total		450	450			35

* 1/3 × 450

Volume variance. The volume variance can be calculated by subtracting the mix variance from the combined mix and volume variance. This is $150,000 minus $35,000 or $115,000. It can also be calculated for each product as follows:

Volume variance

= [(Total actual volume of sales)(Budgeted percentage) − (Budgeted sales)][Budgeted unit contribution]

The calculation of the volume variance for the ABC Division is shown in Exhibit 11–7.

Other revenue analyses. If information is available, revenue variances may be further subdivided. For example, revenue variances can be calculated by market area, by product line, or by both market area and product line. In our example, we have not provided informa-

EXHIBIT 11–7 Calculation of Volume Variance, January 1984 ($000)

(1) Product	(2) Budgeted mix at actual volume	(3) Budgeted volume	(4) Difference (2) − (3)	(5) Unit contribution	(6) Volume variance
A	150	100	50	$0.20	$ 10
B	150	100	50	0.90	45
C	150	100	50	1.20	60
Total	450	300	150		115

tion on market area. We do, however, have the information by product. An analysis of the revenue variances by product for the ABC Division is shown in Exhibit 11–8.

EXHIBIT 11–8 Calculation of Revenue Variances by Product, January 1984 ($000)

	Product			
	A	*B*	*C*	*Total*
Price variance	$(10)	$ 10	$(75)	$ (75)
Mix variance	(10)	45	—	35
Volume variance	10	45	60	115
Total	(10)	100	(15)	75

Market penetration and industry volume. One common variation in revenue analysis is to separate the mix and volume variance into the amount caused by differences in market share and the amount caused by differences in industry volume. The principle is that the divisional manager is responsible for market penetration, but is not responsible for the industry volume because this is largely influenced by the state of the economy. To make this calculation, industry sales data obviously must be available, and many companies cannot obtain such data. This calculation is described below.

Exhibit 11–9 provides details with respect to the assumptions made

EXHIBIT 11–9 Analysis of Budgeted Sales Volume ($000)

	Product			
	A	*B*	*C*	*Total*
Estimated industry volume (units):				
Annual	10,000	6,000	20,000	36,000
Monthly	833	500	1,667	3,000
Budgeted market penetration	12%	20%	6%	10%
Budgeted (1984) volume (units):				
Annual (Exhibit 11–2)	1,200	1,200	1,200	3,600
Monthly (Exhibit 11–5)	100	100	100	300

in the original budget shown in Exhibit 11–2, and Exhibit 11–10 provides details on industry volume and market penetration for the month of January 1984.

EXHIBIT 11–10 Analysis of Actual Sales, January 1984

	Product			
	A	*B*	*C*	*Total*
Industry volume	1,000	1,000	1,000	3,000
Actual sales	100	200	150	450
Market penetration	10%	20%	15%	15%

The following equation is used to separate the effect of market penetration from industry volume on the mix and volume variance:

Market penetration variance
= [(Actual sales) − (Industry volume) (Budgeted market penetration)] [Budgeted unit contribution]

The calculation for market penetration variance for the ABC Division is shown in Exhibit 11–11.

EXHIBIT 11–11 Calculation of Variance Due to Market Penetration, January 1984 ($000)

	Product			
	A	*B*	*C*	*Total*
(1) Actual sales (units)	100	200	150	450
(2) Budgeted penetration at industry volume	120	200	60	380
(3) Difference (1 − 2)	(20)	—	90	70
(4) Unit contribution (budget)	$0.20	$0.90	$1.20	
(5) Variance due to market penetration (3 × 4)	(4.00)	—	108.00	$104

This means that $104,000 of the favorable mix and volume variance of $150,000 resulted from the fact that market penetration was better than budget. The remaining $46,000 resulted from the actual industry dollar volume being higher than budget.

The $46,000 industry volume variance can also be calculated as follows:

Industry volume variance
= (Actual industry volume − Budgeted industry volume)(Budgeted market penetration) (Budgeted unit contribution)

This calculation of variance due to industry volume for the ABC Division is shown in Exhibit 11–12.

EXHIBIT 11–12 Calculation of Variance Due to Industry Volume, January 1984 ($000)

	Product			
	A	*B*	*C*	*Total*
(1) Actual industry volume	1,000	1,000	1,000	3,000
(2) Budgeted industry volume	833	500	1,667	3,000
(3) Difference (1 − 2)	167	500	(667)	—
(4) Budgeted market penetration	12%	20%	6%	
(5) (3) × (4)	20	100	(40)	
(6) Contribution—unit	$0.20	$ 0.90	$ 1.20	
(7) Total (5 × 6)	4.00	90.00	(48.00)	$46

Notes on Revenue Variances

Note that revenue variances in the above examples are calculated using the *budgeted* unit contribution. Any difference between the budgeted unit contribution and the actual unit contribution is shown as a cost variance. This assumes that selling prices are not expected to change during the period *because* of changes in cost. If the marketing department is responsible for changing selling prices as costs change, then the price variance as computed in Exhibit 11–4 would not reflect this responsibility. In these circumstances, a different set of calculations would be made. Instead of the price variance, the difference between budgeted and actual unit contributions would be computed. During an inflationary period, this would show the extent to which increases in costs were covered by increases in selling prices.

Revenue variances are interrelated and variance equations are somewhat arbitrary. Other methods than shown in the text will therefore result in different amounts. However, the magnitudes of the differences are not usually significant.

Cost Variances

Fixed costs. Variances between actual and budgeted fixed costs can be obtained simply by subtraction, since these costs are not affected by either the volume of sales or the volume of production. This is shown in Exhibit 11–13.

Variable costs. Variable costs are those costs that vary directly and proportionately with volume. Consequently the budgeted variable manufacturing costs must be adjusted to the actual volume of production. Assume the January production was as follows: product A,

EXHIBIT 11–13 Calculation of Fixed-cost Variances, January 1984 ($000)

	Actual	*Budget*	*Favorable/ (unfavorable) variances*
Fixed overhead	$ 75	$ 75	$—
Selling expense	55	50	(5)
Administrative expense	30	25	(5)
Total	160	150	(10)

150,000 units; product B, 120,000 units; product C, 200,000 units. Assume also that the variable costs incurred in January were as follows: material, $470,000; labor, $65,000; variable manufacturing overhead, $90,000. Exhibit 11–2 shows the standard unit variable costs.

The budgeted manufacturing expense is adjusted to the amount that should have been spent at the actual level of production by multiplying each element of standard cost for each product by the volume of production for that product. This calculation is shown for the ABC Division as Exhibit 11–14.

EXHIBIT 11–14 Calculation of Variable Manufacturing Expense Variances, January 1984 ($000)

	Product					
	A	*B*	*C*	*Total*	*Actual*	*Favorable/ (unfavorable) variances*
Material	$ 75	$ 84	$300	$459	$470	($11)
Labor	15	18	20	53	65	(12)
Overhead (variable)	30	30	40	100	90	10
Total	120	132	360	612	625	(13)

This exhibit shows that net variable manufacturing costs had an unfavorable variance of $13,000 in January. This is called a ''spending'' variance because it results from spending $13,000 in excess of the adjusted budget. It consists of unfavorable material and labor variances of $11,000 and $12,000, respectively. These are partially offset by a favorable overhead spending variance of $10,000.

Reporting Variances

The separate revenue and cost variances are assembled into a report for management. There are two principal methods of reporting variances: (1) a report that summarizes variances only, and (2) a report that compares the actual and budgeted figures. In some systems both types of reports are used. Each is illustrated below.

Summary of variances only. Using the information developed in the preceding section, the variance report for ABC Division would be as shown in Exhibit 11–15.

EXHIBIT 11–15 Summary Performance Report, January 1984 ($000)

Actual profit (Exhibit 11–1)	$132
Budgeted profit (Exhibit 11–1)	80
Division variance	$ 52
Analysis of variance—favorable/(unfavorable)	
Revenue variances:	
Price (Exhibit 11–4)	$ (75)
Mix (Exhibit 11–6)	35
Volume (Exhibit 11–7)	115
Net revenue variances	75
Variable-cost variances:	
Material (Exhibit 11–14)	(11)
Labor (Exhibit 11–14)	(12)
Variable overhead (Exhibit 11–14)	10
Net variable cost variances	(13)
Fixed-cost variances:	
Selling expense (Exhibit 11–13)	(5)
Administrative expense (Exhibit 11–13)	(5)
Net fixed-cost variances	(10)
Division variance	$ 52

Comparison of actual with budgeted costs. The same variance information could be shown in the format illustrated in Exhibit 11–16.

EXHIBIT 11–16 Performance Report, January 1984 ($000)

	Actual	*Budget**	*Actual better/ (worse) than budget*
Sales	$875	$950	$ (75)
Standard variable cost of sales	570	570	—
Material variance	11		(11)
Labor variance	12		(12)
Variable overhead variance	(10)†		10
Total variable cost	583	570	(13)
Contribution	292	380	(88)
Fixed manufacturing cost	75	75	—
Gross profit	217	305	(88)
Selling expense	55	50	(5)
Administrative expense	30	25	(5)
Profit at actual volume and mix	$132	$230	$ (98)
Mix variance			$ 35
Volume variance			115
Division variance			$ 52

* Budgeted prices and costs at actual sales volume and mix.

† The standard variable cost of sales is calculated using the volume of *sales*. The cost variances are calculated using the volume of *production*. The actual cost of sales, therefore, is equal to the standard cost of sales plus or minus the variances. The difference between units sold and units produced is added to or subtracted from the inventory.

ANALYSIS OF VARIANCE—FULL COST SYSTEM

This part of the chapter describes the methods for analysing variances when a full standard cost system is used.

Under a full cost system, both the variable and fixed manufacturing cost are assigned to the products produced. The unit standard full costs for Products A, B, and C would be as follows (from Exhibit 11–2):

	Product		
	A	*B*	*C*
Material	$0.50	$0.70	$1.50
Labor	0.10	0.15	0.10
Variable overhead	0.20	0.25	0.20
Fixed overhead*	0.25	0.25	0.25
Total	1.05	1.35	2.05

* $300 total fixed overhead for each product divided by 1,200 units.

Assuming that everything was the same except that the budget and actual data were prepared using full costs rather than variable costs, the budget report that corresponds to Exhibit 11–1 would be as shown in Exhibit 11–17.

EXHIBIT 11–17 Performance Report, January 1984 ($000)

	Actual	*Budget*	*Actual better/ (worse) than budget*
Sales	$875	$600	$ 275
Cost of sales	653[a]	445	(208)
Gross profit	222	155	$ 67
Selling expense	55	50	(5)
Administrative expense	30	25	(5)
Net profit	$137	$ 80	$ 57[b]

[a] This is the standard full cost of sales net of variances. The composition of this figure is shown in Exhibit 11–20.

[b] This $57,000 profit differs from the $52,000 under the direct cost system due to the inclusion of $5,000 of fixed costs as part of the standard cost of the unsold production, explained later but computed as follows:

	Product (000)			
	A	*B*	*C*	*Total*
Units produced	150	120	200	
Units sold	100	200	150	
Unsold production	50.	(80.)	50.	
Standard fixed cost ($ per unit)	.25	.25	.25	
Amount of fixed costs	$ 12.5	$ (20)	$ 12.5	$5

Revenue Variances

Price variance. The price variance is the same as under the direct cost system. It is $75,000 unfavorable.

Mix and volume variances. The method of calculating the mix and volume variance is the same as described in the first part of the chapter except that the standard unit gross profit is substituted for the standard unit contribution. Since the fixed cost per unit is $0.25 for each product, the unit contribution will be $0.25 less than the amounts used in the preceding calculation. Mix and volume variances are calculated in Exhibit 11–18.

EXHIBIT 11–18 Mix and Volume Variance, January 1984 ($000)

(1)	(2)	(3)	(4)	(5)	(6)
	Actual volume at budgeted	Mix variance			Mix
Product	mix	Actual sales	Difference (2) − (3)	Gross profit	variance (4) × (5)
A	150	100	$(50)	$(0.05)	$ 2.5
B	150	200	50	0.65	32.5
C	150	150	—		
Total	450	450			35.0

	Volume variance				
Product	Actual volume at budgeted mix	Budgeted volume	Difference (2) − (3)	Gross profit	Volume variance (4) × (5)
A	150	100	50	$(0.05)	$ (2.5)
B	150	100	50	0.65	32.5
C	150	100	50	0.95	47.5
Total	450	300	150		77.5

Cost Variances

Selling expense and administrative expenses are not affected by the type of cost system used. Consequently, the variances for these two expense categories will be identical to those calculated for the direct cost system. Also, the material and labor variances will be the same as in the direct cost system. It is only the overhead expense variances that are different. At this point, we need some new definitions.

Absorbed cost. Absorbed cost is the amount of material, labor, and overhead costs absorbed (included) in the cost of the goods produced. These goods are transferred to inventory at their full standard cost. In the example, the ABC Division produced 150,000 units of product A, 120,000 units of product B, and 200,000 units of product C.

These units were transferred to finished goods inventory. The standard full cost of the goods produced and transferred to finished goods inventory is $729,500, as calculated in Exhibit 11–19.

EXHIBIT 11–19 Calculation of Standard Cost of Goods Produced, January 1984 ($000)

	150 Product A		*120 Product B*		*200 Product C*		
	Unit	*Total*	*Unit*	*Total*	*Unit*	*Total*	*Total*
Material	$0.50	$ 75.0	$0.70	$ 84.0	$1.50	$300.0	$459.0
Labor	0.10	15.0	0.15	18.0	0.10	20.0	53.0
Overhead*	0.45	67.5	0.50	60.0	0.45	90.0	217.5
Total	1.05	157.5	1.35	162.0	2.05	410.0	729.5

* Variable overhead cost plus $0.25 per unit fixed cost.

Budgeted cost. For material and labor, the budgeted cost is the unit budgeted cost multiplied by the units produced. The budgeted overhead cost is calculated by the following formula:

Budgeted overhead costs
= Total budgeted fixed costs + (Units produced) (Budgeted variable overhead cost per unit)

In our example, this would be as follows:

Budgeted overhead
$= \$75 + (150 \times 0.20) + (120 \times 0.25) + (200 \times 0.20)$
$= \$175$

Variances. The actual manufacturing costs were (as given above):

Material		$470
Labor		65
Overhead:		
Variable	90	
Fixed	75	165
Total		700

The total manufacturing variance is equal to the absorbed cost minus the actual cost: $729,500 − $700,000 = $29,500. This means that in the month of January, the ABC Division spent $29,500 less than budgeted in producing products A, B, and C.

The overhead portion of this variance is the result of two factors. First, the division could have spent more or less than the budgeted overhead in producing products A, B, and C. This is the *spending* variance. Second, the division could have produced more or less than standard volume in January. This is the *volume* variance. It is necessary to separate these variances for management, because each has a different cause and may be the responsibility of different people. These two overhead variances are calculated and added to the material and labor variance to arrive at the manufacturing variance, as follows:

Overhead spending variance	= Budgeted cost (at actual volume) − Actual cost		
Volume variance	= Absorbed cost − Budgeted cost		
Spending variance	= $175 − 165 =	$10	favorable
Volume variance	= $217.5 − 175.0 =	42.5	favorable
Total overhead variance		$52.5	favorable
Material variance (from Exhibit 11–14)		(11.0)	unfavorable
Labor variance (from Exhibit 11–14)		(12.0)	unfavorable
Net manufacturing variance		$29.5	favorable

Reporting Variances

The variance report in the full cost system is shown in Exhibit 11–20. Note that the total variance differs from that shown in Exhibit 11–16. This difference (between $57,000 and $52,000) arises because, in a direct cost system, fixed costs are charged as current period expenses, whereas in a full cost system they become part of product costs and are carried into inventory. Since production volume exceeded

EXHIBIT 11–20 Analysis of Variances, January 1984 ($000)

	Actual	*Budget**	*Actual better/ (worse) than budget*
Sales	$875.0	$950.0	$(75.0)
Standard cost of sales	682.5†	682.5†	—
Spending variances	(13.0)		(13.0)
Volume variance (overhead)	42.5		42.5
Gross profit	222.0	267.5	(45.5)
Selling expense	55.0	50.0	(5.0)
Administrative expense	30.0	25.0	(5.0)
Profit	$137.0	$192.5	(55.5)
Mix variance			35.0
Volume variance (revenue)			77.5
Net variance			$ 57.0

* Budgeted prices and costs at actual sales volume and mix.
† Standard unit costs multiplied by the actual volume of sales:

Product	*Units sold*	*Standard unit costs*	*Standard cost of sales*
A	100	$1.05	$105.0
B	200	1.35	270.0
C	150	2.05	307.5
Total	450		682.5

Note: There are two volume variances. The revenue volume variance results from *selling* a greater number of units than was budgeted. The cost variances result from *producing* a greater number of units than was budgeted.

sales volume in the illustration, $5,000 of fixed costs remain in inventory. (Actual production of 470,000 units exceeded actual sales of 450,000 units by 20,000 units. These 20,000 units in inventory carry a fixed overhead cost of $0.25 each, or $5,000 in total.)

USE OF VARIANCE CALCULATIONS

The examples of variance analysis in this chapter are simplified. In actual practice, variances are identified by organization unit down to the lowest responsibility center. Variances by causal factor can be subdivided further from those described in the chapter. For example, material cost variances can be divided between price and usage and further subdivided by type of material. Overhead spending variances can be identified by type of expense and further subdivided by department responsibility.

The entire process of variance analysis is hierarchical. The greatest detail (i.e., subdivision of the variances) is at the lowest organization level reported. The variance analyses are increasingly condensed at each higher level in the organization.

Variances can be analyzed in such a way as to identify the responsible organizational unit and the causes of the variances with a precision that is limited only by the depth with which the original budget was prepared. A good budgetary system can identify variances with considerable objectivity. Management, however, also needs to know the causes of the variances, what is being done to correct them, and how long it is going to take. This information may not only be subjective but also it is influenced by the biases of the preparer. The higher a manager is in the organization, the greater the dependency on these explanations. For example, a plant manager usually does not have problems with identifying the real causes of cost problems in the plant. Higher organizational units (divisional manager or group vice president) may have to rely almost entirely on the explanations prepared at the plant. Thus, even the best variance analysis system may be deficient if sufficient emphasis is not placed on insuring the integrity of the explanation portions of the budget reports. This problem is discussed further in Chapter 12.

QUANTITATIVE TECHNIQUES IN VARIANCE ANALYSIS

One of the problems in variance analysis is to decide when a variance is significant. A related problem is to decide when a variance requires managerial action. (Not all significant variances require management action because some arise from uncontrollable causes.) Mathematical techniques have been developed to solve this type of problem. For example, using probability distributions, it is at least theoretically possible to decide whether a variance was most likely caused by the actual situation being different from budget or whether it was caused by the inherent inaccuracies of the measurement estimate. Other mathematical models have been used to determine the point where the cost of investigating and correcting a variance by the manager when a variance occurs is less than the potential benefits from such involvement.

To date these techniques have been principally of academic interest. The limitation of mathematical models and the lack of information that would be required has limited their application in real-world situations. A bibliography of some of these quantitative techniques is included below.

SUGGESTED ADDITIONAL READINGS

Balman, S., and **Demski, J.** "Variance Analysis Procedures as Motivational Devices." *Management Science,* August 1980, pp. 840–48.

Demski, Joel S. "Optimizing the Search for Cost Deviation Sources." *Management Science,* April 1970.

Dyckman, J. R. "The Investigation of Cost Variances." *Journal of Accounting Research,* Autumn 1969.

Horgren, Charles T. *Cost Accounting: A Managerial Emphasis.* 5th ed. Englewood Cliffs, N.J.: Prentice-Hall, 1982, Chapters 24 and 25.

Jensen, Daniel L., and **McKeown, James C.** "Multiplestep Investigation of Standard Cost Variances." *Journal of Business Finance and Accounting,* 2 April 1977.

Kaplan, Robert S. *Advanced Management Accounting.* Englewood Cliffs, N.J.: Prentice-Hall, 1982. Chapters 9 and 10.

Ozan, T., and **Dyckman, T.** "A Normative Model for Investigating Decisions Involving Multiorigin Cost Variances." *Journal of Accounting Research,* Spring 1971.

Sheshai, K. M. El.; Gorden B. Harwood; and **Roger H. Hermanson.** "Cost Volume Profit Analysis with Interger Goal Programming." *Management Accounting,* October 1977.

Shillinglaw, Gordon. *Managerial Cost Accounting.* 5th ed. Homewood, Ill.: Richard D. Irwin, 1982. Chapter 27.

CASE 11–1
Temple Division*

In this case you are asked to analyze the February and March financial performance of the Temple Division of the ABC Company as compared with its budget which is shown in Exhibit 11–2.

* This case was prepared by John Dearden, Harvard Business School.

PART A—FEBRUARY 1983

Below is the data describing the actual financial results of the Temple Division for the month of February 1983:

Sales	$781
Variable cost of sales	552
Contribution	229
Fixed manufacturing costs	80
Gross profit	149
Selling expense	57
Administrative expense	33
Net profit	$ 59

Sales

Product	*Unit sales*	*Price*	*Dollar sales*
A	120	$0.95	$114
B	130	1.90	247
C	150	2.80	420
Total	400		781

Production

		Manufacturing cost			
Product	*Units produced*	*Material*	*Labor*	*Variable overhead*	*Total*
A	150	$ 80	$20	$ 40	$140
B	130	91	21	35	147
C	120	190	15	30	235
Total	400	361	56	105	522

Questions

1. Prepare an analysis of variance from profit budget assuming that the Temple Division employed a direct standard cost accounting system.

2. Prepare an analysis of variance from profit budget assuming that the Temple Division used a full standard cost accounting system. Under this assumption, the cost of sales amount would be $632,000. (Can you derive this figure?)

3. Industry volume figures are presented below. Separate the mix and volume variance into the variance resulting from differences in market penetration and variance resulting from differences in industry volume. Make the calculation for the direct cost system only.

Industry volume, February 1983:

	Units (000)
Product A	600
Product B	650
Product C	1,500

PART B—MARCH 1983

Below are the data describing the actual financial results for the Temple Division for the month of March 1983:

Income statement

Sales	$498
Variable cost of sales	278
Contribution	220
Fixed manufacturing costs	70
Gross profit	150
Selling expense	45
Administrative expense	20
Net profit	$ 85

Sales

Product	*Unit sales*	*Price*	*Dollar sales*
A	90	$1.10	$ 99
B	70	2.10	147
C	80	3.15	252
Total	240		498

Production

		Manufacturing costs			
Product	*Units produced*	*Material*	*Labor*	*Variable overhead*	*Total*
A	90	$ 40	$ 8	$17	$ 65
B	80	55	10	18	83
C	100	150	8	19	177
Total	270	245	26	54	325

Questions

Answer the same questions included in Part A. The actual cost of sales using full standard costing would be $340.5 in March. Industry volume for March was:

	Units (000)
Product A	500
Product B	600
Product C	1,000

CASE 11–2
Crocker Company*

The profit budget for the Crocker Company for January 1983 was as follows:

		(000)
Sales		$2,500
Standard cost of sales		1,620
Gross profit		880
Selling expense	$250	
Research and development expense	300	
Administrative expense	120	
Total expense		670
Net profit before taxes		$ 210

The product information used in developing the budget was as follows:

	E	*F*	*G*	*H*
Sales—units (000)	1,000	2,000	3,000	4,000
Price per unit	$0.15	$0.20	$0.25	$0.30
Standard cost per unit:				
Material	0.04	0.05	0.06	0.08
Direct labor	0.02	0.02	0.03	0.04
Variable overhead	0.02	0.03	0.03	0.05
Total variable cost	0.08	0.10	0.12	0.17
Fixed overhead ($000)	20	60	60	160
Total standard cost per unit	0.10	0.13	0.14	0.21

The actual revenues and costs for January 1983 were as follows:

		(000)
Sales		$2,160
Standard cost of sales		1,420
Net standard cost of variances		160
Actual cost of sales		1,580
Gross profit		580
Selling expense	$290	
Research and development expense	250	
Administrative expenses	110	
Total expense		650
Net loss		$ (70)

* This case was prepared by John Dearden, Harvard Business School.

Operating statistics for January 1983 were as follows:

		E	F	G	H
Sales (units)		1,000	1,000	4,000	3,000
Sales price		$0.13	$0.22	$0.22	$0.31
Production		1,000	1,000	2,000	2,000
Actual manufacturing costs ($000):					
Material	$360				
Labor	200				
Overhead	530				

Question

Prepare an analysis of variance between actual profits and budgeted profits for January 1979.

CASE 11–3
Wellington Corporation*

The machining department of the Wellington Corporation produced two metal parts that were subsequently incorporated into the company's finished products. In January 1969 the plant superintendent was reviewing the cost performance of the department for the preceding year. A summary of the historical data relating to productivity, labor cost, and material cost is shown below:

	1968
Number of good parts produced:	
Part No. 683	4,451,328
Part No. 845	975,744
Total	5,427,072

Pounds of steel rod used	1,770,739
Cost of steel rod used	$ 460,392
Number of labor hours	34,500
Labor cost	$ 103,500

The machining department operated two types of automatic screw machines. In 1969, the department had 48 Acme machines used to produce Part No. 683, while the Detroit model X7 machines were used for Part No. 845. The Acme machines were faster and more efficient in that they

* This case was prepared by R. F. Vancil, Harvard Business School.

could produce 60 pieces per hour and one operator could serve four machines. The department had 48 Acme machines and during 1968 these machines had been operated at full capacity (40 hours per week for 50 weeks) because of a strong demand for the product which used this part. During the year, therefore, 12 men had always been assigned to the Acme machines and, in order to achieve maximum output, the foreman had always assigned his most highly skilled operators to this equipment. The Detroit machines had a theoretical capacity of 40 units per hour of Part No. 845 and a skilled operator could serve only three of these machines. While there were 24 Detroit machines in the department, full utilization had not been necessary during 1969. The department's normal total work force was 17 men, but this number varied from day to day depending on the production of Part No. 845. Some workers might be temporarily assigned to or from another department to handle these fluctuating requirements. Wellington's contract with the labor union specified that all men assigned to the machining department were to receive the same wage ($3 per hour); for this reason, the payroll accounting department kept track of all temporary transfers, and the machining department was charged only for the time spent by men actually assigned to the department.

A study of the labor efficiency in the machining department, conducted in the fall of 1969, indicated that the machines normally operated about 90 percent of the time. Half of the 10 percent down time was due to regularly scheduled rest periods for the machine operators; the other 5 percent was the time required by a worker of average skill to make adjustments to the machine settings.

Both parts produced by the department were made from the same type of tempered steel rod. Wellington's major domestic supplier had announced a list price for this rod, f.o.b. Wellington's plant, of 28 cents per pound in late 1969. During 1969 however, Wellington's purchasing agent had found that imported rod of equal quality could be purchased on similar terms for 24 cents per pound. By the end of 1969 all of Wellington's rod was being supplied by the foreign producer.

Part No. 683 was smaller than Part No. 845; a finished piece of the smaller part weighed .20 pounds, while a finished unit of the larger part weighed .40 pounds. Because some material was wasted in the machining process, .45 pounds of rod were required to produce one piece of Part No. 845, while .24 pounds were needed for one piece of No. 683. In addition, some of the finished pieces were scrapped because the machine settings tended to become out of adjustment. The company's historical experience had been that Part No. 683, the more complex part, incurred a 20 percent scrappage rate while No. 845 had only a 10 percent scrappage rate. According to the foreman in the department, however, the actual scrappage on Part No. 683 during 1969 had been lower than normal—only 16 percent—because the more skilled workers on the Acme machines were better able to keep the machines in adjustment. The proceeds (10 cents per pound) received from the sale of both metal shavings and scrapped parts were regarded by Wellington's management as "Other Income," and were not credited to the materials cost account of the machining department.

Questions

1. Prepare a statement of estimated or standard prime costs for each part, as of the beginning of 1969. Prime cost is the sum of direct material cost plus direct labor cost. Analyze the actual results for that year in terms of these standards, and compute quantity and price variances in as detailed a manner as is possible with the information available.

2. Wellington's management was considering an opportunity to enter into a one-year supply contract with a major mail-order house for the product which used Part No. 845. The contract would require at least 15,000 units of the part each month. As part of the analysis in deciding what price to offer on this contract, management has asked you to prepare an estimate of prime costs for the coming year which you think would be relevant for this bid.

CASE 11–4
Cotter Company, Inc.*

In preparing its profit plan for 1983, the management of Cotter Company, Inc., realized that its sales were subject to monthly seasonal variations, but expected that for the year as a whole the profit before taxes would total $240,000, as shown in Exhibit 1.

EXHIBIT 1 Budget, 1983

	Amount	*Percent of sales*
Sales	$2,400,000	100%
Standard cost of goods sold:		
Prime costs	960,000	40
Factory overhead	840,000	35
Total standard cost	1,800,000	75
Gross profit	600,000	25
Selling and general overhead	360,000	15
Profit before taxes	$ 240,000	10%

Management defined "prime costs" as those costs for labor and materials which were strictly variable with the quantity of production

* This case was prepared by R. F. Vancil, Harvard Business School.

in the factory. The overhead in the factory included both fixed and variable costs; management's estimate was that, within a sales volume range of plus or minus $1 million per year, variable factory overhead would be equal to 25 percent of prime costs. Thus, the total factory overhead budgeted for 1983 consisted of $240,000 of variable costs (25 percent of $960,000) and $600,000 of fixed costs. All of the selling and general overhead was fixed, except for commissions on sales equal to 5 percent of the selling price.

Mr. Cotter, the president of the company, approved the budget, stating that, "A profit of $20,000 a month isn't bad for a little company in this business." During January, however, sales suffered the normal seasonal dips, and production in the factory was also cut back. The result, which came as some surprise to the president, was that January showed a loss of $7,000 (see Exhibit 2).

EXHIBIT 2 Operating Statement, January 1983

Sales		$140,000
Standard cost of goods sold		105,000
Standard gross profit		35,000
Manufacturing variances:		
		Favorable or (unfavorable)
Prime cost variance	$ (3,500)	
Factory overhead:		
Spending variance	1,000	
Volume variance	(12,500)	$ (15,000)
Actual gross profit		20,000
Selling and general overhead		27,000
Loss before taxes		$ (7,000)

Question

Explain, as best you can with the data available, why the January profit was $27,000 less than the average monthly profit expected by the president.

CASE 11–5 (*A*)
North American Can Company (*A*): The Kokomo Division*

The Kokomo division of the North American Can Company produced a single product: a 12-ounce beer can. Exhibit 1 provides financial

* This case was prepared by John Dearden, Harvard Business School.

EXHIBIT 1 1983 Annual Budget Data

*Item of revenue or cost**	*1983 expected amount†*
Price	$85.20 per unit
Direct material	$28.80 per unit
Direct labor	$5.10 per unit
Manufacturing overhead:	
Indirect labor	$69,000 per year + $3.10 per unit
Indirect material	$1.84 per unit
Utilities	$1.54 per unit
Maintenance	$30,800 per year + $1.25 per unit
Depreciation	$92,500 per year
Property taxes	$30,900 per year
Marketing expense:	
Sales commissions	$4.25 per unit
Salaries	$92,000 per year
Distribution	$0.82 per unit
Administrative costs	$106,000 per year

* All numbers have been disguised and, therefore, may not be representative of actual revenues or costs experienced in a typical can manufacturing plant.

† Expected manufacturing costs are standard costs.

information about the revenues and costs that were projected for 1983 for the Kokomo Division. The total market volume is expected to be 60,000 units for the year. The volume of production and sales for the Kokomo Division is projected to be 12,000 units for the year. A unit is 400 cases. Each case contains 24 of the 12-ounce cans.

Question

Prepare a 1983 profit plan for the Kokomo Division (the profit plan is before income taxes). The Kokomo Division has no beginning or ending inventory accounts.

CASE 11–5 (*B*)

North American Can Company (*B*): The Kokomo Division*

Exhibit 1 provides the actual results of operations for the Kokomo Division for the first quarter of 1983. Kokomo employed a standard full cost system. Sales and production were equal.

* This case was prepared by John Dearden, Harvard Business School.

EXHIBIT 1 Results of Operations—First Quarter, 1983

	Amount
Sales	$275,400
Standard cost of sales	195,145
Variances	(5,780)
Cost of goods sold	189,365
Gross profit	86,035
Marketing expense (Schedule B)	40,000
Administrative expense	26,474
Profit before taxes	19,561
Volume of sales (units)	3,240
Schedule A—Cost of goods sold	
Direct material	$ 81,000
Direct labor	27,216
Indirect labor	27,544
Indirect materials	5,184
Utilities	5,184
Maintenance	12,387
Depreciation	23,125
Property tax	7,725
Total COGS	189,365
Schedule B—Marketing expense	
Commissions	$ 13,770
Salaries	23,476
Distribution	2,754
Total marketing expense	40,000

Questions

1. Compare the actual results with the budgeted amounts prepared in the (*A*) case. (The budget for the first quarter is ¼ of the annual budget).
2. What conclusions can you draw about the first quarter financial performance of the Kokomo Division?
3. What managerial actions would you take as a result of your analysis?

CASE 11–5 (*C*)

North American Can Company (*C*): The Kokomo Division*

Exhibit 1 provides a more detailed description of both budgeted and actual results of operations for the Kokomo Division for the first quarter of 1983.

* This case was prepared by John Dearden, Harvard Business School.

EXHIBIT 1

	Budgeted	Actual
Direct material	.06 cents per square foot (480 square feet per unit)	.05 cents per square foot (500 square feet per unit)
Direct labor.	$10.20 per hour (0.5 hours per unit)	$10.50 per hour (0.8 hours per unit)
Total market . . . . (first quarter)	15,000 units	18,000 units
Sales volume. . . . . (first quarter)	3,000 units	3,240 units

Questions

1. Analyze the causes of the variances from budget and evaluate the first quarter's financial performance of the Kokomo Division.
2. Separate the variances into three classifications:
   a. Largely controllable by management.
   b. Largely uncontrollable by management.
   c. Semicontrollable by management.
3. What managerial actions would you take on the basis of your analysis?

CASE 11–6
Bondsville Manufacturing Company

"Let's face it," said William Haywood, controller of the Bondsville Manufacturing Company to Frederick Strong, the manager of the budget department. "Our budgetary control program is considerably less than a roaring success. As far as I can tell, no one in top management takes any action from our monthly analyses of actual profit performance against budget. Jim [James Smith, Bondsville's president] told me this afternoon that he really cannot use these reports to control the divisions. He said that the variance from budgeted profits always seem to be large, but there always appeared to be reasonable explanations. Further, he pointed out that once a division started to miss its budget, the variances seemed to get larger each month. And Jim wasn't concerned only with unfavorable variances. He says that some divisions are showing favorable variances when he knows darn well that they are doing a poor job."

Frederick Strong was crestfallen. He had come to the Bondsville Manufacturing Company three years before from a large automobile manufacturer, where he had been a budget analyst in one of the divisions. He was responsible for developing and installing the present profit budget system. The system had gone into effect 18 months ago.

For the first year, it was considered experimental. Beginning with the current year (1983) the profit budget was officially installed as the basic tool of management control. Now, after six months, the president of Bondsville was questioning the utility of the budgetary control system and the controller was evidently agreeing.

"I don't understand it," said Strong to Haywood. "The system is similar to the one we used at Universal Motors and they sure paid attention to it. If we missed our budget, we were called on the carpet to explain—and the explanation had to be good."

"Well, it may have worked at Universal," said Haywood, "but it isn't working here. I'll arrange for you to talk with Jim about it. Then, I want you to go over the system and either modify it so that it will work or scrap it and develop something that will." With this last comment, Strong was dismissed to ponder his problems.

Bondsville Manufacturing Company started during World War I as a family-owned manufacturer of cotton textiles for the U.S. Army. The original plant was located in the town of Bondsville, a small village in western Massachusetts. In 1940, the company was taken over from the original family by a group of investors. This group renovated the Bondsville plant, built a knitting plant in nearby Ware, Massachusetts, and purchased a woolen plant in Monson, Massachusetts. During the war, the company prospered and grew until, at the cessation of hostilities, its annual profit was $3 million on a sales volume of nearly $28 million. After World War II, sales increased very slowly and profits declined. In 1970, the stockholders—together with a Springfield, Massachusetts, bank that held a large loan—forced out the incumbent president and appointed James Smith to the post. Smith had been marketing vice president of a large southern textile company, where he had developed a reputation for "getting things done."

Since 1970, the company had prospered. Sales in the three current lines (cotton, knitted goods, and woolens) grew, and by 1980 the company had added two new lines of goods: artificial fiber products (dacron and nylon hosiery, underwear, blouses, etc.) in a plant in Dedham, Massachusetts; and artificial leather in a plant in Milton, Massachusetts. These plants were both acquired by buying the companies that had been operating them. By mid-1983 Bondsville's sales were approaching $100 million a year. Profits, however, still were only about $3 million.

PRODUCTS

Bondsville Manufacturing Company had five product lines. Each line was produced in a separate plant and was marketed by a separate organization.

Each line is described below.

Cotton textiles. The Bondsville plant produced gray goods that were sold directly to jobbers and converters (about 50 percent of the volume) and printed cotton fabrics that are sold to jobbers and also directly to clothes manufacturers.

Knitted goods. The Ware plant produced knitted fabrics and converted these fabrics into clothes. Part of the production was of such standard items as underwear and pajamas. Over 50 percent of the production was in women's clothes, which are style items and seasonal. These were sold directly to department stores by company salesmen.

Artificial fibers. The Dedham plant produced products made of artificial fibers (principally dacron and nylon). The yarn was purchased and the plant wove the cloth and manufactured the garments. These were sold to jobbers and also directly to buyers of large department stores.

Woolen goods. The Monson plant produced woolen cloth of various types. About three quarters of the cloth was sold to finishers by company salesmen. The company finished (dyed) the remaining one quarter of its production and sold this cloth to manufacturers of clothes.

Artificial leather. The Milton plant produced artificial leather for automobile and furniture upholstery. About 50 percent of the production was for automobiles; the remainder was used in a variety of furniture. Artificial leather was sold exclusively by company salesmen directly to manufacturers.

The following are the 1982 sales and gross profits (sales minus manufacturing costs) of each of the product lines:

	Sales (000)	*Gross profit (000)*
Cotton textiles	$42,581	$ 463
Knitted goods	27,862	4,068
Artificial fiber	13,733	716
Woolen goods	10,429	(28)
Artificial leather	5,216	1,582
	$99,821	$6,801

Each of the five operating divisions was headed by a divisional manager. Theoretically, the corporate staff was responsible only for helping the divisions when needed and for coordinating functional activities. In fact, the sales staff vice president and the manufacturing staff vice president had been senior operating people before taking up staff positions. Consequently, they exercised considerable direct control over their functional areas in the divisions. The president also spent several days a month visiting the divisional offices and counseling the managers on their various problems.

THE CONTROLLER'S OFFICE

Exhibit 1 is the organization chart for the controller's office.

EXHIBIT 1 Organization Chart—Controller's Office

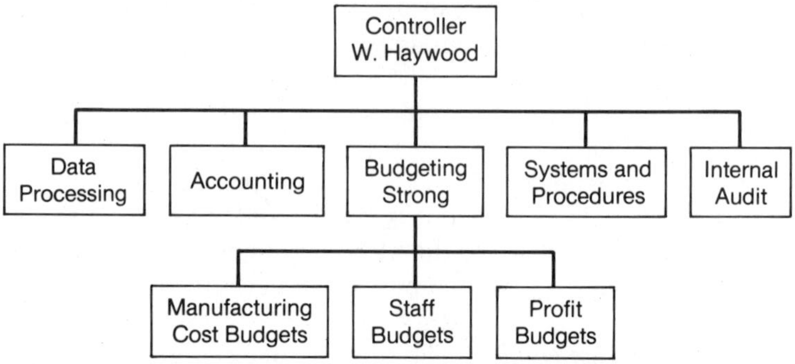

The basic accounting records were maintained at the divisional offices. Each month the divisional balance sheet and profit and loss accounts were submitted to the central office. The central office's accounting department prescribed the company's accounting systems, maintained the central office accounting records, consolidated all of the accounts, and published a company-wide balance sheet and profit and loss statement on the 10th working day after the end of the month.

Each division had its own accounting department. Reporting to the divisional controller, the divisional budget manager was responsible for the budget reports in the division. Each plant manager had a cost analyst who reported directly to him and whose job was to assist the manager by interpreting budget and cost reports and obtaining needed cost information. In addition, the cost analyst was responsible for providing the analysis of budget variances to the divisional budget manager.

The company used a standard cost system to control material and labor and a flexible budget to control manufacturing overhead.

THE BUDGETARY CONTROL SYSTEM

Budget Preparation

Each divisional manager was responsible for preparing and submitting a profit budget in December to cover the succeeding year. The sales department first prepared an estimate of annual sales. This was reviewed and approved by the divisional manager. After sales volume approval, everyone reporting to the divisional manager was responsible for preparing their budgets, based on the indicated volume of sales. The plant budget was based on standard costs for material and direct labor, and the flexible budget for manufacturing overhead. The divisional manager reviewed each budget and approved or adjusted it.

The divisional manager next met with the president, the manufacturing staff vice president, the sales staff vice president, and the corporate controller. (This was the budget approval committee.) In presenting the proposed budget, differences from the current year's actual performance were carefully explained. The committee discussed the proposed budget with the divisional manager and either approved it, adjusted it, or sent it back to be partially redone.

After final approval, the budget became the basis for evaluating actual profit performance.

Each staff vice president also presented a budget for the coming year to the president. After discussion, the budget was either approved or adjusted. The corporate controller's office combined the divisional and staff budgets into a company-wide profit budget, which was presented to the president for final approval. (The president could call for a change in previously approved budgets if the total company profits were not satisfactory.)

Budget Reports

Each month a report was prepared for each division showing actual profits compared to budget. Exhibit 2 is an example of a budget performance report.

EXHIBIT 2 Profit Budget Performance Report, April 1983 ($000)

	Month of April	*Year-to-date*
Actual profit	$(12)	$ (43)
Budgeted profit	42	150
Actual over/(under) budget	(54)	(193)
Analysis of variance—favorable/(unfavorable)		
Revenue items:		
Sales volume	$(65)	$(240)
Selling prices	15	(25)
Product mix	2	10
Cost items:		
Material prices	4	10
Material usage	(3)	6
Direct labor	10	45
Variable overhead	5	30
Advertising and sales promotion	(16)	(35)
Other selling	(1)	(9)
Administration	(5)	15
	$(54)	$(193)

Note: This exhibit was backed up with schedules showing the details of the variances and explanations of the reasons for the variances. The explanations were provided by the various operating executives responsible for these variances.

These budget performance reports were prepared by the divisions and submitted to the central staff on the 12th working day after the end of the month. After review by the corporate budget department, copies were distributed to the president, the sales staff vice president, and the manufacturing staff vice president. The corporate budget department prepared a brief analysis of each report, indicating points that should be brought to management's attention.

The corporate budget department prepared a "Company Profit Budget Report" on the 15th working day after the end of the month. This was a consolidation of the five operating divisions and the six staff offices. Copies of this went to the three executives indicated above.

DISCUSSION WITH SMITH

Frankly, your profit budget performance reports are just about worthless to me. For one thing, we just cannot budget sales revenue with any degree of certainty. All of the budgets show large variances, but what do I do with them? The big variances are almost always in revenue. Either volume has been higher or lower than budget or prices have gone up or down. Furthermore, once a division starts having problems with sales or prices, it might take several months to change the situation. You might have to change your product line, wait until your competitors get tired of losing money and raise prices, or wait until the economy improves. In other words, I look at the budget performance report and say "so what?"

Another thing, I really get no surprises from the budget reports because I know when something has happened long before the budget report reaches me. I get weekly sales reports from each division and I can easily see those divisions that are having trouble with volume or prices. Costs do not usually vary much from month to month. The few times that our costs have gone to hell temporarily, I have known it ahead of time. What I need is a report that will tell me what is going to happen, not one that tells me what I have known for several weeks.

There's a third thing that bothers me, but I'd like you to keep this under your hat. I know for a fact that John Bennett [the manager of the Artificial Leather Division] has been doing a poor job with that division this year, even though his budget performance is the best of the five divisions. Because of quality problems in his plant, he lost one of our best customers in the furniture business. Yet, because automobiles are selling far better than we anticipated, Bennett shows a large favorable sales volume variance. On the other hand, the most capable manager that I have shows the poorest budget performance.

There you are, Fred—three complaints. I can't do anything with the reports: they contain no important information that I did not already know; they do not reflect the true performance of the managers. I had hopes of using profit budget performance as a basis for paying bonuses to the managers. You can see that I can't do this with your system.

You will have to do something about these complaints or discontinue this fancy profit budget system. As it is now, it may have been all right for the big automobile firms but it's no good for us.

Questions

1. What do you think should be done about Bondsville's profit budgeting system?
2. If you believe it should be discontinued, what are company characteristics that have made it unworkable? With what should the system be replaced?
3. In what type of company does a profit budget system work effectively?

CASE 11–7
Modo Company*

August Germain, a director of Modo Company, received the following Exhibits 1 through 4 as part of the packet of material sent in advance of

EXHIBIT 1 Operations Highlights: Net Sales Summary, March ($000)

Current month				*Budget period*		
Budget	*Actual*	*Increase/ (decrease) over budget (percent)*	*Division*	*Budget*	*Actual*	*Increase/ (decrease) over budget (percent)*
$ 2,550	$ 3,816	50%	A	$ 8,345	$10,483	26%
1,155	24	(98)	B	3,398	65	(98)
0	59	0	C	0	276	0
3,274	3,636	11	D	9,443	8,598	(9)
1,761	1,468	(17)	E	4,149	3,874	(7)
2,843	2,692	(5)	F	8,825	9,458	7
6,515	6,101	(6)	G	19,041	16,664	(12)
800	1,067	33	H	2,000	2,912	46
129	0	(100)	J	333	0	(100)
0	0	0	K	0	0	0
591	201	(66)	L	1,966	1,568	(20)
445	567	27	M	1,075	1,363	27
491	615	25	N	1,712	1,357	(21)
4,885	5,574	14	O	12,935	14,277	10
3,514	2,557	(27)	P	11,677	7,986	(32)
4,241	2,200	(48)	Q	10,036	7,354	(27)
492	557	13	R	1,411	1,623	15
33,686	31,134	(8)	Total net sales	96,346	87,858	(9)
(20)	(73)	265	Less: Interdivisional sales	(70)	(326)	366
$33,666	$31,061	(8)%	Consolidated net sales	$96,276	$87,532	(9)%

Note: Unfavorable variances are in parentheses.
All dollar amounts in thousands.

* This case was prepared by R. N. Anthony, Harvard Business School.

EXHIBIT 2 Operations Highlights: Division Pretax Income Summary, March ($000)

Current month				*Budget period*		
Budget	*Actual*	*Variance*	*Division*	*Budget*	*Actual*	*Variance*
$ (4)	$ 213	$ 217	A	$ (10)	$ 502	$ 512
(248)	(103)	145	B	(937)	(418)	519
0	(21)	(21)	C	0	(39)	(39)
362	357	(5)	D	901	550	(351)
471	351	(120)	E	980	937	(43)
377	452	75	F	1,244	1,510	266
772	881	109	G	1,898	1,820	(78)
82	103	21	H	130	185	55
(13)	0	13	J	(41)	0	41
0	0	0	K	0	0	0
(137)	(210)	(73)	L	(265)	(266)	(1)
57	28	(29)	M	88	124	36
(84)	(94)	(10)	N	(130)	(235)	(105)
624	636	12	O	1,440	2,419	979
(122)	(337)	(215)	P	(117)	(776)	(659)
62	(612)	(674)	Q	(493)	(1,467)	(974)
0	38	38	R	0	206	206
8	4	(4)	S	26	65	39
$2,207	$1,686	$(521)	Division pretax income (loss)	$4,714	$5,117	$ 403

Note: Unfavorable variances are in parentheses.

EXHIBIT 3 Operations Highlights: Trade Accounts Receivable, March ($000)

					Number of days sales in receivables*	
Last year	*Budget*	*Actual*	*Variance*	*Division*	*Last year days*	*Actual days*
$ 604	$ 722	$ 4,309	$(3,587)	A	6	41
3,353	3,051	2,631	420	B	65	58
122	—	0	—	C	25	—
3,801	610	4,011	(3,401)	D	37	38
2,590	3,493	3,457	36	E	122	177
13,051	13,810	12,654	1,156	F	161	154
1,632	1,675	1,677	(2)	H and J	61	55
2,113	2,500	2,393	107	K	40	41
8,023	8,474	8,972	(498)	O	59	63
9,077	9,065	8,282	783	P	69	61
8,316	9,213	6,781	2,432	Q	56	46
52,682	52,613	55,167	(2,554)	Total		
12,857	14,634	12,457	2,177	G		
65,539	67,247	67,624	$ (377)	Total		
2,950	—	103		Discontinued divisions	73	77
$68,489	$67,247	$67,727		Total	64	65

* Using net sales for the most recent 12-month period.

EXHIBIT 4 Operations Highlights: Inventories Summaries, March ($000)

Inventories, gross					*Net sales* to ending inventory*	
Last year	*Budget*	*Actual*	*Variance*	*Division*	*Last year times*	*Actual times*
$ 8,857	$ 9,050	$ 7,626	$ 1,424	A	4.1	5.1
5,106	3,412	3,423	(11)	B	3.7	4.8
721	—	0	—	C	2.4	—
9,608	9,702	8,133	1,569	D	3.9	4.8
1,440	1,612	1,427	185	E	5.4	5.0
6,905	7,091	6,480	611	F	4.3	4.6
903	750	889	(139)	H	10.8	12.5
3,031	2,350	3,433	(1,083)	L	6.3	6.2
9,593	12,280	12,241	39	O	5.2	4.3
14,173	14,010	15,419	(1,409)	P	3.4	3.2
11,972	8,540	9,250	(710)	Q	4.5	5.8
72,309	68,797	68,321	476	Total		
14,288	14,016	16,013	(1,997)	International		
86,597	82,813	84,334	$(1,521)	Total		
3,908	—	—		Discontinued divisions	4.5	3.7
$90,505	$82,813	$84,334		Total	4.3	4.5

* Using net sales for the most recent 12-month period.

the April board meeting. As 1 of 15 directors, he thought that in fairness to the others, he should ask not more than three questions about these data.

Question

What questions should he ask?

CASE 11–8
Midwest Ice Cream Company (*B*)*

In 1982, Midwest Ice Cream Company installed a financial planning and control system. (See Midwest Ice Cream Company (*A*), Case 10–2, for details of this system.) After receiving the 1983 operating results, Jim Peterson, president of Midwest, had asked Frank Roberts, marketing vice president, to make a short presentation at the next board of directors meeting commenting on the major reasons for the favorable operating income variance of $71,700. He asked him to draft his presentation in the next few days so that the two of them could go over it

* This case was prepared by John Shank, Harvard Business School.

before the board meeting. Peterson wanted to illustrate to the board how an analysis of profit variance could highlight those areas needing management attention as well as those deserving a pat on the back.

THE PROFIT PLAN FOR 1983

Following the four-step approach outlined in Midwest Ice Cream Company (*A*), the management group of Midwest Ice Cream prepared a profit plan for 1983. The timetable they followed is shown in Table 1.

TABLE 1

		October—1982 (weeks)				*November—1982 (weeks)*			
		1	*2*	*3*	*4*	*1*	*2*	*3*	*4*
I	Variable cost standards		X						
II–A	Sales forecast		X						
II–B	Approval of sales forecast			X					
III–A	Preliminary payroll budget			X					
III–B	Preliminary budget for other operating expenses			X					
III–C	Approval of payroll budget and other expenses budget				X				
IV–A	Preliminary profit plan					X			
IV–B	Approval of profit plan						X		
IV–C	Board of directors meeting							X	

Based on an anticipated overall ice cream market of about 11,440,000 gallons in their marketing area and a market share of 50 percent, Midwest forecast overall gallon sales of 5,720,329 for 1983. Actually, this forecast was the same as the latest estimate of 1982 actual gallon sales. Rather than trying to get too sophisticated on the first attempt at budgeting, Mr. Peterson had decided to just go with

EXHIBIT 1 Profit Plan for 1983

	Standard contribution margin per gallon	*Forecasted gallon sales*	*Forecasted contribution margin*
Vanilla	$0.4329	2,409,854	$1,043,200
Chocolate	0.4535	2,009,061	911,100
Walnut	0.5713	48,883	28,000
Buttercrunch	0.4771	262,185	125,000
Cherry swirl	0.5153	204,774	105,500
Strawberry	0.4683	628,560	294,400
Pecan chip	0.5359	157,012	84,100
Total	$0.4530	5,720,329	$2,591,300

EXHIBIT 1 (*continued*)

Breakdown of budgeted total expenses

	Variable	*Fixed*	*Total*
Manufacturing	$5,888,100	$ 612,800	$6,500,900
Delivery	187,300	516,300	703,600
Advertising*	553,200	—	553,200
Selling	—	368,800	368,800
Administrative	—	448,000	448,000
Total	$6,628,600	$1,945,900	$8,574,500

* The 1983 advertising allowance was 6 percent of sales dollars.

Recap

Sales	$9,219,900
Variable cost of sales	6,628,600
Contribution margin	2,591,300
Fixed costs	1,945,900
Income from operations	$ 645,400

1982's volume as 1983's goal or forecast. He felt that there was plenty of time in later years to refine the system by bringing in more formal sales forecasting techniques and concepts.

This same general approach was also followed for variable product standard costs and for fixed costs. Budgeted costs for 1983 were expected 1982 results, adjusted for a few items which were clearly out of line in 1982. A summary of the 1983 profit plan is shown in Exhibit 1.

ACTUAL RESULTS FOR 1983

By the spring of 1983 it had become clear that sales volume for 1983 was going to be higher than forecast. In fact, Midwest's actual sales for the year totaled 5,968,366 gallons, an increase of about 248,000 gallons over budget. Market research data indicated that the total ice cream market in Midwest's marketing area was 12,180,000 gallons for the year, as opposed to the forecasted figure of about 11,440,000 gallons. The revised profit plan for the year, based on actual volume, is shown in Exhibit 2.

The fixed costs in the revised profit plan are the same as before, $1,945,900. The variable costs, however, have been adjusted to reflect a volume level of 5,968,000 gallons instead of 5,720,000 gallons, thereby eliminating wide cost variances due strictly to the difference between planned volume and actual volume. Assume, for example, that cartons are budgeted at 4 cents per gallon. If we forecast volume of 10,000 gallons the budgeted allowance for cartons is $400. If we actually sell only 8,000 gallons but use $350 worth of cartons, it is misleading to say that there is a favorable variance of $50. The variance is clearly unfavorable by $30. This only shows up if we adjust the budget to the actual volume level:

Carton allowance	= $0.04 per gallon
Forecast volume	= 10,000 gallons
Carton budget	= $400
Actual volume	= 8,000 gallons
Actual carton expense	= $350
Variance (based on forecast volume)	= $400 − $350 = $50 Favorable
Variance (based on actual volume)	= $320 − $350 = $30 Unfavorable

For costs which are highly volume-dependent, variances should be based on a budget that reflects the volume of operations actually attained. Since the level of fixed costs is independent of volume anyway, it is not necessary to adjust the budget for these items for volume differences. The original budget for fixed cost items is still appropriate.

EXHIBIT 2 Revised Profit Plan for 1983—Budgeted at Actual Volume

	Standard contribution margin per gallon	*Actual gallon sales*	*Forecast contribution margin*
Vanilla	$0.4329	2,458,212	$1,064,200
Chocolate	0.4535	2,018,525	915,400
Walnut	0.5713	50,124	28,600
Buttercrunch	0.4771	268,839	128,300
Cherry swirl	0.5153	261,240	134,600
Strawberry	0.4683	747,049	349,800
Pecan chip	0.5359	164,377	88,100
Total	$0.4539	5,968,366	$2,709,000

Breakdown of budgeted total expenses

	Variable	*Fixed*	*Total*
Manufacturing	$6,113,100	$ 612,800	$6,725,900
Delivery	244,500	516,300	760,800
Advertising	578,700	—	578,700
Selling	—	368,800	368,800
Administrative	—	448,000	448,000
Total	$6,936,300	$1,945,900	$8,882,200

Recap

Sales	$9,645,300
Variable cost of sales	6,936,300
Contribution margin	2,709,000
Fixed costs	1,945,900
Income from operations	$ 763,100

Exhibit 3 is the 1983 earnings statement. The figures for December have been excluded for purposes of this case. Exhibit 4 is the detailed

EXHIBIT 3

Earnings Statement,
December 31, 1983

	Month		Year to date	
	Actual	*Budget*	*Actual*	*Budget*
Sales—net			$9,657,300	$9,645,300
Manufacturing cost of goods sold—Schedule A–2*			6,824,900	6,725,900
Delivery—Schedule A–3			706,800	760,800
Advertising—Schedule A–4			607,700	578,700
Selling—Schedule A–5			362,800	368,800
Administrative—Schedule A–7			438,000	448,000
Total expenses			8,940,200	8,882,200
Income from operations			717,100	763,100
Other income—Schedule A–8			12,500	12,500
Other expense—Schedule A–9			6,000	6,000
Income before taxes			723,600	769,600
Provision for income taxes			361,800	
Net earnings			$ 361,800	

* Schedules A–3 through A–9 have not been included in this case. Schedule A–2 is reproduced as Exhibit 4.

Analysis of variance from forecasted operating income:

	Month		Year to date	
	Actual	*Budget*	*Actual*	*Budget*
(1) Actual income from operations			$717,100	
(2) Budgeted profit at forecast volume			645,400	
(3) Budgeted profit at actual volume			763,100	
Variance due to sales volume—[(3) – (2)]			117,700F	
Variance due to operations—[(1) – (3)]			46,000U	
Total variance—[(1) – (2)]			71,700F	

expense breakdown for the manufacturing department. The detailed expense breakdowns for the other departments have been excluded for purposes of this case.

ANALYSIS OF THE 1983 PROFIT VARIANCE

Three days after Jim Peterson asked Frank Roberts to pull together a presentation for the board of directors analyzing the profit variance for 1983, Roberts came into Peterson's office to review his first draft. He showed Peterson the following schedule (Table 2).

Roberts said that he planned to give each member of the board of directors a copy of this schedule and then to comment briefly on each of the items. Peterson said he thought the schedule was okay as far as it went, but that it just didn't highlight things in a manner that indicated what corrective actions should be taken in 1984 or that indicated the

TABLE 2

Favorable variance due to sales:		
Volume	$117,700F	
Price*	12,000F	$129,700F
Unfavorable variance due to operations:		
Manufacturing	99,000U	
Delivery	54,000F	
Advertising	29,000U	
Selling	6,000F	
Administration	10,000F	58,000U
Net variance—favorable		$ 71,700F

* This price variance is the difference between the standard sales value of the gallons actually sold and the actual sales value (9,657,300 − 9,645,300).

real causes for the favorable overall variance. He suggested that Roberts try to break down the sales volume variance into the part attributable to sales mix, the part attributable to market share shifts, and the part actually attributable to volume changes. He also suggested breaking down the manufacturing variance to indicate what main corrective actions are called for in 1984 to erase the unfavorable variance. How much of the total was due to price differences versus quantity differ-

EXHIBIT 4 Manufacturing Cost of Goods Sold, December 31, 1983

	Month		Year to date	
Variable costs	*Actual*	*Budget*	*Actual*	*Budget*
Dairy ingredients			$3,679,900	$3,648,500
Milk price variance			57,300	—
Sugar			599,900	596,800
Sugar price variance			23,400	—
Flavoring (including fruits and nuts)			946,800	982,100
Cartons			567,200	566,900
Plastic wrap			28,700	29,800
Additives			235,000	251,000
Supplies			31,000	35,000
Miscellaneous			3,000	3,000
Subtotal			6,172,200	6,113,100
Fixed costs				
Labor—cartonizing and freezing			$ 425,200	$ 390,800
Labor—other			41,800	46,000
Repairs			32,200	25,000
Depreciation			81,000	81,000
Electricity and water			41,500	40,000
Miscellaneous			1,500	30,000
Spoilage			29,500	
Subtotal			652,700	612,800
Total			$6,824,900	$6,725,900

ences, for example? Finally, he suggested that Roberts call on John Vance, the company controller, if he needed some help in the mechanics of breaking out these different variances.

As Roberts returned to his office he considered Peterson's suggestion of getting Vance involved in revising the schedule to be presented to the board. Roberts did not want to consult Vance unless it was absolutely necessary, because Vance always went overboard on the technical aspects of any accounting problem. Roberts couldn't imagine a quicker way to put the board members to sleep than to throw one of Vance's number-filled, six-page memos at them. "Peterson specifically wants a nontechnical presentation for the board," Roberts thought to himself, "and that rules out John Vance. Besides, you don't have to be a CPA to just focus in on the key variance areas from a general management viewpoint."

Questions

1. Review the variance analysis in Exhibit 3, being certain you understand it. (This is the same idea as in Exhibit 7 of Midwest Ice Cream Company *(A),* Case 10–2.)
2. Calculate the gross margin mix variance for 1983, using the approach shown in the lower portion of Exhibit 5 of Case 10–2. Then calculate a detailed (i.e., flavor-by-flavor) mix variance. For what purposes would the detailed analysis be more useful than the aggregate mix variance calculation?
3. How would you modify Frank Peterson's variance analysis before explaining the $71,700F profit variance to the board of directors?
4. Considering both this case and Case 10–2, evaluate Midwest's budgetary control system.

CHAPTER 12

The Profit Budget in the Control Process

In Chapter 10, we stated that a budget is used for both planning and control, and we discussed its use for planning purposes. In this chapter we discuss its use in the control process.

The profit budget is used for control by top management in two ways.

First, budget reports, comparing actual results with budget, together with analyses of variances, explanations of the causes of variances, an explanation of corrective actions being taken, and a current annual forecast are used to keep management informed on what is happening in the divisions. They function as early warning devices so management can take appropriate action when necessary.

Second, the budget system is used to help top management appraise the performance of the individual manager. The profit budget is usually considered to be a management commitment. A manager, therefore, can be judged according to how well this commitment is met, subject to the qualifications discussed later.

LIMITATIONS OF THE PROFIT BUDGET

In this part of the chapter we describe the principal limitations of the profit budget as a basis for performance appraisal and as an early warning system. We believe it is important that management understand these limitations and take appropriate action to avoid the undesirable consequences that might occur if the control process is overly dependent on the profit budget system.

Performance Appraisal

There are several problems associated with the use of the profit budget, alone, to evaluate managerial performances.

First, profits are affected by so many complex variables that it is impossible to provide an exact answer to the question: How much should this profit center earn this year? Consequently, subjective judgment is required in setting an annual profit objective for a profit center. It follows that annual profit objectives will involve a considerable range of difficulty, even in the best of circumstances. In the usual review process, where a dozen or more divisional budgets might be reviewed in less than a month, time may not permit a thorough analysis. It can happen that the most persuasive manager ends up with the easiest profit objective. In general, the profit objectives of the various profit centers are likely to vary considerably with respect to the ease or difficulty of attaining them.

Second, in arriving at a profit objective, it is necessary to predict the conditions that will exist during the coming year, some of which are entirely or almost entirely beyond the control of the profit center manager. Two of the most important conditions are the economic climate and the competitive situation. If the predictions of these are incorrect, the profit objectives will also be incorrect. Thus, even if one started with a completely equitable profit objective, as soon as the assumptions on which it was based turned out to be incorrect, the profit objective would no longer be equitable.

This situation can be particularly frustrating because the assumptions that affect revenues usually are much more uncertain than the assumptions that affect costs: yet changes in revenues usually have a much greater impact on profits than changes in costs. More than one manager has found that the results of successful cost reduction programs have been overshadowed by unfavorable variances from budget in the volume or mix of sales. The variance between actual and budgeted profit, therefore, is sometimes affected more by the ability to forecast than by the ability to manage.

It is possible, in some instances, to identify noncontrollable revenue variances. To the extent this can be done, the problem is less severe. In many instances, however, a clear identification is not possible and the extent of controllability is, at best, a rough estimate. It is important, however, to make every effort to separate forecast variances from performance variances.

Factors Affecting Performance Appraisal

The ability of a division to set equitable annual profit goals and to perform so as to attain these goals depends on four factors:

1. The degree of discretion that the divisional manager can exercise.
2. The degree to which the critical performance variables can be controlled by the divisional manager.
3. The degree of uncertainty that exists with respect to the critical performance variables.
4. The time span of the impact of the manager's decisions.

Degree of discretion. The degree of discretion that a manager can exercise depends on two things:

1. The nature of the job. The more complex the job, the greater the discretion required to manage it effectively.
2. The degree of delegation. The greater the degree of delegation, the greater the discretion that the divisional manager can exercise.

The greater the degree of discretion that a divisional manager can exercise, the more difficult it is to set precise goals. The number of alternative courses of action that are open to a manager is greater and one cannot determine ahead of time which particular courses of action are best and what the financial impact of these actions should be. For example, if a plant manager is held responsible for keeping actual costs in line with standard costs, but has relatively little discretion in deciding what will be produced, how it will be produced, and how much the labor force will be paid, it may be a relatively simple task to set a reasonable financial objective. By contrast, a divisional manager who is responsible for product development, marketing, production and procurement, and development of personnel has a large number of variables to control directly or indirectly. The optimum financial goal, therefore, is much less certain.

Degree of controllability. The greater the degree of control that a divisional manager can exercise over the critical performance variables, the easier it is to develop an effective budgetary control system. The difficulty in measuring the performance of a divisional manager is directly related to the number and type of noncontrollable or semicontrollable performance variables that exist. In general, external marketing variables are much more difficult to control than internal production variables, because a divisional manager has limited control over competitive activity or the general level of the economy. Thus, it is much easier to set a profit objective and to judge performance against this objective for a division where sales are limited by production capacity (where everything that can be produced can be sold) than for a division that sells in a highly competitive or volatile market and has ample production capacity.

Degree of uncertainty. The greater the uncertainty, the more difficult it is to set satisfactory goals and to measure performance against these goals. Like controllability, uncertainty is much greater with respect to external variables than to internal variables. Also, the degree of uncertainty tends to be related to the degree of innovation. The more innovative the division, the greater will be the uncertainty of its annual profitability.

Time span. If a budget is to provide an exact basis for judging performance, it must measure the real accomplishments of the manager during the period under review. This never happens. Many decisions that a manager makes today may not be reflected in profitability until some future period. Conversely, current profitability reflects in part the impact of decisions made in some past period. If the profit budget system were perfect, it would take into account the impact of past decisions, but this can rarely be done accurately. If it could be done, budgeted profit would reflect satisfactory managerial performance, given the situation that existed at the beginning of the year, and the performance reports would measure the effectiveness of those managerial decisions that affect current profitability. The performance measurement would still be incomplete, however, because it would not measure the soundness of current decisions that affect future profits; such decisions are often extremely important.

Summary. The limitations of the financial control system to measure accomplishment in the short run are less serious when the following conditions exist:

1. The degree of discretion exercised by the divisional manager is restricted.
2. The number and degree of either noncontrollable or uncertain variables are limited.
3. The time span of the manager's job is relatively short.

For example, divisions that sell established products or services in established markets and produce these products or services with established facilities can, with considerable confidence, use a profit budget system as a means for evaluation and control. The further divisional characteristics differ from those listed above, the less effective the profit budget is likely to be an aid to divisional evaluation and the more necessary it becomes, therefore, to use supplementary methods.

Early Warning

For two reasons, senior management should not depend entirely, or nearly entirely, on profit budget reports to provide an early warning of impending problems.

First, problems can develop that do not affect the financial statements significantly until long after management should be aware of their existence.

Second, as we explained in Chapter 11, although the description of the causes of variance, the timing of corrective action, the annual forecast, and the action being taken to correct unfavorable variances are an important part of the budget reports, these parts of the report may be largely subjective and normally prepared by the responsible divisional manager. Consequently, if problems exist, there is the possibility that the reports will be overoptimistic. If divisional managers are pessimistic about their ability to correct a problem, they may appear to be not completely dedicated. In addition to overoptimism, there may also be a tendency to downplay controllable variances and emphasize noncontrollable variances. At worst, a serious condition could be covered up in the hope that it might be corrected before it affects the financial statements.

PROFIT BUDGET ADMINISTRATION

Most companies use similar techniques for preparing and reviewing the profit budget and in the subsequent reporting against the approved budget. Profit budget systems differ widely, however, in the way they are administered, particularly in the degree to which the profit budget is used to monitor divisional activity. If senior management constantly monitors divisional activity during the year, we say it is exercising "tight control." If senior management does only limited monitoring of divisional activity during the year, we say it is exercising "loose control." Note that the distinction between tight control and loose control refers to the extent of monitoring, not the degree of delegation. Although tight control is often accompanied by more limited delegation than loose control, this is not always the case.

All profit budget systems have the limitations described earlier, regardless of the method of administration. The intensity of these problems differ with methods of administration. In this part of the chapter, we describe how tight and loose control can affect the problems of early warning and performance evaluation.

Tight Control

Tight control is based on the management philosophy that:

1. Divisional managers work most effectively when they are required to meet specific short-term goals, typically, one year.
2. Senior management can assist divisional management in solving many day-to-day problems. Put another way, divisions make better day-to-day decisions if top management participates in the decision-making process.

Under tight control, the profit goal of a divisional manager is considered to be a firm commitment against which he or she will be measured and, to a considerable extent, evaluated. Each month, performance to date and the expected performance for the year are analyzed in detail, variances are explained, and courses of corrective action considered when there is a likelihood that the budgeted goals will not be met. Variances from budget, therefore, are a means of reviewing monthly operating results in detail.

Effective implementation of a tight control system requires the following:

1. Complete management involvement in the budgeting and reporting system. This usually requires face-to-face discussions every period with divisional managers, an intimate knowledge of the operations being reviewed, and an ability to analyze and interpret financial data.
2. A capable accounting, budgeting, and analytical staff to make the financial information as reliable as possible and to assist management in using this information.
3. An understanding that management shares responsibility for results.

To demonstrate that these factors are necessary to make a budget system effective, let us consider two problems that tight control intensifies. First, short-term actions that are not in the long-term interests of the company may be encouraged. The more pressure that is applied to meet current profit goals the more likely the divisional manager will take short-term action that may well be wrong in the long run. The greater the amount of discretion delegated to the manager, the greater will be the danger of encouraging uneconomic short-term actions (errors of commission) and discouraging useful long-term actions (errors of omission).

Second, the use of budgeted profit as the sole objective can distort communications between the divisional manager and top management. If divisional managers are evaluated on the basis of their profit budget, they will be tempted to try to sell profit targets that are easily met. This leads to confusion in the planning process prior to the beginning of the year, since the budgeted profit may be less than that which could really be achieved. Also, divisional managers may be reluctant to admit, during the year, that they are likely to miss their profit budget until it is evident that they cannot possibly attain it. This could delay corrective action.

The following additional arrangements can mitigate these problems:

1. Proposed corrective actions are reviewed in detail with divisional managers. This lessens the likelihood of uneconomic short-term action.
2. Senior management evaluates divisional management on the basis of personal observations as well as on profit budget performance reports. The performance of divisional managers can be judged in part on the basis of the *quality* of their decisions. It is not necessary to wait until the impact of these decisions is reflected in profits.

3. Top management can establish the philosophy that a divisional manager who delays informing top management about incipient problems is committing a serious sin. This attitude, supported by extensive analytical efforts on the part of the finance staff, can improve the quality of the information submitted by the divisions.

The insistence by senior management on accurate and immediate communication of problems, together with management's intimate knowledge of individual operations, reduces significantly the likelihood that unexpected adverse situations will develop. In short, senior management can use the budget system as a means of requiring division management to make a commitment, and, subsequently, as a means of getting involved in divisional problems and helping to solve them. Evaluation and control are exercised by senior management through personal observation and nonfinancial information, in addition to the accounting reports. The key to successful operation is senior management's participation in divisional operations. In such a system *all* divisions are reviewed in detail each period. The profit budget is not used as a basis for "management by exception."

Loose Control

Loose control is based on a management philosophy different from tight control. This philosophy is illustrated by the statement: "I hire good people, and I leave them alone to do their jobs."

Under loose control, the budget is used essentially as a communication and planning tool. Annually, budgets are prepared, reviewed by senior management, adjusted where management deems appropriate, and approved. Monthly, or quarterly, actual results and a forecast for the year are compared to the budget, and differences are analyzed and explained. The budget is not considered a management commitment; instead, it is assumed to be the best estimate of profitability at the time that it was prepared. Subsequently, as conditions and expectations change, these are communicated to top management in the form of revised estimates, which are compared to the original budget and differences explained. The fact that the original profit goal has not been met does not necessarily indicate poor performance. Further, the cause of variances, the corrective actions being taken, and the timing of these actions are not reviewed in detail during the year by top management, unless something is clearly amiss.

A budget system administered in this way reduces some of the problems intensified by using the profit budget as an inflexible management commitment. First, there is much less pressure for immediate short-term actions to increase profits. Second, since the emphasis is placed on communication and planning, rather than on performance evaluation, there should be less tendency to withhold unpleasant information. Third, top management does not evaluate divisional performance by comparing it with budgeted profits, thereby avoiding the incomplete or misleading conclusions that are possible when the budget is used for this purpose.

Although a loose control system provides a good basis for planning, it does not satisfy management's need for control. Specifically, it may not:

1. Signal when a divisional manager is performing unsatisfactorily.
2. Provide a means of evaluating divisional management.

Early warning system. In loose control, the budget system does not assure that top management is informed about all important events because there is little top management involvement in divisional activities. Some type of early warning system that signals when something requiring management attention is occurring in one of the divisions is, therefore, necessary. One conclusion we can safely draw is that the *accounting and budgeting system does not provide a reliable early warning system* for a complex organization. The accounting and budgeting system provides an early warning system only for a limited set of unsatisfactory situations, namely, those that are reflected quickly in profit performance. It does not provide an early warning of unsatisfactory managerial action where the impact of these actions on accounted profit is deferred.

Evaluation. Since the profit budget is considered more of a forecast than a commitment, management's performance against the budget is not intended to measure efficiency or effectiveness.

Senior management, therefore, must employ some additional devices for both early warning and performance appraisal. In general, this will involve monitoring divisional activities during the year. The monitoring, however, will differ from that in tight control because it will be less formal and probably performed by someone below top management. Supplementary methods for accomplishing adequate control are considered later in the chapter.

Modified Administration

Most companies employ neither an extremely tight nor an entirely loose control system. It is useful, therefore, to place the administration of the control system of a company at some point on a continuum between entirely tight and entirely loose control. In this way, one can determine the extent of possible problems and management can, then, decide on which other devices will be employed to mitigate the problems that might be occurring as a consequence of the system of administration.

The closer the administration system is to the tight control end of the continuum, the more management has to consider the problems of: (1) short-term suboptimal action on the part of divisional managers, (2) the integrity of the information system, and (3) the overemphasis of profit budget performance in the evaluation of the divisional manager. On the other hand, the closer that the administrative system is to the loose control end of the continuum, the more management has to consider the problems of early warning and evaluation.

SUPPLEMENTARY CONTROL TECHNIQUES

In this part of the chapter, we describe certain techniques that may be used to supplement the profit budget and the related reporting system in controlling divisional operations. These techniques are applicable to any control system regardless of the way it is administered. In a loosely administered system, however, they play a more important role.

Organizational Arrangements

In most instances, effective management control depends upon the informed judgment of an individual who is: *(a)* knowledgeable in the area that is being evaluated, *(b)* familiar with the situation, and *(c)* independent. This means that either senior management or someone between senior management and the divisional manager must perform this function. In smaller or relatively integrated companies, the president is often able to do this effectively. In a large diversified corporation, only a very unusual top manager is able to rely on personal observations and judgment to monitor divisions constantly to detect unsatisfactory activity and to evaluate the performance of divisional managers. In the tight control system, the exercise of managerial judgment is an integral part of the monitoring process. In the absence of the detailed monitoring that is characteristic of tight control, the following organization arrangements might be employed:

1. Appropriate staff offices may be assigned the responsibility for monitoring divisional activity in their respective fields. For example, the marketing staff could be responsible for monitoring the marketing activities, the manufacturing staff for production, and the research staff for research and development. When the staff believes that a divisional manager is making questionable decisions in its area, it would alert top management. Once alerted, top management would take whatever action it deems necessary. This arrangement is not without problems, however. If the monitoring is not done tactfully and carefully, the staff groups might be looked upon as spies by operating management, and this, of course, limits their effectiveness.

2. Instead of just one or two persons in the senior executive group there may be several, and the group may be designated by a title such as "Office of the President." Each division is assigned to one of these executives. The executive monitors the divisional activity and takes appropriate action when he or she feels it is necessary.

3. A committee of senior executives, without line authority, may review divisional activity periodically. These persons are chosen for their expertise and are provided with the necessary time to become familiar with divisional activities. The Du Pont Executive Committee is an example of this type of organization arrangement.

4. The company may be divided into groups of divisions, each headed by a group executive responsible for the operations of the divisions within the group. This arrangement may not be as effective as the other three because the group executive is *responsible* for the effectiveness of the divisions. The group executive tends, therefore, not to be completely independent. If a person is held responsible for an activity, he or she may become a filter that blocks unpleasant information concerning this activity from reaching top management.

Whatever the form of organization that is used to provide top management control over divisional operations, management should recognize that the financial control system, or any system, will not always provide adequate early warning information or reliable evaluation of divisional activities. If senior management believes that it cannot monitor divisional activity adequately alone, it should be sure that someone with the necessary time, ability, and objectivity be assigned that responsibility.

Periodic Financial Evaluation

As described earlier, two of the principal problems with using the profit budget to appraise managerial performance are: (1) the time span that elapses before many important decisions are reflected in financial performance is greater than the time covered by the budget, and (2) the budget uses forecasts of expected conditions that often turn out to be inaccurate. As a result, actual performance against the profit budget may be a poor measure of managerial performance. One technique for overcoming these problems is an after-the-fact analysis of financial results. This analysis is based on two principles: *(a)* the time period covered should be long enough to make the evaluation valid, which involves using a time equal to the time span of divisional managers; and *(b)* the evaluation should be made solely on the basis of what has actually been accomplished.

Evaluation would take place under three conditions:

First, a time period adequate for fair evaluation should be established for each profit center. Evaluation would then take place at the end of this period. The period would generally be between three and five years, although some profit centers could be evaluated more frequently. For example, a year may be reasonable for a profit center in an integrated company that sells its products exclusively within the company; it is really responsible only for manufacturing costs, and these costs lend themselves to control through an annual budget.

Second, when a manager leaves a division, a terminal evaluation would normally be made. This would not only ensure that the departing manager had been appropriately evaluated, but it would also protect the incoming manager. For example, if the new manager is inheriting problems created by a predecessor, this fact should be evident from the evaluation.

Third, whenever top management becomes concerned about a particular profit center, an evaluation of performance could be requested. This would protect the company should conditions deteriorate sufficiently during the evaluation period to make it obvious that managerial performance was below par.

The evaluation would be conducted by the central finance staff with the assistance of other staff offices. Although the main thrust of the evaluation would be on financial performance, it would also be necessary to evaluate marketing and product positions and organizational and personnel development.

The periodic evaluation, would, of course, not exclude other evaluation processes. It would be unrealistic to expect top management to allow a divisional manager to operate between three and five years with no evaluation. If, in the interim, it appeared that performance was submarginal, the divisional manager could be replaced at any time. The periodic review, however, is a formal, comprehensive financial review, superimposed on interim reviews. Because of its comprehensiveness, it is an important element in the evaluation process.

Nonfinancial Measures

After World War I, when General Motors and Du Pont were developing their now-famous decentralized organizations, the formal measurement of performance was almost exclusively financial.

The first major company to deviate formally from the idea of a single measure of performance was the General Electric Company in the 1950s. When General Electric decentralized, it identified eight measures of divisional performance.[1] Although there is some disagreement about which result areas to measure and how to measure them, there appears to be general agreement that profitability, as a single measure

---

[1] For a description of these eight measures, see the General Electric Company *(A)* case in Chapter 3.

of divisional performance, is not adequate for evaluating divisional managers in most instances.

The principal differences among companies in measuring divisional management's performance in nonfinancial areas is the degree of formality employed. At one extreme, the measurements are entirely informal and subjective. At the other extreme, these measurements are detailed and formal, in which case we have a system of "management by objectives."

Management by Objectives[2]

Management by objectives is a system of performance appraisal having the following characteristics:

1. It is a formal system in that each manager is required to take certain prescribed actions and to complete certain written documents.
2. The process involves five steps:
   a. The manager discusses with the subordinate the subordinate's description of his or her own job.
   b. The manager and the subordinate agree to short-term performance targets.
   c. The manager and the subordinate discuss periodically the progress made toward meeting the targets.
   d. The manager and the subordinate agree to a series of checkpoints that will be used to measure progress.
   e. At the end of a defined period (usually one year), the manager discusses with the subordinate an assessment of the results of the subordinate's efforts.

A management-by-objectives system is much broader than a budgetary control system. Indeed, the budgetary control system is a *part* of the management-by-objectives system. We are concerned here, however, only with management by objectives as it applies to the evaluation of divisional performance.

The divisional manager's job tends to be more clearly defined than, say, that of a staff executive, and formal reports on many aspects of the manager's performance (e.g., profits and sales) are usually available. Consequently, the initiation of a management-by-objectives system for divisional managers does not usually involve the amount of innovation

---

[2] There have been a great many articles and books written about management by objectives (MBO). The literature provides many different definitions of MBO and describes many different techniques for implementation. In this book, we are primarily concerned with the inclusion of MBO techniques in the formal annual review and approval of divisional budgets.

that would be required for many other types of jobs. The profit budget system would remain the same as before.

Typically, the divisional manager meets with top management to review his or her proposed budget. Under a management-by-objectives system, other specific objectives in such areas as sales, product development and personal development are also reviewed. Management by objectives, therefore, as it applies to divisional management, extends the profit budget presentation to include specific objectives in nonfinancial areas and to provide checkpoints for measuring the progress toward meeting these objectives. Performance reviews would now include the divisional manager's progress toward meeting these objectives.

In performance appraisal, there is one very important difference between the way management by objectives applies to a divisional manager and the way it applies to an executive with limited budget responsibility. The *profitability of a division is so important that it tends to overshadow other objectives*. This means that divisional managers may be expected to earn a satisfactory profit *in addition* to meeting their other objectives. If top management perceives that a divisional manager's profit performance is less than satisfactory, the fact that the manager has met the other objectives may not be given much weight. Conversely, if divisional managers are perceived to be performing well in the area of profitability, the fact that they have not met some of their objectives may not be held too much against them, unless it is clear that the failure to meet the other objectives will have a serious effect on future profits. It is important that a company using management by objectives for divisional performance evaluation keep this situation in mind. If profits are emphasized to the exclusion of other goals, a management-by-objectives system does not exist. Consequently, it is important that top management take a balanced position in evaluating divisional performance. If this is done, the general approach of setting objectives in other areas in addition to profitability improves the ability of senior management to control divisional operations.

SUGGESTED ADDITIONAL READINGS

Argyris, Chris. "Double Loop Learning in Organizations." *Harvard Business Review,* September–October 1977.

Hofstede, G. "People and Techniques in Budgeting." *Quantitative Methods in Budgeting*. C. B. Tilawus, E. P. Marttnus Nighoff Social Sciences Division. London, 1976.

——. "The Poverty of Management Control Philosophy." *Academy of Management Review,* July 1978.

Odiorne, George S. "MBO: A Backward Glance." *Business Horizons,* October 1978.

Vancil, Richard F. *Decentralization: Management Ambiguity by Design*. New York: Financial Executives Research Foundation, 1979.

CASE 12–1
Del Norte Paper Company*

In early July 1983, Frank Duffy, managing director of the Italian subsidiary of the Container Division of Del Norte Paper Company (DNP-Italia), was sitting in his Torino office thinking about a recent informal discussion held between himself, two case writers, and certain members of his staff. The topic of the discussion had been the problems of applying the corporate budgeting and reporting system (known within the company as the Budget Analysis Program, or BAP) to a foreign subsidiary such as DNP-Italia.

At approximately the same time, Hans Lowenstein, managing director of the German subsidiary of the Container Division (DNP-Deutschland), was sitting in his Frankfurt office thinking about a very similar meeting in which he had recently participated. Once again, the discussion had been focused on Del Norte Paper Company's BAP system and its impact on a foreign subsidiary.

Duffy and Lowenstein had held their respective meetings to prepare themselves for an August meeting on the same topic with John Powell, general manager, International Operations of the Container Division. Both Duffy and Lowenstein believed that Del Norte Paper's system, which originally had been designed primarily for domestic (U.S.) use, had serious weaknesses when applied to the international subsidiaries. Duffy and Lowenstein had been asked by Powell to prepare a list of recommendations, which were to be discussed at the August meeting.

Del Norte Paper Company

Del Norte Paper Company was a large integrated paper producer. In 1982, total sales were approximately $2.8 billion while net income was $223 million. In terms of sales, Del Norte Paper was among the 75 largest industrial concern in the United States.

The Container Division was one of Del Norte Paper's 22 major product divisions. The Container Division was divided into two segments, one domestic and one international. Within the international segment, there were five geographic regions: Germany, Italy, France,

* This case was prepared by M. Edgar Barrett, Harvard Business School.

United Kingdom, and the Caribbean. It was an acknowledged goal of Del Norte Paper to expand its international operations substantially over the next 10 years.

Del Norte Paper Organization Structure

Del Norte Paper had essentially a product line management structure. The company was divided into seven broad product lines called Strategic Product Groups, each headed by a corporate vice president. The Strategic Product Group was further divided into more narrowly defined product divisions, each headed by a division vice president. For example, the Container Division was structurally part of the Container-Containerboard Strategic Product Group. Thus, G. T. Hendrick, vice president of the Container Division, reported directly to R. B. Manning, vice president of the Container-Containerboard Product Group (see Exhibit 1).

The product divisions were comprised of several geographical regions, each headed by a regional manager. In the Container Division, a distinction was also made between the international and the domestic operations. The former were headed by John Powell, general manager, International Operations, who reported directly to the vice president of the Container Division.

The international segment of the Container Division was divided into five regions, each headed by a managing director. Each region in turn was comprised of several plants serving different sales territories. Thus, each plant was responsible for both production and marketing. The plants were headed by a plant manager.

At each level in the Del Norte Paper management structure, the general managers were supported by a functional staff. Thus, at the top management level there was a corporate vice president of finance, a corporate controller, a corporate vice president of manufacturing, etc. Approximately the same functional representation existed at the Strategic Product Group, the product division, the regional subsidiary, and the plant levels. Each functional manager was responsible both to the general manager at his level and to the functional managers at levels above his own (see Exhibit 2 for partial organization charts of DNP-Italia and DNP-Deutschland, two regional subsidiaries of the Container Division).

DNP–Italia and DNP–Deutschland

DNP–Italia, with headquarters in Torino, had six container plants. In 1982 sales were approximately $56 million, while net income after an adjustment reflecting a switch to LIFO accounting was around $2.9 million. In contrast to the performance in 1982, 1983 sales were expected to decline, due to the economic recession, and an operating loss was probable.

Each plant had a marketing staff and was entirely responsible for the sales territory around the plant. The only exception was the two plants near Torino which were consolidated into one sales territory. Each sales territory had a substantially different product mix.

The Italian box market was very competitive. At least in part, this was due to the fact that there were no less than 100 significant producers of boxes in Italy. Most of these companies were family owned and quite small. While Del Norte Paper believed it was the third largest company in the market, it supplied well under 10 percent of the country's box needs.

DNP–Deutschland, with headquarters in Frankfurt, had four container plants. The 1982 sales were approximately $63 million, and net income after an adjustment reflecting a switch to LIFO accounting was about $5.0 million. The recession was having a less drastic impact on DNP–Deutschland than on DNP–Italia. Thus, 1983 sales were expected to increase slightly and net income was expected to decline only a small amount from record 1974 levels.

Once again, each of DNP–Deutschland's four plants was responsible for a different sales territory. A major market for the company, Essen, did not have a local plant. Containers were allocated to the Essen market by whichever of two of Germany's plant had the needed capacity.

Competition also existed in the German market. However, the major competition consisted less of small family owned companies and more of large multinational, integrated paper companies. DNP–Deutschland's most important competitors were Bowater, International Paper, Mead Corporation, Unilever, and Union Camp.

THE FORMAL CONTROL SYSTEM

The formal control system at Del Norte Paper was comprised of three separate but interrelated parts: the BAP budgeting system, the BAP reporting system, and the capital budgeting system. The focus of this case is on the two BAP systems.

In the mid-1970s, Del Norte Paper's Container Division had developed a complete budgeting and reporting system known as the Budget Analysis Program (BAP). The system had changed very little from 1973 to 1983.

The BAP Budgeting System

The BAP budget was a complete operational plan developed through a process of negotiation between the general manager at each level in the organization and his immediate superior. The process began at the plant level.

This negotiation process continued until a complete, consolidated operating plan was submitted to the board of directors for their approval. Once approved, the BAP plan became the basis for reporting and performance evaluation during the year.

At the foundation of the BAP budget was a standard cost system. All budgeting was done using updated standard cost estimates.

Every year, the plant general manager and his staff prepared a series of standardized forms. The required budgeting forms are listed below:

BAP Budget Forms

Document	*Title*
BAP 2	Sales and production forecast
BAP 3	Direct labor budget
BAP 6	Direct cost conversion budget
BAP 7	Manufacturing facility expense budget
BAP 8	Selling expense budget
BAP 9	Administrative operating results
BAP 10	Planned operating results
BAP 90	Analysis of planned operating results
BAP 49	Preliminary operating results
BAP 48	Balance sheet forecast
BAP 36	Planned variances*

* Planned differences between the industrial engineering department standards and the level of efficiency implicit in the budget (Editor).

BAP Budgeting Cycle

The preparation of the budget began in June of the year before the budget year.[1] The month of June was basically devoted to organizing the budgeting effort. For example, it was in June that regional economic forecasts were prepared by the regional staff. The first concrete step in the process at the plant level came in early July when the general managers, the sales managers, and the sales staffs of each plant began to prepare volume forecasts. Each individual salesman was given a form on which was shown the sales volume broken down by major customer for the previous year and for the first six months of the then current year. The salesman was asked to make a projection (also by major customer) for the next calendar year. These forecasts were then consolidated into a plant (territory) sales forecast.

In the middle of July, the regional managing director and his staff reviewed the volume forecasts submitted for each plant. All the plant

[1] Del Norte Paper operated on a calendar (January–December) year.

general managers and the plant sales managers then came to regional headquarters for separate one- to two-hour meetings with the regional managing director and his controller. The volume forecasts could possibly be revised at this meeting.

After the volume forecasts for each sales territory were accepted, then the production planning process was started. The plant general managers and the plant production managers decided what their labor requirements would be, how many shifts would be needed, and so on. Detailed estimates were also made of certain variable and fixed-cost items, such as supplies, utilities, and depreciation.

By the end of July, the regional headquarters office had a detailed preliminary projection of profit for each plant. At this point, the regional managing director and several members of his staff reevaluated the budget. Once again, revisions were possible.

In the middle of August, the regional subsidiaries were required to send to the general manager, International Operations, a preliminary budget summary form (known as BAP 49) for each plant and for the entire region.[2] The general manager of International Operations then reviewed the plan with his immediate superior, the Container Division vice president. Shortly thereafter, the Container Division submitted to the Container-Containerboard Strategic Product Group vice president the individual regional preliminary budget forms. As always, this review could result in budget revisions.

On approximately August 22, the regional subsidiary was supposed to be advised by the Container Division of the acceptability of its preliminary budget.[3] If any changes were necessary, they were made at this point.

In early September, the complete proposed profit plan for each regional subsidiary was resubmitted to Container Division in order that it could be put into computerized format. The computerization was required so as to facilitate revisions at a later date.

In later September, the regional managing director and the regional controller for each subsidiary went to Container Division headquarters in San Francisco for a final review of the profit plan with the general manager, International Operations, and the Container Division controller. Each regional subsidiary was allocated one-half day to make a presentation of its profit plan.

After the profit plan meeting in late September, the general manager of International Operations again reviewed the profit plans with the Container Division vice president. Shortly thereafter, the profit plans

[2] The budgets at the plant and regional levels were derived using the local currency. When the plans were submitted to the Container Division, they were denominated in U.S. dollars. The regions were held responsible for their dollar results.

[3] In 1983, this communication took place on August 29.

were reviewed with the Strategic Product Group vice president. After this review, in late October, the Strategic Product Group vice president presented the final profit plan to the Del Norte Paper senior management and the board of directors. If accepted, this profit plan became the budget for the next year.

Other Aspects

Revisions. Ordinarily, the budget was prepared only once a year. However, in the last few years Del Norte Paper had found it necessary to revise the budget during the budget year. Indeed, DNP–Italia and DNP–Deutschland had been required to change the 1983 budget several times.

In 1982, when the 1983 plan was being prepared, the DNP–Deutschland plan had to be revised two times and DNP–Italia's one time. The first change at DNP–Deutschland occurred because of a change in the U.S. dollar/Deutschmark exchange rate. The second change came in December 1982, at which time the economic outlook was very different than had been anticipated. DNP–Italia's plan was also changed at this point.

The 1983 budget was also changed in April 1983. Once again, the reason for the revision was a changed economic outlook. However, the April change was only done within the Container Division. The December 1982 budget for 1983 still remained the budget for which the overall Container Division was held responsible.

Other documents. In addition to the one-year BAP budget, each regional subsidiary was required to submit two other documents. The first was a long-range (five-year) plan. This had not been used every year by the international subsidiaries. It was, however, expected to become more important with time.

The second document required was a free form list of regional objectives and programs to achieve the objectives. This document was known as the "Standards of Performances." Both this document and the five-year plan were presented to the general manager–International Operations at the late September meeting at Container Division headquarters in San Francisco.

The BAP Reporting System

The BAP reporting system had also been developed by the Container Division in the mid-1970s. The purpose of the reporting system was to allow the general manager at each level to identify problems which needed corrective action.

The BAP reports relied heavily on the standard cost system imbedded in the BAP budgeting system. Essentially, the reports were intended to identify the size and origin of variances from the standards which had been used in the budgeting process.[4] Thus, the reports were designed to identify such things as price, efficiency, and volume variances, as well as to provide some overall indication of the goodness of the original budget estimates for pricing purposes. The relevant general manager would then use the data provided as an indication of where attention was needed.

The required BAP reporting forms are listed below:

BAP Reporting Forms

Document	*Title*
BAP 15	Statement of operating results
BAP 16	Sales and cost analysis
BAP 17	Direct conversion
BAP 18	Manufacturing facilities
BAP 19	Selling expense
BAP 20	Administrative expense
BAP 21A	Analysis of operations
BAP 55	Balance sheet analysis

In addition to these standardized BAP forms, each month the regional subsidiaries were required to send a free form "Commentary on Operations." This report was prepared by the regional managing director with the assistance of his staff. The report dealt with general economic trends, the competitive situation, and a number of other similar issues. Copies of the report were sent to the general manager–International Operations, the Container Division controller, the Container Division vice president, and to the division vice president, Manufacturing.

The BAP Reporting Cycle

On the 25th day of each month, Del Norte Paper's foreign subsidiaries "closed their books"; that is, they began to derive consolidated income statements and other financial reports. On the third working day of the following month, the regional subsidiaries were required to telex to Container Division headquarters a summary of production and deliveries during the preceding month at each plant and for the entire region. The plant reports were telexed directly by the plants to division headquarters as well as to regional headquarters. On the fourth work-

[4] In their budgeting forms, the regional subsidiaries had a number of "planned" variances. Thus, the budget (plan) included a certain amount of variance. An example was indirect labor, in which the standard was set at 100 percent efficiency, but the plan was set at 80 percent efficiency. The variances in the reporting forms related to the 80 percent, not the 100 percent.

ing day of the same month, the subsidiaries were required to telex to San Francisco a complete profit and loss statement for the previous month for each plant and for the entire region.

On the fourth working day, the regional plants and the subsidiary were required to telex a copy of BAP 15 to Container Division headquarters. A complete balance sheet for each plant and for the region was also telexed to Container Division on that date.

Also on the fourth working day of the month, the monthly commentary on the last month's operations by plant and for the region was telexed to San Francisco. Hard copies of these commentaries were due on the 14th working day of the month.

Finally, written copies of the BAP reporting forms described previously (BAP 15, 16, 17, 18, 19, 20, 21A, and 55) were due by the middle of the month after the month for which the forms were applicable. Copies of these reports were mailed to the general manager, International Operations, and to the Container Division controller.

In addition to the BAP reports listed above and the monthly commentaries on operations, each regional subsidiary and its plants[5] was required to submit a number of other scheduled reports to Container Division headquarters.

Other Aspects

A second set of scheduled reports was focused on the manufacturing side of the business. Each plant was required to submit detailed analyses of manufacturing operations each month. The reports were originated at the plant level by the plant general manager and the plant production manager, and were mailed to the manufacturing staff of the Container Division. A regional report was also sent by the director of operations of the regional subsidiary.

The final series of scheduled reports were updated monthly forecasts by plant and for the consolidated region of the expected operating results for the next three months. These forecasts were submitted in the middle of each month to the general manager–International Operations.

In addition to the scheduled reports listed above, the regional subsidiaries also had to submit a number of unscheduled reports. There were two types of unscheduled reports. The first was in response to specific requests by someone at Container Division or higher in the Del Norte Paper organization. An example might be a summary of marketing programs planned during the next few months.

[5] In all cases, copies of the reports were mailed by the plans first to regional headquarters and then to the responsible manager in San Francisco.

The second type of unscheduled reports was represented by those addressed to issues raised about the BAP reporting forms or the other reports submitted. For example, if the general manager–International Operations identified problem areas in the reports submitted, he would telex the regional subsidiary asking for an explanation or a summary of the program undertaken to correct the problem. Similar requests came from other members of the Del Norte Paper organization back in San Francisco.

Performance Evaluation at Del Norte Paper

Each Strategic Product Group, each product division, each regional subsidiary, and each plant was evaluated by Del Norte Paper as a profit center. Return on investment and cash flow to the parent company were also important evaluation factors.

The performance of the general manager at each level was evaluated on the basis of a number of criteria. The first and most important criterion was the general manager's profit results relative to the budget which had been negotiated between him and his superiors.

At Del Norte Paper there were four different ways of calculating profit for evaluation purposes: net after tax, integrated profit after allocation of corporate and division overhead; net after tax, nonintegrated profit after allocation of corporate and division overhead; net after tax, nonintegrated profit before allocation of corporate and division overhead; and, nonintegrated profit before tax and before allocation of corporate and division overhead. Integrated profit included an allocation of "upstream" profits, which were those profits made at the mill level on orders placed by the relevant converting plant. Nonintegrated profits were before the allocation of upstream profits.

While precisely which executives used which measurement methods in evaluating the performance of managers or subsidiaries was not entirely clear, all four methods were used in some manner. The integrated profit figures were said to be monitored closely by the chairman of the board and the president of Del Norte Paper Company. The net, nonintegrated and fully allocated figures were also said to be watched closely by the chairman of the board and certain board members.

The net, nonintegrated, nonallocation-of-overhead figures were the ones routinely reported under the international version of the BAP system. Thus, these were also widely distributed throughout the company. Finally, the nonintegrated profit before tax and before overhead allocation figures were said to be those used primarily for the evaluation of a regional managing director's performance. For example, the bonus was based primarily on this set of figures.

All three of the non-BAP sets of figures were sent monthly to the regional managing director's home. The integrated profit figures, however, were only for his information so as to maintain a legal, arm's-length business relationship.

Finally, in addition to these profitability criteria, performance was also judged on actual results relative to the "Standards of Performance" documents negotiated between the general managers and their superiors. The bonus of the regional managing director, for example, was partly based on his performance relative to the "Standards of Performance."[6]

The Informal Discussion at DNP–Italia

Late on June 27, 1983, several members of the management team at the Torino office of DNP–Italia gathered for a discussion of the corporate budgeting and reporting system. Present throughout the meeting were: Frank Duffy, regional managing director; B. Rizzo, director of Operations; R. Angelo, director of Business Systems; L. Guppi, controller; D. Corleone, Engineering Manufacturing Service manager; G. Pruitt, a marketing executive who was just in the process of being transferred from Del Norte Paper's Seattle office to DNP–Italia; and, the two case writers. The discussion was begun by a case writer asking Frank Duffy his view of the BAP system. The following is a paraphrased summary of that meeting:

Duffy: I think that one has to talk about the BAP budgeting system and the BAP reporting system separately. First, with respect to budgeting, BAP is basically very strong. The budgeting process trains the plant manager, in particular, to focus on key variables. He really has to understand all aspects of the container business from marketing to production in order to work with the BAP budgeting forms. Also, because the budget sets a solid objective for the manager, he is more motivated, I believe, than he would be without a strong budgeting system.

However, there are problems in the use of the BAP budgeting system in a subsidiary such as DNP–Italia. First, we have very different labor situation here in Italy than in the United States. Whereas manufacturing labor in the U.S. is a variable cost and is treated as such on the BAP budget forms, all labor in Italy is essentially a fixed cost. We simply cannot fire workers if business slows down; and, even if we put our workers on reduced work weeks, we have to pay a very substantial portion of the full-time wage cost. The fixed-cost nature of labor makes it important to modify our approach to business in Italy.

Rizzo: We have also had another problem with the budget system. As you know, the BAP budgets are built around a standard cost system. In the past few years, because of the economic volatility we've seen in Italy, it has been very difficult to base our marketing and production decisions on the standard costs built into the BAP budgets. The problem has been especially

[6] The bonus of regional managing director also depended in part on the profitability of the Strategic Profit Group, the division, and the overall corporation.

troublesome in the area of determining the correct raw materials paper cost on which to base our pricing decisions.

The price of paper has been extremely volatile here in Italy, more so than in the United States. The problem is complicated by the fact that we use 12 different grades of paper, which is also more than in the U.S. These two facts combined have made it very difficult to make consistent pricing decisions.

As a result, there has been very little correlation between our original estimates of contribution for each box order and the end-of-the-month actual contribution figures after taking into account price and efficiency variances.

Angelo: I agree with Benito that this has been a problem. We have tried to address that problem by using updated forecasts of paper prices in making our pricing decisions instead of the standard cost in the budget. In spite of our best efforts, I must admit it has been very difficult to make accurate forecasts.

Pruitt: Staying on this pricing decision issue for a minute, it seems to me that the fixed versus variable manufacturing labor cost issue is very important. Depending on how you resolve the controversy, your contribution calculations are going to be significantly impacted. In a recession such as we are now experiencing, the contribution calculations are especially crucial.

Case writer: Are there any other major problems with the BAP budgeting system?

Duffy: There is one other problem I should mention. The budget is supposed to be a goal for the plant manager and his workers. If he meets or exceeds his budget, he should be rewarded. The problem is that we cannot really have an incentive pay system here in Italy because of the labor laws. We can give bonuses; but once a worker's pay is increased, we are not allowed to decrease his total wages. This takes some of the power out of a strong goal-setting budgeting process.

Case writer: Frank, you mentioned that the BAP reporting system should be viewed separately from the budgeting system.

Duffy: Yes. I believe the BAP reporting system is quite strong at the plant level. Each of the BAP forms provides information to the plant manager that he needs, though some of the information is not so useful.

For example, the fixed-cost nature of labor should be incorporated into the BAP reporting forms. The plant manager should only be held responsible for the items he can control.

Going above the plant level, the BAP reporting system becomes increasingly less useful. At the regional managing director level, I can't use all the information provided in the BAP forms. I need more summary information, though it has been useful to have the BAP reports as a supporting material when I am talking to the plant manager.

The problem arises that the BAP forms, which were always intended to be used primarily at the plant level, presently are used as our reporting system back to Container Division. They can't possibly analyze all the information sent to them. In fact, I feel there are real dangers in having them try to look at the minute details of the BAP system, in that these details are sometimes misleading in the short run.

Angelo: Generating the volume of information required by San Francisco is also very expensive, particularly when one considers that most of the information has to be generated by hand. This problem is due, at least in part, to our limited computerization capabilities. Fortunately, we are improving our data processing systems, so this won't be as big a problem in the future.

Guppi: You have to remember that the BAP reports represent only part of the total reports sent to headquarters. We have separate marketing and production reporting systems, for example. A lot of the information we send is duplicative. If the various division functions would work together, it would save us a great deal of time and money. We could manage our business better if we didn't have such onerous reporting requirements.

Duffy: Another problem with the BAP reporting system from the foreign subsidiary to the division headquarters is that the information is no longer relevant by the time they get a chance to analyze it. This makes their requests for explanation out of date and our responses even more so. By the time they identify a problem, the plant manager should already be attempting to correct it.

The Informal Discussion at DNP–Deutschland

Late on June 30, 1983, several members of the management team of DNP–Deutschland gathered in the Frankfurt office of the managing director, Hans Lowenstein, for a discussion of the Del Norte Paper corporate BAP budgeting and reporting system and its effects on DNP–Deutschland's operations. Present through the meeting were: Hans Lowenstein, managing director; Alex Stuart, regional controller and director of administration; and Thomas Buskey, planning manager.

The discussion began when one of the case writers asked Mr. Lowenstein for his opinion about the BAP system. The following is a paraphrased summary of that discussion:

Lowenstein: In my opinion, the weakest part of BAP is the reporting system. San Francisco requires so much information, much of it duplicative, that it interferes with our ability to manage in Germany. In addition, the volume of reporting imposes an unnecessary cost burden on us because we are not yet completely computerized.

You know, I wouldn't mind sending in so many reports if I thought headquarters could use the information and give us some help. But it's just too much data for them to analyze in a useful way.

Stuart: I agree with you, Hans. The BAP reporting system is not very useful as a form of communication with corporate headquarters. They just don't have the staff to analyze all the reports.

At the plant level, however, I think we all agree that BAP is a fairly good system. The BAP reports provide the plant manager with the information he needs to manage effectively. We don't have many complaints about BAP at this level.

Case writer: Do you get any complaints from the plant managers about BAP?

Lowenstein: No line manager has ever liked to fill in lots of reports. As a result, we do get some gripes about the volume of information requested. You have to remember that these guys have a large number of other reports to fill out—such as the monthly manufacturing summary, etc. Another problem is that many of these reports ask for the same information but in a different format. The plant people feel this kind of duplication wastes time.

Stuart: We also get some complaints about having to file the reports using U.S. dollars and American units of measurement—square feet, tons, etc. While it's simple to make the translation, it is a tedious job for the plant people.

Case writer: Do you have any other problems with the BAP reporting system?

Lowenstein: As we've said, we think the standardized BAP reports are pretty good as an operating tool at the plant level, but not very good as a reporting system with corporate headquarters.

The monthly "Commentary on Operations", which is sent both by the plant managers and by me at the regional level, attempts to address the reporting deficiencies of the BAP reports. The problem is that it is very difficult to get enthusiastic about writing the commentary when you aren't sure anyone pays any attention to them back in San Francisco. The plant managers don't at all like the fact that I have them write commentaries.

Stuart: You know, about a year ago, one of our plant managers sent three of his monthly commentaries back to San Francisco in German—and we never did receive any comment from San Francisco.

Oh, I should mention one other difficulty. San Francisco requires the region and each plant to send in BAP 15 on the fourth working day of the month. The problem is that there is not enough time for me to do any analysis of the operating results before the plants send the forms on to San Francisco. I can't even check for clerical errors. I wish they could delay the deadline for at least a few days.

Case writer: Hans, what do you think of BAP budgeting system?

Lowenstein: In general, I think it's a reasonably good system. But it has some of the same inherent difficulties as the BAP reporting system. It's an American system designed for use in our U.S. plants. Inevitably, there are going to be problems in applying a domestic system to a foreign subsidiary.

Case writer: For example?

Lowenstein: One problem is that the budget is denominated in dollars, rather than Deutsche Mark. We are held responsible for our dollar results though we obviously have absolutely no control over foreign exchange rates.

Stuart: Of the three times we had to change the 1983 budget, one revision was due primarily to a changed exchange rate. The plant managers don't see how they can be held responsible for dollar-dominated results.

Also, with respect to the three budget changes I mentioned before, the last one was caused by a changed economic environment. Container Division asked us to start from scratch and make a completely new budget. Only after we put in a tremendous amount of work did we find out that the budget revision was only for Container Division use. Container still kept the same budget for reporting purposes above. A lot of the work we put in was really unnecessary.

Lowenstein: Another problem, which is not peculiar to the foreign subsidiaries, is the relationship between the capital expenditure budget and the BAP budget. We don't receive final approval for our capital budget until January or February, but we have to submit our final profit budget well before that time. We have to budget for the probable results of our investments even before we know whether we can make them. If the investment projects are eventually turned down, we are not allowed to change the budget. For small projects the effect is negligible, but for large projects the effect can be quite significant.

Case writer: Any other aspects of the budgeting system you want to talk about?

Buskey: There is one thing I would like to mention. This year we really made an effort to build a good five-year plan. Long-range planning has not been really emphasized before in Container Division. After we put in a huge amount of work, we found out that the five-year plans were not going to be emphasized this year. There were too many other pressing problems. The effort was very worthwhile for DNP–Deutschland, but it is somewhat frustrating to work so hard on a project and find out divisional headquarters doesn't think it's very important.

EXHIBIT 1 Organizational Chart

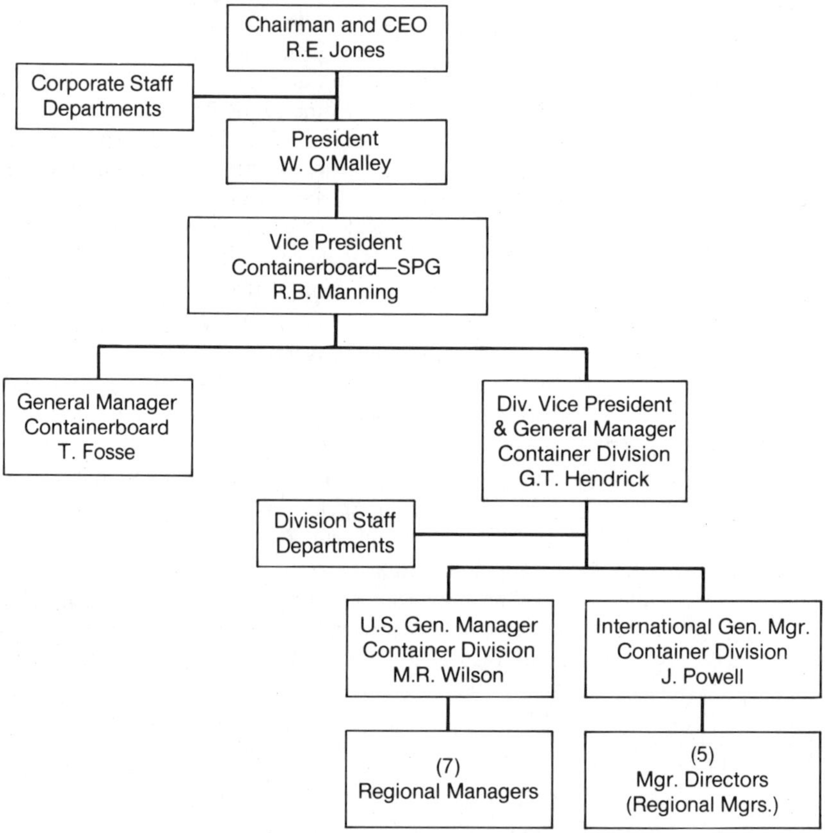

EXHIBIT 2 Partial Organization Charts: DNP–Italia and DNP–Deutschland

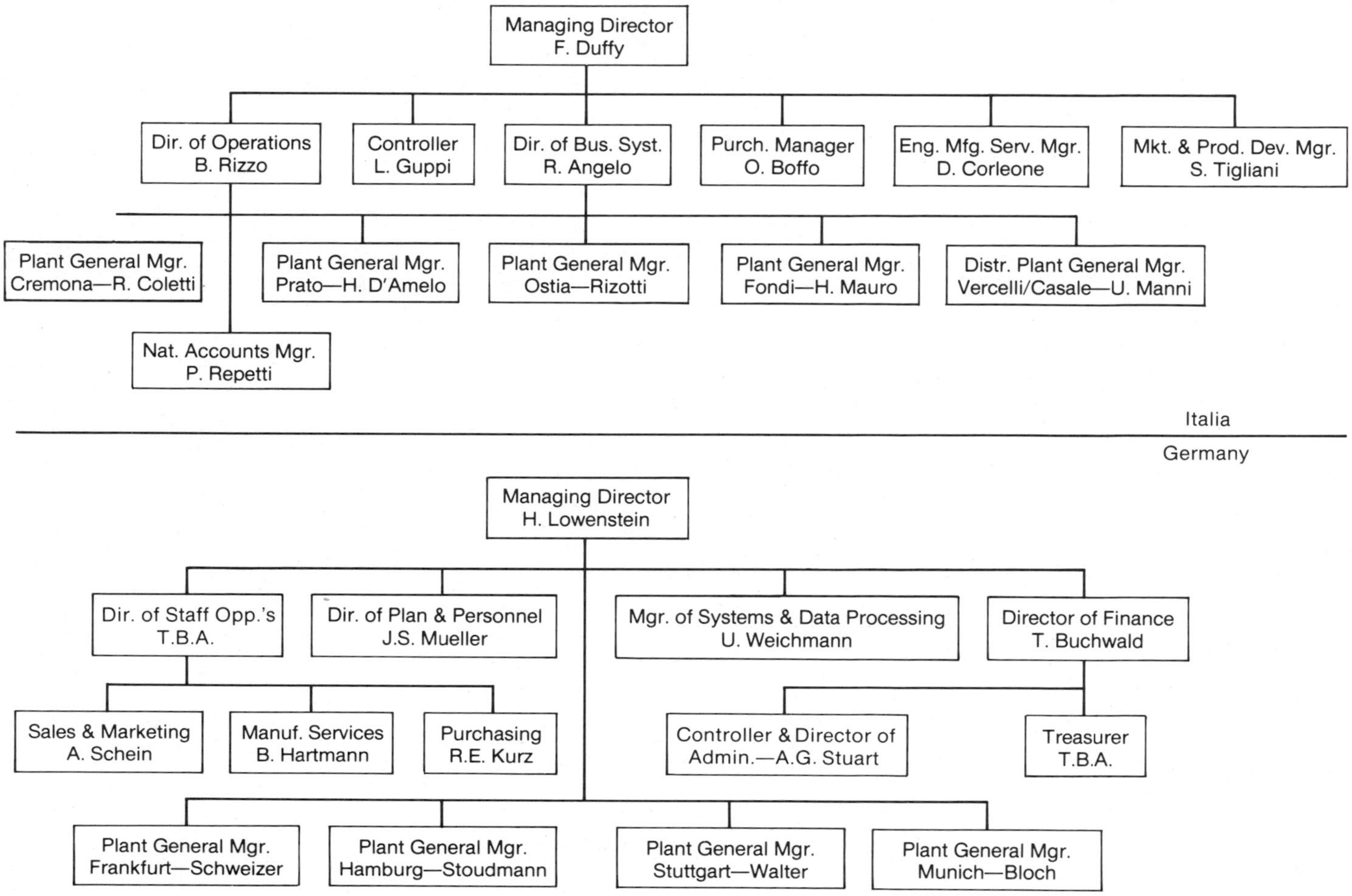

CASE 12–2
Galvor Company

When M. Barsac replaced M. Chambertin as Galvor's controller in April of 1974, at the age of 31, he became the first of a new group of senior managers resulting from the acquisition by Universal Electric. It was an accepted fact that, in the large and sprawling Universal organization, the controller's department represented a key function. M. Barsac, who was a skilled accountant, had had 10 years' experience in a large French subsidiary of Universal.

He recalled his early days with Galvor vividly and admitted they were, to say the least, hectic:

> I arrived at Galvor in early April 1974, a few days after M. Chambertin had left. I was the first Universal man here in Bordeaux and I became quickly immersed in all the problems surrounding the change of ownership. For example, there were no really workable financial statements for the previous two years. This made preparation of the Business Plan, which Mr. Hennessy and I began in June, extremely difficult. This plan covers every aspect of the business, but the great secrecy which had always been maintained at Galvor about the company's financial affairs made it almost impossible for anyone to help us.

M. Barsac's duties could be roughly divided into two major areas: first, the preparation of numerous reports required by Universal, and, second, supervision of Galvor's internal accounting function. While these two areas were closely related, it is useful to separate them in describing the accounting and control function as it developed after Universal's acquisition of Galvor.

To control its operating units, Universal relied primarily on an extensive system of financial reporting. Universal attributed much of its success in recent years to this system. The system was viewed by Universal's European controller, M. Boudry, as much more than a device to "check up" on the operating units:

> In addition to measuring our progress in the conventional sense of sales, earnings, and return on investment, we believe the reporting system causes our operating people to focus their attention on critical areas which might not otherwise receive their major attention. An example would be the level of investment in inventory. The system also forces people to think about the future and to commit themselves to specific future goals. Most operating people are understandably involved in today's problems. We believe some device is required to force them to look beyond the problems at hand and to consider longer range objectives and strategy. You could say we view the reporting system as an effective training and educational device.

THE BUSINESS PLAN

The heart of Universal's reporting and control system was an extremely comprehensive document—the Business Plan—which was prepared annually by each of the operating units. The Business Plan was the primary standard for evaluating the performance of unit managers, and everything possible was done by Universal's top management to give authority to the plan.

Each January, the Geneva headquarters of Universal set tentative objectives for the following two years for each of its European operating units. This was a "first look"—an attempt to provide a broad statement of objectives which would permit the operating units to develop their detailed Business Plans. For operating units which produced more than a single product line, objectives were established for both the unit as a whole and for each product line. Primary responsibility for establishing these tentative objectives rested with eight product-line managers located in Geneva, each of whom was responsible for a group of product lines. On the basis of his knowledge of the product lines and his best judgment of their market potential, each product-line manager set the tentative objectives for his lines.

For reporting purposes, Universal considered that Galvor represented a single product line, even though Galvor's own executives viewed the company's products as falling into three distinct lines—multimeters, panel meters, and electronic instruments.

For each of over 300 Universal product lines in Europe, objectives were established for five key measures:

1. Sales.
2. Net income.
3. Total assets.
4. Total employees.
5. Capital expenditures.

From January to April, these tentative objectives were "negotiated" between Geneva headquarters and the operating managements. Formal meetings were held in Geneva to resolve differences between the operating unit managers and product-line managers or other headquarters personnel.

Negotiations also took place at the same time on products to be discontinued. Mr. Hennessy described this process as a "sophisticated exercise which includes a careful analysis of the effect on overhead costs of discontinuing a product and also recognizes the cost of holding an item in stock. It is a good analysis and one method Universal uses to keep the squeeze on us."

During May, the negotiated objectives were reviewed and approved by Universal's European headquarters in Geneva and by corporate headquarters in the United States. These final reviews focused primarily on the five key measures noted above. In 1976, the objectives for total capital expenditures and for the total number of employees received particularly close surveillance. The approved objectives provided the foundation for preparation of Business Plans.

In June and July, Galvor prepared its Business Plan. The plan, containing up to 100 pages, described in detail how Galvor intended to achieve its objectives for the following two years. The plan also contained a forecast, in less detail, for the fifth year hence—e.g., for 1981 in the case of the plan prepared in 1976.

SUMMARY REPORTS

The broad scope of the Business Plan can best be understood by a description of the type of information it contained. It began with a brief one-page financial and operating summary containing comparative data for:

Preceding year	(actual data).
Current year	(budget).
Next year	(forecast).
Two years hence	(forecast).
Five years hence	(forecast).

This one-page summary contained condensed data dealing with the following measures for each of the five years:

Net income.
Sales.
Total assets.
Total capital employed (sum of long-term debt and net worth).
Receivables.
Inventories.
Plant, property, and equipment.
Capital expenditures.
Provision for depreciation.
Percent return on sales.
Percent return on total assets.
Percent return on total capital employed.
Percent total assets to sales.
Percent receivables to sales.
Percent inventories to sales.
Orders received.

Orders on hand.
Average number of full-time employees.
Total cost of employee compensation.
Sales per employee.
Net income per employee.
Sales per $1,000 of employee compensation.
Net income per $1,000 of employee compensation.
Sales per thousand square feet of floor space.
Net income per thousand square feet of floor space.

Anticipated changes in net income for the current year and for each of the next two years were summarized according to their cause, as follows:

Volume of sales.
Product mix.
Sales prices.
Raw material purchase prices.
Cost reduction programs.
Accounting changes and all other causes.

This analysis of the causes of changes in net income forced operating managements to appraise carefully the profit implications of all management actions affecting prices, costs, volume, or product mix.

FINANCIAL STATEMENTS

These condensed summary reports were followed by a complete set of projected financial statements—income statement, balance sheet, and a statement of cash flow—for the current year and for each of the next two years. Each major item on these financial statements was then analyzed in detail in separate reports, which covered such matters as transactions with headquarters, proposed outside financing, investment in receivables and inventory, number of employees and employee compensation, capital expenditures, and nonrecurring write-offs of assets.

MANAGEMENT ACTIONS

The Business Plan contained a description of the major management actions planned for the next two years with an estimate of the favorable or unfavorable effect each action would have on total sales, net income, and total assets. Among some of the major management actions described in Galvor's 1966 Business Plan (prepared in mid-1965) were the following:

Implement standard cost system.

Revise prices.

Cut oldest low-margin items from line.

Standardize and simplify product design.

Create forward research and development plan.

Install punch card inventory system.

Implement product planning.

Separate plans were presented for each of the functional areas—marketing, manufacturing, research and development, financial control, and personnel and employee relations. These functional plans began with a statement of the function's mission, an analysis of its present problems and opportunities, and a statement of the specific actions it intended to take in the next two years.

Among the objectives set for the control area in the 1976 Business Plan, M. Barsac stated that he hoped to:

Better distribute tasks.

Make more intensive use of IBM equipment.

Replace nonqualified employees with better-trained and more dynamic people.

The Business Plan closed with a series of comparative financial statements, which depicted the estimated item-by-item effect if sales fell to 60 percent or to 80 percent of forecast or increased to 120 percent of forecast. For each of these levels of possible sales, costs were divided into three categories: fixed costs, unavoidable variable costs, and management discretionary costs. Management described the specific actions it would take to control employment, total assets, and capital expenditures in case of a reduction in sales, and when these actions would be put into effect. In its 1976 Business Plan, Galvor indicated that its program for contraction would be put into effect if incoming orders dropped below 60 percent of budget for two weeks, 75 percent for four weeks or 85 percent for eight weeks. It noted that assets would be cut only to 80 percent in a 60 percent year and to 90 percent in an 80 percent year "because remodernization of our business is too essential for survival to slow down much more."

APPROVAL OF PLAN

By midsummer, the completed Business Plan was submitted to Universal headquarters; and beginning in the early fall, meetings were held in Geneva to review each company's Business Plan. Each plan had to be justified and defended at these meetings, which were attended by senior executives from both Universal's European and American headquarters and by the general managers and functional managers of many of the operating units. Universal viewed these meetings as an important element in its constant effort to encourage operating managements to share their experiences in resolving common problems.

Before final approval of a company's Business Plan at the Geneva review meeting, changes were often proposed by Universal's top management. For example, in September 1976, the 1977 forecasts of sales and net income in Galvor's Business Plan were accepted; but the year-end forecasts of total employees and total assets were reduced about 9 percent and 1 percent, respectively. Galvor's proposed capital expenditures for the year were cut 34 percent, a reduction primarily attributable to limitations imposed by Universal on all operating units throughout the corporation.

The approved Business Plan became the foundation of the budget for the following year, which was due in Geneva by mid-November. The general design of the budget resembled that of the Business Plan, except that the various dollar amounts, which were presented in the Business Plan on an annual business, were broken down by months. Minor changes between the overall key results forecast in the Business Plan and those reflected in greater detail in the budget were not permitted. Requests for major changes had to be submitted to Geneva no later than mid-October.

REPORTING TO UNIVERSAL

Every Universal unit in Europe had to submit periodic reports to Geneva according to a fixed schedule of dates. All units in Universal, whether based in the United States or elsewhere, adhered to essentially the same reporting system. Identical forms and account numbers were used throughout the Universal organization. Since the reporting system made no distinction between units of different size, Galvor submitted the same reports as a unit with many times it sales. Computer processing of these reports facilitated combining the results of Universal's European operations for prompt review in Geneva and transmission to corporate headquarters in the United States.

The main focus in most of the reports submitted to Universal was on the variance between actual results and budgeted results. Sales and expense data were presented for both the latest month and for the year to date. Differences between the current year and the prior year also were reported because these were the figures submitted quarterly to Universal's shareholders and to newspapers and other financial reporting services.

DESCRIPTION OF REPORTS

Thirteen different reports were submitted by the controller on a monthly basis, ranging from a statement of preliminary net income, which was due during the first week following the close of each month, to a report on the status of capital projects due on the last day of each month. The monthly reports included:

Statement of preliminary net income.
Statement of income.
Balance sheet.
Statement of changes in retained earning.
Statement of cash flow.
Employment statistics.
Status of orders received, canceled and outstanding.
Statement of intercompany transactions.
Statement of transactions with headquarters.
Analysis of inventories.
Analysis of receivables.
Status of capital projects.
Controller's monthly operating and financial review.

The final item, the controller's monthly operating and financial review, often ran to 20 pages or more. It contained an explanation of the significant variances from budget, as well as a general commentary on the financial affairs of the unit.

In addition to the reports submitted on a monthly basis, approximately 12 other reports were required less often, either quarterly, semiannually, or annually.

COST OF THE SYSTEM

The control and reporting system, including preparation of the annual Business Plan, imposed a heavy burden in both time and money on the management of an operating unit. M. Barsac commented on this aspect of the system in the section of Galvor's 1976 Business Plan dealing with the control functional area:

> Galvor's previous administrative manager [controller], who was a tax specialist above all, had to prepare a balance sheet and statement of income once a year. Cost accounting, perpetual inventory valuation, inventory control, production control, customer accounts receivable, control, budgeting, etc. did not exist. No information was given to other department heads concerning sales results, costs, and expenses. The change to a formal monthly reporting system has been very diffi-

cult to realize. Due to the low level of employee training, many tasks, such as consolidation, monthly and quarterly reports, budgets, the Business Plan, implementation of the new cost system, various analyses, restatement of prior years' accounts, etc. must be fully performed by the controller and chief accountant, thus spending 80 percent of their full time in spite of working 55–60 hours per week. The number of employees in the controller's department in subsequent years will not depend on Galvor's volume of activity, but rather on Universal's requirements.

Implementation of the complete Universal Cost and Production Control System in a company where nothing existed before is an enormous task, which involves establishing 8,000 machining and 3,000 assembly standard times and codifying 15,000 piece parts.

When interviewed early in 1977, M. Barsac stated:

Getting the data to Universal on time continues to be a problem. We simply don't have the necessary people who understand the reporting system and its purpose. The reports are all in English and few of my people are conversant in English. Also, American accounting methods are different from procedures used in France. Another less serious problem concerns the need to convert all of our internal records, which are kept in francs, to dollars when reporting to Universal.

I am especially concerned that few of the reports we prepare for Universal are useful to our operating people here in Bordeaux. Mr. Hennessy, of course, uses the reports, as do one or two others. I am doing all that I can to encourage greater use of these reports. My job is not only to provide facts but to help the managers understand and utilize the figures available. We have recently started issuing monthly cost and expense reports for each department showing the variances from budget. These have been well received.

Mr. Hennessy also commented on meeting the demands imposed by Universal's reporting system:

Without the need to report to Universal, we would do some things in a less formal way or at different times. Universal decides that the entire organization must move to a certain basis by a specified date. There are extra costs involved in meeting these deadlines. An example was applying the punch card cost system to our piece parts manufacturing operation before we were really ready to tackle the job. It should be noted, also, that demands made on the controller's department are passed on to other areas, such as marketing, engineering, and production.

M. Boudry, Universal's European controller, acknowledged that the cost of the planning and reporting system was high, especially for smaller units:

The system is designed for a large business. We think that the absolute minimum annual sales volume for an individual unit to support

> the system is about $5 million; however, we would prefer at least $10 million. By this standard, Galvor is barely acceptable. We really don't know if the cost of the system is unnecessarily burdensome in the sense that it requires information which is not worth its cost. A reasonable estimate might be that about 50 percent of the information would be required in any smartly managed independent business of comparable size, another 25 percent is required for Universal's particular needs, and 25 percent is probably "dead underbrush" which should be cleaned out. Ideally, every five years we should throw the system out the window and start again with the essentials.

As an indication of some of his department's routine activity, M. Barsac noted that at the end of 1976 Galvor was preparing each working day about 10,000 punch cards and 200 invoices. At that time the company had approximately 12,000 active customers.

EXHIBIT 1 Organization of Controller's Department (January 1977)

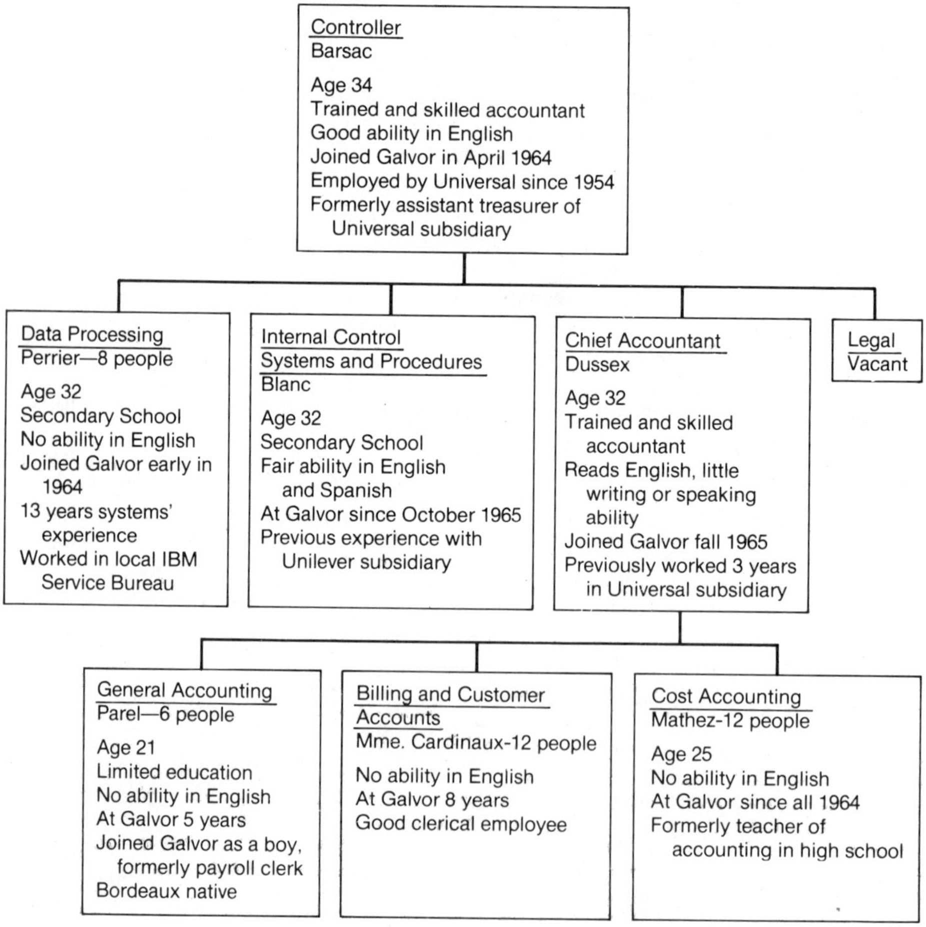

Early in 1977, 42 people were employed in the controller's department, about 6 percent of Galvor's total employees. The organization of the department is described in Exhibit 1.

HEADQUARTERS PERFORMANCE REVIEW

Galvor's periodic financial reports were forwarded to M. Boudry in Geneva. The reports were first reviewed by an assistant to M. Boudry, one of four financial analysts who together reviewed all reports received from Universal's operating units in Europe.

In early 1977, M. Boudry described the purpose of these reviews:

> The reviews focus on a comparison of performance against budget for the key measures—sales, net income, total assets, total employees, and capital expenditures. These are stated as unambiguous numbers. We try to detect any trouble spots or trends which seem to be developing. Of course, the written portions of the reports are also carefully reviewed, particularly the explanations of variances from budget. If everything is moving as planned, we do nothing.
>
> The reports may contain a month-by-month revision of forecasts to year-end, but if the planned objectives for the year are not to be met we consider the situation as serious.
>
> If a unit manager has a problem and calls for help, then it becomes a matter of common concern. He can probably expect a bad day in explaining how it happened, but he can expect help, too. Depending on the nature of the problem, either Mr. Forrester, Galvor's product-line manager, or one of our staff specialists would go down to Bordeaux. In addition to the financial analysts, one of whom closely follows Galvor's reports, we have specialists on cost systems and analysis, inventory control, credit, and industrial engineering.
>
> We have not given Galvor the help it needs and deserves in data processing, but we have a limited staff here in Geneva and we cannot meet all needs. We hope to increase this staff during 1977.

With reference to Galvor's recent performance, M. Boudry stated:

> Galvor is small and we don't give it much time or help unless its variances appear to be off. This happened in the second half of 1976 when we became increasingly concerned about the level of Galvor's inventories. A series of telexes on this matter between Mr. Hennessy and M. Poulet, our director of manufacturing here in Geneva, illustrate how the reports are used. [See Exhibits 2 through 5.]
>
> We feel the situation is under control and the outlook for Galvor is okay despite the flat performance between 1973–75 and the downturn in 1976. The company has been turned about and 1977 looks promising.

Although the comprehensive reporting and control system made it appear that Universal was a highly centralized organization, the managements of the various operating units had considerable autonomy.

EXHIBIT 2 Telex from Poulet to Hennessy, Concerning Level of Inventory

TO: HENNESSY—GALVOR
FROM: POULET—UE
DATE: SEPTEMBER 26, 1976

FOLLOWING ARE THE JULY AND AUGUST INVENTORY AND SALES FIGURES WITH THEIR RESPECTIVE VARIANCES FROM BUDGET.

THOUSANDS OF DOLLARS	*ACTUAL*	*JULY BUDGET*	*VARIANCE*	*ACTUAL*	*AUGUST BUDGET*	*VARIANCE*
INVENTORY	2,010	1,580	(430)	2,060	1,600	(460)
SALES TO DATE	3,850	3,900	(50)	4,090	4,150	(60)

LATEST AUGUST SALES FORECAST REFLECTS DECREASE IN YEAR-END SALES OF 227 VERSUS INCREASE OF 168 IN YEAR-END INVENTORIES OVER BUDGET.

REQUEST TELEX LATEST MONTH-BY-MONTH INVENTORY AND SALES FORECAST FROM SEPTEMBER TO DECEMBER, EXPLANATION OF VARIANCE IN INVENTORY FROM BUDGET AND CORRECTIVE ACTION YOU PLAN IN ORDER TO ACHIEVE YEAR-END GOAL. INCLUDE PERSONNEL REDUCTIONS, PURCHASE MATERIAL CANCELLATIONS, ETC.

POULET

EXHIBIT 3 Telex from Hennessy to Poulet Concerning Level of Inventory

TO: POULET—UE
FROM: HENNESSY—GALVOR
DATE: SEPTEMBER 27, 1976

YOUR 26.9.76
MONTHLY INVENTORY FORECAST SEPTEMBER TO DECEMBER BY CATEGORY AS FOLLOWS:

THOUSANDS OF DOLLARS	*SEPT. 30*	*OCT. 31*	*NOV. 30*	*DEC. 31*
RAW MATERIALS	53	51	50	50
PURCHASED PARTS	180	185	190	195
MANUFACTURED PARTS	95	93	93	91
WORK-IN-PROCESS	838	725	709	599
FINISHED GOODS	632	694	683	705
OTHER INVENTORIES	84	84	82	80
ENGINEERING IN PROCESS	55	58	48	44
RESERVE	(14)	(14)	(14)	(20)
INDICA	50	52	55	55
TOTAL	1,973	1,928	1,896	1,799

THE MAIN EXPLANATIONS OF PRESENT VARIANCE ARE THREE POLICIES ADOPTED END OF 1965 AND DISCUSSED IN MONTHLY LETTERS BUT WHICH LEFT DECEMBER 1966 BUDGET OPTIMISTICALLY LOW. FIRST WAS TO HAVE REASONABLE AMOUNTS OF SELLING MODELS IN STOCK WITHOUT WHICH WE COULD NOT HAVE ACHIEVED 19 PERCENT INCREASE IN SALES WE ARE MAKING WITH OUTMODED PRODUCT.

SECOND POLICY WAS TO MANUFACTURE LONGER SERIES OF EACH MODEL BY DOUBLE WHEREVER SALES WOULD ABSORB IT, OTHERWISE MANY OF OUR COST REDUCTIONS WERE NEARLY ZERO. THIS MEANS OUR MANUFACTURING PROGRAM ANY MONTH MAY CONTAIN FIVE MONTHS WORTH OF 15 MODELS INSTEAD OF 10 WEEKS WORTH OF 30 MODELS (OUT OF 70). THIRD WAS NEW POLICY OF REDUCING NUMBER OF PURCHASE ORDERS BY MAINTAINING A MINIMUM STOCK OF MANY THOUSANDS OF LOW VALUE ITEMS WHICH YOU

EXHIBIT 3 (*concluded*)

AGREED WOULD AND DID INCREASE STOCK UPON FIRST PROCUREMENT BUT WE ARE ALREADY GETTING SLIGHT REDUCTION. CORRECTIVE ACTIONS NUMEROUS INCLUDING RUNNING 55 PEOPLE UNDER BUDGET AND ABOUT 63 BY YEAR END PLUS REVIEWING ALL PURCHASE ORDERS MYSELF PLUS SLIDING A FEW SERIES OF MODELS WHICH WOULD HAVE GIVEN SMALL BILLING IN 1976 INTO 1977 PLUS THOSE POSTPONED BY CUSTOMERS. THIS WILL NOT HAVE DRAMATIC EFFECT AS NEARLY ALL THESE SERIES ARE PROCURED AND HAVE TO BE MADE FOR RELATIVELY SURE MARKETS BUT SOME CAN BE HELD IN PIECEPARTS UNTIL JANUARY. WE ARE WATCHING CAREFULLY STOCKS OF SLOW MOVING MODELS AND HAVE MUCH CLEANER FINISHED STOCK THAN END 1975.

FINAL AND GRAVE CONCERN IS ACCURACY OF PARTS, WORK IN PROCESS, AND FINISHED GOODS VALUATION SINCE WE BEGAN STANDARD COST SYSTEM. INTERIM INVENTORY COUNT PLUS VARIANCES VALUED ON PUNCH CARDS STILL DOESNT CHECK WITH MONTHLY BALANCE USING CONSERVATIVE GROSS MARGINS BUT NEARLY ALL GAPS OCCURRED FIRST FOUR MONTHS OF SYSTEM WHEN ERRORS NUMEROUS AND LAST 4 MONTHS NEARLY CHECK AS WE CONTINUE REFINING. EXTENSIVE RECHECKS UNDERWAY IN PARTS, WORK IN PROCESS, AND FINISHED GOODS AND CORRECTIONS BEING FOUND DAILY.

YOUR INVENTORY STAFF SPECIALISTS ARE AWARE OF PROBLEM AND PROMISED TO HELP WHEN OTHER PRIORITIES PERMIT. WILL KEEP THEM INFORMED OF EXPOSURE WHICH STARTED WITH RECORDING ALL PARTS AND BEGINNING NEW BALANCES WITH NEW STANDARDS AND APPEARS CLOSELY RELATED TO ERRORS IN THESE OPERATIONS. WE CAN ONLY PURGE PROGRESSIVELY WITHOUT HIRING SUBSTANTIAL INDIRECT WORKERS.

HENNESSY

EXHIBIT 4 Telex from Poulet to Hennessy Concerning Level of Inventory

TO: HENNESSY—GALVOR
FROM: POULET—UE
DATE: NOV. 10, 1976

SEPTEMBER INVENTORY INCREASED AGAIN BY 64,000 COMPARED TO AUGUST WHILE SEPTEMBER SALES WERE 145,000 UNDER BUDGET REFERRING TO YOUR LATEST TELEX OF SEPTEMBER 27 IN WHICH YOU HAVE A BREAKDOWN OF THE SEPTEMBER FORECAST. REQUEST DETAILED EXPLANATION FOR NOT MEETING THIS FORECAST IN SPITE OF YOUR CURRENT CORRECTIVE ACTIONS.

SEPTEMBER	*YOUR FORECAST*	*ACTUAL*	*VARIANCE*
RAW MATERIALS	53	96	(43)
PURCHASED PARTS	180	155	25
MANUFACTURED PARTS	95	108	(13)
WORK-IN-PROCESS	838	917	(79)
FINISHED GOODS	632	723	(91)
OTHER INVENTORIES	84	87	(3)
ENGINEERING IN PROCESS	55	52	3
RESERVE	(14)	(14)	—
INDICA	50	51	(1)
TOTAL NET	1,973	2,175	(202)

IN ORDER TO MEET YOUR DECEMBER FORECAST OF 1,799 YOUR WORK IN PROCESS HAS TO BE REDUCED BY 318. THIS MEANS A REDUCTION OF ABOUT

EXHIBIT 4 (*concluded*)

100 PER MONTH FROM SEPTEMBER 30 TO DECEMBER 31. THEREFORE, I ALSO WOULD LIKE ACTUAL ACHIEVEMENTS AND FURTHER REDUCTION PLANS DURING OCTOBER, NOVEMBER, AND DECEMBER CONCERNING THE POINTS MENTIONED IN YOUR SAME TELEX OF SEPTEMBER 27. CONSIDER AGGRESSIVE ACTIONS IN THE FOLLOWING SPECIFIC AREAS:

1. REALISTIC MASTER PRODUCTION SCHEDULES.
2. SHORT-TERM PHYSICAL SHORTAGE CONTROL TO INSURE SHIPMENTS.
3. WORK-IN-PROCESS ANALYSIS OF ALL ORDERS TO ACHIEVE MAXIMUM SALABLE OUTPUT.
4. MANPOWER REDUCTION.
5. ELIMINATION OF ALL UNSCHEDULED VENDOR RECEIPTS. HAVE YOU ADVISED OTHER UNIVERSAL HOUSES NOT TO SHIP IN ADVANCE OF YOUR SCHEDULE UNLESS AUTHORIZED?
6. ADVISE FULL DETAILS ON ALL CURRENT SHORTAGES FROM OTHER UNIVERSAL HOUSES WHICH ARE RESPONSIBLE FOR INVENTORY BUILD-UP.

POULET

EXHIBIT 5 Telex from Hennessy to Poulet Concerning Level of Inventory

TO: POULET—UE
FROM: HENNESSY—GALVOR
DATE: NOV. 15, 1976
YOUR 10.11.76

WE NOW HAVE OCTOBER 31 FIGURES. OUR ACTUAL ACHIEVEMENTS FOLLOW: RAW MATERIALS 54 VARIANCE PLUS 3, PURCHASED PARTS 173 VARIANCE MINUS 12, MANUFACTURED PARTS 110 VARIANCE PLUS 17, WORK IN PROCESS 949 VARIANCE PLUS 224, FINISHED GOODS 712 VARIANCE PLUS 18, OTHER 82 VARIANCE MINUS 2, ENGINEERING 54 VARIANCE MINUS 4, RESERVE MINUS 14 VARIANCE NIL, INDICA 55 VARIANCE PLUS 3, TOTAL 2,175 VARIANCE PLUS 247. EACH ITEM BEING CONTROLLED AND THE ONLY SIGNIFICANT VARIANCES 224 WORK-IN-PROCESS AND 18 FINISHED GOODS ARE MY DECISION UPON SALES DECLINE OF SEPTEMBER AND OCTOBER OF 311 TO DELAY COMPLETION OF SEVERAL SERIES IN MANUFACTURE IN FAVOR OF ANOTHER GROUP OF SERIES, MOSTLY GOVERNMENT, WHICH ARE LARGELY BILLABLE IN 1976 IN ORDER TO PARTLY REGAIN SALES. LAST EIGHT DAYS ORDERS AND THEREFORE SALES ARE SHARPLY UP AND NONE OF THIS WORK IN PROCESS WILL BE ON HAND MORE THAN 3 TO 6 WEEKS LONGER THAN WE PLANNED.

NEVERTHELESS YOU SHOULD BE AWARE WE MANUFACTURE 4 TO 8 MONTHS WORTH OF MANY LOW VOLUME MODELS AN EXAMPLE OF HOW WE DETERMINE ECONOMIC SERIES WAS FURNISHED YOUR STAFF SPECIALIST THIS WEEK. WE CANNOT MAKE SIGNIFICANT COST REDUCTIONS IN A BUSINESS WHERE AT LEAST 70 OF 200 MODELS HAVE TO BE ON SHELF TO SELL AND TYPICAL MODEL SELLS 15 UNITS MONTHLY. REGARDING YOUR 5 SUGGESTIONS AND TWO QUESTIONS WE ARE CARRYING OUT ALL 5 POINTS AGGRESSIVELY AND HAVE NO INTERHOUSE SHORTAGES OR OVERSHIPMENTS.

HENNESSY

For example, Mr. Hennessy, who was judged only on Galvor's performance, was free to purchase components from other Universal units or from outside sources. There were no preferred "in-house" prices. A slight incentive was offered by Universal to encourage such transactions by not levying certain headquarters fees, amounting to about 2 percent of sales, against the selling unit.

Similarly, Universal made no attempt to shift its taxable income to low-tax countries. Each unit was viewed as though it were an independent company subject to local taxation and regulation. Universal believed that this goal of maximizing profits for the individual units would in turn maximize Universal's profits. Forcing every unit to maximize its profits precluded the use of arbitrary transfer prices for "in-house" transactions.

RECENT DEVELOPMENTS AT GALVOR

A standard cost system, which included development and tooling costs as well as manufacturing and assembly, had been in effect since March 1976.

According to Mr. Hennessy:

> We had hoped to start in January, but we were delayed. On the basis of our experience in 1976, all standards were reviewed and, where necessary, they were revised in December. We now have a history of development and tooling experience, which we have been accumulating since 1975. This has proved extremely useful in setting cost standards. Simultaneously, we have integrated market and sales forecasts more effectively into our pricing decisions.

Before Universal acquired Galvor, a single company-wide rate was used to allocate factory overhead to the costs of products. For many years this rate was 310 percent of direct labor. In a discussion of his pricing policies in 1972, Mr. Latour said: "I have been using this 310 percent for many years and it seems to work out pretty well, so I see no reason to change it."

M. Chambertin had long argued that the less-complex products were being unfairly burdened by the use of a single overhead rate, while electronic products should bear more.

Mr. Latour's response to this argument was:

> I have suspected that our electric products are too high-priced, and our electronic products are too low-priced. So what does this mean? Why should we lower our prices for multimeters and galvanos? At our current prices, we can easily sell our entire production of electric products.

M. Chambertin remained convinced that eventually Galvor would be forced by competitive pressures to allocate its costs more realistically.

In 1976, as part of the new standard cost system, Galvor did indeed refine the procedure for allocating overhead costs to products. Fifteen different cost centers were established, each with a separate burden rate. These rates, which combined direct labor cost and overhead, ranged from 13.19 francs to 38.62 francs per direct labor hour.

Concluding his comments about recent developments, Mr. Hennessy said:

> A formal inventory control system went into effect in January 1967. This, together with the standard cost system, allows us for the first time to really determine the relative profitability of various products, and to place a proper valuation on our inventory.
>
> We are installing a new IBM 6400 in February, which we will use initially for customer billing and for marketing analysis. We hope this will reduce the number of people required in our customer billing and accounts receivable operations from 12 to 6 or 7.

CASE 12–3
Binswanger & Steele, Inc.*

Alvin Binswanger, president of Binswanger & Steele, Inc., which manufactured office equipment, had introduced a new system for appraising the performance of his top executives in 1979. During 1980, he decided the system, which was called "management by objectives," might help solve some problems in the sales area, and in 1981, the system was extended to the national sales manager and the eight regional sales managers. After the 1981 performance, appraisals had been submitted and reviewed, and several of the company's managers discussed the desirability of extending the system to lower levels of management.

THE MANAGEMENT BY OBJECTIVES SYSTEM

The management by objectives system of performance appraisal was based on the concept that evaluation of executives should depend on how the results they achieved compared with their objectives; that is, with reasonable estimates of what was possible.

In October 1978, Binswanger decided to test the system on his key

* This case was prepared by J. S. Livingston, Harvard Business School.

executives. If the system proved successful, he planned to instruct these executives to extend it to the managers who reported to them. The appraisal system then would be introduced to successively lower levels of management each year until it included all employees.

During the first week of October 1978, Binswanger and his key executives met privately to determine their key objectives for their own satisfactory performance for fiscal 1979, beginning November 1, 1978. They agreed that, if they exceeded their objectives, they would consider their performance outstanding. If they merely met their objectives, they would consider their performance satisfactory. If they failed to meet their objectives, they would consider their performance unsatisfactory. Bonuses and raises were to be awarded only to the men who exceeded their key result targets.

In December of 1979, at the end of the one-year trial period, each executive met privately with Binswanger to review his individual performance. Each manager's performance exceeded his stated objectives for 1979.

EXTENSION TO THE SALES DIVISION

In June 1980, Binswanger and Steele's executive committee met to discuss the increasing turnover and evidence of low morale among the company's salesmen. Sales Vice President Ben Weddels attributed these problems to several factors, including management problems generated by the expansion of the sales force from 300 salesmen in 1975 to 500 in 1980 and the increased complexity of the selling jobs caused by a large number of new and more complex products which had been added to the company's line in recent years. Weddels was concerned that he and Ted Forman, the national sales manager, might have inadequate control over the sales force. Weddels believed that the management by objectives system would be useful in tightening up this control. The executive committee approved Weddel's suggestion that the system be applied to the national sales manager and his eight regional sales managers during fiscal 1981.

In July 1980, Weddels called in Ted Forman to explain the performance appraisal system. Ted Forman, 55 years old, had been with Binswanger & Steele since 1947. During that time he had been a salesman, branch sales manager in four different areas of the country, and regional sales manager in New England for six years before being selected as national sales manager in 1980.

Weddels and Forman agreed to appraise Forman's 1981 performance on the basis of satisfactory performance of his regional sales managers. Forman, in turn, was to explain the system to the regional managers and to negotiate objectives for the year with each of them. Weddels gave Forman a memorandum setting forth guidelines for implementing the performance appraisal system (see Exhibit 1).

EXHIBIT 1 Memorandum

July 15, 1980

TO: Ted Forman

FROM: Ben Weddels

SUBJECT: Management by Objectives Performance Appraisal System

In the fall, the supervisor should invite his immediate subordinates to submit to him what they believe to be their key result targets for the coming year. The supervisor should meet with each subordinate in closed conference and negotiate the subordinate's key result targets. The supervisor should not accept his subordinate's targets without questioning them, and the subordinate should be encouraged not to accept his superior's targets until he understands the complete logic behind them.

During the year, the supervisor should discuss with each subordinate any of his key result targets that do not appear to be on schedule. A plan for attaining off-schedule key result targets should be worked out between superior and subordinate. At the end of the year, the subordinate and supervisor should review the subordinate's key result targets and his actual achievements on a simple work sheet called a Manager Performance Statement.

The supervisor should send the work sheet to the subordinate prior to the appraisal interview and ask him to enter his results next to his agreed-upon targets. The subordinate returns a copy of the work sheet to the supervisor prior to the appraisal interview.

The purpose of the appraisal interview is to give supervisor and subordinate an opportunity to review the subordinate's performance in detail and to help the subordinate understand his strengths and weaknesses so that he can concentrate on improving himself. If a subordinate does not achieve key result targets because of circumstances outside of his control, such as an unanticipated increase in price or a shortage of supply, that fact should be noted in the supervisor's comment column. Such factors should not be counted against a subordinate in his appraisal. Normally, an appraisal interview takes two to four hours.

A supervisor-subordinate meeting is scheduled, during which a plan of action should be drafted for the subordinate to use in the coming year to improve his areas of weakness. This plan of action should be incorporated into the subordinate's key result targets for the coming year. These new targets should be presented about four weeks after the appraisal interview.

Bonuses and raises will be awarded only to those men who exceed their key result targets. One of the most useful indications a supervisor's manager can have of a supervisor's effectiveness is the Manager Performance Statements for the supervisor's subordinates. In other words,

EXHIBIT 1 (*concluded*)

Ted, I'll be looking at your regional manager's performance appraisals in order to evaluate your performance for 1981.

Ben Weddels

In September 1980, Forman wrote each of his regional sales managers and asked them to draft their own key result targets (objectives) for the fiscal year ending October 31, 1981. He defined "key result target" as a critical business accomplishment required of a regional sales manager, and suggested the following areas as some of those to be defined carefully: net sales, gross profit, gross percentage, operating expenses, branch pretax profit, year-end inventory level, and year-end inventory turnover.

THE MIDWEST SALES REGION

One of Binswanger's regional managers was 40-year-old Ed Michelson, the Midwest regional sales manager. Ted Forman was

EXHIBIT 2 Performance of Midwest Region and Selected Districts

District and year	*Net sales ($000)*	*Gross profit ($000)*	*Percent gross profit to net sales*	*Operating expenses*	*Pretax profit*
Chicago (June 1970)*					
1968	$ 759	$ 128	16.9%	$ 107	$ 21
1969	982	133	13.5	115	18
1970	655	94	14.3	111	(17)
St. Louis (April 1970)					
1968	760	114	15.0	88	26
1969	712	96	13.5	96	0
1970	552	78	14.2	111	(33)
Detroit (September 1969)					
1968	1,940	242	12.5	197	45
1969	1,470	212	14.4	316	(104)
1970	1,990	275	13.8	277	(2)
Dayton (December 1967)					
1968	796	116	14.6	94	22
1969	1,103	152	13.8	112	40
1970	1,226	188	15.3	137	51
Midwest region Total (9 branches)					
1968	10,637	1,517	14.2	1,219	298
1969	10,576	1,495	14.1	1,455	39
1970	10,038	1,457	14.5	1,415	42

* Date district manager appointed.

aware that Ben Weddels considered Michelson the most effective and promising of the company's regional sales managers. Since Forman was eager to please Weddels, he decided to pay special attention to Ed Michelson's key result targets for fiscal 1981.

When Michelson received Forman's letter asking for key result targets, Michelson went to the files and reviewed midwestern sales data for the past three years to arrive at key result targets for his branches. Meanwhile, Forman reviewed his personal copies of the same data. (Exhibit 2 gives these data).

THE FORMAN-MICHELSON CONFERENCE

Forman and Michelson met in October 1980 to negotiate Michelson's key result targets for fiscal 1981. During the meeting, there was a cordial atmosphere, but Forman reserved the right ultimately to determine Michelson's objectives. Michelson and Forman agreed that the Midwest region had shown little sales improvement in the past few years. Both men suspected that a business recession may have affected sales, but there was no indication that the recession would affect sales in 1981. Forman got the impression that Michelson's sales estimates were highly conservative and his requests for sales expenses were overly liberal. When the men disagreed, Forman made reference to corporate level marketing data, unavailable to Michelson, that substantiated Forman's claims. Michelson claimed that he did not believe it would be possible to produce the sales volume Forman desired, given the imposition of such low sales expenses. Michelson was not pleased with his conference and said he did not know how he was going to achieve the key result targets budgeted for 1981.

Forman also incorporated into Michelson's 1981 key result targets several items about which Michelson had no previous notice. Forman said that his list of specific targets which would apply to all regional managers had been delayed in preparation. He explained that the specific targets, such as improving sales mix and the market share and sales volume of particular product lines, were intended to help regional sales managers direct their efforts toward areas considered important by top management. Michelson did not argue with Forman's specific targets, but complained that he had had no prior opportunity to determine his region's current status and the feasibility of meeting Forman's targets.

SALES RESULTS—MIDWEST REGION

During 1981, Michelson spent much of his time traveling to the branch offices in his region and working out problems with his branch sales managers. He did not have an opportunity to work out an account analysis with his managers and intended to do this as soon as there was sufficient time. When the fiscal year ended in October, Forman was unable to meet with Michelson for a performance appraisal interview. Instead, Michelson was sent a Manager Performance Statement with the 1981 key result targets and budgeted figures for each target, with instructions to fill in the 1981 actual results. When he completed this task, Michelson returned the work sheet to Forman.

The two men met in early November and, in an hour, reviewed Michelson's Manager Performance Statement. Forman jotted his notes of the meeting in the space provided "for use of executive making appraisal." After the review, he instructed Michelson to prepare 1982 key result targets for the Midwest region, and to study the possibility of introducing the management by objectives performance appraisal system to his branch sales managers.

In the meantime, Ben Weddels had seen preliminary 1981 sales figures for the Midwest region, which indicated a decline in both net sales and gross profit. He was concerned about this decline, and in mid-November, asked Ted Forman to send Michelson's Manager Performance Statement to his office. Forman was surprised to receive Weddels' request. He had filed Michelson's materials and forgotten about them, but was under the impression that Ed Michelson had done as well as or better than any of the other regional managers in meeting his key result targets. To prove this, Forman prepared an analysis showing which of the regional sales manager's actual results had exceeded their targeted results by 5 percent or more. Of 63 branches, 8 had exceeded their gross profit target, and about 12 each had exceeded their net sales, gross profit percentage, branch operating expense, or branch pretax profit target. More branches in the Midwest region exceeded each of these targets than in any other region except the South Central region. He submitted the details of this comparison analysis with Michelson's performance appraisal (see Exhibit 3) to Ben Weddels.

EXHIBIT 3 Manager Performance Statement*

Name:	Ed Michelson	*Position:*	Regional Manager
Region:	Midwest	*For Period:*	1981

Key Results Expected

1. Achieve at branch level 1971 budgeted components in the following categories:
   a. Net sales.
   b. Gross profit.
   c. Gross profit percentage.
   d. Branch operating expenses.
   e. Branch pretax profit.

Key Results Achieved (include appropriate supporting comment)

EXHIBIT 3 (*continued*)

	1981 est. (Michelson)	*1981 Budget (Michelson–Forman)*	*1981 actual*
Chicago branch:			
a. Net sales	$ 690	$ 820	$ 628
b. Gross profit	99	127	68
c. Gross profit percentage	14.4%	15.5%	10.9%
d. Branch operating expenses	125	110	91
e. Branch pretax profit	(26)	17	(23)
St. Louis Branch:			
a. Net sales	560	720	562
b. Gross profit	84	110	93
c. Gross profit percentage	15.0%	15.3%	16.5%
d. Branch operating expenses	125	100	87
e. Branch pretax profit	(41)	10	6
Detroit branch:			
a. Net sales	2,000	2,080	2,151
b. Gross profit	300	300	325
c. Gross profit percentage	15.0%	14.4%	15.1%
d. Branch operating expenses	260	250	257
e. Branch pretax profit	40	50	68
Dayton branch:			
a. Net sales	990	1,190	1,051
b. Gross profit	150	190	142
c. Gross profit percentage	15.1%	16.0%	13.5%
d. Branch operating expenses	140	132	117
e. Branch pretax profit	10	58	25
Regional total (9 branches):			
a. Net sales	9,890	10,970	9,792
b. Gross profit	1,448	1,652	1,456
c. Gross profit percentage	14.7%	16.5%	14.9%
d. Branch operating expenses	1,435	1,329	1,224
e. Branch pretax profit	13	323	232

Comment (for use of executive making appraisal):

Net sales off slightly more than 10 percent for region which was below expectations; however, two branches did exceed budget. Dollar gross profit was severely affected, but again, same two branches were above or near budget. Expense reduction was made, but in my opinion, action was not taken soon enough. Even though Chicago attained expense budget, additional profit should have been realized through closer control of expenses. Profit was disappointing, partially contributed to by chaotic conditions. Greater profit could have been obtained through better planning and expense control.

Key Results Expected

2. Improve sales mix between commercial, institutional, and military. Emphasize new business and re-equipment sales.

Key Results Achieved (include appropriate supporting comment)

EXHIBIT 3 (*continued*)

	Gross sales ($000)				
	Chicago	*St. Louis*	*Detroit*	*Dayton*	*Total (9 branches)*
Commercial:					
1970	$553	$502	$ 924	$1,152	$ 7,055
1971	500	403	813	784	5,763
Difference	(53)	(99)	(111)	(368)	(1,292)
Institutional:					
1970	132	74	932	157	2,605
1971	118	125	1,271	223	3,116
Difference	(14)	51	339	66	551
Military:					
1970	9	4	205	0	$ 802
1971	5	12	158	10	778
Difference	(4)	8	(47)	10	(24)
Government:					
1970	1	0	19	14	124
1971	36	53	21	94	627
Difference	35	53	2	80	503

Comment (for use of executive making appraisal):
Satisfactory on institutional and government. Held steady in military but too great a decline in commercial.

Key Results Expected
3. Increase average gross profit realization to 15.8 percent or better.

Key Results Achieved (include appropriate supporting comment)

Overall gross profit percentage:
1981 Budget—15.1%
1981 Actual—13.9%
(See Target No. 1, *Key Results Expected,* for gross profit percentages of individual branches.)

Comment (for use of executive making appraisal):
15.8 percent was for all eight regions. Your measurement should be based on your budgeted regional level of 15.1 percent. Actual percentage attained was 13.9 percent, which was not satisfactory. However, it is recognized that improvement is difficult under severe competitive conditions, but you must watch this phase closely in the affected areas.

Key Results Expected
4. Institute an inventory of manager development requirements for all branch managers, as well as inaugurate an individual on-the-job development action program for three prospective branch managers.

Key Results Achieved (include appropriate supporting comment)
Inventory of developmental requirements taken for all managers in the Midwest region and action program prepared for three.
Action program postponed because of press of business in last quarter 1981.

Comment (for use of executive making appraisal):
This should be your personal target to continue some training of managers to correct their weaknesses during 1982.

Key Results Expected
5. Improve market share of corporate products. Achieve 5.7 percent share of market for Exec-Q-Tote portable dictating machine at each branch.

Key Results Achieved (include appropriate supporting comment)

EXHIBIT 3 (*concluded*)

	Exec-Q-Tote 10 months' net sales ($000)		
	5.7 percent share (estimated)	*1971 actual (10 months)*	*Difference*
Chicago	$ 22	$ 22	—
St. Louis	84	50	($34)
Detroit	108	92	(16)
Dayton	104	87	(17)
Regional total (9 branches)	605	532	(82)

Comment (for use of executive making appraisal):
Share of market not a satisfactory measurement and you agree that sales of these products need serious attention in 1982.

Key Results Expected
6. Improve sales volume of noncorporate products. Achieve overall 5 percent or more increase in sales of typewriter ribbons and supplies.

Key Results Achieved (include appropriate supporting comment)

	Typewriter ribbons and supplies ($000s)		
	1981 unit objective	*Dollar sales to 10/31*	*Percent achievement*
Chicago	$ 292	$ 270	92%
St. Louis	124	156	126
Detroit	751	878	117
Dayton	423	396	93
Regional total (9 branches)	3,438	3,639	106

Comment (for use of executive making appraisal):
Generally satisfactory.

* Detail on five branches omitted.

Weddels was not happy with the results reported by Forman. According to the performance appraisal system, most of the regional managers, including Ed Michelson, were "below standard." On the other hand, he knew that many of them had faced competitive conditions which could not have been predicted with accuracy.

ALVIN BINSWANGER'S MEMORANDUM

Shortly thereafter Ben Weddels received the following memorandum:

November 22, 1981

TO: Ben Weddels

FROM: Alvin Binswanger

SUBJECT: Management by Objectives Performance Appraisal System—1981 Results

Happy Thanksgiving, but no relaxation for managers. We must get together soon to work out our 1982 plan for appraising managers. I am still excited about the management by objectives performance appraisal system, and eventually, I would like to extend the system to all levels in the organization and broaden its concept to tie in directly with compensation and development. I would like to hear your views on the system's effectiveness last year. I would appreciate it if you would dig up some answers to the following questions before we meet:

1. Were the key result targets realistic and challenging? Do you think they motivated the men to improve their performance?
2. Did the system help the managers appraise the strengths and deficiencies of their subordinates? Did they use the system to develop plans for improvement? If not, was it the fault of the system or the way the system was applied?
3. What can we do to improve the system?
4. Are we ready at this time to extend the system to the branch sales managers? If so, what steps should we take?

Alvin Binswanger

Alvin Binswanger

CASE 12–4
Performance Rating for Divisional Control

Exhibit A is an article that appeared in the *Financial Executive* in March 1975.

Question

Evaluate the system of divisional measurement described in this article. In particular, what are its strong points? What are its weak points? How, if at all, would you change this system?

EXHIBIT A*

PERFORMANCE RATING FOR DIVISIONAL CONTROL

For over 10 Years USI Has Inspired—and Measured—Its Divisional Executives' Performance with Its Performance Rating System

By Frank J. Tanzola, Senior Vice President and Corporate Controller, U.S. Industries, Inc.

The executives of large multidivisional companies are invariably asked two questions: how do you manage so many diverse businesses and how do you motivate the people running the businesses, many of whom are independently wealthy because they have sold their businesses to the conglomerate? The answers to these questions are found in organization structure, comprehensive planning, and accountability in the form of budgeting and monthly reporting, pooling expertise and business acumen, financial and other incentives, and, at times, downright toughness.

USI is no exception. (USI has quite a history of successful acquisition. The company has acquired nearly 100 companies since 1965, with a substantial increase in net income—from $2 million in 1965 to $81 million in 1972. However, due to a worsening economy and setbacks at certain of its operations, net income has declined in the last two years.)

USI incentives for good performance have been broad. They have included contingency arrangements, whereby the total consideration paid for an acquired business depends on its profits during a number of years subsequent to the acquisition; a bonus system based on profits after a return on the corporation's investment; a stock option plan; base salary levels commensurate with position, responsibilities, and achievement; and a preference for internal promotion to higher level positions. Nevertheless, during discussions of these methods, one technique never fails to excite the questioners' interest and curiosity—USI's performance rating system.

Division Performance Rating

USI's performance rating system (we also refer to it as our achievement of objectives system) is a quantification of progress against agreed-upon standards as good, prudent measures of operating results.

* From *Financial Executive*, March 1975. Used with permission.

The rating system has been in use at USI for more than 10 years, predating the acquisition period I mentioned earlier, but it proved to be easily adaptable to a growing number of diverse businesses.

Each year the group operating executives solicit the idea of their division management about appropriate measurement standards. Common standards are adopted by agreement of the group executives and corporate management. The powers assigned to standards reflect those areas management decides require special attention.

Basis for Measurement

The standards and point assignments are part of USI's management guide, which sets forth the corporation's policies and objectives. The guide is distributed to all top executives throughout the corporation. With the guide, all managers have a clear understanding of the challenge presented to their operation. The latest point system is outlined in Exhibit 1.

As can be seen from Exhibit 1, the measure of performance is in three broad areas:

1. Profits are compared to the former year in absolute dollars,

EXHIBIT 1 Standards and Point Assignments

Doing better than last year	
Pretax dollar profit:	
—exceeds same period prior year	1 Point
—exceeds same period prior year by 15% or more	1 Point
—exceeds same period prior year by 25% or more	1 Point
Pretax profit percentage on sales:	
—exceeds same period prior year	1 Point
Return on average investment:	
—exceeds same period prior year	1 Point
Planning realistically	
Pretax dollar profit for period:	
—not less than 90% nor more than 125% of budget	1 Point
Pretax percent profit on sales for the period:	
—equals or exceeds budget	1 Point
Return on average capital employed for period:	
—not less than 90% of budget	1 Point
Managing cash and capital	
Investment criteria:	
—number of months' sales in receivables equals or less than budget*	1 Point
—number of months' cost of sales in inventory equals or less than budget*	1 Point
Cash transfers to headquarters:	
—at least 75% of prior 12 months' pretax profits	1 Point
—equals or exceeds year-to-date budgeted transfers	2 Points
Maximum per period	13 Points**

* Provided return on capital employed is better than prior year.
** 12 points achieves standard of excellence.

margins, and return on investment. The investment community applies these yardsticks in evaluating the company as a whole.

2. Profits are compared to budget. Note that a point is lost for dollars of profit either too far below or too far above the amount budgeted. This is one way of discouraging divisional budgets which are either too cozy or too aggressive. Realistic divisional budgets serve as a norm to identify good or poor performers or shifts in business conditions. They also provide the firm basis required for corporate planning.

3. Managing cash and capital. The emphasis here is on good management of inventory and receivables. Sales turnover ratios are used to allow for better-than or worse-than-expected business conditions and to measure management reaction to the changed conditions. Cash, of course, is the ultimate end product of business activity; its emphasis here needs no rationale other than to provide incentive to produce it so that it can be kept at work in the overall corporate structure.

It should be noted that this approach also affords a good performance evaluation of the management of a business operating in a depressed market. While admittedly, through no fault of their own, they may not be able to earn the points based on profit comparisons to the prior year, they could nevertheless earn the points for good management of cash and capital and, to the extent they had the foresight, the points based on budgeted amounts. Thus, the management of such a business would not be rated as poorly as they might be if they were to be judged solely on comparative profit results.

Performance Report

Each quarter, every division rates itself on a form devised and provided for that purpose and with reference to the management guide point standards. These forms are forwarded to corporate headquarters, where they are reviewed and the divisions ranked, according to points earned, among all divisions in the company. Where divisions have earned the same number of points, ranking in the quarterly report is according to the percent improvement of dollar profits over the prior year period. A sample of the quarterly rating form is shown in Exhibit 2.

Giving Visibility to Performance

When this information has been assembled and divisions ranked at corporate headquarters, a performance standing report is prepared and distributed throughout the company to all management guide holders during the third week following each quarter. A sample of a performance standing report is shown in Exhibit 3. The names used are not the actual USI divisions, nor are the points shown necessarily indicative of ratings on any actual USI quarterly report.

EXHIBIT 2

COMPANY________________

GROUP

PERFORMANCE MEASUREMENT REPORT

(SUBSIDIARY/DIVISION)

(DATE)

	This Year Actual	This Year Budget	Last Year's Actual	This Year % of Budget	This Year vs. Last % Incr.	Points Current Quarter	Points Year to Date
	(Dollars Amounts in Thousands)						
Profit objectives							
Pretax profit:							
—Current quarter	$......	$......	$......	.....%	.....%	☐	
—Year to date	$......	$......	$......	.....%	.....%		☐
Net sales:							
—Current quarter	$......	$......	$......				
—Year to date	$......	$......	$......				
Pretax profit %:							
—Current quarter	.....%	.....%	.....%			☐	
—Year to date	.....%	.....%	.....%				☐
Average investment	$......	$......	$......				
Return on average investment	.....%	.....%	.....%	.....%		☐	☐
Investment criteria							
Receivables	$......	$......					
Average sales—last 3 months	$......	$......					
Number of months sales in receivable	......	......				☐	☐
Inventories	$......	$......					
Average cost of sales—last 3 months	$......	$......					
Number of months cost of sales in inventory	......	......				☐	☐
Cash transfers							
Pure cash transfers equal to budget-year to date	$......	$......				☐	☐
Pure cash transfers and equivalents* as % of most recent 12 months' pretax profits:	12 Mos. Cash	12 Mos. Equiv.	12 Mos. Total	12 Mos. PTP	12 Mos. Percent		
	$......	$......	$......	$......	.....%	☐	☐
				Total performance points		____	____

* Consists of any direct payments for income taxes or debt.

EXHIBIT 3 USI Management Guide: Performance Standing (three months ended March 31, 19xx, ranked in accordance with USI management)

Rank	Top 25% Division (and points)
1	Apex (12)
2	Dural (12)
3	AE Wire & Cable (12)
4	Nashville (12)
5	Rolled Steel Products (12)
6	Daly Baking (12)
7	Hudson Chemical (12)
8	Super Automatic (12)
9	Bovy Products (12)
10	Lingus Linens (12)
11	Minute Fjoods (12)
12	Harvey Fasteners (12)
13	Burkey's (12)
14	Atwell (12)
15	Giner Products (12)
16	Agrol (11)
17	Mann's Supply (11)
18	Hyko (11)
19	Remson (11)
20	Warston (10)
21	Philippsburg (10)
22	Hartwell (10)
23	Prince Charming (10)
24	Eastern Window (10)
25	Royal (10)
26	Keystone (10)
27	Southern Aire (10)
28	Brown Company (9)

Rank	Second 25% Division (and points)
29	Scatter Chain (9)
30	Boggs Ewell (9)
31	West-Link (9)
32	Duralee (9)
33	Specto (9)
34	Revere (9) points
35	Tacco (9) ducts
36	Springdale (9) (2)
37	Dusco (9) (
38	Buliog-Art dle (2)
39	Greenco Pack (2)
40	Halfield (2)
41	Relay po (2)
42	Duby Tel (2)
43	Rel aliant (2)
44	B ducto (2)
45	D El-Con (2)
46	Karpo (2)
47	Bel-Tone (2)
48	
4	
	House (3)

Rank	Division (and points)
3	Brookings (2)
99	Konsort (2)
100	Gurnay (2)
101	El Paso (2)
102	Holsum Kraft (2)
103	Centrex Leasing (2)
104	D & W Fixtures (2)
105	National Abroding (2)
106	Thompson (2)
107	Portland (2)
108	Southwest Reduction (2)
109	Revolvo (2)
110	Timer Tones (2)
111	Holgren (2)
112	Culver (2)

The same system is applied to the four USI operating groups and they, too, are rated and ranked, but separately among themselves.

To provide increased visibility for performance and additional incentives and to foster the competitive spirit implicit in the system, 12-pointers are presented excellence awards in the form of "E" flags each quarter. The division and group with the highest cumulative points for the year each receives the annual first-place award—a bronze plaque. We also distribute a quarterly "Performance Awards" brochure. A full page is devoted to each of the winning organizations with photos of the key executives together with an announcement of the award and a write-up of their division or group. The first page of this brochure is a letter of congratulations from the chairman and president. What I am saying is this: It isn't enough to merely tabulate performance statistics. The results must be widely publicized and the system must have the interest and support of top management. Additional importance is attached to it when high point achievement is given weight in annual bonus considerations.

Has It Been Effective?

Managing a giant corporation from the top can be a very lonely and, at times, a frustrating and thankless job. The question of how to get line management to function most effectively in areas of corporate concern and benefit has no easy answer. The fields of employee motivation and management science are broad. Their volumes and practitioners offer many varied approaches adaptable to particular circumstances. At USI, we employ many of the usual approaches, but the rating system which I have described has contributed surprisingly well to our motivational efforts. I say surprisingly because at first blush it may seem schoolboyish and unlikely to interest the sophisticated, successful businessmen. On the contrary, however, we have witnessed that extra effort, that special attention to achieving goals by both our professional managers and entrepreneurs to come away with the honors of the awards for their divisions or to gain a respectable ranking among all divisions. It reaffirms for us that pride and the competitive spirit are potent human drives. A motivational or incentive package which ignores or underrates them is missing a fundamental.

Side Benefits

At the risk of claiming too much for the system, it is important to list some of its secondary benefits. Starting out with the premise that the agreed-upon standards are good, prudent business measures of operating results, it follows that:

—Management can see by a glance at the performance standing report which divisions are performing well and which not so well.

—The lost points act as red flags directing management's attention to those areas.

—Among the required agenda items for monthly division executive meetings is a discussion of the areas where points were lost, the reasons, and corrective actions taken. This often leads to in-depth discussion of business conditions and operating problems. Minutes of these meetings are forwarded to group and corporate headquarters where they are read by all key executives.

—Included in the internal audit review scope is a procedure where the auditor satisfies himself as to the stated reasons for the division's lost points. This can lead the auditor to important findings which might otherwise escape his attention.

Flexibility

The system has flexibility in regard to shifting management emphasis. It is also flexible as to its application to organizational units other than the operating division, such as departments or even business segments. In fact, a good example of adapting it for both shifting emphasis and different organization units is currently underway at USI. Management has determined that with post-acquisition earnout periods largely past, and for reasons related to concentrating business expertise and operating efficiencies, the company would now be better served if it were to reorganize divisions into much fewer but larger operating units along product lines. Added benefits expected from the more simplified structure are better investor understanding of the company and better market identification. This necessitates a complete revision of the rating system to adapt it to the new structure. Nevertheless, we fully expect that the revised system will be fully operational and will be serving us as well in the future as it has in the past.

CHAPTER 13

Executive Incentive Compensation Plans

Executive incentive compensation plans can be roughly divided into two types: those that relate compensation to the profits earned by the company or a segment of the company, and those that relate compensation to the market price of the company's common stock. We discuss each of these types of plans in this chapter.

PROFIT SHARING

Executive profit-sharing plans (hereafter called "bonus plans") have two characteristics: (1) participation is limited to managers high enough in the organization to be able to affect policy; and (2) the size of the bonus is calculated by a formula that in some way relates it to the amount of profits earned during a specified period, usually a year.

The purpose of a bonus plan, of course, is to encourage high performance by allowing managers to participate financially in the results of their accomplishments. Such a plan can be classified into two broad categories: plans based on company-wide profitability and plans based on divisional profitability. Each is discussed in this part of the chapter.

Company-wide Plans

All bonus plans must to some extent be based on total corporate profitability because there will always be a number of executives whose bonuses are directly related to total company profits. We shall first describe the principal options open to a company when it adopts a new or revised bonus plan. Because bonus plans usually must be approved by stockholders, changes often are difficult to make. Consequently, it is important that the implications of all elements of the plan be carefully considered before it is submitted to the stockholders for approval.

The total fund. A decision must be made as to the size of the bonus fund. Usually the overriding consideration is to make the total executive compensation package competitive. Consequently the board of directors arrives at an amount of incentive compensation that appears to be the best "fit," given the company's level of base salary, fringe benefits, and other compensation, such as stock options, relative to competitive compensation levels.

The bonus formula. Once the total bonus has been estimated, the next problem is to determine the bonus formula. The simplest method is to make the bonus equal to a set percentage of the profits. For example, assume that profits of $50 million represented an average profitable year. If the board had already decided that a $1 million bonus fund was required to make the executive compensation package competitive, the bonus formula could then be set up to pay 2 percent of the net profit in bonuses.

Many companies find this method undesirable because it means paying a bonus even at low levels of profitability. Moreover, it fails to reflect additional investments; thus profits and, consequently, bonuses can increase simply as a result of new investments, although the performance of the company may be static or even deteriorating. Many companies, therefore, use formulas that pay bonuses only after a specified return has been earned on capital. There are several ways of accomplishing this.

Several large U.S. companies, for example, define capital as net worth plus long-term liabilities. The bonus allowance is equal to a percent of the profits before taxes and interest on long-term debt minus a capital charge on both net worth and long-term debt. They reason that managerial performance should be based on employing corporate net assets profitability. Since long-term debt is determined by financial policy, it should not influence operating performance.

Another method is to define capital as equal to stockholders' equity, although this approach could reward or penalize managers for financial leverage, even though they had no influence on the financial structure. One difficulty with this approach is that a loss year reduces stockholders' equity and, thereby, could increase the amount of bonus to be paid in profitable years. A series of losses would make an even higher bonus possible when a profit finally is earned.

A third method is to base the bonus on a percent of profits after a predetermined level of earnings per share has been attained. Using our earlier example, assume the following situation:

1. Estimated level of satisfactory profitability: $50 million.
2. Desired amount of bonus at the above level of profitability: $1 million.
3. Number of shares outstanding: 10 million.
4. Minimum earnings per share before bonus payments: $2.50.
5. Bonus formula: 4 percent of profits after subtracting $2.50 per share.

This method, however, does not take into account increases in investment from reinvested earnings. The objection can be overcome by increasing the minimum earnings per share by a percentage of the annual increase in retained earnings. In the example above, assume that the profits for the year were $50 million before bonuses and that dividends were $30 million. Also assume that the board of directors has decided that a 6 percent return must be earned on additional investments before any additional bonuses are paid. The $2.50 minimum earnings per share would thus be adjusted for the coming year in the following manner:

Increase in retained earnings:

$50,000,000 (profit) − $500,000 (bonus after taxes) − $30,000,000 (dividends) = $19,500,000.

Increase in required earnings before bonus:

Total = $19,500,000 × 0.06 = $1,170,000
Per share = $1,170,000 ÷ 10,000,000 = $0.117

Adjusted minimum earnings per share:

$2.50 + $0.12 = $2.62

Note that no reductions in the required earnings per share are normally made when the company experiences a loss; however, the required earnings would not be increased until retained earnings had exceeded its preloss level.

There are other, less common, methods of calculating the bonus. A few companies base the bonus on increase in profitability of the current year over the preceding year. This not only rewards a mediocre year that is followed by a poor year, but it also fails to reward a good year if it happens to follow an excellent one. This problem can be partially corrected by basing the bonus on an improvement in the current year that is above a moving average of the profits in a number of past years.

Another method bases bonuses on company profitability relative to industry profitability. Obtaining comparable industry data may be difficult, however, as few companies have the same product mix or employ identical accounting systems. This method could also result in a high bonus in a mediocre year because one or more of the industry components had a poor year.

Yet another method uses the degree to which profit goals are attained to calculate the bonus. As this method is most often used in systems based on divisional profitability, we will discuss it later in that context.

The bonus formula must also take into consideration some or all of the following factors:

1. What items, if any, should be excluded from profits (e.g., extraordinary gains or losses, gains or losses from discontinued operation, or income taxes).
2. The maximum size of the bonus pool.
3. Whether to use a sliding scale, such as using different percentages for different levels of profit.

Individual rewards. After developing a formula for the total bonus fund, a method for distributing the fund to individual executives must be devised. This requires: (1) deciding on a formula for calculating the standard bonus of each executive, and (2) establishing a review and approval procedure for awarding individual bonuses.

Individual bonus formula. A common method for developing individual bonus formulas is to base them on a percentage of base salary. The simplest formula is the ratio of the total bonus fund to the total salaries of eligible executives. This ratio then is used to determine the individual bonus awards. For example, if the total bonus amount is $1 million and the total salaries of eligible executives is $2 million, then each executive will receive a bonus equal to 50 percent of his or her salary. A problem with this approach is that salary level alone may not be an accurate measurement of an executive's contribution to profits.

A more complicated method uses different percentages for different salary levels; the higher the salary, the higher the percentage of bonus to salary. For example, a company's bonuses might vary from 20 percent of salary at the lowest level to 100 percent of salary at the top level. The advantage of this method is that it provides relatively larger incentive compensation for the executives who have the greatest influence on profitability—assuming, of course, that the higher the salary, the greater the effect an executive has on company profitability.

Less frequently the total bonus is distributed not according to salary but on the basis of "bonus points." This incentive system has several variations, but its main feature is the assignment of a number of bonus points to every job. A bonus point represents a share of the bonus fund. Each year the total bonus fund is divided by the total number of bonus points outstanding, which yields a standard bonus amount for each point. An individual's bonus is calculated by multiplying the standard amount per point by the number of bonus points assigned the position.

Bonus point systems tend to be more flexible than salary-based methods because bonus points can be assigned in relation to the direct impact of a position on company profitability. Thus, line managers, who make decisions directly affecting profits, can be assigned relatively more bonus points than staff managers, who act more in an advisory role. The total compensation for staff positions, therefore, will consist of relatively less bonus than that of line positions, even though the average total compensation is the same for both groups. In short, the use of a bonus-point system allows top management to utilize two relatively independent systems of compensation.

Review procedures. Although some companies simply pay each executive according to the bonus formula, many authorities believe that such automatic bonuses lead to an abdication of one of management's most important responsibilities—the evaluation of performance. If each manager exercises some judgment regarding the bonuses of subordinates, executive bonuses will be more closely related to individual performance.

One approach is simply to give senior managers the freedom to distribute the total of the bonuses computed for their subordinates in any way they please, subject only to the approval of their superior. Such a system obviously gives considerable authority to a senior manager. In fact, when bonuses are relatively large, the authority for awarding bonuses can have a significant impact on a subordinates' total compensation. For this reason, most systems place some restrictions on executive authority to set bonus amounts. One method is to reduce the standard bonuses by a given percentage—say 25 percent—and then give the manager freedom to distribute this amount. For example, assume that a manager had five subordinates with a total standard bonus award of $100,000. Each subordinate would get a standard bonus of 75 percent of the standard award plus whatever distribution of the remaining $25,000 that the senior manager deemed appropriate.

Cutoff levels. Two important decisions here are the level of profit at which a maximum bonus is reached and, conversely, the level below which no bonus awards will be made because such cutoff levels may produce undesirable side effects. When executives recognize that either the maximum bonus has been attained or that there will be no bonus at all, the motivational effect of the bonus system may be contrary to corporate goals. Instead of attempting to optimize profits in the current period, executives may be motivated to decrease profitability in one year to set up an opportunity for a high bonus in a later period. Although this would principally affect only the timing of expenses, such action could certainly be undesirable. Moreover, such a system may be unfair to executives in that it is based on a single year. This objection can be met simply by carrying over the excess or deficiency into the following year. Thus, the bonus available for distribution in a given year would be the amount of bonus earned during that year plus any excess, or minus any deficiency, from the previous year.

There is another, more flexible technique for eliminating absolute cutoffs. Instead of paying the earned bonus automatically, this system features annual carry-over of an amount determined by the bonus formula. The amount is positive if the earnings are above the minimum required in the bonus formula. The carry-over amount may be negative if the earnings are below the minimum, although this practice is unusual. Each year a committee of the board of directors decides how much to pay from the carry-over account. Typically, the committee can pay as much of the carry-over as it chooses, the only restriction being the total positive amount available. This method has two advantages over the absolute cutoff method: (1) it offers more flexibility, since payment is not determined automatically by a formula, and the board of directors can exercise its judgment; and (2) it can reduce the magnitude of the swings that occur when the bonus payment is based strictly on the formula amount calculated each year. For example, in an exceptionally good year the committee may decide to pay out only a portion of the bonus. Conversely, in a relatively poor year, the committee may decide to pay out more than the amount added to the carry-over bonus account if a surplus has accrued. The disadvantage of the method is that the bonus relates less directly to current performance.

Deferred payments. Points raised in the foregoing section lead to a final important decision: whether to pay the total bonus award each year or to spread payments over a period of time, perhaps three to five years. Under a five-year deferred system, executives receive only one fifth of their bonus in the year in which it was earned. The other four fifths are paid out equally over the next four years. Thus, after the executive has been working under the plan for five years, the bonus consists of one fifth of the bonus for the current year plus one fifth of each of the bonuses for the preceding four years. This deferred payment method offers a number of advantages:

1. Executives can estimate, with reasonable accuracy, their cash income for the coming year.
2. Deferred payments smooth an executive's receipt of cash, because the effects of cyclical swings in profits are averaged in the cash payments.
3. An executive who retires will continue to receive payments for a number of years; this not only augments retirement income but also usually provides a tax advantage as income tax rates after retirement are likely to be lower than during working life.

Deferred bonus plans have the disadvantage of not making the deferred amount available to the executive in the year earned. (In some cases the deferred amount may earn interest for the executive to offset this disadvantage.) As deferred bonus payments are not directly related to current performance, they may have questionable value as incentives.

Vesting. When bonus payments are deferred, a decision must be made on when the deferred amount vests. In some instances, an executive will not receive the deferred bonus if he or she leaves the company before it is paid. In other cases, restrictions are placed on the payment.

For example, some companies do not pay deferred bonuses to executives who depart to work for a competitor; other companies require executives to leave their work in orderly condition and to remain available for a limited amount of consulting.

Divisional Bonuses

In companies with profit centers, management must decide whether divisional managers' bonuses should be based on company-wide profits, division profits, or some combination of each. Proponents of basing the award on divisional profitability argue that such bonuses are more likely to motivate managers and are fairer than bonuses based on company-wide profits. They state that a company-wide plan can unfairly penalize operating divisions. For example, even in a poor profit year for the company, a division that turns in an outstanding performance will not be adequately rewarded if bonuses are based on company-wide profits. In some companies, bonus plans based on division profitability appear to work well, while in others they do not.

The advisability of basing bonuses on divisional profitability is closely related to a company's product lines, management philosophy, and organization. It is useful to conceptualize decentralized companies as falling within a spectrum that has two extremes. At one end is the loosely held, venture-capitalist conglomerate. This type of company is characterized by diversification, little integration among divisions, few interdivisional transactions, a small central staff, and a minimum of centralized policies and procedures. At the other end is the dominant-product company. This type of organization is characterized by a limited number of product lines, significant integration among divisions, numerous interdivisional transactions, a large central staff, and a high degree of policy and procedural centralization.

In general the problems of company-wide bonus plans described in the first part of this chapter also crop up with division plans, and their development is similar. The major difference is in corporate versus divisional application.

The venture capitalist. The closer a company is to the loosely held, venture-capitalist extreme, the more feasible is a bonus system based on division profitability. The general idea is to give the division manager a "piece of the action." If the divisions are successful, the managers share in that success; if they are not, the managers receive little or no bonus. The purpose is to motivate managers to act as though the division were their own company.

At this end of the spectrum, separate incentive compensation plans may be worked out for each division or subsidiary. This has the additional advantage of allowing bonus plans to be consistent with competitive practices. Many of these plans provide for a share of the profits, after a capital charge is deducted. But here, as in company-wide systems, a great deal of care must be taken in defining "investment." All the problems associated with measuring divisional performance on the basis of return on investment are intensified if the bonus is affected by the investment base.

The dominant-product company. In contrast to the venture-capitalist, an executive bonus system based on division profitability has problems in the dominant-product company.

Establishing the bonus amount. Venture-capitalist bonus plans are usually based on providing a percent of actual divisional profits after a deduction of a capital charge. This is usually not a satisfactory basis for divisional bonuses in dominant-product companies. If absolute profitability is used as the measure, the managers of the most profitable division will receive the largest bonuses; yet the amount of profit earned by a division may bear no relationship to the difficulty of a given job or to the accomplishments of a particular manager. The reverse is often true—the most difficult management assignments may be in low-profit divisions. Therefore, absolute profitability usually results not only in inequitable compensation but also in a condition that makes the best managers reluctant to accept the challenge to turn around a division in difficulty. In short, it reduces the flexibility of central management to move executives to the place where they are most needed by the company.

Because of this problem, many companies base bonuses on the degree to which division managers have met their profit budget commitments. The use of profitability compared with budget, however, can also create problems, some of which were described in Chapter 12. For example, a typical profit budget includes both a commitment to certain management actions and a forecast of expected conditions. In general, companies wish to reward their division managers on how well they have managed, not on their ability to forecast economic and competitive conditions. (In many instances, the economic forecasts are given to division managers.)

An alternative to strict budget-based bonuses would adjust the performance measures for noncontrollable factors. This is difficult to do because the distinction between controllable and noncontrollable performance factors is frequently not clear. Considerable debate between division managers and top management is likely to ensue, with positive adjustments being made in the bonuses of the most articulate managers. The annual budgeted profit can be an unreliable measure of division accomplishment and should be used with great caution.

Another approach is to use some form of management by objectives and base the bonus award on the degree that these objectives have been met. R. J. Walters Company *(A)* (Case 13–2) is an example of this method.

Another method is to base the divisional award on top management's judgment as to *how well* the division has performed. Finally, some companies employ a combination of the above methods.

Incongruence of goals. In many companies it is very difficult to develop a system of interdivisional relationships in which there is complete congruence between the goals of the divisions and the goals of the company. We have described in earlier chapters how division managers can increase their own profitability by taking certain actions that are contrary to the interests of the company. Of course, division managers are generally expected to act in the best interests of the company, even though their division's profits may be affected adversely. It is less realistic to expect such actions if a manager's bonuses are adversely affected.

Short-term rewards. Divisional accomplishments are not always reflected in short-term profits. For example, product or personnel development may not affect profits for several years. In dominant-product companies with centralized personnel policies, personnel development may never benefit the managers responsible because the people they develop are often transferred to other divisions. By the same token, if division managers are changed frequently, the positive effects of their long-term actions are not likely to be reflected in their own bonuses.

In short, annual divisional profitability often does not reflect the accomplishments of the division manager, and bonuses based solely on division profitability may not only result in inequities in the amount of compensation but could also produce strong motivation toward short-term action.

Decisions to be made. In spite of these problems, many companies do decide to base the bonus on divisional profitability. In that situation, management must make four decisions:[1] (1) whether to have a single companywide plan or a separate plan for each division; (2) what quantitative measure to use; (3) what impact corporate profits should have on divisional bonuses; and (4) what role judgment should play in the bonus award.

In general, divisional bonus plans depend on the type of business. In the venture-capitalist type of business, it is practical to have a different plan for each division or subsidiary, to base the bonus on absolute profitability, to have the bonus decided entirely by formula, and to base the bonus entirely on division profits. The dominant-product company, on the other hand, would be more likely to have a single plan for all divisions, to base the bonus formula on actual profits compared to

[1] For a more complete discussion of these decisions, see David Kraas, "Making Executive Incentives Effective in Diversified Companies," *Financial Executive,* June 1977.

budget, to use some judgment in making the bonus award, and to award part of the bonus on the basis of company profits.

As with company systems, the goal should be to devise a system that is most appropriate to the characteristics of the industry, the company, and the executive group.

Why Incentive Plans Fail

The purpose of a bonus system is to provide managers with an incentive for high performance. Since companies with bonus systems tend to pay out more in executive compensation than companies without them, the stockholders should be assured that the bonus system does actually increase executive performance. A logical question, therefore, is: Why do some incentive plans fail? Arch Patton, writing in the *Harvard Business Review,* lists three reasons for failure: (1) industry characteristics. (2) misused bonus mathematics, and (3) administrative flaws.

Industry characteristics. One reason why incentive plans fail is that some industries are not readily adaptable to incentive compensation systems.

The pattern of incentive plan use indicates that some industries are more disposed to employ this form of executive motivation than are others. Indeed, whole groups of industries largely use or shun executive incentives. Consider the incentive-use spectrum:

1. At one extreme, virtually every large company in the automotive, retail chain, department store, electric appliance, office equipment, textile, chemical, and pharmaceutical industries had an executive incentive program.
2. At the other extreme, relatively few incentive plans are found among the large public utility, banking, mining, railroad, and life insurance companies.[2]

Mr. Patton goes on to describe the characteristics of a natural incentive industry: (1) profits can be affected by numerous, short-term decisions; (2) decentralized organizations are typical; (3) budget variances, market-share data, and economic analysis are used to judge performance; and (4) a great deal is demanded from management. By contrast, marginal incentive industries are characterized by: (1) a few long-term decisions that have the greatest profit impact; (2) functional organization; (3) absence of sophisticated market and economic research tools to judge performance; and (4) lower executive-stress fac-

[2] Arch Patton, "Why Incentive Plans Fail," *Harvard Business Review,* May–June 1972, p. 59.

tors. Mr. Patton states: "Of course, it is *possible* to have a highly productive incentive plan in a marginal industry company, but the difficulties are so numerous that relatively few are found."[3]

Misused bonus mathematics. All bonus systems have their disadvantages. Some are too rigid, while others are too flexible, changing widely from year to year. Some bonus formulas may underreward executives and others may overreward them. Thus a second reason bonus plans fail is that the method for calculating the bonus does not fit the characteristics of the industry, the company, or the executive group.

Administrative flaws. The third reason for the ineffectiveness of bonus plans is the presence of administrative flaws. Bonus plans are most effective when they are based on difficult short-term goals, and when the reward is tied directly to the accomplishment of these goals. Providing the same reward for low accomplishment as for high accomplishment will tend to make a bonus system ineffective. Consequently, top executives must conduct the awarding of bonuses in such a way that the recipients will believe they are being rewarded fairly. Otherwise, the bonus system will not motivate managers to optimum performance and could even discourage efforts to be efficient and effective.

STOCK AWARD SYSTEMS

Stock award systems reward executives by allowing them to acquire shares of stock in the company at favorable rates, or otherwise to gain from an increase in the share prices. These can roughly be divided into two types: those in which the executives *buy* the shares at a favorable price and those in which managers are awarded the shares. A complete treatment of the subject of stock award systems is outside the scope of the book because of the complexities of the tax laws, the accounting rules, and the Securities and Exchange Commission regulations. But the central purpose of them all is to motivate managers to work for the long-term growth of the entire company. In this part of the chapter, we describe the principal types of stock award systems.

Stock Options

A stock option is a right to buy a number of shares of stock at a given price during a specific period in the future. Stock options have been widely used since the 1950s.

Qualified stock options. A qualified stock option plan is one that is accorded favorable tax treatment. Executives can exercise the option

[3] Ibid., p. 61.

and, if they sell the stock, the difference between the exercise price and the selling price is taxed as a capital gain. As long as the stock is held there is no tax at all, even though the executive might have purchased the stock at well below the current market price.

A qualified plan requires that the exercise price of an option be set close to the market price of the stock at the date of the award and that executives hold the stock for at least three years after exercising the option.

Nonqualified option plans. Nonqualified plans are those that do not qualify for favorable tax treatment. A nonqualified option can be awarded at a price below current market at the date of the award, and it does not have to be held more than the six months required by the Securities and Exchange Commission. On the other hand, when exercised the difference between the market price and the option price at the date of exercise is taxed as regular income to the executive. Also, this amount must be treated as an expense to the company on its financial statements.

Decline in popularity of stock option plans. By the end of the 1970s, the advantage of qualified stock option plans declined significantly. First, the Tax Reform Act of 1969 reduced the advantage of capital gains tax treatment. Second, the stock market performance was such that option prices were often significantly higher than the current market price. Third, the increase in interest rates made it more expensive for executives to finance stock purchase. In any event, the Tax Reform Act of 1976 ended new qualified stock option plans.

Incentive stock options. The Economic Recovery Act of 1981 has revived some of the popularity of stock options. This act legalized a new qualified stock option, called "incentive stock options," that allows executives to take part of their compensation in long-term capital gains that are taxed at 20 percent.

There are eight conditions that must be met to qualify for an incentive stock option. Among these conditions are that the option price must be at least equal to the fair market value of the stock on the date the option is granted, that only $100,000 in stock can be optioned to any one employee each year, and that options be exercised in the order they were granted.

Any employee stock option plan that satisfies these conditions allows the recipient to take a capital gain on any increase in the value of the optioned stock when sold.

Although stock option plans, either qualified on unqualified, are still used widely, other approaches are being used to motivate or encourage executives to participate in development of the growth and profitabilities of the companies they manage. Two of the principal methods are described in the next part of this chapter.

Nonoption Stock Plan

Phantom shares. The principle of a phantom stock plan is to award the executives a number of shares for bookkeeping purposes only. At the end of a specified period (say, five years) the executive is entitled to receive an award equal to the *appreciation* in the market value of the stock since the date of award. This award may be in cash, shares of stock, or both.

Although there is no preferential tax treatment, the phantom stock plan does not involve any downside risk on the part of the executive. Also, no financing costs are involved. For an example of a phantom stock plan see R. J. Walter's Company *(B)* (Case 13–3).

Performance shares. A performance share plan awards a given number of shares to an executive when specific long-term goals have been met. These goals may be corporate, divisional, or individual job results. This plan has the advantages over either stock option or phantom stock plan in that the award is based on performance that can be controlled, at least partially, by the executive. Also, the award is not dependent upon a gain in stock prices, although the more a stock gains in market value the more the award is worth.

SUGGESTED ADDITIONAL READINGS

Baker, John C. "Are Corporate Executives Overpaid?" *Harvard Business Review,* July–August 1977.

———. "Are Executives Overpaid? Readers Respond." *Harvard Business Review,* July–August 1978.

Carey, James F. "Successors to the Qualified Stock Option." *Harvard Business Review,* January–February 1978.

———. "Third Dimension for Executive Incentives." *Financial Executive,* January 1978.

Kaplan, Robert S. *Advanced Management Accounting.* Englewood Cliffs, N.J.: Prentice-Hall, 1982. Chapter 16.

Sommerfeld, Ray M. *Federal Taxes and Management Decisions, latest Edition.* Homewood, Ill.: Richard D. Irwin, 1983. Chapter 7.

Stata, Ray, and **Modestana Maidque.** "Bonus Systems for Balanced Strategy." *Harvard Business Review,* November–December, 1980.

CASE 13–1
Pullen Lumber Company*

John Pullen, founder and president of Pullen Lumber Company, was considering an incentive compensation plan for his managers which had been prepared at his request. Currently, the 700 Pullen employees were paid a straight salary (plus overtime when applicable). They were also paid an annual bonus equal to two weeks' salary. The proposed plan would apply only to the 43 managers of lumber yards, the 5 district managers, and 5 senior managers at headquarters. Instead of the annual bonus, these managers would be eligible for a bonus according to a proposal described later in the case.

EXHIBIT 1

PULLEN LUMBER COMPANY
Balance Sheet
As of 12/31/82

Assets		
Current assets:		
Cash and short-term investments		$ 1,346,000
Accounts receivable	$ 5,386,000	
Less: Allowance for doubtful accounts	56,000	5,330,000
Inventory		11,260,000
Total current assets		17,936,000
Fixed assets:		
Trucks, automobiles and equipment	3,450,000	
Less: Accumulated depreciation	1,260,000	2,190,000
Land and buildings	10,040,000	
Less: Accumulated depreciation	4,020,000	6,020,000
Total fixed assets		8,210,000
Other assets		2,900,000
Total assets		$29,046,000
Liabilities and Owners' Equity		
Current payables		$ 5,478,000
Long-term note payable, 8%		5,000,000
Total liabilities		10,478,000
Owners' equity:		
Capital stock ($40 par; 250,000 shares issued and outstanding)		10,000,000
Retained earnings		8,568,000
Total owners' equity		18,568,000
Total equities		$29,046,000

* This case was prepared by C. J. Casey, Jr., Harvard Business School.

THE COMPANY

Pullen Lumber company operated 43 lumber yards located in four midwestern states. Few interdependencies existed among the yards and each carried a line of lumber, plywood, roofing materials, doors, windows, tools, paint, flooring, and builders' supplies. Sales were made to contractors, homebuilders, and to individual homeowners and hobbyists. The lumber yards were supervised by five district offices. Each district office also had a sales force that solicited business from large contractors. As a service, the district offices sometimes aided contractors in preparing the material components in bids and gave informal advice on the material best suited to a job. Yard managers also gave this advice to smaller contractors.

There was a fixed budget for each yard and each district, showing planned revenues and expenses. Actual revenues and expenses were reported annually. Data on the company's financial condition and performance for the year are provided in Exhibits 1 and 2.

The company had enjoyed profits the past few years which were considerably greater than those of its competition, for whom the aver-

EXHIBIT 2

PULLEN LUMBER COMPANY
Income Statement
For 1982

Sales (net)		$56,127,000
Service revenue		2,148,000
		58,275,000
Less: Cost of sales		41,458,000
Gross margin		16,817,000
Operating expenses:		
Payroll	$6,705,000	
Property expense*	1,688,000	
Advertising	1,312,000	
Bad debt expense	836,000	
Equipment expense†	1,127,000	
Other expenses	1,529,000	
Total operating expenses		13,197,000
Operating income		3,620,000
Nonoperating items:		
Interest expense	400,000	
Loss on sale of equipment	32,000	432,000
Income before taxes		3,188,000
Provision for income taxes		1,476,000
Net income		$ 1,712,000

* Property expense includes real estate taxes, rentals, depreciation, and utilities expense.

† Equipment expense includes depreciation, maintenance and repairs, and routine operating expenses.

age aftertax return on investment in total assets was approximately 6 percent. Although the company as a whole had done well in the opinion of the company president, some of its yards and districts had incurred operating losses. Meanwhile, competitive pressures had been growing and the differences in profits among Pullen Company and its competitors had narrowed significantly. Because of this, the individual differences in the performances of the yards, and Mr. Pullen's often expressed desire to gain a larger market share in each of the company's lines of business, the proposed bonus plan assumed added significance.

BACKGROUND OF THE PLAN

At an Executive Committee meeting in September, Mr. Pullen introduced the idea of a bonus plan, and it seemed to be favorably received. At the end of this meeting he appointed a committee to draft a bonus plan. It consisted of the controller, who was to serve as a chairman, the general sales manager, and the director of purchases. The first problem they tackled was identification of the persons to whom the plan should apply. Three groups were initially considered: (1) district salesmen, (2) buyers, and (3) managers.

The sales manager foresaw great difficulties in identifying improved sales volume with individual salesmen. Many of the company's best customers had dealt with the company for years, and no substantial selling effort was required. Furthermore, personal friendships existed between the top officers of some companies which were good customers and the top officers of Pullen Lumber Company. These conditions made it relatively unimportant which salesman called upon and serviced the account. The volume of business from these customers would remain virtually unchanged, regardless of the salesmen's efforts.

The director of purchases also foresaw problems in attempting to recognize and reward individual buyers. The discounts obtained on an order related to factors over which the buyer had so little control as not to be a valid basis for a bonus award.

The committee therefore decided that the bonus plan should be limited to managers—the managers of individual lumber yards, the district managers, and the senior management group at headquarters.

In considering the managers' responsibility for profit performance, the committee agreed generally on the following points:

1. The yard manager is the primary factor in influencing customers' loyalty toward Pullen, by giving good service, by having the goods on hand when the customer wants them, and by his supervision of yard personnel.

2. Although standard selling prices are set by the central purchasing department, the yard manager has latitude in reducing prices to

meet competition and in the markdowns he allows for defective or old merchandise.

3. The yard manager is responsible for inventory, both to replenish stocked items and to decide what items should be added to or deleted from inventory within limits specified by headquarters.

4. The yard manager has major responsibility for bad debts, although for large accounts he is expected to ask headquarters for a credit check.

5. An aggressive yard manager will generate new business by calling on prospective customers.

6. The yard manager has considerable discretion in advertising, although the artwork and much of the copy of space advertising is prepared at headquarters. Catalogs and direct-mail pieces are also prepared at headquarters.

7. The yard manager is responsible for expense control.

8. The district manager is generally responsible for the yards in his district.

9. The district office also helps profitability by the services it renders to large customers. Orders from these customers are shipped from the yard nearest to the job.

10. Sales volume varies with construction activity in the territory served by the yard.

Most of the yard managers had only a high school education; in the opinion of the controller, they understood very little of the relationship between their performance and the profitability of their yards. It was the controller's view that a concentrated management training program for managers, supplemented by a bonus plan, would make them conscious of the necessity of increasing profits through better management and would furnish them the incentive to put better practices into effect.

When the committee reported back to the president, it was their consensus that the controller should devise a bonus plan along the lines outlined above. Shortly thereafter, the controller submitted the following proposed bonus plan:

GENERAL STATEMENT OF PLAN

This bonus plan is designed to provide company managers with an opportunity to earn additional compensation for improved performance as reflected by an increased return on the company's investment at the yards under their management.

DEFINITION OF TERMS

A. *Investment* at each location will include the annual average of the following:

1. Month-end cash balances.
2. Month-end inventory, at cost, excluding central stocks placed at a given location by the purchasing department.
3. Month-end accounts receivables associated with bonusable sales.
4. Investment in automobiles and trucks assigned to the location, at depreciated cost.
5. Investment in equipment, furniture, and fixtures assigned to the location at depreciated cost.
6. Land and buildings at depreciated cost assigned to the location (if property is rented, the rent will show up as an expense).

B. *Bonusable sales* are all shipments made from the location except sales orders written by district or headquarters sales personnel. These orders will be coded as written and deducted from the gross sales of the yard.

C. *Expenses* include:

1. Cost of goods sold on bonusable sales.
2. Operating expenses of the yard, including rental and depreciation.
3. Actual cost of services provided by district offices to the yard and to customers of the yard. (If the customer cannot be identified with a specific yard, these costs will be included in district office cost.)
4. Actual cost of credit investigations and collection efforts for the benefit of the yard.
5. Advertising material, catalogs, and other material supplied to the yard at actual cost.

   Note: Costs of district advertising (space and TV) for items not carried in a given yard will not be charged to that yard.
6. Pro rata share of office expenses for purchasing. This will be determined on the basis of the yard's receipts into inventory as a proportion of total company receipts into inventory.
7. Pro rata share of district office and headquarters expenses not charged directly to a yard. This will be determined on the basis of each yard's gross sales as a proportion of total company sales.
8. The following operating losses will be charged to the yard when the district manager determineds that these are the responsibility of the yard manager:
   a. Inventory shortages.
   b. Cost of repairing damaged property.
   c. Loss on sale of fixed assets.
   d. Bad debt losses.

D. *Bonusable profit* is bonusable sales minus expenses.

E. *Return on investment* is bonusable profit divided by investment in total assets.

CALCULATION OF THE BONUS

A. The total bonus pool will be $90,000 plus 5 percent of the corporation's income in excess of $2 million before income taxes.

B. The total bonus pool will be divided as follows:

Yard managers	65%
District managers	15
Senior management	20

C. The yard managers' bonus pool will be divided among yard managers on the basis of the number of bonus units that they earn. The manager of a yard whose return on investment is 5 percent will earn one bonus unit. For each full percentage point above 5, the manager will earn an additional bonus unit, up to a maximum of six bonus units. The monetary value of one bonus unit is found by dividing the total dollar amount in the yard managers' pool by the total number of bonus units earned by all yard managers.

D. The bonus units awarded by any yard manager who has been in that position for less than one year will be decided by his district manager, applying the above principle as closely as is feasible.

E. The district managers' bonus pool will be divided among district managers in relation to the total bonus units earned by the yards in their district as a proportion of the total bonus units earned by all yards.

F. The headquarters' bonus pool will be divided as decided by the president.

G. Bonuses will be paid in cash as soon after the end of the year as they can be calculated.

Mr. Pullen looked over the plan quickly and observed that it was drawn to include only managers. He said, "You can bet your bottom dollar that the district salesmen aren't going to be happy when they hear about a bonus plan for yard managers. What does the sales manager have to say about the proposed plan?"

The sales manager explained that the committee recognized the role of the district sales and sales service personnel but that there was no practical way of measuring their contribution to profitability because actual sales werre booked through the yards that made delivery.

The controller also explained the rationale behind the recommended size of the bonus pool. The elimination of the annual bonus for the 53 managers in the plan would create $40,000 of available funds. In addition, the usual annual salary increase to these managers of about

$50,000 would not be given. Thus, at the current level of profits, a bonus of $90,000 would not affect costs. If the plan resulted in profits greater than $2,000,000 before taxes, the bonus would be correspondingly higher.

Questions

1. Evaluate the proposed bonus plan which Mr. Pullen is considering. Does your evaluation suggest any generalization for exercising management control through payment schemes?
2. How, if at all, would you modify the proposed plan?

CASE 13–2
R. J. Walters Company *(A)**

In April, Mr. James Walters, president of R. J. Walters Company, began his annual review of compensation to his key managers. The company, which was engaged in the spinning, selling, and retailing of industrial and consumer sewing thread and stitchcraft kits, had just completed another year of continued growth in sales and profits in both its domestic and overseas operations. (See Exhibit 1.)

EXHIBIT 1 Growth in Sales and Profits ($ million after tax)

Year ended	*Assets*	*Sales*	*Profits*
3/71	28.7	55.1	2.3
3/72	30.9	59.5	3.0
3/73	38.6	81.5	3.4

In undertaking the review, Mr. Walters recognized several related problems. Some of the senior executives were questioning the organizational structure (Exhibit 2) in support of which the compensation system had been developed. The questioning had come in the face of increasing competition at the low-price end and rising sales, distribution, and handling costs. Second, the company was growing rapidly, with lean general management at the top coming under increasingly severe strain. The time required to find and attract experienced senior managers from outside was long. Besides, the problems involved in assimilating such new talent had not been fully realized until the exit of a senior manager, who had recently been recruited from outside. The

* This case was prepared by M. S. Salter, Harvard Business School.

EXHIBIT 2 Partial Organizational Chart

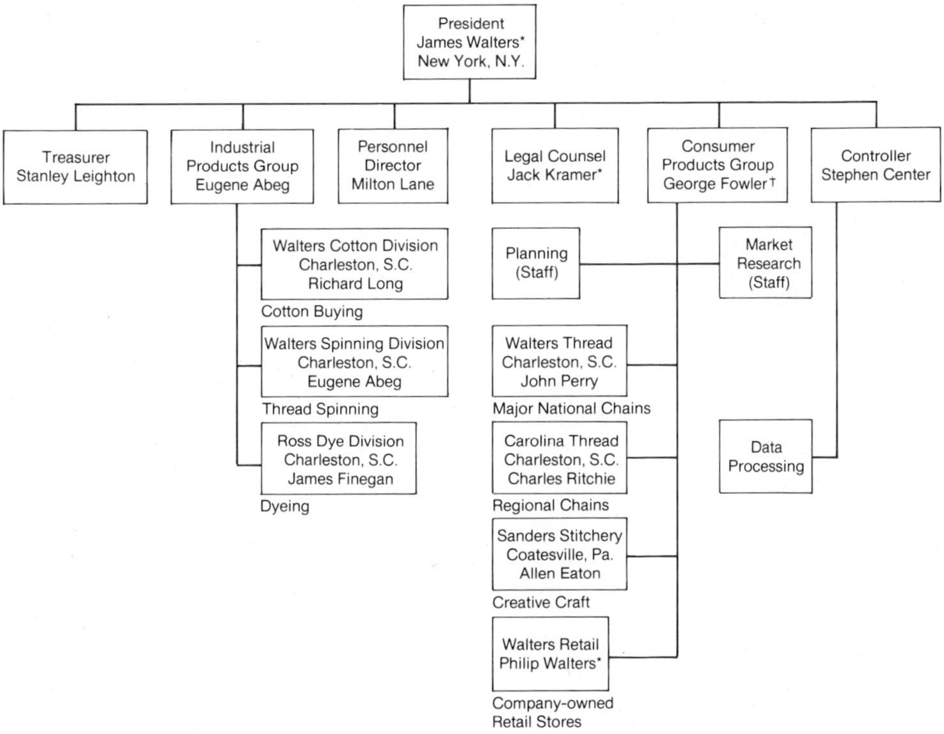

As of April:
* Family members.
† Vacant since the exit of Mr. Fowler.

scope for internal promotions was limited because of the long functional training and outlook of some of the present executives and the thinness of middle management. Mr. Walters wondered what changes were appropriate in the compensation system, in the instruments, such as bonus and stock options, and in the performance evaluation practices of the company.

EARLY HISTORY

The company was set up as a commission sales agency in 1911 by Mr. R. J. Walters, father of Mr. James Walters, and a salesman for a midwestern thread company. As the sales agency business grew, Mr. R. J. Walters set up his own office in New York. In 1918, he acquired a mill in Charleston, South Carolina, to cover the loss of a major account and to provide an assured source of thread supply. By 1929, the spinning unit had reached sizable proportions with sales of over $1 million. To meet the postwar scarcity of cotton, the company successfully introduced several blended threads. During the 1950s the company strengthened its manufacturing capacity, by adding new units in Coatesville, Pennsylvania. Its modern manufacturing facilities and the expertise in mixed threads, came in handy when Du Pont was looking for spinners of nylon staples; the company continually shared the growth in synthetic fibers. Aggressive in its sales policies, the company supplied home sewing thread with private labels, successfully exploiting a vacuum created by the reluctance of the leading thread manufacturers of the day to supply under a private label in competition with their own brands. In addition, the company changed its emphasis from thread for industrial customers to home sewing threads for final customers. Building on these opportunities, the company expanded geographically, with sales in the East Coast, Midwest, and West Coast. In recent years, the company had kept pace with new synthetic fibers, as also with the changing trends in leisure-time activities of consumers through its product development policies, in the sewing notions, and stitchcraft areas.

CURRENT STRATEGY

R. J. Walters Company was a sizable family-owned company with sales revenues of over $80 million and employing over 2,400 people in the United States. The company had expanded its overseas operations through a series of joint ventures in the Netherlands, Switzerland, Greece, and Belgium. During one decade, the company made several acquisitions. The most successful one was a conversion and thread sales business similar to the Charleston operations. The stitchcraft business acquisition was being turned around but had taken much longer than anticipated. The spinning, threads, and dye business acquired earlier had been integrated fully with the Charleston operations.

Within the United States, the company sold sewing thread and stitchcraft kits to several national and regional chains of department and discount stores. In addition, the company sold industrial thread directly to apparel manufacturers, and sewing products to the public through its own specialty retail outlets in several cities. The development of the stitchcraft kit business and the retail store business represented a recent step in a continuing effort to move away from a strictly industrial orientation and to participate in the growing leisure-time and sewing notion market.

Mr. James Walters commented on the future of the company as follows:

> I definitely want to maintain our current rate and direction of growth. We can only achieve those goals by being responsive to the changing needs of the consumer and the marketplace. To support this effort we need a structure and systems of management that will allow us both to retain our ability to make quick decisions at the business

level and to support the rapid growth planned for future years. In addition, I want to continue my disengagement from daily operating problems so that I will have more time to concentrate on systematic corporate planning and some of my outside activities.

ORGANIZATIONAL STRUCTURE

The company was formally organized along divisional lines. (See Exhibit 2.) The two major groups were the Industrial Products Group and the Consumer Products Group. The several units in the Industrial Products Group were operated as profit centers and sold the bulk of their output to the selling divisions in the Consumer Products Group. These units bought raw fiber from the market and processed it into a variety of threads. The Walters Cotton Division bought cotton from the market and processed it into a semimanufactured form which was sold to the Walters Spinning Division. The Walters Spinning Division bought synthetic staple from the market in addition to cotton and spun it into a variety of blended threads. The Ross Dye Division in the Industrial Products Group dyed the bulk staple or the spun threads.

The Walters Spinning Division also bought thread directly from the market and also sold certain varieties to the market. The managers of the divisions in the Industrual Products Group felt that this continuous exposure to the market helped them to maintain efficient operations. However, nearly 80 percent of their sales were to the divisions in the Consumer Products Group. The two major divisions in the Consumer Products Group, Walters Thread and Carolina Thread, bought nearly 95 percent of their needs from the Industrial Product Group. These two divisions converted, packaged, and sold thread to major national and regional chains of department and discount stores. The Sanders Stitchery Division in the Consumer Products Group designed and marketed sewing notions and creative stitchcraft kits through all chains in addition to selling its own brand of sewing thread. The Walters Retail Division operated specialty retail stores in various cities selling directly to the consumers, fabrics, home sewing thread, notions, and stitchery items.

Interdivision product transfers were priced at the division's most recent price to outside customers or at market prices. The Industrial Products Group kept a close touch with the market, selling surplus or buying requirements in periods of scarcity. The Consumer Products divisions were organized to serve specific customer groups. They had their own conversion and packaging equipment and other resources to enable them to respond to the customer needs promptly. Although the sales divisions bought their requirements almost entirely from the Industrial Products Group, they could buy from outside at a lower price after giving the selling division an opportunity to match the outside offer, and if provision for outside purchase had already been made in the corporate budget. Corporate staff handled differences on transfer prices.

There was close coordination between the two groups. The Industrial and Consumer Products Group managers reviewed and finalized the production plans of the spinning and dye divisions each month on the basis of a quarterly revolving forecast.

A key measure used in the evaluation of performance of divisions and profit centers was the percent return on assets used (ROAU). The asset base was defined as inventory, plus receivables, plus fixed assets before depreciation *less* accounts payable. The divisions were charged for the assets they used at 1 percent above the prime rate. Corporate staff services were not allocated to the divisions. They were charged based on their use. In determining the assets used, capital expenses on new projects were excluded during the "start-up" period.

Capital requests of the divisions were approved by the President James Walters; appropriation requests were prepared for investments above $5,000.

EXECUTIVE COMPENSATION

The compensation structure at Walters consisted primarily of salary, including a nondiscretionary Christmas bonus, and a performance bonus. The company also had a profit-sharing plan, which was basically a retirement income scheme. Not all executives were eligible for bonus. Eligibility was based on whether the executive could directly contribute to division or corporate profits. The number of executives eligible was 42, of which 11 were corporate staff members. Mr. James Walters reviewed the salaries and bonuses for all executives.

a. Salary and Christmas bonus. An attempt was made in these annual reviews to insure that the total compensation of an executive (assuming an average performance bonus), was comparable to the average for a comparable job in a similar-sized company in the industry. The industry averages used were those published by the American Management Association. The comparison of size was based on sales, number of employees, and particular indexes, such as the number of plants in the case of a production manager. (See Exhibit 3.)

The Christmas bonus was a lump-sum amount paid to every employee just before Christmas. Most of the executives received $1,000 as a Christmas bonus. Mr. Walters commented on the Christmas bonus as follows:

> The practice of giving a Christmas gift goes back to my father's days. A few years ago, I proposed doing away with the Christmas bonus by merging it with the base salary. There was so much protest against the proposal that we are still continuing the practice as before. It has probably no place in our wage structure given the present size,

EXHIBIT 3 Procedure for Annual Review of Salary and Total Compensation

1. Adjusting total compensation to industry averages:

	*AMA**	*Company example*	*AMA**
Division sales ($ million)	$7.2	$10.0	$15.5
Employees	297	310	481
Number of plants	2	1	3
Total compensation	23,600	$24,300	25,500

2. Determining base salary given total compensation and assuming "normal" bonus:

Base salary	$20,000
Christmas bonus	1,000
Salary + Christmas bonus	21,000
Normal bonus 16% of salary plus Christmas bonus (see Exhibit 5)	3,300
Total compensation. Should equal AMA adjusted for size as shown above, company example	24,300

If the base salary for this executive is $20,000 his total compensation, assuming normal hours, would be $24,300, which is equal to the AMA averages after adjusting for the magnitude of the job.

3. Add 5.5 percent (of $20,000), the average increase in salaries, to arrive at the base salary figure.

* From the 1971 annual survey of the American Management Association.

geographically dispersed operations, and the general climate of all our organizational practices.

b. ***Executive bonus awards.*** The individual bonus awards were based on an evaluation of each executive's performance. Considerable judgment was involved in the classification of overall rating of individual performance into Exceptional (A), Superior (B), Satisfactory (C), Good (D), and Adequate (E). The work sheet used for this purpose is shown in Exhibit 4, and gives an idea of the factors considered. Satisfactory performers were given a "normal bonus." The normal bonus percentage depended on the salary level ranging from 60 percent at the level of $100,000 basic salary per year to 10 percent at the salary level of $15,000. Exceptional performers were awarded 1.5 times the normal bonus, and adequate performers only half the normal bonus. The factor was 1.25 to "Superior" performers and 0.75 to "Good" performers. (See Exhibit 5.)

Mr. James Walters described his views on performance evaluation as follows:

> I think nobody has a good system. Although we have developed a fairly detailed plan, in practice, much of our evaluation centers around the divisional ROAU. If the divisional ROAU gets a "B" rating, all the managers in the division get a "B" for their individual performance.

EXHIBIT 4

Confidential Executive Work Sheet
(See Procedure Manual Section II, pp. 50 to 55)

		April 1973
Name	John Perry	Date
Position	Division Manager	Rating A to Zero
Division	Walters Thread	(See Section II, pp. 54–55)

	Last Year	This Year	Rating
I. Division Performance			
A. Profit:			
1. % ROAU	11.3	23.8	B–
2. Total $ Profit	889	1535	B–
3. % Change ROAU		111%	B–
4. $ Change Total $ Profit		73%	B–
B. Change in Market Share.			C
C. Qualitative factors that could involve future profits:			
1. Management			E
2. Markets			B/C
3. Product Line			B
4. Facilities			C
5. Quality			E
6. Miscellaneous			E
Overall Rating of Division Performance			B/C
II. Individual Performance			
A. Objectives for this just completed year:			
1. How did he see the problems and opportunities?			C
2. How challenging were the objectives set?			C
3. Were the objectives achieved?			C
B. Degree of supervision required.			D
C. Promotability.			E
Overall Rating of Individual Performance			C–

EXHIBIT 5 Guide for Determining Individual Bonus Awards

Base salary ($000)	*"Normal" percent bonus*
200	100
150	75
100	60
75	50
40	30
30	25
25	20
20	15
15	10

Individual performance		*Bonus factor*
A	Exceptional	$1.50 × normal bonus
B	Superior	1.25 × normal bonus
C	Completely satisfactory	1.00 × normal bonus
D	Good	0.75 × normal bonus
E	Adequate	0.50 × normal bonus

This may be alright in the case of divisional managers, and well-tailored to our strategy and structure, but at levels below the divisional managers the problem becomes extremely difficult. At these levels, and even at the division manager level, the argument for using objectives and to relate these objectives to individual bonuses is very strong. But there are qualitative and uncertain factors, such as product quality, unforeseen events, and genuine difficulties in judging the quality of the objectives set, which will render the implementation of objective-related bonuses highly subjective.

One of the attractions our structure provides is the opportunity for our executives to take risks and challenging objectives and the ability to take quick decisions in meeting those objectives. This, I would say, is a big plus for our present structure and performance evaluation system.

Our progress in implementing a system of Management by Objectives has been slow. Although I accept the principle of tying bonuses to objectives, I am not sure we have yet reached a stage where we can do so effectively. We may end up rewarding activities completed rather than those which directly contribute to profits.

The guideline followed by Mr. Walters on the total amount of bonus available for distribution was 8 percent of before-tax domestic profits after allowing for 7 percent return on beginning equity. Although this guideline on the total available bonus fund existed, greater reliance was placed in practice on individual bonuses rather than looking at the problem as one of allocation. Very often the aggregate of individual bonuses came close to the total available fund, but no attempt was made to match it. Exhibit 6 provides a partial list of bonus awards for

EXHIBIT 6 A Partial List of Bonus Awards

Person and position	*Age*	*Item*	*Year A*	*Year B*	*Factors in performance evaluation*
Mr. Charles Ritchie, division manager, Carolina Thread	33	Salary*	$28,000	$33,000	Division selling specialties to a segment of market. Small division. Met its objectives. Division performance rated A because of percent ROAU. The quality of objectives set was, however, considered satisfactory but not excellent enough or challenging. Although overall individual performance considered satisfactory, bonus for Year B is 1.5 times the normal or is an exceptional bonus.
		Extra bonus	10,000	12,500	
		Total	38,000	45,500	
Mr. Philip Walters, division manager, Walters Retail	57	Salary*	$40,000	$50,000†	Division performance considered E, or adequate. The division is in a developmental stage but, even excluding development cost, the operating results were not satisfactory. However, after discussion with division manager, a rating of "D" was agreed upon in view of target fulfillment. Mr. Philip Walters is a stockholder and also supervises the corporate traffic functions.
		Extra bonus	20,000	25,000	
		Total	60,000	75,000	
Mr. Richard Long, division manager, Walters Cotton	55	Salary*	$33,000	$33,000	With company for over 20 years. Specialized job requiring judgment. However, market conditions, beyond control of manager, affect division performance. "A" bonus because of excellent division performance.
		Extra bonus	10,000	13,200	
		Total	43,000	46,200	
Mr. Eugene Abeg, division manager, Industrial Products Group	45	Salary*	$35,000	$42,000‡	Capital intensive business. Long-range decisions affect performance, cyclicality and over- and under-capacity affect division performance. Continuously good personal record. Loyal to company. President rated "B" for individual and division performance.
		Extra bonus	7,000	16,700	
		Total	42,000	58,700	
Mr. John Perry, division manager, Walters Thread	50	Salary*	$44,000	$44,000	With company for over 16 years. Good salesman. Does not pay adequate attention to production, inventory or finance. But has good business sense and entrepreneurial outlook. Performance rated "C" by president. Division performance rated "B". Bonus for Year B is based on the "B" rating.
		Extra bonus	8,500	16,800	
		Total	52,500	60,800	
Mr. Edward Myers, sales manager, Walters Spinning	55	Salary*	$32,000	$35,000	With company for 20 years. Concerned with product development and materials pricing in addition to sales. The profit center was rated "C." For Year B, the division manager recommended "A." President compromised on a rating of "B."
		Extra bonus	10,000	11,000	
		Total	42,000	46,000	
Mr. Allen Eaton, sales manager Sanders Stitchery	40	Salary*	$26,000	$30,000	Division turned around from a poor level of performance to low level of performance, which was still considered inadequate. Division Manager recommended a "B" bonus. President, who had favored no bonus, compromised on an "E" bonus.
		Extra bonus	—	2,700	
		Total	26,000	32,700	

* Including Christmas bonus of $1,000. † Salary increased from December 1. ‡ Salary increased from January 1.

1971–72 and 1972–73 to some executives and the factors involved in their performance evaluation.

Mr. Stephen Center, corporate controller, commented on the compensation system as follows:

> There is no compensation problem as such. There is no formula but there is a logic behind the bonuses. It is only in extreme cases when the bonus is zero or when the percent ROAU is very high that I can be clear about the process of determining bonuses. Inevitably there is a lot of judgment. But as we grow larger, I think we will have to follow the track of evaluating goal setting and relating goals to bonuses in advance.
>
> There is another area which needs attention. At the functional and staff levels below the divisional manager there is a good deal of dissatisfaction about the process of evaluation—an area which is very difficult at best.

The division managers had a wide range of views on the compensation system from complete approval to serious doubts about it.

One of the division managers raised several questions. His evaluation of the system was as follows:

> The compensation system is closely related to our structure and our goals. Unless we are clear on goals, and design a structure to achieve those goals, we cannot be sure how good our compensation system is.
>
> The present structure and the profit and growth targets push us in certain directions. I am not sure whether those directions and the attendant risks are what the executive group and the stockholders want.
>
> Given the nature of our operations the compensation system poses several problems. With the high volume of interdivisional transactions, the divisional percent ROAU is more an accounting result than a measure of the excellence of the managerial job. There is a tendency to argue that the price being charged by the Industrial Products Group is too high. A considerable amount of executive time and effort is wasted in arriving at a price.
>
> Another problem relates to who should be eligible for executive bonus. Because of differences in both size and the nature of operations between divisions, a job may become eligible for executive bonus in one division but not in another. Further, I do not see why we cannot allocate to each division a sum of money, based on the size and performance of the division, for distribution as bonus to divisional executives.

THE REVIEW PROCESS

There were no formal performance review sessions in the company. Mr. James Walters discussed the bonus awards with the corporate staff and the divisional managers individually. However, these discussions were informal and had no format. The discussion depended on the nature of the relations between the president and the executive concerned.

Mr. John Perry, division manager, Walters Thread Division, described his meeting with Mr. Walters as follows:

> Our meetings are candid and forthright. This year I was a bit unhappy about my salary. Jim argued that it was higher than the AMA average, and, therefore, decided to continue with the same salary for another year. This actually means a cut in my salary given the increasing cost of living.
>
> My division spent a lot of effort last year in product development. The results of this product development were not evident last year because of the scarce supply conditions. But in conditions of poor demand and excess capacity in the industry, these efforts will pay off. I am not clear how this activity has been evaluated.
>
> Ours is a family company. We have our differences, but fortunately, they do not prevent us from cooperating in a friendly way. My division has grown in these 16 years severalfold. My compensation has kept pace and I am happy. I prefer staying with the division rather than work as a corporate staff member.

The divisional managers recommended to the president bonus awards to their executives. There were several instances of differences of opinion on the ratings on individual performance between the president and the divisional managers. One of the division managers described these meetings as follows:

> Sometimes, we have promises to fulfill. These are bonus promises if agreed-upon targets are achieved. Because of the heavy weight given to the divisional performance rating in determining individual bonus awards, it is difficult to fulfill these promises when divisional performance rating is very different from that promised to the individual. Such cases come to the fore at these meetings. We usually compromise. In some cases the compromise is on the individual's rating. In others, the salary is adjusted upward after a review of the responsibilities and the degree of applicability of AMA averages; the total compensation to the individual executive is not allowed to go too far out of line from reasonable expectations of the divisional manager or the executive concerned.

Meetings of the divisional managers with their executives to review the bonus awards also were personal and informal. However, there was much less leeway in such meetings for immediate changes in salary or bonus awards for that year. The degree of secrecy or openness about the bonus recommendations or actual awards differed from division to division, depending upon the management style and personality of the division manager.

Mr. James Walters commented on the review process as follows:

This is the last year that I will personally award bonuses to all the key executives. From next year on I want my divisional managers to *evaluate their executives* and award bonuses. In transferring a major part of the bonus responsibility, I want to ensure that the process retains several qualitative and judgmental aspects.

I want to ensure that the system does not become mechanical. Formula methods, although they appear objective, have severe problems. For example, 1966 was a bad year for us domestically. We gave no bonus to any of our employees. Yet our managers worked harder during that year than in the previous one when we gave a bonus. That experience has highlighted the inadequacies of a formula approach. Another thing that should be avoided is what I call "economic windfalls," a situation where a manager gets rewarded on results that were fortuitous rather than results that he achieved through his own effort.

There is great pressure for an objective approach to performance evaluation which increases my reliance on year-end percent ROAU figures. Six years ago, we introduced a system of management by objectives. But we have made very little progress so far in implementing it widely or in making it a part of the way we operate.

OPERATIONS AT THE DIVISIONAL MANAGER LEVEL

The close coordination between the Industrial Products Group and the selling divisions was facilitated by the fact that the managers for the Industrial Products Group, for Walters Thread, the biggest sales division, and for Carolina Thread, a small but growing division, were all located in the same small town. They were in contact on a daily basis in coordinating their operations. Further, the division managers had been with the company from the days of Mr. R. J. Walters and acquired a perspective that went beyond their formal structural boundaries and compensation system. Their own personal growth along with that of the company made promotion and divisional size the bigger part of the incentive package.

Mr. Abeg, manager of the Industrial Products Group, commented as follows:

I have been with the company for 20 years. I am, in fact, shortly getting a 20-year service ring from the company.

I was a plant manager only 18 months ago. Now I am a division manager in charge of several plants and the operations of the entire Industrial Products Group. I do not make my decisions with an eye on what effect it will have on my divisional percent ROAU. I make the decisions from the point of view of the company, as a whole. I do not care if a decision reduces my percent ROAU by a few points as long as it is the right decision for the company.

Some time ago, for example, we developed a cotton/polyester core thread with imported, low-priced staples. We had a product better than

> what one of our sales divisions was buying from outside. Our price was lower too because we picked up some savings in dyeing and other operations. Based on the projections of John Perry [Walters Thread manager] I built up a lot of inventory, nearly $500,000 worth. Recently, John has been revising his estimates downwards because he does not see much of a market for the product. However, we have borne the bulk of the inventory burden. In a seasonal and competitive market such as ours we will be missing out on opportunities if we fail to build inventory for fear that it may affect the divisional percent ROAU. As R. J. Walters Company, we have to take certain risks irrespective of how it affects divisional performance. Without such risk-taking we would not have had the Slitter thread, one of our outstanding successes, a product on which we are sometimes unable to meet the demand.
>
> Jim [James Walters, president] believes that the divisional structure is a big plus, bringing out the entrepreneur in us, so that if each division took care of its percent ROAU, corporate performance will take care of itself. But I am not so sure.
>
> Our volume is much larger now than it was when the divisional structure was introduced. While sensitivity to customer and faster decision making are great, when the volume is big the risks are high. Our distribution and handling costs are increasing. There is considerable additional handling and transportation cost because of the present structure. We buy in North Carolina, dye in South Carolina, ship it to Pennsylvania for conversion, packaging and dispatch to the customer.
>
> The problems of coordination are many. And the organization lacks a chief operating officer; Jim is a strategist and is busy with overseas operations, relations with bankers, etc. He does not have the time to get involved in operational details.
>
> Mr. George Fowler, manager of the Consumer Products Group, was hired recently from a large, professional organization. Located in New York, he was acting as a chief operating officer in planning and coordination. However, the company has had great difficulty in fully absorbing him as a member. There were several personality conflicts because of which he had to leave the company's services. This has left a vacuum as far as operational leadership is concerned.

Mr. John Perry, division manager and sales manager for Walters Thread, who had been with the company for over 16 years, was considered an excellent salesman by the other executives. He commented as follows:

> The divisionalized structure was introduced in 1966 after we had a couple of cool years. I think it has worked well for us so far because of increasing demand. But now I look at it with some reservation. The divisionalized structure is pushing us toward the high-price end of the market. Each division—the Spinning Division, the Dye Division, the Conversion, Packaging and Sales Division—wants a markup. The result has been that we are squeezing ourselves out of the low-price

end. According to a recent consumer survey, the low-price end of the market has increased its share in a growth year from 27 percent in the first quarter of 1972 to 40 percent in the first quarter of 1973. Those who are operating in the low-price end on low margins will in time be big competitors for us, especially in buyers' market conditions, over the whole product line.

The structure is a hindrance at this point. The flexibility to react to the business conditions does not exist because I just cannot compete at the low-price end, a market that is substantial and growing. I wonder whether we can afford to ignore that market for long without endangering our potential competitive strength. Besides, we possess the advantages to compete in the low-price end of the market being a vertically integrated company.

Mr. Charles Ritchie, division manager of Carolina Thread, had joined the company soon after school. He was the recipient of a R. J. Walters Company scholarship before becoming divisional manager. He commented as follows:

Ours is a small division. We have been meeting our targets very well for the last several years. I have not worked with any company other than the Walters Company. And I have been with the company for 18 years. I like the divisional structure because it gives me autonomy and the ability to make quick decisions. I do not know what I will be in a functional, centralized structure. I wonder if I would work for such a company. No doubt there are problems with the divisional structure, such as duplication of sales effort and transfer pricing. But while they need to be overcome, their costs are minor compared to the benefits from the divisional structure, through increased motivation and opportunity.

Mr. Philip Walters, brother of Mr. James Walters and manager of the Walters Retail Division, commented as follows:

Our operations at the Walters Retail Division are different from those of the other divisions. Ours is a developmental situation. We operate off a budget and we do not expect to be in the black for another three years. For purposes of performance evaluation, the divisional ROAU for my division is calculated after excluding the pre-opening expenses.

I think the main problem with executive compensation is one of communication. We need to get an agreement between the top management and the divisional management on the qualitative factors. Given our structure and operations, I think it is better to award bonuses to divisional managers based on corporate performance and to the executives below them based on division performance.

Top management is shortsighted in judging performance solely based on the bottom line. We have had cases this year where my evaluation of my managers had to be compromised because the president's evaluation of the divisional performance got the higher weight.

> This creates serious problems at my level because I am trying to motivate these people to meet their targets. Besides, this puts me in a very bad situation.

Mr. David Scott, a member of the family, and recently transferred to the corporate staff, commented as follows:

> If we compare our executive strength with other firms of similar size in the industry, we find that we have far fewer managers. Further, many of our managers have risen through functional expertise in production or sales. They are busy and do not have enough time to train general managers from the ranks. This makes operations on a divisional basis very difficult. It also raises some questions as to the proper executive staffing, training, and compensation.

CONSULTANTS' EVALUATION OF EXECUTIVE COMPENSATION POLICIES

Mr. Walters hired a well-known firm of consultants to evaluate the company's compensation structure and come up with recommendations.

The consultants made a survey of companies in the industry and gathered available published material. They found that the salary structure of Walters was comparable to industry for most of the benchmark positions that they evaluated. The short-term annual incentive compensation, or the percentage bonuses, were found to be about a third higher than industry levels. However, the lack of longer-term incentives, such as stock options, resulted in a total compensation level that was about 10 percent below that in industry.

The consultants recommended maintaining the incentive compensation about one third higher than industry levels in view of the nature of the company's operations and its family ownership. The longer-term income, such as that through stock or phantom-stock options, could be kept below industry levels to an equivalent extent. The main argument for this compensation policy was that, in privately owned companies, most of the longer-term decisions were made by the top executive. Second, given the nature of Walters' operations, second- and third-level managers contributed substantially to the company's profits through short-term operational decisions.

Based on the company's percent ROAU objectives, the consultants recommended determining the total bonus fund by a formula depicted in Exhibit 7. The logic of this formula was the following:

> A normal bonus for all eligible executives required a sum of \$320,000. This is what is shown as the target bonus and is related to earning the goal of 20 percent ROAU. Around this level the bonus fund varies sharply at the rate of \$35,000 for every percent ROAU, between 15 percent ROAU and 30 percent ROAU.

EXHIBIT 7 Bonus Fund Formula

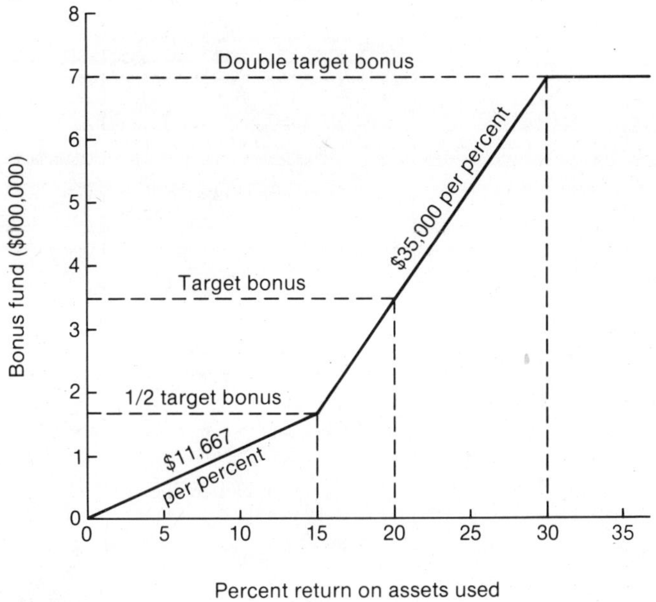

When the ROAU is 10 percent or less, the formula provides a bonus fund at the rate of $11,667 for each percentage point. This modest bonus fund is to retain the ability to reward exceptional invididual performance even when the corporate performance is considered below normal.

The consultants proposed determining individual bonus awards based on a composite of individual, divisional and corporate performance as follows:

$$\text{Individual actual bonus} = \text{Individual target bonus} \times \frac{\text{Corporate actual bonus fund}^{2}}{\text{Corporate target bonus fund}^{3}}$$

$$\times \frac{\text{Division actual percent ROAU}}{\text{Division target percent ROAU}} \times \frac{\text{Individual actual performance}}{\text{Individual target performance}}$$

The working of this formula is illustrated in Exhibit 8. The consultants also recommended the evaluation of individual performance against predetermined goals. In addition, their proposed system called for establishing different percent ROAU goals for different divisions and an overall corporate percent ROAU target.

[2] Based on Exhibit 7, actual percent ROAU, and target percent ROAU.

[3] Ibid.

EXHIBIT 8 Year-end Bonus Calculations ($000)

Division	*Employee*	*Salary grade*	*Salary midpoint*	*Target bonus*	*Company performance factor**	*First adjustment bonus*	*Division performance factor†*	*Second adjustment bonus*	*Individual performance factor‡*	*Final bonus*
A	D	29	$36.0	$10.7	1.14	$12.2	1.2	$14.6	1.2	$17
	E	26	27.0	6.7	1.14	7.6	1.2	9.1	1.0	9
	F	23	20.4	4.2	1.14	4.8	1.2	5.8	0.8	4
B	G	29	36.0	10.7	1.14	12.2	1.0	12.2	1.0	
	H	26	27.0	6.7	1.14	7.6	1.0	7.6	0.8	
	I	23	20.4	4.2	1.14	4.8	1.0	4.8	1.2	
C	J	29	36.0	10.7	1.14	12.2	0.8	9.8	0.8	
	K	26	27.0	6.7	1.14	7.6	0.8	6.1	1.2	
	L	23	20.4	4.2	1.14	4.8	0.8	3.8	1.0	

* Assured ROAU achieved = 16; actual bonus fund; $400,000; target fund, 350,000; factor 400/350 = 1.14.
† Assumed 120 percent, 100 percent, 80 percent for Divisions A, B, and C, respectively.
‡ Assumed division managers (employees D, G, J) received same rating as the division.

CASE 13–3
R. J. Walters Company (*B*)*

In April 1973, Mr. James Walters, president of R. J. Walters Company, had to evaluate a recommendation to introduce a Phantom-Stock Appreciation Plan for his key executives. A New York firm of consultants had just completed a study of the company's Executive Compensation System and had recommended the introduction of a Phantom-Stock Appreciation Plan. Mr. Walters wondered how he might present the benefits of the plan to the board of directors.

The R. J. Walters Company *(A)* (Case 13–2) describes the organizational structure, performance evaluation, executive compensation system, and the internal operations of the company. The present *(B)* case outlines the objectives of the proposed Phantom-Stock Appreciation Plan and the organizational context in which it was to operate. The company was engaged in the manufacture, selling, and retailing of a variety of industrial and home sewing threads, notions, and stitchery kits.

BRIEF BACKGROUND

The company was set up as a commission sales agency in 1911 by Mr. R. J. Walters, father of Mr. James Walters, who was a thread salesman. Through the years, the company had expanded its operations by acquiring a mill, by introducing new blends, and by following aggressive sales policies. During the late 1960s, the company acquired three companies—in the thread manufacture, dyeing, and stitchery businesses.

In spite of the heavy finances required for this growth, the family had retained firm control of the ownership. A family trust controlled 71 percent. Mr. James Walters and the company's legal counsel, Mr. Jack Kramer, were the trustees. Just over 20 percent was held by Mr. Bruce F. Failing, Jr., who had inherited the stock from his father. The rest of the stock was owned by various members of another family. Some of the shareholders wanted to sell their stock for cash.

CURRENT OPERATIONS

In fiscal 1973, R. J. Walters Company had domestic U.S. sales of over $80 million and employed over 2,400 people. It had two manufacturing units in Charleston, South Carolina, one in Coatesville, Pennsylvania, and a modern spinning mill was being set up in South Carolina.

EXHIBIT 1 Partial Organizational Chart

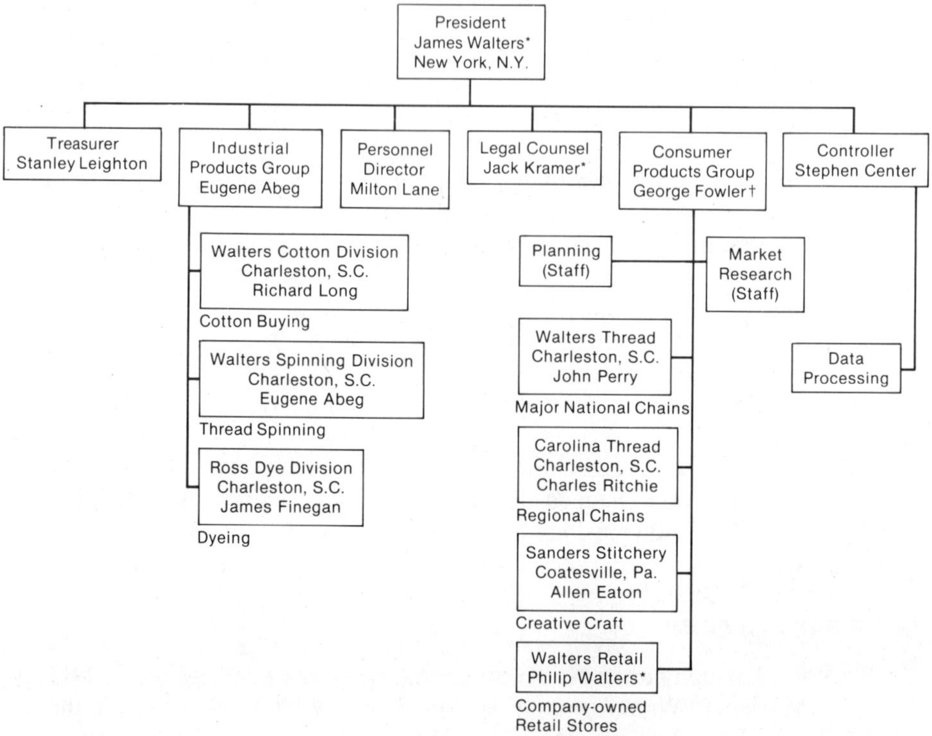

As of April 1973:
* Family members.
† Vacant since the exit of Mr. Fowler.

The company was organized along divisional lines (Exhibit 1). The sales divisions specialized in serving specific groups, although differences between divisions as regards the types of customers they served had lately diminished. The Industrial Products Group sold most of its output to the sales divisions in the Consumer Products Group, who had their own conversion, packing, and labeling equipment. The Industrial Products Group kept in close touch with the thread market, selling certain varieties and buying substantial quantities during periods of high demand. The major sales divisions bought nearly 95 percent of their thread needs from the Industrial Products Group. Within the Industrial Products Group, the output was transferred 100 percent from the Walters Cotton Division, to the Walters Spinning Division and then on to the Ross Dye Division. Interdivision transfers were negotiated around market prices.

In addition to the domestic operations, the company had joint ventures in several countries in Europe and South America.

CORPORATE STRATEGY

Mr. James Walters described his strategy as follows:

> In recent years, we have achieved sales and earnings growth rate of over 20 percent. Although the market conditions were very favorable, we pursued our interests by maintaining quality and sensitivity to customer needs and deadlines. My strategy is to build on the company's ability to move quickly in the market, through successful product development and concentrating on the growth segments. My target is to continue the growth rate of 20 percent in earnings per share.

EXECUTIVE COMPENSATION

a. Salary and bonus determination. Executive compensation consisted mainly of salary and bonus. Recently, 42 executives were eligible for bonus awards, including 11 corporate staff members. Eligibility for bonus awards was based on the ability to contribute to profits.

The total compensation (salary plus a normal bonus) of an executive was evaluated each year so as to make it comparable to the average paid for a similar job in a similar-sized company in industry. This was accomplished by using published American Management Association (AMA) average figures. Although the AMA averages presented some problems of comparability, gross dissatisfaction with salary levels was rare. Once the total compensation was determined, the salary level was obtained after deducting an amount of bonus applicable to normal or satisfactory performance. Normal bonus percentages increased with base salary from 10 percent at a base salary of $15,000 a year to 60 percent at a base salary of $100,000.

A key measure in determining individual bonuses was the divisional (or corporate) percent return on assets used (percent ROAU). The percent ROAU was the contribution to profits divided by the total of inventory, accounts receivable, fixed assets (before depreciation), and excluding accounts payable. The divisions were charged for the assets they used at 1 percent above the prime rate. Staff services were allocated in proportion to use. Interdivisional accounts receivable were included in percent ROAU calculations.

The evaluation of individual performance depended heavily on percent ROAU of division for division executives and that of the company for corporate staff. Mr. James Walters evaluated the division and corporate performance taking into account the percent change in ROAU from previous year, the absolute level of percent ROAU, and the absolute dollar profit figure. Although evaluation of individual performance included such factors as change in market share and the qualitative factors affecting profit potential, the division or corporate performance rating was a dominant factor for determining executive bonuses. A division rating of "B" usually implied a "B" for all division executives. The ratings were: A (Exceptional, 1½ times normal bonus), B (Superior, 1¼ times normal bonus), C (Satisfactory, normal bonus), D (Good, ¾ times normal bonus), and E (Adequate, half the normal bonus).

b. Compensation policies. A New York consulting firm had recently studied the executive compensation system at R. J. Walters Company. They made a comparison of the company's compensation data with the levels in competing companies obtained through proxy statements, surveys, and published material. They found that salary levels at Walters were about comparable to those in industry. Short-term incentive compensation, or bonus, was about one third higher than industry. But in the absence of longer term incomes, such as those from stock options, total compensation at R. J. Walters Company was about 10 percent lower than in industry.

The consultants observed the following:

> The business at R. J. Walters Company is one where short-term operational decisions of second- and third-level managers have relatively greater impact on the success of the enterprise than any long-term strategic decisions that they might make.

The consultants, therefore, recommended a strategy of maintaining the one-third higher percentage bonuses in order to be able to motivate executives to achieve short-term results. Inasmuch as the longer-term decisions were made mostly by the top executive, usually also the major stockholder in family-owned companies, they thought the extent of emphasis on stock options could be correspondingly reduced. Hence, they recommended a Phantom Stock Appreciation Plan with projected incomes from appreciation about 25 percent less than the average longer-term income levels for executives in other firms in the industry.

THE PROPOSED PHANTOM STOCK APPRECIATION PLAN

Eligibility for the Phantom Stock Appreciation Plan was restricted to 19 executives, in relation to 42 who were eligible for bonuses. The eligibility for the plan was based on organization level and salary grade. Among those eligible were 7 corporate staff members, including the president, and 12 divisional executives. Included among the divisional executives were three sales managers, three plant managers, one purchase manager, and five division managers. The projected annual phantom stock plan income to participants ranged from $3,500 to $36,000, amounting to a total of $140,000.

The value of the phantom shares to be awarded was determined to be about equal to the annual incentive bonuses. To the extent that the

EXHIBIT 2 Stock Incentive Plan—Example for Salary Grade 28

Year	Salary grade	Salary midpoint	A Strategic incentive compensation*	B Projected stock price	C (C = A ÷ B) Phantom shares awarded	D Increase in stock price	E (E = C × D) Increase in value of phantom shares	F (F = E ÷ B) Shares of common stock awarded	Value at end of eight years
1972	28	$32,700	$9,200	$13.50	681				
1973				16.20					
1974				19.20					
1975				22.60					
1976				26.80					
1977				31.60		$18.10	$12,326	390	
1978				35.60					
1979				40.00					
1980				45.00					$17,550
					Earned income		12,326		
					Capital gain		5,224		
					Total value		17,550		

* Compensation other than salary and bonus, usually stock-related longer-term income.

bonus scheme was related to individual performance, the Phantom Stock Appreciation Plan was, too. Each year the account of each eligible executive was to be credited with phantom shares equal to his actual short-term incentive bonus for the year divided by the price of R. J. Walters Company common stock, valued at 15 times that year's earnings per share (EPS) (Exhibit 2). The executive would be eligible to receive only the actual appreciation in the value of these phantom shares at the end of five years, the price of a share being 15 times the EPS for that year. At his choice, the executive could receive up to 50 percent of this appreciation in cash and the rest in common stock of R. J. Walters Company. After the first five years, there would be five active plans and the executive would receive each year the appreciation, if any, on the phantom stock awarded to him five years earlier (Exhibit 3).

The phantom stock plan was designed to provide approximately the same net income (after taxes) to the executive as under a conventional stock option plan; the benefits from the stock option plan were set at about 25 percent below the industry average long-term income levels. Exhibit 4 shows the working of a typical stock option plan for the salary level of $33,000 a year, assuming that the executive exercised the option at the end of five years and sold the stock at the end of eight years. Exhibit 5 shows the tax comparison between stock options and the Phantom Stock Appreciation Plan. The net income after tax under the Phantom Stock Appreciation Plan is about 8 percent more than in the conventional stock option plan. This difference was considered within the range of error of the projected stock prices.

The consultants suggested valuing the Walters Company common stock at a P/E multiple of 15. They recommended a multiple less than what Mr. Walters expected for a public offering in order to associate some gain to executives when the company went public and to motivate them to maintain a higher P/E multiple than 15.

ADVANTAGES OF PHANTOM STOCK OVER QUALIFIED STOCK OPTIONS

The Phantom Stock Appreciation Plan had many advantages from the point of view of the executives. In contrast to stock option plans, which qualified for preference tax under the IRS Code, the executive bore less risk especially in a privately held company, such as the R. J. Walters Company, with an unlisted stock. No investment was required to be made by the executive. He would possess the stock immediately, rather than wait for five years to exercise his stock option. The rewards were keyed to the objective gains in earnings per share, rather than to unpredictable market fluctuations.

The tax treatment of the two plans was different. Stock appreciation paid to the executive was treated as a compensation expense for

EXHIBIT 3 Effect of Multiple Phantom Stock Grants—Example for Salary Grade 28

	Shares of stock awarded from plan number										
Year	*1*	*2*	*3*	*4*	*5*	*6*	*7*	*8*	*Cumulative shares awarded*	*Projected stock price*	*Cumulative share value*
1										$16.20	
2										19.20	
3										22.60	
4										26.80	
5	390								390	31.60	$ 12,324
6		330							720	35.60	25,632
7			281						1,001	40.00	40,040
8				242					1,243	45.00	55,935
9					201				1,444	50.00	72,200
10						175			1,619	57.00	92,283
11							163		1,782	64.00	114,048
12								154	1,936	72.00	139,392

Note: An executive who leaves the company during Year 9 forfeits the shares within the dotted lines—a total of 693 shares worth $49,900 in Year 12.

EXHIBIT 4 Typical Stock Option Plan—Example for Salary Grade 28

			A	B	C (C = price in 1977 − price in 1972)	D (D = A ÷ C)		
Year	*Salary grade*	*Salary midpoint*	*Proposed strategic long-term income**	*Projected stock price*	*Projected spread*	*Estiamted shares granted*	*Value at exercise*	*Value at end of 8 years*
1	28	$32,700	$5,900†	$13.50	$18.19	326		
2				16.20				
3				19.20				
4				22.60				
5				26.80				
6				31.60			$10,300	
7				35.60				
8				40.00				
9				45.00				$14,700

* Compensation other than salary and bonus, usually stock-related long-term income.

† This amount ($5,900) is 18 percent of $32,700. The industry average long-term income was 25 percent at this salary level. Under the proposed strategy, this percentage was reduced to 18 percent for R. J. Walters Company.

Company contribution	$ 5,900
Executive contribution	4,400
Appreciation	4,400
Value at 8 years	14,700
Capital gain	10,300

EXHIBIT 5 Tax Comparison between Stock Incentive Plan and Stock Options

Salary grade 28	*Stock options*	*Stock incentive plan*
Salary midpoint	$32,700	$32,700
Bonus	9,200	9,200
Other earned income		12,326
Capital gain	10,300	5,224
Total income	52,200	59,450
Total taxes	10,900	14,979
Net income after tax	41,300	44,471
Difference = $3,174 = 7.7%		

corporate tax purposes, while the individual executive paid taxes at earned income rates. Under qualified stock options, no allowance was given for corporate tax purposes if the executive held the stock for at least three years after exercise. But the executive paid only capital gains taxes if and when he sold them (provided he held the stock for the statutory period of three years after exercise).

FACTORS INFLUENCING THE DECISION OF THE PHANTOM STOCK APPRECIATION PLAN

Mr. James Walters pondered on the factors influencing his decision as follows:

> The need for some form of stock options became evident, recently, when we were in the market for a senior executive. At the time we recruited Mr. George Fowler, manager, Consumer Products Group, we found that we had fewer compensation instruments than companies from whom we were trying to attract executives. Mr. Fowler was a senior executive in a large industrial firm and sought options from us. Mr. Fowler has since left the company because of severe personality conflicts between him and the continuing executive group.
>
> I now wonder what role a stock-oriented, long-term incentive plan has in our company. Several large firms, particulary the big conglomerates, have recently evinced interest in our industry and two have actually acquired smaller firms. If we have to compete with them in attracting new talent or in retaining existing talent we may find the Phantom Stock Appreciation Plan of some use. However, there may be better alternatives than a Phantom Stock Appreciation Plan for this purpose. Besides, the response from my key executives to the Plan is by no means overwhelmingly favorable.
>
> One of the difficult problems is how are we going to price the stock? Right now, several good stocks, such as Chrysler, have a low P/E. We are planning to go public and we probably will not do so unless we get a P/E of about 20. The consultants have recommended a P/E of 15. If we

> go public at a P/E of 20 soon, our executives will have windfall benefits unrelated to their contribution to increasing the market value of the company.
>
> I am, therefore, considering several alternatives, such as a deferred long-term incentive plan payable in cash rather than in stock. In such a deferred plan, we could relate the amount to be paid to the executive to specific earnings per share targets, if necessary, on a cumulative EPS basis. Such a plan would have most of the advantages of the Phantom Stock Appreciation Plan, from a tax viewpoint. It would not require any investment by the executive. Further, a deferred plan would be economical, if investment returns on the funds retained with the company are taken into account. However, it would not bring as powerful a feeling of ownership and identity of interests between the stockholders and the executives as the Phantom Stock Appreciation Plan.
>
> By introducing the proposed Phantom Stock Appreciation Plan, we would be diluting the ownership by about 1 percent. By this I mean, that by 1978–79 the executives receiving stock options would own about 1 percent of the company if they opted for 100 percent of the appreciation to be awarded in stock. That dilution may be well worth its price if we can increase the total value of the company by a factor of two.

Mr. Jack Kramer, the company's legal counsel and a trustee of the family stockholding trust, commented on the Phantom Stock Appreciation Plan as follows:

> I think we will be deceiving the executives by giving them unlisted stock. It would be meaningless to them and of questionable incentive value unless there is a market for the stock they possess. What P/E multiple will the market give to our stock? One way to avoid this problem may be for the company to buy back the stock from the executives in case they leave the company, or in case of death, thus creating an internal market based on book values or on fixed P/E ratios. This would also avoid any dilution in ownership. Another alternative would be a straightforward deferred bonus scheme.
>
> When I see what has happened to some of the executives who exercised their stock options in large companies, such as Brunswick, I wonder what incentives stock option plans provide.

CASE 13–4
Empire Glass Company *(B)*

During the first 10 months of 1963, one of Empire Glass Company's Glass Products Division's plants performed slightly better than budget in all categories of cost and revenue. If the plant could maintain this performance to the end of the year, the plant management (all people have assistant foremen, as shown in Empire Glass Company *(A)*, Case 4–1) could expect to receive a bonus.

The expected bonus would be calculated as follows: For bettering the budgeted manufacturing efficiency rate and budgeted cost reductions, the plant supervisory staff could receive as much as 25 percent of their base salary. However, to qualify for this portion of the bonus the plant must make at least 90 percent of its budgeted profit. If the plant exceeds its budgeted profit, the plant management group will receive an additional bonus of up to 10 percent of their base salaries.

The plant's 1963 budgeted annual sales volume was 100 million units at an average price of 5 cents. The budgeted contribution was 35 percent of gross sales. Variable costs, which were 70 percent of total costs, consisted of 30 percent direct labor, 60 percent direct material, and 10 percent direct variable overhead. Budgeted fixed costs accounted for the remaining 30 percent of total costs. These fixed costs included $393,000 of programmed costs. In addition, the plant anticipated it would realize the following additional revenue during 1963: $150,000 from budgeted cost reductions and $50,000 from budgeted sales of seconds.

During the last two months of 1963, due to several unexpected and drastic snowstorms in October, the sales of glass bottles declined throughout the industry. Under these new conditions, on November 1 the plant manager estimated that actual 1963 sales would be 98 million units, rather than the original estimate of 100 million, and that the average price would decline slightly from 5 cents. Consequently, actual 1963 dollars sales volume was not expected to be 97 percent of the budgeted dollar sales volume.

Questions

1. Would this plant management be eligible for any bonus if, during the remainder of the year, the following conditions prevailed: the plant continued to operate at slightly better than the standard manufacturing costs; the budgeted fixed costs remained constant; the budgeted cost reductions and seconds sales were realized; the actual dollar sales were 97 percent of budgeted sales?
2. What organizational problems do you predict might arise at this plant during the last two months of 1963?
3. Would you recommend a different incentive bonus plan for plant managers and their staffs? What is the objective of your suggested plan?

PART FOUR

Special Management Control Situations

Although the management control process occurs in organizations of all types, in the preceding chapters we have tended to focus on the process as it occurs in industrial companies.

Chapter 14 describes certain control problems that are peculiar to multinational organizations, particularly the appropriate transfer pricing policy for international transactions and problems relating to fluctuations in monetary exchange rates.

Chapter 15 discusses the special problems of service organizations; that is, organizations that produce and sell services, rather than tangible goods. Two types of such organizations are discussed in some detail: (1) banks and similar financial institutions, and (2) professional organizations.

Chapter 16 discusses nonprofit organizations. The principal difference between these organizations and profit-oriented organizations arises from the absence of a profit measure. Profitability provides both an easily understood criterion for evaluating proposed programs and a good way of motivating and measuring performance. In nonprofit organizations, the task of finding suitable alternatives to the profit measure is difficult.

Chapter 17 discusses the control of projects. The management control of projects differs from the management control that focuses on responsibility centers in several important respects. The chapter discusses these and, also, the problems of management control in a matrix organization; that is, an organization in which persons have responsibilities both to a project and to a functional responsibility center.

CHAPTER 14

Multinational Companies

In this chapter we describe management control problems and practices in multinational organizations. Many of the aspects of controlling foreign operations are similar to those for controlling domestic operations, and these are discussed only briefly. There are, however, two problems that are unique to foreign operations, and most of this chapter is devoted to these problems. Although our discussion is stated in terms of a U.S. corporation and its foreign subsidiaries, the same general problems exist with respect to the parent company in any country and its foreign subsidiaries.

SIMILARITIES

In general, foreign operations may be organized as expense centers, revenue centers, profit centers, or investment centers, and the considerations that govern the choice of a particular type of responsibility center are in most respects similar to those for domestic operations. One important difference, however, is that even if a foreign operation is an expense center or a revenue center for control purposes, it is often a profit center for accounting purposes. Many foreign operations are legal entities, incorporated in the host country, and must therefore maintain a complete set of accounting records for legal and tax reasons.

Most U.S. companies maintain management control systems for foreign operations that are essentially the same a those they maintain for domestic operations. One study showed that 90 percent of large U.S. multinational corporations responding to a questionnaire used profit budgets in controlling foreign operations, and that virtually all of these companies (97 percent) used the same, or essentially the same, system for budgeting and reporting as was used for domestic divisions.[1]

[1] Edward C. Bursk; John Dearden; David Hawkins; and Victor Longstreet, *Financial Control of Multinational Operations* (New York: Financial Executive Research Foundation, 1971), pp. 22–24.

One difference in control practices was that return on investment was used as a measure of performance by only 29 percent of the companies, which is much less than the comparable percentage for domestic operations.[2]

In general, the same problems of early warning and evaluation are experienced in controlling foreign operations as were described in Chapter 12 for domestic operations. As might be expected, although the problems are similar, their solution tends to be more difficult because headquarters managers tend to be unfamiliar with the environment in various foreign countries.

There are differences in the culture of various countries, and the management control system in a given country must be adapted to these differences. That these differences exist is well known in a general way, and in recent years there have been some attempts to identify them. For example, Hofstede conducted attitude surveys of employees of a single multinational corporation that had subsidiaries in 40 countries.[3] He asked questions of middle-management employees in each subsidiary designed to show: *(a)* the percentage of subordinates who *perceived* that their superiors acted in an autocratic rather than a persuasive way, *(b)* the percentage of subordinates who *preferred* that their superiors act in an autocratic rather than a persuasive way, and *(c)* the extent to which employees were afraid to disagree with their superiors. From the answers he constructed a "power distance index," showing the perceived distance between employees and their superiors. As compared with the United States, France, Belgium, Japan, and Italy, most developing countries had a high power distance index. Other industrialized countries had about the same or lower index than the United States, with the lowest in Denmark, Israel, and Austria.

TRANSFER PRICING

Of all aspects of management control, transfer pricing represents the greatest difference between controlling domestic and foreign operations. In domestic operations, the criterion for the transfer price system is almost exclusively goal congruence; that is, the principal objective is to develop a transfer price system that insures that actions taken by the divisional manager will be consistent with the best overall interests of the company. Total company profits should change, as the result of any decision, in the same direction and often in the same

---

[2] Ibid., p. 25.

[3] Geert Hofstede, *Cultural Determinants of the Exercise of Power in a Hierarchy*, Working Paper 77–8 (Brussels: European Institute for Advanced Studies in Management, 1977).

amount as divisional profits change. In some instances, divisions may be allowed complete freedom in sourcing, and this may result in some products being produced outside of the company even though inside capacity exists. Freedom in sourcing may be permitted because top management believes that the short-run loss in profits will be more than offset by long-run gains resulting from the impact of competitive pressures on the selling division.

In foreign operations, however, considerations other than goal congruence are important in arriving at the transfer price. The most important of these are:

1. Effective income tax rates can differ considerably among foreign countries. A transfer price system that results in assigning profits to low-tax countries can reduce total income taxes.
2. Tariffs are often levied on the import value of a product. The lower the price, the lower will be the tariff.
3. A company may wish to accumulate its funds in one country rather than another. Transfer prices are a way of shifting funds into or out of a particular country. Profits can be affected by differing interest rates, changes in exchange rates, different degrees of inflation, and so forth.
4. Government regulations, both United States and foreign, affect the way in which the transfer price can be calculated.

Note that the first and second factors—income taxes and tariffs—tend to work in opposite directions. Although tariffs for goods shipped to a given country will be low if the transfer price is low, the profit recorded in that country—and hence the local income tax on the profit—will be correspondingly high. Thus, the net effect of these factors must be calculated in deciding on the appropriate transfer price. The results of this calculation may be modified by the effect of the third and fourth factors.

In addition to the transfer prices for goods sold by one profit center to another, profits and funds can also be affected by royalties and service charges made between profit centers and funds loaned by one company unit to another.

Legal Considerations

Almost all countries place some constraints on the flexibility of companies to set transfer prices for transactions with foreign subsidiaries. The reason is to prevent the multinational company from avoiding the host country's income taxes. Regulations for the United States are basically set forth in Section 482 of the Internal Revenue Code.

In general, Section 482 tries to ensure that financial transactions between the units of a "controlled taxpayer" (a company that can control transactions between domestic and foreign profit centers) are conducted as if the units were "uncontrolled taxpayers" (independent entities dealing with one another at arm's length). In the words of this regulation:

> The purpose of Sec. 482 is to place a controlled taxpayer on a tax parity with an uncontrolled taxpayer, by determining, according to the standard of an uncontrolled taxpayer, the true taxable income from property and business of a controlled taxpayer. . . . The standard to be applied in every case is that of an uncontrolled taxpayer dealing at arm's length with another uncontrolled taxpayer.

In case of a dispute, Section 482 permits the Internal Revenue Service to calculate what it believes to be the most appropriate transfer price, and the burden of proof is then on the company to show that this price is unreasonable. This is in contrast with most provisions of the Internal Revenue Code, which permits the company to select whatever permissible alternative it wishes, and places the burden of proof on the Internal Revenue Service to show that the company's method is wrong. The wording is as follows:

> In any case of two or more organizations, trades or businesses (whether or not incorporated, whether or not organized in the United States, and whether or not affiliated) owned or controlled directly or indirectly by the same interests, the Secretary or his delegate may distribute, apportion or allocate gross income, deduction, credits, or allowances between or among such organizations, trades or businesses, if he determines that such distribution, apportionment, or allocation is necessary in order to prevent evasion of taxes or clearly to reflect the income of any of such organizations, trades or businesses.

Section 482 regulations provide rules for determining an arm's length price on sales between members of the controlled group. Acceptable intercompany pricing methods, listed in descending order of priority, are as follows:

1. Comparable uncontrolled price method. An arm's length price will be ascertained from comparable sales where either or both the buyer and seller are not members of a controlled group. Comparability is based on the similarity of the controlled and uncontrolled sales with respect to the physical properties and factual circumstances underlying the transactions. An uncontrolled sale will be considered comparable if the differences are such that they can be reflected by an adjustment of the selling price (e.g., where the difference is accounted for by a variance in shipping terms). However, a sale will not be considered comparable if it represents an occasional or marginal transaction or is a sale at an unrealistically low price.

Circumstances which may affect the price include the quality of the product, terms of sale, market level, and geographical area in which the item is sold; but quantity discounts, promotional allowances, and special losses due to currency exchange and credit differentials are excluded.

Lower prices, and even sales at below full cost, are permitted in certain instances, such as during the penetration of a new market or maintaining an existing market in a particular area.

2. *Resale price method.* Where comparable sales are not available, the next preferred method is the resale price method. Under this method, the taxpayer works back from a predetermined price at which property purchased from an affiliate is resold in an uncontrolled sale. This "resale price" is reduced by an appropriate markup percentage based on uncontrolled sales by the same affiliate or by other resellers selling similar property in a comparable market. Markup percentages of competitors and industry averages are also helpful in this connection.

The Regulations require that this method be used (1) if there are no comparable uncontrolled sales, (2) the resales are made within a reasonable time before or after the intercompany purchase, (3) the reseller has not added significant value to the property by physically altering it, other than packaging, labeling, and so forth, or by the use or application of intangible property.

3. *Cost-plus method.* Under this method, the lowest priority of the three prescribed methods, the starting point for determining an arm's length price is the cost of producing the product, computed in accordance with sound accounting practices. To this is added an appropriate gross profit expressed as a percentage of cost and based on similar uncontrolled sales made by the seller or other sellers or, finally, an industry rate.

A schematic representation of these three methods appears as follows:

1. *Comparable uncontrolled price method:*

Transfer price = Price paid in comparable uncontrolled sales ± Adjustments.

In a controlled sale, the transaction is between members of a controlled group. In an uncontrolled sale, one of the parties is not a member of the controlled group.

2. *Resale price method:*

Transfer price = Applicable resale price − Appropriate markup ± Adjustments.

Applicable resale price is the price at which property purchased in a controlled sale is resold by the buyer in an uncontrolled sale.

Appropriate markup = Applicable resale price × Appropriate markup percent.

Appropriate markup percent = Percent of gross profit (expressed as a percent of sales) earned by the buyer (reseller) or by another party in an uncontrolled purchase and resale similar to controlled resale.

3. Cost-plus method:
Transfer price = Costs + Appropriate markup ± Adjustments.

Appropriate markup = Cost × Appropriate gross profit percent. *Appropriate gross markup percent* = Gross profit percent (expressed as a percent of cost) earned by seller or another party on uncontrolled sale similar to controlled sale.

In lieu of one of these three specified methods, the taxpayer is permitted to use another method if he or she can establish that, in view of all the circumstances, this other method is "clearly more appropriate."

Puerto Rico. Although not a foreign country, Puerto Rico makes income tax concessions to American companies that manufacture products there, and transfer price problems therefore arise for products shipped out of Puerto Rico that are similar to those involved in international companies. Companies can use either the rules set forth in Section 482, or those in Revenue Procedure 63–10, which shows alternative ways of arriving at the price for Puerto Rican transfers.

Implications of Section 482

From a management control point of view, there are two important implications of Section 482:

1. Although there are legal restrictions on a company's flexibility in transfer pricing, there is considerable latitude within these restrictions.
2. In some instances, the legal constraints may dictate the type of transfer prices that must be employed. Each of these is discussed below.

Latitude in Transfer Prices

In many multinational companies there is a difference between the transfer prices that management would use purely for control purposes and those legally allowable transfer prices that minimize the sum of the tax and tariff impacts.[4] Since a certain amount of subjectivity is in-

[4] Throughout this discussion, we assume that corporations are using transfer prices that comply with Section 482.

volved in applying Section 482 to many goods and services, there can be a considerable range in the permissible transfer price for a particular good or service. Management can minimize the sum of income taxes and tariffs by maintaining transfer prices as far as possible at the appropriate end of the range. For example, if a U.S. parent company sells a product to a subsidiary in a country with materially lower income taxes than the United States, profits can be shifted to the foreign subsidiary by keeping the transfer price as low as is legally allowable. This practice, however, may cause a problem in control because profits in the foreign subsidiary would be reported as being higher, and profits in the American profit center would be reported as being lower, than would be the case if the transaction took place between independent entities.

There are two extremes of policy in dealing with this problem. Some companies permit profit centers to deal with each other at arm's length and let the impact of taxes fall where it may. With this policy, there is no question about the legality of transfer prices because the subsidiaries are trying to do exactly what the regulations say they should do—deal at arm's length. Under this policy, foreign transfer pricing will be essentially the same as domestic transfer pricing; that is, the objective will be goal congruence. Consequently, the transfer price system supports the management control system. On the other hand, the policy could result in higher total tax costs.

At the other extreme, foreign transfer prices may be controlled almost entirely centrally with the purpose of attempting to minimize total corporate costs or maximizing dollar cash flow. For example:

> In Company 62, an executive explains that the objective is to get as much profit home as possible, so long as foreign subsidiaries' payments are deductible for local tax purposes. He prefers to repatriate funds as royalties rather than as dividends, because royalties are often deductible overseas and because they are classified by the United States as foreign source income—thereby raising the limitation on foreign tax credit. Actually, he feels, there is little basis for charging royalties overseas, because his company's intangibles have little value to the foreign subsidiaries until the subsidiaries themselves develop them.
>
> "The best way to bring money back varies with the situation," he explains. "Some countries allow royalties to be deducted, but are tough on service fees. Others are the other way around. Some have a progressive withholding rate. We call the payments whatever seems best under the circumstances."[5]

Such a policy has the advantages of possibly reducing total costs and in controlling cash flow. It can severely restrict the usefulness of the control system, however, because in some instances the transfer prices may bear little relationship to the prices that would prevail if the

[5] Michael G. Duerr, *Tax Allocation and International Business* (New York: The Conference Board, 1972), p. 32.

buying and selling units were independent. If this policy is followed, the question of what to do about the control system arises.

One possibility is to adjust profits for internal evaluation purposes so as to reflect competitive market prices. For example, the total differences between the prices actually charged and those that would have been in effect had taxation not been a consideration could be added to the selling subsidiary's revenue and the buying subsidiary's costs when profit budget reports are analyzed. This is a questionable practice, however, and few companies use it. If asked, a company would be required to disclose these adjustments to the Internal Revenue Service, and their existence of course would raise questions concerning the validity of the transfer prices being used for tax purposes.

Most companies that price to minimize taxes and tariffs use the same transfer prices for profit budget preparation and reporting as are used for accounting and tax purposes. The approved budget reflects any inequities arising from the transfer prices. For example, a subsidiary that sells for lower than normal prices might have a budgeted loss. If reports of performance show that the subsidiary loses less than budget, its performance is considered to be satisfactory. In short, the transfer prices are considered both in approving the budget and in analyzing results.

If profit budgets and reports reflect uneconomic transfer prices, care must be taken to be sure that profit center managers are making decisions that are in the best interests of the company. For example, suppose that subsidiary A purchases a line of products from subsidiary B at a price that gives B most of the profit. In these circumstances, Subsidiary A can improve its reported profit performance by not selling B's products aggressively and by concentrating its marketing effort on products that add to its reported profits. Such a practice could be contrary to the best interests of the company as a whole. If uneconomic transfer prices are used in budgeting, therefore, it is important to guard against such situations. It may be necessary to use other measures of performance than profitability or, at least, other measures *in addition* to profitability, such as sales volume or market share.

Legal Constraints on Transfer Pricing System

In some instances, legal constraints may require that a particular transfer pricing system be used, or that a preferred transfer system may not be used. For example, the two-step transfer price system described in Chapter 7 might be questioned by the tax authorities simply because it is not mentioned in Section 482 and is not widely known about.

Some constraints are caused by the nature of the product being transferred. For example;

> In the oil industry (the biggest single multinational organized industry) the posted price system limits transfer pricing, removes it from the control of the companies and indeed exploits it in favor of the exporting countries. With many other primary products, transfer pricing is either organized by the exporting country through state trade or similar regulation (e.g., Chilean and Peruvian copper exports) or severely limited by specific taxes (e.g., tonnage levies on output or exports).[6]

In other instances, the "full cost" approach implicit in Section 482 may limit a company's ability to transfer some products at less than full costs. For example;

> An executive of another large multinational firm suggests that the arm's length concept introduces an air of unreality to management decision making. He explains, "Internal accounting recognizes management objectives and intracompany negotiations, but the IRS accounting does not; and this is what causes much of the trouble with Section 482. For example, management may want to sell a new product without burdening it with parent company overheads. Incremental costing may make perfect sense from the marketing standpoint, but the IRS says the overhead must be allocated."[7]

If legal constraints require the use of transfer prices different from the ones that would be used for control purposes, a company is in the same position as the company that uses one set of transfer prices for taxation and another for control, except that such a company can safely adjust profit center revenues and costs for differences between the legal transfer price and the preferred transfer price in most cases. Since the company presumably would have no objection to using the preferred transfer price for legal purposes, no harm comes from, in effect, keeping two sets of books. A company contemplating such a system should consider the possibility that it might be required to use a different price in two different countries for the same type of transaction.

Domestic International Sales Corporations

In order to encourage U.S. companies to develop increased amounts of foreign trade, the Congress has authorized the use of Domestic International Sales Corporations (hereafter referred to as DISC). A DISC receives favorable tax treatment both with respect to the timing of tax payments and the total amount of taxes paid.

A DISC is a separate corporation that buys goods from a U.S.

---

[6] Malcolm Crawford, "Transfer Pricing in International Transactions," *Multinational Business*, September 1974, p. 1.

[7] Michael G. Duerr, *Tax Allocation and International Business* (New York: The Conference Board, 1972), p. 67.

corporation and sells such goods abroad. The physical handling of the goods can be identical to that used before the DISC was formed. The existence of the DISC simply changes the accounting. It is to the advantage of a parent company to charge the lowest price possible to the DISC, since the DISC's income tax rates are lower than those of the parent company. Consequently, the transfer price to the DISC is of interest both to management and the Internal Revenue Service.

The rules for transfer pricing between a DISC subsidiary and its parent company are as follows:

Regardless of the actual transfer price charged, the transfer price in intracompany sales to (but not by) a DISC is the transfer price that results in the *largest* amount of taxable income under three rules:

1. Taxable income based on the actual price but subject to Section 482 adjustment.
2. Four percent of qualified export receipts on resale plus 10 percent of export promotion expense.
3. Fifty percent of the combined taxable income of the DISC and the related supplier derived from the entire transaction plus 10 percent of the export promotion expense.

Under rules 2 and 3, income must *not* be allowed to the DISC to the extent that the allocation causes the supplier to realize a loss on the sale.

Minority Interests

The foregoing discussion has assumed that the intracompany transfers were between divisions or wholly owned subsidiaries. The problem becomes more difficult if minority interests are involved, for in these circumstances top management's flexibility in distributing profits between subsidiaries is severely restricted. In this event, it would seem almost mandatory that subsidiaries deal with each other at arm's length, to the extent possible.

There are no easy answers to the transfer price problem. The important point is that management must recognize the problem and consider what it should do. This is a top management policy decision, not one that can be delegated to the controller. Furthermore, such a decision cannot be made in the abstract. A realistic estimate of the costs to the company of ignoring taxes, tariffs, or cash flow will have to be made.

FOREIGN EXCHANGE TRANSLATION

A second problem, unique to foreign subsidiaries, occurs because foreign subsidiaries maintain their accounting records in the monetary unit of the foreign country where they are located. To consolidate the accounting results of foreign subsidiaries with the accounting results of the parent, subsidiary financial statements must be translated into dollars. This is a financial accounting problem. As long as activities of foreign subsidiaries are measured in terms only of local currency, exchange translation is not a problem in management control. Most United States companies, however, measure results in terms of dollars. Also, many foreign subsidiaries must translate the results of foreign transactions of their own (e.g., a French subsidiary dealing with a German company in marks). It is necessary, therefore, to understand the principles of exchange translation. This part of the chapter describes such principles.

Exchange Rates

An exchange rate is the relationship between two currencies. In the situation we will discuss, it is the relationship between the dollar and a foreign currency. For example, the exchange rates on June 16, 1983 for several types of foreign currency are shown in Exhibit 14–1.

EXHIBIT 14–1 Exchange Rates for Various Foreign Currencies on June 16, 1983

Country	*Monetary unit*	*Value of foreign monetary unit in U.S. dollars*	*Number of foreign monetary units equal to U.S. $1*
Argentina	peso	.1284	7.7905
Australia	dollar	.8770	1.1402
Brazil	cruzeiro	.0020	491.15
Britain	pound	1.5260	.6553
France	franc	.1304	7.6670
Japan	yen	.00416	289.85
Switzerland	franc	.4730	2.1140
West Germany	mark	.3920	2.5510

The schedule indicates that on this date a dollar was worth 2.1140 Swiss francs, 7.6670 French francs, 2.5510 West German marks, and so forth. This means that banks in foreign countries will accept U.S. dollars at these rates and, conversely, they will convert dollars into foreign currencies at these rates. Under the system currently in operation, the rate of exchange of the dollar with other currencies can vary significantly over the course of a year. Also, the magnitude of changes in rates can be different for different currencies. For example, during a given year, the value of the dollar could increase relative to the pound sterling and decrease relative to the West German mark. At one time the rate of exchange of the currencies of most developed countries was fixed within small limits because the value of each currency was based on a specific amount of gold. Consequently, significant changes in exchange rates were generally confined to third-world currencies and an occasional revaluation by one of the developed countries, for example, the British pound in 1967 and the French franc in 1969. At present currencies are not tied to gold. As a result, their values fluctuate with supply and demand. Also, speculative activities can affect exchange rates in somewhat the same way that stock prices fluctuate with buyer and seller expectations. This situation makes the conversion problem considerably more important to the manager now than has been true in the past.

Methods of Conversion

There are three principal methods for translating financial statements of foreign subsidiaries into the monetary unit of the parent company. These methods are described in this part of the chapter.

Temporal method. Under the temporal method, each item on the balance sheet that is expressed in terms of market value is translated at the exchange rate in effect on the balance sheet date. (This is called the "current rate.") Other items on the balance sheet are translated at historical rates. The historical rate is the rate of exchange that existed at the date the asset was acquired or the liability incurred. The temporal method translates all monetary assets and monetary liabilities at the current rate. (A monetary asset is cash or the right to receive a specific amount of cash, for example, accounts receivable. A monetary liability is the obligation to pay a specific amount of cash, for example, accounts payable, bank debt, or loans payable.) Fixed assets are translated at historical rates. Inventories are generally translated at historical rates, but occasionally may be translated at the current rate if they are valued on the local balance sheet at their market value. The income statement is translated at the average exchange rate in effect during the period, except for those items that are related to assets translated at historical rates, such as depreciation. These are translated at historical rates.

The rationale for the temporal method is that only monetary assets and liabilities, or those expressed in terms of current value, are exposed to gains or losses from currency fluctuations.[8] The value of

[8] The term *exposure* is used to designate that an asset or a liability is subject to a potential gain or loss when the balance sheet is translated into the home country currency. Assets and liabilities that are translated at current rates are exposed.

nonmonetary assets expressed in home country currency will not change as a result of foreign currency fluctuations. For example, if the value of a currency decreases, the fixed assets will be worth more in that currency and will have approximately the same value when expressed in home country currency.

The rationale for the temporal method probably comes from the United States experience during the two decades following World War II. The main currency fluctuations during that period were caused by the continual devaluation of certain third-world currencies. This devaluation was always accompanied by a high inflation. Thus, physical assets would maintain their value in terms of dollars while the value of monetary assets would be reduced continuously.

The temporal method was required in the United States under the Statement of Financial Accounting Standards (SFAS) No. 8 from 1976 until 1982.

The all-current method. Under the all-current method, all items on the balance sheet are translated at the rate in effect on the balance sheet date. The income statement also is usually translated at the current rate, with the result that all items on the subsidiary financial statements are translated at the same rate.

The rationale for the all-current method is that a company's exposure in a foreign subsidiary is equal to the amount that has been invested in that subsidiary. If the local currency of the foreign subsidiary is devalued, the income earned by that subsidiary would be smaller in terms of the home country currency and, thus, the investment would be worth less.

The all-current method is used almost exclusively in the United Kingdom and all countries that generally follow United Kingdom accounting practices. This includes most of the Commonwealth or former Commonwealth countries, excluding Canada.

The current-noncurrent method. Under the current-noncurrent method, all current assets and current liabilities are translated at current rates. All other assets and liabilities are translated at historical rates. (Note that, in the current-noncurrent method, the term *current* refers to current assets and current liabilities—*not* to the current exchange rate.)

The rationale for the current-noncurrent method is that only current assets and current liabilities are exposed. Noncurrent assets are not exposed because they represent real value, independent of the exchange rates. Noncurrent liabilities are not exposed because they will not have to be paid until some future time and, even then, may not be paid with home country currency.

The current-noncurrent method is used by most companies in Europe, except the United Kingdom and Ireland.

Comparison of Methods of Translation

The following is a comparison of the three methods just described.

	Temporal	*All current*	*Current noncurrent*
Cash	C	C	C
Accounts receivable	C	C	C
Inventories	H*	C	C
Investments	H*	C	H
Fixed assets	H	C	H
Accounts payable	C	C	C
Long-term debt	C	C	H

* Unless these items are shown at current market value.
C = Current rate.
H = Historical rate.

Translation gains and losses. From a management point of view, the overriding problem is that the exchange translation process creates a gain or a loss. For example, if the value of the local currency increases from one accounting period to the next, compared with the U.S. dollars, the assets that are translated at the current exchange rates will increase in value in terms of the home country currency. This results in an exchange gain. On the other hand, liabilities will also increase in terms of the home country currency, which create an exchange loss. If the exposed assets exceed the exposed liabilities, we say that the exposure is "long." This means that if the local currency increases in value relative to the home country currency, there will be a gain. This is somewhat similar to the same expression used in stock market trading. One is "long" if one owns stock in the expectation that it will increase in value. Conversely, if the exposed liabilities exceed the exposed assets, we say that the exposure is "short" because an exchange gain will be realized if the local currency decreases in value.

Effect of different methods of translation. Using the temporal method, the exposure can be either long or short. However, it will tend to be short by the amount of long-term debt, because the monetary assets (cash and receivables) will tend to offset the current liabilities. Thus, the exposure will usually be determined by the amount of local debt. On the other hand, the exposure using the all-current method will always be long and equal to the net worth of the foreign subsidiary. The exposure using the current-noncurrent method will also be long but by the amount of the net working capital. (These statements assume that the foreign subsidiary will always have a positive net worth and a positive net working capital.) The depreciation of the local currency will usually show an exchange gain if the temporal method is used, but will show a loss if either the all-current or the current-noncurrent method is used. An appreciation of the local currency will, of course, have the opposite effect. Furthermore, the treatment on the income statement tends to differ. In the United States, SFAS No. 8 required that *all* exchange gains or losses be reflected in the income statement in the period in which they were incurred. In Europe, it is usual to charge the gains or losses from balance sheet translation directly to retained earnings, thus avoiding the income statement.

The income statement. Translation gains or losses result from the translation of the balance sheet. If the rate of exchange of a foreign currency and the home country currency changes during a year, it will also affect net income, but not in terms of an exchange gain or loss. For example, if the local currency declines in value relative to the home country currency, the amount of profits expressed in terms of the home country currency will decrease accordingly. Thus, a reduction in consolidated profits could occur between two years solely as a result of changes in the rate of exchange. Changes in consolidated net income as the result of changes in the exchange rates may not be identified on the consolidated income statement. The consolidated income is increased or decreased as the case may be, but the change is not reflected as an exchange gain or loss. Unless the amount was disclosed in a footnote, therefore, one could be unaware of it.

SFAS No. 52—Foreign Currency Translation

The FASB published SFAS No. 8, *Accounting for Translation of Foreign Currency Transactions and Foreign Currency Financial Statements,* effective in 1976. This standard required that United States companies use the temporal method of translation and include translation gains or losses in income each quarter. SFAS No. 8 was a most controversial and a highly criticized accounting standard. The reason for the intense opposition was that it resulted in most United States multinational companies showing large translation losses, and these fluctuated widely from quarter to quarter. As explained earlier, the temporal method usually results in short exposure equal to the local borrowing. During the late 1970s and early 1980s, the dollar was generally falling. Foreign liabilities were thereby increased in dollar terms, and this resulted in a translation loss. Since losses were taken into income quarterly, even random fluctuations in the value of the dollar could create fluctuations in profits that might be misunderstood by the reader of financial statements. As a result of these problems, the FASB, after an extensive review, published SFAS No. 52 in late 1981, effective for fiscal year beginning December 15, 1982.

SFAS No. 52 made two basic changes in the methods of exchange translation. First, it required the use of the all-current method for translating the balance sheet. Second, conversion or translation losses were no longer included in income, but were reported separately and accumulated in a separate component of equity. These changes made foreign exchange translation in the United States similar to that used in the United Kingdom. The income statement is translated at the exchange rate in effect on the date when the income or expense items are recognized. The Financial Accounting Standards Board, however, allows the use of a weighted average exchange rate for the period, because the use of actual exchange rates might involve excessive record-keeping.

Appendix A provides an example of exchange translation under SFAS No. 52.

Management Considerations

Management must decide the extent to which the effects of exchange translation should affect the financial performance of the subsidiary manager. SFAS No. 52 eliminated the effect of balance sheet translation from the income statement, so this is no longer a matter of contention. However, the translation of the income statement *will* effect the profitability of a subsidiary to the extent that the actual exchange rate of the local currency differs from that used in preparing the budget.

Let us take the simplest example. Assume a United States corporation had a Swiss subsidiary that dealt entirely within Switzerland. Suppose that this subsidiary had an approved budgeted profit for 1984 of SF 10 million. The budget projected an exchange rate for the Swiss franc of $.60 so the budgeted profits in dollar terms was $6 million. During 1984, the Swiss subsidiary met its budget objective exactly. The exchange rate of the Swiss franc relative to the dollar fell, however, to $.45. Although the profit objective was met in Swiss francs, it was 25 percent below that objective in dollar terms, and the lower profit would be reported on the consolidated financial statements.

There are at least four ways of accounting for this situation:

1. Measure the financial performance of the subsidiary in Swiss francs.
2. Measure the financial performance in dollars but eliminate the exchange rate variance from the performance evaluation.
3. Measure performance in terms of dollars but adjust the dollar budget to the actual exchange rate experienced during the period.
4. Make no specific adjustment and, at least nominally, hold the subsidiary manager responsible for meeting dollar profit objectives.

Method 2 would seem to be the most satisfactory means of doing this. However, many United States companies use Method 4. Part of the reason for this could be that most of these control systems were developed in the 1950s and 60s when exchange rates were fixed. Another possible reason may be that many companies do not distinguish between the financial performance of the manager and the financial performance of the subsidiary. Still another reason may be that the company reports to its stockholders in dollars, and that is the monetary unit for which all managers are responsible.

Many foreign subsidiaries also deal with buyers or sellers in other foreign countries. These transactions generate exchange gains and losses. If the foreign transactions are controlled by the subsidiary manager, it is appropriate that gains and losses be reflected in the financial performance of the subsidiary.

Foreign subsidiaries of the same company frequently deal with each other, and the settlement of these transactions results in an exchange gain or loss. If the transactions are carried out at competitive price levels, the exchange gains or losses should also reflect competitive conditions. That is, gains or losses should be booked as if the parties were independent. These appear on the consolidated income statement.

See Bulova Watch Company (Case 14–5) for examples of some foreign exchange problems.

SUGGESTED ADDITIONAL READINGS

Battersby, Mark E. "Swapping Risk for Reward." *Financial Executive,* May 1975.

Coborn, David L., and **Ellis, Joseph R., III.** "Dilemmas in MNC Transfer Pricing." *Management Accounting,* November 1981.

Cowen, Scott S. "Multinational Transfer Pricing." *Management Accountant,* January 1979.

Granick, David. "International Differences in Executive Rewards Systems: Extent, Explanation, and Significance." *Columbia Journal of World Business,* Summer 1978.

Horovitz, Jacques H. "Management Control in France, Great Britain and Germany." *Columbia Journal of World Business,* Summer 1978.

Malmstrom, Duane. "Accommodating Exchange Fluctuations in Intercompany Pricing and Inventory." *Management Accounting,* September 1977.

Robbins, Sidney M., and **Stobaugh, Robert B.** "Some Financial Dilemmas of the Multinational Enterprise." From J. Fred Weston, ed., *Large Corporations in a Changing Society.* New York: New York University Press, 1974.

Tang, Roger Y. W.; Walter, C. K.; and **Raymond, Robert H.** "Transfer Pricing—Japanese vs. American Style." *Management Accountant,* January 1979.

APPENDIX A
Example of Exchange Translation

Assume that a United States corporation had a Swiss subsidiary with the following financial statements, expressed in Swiss francs (SF):

Beginning Balance Sheet

	December 31, 1983
Assets	SF 100,000
Liabilities	SF 60,000
Capital stock	20,000
Retained earnings	20,000
	SF 100,000

During 1984, the subsidiary had the following transactions:

(1) Borrowed SF 10,000 from a local bank. The journal entry was:

1984 Transactions

Assets	SF 10,000	
Liabilities		SF 10,000

(2) Earned SF 5,000 from operations:

Revenues	SF 15,000
Expenses	10,000
Profit	SF 5,000

The impact of (2) is to increase assets by SF 5,000 and retained earnings by SF 5,000.

Ending Balance Sheet

	December 31, 1984
Assets	SF 115,000
Liabilities	SF 70,000
Capital stock	20,000
Retained earnings	25,000
	SF 115,000

Assume that the Swiss franc was worth $.60 on December 31, 1983, and $.50 on December 31, 1984. The average value during 1984 was $.55.

Problem

Translate these following statements into dollars so the subsidiary results can be consolidated with the parent company's financial statement.

Beginning Balance Sheet

	December 31, 1983
Assets (SF 100,000 × .6)	$60,000
Liabilities (SF 60,000 × .6)	$36,000
Capital stock (SF 20,000 × .6)	12,000
Retained earnings (SF 20,000 × .6)	12,000
	$60,000

Income Statement

Revenues (SF 15,000 × .55)	$ 8,250
Expenses (SF 10,000 × .55)	5,500
Profits	$ 2,750

Ending Balance Sheet

December 31, 1984

Assets (SF 115,000 × .5)	$57,500
Liabilities (SF 70,000 × .5)	$35,000
Capital (SF 20,000 × .5)	10,000
Retained earnings (SF 25,000 × .5)	12,500
	$57,500

Reconciliation of Retained Earnings in Dollars

Beginning balance	$12,000
Profits	2,750
Indicated ending balance	14,750
Actual ending balance	12,500
Translation loss	$ 2,250

The United States corporation will include profits of $2,750 in its consolidated income statement and a reduction of $2,250 in a segregated part of retained earnings. This represents the financial effect of the fall in the Swiss franc; put another way, the rise in value of the dollar.

CASE 14–1
Macomber Corporation*

Macomber Corporation consisted of 10 U.S. operating divisions and several foreign subsidiaries. Each division was responsible for both manufacturing and marketing its product lines. There was some transfer of finished goods among divisions, but it was relatively minor. Each division and subsidiary was operated as a profit center. The firm's compensation plan was structured such that the incomes of key line managers were heavily influenced by the pretax incomes of their divisions.

In the early 1960s the Mendell Division, with the approval of corporate management, decided to open a plant in Puerto Rico. Within the firm, opinion was mixed as to the success of the venutre. While it appeared successful in terms of reported net income and return on investment, there were certain aspects of the Puerto Rican tax laws which some felt obscured the plant's true profitability.

PUERTO RICO

The citizens (individual and corporate) of the Commonwealth of Puerto Rico govern themselves and also enjoy the advantages of U.S. citizenship without bearing many of the costs. Puerto Ricans are protected by the U.S. Constitution, are serviced by the U.S. postal and judicial systems, and use U.S. currency. They are subject to the same tariff regulations (with certain minor exceptions) as are other U.S. citizens. Unlike other U.S. citizens, however, they are exempted from paying federal income taxes.

The Commonwealth itself does levy a tax on profits, ranging from 22 to 48 percent for corporations. However, as an incentive to new industry it exempts from this tax income earned in the first 10 years of operations. Such exemptions also apply to new or expanded divisions of firms previously doing business in Puerto Rico.

In 1949 the Commonwealth's gross national product was approximately \$750 million. Annual per capita income was \$256. There was virtually no industry. Average life expectancy was 46 years. The leaders of the island began a program, which they called "Operation Bootstrap," intended to bring an end to economic privation and to improve substantially the quality of life on the island. Due in large part to incentives provided by the government and a spirit of cooperation among government, labor, and industry, the GNP in 1974 was approximately \$6.5 billion and per capita income almost \$2,000. Average life

* This case was prepared by R. N. Anthony, Harvard Business School.

expectancy in 1974 exceeded 70 years, 90 percent of the population was literate, and the median education level of employed persons was 11 years.

The island has a well-developed infrastructure with good roads (over 6,500 miles of expressways and superhighways), port facilities, an airport (38 flights daily from the United States), and communication facilities comparable with those on the U.S. mainland.

Puerto Rican firms also received government assistance in the areas of site development, labor training, and debt financing. Sites were generally available throughout the island in currently developed industrial parks, portfront locations, and elsewhere. A government agency maintained an inventory of factory buildings adaptable to individual requirements for light or moderately heavy industry.

Unemployment on the island was generally around 15 percent. As a result, wage rates were relatively low. In 1974 the average hourly wage for a manufacturing worker was $2.43. In the U.S. mainland the average was $4.42, and in South Carolina, $3.45.

Currently, the government was attempting to reduce unemployment, and to this end was subsidizing vocational and technical schools and sharing the cost of various employment training programs. The educational and training programs, together with the conditions of the labor market and cultural values on the island, combined to provide an environment which many firms considered attractive: relatively high skill levels, high morale, low turnover, low absenteeism, and low wages.

The island was served by numerous commercial banks (including large New York banks) and several investment banking houses. New industry financing obtained through these sources was frequently supplemented by financing from the Government Development Bank. Furthermore, if a new firm located a facility in an economically undeveloped area, the government would provide financing for up to 90 percent of the firm's fixed assets and working capital with repayment schedules of up to 25 years.

TRUEDALE DIVISION PROPOSAL

After the normal delays in getting started, the Mendell Division plant began operating very efficiently in terms of cost, quality, and delivery. As a result, other divisions began to consider moving some operations to the island. In 1970 the Truedale Division did a feasibility study analyzing the possibility of manufacturing part of its Trudy product line, a branded consumer product, in Puerto Rico. Additional manufacturing facilities were required to accommodate the expanding sales volume of this line. Estimated income statements, based on a 10-year tax holiday, are shown in Exhibit 1.

EXHIBIT 1 Estimated Income Statement, Expansion of Trudy Product Line ($000)

	If manufactured in U.S.A.	*If manufactured in Puerto Rico*
Revenue	$1,190	$1,190
Cost of sales (all manufacturing and shipping costs)	880	720
Gross margin	310	470
Selling expense (USA)	130	130
Pretax income	180	340
Income tax*	86	86
Net income	$ 94	$ 254

* It was assumed that goods would be transferred from Puerto Rico to the United States at a price that approximated the American total manufacturing cost, and the U.S. income tax would be levied on net income as computed on the basis of this cost. Therefore, U.S. income tax would be approximately the same under either alternative.

Top management of the Macomber Corporation encouraged such moves if they actually were profitable. Questions arose about the effect of such actions on divisional profitability, however.

The first related to the fact that income generated in Puerto Rico became taxable if it were remitted to the United States within 10 years. The tax rate was the sum of the 48 percent U.S. rate plus a special 15 percent Puerto Rico rate. As a result of this restriction, Macomber Corporation already had sizable amounts of cash tied up in Puerto Rico, resulting from the operations of the Mendell Division. The corporation could make good use of this cash for expansion of U.S. operations and for acquisitions. In fact, it could not raise equity money (or use stock for acquisitions) because its price/earnings multiple was temporarily low, and it could not borrow without issuing a corresponding amount of equity. The financial vice president, therefore, believed that some cost should be assessed to the Trudy Division to discount Puerto Rico earnings at the present value of the cash when it was released 10 years hence. At an annual rate of 10 percent, this would mean that each dollar of Puerto Rico cash earnings in the first year would be given a value of 40 cents.

Offsetting this, in part, was the fact that Puerto Rican cash could be used to build and equip Puerto Rican plants. Thus, the Truedale Division argued that, if its earnings were discounted, the book value of plant and equipment should be discounted at the same rate, and annual depreciation would be correspondingly lower. Furthermore, Macomber liquid funds in Puerto Rico could be invested in local, well-secured loans at a return of approximately 6 percent. (These were short-term investments because the possibility existed that the political climate in

Puerto Rico might change unfavorably, and corporate management regarded long-term investments as unduly risky.)

The Truedale plant would be leased from the government development agency, and the division would install $300,000 worth of new equipment, which it would purchase using Macomber Corporation excess funds available in Puerto Rico. The manufacturing cost on Exhibit 1 included $30,000 depreciation on this equipment.

The working capital requirements for the Puerto Rican plant, consisting primarily of inventory, were expected to be approximately $200,000.

If the goods were manufactured in the United States, the plant would be leased, its equipment would cost $300,000, and working capital requirements would be about $200,000. (The lower cost content of inventory in Puerto Rico was offset by the necessity for carrying larger raw material inventory quantities because of delivery uncertainties.)

Finally, the Truedale Division suggested that divisional profitability should henceforth be measured on the basis of aftertax income so that the division would be given credit for the income tax saving it would produce for the corporation.

Questions

1. Should the additional goods for the Trudy product line be manufactured in the United States or in Puerto Rico?
2. Should the financial value of the Trudy line to Macomber be assessed in terms of pretax income, aftertax income, return on investment, or some other measure?
3. On what basis should the calculation of the Trudy Division manager's bonus be made?

CASE 14–2
Longwood Manufacturing, Inc.*

Wallace Burnham, chairman of the board of Longwood Manufacturing, Inc., opened the January 30, 1983, board meeting with the statement, "Gentlemen, Longwood now has its foreign subsidiaries—and it looks as if our problems are just beginning."

Longwood manufactured industrial equipment for the garment trades. It produced three models of sewing machines, but was primarily noted for its specialized machinery for buttonholes, blind stitching, and machine embroidery. Established in 1926, its growth had been

* This case was prepared by Mary M. Wehle, Harvard Business School.

steady until recently. Sales had stabilized in the $160 million range from 1967–72. Although the company had increased domestic sales in this period, the increase was offset by loss of overseas distribution. In 1971, Longwood management decided that maintaining foreign sales would require overseas manufacturing facilities, and instigated a search for acquisition candidates. By mid-1972 the search had been narrowed to two overseas manufacturers, Peluffo in Argentina and Halm in Switzerland. Both were small manufacturers with their own sales force. Halm was noted for its production of a binding machine for which Longwood was the U.S. distributor. Peluffo's market potential was considered outstanding, although this advantage was offset by the continual inflation in Argentina. Final arrangements to acquire the companies were completed in November 1972, and actual transfer to be effective January 1973.

Mr. Burnham continued his explanation to the board:

Now that we have purchased both Halm and Peluffo, we must decide how they are to be managed. Up to now, we have not had much of a formal control system, since we have only one plant here in Philadelphia, which is well managed by our president, Mr. Robinson. We have arranged to have the managers of the new subsidiaries continue to operate the plants, but Mr. Moore, our controller, has suggested that we send one of his men to each plant as controller. He thinks this will help get the financial information to us sooner. We just got the subsidiaries December 31 financial statements.

We have to decide what kinds of goals we want to set for the subsidiary managers. We've told them that we'll include them in our bonus plan just as soon as we can figure out some standards of reasonable performance. Right now, our bonus plan is based on meeting the ROI objective of 22 percent before tax. One of the questions is whether 22 percent would be appropriate, or whether we should set a separate figure for them.

A bigger question is whether we should set ROI in terms of their currency or U.S. dollars. What shows up in our financial statements is the dollars the subs have earned for us, not the marks or pesos. Mr. Moore tells me that if we want to set the goals in terms of dollars, we'll have to get into some accounting questions. We've never had this problem before; we've always just used our accounting figures to calculate the return on investment, even including the net book value of fixed assets. But there's more than one way to calculate the dollar equivalent of the subsidiary's investment; as a matter of fact, there are four different ways. Mr. Moore's staff has put together some summary figures for the subs showing the results under two of these methods. Also, there's another complication. The dollar was floated again this month, and the figures change because the exchange rate changed. So they've calculated the figures before and after the dollar float.

There's one other question I just didn't expect quite so soon. Peluffo wants to buy binding machines from Halm, but wants a 20 percent

EXHIBIT 1 Memorandum

TO: Board of Directors

FROM: Richard Moore, Controller

The following summary shows the effect of the recent exchange rate change and the different accounting methods on Halm and Peluffo. The accounting methods differ only in the exchange rate applied to the assets and liabilities.

Peluffo (000)

			After dollar float (5 pesos = $1)	
	Pesos	*Before dollar float (4 pesos = $1)*	*Current/ noncurrent*	*Current rate*
Current assets	720	$180	$144	$144
Fixed assets (net)	1,080	270	270	216
	1,800	$450	$414	360
Current liabilities	120	30	24	24
Long-term liabilities	240	60	60	48
Stockholders' equity	1,120	280	280	280
1972–73 earnings:				
Profit	320	80	80	80
Translation			(30)	(72)
	1,800	$450	$414	360

Halm (000)

			After dollar float (3 francs = $1)	
	Francs	*Before dollar float (4 francs = $1)*	*Current/ noncurrent*	*Net asset*
Current assets	720	$180	$240	$240
Fixed assets (net)	1,080	270	270	360
	1,800	$450	$510	$600
Current liabilities	900	$225	$300	$300
Long-term liabilities	360	90	90	120
Stockholders' equity	220	55	55	55
1972–1973 earnings:				
Profit	320	80	80	80
Translation (loss)			(15)	45
	1,800	$450	$510	$600

discount off the usual wholesale price to allow them to do some marketing. The Halm sales manager has refused, but since Argentina is in our license territory, has suggested that Longwood might care to make such a concession.

Here are Mr. Moore's figures on the subsidiaries.

Now, gentlemen, what are your thoughts?

CASE 14–3
Universal Data Corporation

The scene is a conference room in the head office in Geneva of Universal Data Corporation's European operations. The time is shortly after lunch on a winter day in 1982. Three men are finishing cups of coffee, which have been served by a secretary.

Seated at the head of the table is Clive Price, age 45, British by nationality and president of UDC–Europe. The other two are David Simmons, 39, Swiss, and vice president—finance; and Clinton Salter, 48, American and vice president in charge of sales. (Two other officers of UDC–Europe mentioned in the conversation that follows are William O'Shaughnessy, general manager of the British Isles subsidiary, and Christian van Rhijn, general manager of the Belgian subsidiary.) UDC—its operations and its management control system—is briefly described in the appendix.

Price: You chaps know why we're here. We've got problems related to pricing at our British and Belgian subsidiaries, and both of them require our immediate attention.

Simmons: I'm familiar with the Belgian matter, but not with the British one. What's wrong in England?

Salter: It's that recent shipment of U-64s to Amalgamated Metals, the one we invoiced directly from our Spanish plant as a means of getting around the British Price Commission.

Simmons: And a fine idea at that! Any time we can pick up an extra $200,000 by using Continental European prices, I shall support it. I wish we had thought of it earlier. What is the problem? Are the machines printing in Spanish?

Price: No. But apparently they're having service problems with them. Carlos Navarro, at our Spanish subsidiary, rang up yesterday. He says that the people at Amalgamated telephoned him to say it's been almost impossible to get anyone in England to service the machines.

Salter: The same old story.

Price: I rang up O'Shaughnessy right away. He admits that there's been a delay. However, he claims that his systems engineers have been tied up at

ICI on a new project. Besides, he said, if Carlos was so concerned, he could have sent one of his own men down. After all, the Spanish subsidiary got credit for the sale.

Simmons: I beg to differ, Clive. We charged a commission against Spain's recorded profit, and we showed the same amount of commission as an additional revenue item on Britain's monthly operations report.

Salter: Maybe O'Shaughnessy missed that line on the report. What's the story in Belgium?

Simmons: We received a telex from the controller of the Belgian subsidiary this morning. Here, I made a copy for each of you.

[He gives Price and Salter each a sheet of paper, which they read. The text of the telex follows.]

ATTN: D P SIMMONS

PAPERWORK ON FIRST SHIPMENT U82/15 ENROUTE FROM IRELAND RECEIVED TODAY. FIVE MACHINES ENROUTE TO BRUSSELS AT FOB $41,000 EACH.

WE DO NOT WANT TO CLEAR THESE MACHINES THROUGH CUSTOMS AS SHIPMENTS FROM FRANCE HAVE BEEN ARRIVING AT FOB $32,000 AND FROM USA AT FOB $35,200.

PLEASE INSTRUCT IRELAND TO ISSUE REVISED INVOICES AT FOB $32,000 EACH SO WE CAN CLEAR THIS SHIPMENT WITHOUT CREATING VERY DANGEROUS SITUATION WITH LOCAL CUSTOMS.

WE AWAIT URGENT REPLY TO REQUEST.

DAG ERICSSON
UDC-BRUSSELS

Simmons: You see, our Belgian controller is worried about the reaction of the customs authorities. He thinks they won't understand why the same model is arriving from three different sources at three different prices.

Price: Pardon me, David, but doesn't the real risk involve dumping? After all, seeing the same model come in at three prices may lead customs to conclude that some of the machines were dumped—particularly the American ones. If that happens, wouldn't we be slapped with higher duty charges on the American machines?

Simmons: I fear you're right, Clive. They might decide to put higher duty charges on all our American-made imports. With a duty on them of 8.4 percent, it would take little change in the assessed value of the goods to rack up a substantial tax bill. And it could get worse. We think that the Belgian officials trade data with their counterparts in other countries. Imagine the mess if all the Common Market countries began to investigate our transfer pricing.

Salter: Well, the answer to this one seems simple enough. Let's lower the incoming price to the French level. It's only a bookkeeping entry anyway.

Price: It's not that simple. The machines were diverted to Brussels at the

EXHIBIT 1 Profitability of British Sales (estimated per unit of Model U-64*)

General data		
Manufactured in	Spain	United Kingdom
Sold to customer in	United Kingdom	United Kingdom
Selling subsidiary	Spain	Britain
UDC-Europe		
Retail price	$62,000	$42,000
Cost of goods sold	23,000	24,500
Gross margin	39,000	17,500
All other expenses†	18,000	16,000
Profit before tax	21,000	1,500
Tax‡	1,520	780
Profit after tax	$19,480	$ 720
British subsidiary only		
Retail price or sales commission earned	$11,000	$42,000
Cost of goods sold	0	24,500
Gross margin	11,000	17,500
All other expenses	10,000	16,000
Profit before tax	1,000	1,500
Tax‡	520	780
Profit after tax	$ 480	$ 720
Spanish subsidiary only		
Retail price	$62,000	N.A.
Cost of goods sold	23,000	
Gross margin	39,000	
Sales commission paid	11,000	
All other expenses	8,000	
Profit before tax	20,000	
Tax‡	1,000	
Profit after tax	$19,000	

N.A. = Not available.

* Data are on a per-machine basis. Actual exchange rates and cost figures from most recent monthly operations reports are employed. The Amalgamated Metals order was for 10 machines.

† A combination of freight charges, duty charges, and differences in national cost structures accounts for the disparity between the two columns.

‡ Based on local tax rates. Funds are not expected to be repatriated to parent for many years. Spanish figures reflect a tax rate of 35 percent and the benefits of a 15 percent export incentive computed on the Spanish added value of goods exported from Spain.

request of the Belgian subsidiary. Christian van Rhijn agreed to take the machines, at $41,000 each, from the Irish plant.

Salter: I'm confused. Why would he do that?

Simmons: The story goes back several months now. During the spring, Clive received a telephone call from Christian demanding to know whether we actually planned to allow Galway to bill Belgium at an above-budget price for these extra machines. In addition, he complained about the 10 percent premium he had had to pay in order to get several extra machines from the United States.

EXHIBIT 2 Profitability of Belgian Sales (estimated per unit of Model U-82/15*)

General data		
Manufactured in	Ireland	Ireland
Sold to customer in	Belgium	Belgium
Selling Subsidiary	Belgium	Belgium
	High transfer price	*Low transfer price*
UDC-Europe		
Retail price	$60,000	$60,000
Cost of goods sold	27,000	27,000
Gross margin	33,000	33,000
All other expenses†	18,000	17,700
Profit before tax	15,000	15,300
Tax‡	2,400	6,900
Profit after tax	$12,600	$ 8,400
Belgian subsidiary only		
Retail price	$60,000	$60,000
Transfer price in	41,000	32,000
Gross margin	19,000	28,000
All other expenses†	14,000	13,700
Profit before tax	5,000	14,300
Tax‡	2,400	6,900
Profit after tax	$ 2,600	$ 7,400
Irish subsidiary only		
Transfer price out	$41,000	$32,000
Cost of goods sold	27,000	27,000
Gross margin	14,000	5,000
All other expenses	4,000	4,000
Profit before tax	10,000	1,000
Tax‡	0	0
Profit after tax	$10,000	$ 1,000

N.A. = not available.

* Data are on a per-machine basis. Actual exchange rates and cost figures from most recent monthly operations reports are employed. This shipment involves five machines. The agreement between the two subsidiaries covered a total of 40 machines.

† Differences in incoming duty payments account for the disparity between the two columns. The duty payments are based on the invoiced (transfer) price.

‡ Based on local tax rates.

Price: David and I explained to him that the high price resulted from three things—the increased demand for this model, higher than usual start-up costs in Galway, and the favorable tax deal we obtained from the Irish government. As you remember, we have a 16-year exemption from income tax on all export sales.

Simmons: Christian wasn't exactly enthralled with our explanation. He thought the Irish were taking advantage of the tight supply situation. He saw no reason why Belgium should absorb Galway's production inefficiencies. Moreover, he insisted that his reported results and his own annual bonus should not be affected by some quirk in the tax laws.

Price: So I rang up O'Shaughnessy and asked whether he could bring the price down. He mentioned the tax arrangement, saying it would be sheer folly to transfer any more profit to a high-tax area like Belgium. Then he reminded me that Belgium had no alternative source and Ireland could place the machines elsewhere. Besides, he said, the Brussels operation would still show a small profit on the transactions.

Simmons: I finally telexed Brussels that the final decision on price was up to them and O'Shaughnessy's group. I did note, however, that the Irish tax savings were substantial. They settled on the price of $41,000 each, f.o.b. Brussels.

Salter: You know, I'm not wild about *your* explanation either. It seems to me that this creative transfer pricing is bound to blow up in our faces. In fact, my eyebrows feel a little warm right now.

Price: Now now, Clint, tax minimization is part of the game. You know very well that the decision to locate in Galway was heavily influenced by its cash flow advantages.

Simmons: Clive's right, Clint. We all agreed to the Galway plant decision. Besides, we're in business to earn a profit for our shareholders. Contributing corporate cash to the British or Belgian government is not high on UDC's list of priorities.

Salter: Well, I'm still not convinced. Don't you think we ought to forget the fancy footwork and stick to what we know best—building and selling computers?

APPENDIX
Facts about UDC–Europe

The company, founded in 1972, is a U.S.-based manufacturer of minicomputers and peripheral hardware. It sells, leases, and services its equipment worldwide. Of its $800 million in revenues, the European operations contribute $185 million.

UDC–Europe, a wholly owned subsidiary, was founded in 1976. It is very profitable and enjoys a great deal of autonomy from the parent company. General managers of its 10 geographically organized subsidiaries are administrative umbrellas for two or more legal entities created to meet national legal and tax requirements. Four subsidiaries (the Spanish, the French, the British, and the Irish) have manufacturing as well as marketing operations.

UDC–Europe treats each subsidiary as a profit center for purposes of managerial control and evaluation. It sets annual budgets in terms of pretax profit and judges local managers largely on their ability to meet or beat the targeted figures. UDC–Europe prices intracompany transfers at levels determined at the annual budget meeting except under special circumstances, such as unexpectedly higher volume or a complex tax situation. In the former case, the subsidiary manager is expected to negotiate a price. In the latter case, management at Geneva may set the price.

CASE 14–4
Bulova Watch Company, Inc.*

"We don't have too many control problems with our domestic operations, but we certainly have some with our overseas operations." During a conversation in the summer of 1973, John Chiappe, vice president and controller, was describing Bulova's control system. "Let me show you an example of one type of problem we are up against." The controller started to jot down some figures. "These figures are purely hypothetical and I've simplified them to get my point across, but they are indicative of what actually happens." The paper he passed across the table showed the following:

France—Fiscal 1973 (000 francs)

	Budgeted	*Actual*
Sales	1,000	1,000
Cost of goods sold:		
Local costs	300	290
Imported goods	300	315
Gross profit	400	395
General and administration	300	300
Operating profit	100	95

The controller started to explain:

Assume that these figures were taken from the budgeted and actual income statements for our French marketing subsidiary. I've ignored taxes as that just complicates things further. Now, we treat our marketing subs as profit centers, and we evaluate them on a local currency basis. So we'll say that French management's profit center goal for the year was 100,000 francs. Now, picture something else. I'm sitting in Switzerland a couple of months ago with the manager of our French

* This case was prepared by F. T. Knickerbocker, Harvard Business School.

sub and the head of our Swiss manufacturing operations. What sort of thing goes on?

I note that France ended the year at 95 percent of its planned franc profit. Our French general manager acknowledges this, but says that it doesn't mean anything. He points out that when the budget was put together, the 100,000 francs profit was, let's see, worth about U.S. $19,900; now the 95,000 francs profit is worth about $20,900 or 5 percent over plan. He adds, giving me the needle, that notwithstanding all our talk about being an international company, we are really interested in earning dollars.

I agree but point out that the higher dollar figure was, from his standpoint, luck. During the year the dollar devalued against the franc, or the franc appreciated against the dollar, depending on how you want to look at it. He didn't bring about the exchange rate shift, however. Immediately he replies with his second line of argument. He points out that the French sub reached its sales target, cut its local cost of goods sold under the planned figure, and didn't overspend on its selling and administrative expenses. What hurt him, he adds, was the higher cost, in terms of French francs, of the movements he imported from our factories in Switzerland. During the year the Swiss franc appreciated against the French franc by almost 8 percent, with the result that—after the imported materials flowed through his local production process—this part of his cost of goods sold went up by 5 percent. If this exchange rate shift hadn't occurred, he says, he would have ended the year with a profit of 110,000 French francs. Actually, he says, he was helping out our Swiss manufacturing branch.

That brings the head of Swiss production into the act. He asks how did France help them out. At the beginning of the year France had told him they needed *X* number of movements, and these were worth about 230,000 Swiss francs. During the year the Swiss plants shipped him exactly *X* number of movements and billed him exactly 230,000 Swiss francs. So, how did France help him?

Our general manager in France, who's no slouch, has already thought that one through. He points out that the 230,000 Swiss francs were worth, at the beginning of the fiscal year, U.S. $59,600. At year end, they were worth $71,000, so companywide we were $11,500 better off thanks to his efforts.

Again, I say this was an accident. During the year the Swiss franc appreciated against the dollar, even more so than the French franc, but our Swiss plants couldn't take the credit for that.

About then, our French general manager throws up his hands in exasperation. Look, he says, you started off with this business about France ending the year with profits 5 percent under plan, when you know by looking at our income statement that we outperformed the budget in every respect. Then every time I try to explain the difference from budget, you say it was an accident. All I know is that I did what I said I was going to do and that somehow we are all better off than we expected. With all the shifting going on between the dollar and the French franc and the Swiss franc, the reports don't mean much anyway. Let's talk about next year.

The controller paused for a moment.

> Let's face it, I've been exaggerating and the episode I've just described never took place. However, it's typical of the sort of control problem we live with every day. And actually, when you get all the figures out, a lot more than in my simple example, matters can really get confused sometimes.
>
> Of course, when our subsidiaries put their annual budgets together, they try, with our assistance, to predict exchange rate shifts to alleviate problems like this, but you seldom hit the changes on the button. And, of course, we can and do isolate and break out for reporting purposes the effects of exchange rate shifts on our subsidiaries' inventories and cost of goods sold.
>
> Still we are trying to run the company on a profit center basis. If we constantly adjust figures or reassemble them, then commitment to profit goals becomes a joke after a while. Given the way goods in process move around within Bulova, there's no doubt that it is tough to push our operating managers for profit responsibility. Maybe there's a better way of doing things?

Bulova's controller went on to describe the highlights of the company's control system and some of the features of the company's operations that complicated the control process. His comments are summarized in the next few pages.

MANUFACTURING

Above all else, Bulova's control system had to take into account the rather unusual features of the company's manufacturing operations. In 1973, the company made its products in 21 plants, 12 located in the United States, 9 overseas. Though the number and size of the plants, compared to what was common in other industries, was not large, the degree to which output moved around the world and from one plant to the next was out of the ordinary. Exhibit 1 gives a rough picture of the product flows within the Bulova manufacturing system.

The description of manufacturing flows pinpointed one fact. Within Bulova, intercompany sales and/or purchases were frequent and important. The best example of this was the domestic company's reliance on overseas production. In the early 1970s, of all the watches sold by Bulova in the United States, about 85 percent contained movements imported from abroad. In some instances, from the time components were manufactured at a foreign site to the time finished watches were ready for sale in the United States, as many as five intercompany transactions took place.

Bulova's policy was to have all intercompany transfers billed at standard cost plus 10 percent. Exceptions to this policy were rare. Bulova operated on the basis of a standardized, world-wide cost accounting system. The standard costs for manufacturing subsidiaries

EXHIBIT 1 Manufacturing Flows within Bulova for Consumer Products*

Source	*Product*	*Destination*
Swiss plants (including that of Bulova's subsidiary, Universal Geneve).	Movements and finished watches.	Bulova's 8 and Universal Geneve's 7 foreign marketing subsidiaries.
	Finished watches.	Bulova's and Universal Geneve's third-party distributors.
	Finished watches.	Bulova's Hong Kong and Tokyo distribution centers.
	Components.	Bulova's Virgin Islands and American Samoa assembly plants.
Bulova's Virgin Island plant.	Assembled movements.	Bulova's Flushing, N.Y., plant.
Bulova's American Samoa plant.	Assembled movements.	Bulova's Flushing, N.Y., plant.
Bulova's joint-venture Taiwan plant.	Watch cases.	Bulova's Flushing, N.Y., plant; Toyo Corp., Japan; and third-party customers.
Bulova's joint-venture Japan plant.	Finished tuning fork, watches.	Bulova brand products: all world markets except the United States. Citizen brand products: Japan and other selected markets, especially the Middle East.
Citizen Watch Co., Japan (independent supplier to Bulova for 13 years).	Components, movements.	Bulova's Virgin Islands; Flushing, N.Y.; and Toronto, Canada, plants.
Bulova's Flushing, N.Y., plant.	Finished tuning fork, quartz, and conventional jeweled-lever watches.	Bulova's U.S. marketing subsidiaries; Bulova's overseas marketing subsidiaries: Accuquartz watches only.
	Tuning fork movement subassemblies.	Bulova's Swiss plants during start-up phases of production.
Bulova's two U.S. watch case plants.	Cases.	Bulova's Flushing, N.Y., and Swiss plants and its marketing subsidiary in Canada.

* This list ignores manufacturing flows within Bulova for industrial defense products. With very minor exceptions, all such products were made and sold in the United States. As of 1973, industrial defense production took place in eight plants. In five of the eight, Bulova also manufactured consumer products: watch movements, cases, clocks, etc.

were based on a full costing system with the standards set by the production engineering department with the assistance of the cost accounting department. Management did not regard intercompany pricing as an issue that was negotiable among subunits.

A second implication of Bulova's manufacturing flows was that the company was almost always moving products across national boundaries and hence across currencies.[1] With watches, for example, in

[1] A third implication, not discussed here, was that Bulova was almost always moving products across tariff barriers.

nearly 8 cases out of 10 all or a major part of the costs associated with their production were accumulated in one currency while the revenues associated with their sale were generated in a second currency. Only four operations within Bulova did not involve a currency shift between costs and revenues, but three of the four were not, as of the early 1970s, of great importance to the firm: (1) Bulova made and sold a few watches within Switzerland, (2) it made watches in Switzerland for export, billed in Swiss francs, to third-party distributors, and (3) its joint venture made and sold watches in Japan. Of course, these three operations eventually involved a second type of cross-currency transaction when profits, upon remittance to the parent company, were converted into U.S. dollars. The one important watch activity within Bulova that did not involve cross-currency transactions was the manufacture and sale of watches in the United States. This activity generated about 25 percent of Bulova's total *domestic* consumer business by fiscal 1973.

Bulova's controller summed up the matter this way:

> Many of the large multinational firms don't face the cross-currency complexities we do. They have numerous subsidiaries that make and sell products within single countries. Thus, they are largely operating within single currencies. Only when profit remittance comes up do they face, as of course we do, the problem of converting currencies.

He added:

> Looking at the company as a whole, you might say that our income statement is made up of sales denominated in one bundle of currencies while cost of goods sold and expenses enter the statement denominated in a second bundle of currencies. Thus, exchange rate considerations play a part in practically every control matter we handle.

OPERATIONS IN THE U.S. VIRGIN ISLANDS AND AMERICAN SAMOA

Within Bulova's manufacturing system, its movement assembly operations in the Virgin Islands and American Samoa raised special problems. Since, in unit terms, the number of movements flowing through the Virgin Islands and Samoan plants was approaching 30 percent of Bulova's annual domestic requirements, close control of these activities was obviously critical. But there were complications.

First, in order to gain the tariff advantages associated with production at the island sites, Bulova had to ensure that local value added exceeded 50 percent of the selling price of the assembled movements.[2]

---

[2] The U.S. tariff law stipulates that goods can be imported duty free into the United States from its insular possessions (the U.S. Virgin Islands, American Samoa, and

Four different sets of prices or cost were involved: (1) transfer prices for incoming components from Bulova's Swiss plants, (2) purchase prices for incoming components from Bulova's Japanese supplier, (3) locally generated costs, and (4) transfer prices for sales between the two island plants and Bulova's domestic operations.

Second, in the case of the Samoan operation, though not the Virgin Islands one, Bulova had a 10-year exemption from taxation. Naturally, the company wanted to take advantage of the exemption to the greatest extent possible.

The two island operations were profit centers, but whether it made sense at all to treat them as such represented one side of the control problem. Yet, given their importance to the whole manufacturing system, how to exert pressure on their local managers for better performance constituted the other side of the control problem.

SWISS MANUFACTURING AND THE FOREIGN MARKETING SUBSIDIARIES

Other factors complicating the control process arose out of the relationships between the Swiss manufacturing plants and the foreign marketing subsidiaries. As of the early 1970s, about 40 percent of the output from Bulova's Swiss plants was shipped to its overseas marketing subs or to third-party customers in foreign countries. The remainder was shipped, directly or indirectly, to Bulova–United States.

The usual arrangements between Swiss manufacturing and the foreign marketing subsidiaries were as follows: The Swiss plants sold the subsidiaries on open account. That is, the intercompany billings had no stipulated repayment time. Management had adopted this practice as a means to finance, in an indirect way, the growth of the fledgling marketing subsidiaries. The billings were denominated, of course, in Swiss francs, and as per company policy, the Swiss plants billed the subsidiaries at standard cost plus 10 percent.

Management had also decided that the foreign marketing subsidiaries should have a high degree of purchasing autonomy. The subsidiaries were required to purchase movements, either jeweled-lever or tuning fork, from Bulova's Swiss plants, but they were not obliged to accept what the plants offered in the way of finished watches. The subsidiaries could buy all the exterior components of watches from outside suppliers and finish the watches in their own local assembly facilities. Moreover, if the subsidiaries bought finished watches from

---

Guam) provided that local value added exceeds 50 percent of the selling price in the islands. Bulova established a subsidiary in the Virgin Islands; six years later, it established one on American Samoa. In the case of Samoa, Bulova received the 10-year tax exemption as an investment inducement.

the Swiss plants, they had the option of returning them to Switzerland if they did not sell in local markets. According to management, this policy was designed to ensure that market pressures worked their way back to Swiss manufacturing. As Bulova's president put it, the system guaranteed that Bulova manufactured what could be sold, rather than sold what could be manufactured. From the control standpoint, though, the policy made it a good bit more difficult to measure how well the Swiss plants planned their production and managed their inventories.

CONTROL SYSTEM

During the 1960s, Bulova developed a formal annual budgeting program, and this became the key to its control system.[3] Since little about the mechanics of the system was unusual, only a few of its main characteristics will be mentioned here. Foremost of these characteristics was management's attempt to use the profit center concept to the maximum extent possible.

As of 1973, Bulova was composed of 32 operating subunits, each with its own profit responsibility. Of the total number of profit centers, 22 were located outside the United States. They were:

15 marketing subsidiary profit centers.

3 manufacturing profit centers in Switzerland.

2 profit centers, one each in the Virgin Islands and American Samoa.

2 joint venture profit centers, one each in Japan and Taiwan.

Each of these was a separate planning and reporting unit responsible for performance down to the profit-aftertax level.

When asked about what led management to focus heavily upon the profit center concept in Bulova's foreign subunits, the corporate controller responded that the manufacturing and foreign marketing subsidiaries were separate corporations or taxable entities. He further noted that these subunits operated under the laws of countries which require that they be legally constituted and taxable therein. There was no way, he said, that they could exist except as separate profit centers.

At home, 11 of Bulova's 12 manufacturing plants were organized into four profit centers, each responsible for performance down to the

[3] Most, though not all, of the budgeting and reporting system was formalized. Management did not disseminate performance goals in a formal way. Generally, line management learned about management's performance expectations in meetings conducted by Bulova's president or in conversations between individual managers and the president.

profit-before-tax level.[4] On the marketing side, the company was organized into six product divisions, each held for performance down to the operating profit level. General administrative expenses were allocated to both the manufacturing operations and the product divisions. Only general corporate expenses (e.g., interest expense) were not charged to the domestic profit centers.

The budgeting and reporting procedures followed by the domestic operations were fairly routine, and, because the profit centers were near at hand, headquarters management could easily get supplementary facts or explanations whenever needed. The flow of information from overseas was somewhat less detailed and frequent. The foreign marketing subsidiaries prepared and forwarded to New York these reports:

Annually	*Quarterly*	*Monthly*
Income statements Balance sheets Cash flow statements for the forthcoming year	Income statements Balance sheets Cash flow statements; actual for last quarter and revised for the remaining quarters of the year	Trial balances Sales reports by product and territory Statements of intercompany cash remittances

On an annual and quarterly basis, the three Swiss-based manufacturing profit centers submitted to New York the same reports as those sent in by the marketing subsidiaries.[5] On a monthly basis they submitted reports, beyond those listed above, on shipments, sales by product and destination, and intercompany payables and receivables. Among other things, this reporting system made it possible to centralize cash flow management in New York.

As regards data on the manufacturing costs of the Swiss plants, headquarters received a complete report only once a year. Bulova's controller stated that headquarters did not get into the detail of manufacturing costs, but rather left that up to the managers of the three profit centers in Switzerland. He explained that the real mechanism by

[4] In those domestic plants where joint production of consumer products and industrial defense products took place, overhead, general expenses, etc., were allocated to the various product lines on the basis of direct labor costs. One Bulova plant was run on a fee basis for the U.S. government.

[5] On an annual basis, all manufacturing profit centers, domestic and foreign, also submitted capital expenditure budgets, which went to the board of directors for approval. How changes from budget were handled differed depending on whether the changes arose in foreign or domestic profit centers. Overseas units were permitted to modify the composition of their capital budgets so long as they stayed within their total approved limits. All changes taking them beyond their approved limits had to be forwarded to New York for review. In the case of domestic units, any change from budget had to be forwarded to headquarters for review.

which headquarters controlled manufacturing costs in Switzerland was through exerting competitive pressures on the Swiss plants. That is, headquarters kept the Swiss plants well-informed of the intercompany prices the domestic company could afford to pay for movements. These prices were derived from predicted competitors' retail prices in the United States. As Bulova's controller put it:

> Our Swiss plants know a year or so in advance what sort of manufacturing costs they will have to meet for movements if we are to stay competitive in the U.S. marketplace. They are expected to meet these targets. How they do it is the job of the managers in Switzerland.

By and large, the various other overseas manufacturing operations within Bulova, the plants in the Virgin Islands and Samoa, the Japanese and Taiwanese joint ventures, followed the same budgeting and reporting procedures, though the joint ventures did submit monthly income statements, balance sheets, and so on.

Since all information and documentation flowed to New York, the overall picture was one of a highly centralized control system. In effect, no layers of management intervened between the field profit centers and headquarters.

Bulova did not have a long-range budgeting system. Domestic and foreign profit centers budgeted only for the forthcoming fiscal year; and as the budget year progressed, they revised their plans only to the end

EXHIBIT 2 Estimated Manufacturing and Distribution Costs for a Quality Jeweled-lever Watch

U.S. jeweler's selling price		$100.00
U.S. jeweler's markup		50.00
Manufacturer's selling price		50.00
Manufacturer's markup		18.75
Manufacturer's assembled cost		31.25
Materials and labor cost for adding, in the United States, the case, dial, bracelet, and packaging		15.00
Manufacturer's landed cost of movement:		16.25
Duty	$ 2.70	
Transportation and insurance	0.10	2.80
Manufacturer's movement cost f.o.b. Switzerland		13.45
Manufacturing markup		2.50
Total movement cost, of which:		10.95
Direct labor	4.10	
Indirect labor and overhead	5.75	
Materials	1.10	
	10.95	

Notes: The assumed watch is a 17-jewel watch, containing a Swiss-made automatic movement, with a day and date display and a stainless steel case and bracelet.

The figures are not actual data taken from any one firm. Rather, they indicate what might be regarded as industry-typical numbers starting from an assumed jeweler's U.S. selling price of $100.

of the current fiscal year. Yet, separate from the control system, Bulova carried out a type of long-range planning.

BUSINESS PLANS

Each year, the managers of all profits centers submitted directly to Bulova's president a business plan that extended beyond the next fiscal year. Usually, these covered two years though some, upon the request of the president, carried planning five years forward. Year 1 of the business plans matched each subunit's budget for the next fiscal year. Years 2 and on of the business plans presented, largely in narrative form, the goals and programs of the profit centers. More often than not, the plans concentrated on marketing objectives, such as growth goals, and on market share goals. Executives in Bulova described these reports as personal plans of the profit centers managers, and they were viewed as private interchanges between these managers and Bulova's president.

MEASUREMENT AND REWARDS

Though Bulova was organized, for control purposes, around profit centers, the performance criteria that operating managers seemed to follow most closely were gross margins and the levels of inventories and receivables. Still, top management kept a careful eye on the bottom line.[6] When asked if the profit center system had any teeth in it, the controller observed, "Those managers who haven't been able to meet their profit goals haven't stayed around in the company very long. I can think of three or four instances of this in the last few years."

Complicating this picture, however, was the nature of the company's reward system for its managers. In the mid-1960s, Bulova's management had instituted a version of management by objectives. Individual managers, in consultation with Bulova's president, set specific goals for the forthcoming year or two (e.g., share of market for a new watch line). Attainment of these goals was factored into the performance review of each manager. However, there was more to the reward system than this. As a general policy, therefore, all the more important line and staff managers of the company, domestic and foreign, were rewarded on the basis of the company's overall performance. According to Bulova's president, the nature of the company's operations precluded any other sort of reward system.

---

[6] Top management, naturally, also measured progress against return on investment; but, given the nature of the company's operations, managers under the top echelon seemed to give little attention to the ROI criterion. Rather, they focused more on managing current assets, largely by applying certain rules of thumb to determine acceptable levels of receivables and inventories.

THE QUESTION

Bulova's controller summed up his comments:

We think our control system, and our commitment to profit centers, makes good sense. Yet, for a number of reasons, I think our control problems are tougher than a lot of firms face. For one thing, we are not only a highly integrated company but also we are a highly international company.

Sure, so are all the oil companies, some of the other mineral companies, some of the metal companies, so why should our control problems be special? I'll tell you. First, we're in the fashion business, so we are constantly facing market instability. And second, our entire industry is a drop in the bucket compared to these other industries. We simply don't have the resources for elaborate administrative systems.

I suppose what bothers me is that we have pushed the profit center concept pretty far in our company. Maybe too far? I'd love to have somebody take a good look at us and suggest alternative ways of controlling the company. Got any ideas?

CASE 14–5
SKA, Ltd.*

In July 1980, the management of SKA, Ltd., were considering how to reply to a proposal, received from their parent company, to implement a system of measuring the amount of resources either contributed or used by each business area and product throughout the world.

SKA, Ltd., was a wholly owned Australian subsidiary of Svenska Kemisk Akiebolag (hereafter called SKA–Sweden). SKA–Sweden was a large, multinational manufacturer of chemicals and related products with headquarters based in Uppsala, a city in the southeast part of Sweden. SKA, Ltd., located in Newtown, Australia, manufactured fertilizers and related chemical products, which were sold in Australia, New Zealand, and other countries in the Far East.

PRODUCTS AND ORGANIZATION

SKA, Ltd., was divided into three business areas as follows:

1. Agricultural products.
2. Industrial products.
3. Services (e.g., power, water, and steam).

* This case was prepared by John Dearden, Harvard Business School.

Each of the business areas had its own plants and its own marketing organization. Most of the SKA, Ltd., production facilities were located in a large industrial complex in Newtown, although three other smaller plants were located in southeastern Australia. The corporate staffs and the central research department were also located in Newtown.

Each business area was a profit center. Except for marketing, almost all managers had a dual reporting responsibility. For example, all plant managers reported to the production management at the staff level on a functional basis and to the business area manager on a line basis. A similar dual relationship existed for accounting, personnel, research, industrial engineering, and so forth. A unique feature of the organization was that many managers held two positions. For example, the production manager was also the general manager of the fertilizer business area.

COST ACCOUNTING

SKA, Ltd., used a process cost accounting system. Costs were accumulated by each production department and transferred to subsequent departments as the product was transferred. Thus, at all points in the production process, all costs incurred in the manufacture of a product to that point had been charged to it.

Dual Systems

SKA, Ltd., maintained two parallel systems. One system collected the actual costs incurred by each department and transferred these costs to subsequent departments; this was called the "roll-through system." A second system transferred certain intermediate products at a transfer price; this was called the "transfer-price" system. The products transferred at a price were independent products (e.g., ammonia and nitric acid) that were normally traded in the market. The market price determined the transfer price.

A dual system was maintained because the management of SKA, Ltd., exercised two types of control. First, control over products was exercised through a system of product profitability analysis. The roll-through was used for product control. Second, operating control was exercised through a profit budget. The transfer price system was used for operating control.

Standards

Standard costs were set for all products. As explained above, however, products were transferred through the system at actual costs, contrary to many standard cost systems. Standard costs were calculated for the products produced—and then the total standard costs were compared to the actual costs incurred *outside* of the books of account. Inventories, however, were maintained at standard costs.

PRODUCT PROFITABILITY ANALYSIS

Annually, and sometimes twice a year, the profitability of all product groups were analyzed. A unique feature of this analysis was that it was made on the basis of both historical and inflation adjusted costs (called "current costs" hereafter). Management relied principally on current costs in making product decisions.

Calculating Current Costs

Current costs were calculated by adjusting fixed assets and inventories for the effect of inflation. These adjustments are explained in this part of the case.

Fixed assets. The construction index for the chemical industry was the basic means for adjusting fixed assets for the effect of inflation. However, this was modified for the following circumstances:

1. An independent estimate of replacement cost of each facility was made by the plant engineering department. Where this estimate differed by more than 15 percent from the index adjusted amount, further study was made and the discrepancy resolved.
2. Specific information was used where available. For example, where major new plants have been recently completed, the existing plants were valued on this basis and adjusted for differences in capacity, if appropriate.
3. Where excess capacity existed, only the replacement cost of the capacity being used was included.
4. Antipollution and environmental improvements were excluded in the replacement cost estimate where these were not part of the existing facilities. (This was a rule laid down by Uppsala.)

Two other points on the fixed-asset replacement cost calculations were of importance:

1. In the interests of simplicity, it was decided to do the following:
   a. Replacement costs were calculated on a "site" basis only. For example, calculations would not assume a different plant in a different place or a leased plant instead of a purchased plant. In short, replacement costs assumed the same facilities in the same location.
   b. Adjustments were not made for greater efficiency, more advantageous location, or any other technological change, except for capacity.

2. Current costs reflected the best estimates of the expected lives of the assets. This was important because, in some instances, the historical accounting lives of fixed assets were shorter than the expected lives, partly to offset the effects of inflation.

Inventories. Inventories were valued at standard costs, which approximated the current (replacement) cost of the inventories. Standard costs were changed *each quarter* to reflect expected changes in price levels. (The technique for setting quarterly standard costs is explained later in the case.)

Return on Capital (ROC)

The final result of the profit profitability analysis was a rate of return on capital. This was calculated by business area, product-line, and individual products. All analyses were on a company-wide consolidated basis and were calculated for both historical costs and current costs.

Revenues. The revenues were those actually realized from the sale of the product to outside customers. (Also included were some sales to other subsidiaries of SKA–Sweden.)

Costs. All costs incurred by the SKA, Ltd., including a corporate assessment from Uppsala, were assigned to business segments, except income taxes.

Capital. Investment was equal to the working capital plus fixed assets at gross value. Inventories and fixed assets were included at both historical costs and replacement value.

USE OF PRODUCT PROFITABILITY ANALYSIS

The profitability of business areas and product lines were reviewed periodically by the top management of SKA–Sweden and SKA, Ltd., as well as by all of the managers responsible for individual segment profitability. These analyses had four principal uses.

First, they were used as a guide in setting selling prices. (The prices of all basic products were reviewed and approved by the top management of SKA, Ltd.)

Second, they acted as a discipline to the marketing organization to keep prices in line with inflation.

Third, they were used to identify products that were not earning a sufficient profit.

Fourth, they were used in the analysis of budget proposals. For example, if the ROC was declining, an analysis was made to determine which business areas and products were contributing to this decline and why?

BUDGETING

SKA, Ltd., presented an annual profit budget to top management in Uppsala, Sweden, for review and approval. Monthly reports—showing actual results compared to budget, analysis of variances and, explanations of significant deviations from budget—were submitted monthly to Uppsala.

Within SKA, Ltd., budgets were also used for the day-to-day control of operations. (The transfer price system was used for budgeting.) Each of the business areas prepared a profit budget, which was reviewed and approved by the company management. Staff offices and the research department prepared expense budgets, which were similarly reviewed and approved. Monthly, actual results were compared to budget and deviations analyzed and explained.

Current Costs

A unique feature of the SKA, Ltd., budgeting system was that it took into account the amount of inflation expected during the year. Revenues and nonmanufacturing costs were calendarized by month. Standard costs were projected for each quarter. Thus, four sets of standard costs were incorporated in the budget, and new standard costs were introduced at the beginning of each quarter.

In setting these quarterly standards, the following techniques were used:

1. Estimated average prices were used for commodities in which prices fluctuated randomly throughout the year.
2. Where materials were purchased by contract, an estimate of the new price was phased in at the appropriate time.
3. Other material prices were forecast as follows:
   a. The prices of all major material were estimated individually.
   b. The prices of nonmajor material items was adjusted for the forecast of the wholesale price index.
4. Direct labor was based on the expected changes in the labor contracts.
5. Important overhead costs, such as maintenance, supplies, and power, were forecast individually.

THE PROPOSAL FROM UPPSALA

The top management of SKA–Sweden was concerned with identifying business and products world-wide that were not contributing sufficient cash to enable the company to realize its strategic plans. A study was undertaken by the corporate director of finance to develop a method for systematically identifying such business segments.

A task force, assigned to this project, developed an objective rate of return on capital. Any subsidiary, business area, or product earning less than this return was considered not to be generating its share of the cash required for SKA, world-wide, to accomplish its strategic plans. This part of the case describes how this objective rate of return was developed.

Step 1, the task force prepared a forecast of the amount of cash that must be generated from operations on a world-wide basis if SKA was to have enough financial resources to accomplish its strategic plan.

Step 2, the total noncash expenses (principally depreciation) that would be generated world-wide from all operations were estimated. (These noncash expenses were based on the *current cost* estimates.) This amount was subtracted from the amount calculated in step 1 above.

Step 3, the amount of income taxes expected to be paid world-wide was calculated and *added* to the amount calculated in step 2. Steps 2 and 3, therefore, translated the required cash flow into operating profits before taxes. In other words, if all operations earned a total profit before taxes equal to the amount calculated in step 3, the net cash flow would equal the amount estimated in step 1.

Step 4, the total capital (working capital and gross fixed assets on a current cost basis) that would be employed by all operating units world-wide was calculated.

Step 5, the amount calculated in step 3 was divided by the amount calculated in step 4. This was the objective rate of return that all business segments must earn if they were to contribute their shares to the cash requirements of the company.

It was reasoned, therefore, that any business or product not earning this return was a cash drain, and that the amount of this drain was equal to the capital employed multiplied by the difference between the actual or projected rate of return and the objective. A hypothetical calculation is as follows assuming an objective of 10 percent:

Product A—Thousands of Australian Dollars

	Actual			*Projected*		
	1980	*1981*	*1982*	*1983*	*1984*	*1985*
Profit before taxes	100	90	80	90	100	110
Capital	1,500	1,600	1,800	1,700	1,600	1,500
Rate of return	6.7%	5.6%	4.7%	5.3%	6.3%	7.3%
Excess/(deficiency):						
Percent	(3.3%)	(4.4%)	(5.3%)	(4.7%)	(3.7%)	(2.7%)
Amount	(49.5)	(70.4)	(95.4)	(79.9)	(59.2)	(40.5)

Uppsala proposed that, world-wide, all business segments be evaluated in terms of this objective rate of return, and that excesses or deficiencies represent cash contribution or drain. Segments that were creating a cash drain were to be carefully evaluated to see if the situation could be corrected. If not, there should be valid reasons why the business segment should not be dropped or, at least, curtailed.

SKA, LTD., ANALYSIS

The finance director of SKA, Ltd., was puzzled by the proposal from the Uppsala task force. SKA, Ltd., had been remitting significant amounts of cash to the parent company consistently over the past several years. Yet, on the basis of the standard criteria, most products of SKA, Ltd., were cash drains and, the subsidiary, as a whole, was a significant net cash user. On further reflection and analysis, the finance director determined that four conditions caused this inconsistency:

First, the formula did not take into account capital grants or rapid depreciation. In the part of Australia where SKA, Ltd., was located, it was possible to obtain a 25 percent grant on most investments and to write off the entire investment for tax purposes in the first year. Thus, an investment of A$1,000,000 would include a cash outlay of only A$250,000 (1,000,000 − 500,000 tax savings − 250,000 capital grant).

Second, effective income tax rates differed widely among countries. This was not so much because statutory rates were different but because some countries were more liberal in allowable deduction than others. The finance director believed that Australia had one of the lowest effective tax rates.

Third, the rate of growth differed widely among business segments. The higher the growth rate of a subsidiary or product, the more cash would be required. The Australian company, with its lower growth rate, was subsidizing higher growth segments of the company.

Finally, the proportion of working capital to total capital varied widely among subsidiaries, business areas, and products within business area. Working capital required a constant investment; whereas the actual investment in fixed assets declined over time, because depreciation represented a partial return of the original investment.

SKA, Ltd., being heavily capital intensive, would have a lower real investment than a subsidiary with the same total amount of capital that included a larger percentage of working capital.

Questions

1. Evaluate the product profitability and budgetary control systems of SKA, Ltd. In particular, how do you evaluate their current cost procedures, both in principle and execution? How would you change them—if at all?
2. Evaluate the proposal of the Uppsala task force:
   a. Do you agree with their general method for identifying cash contributors and users?
   b. If you disagree, how would you identify cash contributors and user?
   c. To what extent would you take into account the points raised by the finance director of SKA, Ltd.?

(Remember, the objective is to develop standard criteria that can be applied world-wide to any subsidiary, business area, or product.)

CHAPTER 15

Service Organizations

In the preceding chapters our focus, at least implicitly, has been on organizations that produce and sell tangible goods. In this chapter, we discuss management control in organizations that provide intangible services, with particular attention to organizations that provide professional services.

In the Standard Industrial Classification, service organizations include hotels, restaurants, and other lodging and eating establishments; barbershops, beauty parlors, and other personal services; repair services; motion picture, television, and other amusement and recreation services; legal services; and accounting, engineering, research/development, architecture, and other professional service organizations. Because of the similarity of their management control problems, we also include banks, insurance companies, and other financial institutions. Government agencies, educational organizations, and most other nonprofit organizations are service organizations; but in this chapter we focus on profit-oriented organizations. Nonprofit organizations are discussed in Chapter 16. In the 20th century the fraction of the work force employed in service organizations has been steadily increasing, and in the United States currently more people are employed in these organizations than in organizations that produce goods.

SERVICE ORGANIZATIONS IN GENERAL

Characteristics of Service Organizations

The production and sale of services, as contrasted with tangible goods, has several important implications for the management control process.

Absence of inventory. Goods can be held in inventory, and this inventory is a buffer that dampens the impact on production activity of fluctuations in sales volume. Services cannot be stored. If the services available today are not delivered today the potential revenues from these services are lost forever. Some organizations can smooth out their workload by accumulating a backlog of service requests, but clients ordinarily do not want to wait for their services, so the opportunities for doing this are limited. By contrast, in order to obtain the advantages of long production runs or for other sound reasons, manufacturers often produce goods for which they have no current orders. Up to a point, they need not be concerned that these goods are not sold currently; the revenues should be earned in the near future. Because of inventory, the manufacturer can earn revenue in the future from production capacity that is not sold today, but the service company has no such option.

Even worse, the resources available for sale in many service organizations are essentially fixed. In the short run, a hotel cannot increase the number of rooms that it offers for rent, and it does not reduce costs substantially by closing off some of its rooms. An accounting firm, law firm, or other professional organization could conceivably lay off some of its professional personnel in times of low volume; but, for morale reasons and to avoid the costs of rehiring, managers of such firms are reluctant to do so.

These conditions cause great emphasis to be placed on planning for an amount of available services that is not in excess of what can be sold currently and on marketing efforts to sell these services each day. For various reasons, full utilization of capacity may not be feasible; for example, a hotel has a fixed stock of guest rooms, but its occupancy rate may vary greatly by days of the week and by seasons of the year. The loss from unsold services is such an important factor that occupancy rates and similar indications of success in selling available services are normally key variables in service organizations of all types.

Nonstandard products. In some service organizations, such as fast-food restaurants, products are as standardized as those in a factory. In most, however, each job is different from other jobs so that standard costs, similar to those used in a factory, cannot be developed.

Labor intensive. Service organizations tend to be labor intensive; that is, they tend to require relatively little capital per unit of output. It is more difficult to control the work of a labor-intensive organization than that of an operation whose work flow is paced or dominated by machinery. (Some service organizations are becoming capital intensive as computers replace clerks, and as food preparation and dispensing equipment replaces cooks and waiters.)

Quantity measurement. The quantity of tangible goods moving through the production process, the quantity in inventory, and the quantity moving out to customers, can readily be measured. It is not practical to measure the quantity of many services, however. We can measure the number of patients a physician treats in a day, for example, and even classify these visits by type of complaint, but this is by no means equivalent to measuring the amount of service the physician provides to each of these patients. For many services, the amount provided can be measured only in the crudest terms, if at all.

Quality measurement. The quality of tangible goods can be inspected, and in most cases the inspection can be performed before goods are released to the customer. If the goods are defective, there is physical evidence of the nature of the defect. The quality of most services cannot be inspected in advance; at best, services can be inspected during the time they are rendered to the client. Judgments on the adequacy of the quality of most services are subjective; measuring instruments and objective quality standards do not exist. A public accounting firm can measure the number of hours spent on an audit, but not the thoroughness of the work done during those hours. A consulting firm has no objective way of appraising the soundness of its recommendations. A law firm may leave loopholes or ambiguities in documents it drafts that do not come to light until years later.

Historical development. Cost accounting started in manufacturing companies because of the necessity for valuing work-in-process and finished goods inventories for financial statement purposes. These amounts provided raw data that were easily adapted to use, first for setting selling prices and later for other management purposes. Standard cost systems, separation of fixed and variable costs, and analysis of variances were built on the foundation of these cost systems. Until the last few decades, most books on cost accounting dealt only with practices in manufacturing companies.

Because service organizations have no inventories, they did not have the natural impetus to develop cost data that existed in manufacturing companies. It is only in fairly recent years that they have learned of the usefulness of cost information to management. Since World War II, the development of management control systems in service organizations has been rapid.

The literature on control techniques—standard costs, analysis of variances, statistical quality control, production control, inventory control—still tends to emphasize production situations rather than service organizations. For example, in 1972 the Price Commission placed great emphasis on the importance of increasing productivity as the only noninflationary way of justifying higher wage rates. It was able to establish quantitative annual productivity goals for each manufacturing industry, but no one was able to devise reliable ways of measuring productivity in most service organizations.

Size. With notable exceptions, such as law firms, service organizations are relatively small and operate in a single location. Top management in such organizations can personally observe what is going on and personally motivate employees. Thus, there is less need for a sophisticated management control system, with profit centers and heavy reliance on formal performance reports. (Nevertheless, even a small organization needs a budget, a regular comparison of actual performance against this budget, and the other basic ingredients of a management control system.)

Implications for Management Control

The characteristics listed in the proceeding section suggest differences between management control systems in service organizations and those in manufacturing organizations. These are differences in degree, rather than in kind, however. The essential features are the same in both types of organizations. In both, planning is done in terms of programs and responsibility centers, including profit centers and investment centers for organization units that meet the criteria described in Chapters 6 and 8. The management control process in both organizations involves the steps of programming, budgeting, the measurement of performance, and the evaluation of that performance. Transfer pricing is important in both.

Systems currently found in service organizations tend to be less well developed than those in manufacturing organizations. Because of the difficulty of measuring both the quantity and the quality of output, judgments about both the efficiency and the effectiveness of performance are more subjective than is the case when output consists of physical goods, which means that there is more room for legitimate differences of opinion about performance. Managers are coming to recognize that performance is not easy to measure, and this recognition has led to a search for better measurement tools.

In their details, the management control systems of various types of service organizations vary widely. We shall limit the discussion in this chapter to two types of organizations in which special problems exist, namely, financial institutions and professional organizations.

FINANCIAL INSTITUTIONS

Commercial Banks

In the 1960s, commercial banks began to create profit centers for their branches and for their corporate trust, personal trust, investment, and other revenue-producing units. In doing so, they had to solve problems not faced by industrial companies.

A particularly serious problem is establishing a transfer price for money. Money is obtained by borrowing from other financial institutions, from customers who make savings account deposits ("time deposits"), and from customers who make checking account deposits ("demand deposits"). The interest cost of borrowed funds and of time deposits is readily determined. The cost of demand deposits is difficult to measure, however. Until recently, banks were prohibited by regulatory authorities from paying interest on checking accounts, and in lieu thereof they provided free services to customers. These included processing checks, handling payroll records, accounting for accounts receivable, and providing financial advice. The cost of providing these services is the cost of the money obtained from checking accounts deposits. Moreover, government regulations require that a certain fraction of deposits be held in reserves on which low interest rates, in some cases zero, are earned. These reserves must be taken into account in calculating the cost of the money that is available for lending.

The problem is further complicated because some corporate checking accounts include compensating balances, that is, funds that the corporation is required to leave on deposit as a condition of a loan the bank has made to it. Conceptually, a compensating balance reduces the net amount of funds made available to the borrower and thus increases the effective interest cost and the rate of return to the bank. As a practical matter, the problem of treating compensating balances separately from other checking account balances is so difficult that banks usually do not make the separation in their formal control system, although they may do so in special analyses.

These problems make it difficult to calculate a transfer price for money, that is, a price that determines the revenue of the profit centers that bring in deposits and the "cost of sales" of profit centers that lend money. A transfer price is especially important when the bank has a number of branches, each of which is a profit center. Some branches generate more money in deposits than they loan out; they are "deposit-heavy." Other branches are "loan-heavy." In order to measure the profitability of these profit centers, the cost of money must be correctly calculated. If the transfer price for the cost of money is set too low, the reported profitability of the loan-heavy units will overstate their actual performance; whereas if it is set too high, the profitability of the deposit-heavy units will be overstated.

Measurement of the cost of money is also important in assessing the profitability of loans with different maturities, loans with different risk characteristics (e.g., consumer installment loans versus high-grade corporate loans), and loans to different markets (local, national, and international).

Partly in order to arrive at a sound transfer price, banks have started to analyze carefully the real cost of services they provide to customers and to measure the profitability of individual customer accounts. The Federal Reserve System, to which many banks belong, has facilitated such analyses by its Functional Analysis Program, which collects costs by functions from member banks, computes averages, and makes these available.

Banks also have serious problems in dividing up common costs and common revenues. Accounting and check processing are usually done centrally, and the costs of such work must be equitably assessed to the branches. A customer who maintains an account in one branch may use the services of another branch, or may be induced to use services provided by a headquarters unit. The branches that "sell" such services should be given appropriate credit.

With these important exceptions, the management control systems in commercial banks are similar to those described in earlier chapters.

Insurance Companies

Insurance companies also deal with money. They collect money in the form of premiums, invest it, and subsequently pay out money in the form of claims, death benefits, or annuities. Many years may elapse between the time a policy is written and the time when benefit payments are completed. The profitability of the policy cannot be known with certainty until the last payment has been made; but, for management control purposes, the company cannot wait that long; it needs information currently.

Traditionally, insurance companies measured the performance of their responsibility centers by rough rules of thumb, such as the amount of first-year premiums or the face amount of insurance written. In recent years, they have begun to explore the possibility of measuring the approximate profitability of each policy at the time it is written. For example, the annual premium on an ordinary life policy is arrived at by taking into account life expectancy, estimated investment income, selling costs, and recurring operating costs over the life of the policy. Each of these components is set conservatively; for example, the mortality table used in setting premiums understates the actual life expectancy. The ultimate profitability of the policy arises from the difference between the conservative estimates and the actual amounts experienced. The true expectations can be estimated, and from them the expected present value of the policy can be determined. Thus, a measure of profitability can be calculated at the time the policy is sold.[1]

With this measure of profitability as a starting point, insurance companies can organize their sales branches as profit centers; and they can also measure the performance of the investment, actuarial, and other parts of the company by comparing actual results with those used in the calculations of the present value of a policy's profitability.

---

[1] For a full description, see James S. Hekimian, *Management Control in Life Insurance Branches* (Boston: Division of Research, Harvard Business School, 1965).

PROFESSIONAL ORGANIZATIONS

Research/development organizations, law firms, accounting firms, medical clinics, health maintenance organizations, engineering firms, architectural firms, consulting firms, investment firms, and advertising agencies are examples of organizations whose product is professional services. These firms differ from manufacturing companies and from other service companies in ways that have a substantial impact on management control problems and practices.

Characteristics

Organizational goals. In manufacturing companies, and also in some service organizations, such as hotels, the dominant success criterion is return on assets employed. The organization is successful if it earns a satisfactory return on assets employed, and capital investment decisions are made according to this return on investment criterion. Assets can be measured, and they are reported on the balance sheet. In a professional organization, the amount of tangible assets employed is relatively insignificant. The principal resource of the organization is the skill of its professional staff, and return on assets employed provides neither a basis for measuring success nor a criterion for decision making. Thus, the conceptual foundation on which our discussion of measuring the profitability of profit centers and investment centers in manufacturing companies was based, does not apply to these organizations.

Output measurement. The output of a professional organization cannot be measured in units, tons, or gallons. Revenues earned are one measure of output, but these monetary amounts may relate to the quantity of services rendered, not to their quality, at least in the short run. As noted above, the output of a professional organization is intangible, is therefore not easy to measure in quantitative terms, and is difficult or impossible to evaluate in qualitative terms.

Production standards. The work done by professionals tends to be nonrepetitive. No two consulting jobs or research/development projects are quite the same. This makes it difficult to plan the time required for a task, to set reasonable standards for task performance, and, therefore, to judge how satisfactory the performance was. Some tasks are essentially repetitive; the drafting of simple wills, deeds, sales contracts, and other documents; the taking of a physical inventory, and certain medical and surgical procedures, are examples. The development of standards for such tasks may be worthwhile, although, in using these standards, unusual circumstances affecting them must be taken into account. Although the drafting of a deed for residential property and the related title search may be a cut-and-dried process in the majority of instances, there are enough situations involving ambiguity in the title or special restrictions in the deed that a "standard time" for deed preparation is at best only a general guide.

Some professionals, notably scientists and engineers, are reluctant to keep track of how they spend their time, and this complicates the task of measuring performance. This reluctance seems to have its roots in tradition, and it usually can be overcome if senior management is willing to put appropriate emphasis on the necessity of accurate time reporting.

Marketing. In most professional organizations no clear dividing line exists between marketing efforts and production efforts. In some, such as law, medicine, and accounting, the ethical codes of the profession limit the amount and character of overt marketing efforts. Since marketing is an essential activity in any organization, if it cannot be conducted openly, it takes the form of personal contacts, speeches, articles, golf, and similar activities. These activities are carried on by professionals. In professions which permit explicit marketing efforts, the professional staff is responsible for developing leads, preparing proposals, and carrying on discussions with prospective clients, all of which are activities that would be conducted by the marketing department in an industrial company.

Because marketing is not an identifiable function, and because new business is generated by the part-time activities of professional staff members who are primarily engaged in doing production work, it is difficult to assign appropriate credit to the person responsible for the generation of revenue. In a consulting firm, for example, a new engagement may result from a conversation between a member of the firm and an acquaintance in the client company; from the reputation of one of the firm's professionals, as an outgrowth of an existing engagement; from a speech or article, as well as from an explicit written proposal. Moreover, the professional who is responsible for obtaining the engagement may not personally be involved in doing the work. Thus, the practice of assigning responsibility for obtaining a specified share of the market and of measuring performance against this standard, which is common in an industrial company, is often impossible to use in a professional organization. In professions that frown on marketing, firms tend not to give much, if any, thought to the marketing mix, the proper positioning of the product line, and other fundamental marketing concepts.

Professionals. Professionals often have motivations that are inconsistent with good resource utilization, and their success, as perceived by their professional colleagues, reflects these motivations. Professionals are motivated by dual standards: (*a*) those of their organizations, and (*b*) those of their professional colleagues. The former standards are related to organizational objectives; the latter may be inconsistent with organizational objectives. The rewards for achieving organizational objectives may be less potent than those for achieving professional objectives. For example, scientists in a research/development organization tend to do research that increases their reputation in the profession, without much regard to whether the cost of this research is a worthwhile expenditure from the viewpoint of the long-run profitability of the organization.

Professionals who are departmental managers tend to work only part-time on management activities. They spend a substantial part of their time doing the same work as their subordinates. The head of the surgical department in a hospital does surgery. The senior partner in the local office of an accounting firm participates actively in audit engagements. In organizations not dominated by professionals, management tends to be a full-time job, and managers do not do the same type of work as their subordinates.

Many professionals, by nature, prefer to work independently. Examples are researchers and physicians. Because the essence of management is getting things done through people, professionals with such a temperament are not naturally suited to the role either of managers or of subordinates.

In a professional organization, the *professional quality* of the people is of primary importance, and other considerations are secondary. Therefore, managers in professional organizations spend much of their time recruiting good people and seeing to it that they are kept happy. The manager has correspondingly less time for those aspects of the job that relate to efficiency. In a professional organization, the practice of recruiting many and then weeding out unsatisfactory workers is expensive, so management must concentrate on careful preselection.

Managers in a professional firm are less likely to have come up through the ranks than those in a commercial company. A salesperson can become the sales manager, but a draftsman is unlikely to become a partner in an architectural firm. Except for such professions as accounting and management consulting, professional education usually does not include education in management, and quite naturally stresses the importance of the profession rather than that of management. For this and other reasons, professionals tend to look down on managers. In some hospitals, the administrator's status and pay are below that of all professional people; the chief administrator may not even attend the board of trustees meetings in which the professionals and the trustees decide on policies.

Although the leadership of an organization may require more management skills than professional skills, tradition often requires that the manager be a professional. Traditionally, the head of a research/development organization was a scientist; the president of a university, a professor; the head of a hospital, a physician. This tradition seems to be diminishing, however.

Professionals tend to give inadequate weight to the financial implication of their decisions. The physician feels no limit should be placed on the amount spent to save a human life, although in a world of limited resources such an attitude is unrealistic.

Differences among organizations. The characteristics described above are tendencies which are applicable to varying degrees in most professional organizations. There also are differences among professions and among the firms within a given profession that are relevant for management control.

In some organizations, professionals work as a team on an engagement; in others they tend to work as individuals with perhaps temporary assistance from colleagues. Research/development organizations, accounting firms, engineering firms, and consulting firms are examples of the former type; and physicians, some law firms, and investment advisory firms are examples of the latter. The former type requires a matrix organization and the project controls that are discussed in Chapter 17.

Organizations also vary in the proportion of support personnel to professional staff. In the legal and medical professions, the proportion traditionally has been low; the professional received relatively little staff assistance. In recent years, however, the number of paralegal and paramedical personnel has grown substantially. In accounting firms, engineering firms, and research/development firms, the proportion of support personnel is relatively high. These firms apply the economic principle of division of labor, with its favorable impact on profitability. In essence, if professionals sell only their own time, their income is limited by the number of professional hours in a day; whereas, if they use support personnel for some of the work, their income can be increased by the profit margin of this work.

Pricing

The criterion of return on assets employed both provides a conceptual basis for analyzing and explaining the behavior of the prices of industrial products, in general, and also serves as a practical guide to pricing in individual companies. Since assets, in the conventional accounting sense, are relatively less important in professional organizations, the return on assets criterion does not provide a rationale for pricing in these organizations.

The problem can be seen most clearly in the case of cost-reimbursement government contracts. For contracts that involve the production of physical goods, a price that is equal to cost plus a profit margin based primarily on assets employed is equitable both to the contractor and to the government. If this pricing policy is used for contracts involving professional services, however, the firm would receive only an insignificant amount of profit since it employs relatively small amounts of assets. Clearly, the professional team has a value to the government that is greater than the sum of the compensation paid to individual members of the team. Otherwise, the government would be well advised to hire the persons as individuals, rather than contracting with the professional firm for their services at a higher cost. This higher value of the professional organization arises for any or all of the following reasons:

1. The firm has assembled a group of competent persons. Considerable time and effort would be required for the government to go through the process of recruiting and screening individuals to obtain persons of comparable ability.
2. The firm has identified the skills of these persons, and given them assignments commensurate with these skills. Considerable effort would be required for the government to do this with a group of individuals.
3. The firm has increased the value of these individuals both by skills developed on the job, and by paying for formal training programs.
4. The firm has organized these individuals, taking account not only of professional skills but also of personality "fits," managerial ability, and other factors.
5. The firm has developed policies and procedures that are useful in assuring that work is done efficiently and effectively.
6. The firm accepts responsibility for the quality, cost, and on-time delivery of its product.
7. The firm assumes risks; both the risk of monetary loss if actual costs exceed prescribed limits and also risks to its reputation if the work is not well done.
8. The firm must absorb the costs of professional personnel when they have no revenue-producing work. The government uses the professional resources only for a limited purpose and for a limited time, and pays only for the time that it uses.

If it is granted that a professional organization is entitled to some profit that is unrelated to the amount of assets employed, the question then arises: how should this profit be calculated? No satisfactory conceptual answer to this question has yet emerged.

Many professional firms are organized as partnerships, and the compensation for individual services plus profit winds up eventually as partnership compensation, with the line between these two components being fairly arbitrary. Indeed, for many consulting contracts, the client pays no "profit" as such, although it knows that an amount equivalent to profit is built into the daily rates for professionals that are set forth in the contract.

Professional firms tend to price according to tradition. In each profession, there is a traditional fee structure, the principles of which change relatively little over time. If the profession is one in which members are accustomed to keeping track of their time, the fees are generally related to professional time, and often are built into an hourly billing rate. Investment bankers, by contrast, tend to base fees on the amount of money involved in a security issue, an acquisition, or other type of engagement. Fees vary widely from one profession to another, and in ways that are unrelated to supply-demand relationships. For example, they are relatively low for scientists and relatively high for accountants and physicians.

In some firms, particularly small proprietorships or partnerships, the value of the firm itself can be estimated because similar firms are sold in the marketplace at prices that are publicly available. The market value of such firms can be used as a measure of the value of the owner's investment, and prices can be set to produce a satisfactory return on this investment.

Programming and Budgeting

In general, formal programming and budgeting systems are not so well developed in professional organizations as in industrial companies of comparable size. With respect to programming, part of the explanation is that professional organizations have no great need for a formal programming system. In industrial companies, most program decisions involve commitments to plant and equipment, which have a predictable effect on both capacity and on costs for several years into the future and which, once made, are essentially irrevocable. In a professional organization, the principal assets are people, and although short-run fluctuations in personnel levels are avoided wherever possible, changes in the size and composition of the staff are easier to make and are more easily reversed than changes in the capacity of a physical plant. Furthermore, although there is some specialization of professional personnel in a firm, professionals tend to be more "general purpose" than the machine tools in a typical factory; they can work on a variety of different jobs. Thus, the program of a professional organization tends to consist only of a long-range staffing plan, rather than a full-blown program for all aspects of the firm's organization.

Professional organizations, particularly research/development organizations, do acquire capital assets, and they need a procedure for making capital acquisition decisions and for following up on asset acquisitions similar to that used in industrial companies. The return-on-assets criterion cannot be used for many such decisions, however, so management's intuitive judgment is correspondingly more important.

The fact that budgeting systems are not well developed in professional organizations is difficult to explain, because the need for a formal spending commitment by managers of responsibility centers is as great in these organizations as in industrial companies. Probably the explanation is that professional organizations, like service organizations generally, are late in adopting good management control techniques. In preparing budgets, many professional firms do not make full use of available data: data on past performance in the firm, on costs in other firms that are collected and published by trade associations, and on the behavior of costs as volume changes.

A good budgeting process helps to ensure that departments are in balance with one another, and particularly that support departments are at an optimum size to provide service to the professional staff. The budget determines the size and scope of the firm's operations for the coming year, particularly its capacity to take new business. It identifies the additional staff and other resources that must be acquired. It states permitted levels of spending, and it provides a basis for motivating desired spending performance and for judging actual performance.

An illustrative budget. Exhibit 15–1 shows a budget for a relatively small CPA firm. The starting point in preparing this budget was the desired income of $100,000, calculated as a percentage of the market value of the firm. Salaries were estimated at the anticipated rates in the area in the budget year. Expenses were then estimated. The sum of desired income and expenses is the revenue that must be generated from billings, $1,106,000. Various combinations of billing rates and chargeable hours were calculated until a feasible combination that produces the desired income was found. (The amount in Exhibit 15–1 labeled "special billings" was a reduction in gross revenue from work that was billed at less than standard rates.)

Task Control

Because the products that a professional organization offers for sale are professional services, which cannot be stored in inventory, measures ensuring that these services are used for the highest feasible percentage of the time are especially important in such organizations. Much attention is, or should be, given to scheduling the time of professionals. The *billed time ratio,* which is the ratio of hours billed to total professional hours available, is watched closely. If, in order to use otherwise idle time or for marketing or public service reasons, some engagements are billed at lower than normal rates, the resulting price variance is another variable that may warrant close attention.

The inability to set standards for task performance, the desirability of carrying out work by teams, the consequent problems of managing a matrix organization, and the behavioral characteristics of professionals, all complicate the planning and control of the day-to-day opera-

EXHIBIT 15–1 Budget for a CPA Firm

	Estimated actual year ending 9/1/83				*Budget year ending 9/1/84*			
	Billed hours	*Standard rate*	*Gross revenue*	*Salary*	*Billed hours*	*Standard rate*	*Gross revenue*	*Salary*
Gross revenue:								
Armstrong	1,200	$150	$180,000	$120,000	1,200	$150	$ 180,000	$120,000
Baker	1,500	110	165,000	80,000	1,500	120	180,000	80,000
Colwell	1,500	110	165,000	80,000	1,500	110	165,000	80,000
(Additional)	—	—	—	—	800	100	80,000	40,000
Staff #1	1,800	60	108,000	50,000	1,800	60	108,000	54,000
Staff #2	1,600	60	96,000	40,000	1,800	60	108,000	43,000
Staff #3	1,800	50	90,000	40,000	1,800	55	99,000	43,000
Staff #4	1,700	50	85,000	30,000	1,800	55	99,000	32,000
Staff #5	—	—	—	—	900	50	45,000	25,000
Secretaries (2)	1,000	25	25,000	30,000	1,000	30	30,000	33,000
Clerks (2)	3,000	20	60,000	28,000	3,000	25	75,000	31,000
Total (at standard)	15,100		974,000	498,000	17,100		1,169,000	581,000
Special billings			(46,000)				(58,000)	
Net revenue			928,000				1,111,000	
Expenses:								
Salaries (as above)			498,000				581,000	
Benefits			124,000				145,000	
Controllable costs			164,000				150,000	
Fixed costs			120,000				130,000	
Total			906,000				1,006,000	
Income			22,000				105,000	

tions in a professional organization. When the work is done by project teams, control is focused on projects. There is need for a written plan for each project and for timely reports that compare actual performance with planned performance in terms of cost, schedule, and quality, as described in Chapter 17.

The measurement and control of quality is difficult, and procedures used for this purpose are often inadequate. The current crisis resulting from the tremendous increase in malpractice payments in the medical profession, and the less dramatic but nevertheless significant increase in suits against the accounting profession, are, in part, the result of the failure of these professions to set up adequate quality control procedures. These crises are leading to increased attention to such procedures.

Because quality usually cannot be measured by physical instruments or by other inspection procedures found in industrial companies, special control techniques are needed. A common technique is the progress report. Progress reports are effective if the atmosphere of the organization is such that project leaders are willing to reveal actual or incipient problems to their superiors, rather than hiding them until it is too late. If, however, there is an environment in which unpleasant reports invariably lead to destructive criticism, rather than helpful suggestions, progress reports resemble works of fiction.

Progress reports are paperwork, which professionals tend to dislike, but they are nevertheless essential. Report requirements that lead to voluminous descriptions of trivial matters should, of course, be avoided. In particular, if the project is proceeding without difficulty, extensive documentation of this fact is a waste of time. Setting up a list of a relatively few (say, 10 percent) of the projects that are in trouble and requiring special reports on these projects can be a helpful procedure.

A study of professionals' reactions to control in a large public accounting firm concluded that the following conditions were associated with high performance:

1. Participants understood clearly what they were expected to do.
2. They received prompt feedback from their superior on strengths and weaknesses of their current performance.
3. They participated in setting standards for which they would be held responsible.
4. Their performance was reflected by appropriate rewards.[2]

At best, formal reports are unlikely to provide the principal means of finding out about quality problems. Informal conversations, regu-

---

[2] John T. Todd, "The Management Control Process: A Behavioral Science Approach" (Boston: Harvard Business School, unpublished doctoral dissertation, 1972). Summarized in John T. Todd, Paul H. Thompson, and Gene W. Dalton, "Management Control of Personnel," *The Journal of Accountancy*, February 1974, pp. 34–40.

larly scheduled meetings, and the managers' sensitivity to hints of trouble received from various sources are likely to be much more important.

Especially in professions where public criticism of quality is increasing, internal audit procedures are being introduced as a means of controlling quality. In many accounting firms, the report of an audit is reviewed by a partner other than the one who is responsible for it. The proposed design of a building may be reviewed by architects who are not actively involved in the project.

Performance Measurement and Appraisal

At the extremes, the performance of professionals is easy to measure; that is, it is easy to identify and take appropriate action about professionals who do sloppy, incompetent, or inadequate work on the one hand and those who do brilliant work on the other hand. Appraisal of the large percentage of professionals who are well within either extreme is much more difficult. In some situations, objective measures of performance are available: the recommendations of an investment analyst can be compared with actual market behavior of the securities; the accuracy of a surgeon's diagnosis can be verified by an examination of the tissue that was removed, and skill can be measured by the success ratio of operations. These measures are, of course, subject to appropriate qualifications. In most circumstances, however, the assessment of performance is a matter of human judgment. These judgments may be made by superiors, peers, self, subordinates, or clients.

Most common are judgments made by superiors. Professional organizations are increasingly using formal systems to collect performance appraisals as a basis for personnel decisions and for discussion with the person involved. Some of these systems require numerical ratings of specified attributes of performance and provide for a weighted average of these ratings. Compensation may be tied, in part, to these numerical ratings. In a matrix organization, performance is judged both by the person's project leader and by the head of the functional unit that is his or her organizational "home."

Appraisals by a professional's peers or subordinates, are sometimes part of a formal control system. Occasionally, the individual may be asked to make a self-appraisal. In all cases, information that a superior receives from these sources is an informal input to the judgmental process.

Expressions of satisfaction or dissatisfaction from clients are also an important basis for judging performance, although such expressions may not be forthcoming in many engagements. One firm that sells investment advice to institutional clients keeps a record of letters of commendation or criticism received from these clients, classifies these according to the analysts who made the relevant recommendations, and uses this information as part of its performance evaluation system.

For reasons given earlier, the measurement of the revenue generated by a professional's "marketing effort" often is not feasible. A few firms have a formal system for doing this. At the time an engagement is contracted for, the persons involved agree among themselves on the percentage of the fee that is equitably attributed to each of them, and revenue associated with each professional is developed by applying these percentages to the actual fee earned on the engagement. Such a procedure can be useful if there is goodwill and a minimum of wrangling among the persons involved.

The budget can be used as the basis for measuring cost performance, and the actual time taken can be compared with the planned time. Budgeting and control of discretionary expenses is as important in a professional firm as in a manufacturing company. Such financial measures are relatively unimportant in assessing a professional's contribution to the firm's profitability, however. The major contribution is related to the quality of the work, and its appraisal must be largely subjective. Furthermore, the appraisal must be made currently; it cannot wait until one learns whether a new building or a new control system actually works well or whether a bond indenture has a flaw.

An analysis of the profitability of the various services offered by the firm also is useful. The techniques are similar to those used to analyze product profitability in manufacturing companies.[3]

HUMAN RESOURCE ACCOUNTING

The principal asset of a professional organization is its professional staff. The value of this staff does not appear on its balance sheet, however. From 1967 on, accounting literature contains many references to the desirability of accounting for the asset value of human resources in a way that is analogous to the conventional accounting treatment of physical and financial resources.[4]

The only application of this idea in a real situation reported in the literature was that in a medium-sized industrial company. For several years beginning in 1968 the company prepared and reported supplementary financial statements in which "management assets" were listed as a balance sheet item. The amounts reported were arrived at by assigning estimated recruiting, hiring, and training costs to persons in each level of management from first-line supervisors on up. The com-

[3] See John Dearden, "Cost Accounting Comes to Service Industries," *Harvard Business Review,* September–October 1978, pp. 132–40.

[4] See especially Eric G. Flamholtz, *Human Resource Accounting* (Encino, Calif.: Dickerson Publishing, 1974).

pany no longer does this. Those involved in installing the system stated that it was a basic premise and a testable hypothesis that "decisions will be made differently and human assets will be managed more effectively with the addition of information provided by a human resources accounting system."[5] No evidence of such results has been reported in the literature.

The label "human resource accounting" has been applied to other analytical devices, such as the measurement of the effectiveness of training programs, the cost effectiveness of measures to reduce employee turnover, and the like. There is nothing especially new about these techniques. To reduce ambiguity, it seems desirable to restrict the term *human resource accounting* to accounting; that is, to a formal system for recording the status and flow of economic resources. Viewed in this way, it cannot be said that human resource accounting has had any significant amount of acceptance by business.

The basic weakness in the present approach is that valuing human resources at their hiring and training costs far understates the real value of these resources to a company. Conceptual alternatives, such as what it would cost to replace the organization's human resources or the discounted net cash flows that human resources are expected to generate, are completely impractical, even more impractical than the concept that the value of a physical asset is the present value of its future earnings.

In assessing damages in negligence suits involving loss of life, and in the analysis of certain social issues, the value of a human being is taken as being the present value of the person's expected future earnings. The effect of this approach is to attribute a high value to young people compared with old people, to males compared with females, to whites compared with members of minority groups, and to business executives compared with the clergy and others in low-paying occupations. More importantly, this approach has conceptual weakness—it does not take into account the food, shelter, and other resources that persons consume at the same time they generate earnings. In any event, this approach holds no promise as a way of valuing human resources in an organization.

An alternative approach, which does hold promise, starts with the premise that a person's current earnings are an indication of what that person is worth to the company. Just as an office building that generates $100,000 of net rentals is worth twice as much as one that generates $50,000, so a $100,000 professional can be said to be worth twice as much as a $50,000 professional. The value of the office building can

---

[5] R. Lee Brummet, Eric G. Flamholtz, and William C. Pyle, "Human Resource Accounting: A Tool to Increase Managerial Effectiveness," *Management Accounting*, August 1969.

be found by capitalizing the net rentals at an appropriate rate, which is the cost of capital. By analogy, the value of the professionals might be found by capitalizing their current compensation at an appropriate rate, but no one has so far suggested a rational approach to the determination of this rate. Further, the analogy is weakened by the fact that an organization does not own its professionals as it owns its office buildings, although as a practical matter the probability that a professional will stay with the organization can be estimated sufficiently closely to allow for this difference.

The need for a method of valuing human resources was pointed out in connection with the discussion of pricing in the preceding section. Human resource values would also be useful in many other types of management decisions. Thus, although there have been practically no worthwhile accomplishments to date, the subject is important, and continued research on it is eminently worthwhile.

SUGGESTED ADDITIONAL READINGS

Alou, Susan, and **Roemmich, Roger A.** "Responsibility Accounting for Banks." *Management Accounting,* May 1977, pp. 35–38.

American Institute of Certified Public Accountants. *Management of an Accounting Practice Handbook.* New York: AICPA (looseleaf).

Dearden, John. "Cost Accounting Comes to Service Industries." *Harvard Business Review,* September–October 1978, pp. 132–40.

Hekimian, James S. *Management Control in Life Insurance Branches.* Boston: Division of Research, Harvard Business School, 1965.

Tewes, James A. "Valuing Bank Funds for Allocation and Pricing Decisions." *Marketing Accounting,* November 1976, pp. 27–33.

CASE 15–1
Harley Associates, Inc.*

In 1975 Harley Associates, Inc. was one of America's largest advertising agencies. Advertising agencies are retained by many major corporations to assist them in the development and implementation of campaigns to promote sales. Two of the principal groups of advertising work in which agencies engage are the development of strategy and plans for new products, and the maintenance and improvement of the market share of established products. Generally speaking, the most successful partnership between advertisers and agencies are those of

* This case was prepared by John Yeager, Harvard Business School.

long duration. Harley Associates had worked with many of its present clients for more than 20 years.

Advertising agencies are remunerated by their clients in one of two ways. First there is the commission basis, whereby the agency receives a rebate of 15 percent of gross billings from the medium in which the advertisement is placed.[1] Out of this amount the agency must meet all of its expenses. The other system, called the "fee" system, has many variations, but in general the client is billed for specific amounts of work done on his behalf by the agency. This may be on a cost-plus basis or involve a retainer fee plus a reimbursement of expenditures. Harley Associates had worked under various fee arrangements, but its preference was for the 15 percent commission system since it considered that such a system offered greater benefits to both the client and the agency.

ORGANIZATION

Harley Associates was organized into five divisions of management:

Account management. The account supervisor and his staff formed the principal day-to-day contact between the agency and the client organizations. It was their function to work with the client in the development of the marketing plan. In addition, they acted as a liaison among the other areas of management within the agency to coordinate activities on the client's account.

Creative management. The creative department conceived and developed advertising copy and artwork required for prints and advertisements.

Information management. This group was responsible for planning and conducting copy and market research programs, and for advising on merchandising and product promotion opportunities. It also maintained the agency reference library, and a training group for teaching the sales personnel of clients.

Media management. Within the framework of the market plan developed by the account manager, this group developed a media strategy that set forth the desired objectives, and then developed a media plan aimed at accomplishing the strategy most effectively. The relations between the agency and the advertising media, including the buying of space and time and the planning of advertisements, was the responsibility of this group.

Administrative management. This group was concerned with the

---

[1] For example, if Harley placed a full-page ad for a client's product in a magazine whose full-page rate was $10,000, Harley would collect $10,000 from the client, but would have to pay the magazine only $8,500.

internal management of the agency, dealing with personnel, financial and office services areas.

As noted above, the direct contact between the agency and the client organization was through the account supervisor. It was the function of account management to coordinate the work with the client and map out the marketing, creative, and media strategies to promote the client's product. When an account supervisor was promoted to the position, he would begin with one account, and, as he developed, he would assume the responsibility for additional accounts. There was also a certain amount of turnover of accounts among the account supervisors so that each supervisor seldom stayed on the same account for more than a few years. The turnover required the supervisors to learn all about a new business each time they were transferred. This was obviously an expensive procedure, but Harley Associates considered it to be an excellent investment. The rationale behind it was that if the person was of high quality, he would be continually on the lookout for new challenges.

THE "NEW CLIENT" DECISION

One of the most important decisions faced by the top management of an advertising agency is that of accepting an assignment from a new client. Certain firms have to be excluded from consideration because of the competitive constraint: an agency cannot accept a new assignment involving a good or service (i.e., "product") which is competitive with that of another client.

With the above exception, Harley Associates would consider any new client which satisfied two criteria: if the client had a satisfactory business reputation and was of good standing in the business community generally, and if the product seemed to the agency to be likely to satisfy a consumer need, the agency would be interested in accepting the assignment.

In assessing the profit potential of the assignment, the agency used its experience of past costs. Harley Associates was serving over 150 products for 33 clients in 1975, covering a wide range of product groups. On the basis of the cost data for these, an estimate of the cost of servicing the product under consideration would be made. An estimate would also be made of the amount of advertising required to build up the product to the desired market share, and the amount needed to maintain it thereafter. Since an advertising allowance was usually built into the cost of the product, the agency could determine the amount they were going to be able to spend on the basis of certain volume assumptions. If the advertising allowance seemed to be sufficient to build up and to sustain the product, given the estimates of requirements, there would be a prima facie case for accepting the assignment.

THE INTRODUCTION OF A NEW PRODUCT

When a new product was being considered, the problem of estimating the costs of its introduction was acute. As a first step, the information management group tested the market to determine if there were a consumer need for the product and, if so, to isolate the consumer benefit. This procedure was not the introduction of the product to a limited market (Harley Associates referred to this as test marketing), but rather a gauging of consumer acceptance of the product. To aid in this, Harley Associates maintained a research panel of several thousand ordinary citizens around the country.

If it was satisfactorily established that a consumer need for the product existed, a creative strategy was developed, based largely upon the perceived consumer benefit. The product would then be test marketed in order to test the effectiveness of the execution of the strategy. If the first test was unsuccessful, it was assumed that the selling message had not gotten across to the consumer and a change would be attempted in the execution of the strategy. The creative strategy itself was not subjected to question in this process. Such changes were time-consuming, both for the agency and for the client.

After the test marketing was completed, the agency advised the client of its opinion on the probable outcome of launching the product on a full-scale basis. It was only after the decision to proceed had been taken and the advertising expenditures built up that the agency received significant revenue from the assignment. As well as covering current expenses, this revenue had to recompense the agency for the initial costs, so the management judgment early in the assignment concerning the likelihood of success of the product was extremely critical to the profitability of the agency.

SUPPORT OF AN ESTABLISHED PRODUCT

The advertising strategy involved in the support of an established product differed from that used in introducing a new one. The uncertainty attached to the market performance of a new product was considerably less acute in the case of an established product, although the constant possibility of product obsolescence remained. In essence, the function of advertising in supporting a product was to maintain constant exposure of the product's advantages to the ultimate user. The agency personnel and the client's marketing department were constantly seeking new ways of presenting the product to consumers with the objective of expanding market share.

Typically a new maintenance campaign would be started after the existing campaign had run for a predetermined period of time. Judgment was involved in deciding how often a new campaign should be initiated. In addition, a drop in the product's market share might be a sign that a new campaign was required. Adjusting to meet competitive advances was an important part of the maintenance of a product.

When a new campaign was being planned, the account supervisor would instruct the creative department to prepare plans for a strategy. The account supervisor and his staff would then meet, perhaps several times, with the sales personnel of the client to discuss the plans. Eventually a strategy would be agreed upon and the advertisement, commercial, or other promotional device prepared. The agency's media department would then arrange for the execution of the promotion as specified by the account supervisor.

PROFITABILITY OF AN ASSIGNMENT

An important part of the agency top management's job was the assessment of the profitability of an account.

The most profitable clients to the agency were those using each advertisement frequently. The major expenses involved in the agency's work were incurred preceding the completion of the commercial or the copy. Thereafter, the work involved in placing the advertisement with the media was small compared with the 15 percent commission obtainable. Obviously, the more a given advertisement was used, the greater was the probability that the contribution (commission less placement costs) would amount to more than the cost of the preparatory work. If, on the other hand, the client's marketing strategy required constant development of new copy, which would be used only once or twice before it was considered obsolete, the agency's profits would be smaller.

The size of the client might also affect the profitability of an account. If numerous people in the client's organization had to clear an advertising plan, which was more likely to be the case with larger clients, this took a great deal of agency personnels' time and effort. The repeated conferences and revisions involved might push up the agency's costs to the extent of rendering the account unprofitable.

Other considerations involved in the top management decision on the retention of an account were frequently of greater significance than cost considerations. For example, even if a particular product was judged to be unprofitable to the agency, the agency might continue to carry this product because of the profitability of other products being carried for the same client. Sometimes a certain product line had to be maintained by the client for competitive purposes even though the client was aware that the line was not showing a profit for him. If this were the case, the amounts spent on advertising such a product would frequently be small as the client would not be anxious to promote the sales of a losing product. The agency would continue, in many cases, to handle such an account. At the same time, the agency would attempt to minimize its own expenditures involved in the advertising of such a product.

COST COLLECTION

In an effort to determine the cost associated with servicing a given account, close attention was paid to the amount of payroll costs associated with that account. Typically, payroll would amount to between 60 percent and 65 percent of the gross revenues of the agency. In many agencies, expenses other than payroll ranged from 20–25 percent of gross revenues, leaving the remaining 10–20 percent as profit before tax.

All employees except those in administrative management filed time sheets on which they recorded the time they had spent on specific accounts during the previous week. Anyone in the administrative department whose work could be allotted to a specific account would also file a time sheet. From the time sheets, 85 percent of the total payroll cost could be charged directly to the various accounts. Since 85 percent of the payroll was direct, and 65 percent of total cost was payroll, it followed that about 55 percent of cost was direct payroll. This led to a rule-of-thumb method for judging the profitability of an account. If the direct payroll of the account was less than 55 percent of the gross revenue from the account, it was assumed to be profitable.

Of the nonpayroll expenses, about 20 percent (i.e., 4–5 percent of revenues) were directly chargeable to the job. Included in direct expenses were travel, entertainment, the cost of rough copies, copy research work, and pretesting of copy. Indirect nonpayroll expenses included rent, which was the largest, telephone expenses, and so on. These indirect expenses were allocated to assignments on the basis of direct labor payroll.

One feature of Harley Associates' cost accounting system, which was unusual in the business, was that the figures on the profitability of an account were made available only to the chairman, the president, and the treasurer of the company. This was done so that the enthusiasm of the service personnel for their work would not be affected by the profitability of the account. It was thought that an employee might have less enthusiasm for an unprofitable account, and that the quality of his work might suffer as a result. It was considered to be the job of top management to decide which jobs to carry, and that the function of the creative personnel was to execute their tasks as well as they could.

THE ELECTRON INDUSTRIES SITUATION

Electron Industries was a large manufacturer of industrial products. The company comprised many divisions, each of which was autonomous except for those things which affected the image of the company as a whole, including advertising. Some of the company's divisions were clients of agencies other than Harley Associates.

Until recently, each of the divisions of Electron Industries which were clients of Harley Associates had been considered by the agency to be profitable. Early in 1976, however, the profitability to the agency of Electron's International Division had been subjected to question. The client profit and loss statement for the division for the year 1975 is shown in Exhibit 1.

EXHIBIT 1

Client Profit and Loss Statement

Client = Electron Industries, Inc., International Division
Product = Professional Prod.
Period = Year to 12/31/75

Billing	$348,000
Commissions and fees	$ 61,800
Direct payroll:	
Account management	18,000
Copy	22,000
Art	10,000
Media	3,000
Administrative	1,500
	54,500
Other direct expenses:	
Unbillable costs	600
Travel	200
Entertainment	600
	1,400
Indirect expenses:	
Occupancy	8,000
Employee benefits	3,200
Telephone	2,100
Indirect service departments	14,600
Other indirect	6,800
	34,700
Total expense	90,600
Profit (loss) before taxes	($ 28,800)

The International Division did not advertise through the mass media. It was equipped to do most of its own artwork, so Harley Associates did not have to provide these services to the same extent that they did for other clients. The agency's main functions for this division were the development of advertising copy and the placing of advertisements with the media.

The account supervisor had spent considerable time becoming acquainted with International Division's products, and with Electron Industries' objectives in order to convey in the advertising plan a message which would meet with the approval of corporate management.

Within the agency he had to ensure that the copywriters also were thoroughly familiar with the subject matter and the objectives of the advertising plan, so that the copy would conform to Electron's corporate policy.

Mr. Sykes, a member of the agency's staff at headquarters, had been instructed to prepare a report for a top management meeting at which the profitability to the agency of International Division was to be discussed. The report was to include a statement of all the relevant points at issue, a list of alternative courses of action available to the agency, a brief note on the consequences of each, and Sykes' recommendation.

Questions

1. Describe a management control system that is appropriate for Harley Associates.
2. What points would you include in the report mentioned in the last paragraph of the case?

CASE 15–2
Chemical Bank*

Chemical Bank, with deposits averaging well over $1 billion, was one of the largest banks in the United States. Its banking operations were conducted in a main office and in several dozen branch offices located throughout the New York metropolitan area. A partial organization chart is shown in Exhibit 1.

Branch offices operated as if they were independent banks. They served individual, commercial, and industrial customers by accepting demand, savings, and time deposits, by extending various types of loans, and by performing other services normally expected of a bank. The sizes and operating characteristics of the branches varied over a wide range. Average deposits outstanding ranged from $1 million to over $100 million; average loans outstanding, from no loans to over $100 million. Moreover, the ratio of deposits to loans varied considerably from one branch to another; most branches had more deposits than loans, but a few had more loans than deposits. In brief, both the magnitude and composition of assets and liabilities were significantly different among the different branches. Inasmuch as these differences were related to the geographical location of the branches, the difficulty of

* This case was prepared by R. N. Anthony, Harvard Business School.

EXHIBIT 1 Partial Organization Chart

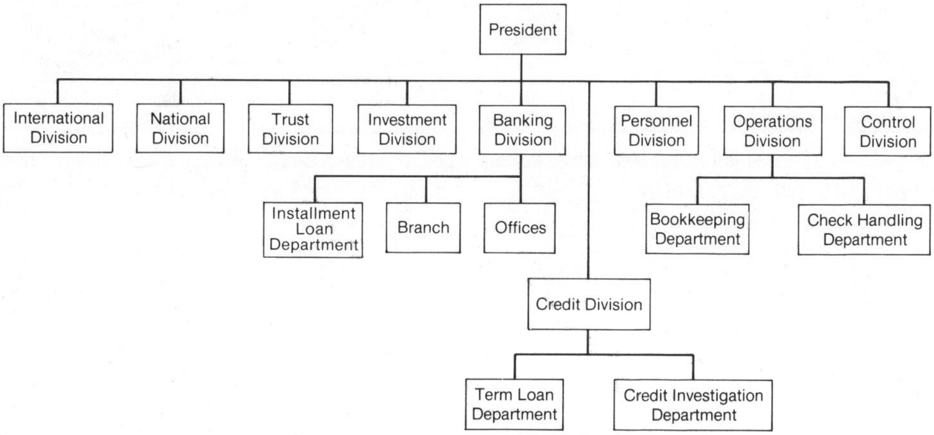

evaluating and comparing the performances of branches for the purpose of overall planning and control was inherent in the situation. The design and operation of a planning and control system for this purpose was the responsibility of the control division.

Among various reports reaching top management, the quarterly comparative earnings statement (see Exhibits 2 and 3) played a central role in the evaluation of branch performance. The report was designed to show the extent to which branches attained three important goals: (1) branches should operate within their budgets, (2) branches should grow in deposits and loans, and (3) branches should earn satisfactory profits. Accordingly, the statement showed for each branch the budgeted and actual amounts of deposits and loans outstanding, and income, expenses, and earnings for the current quarter, the year to date, and the year to date for the preceding year.

BUDGET

In early November, each branch prepared a budget for the following year for submission to headquarters of the banking division and to top management. The branches were furnished a booklet containing sample forms, 24 pages of detailed instructions, and a brief set of policy guides from top management to facilitate the preparation of their budgets. The instructions gave the procedures to be followed in arriving at the budget amounts for specific items. It was, for instance, specified that the starting point for forecasting was to be the prior year's figures on the quarterly basis, that the income item of interest on loans was to be derived from the projected volume of loans and loan rates, that painting cost should not be included in the item for building maintenance expense, and so on.

EXHIBIT 2 Comparative Statement of Earnings, 1960 (Branch A)

3rd quarter			*January 1 through September 30*	
Actual	*Budget*		*Actual*	*Budget*
		Income:		
$ 13,177	$ 12,600	Interest on loans	$ 33,748	$ 35,200
6,373	4,800	Service chgs.—regular A/C's	14,572	14,100
3,816	3,600	Service chgs.—special ck.	11,114	10,700
1,168	1,300	Safe deposit rentals	4,317	4,500
2,237	2,154	Installment loans (net)	5,126	5,406
—	—	Special loans (net)	—	—
1,010	1,200	Fees, comm., other income	3,321	3,300
27,781	25,654	Total direct income	72,198	73,206
104,260	102,148	Interest on excess (borr.) funds	324,434	306,166
132,041	127,802	Gross income	396,632	379,372
		Expenses:		
32,363	32,617	Salaries	96,151	97,164
2,955	2,955	Deferred compensation	8,865	8,865
5,232	4,689	Employee benefits	14,925	14,067
11,485	11,489	Rent and occupancy	34,398	33,947
6,824	7,560	Interest on deposits	20,455	21,780
9,458	8,090	Other direct	25,688	23,930
3,128	3,097	Office administration	9,676	9,725
19,183	17,642	Service departments	57,059	52,399
6,415	5,061	Indirect and overhead	14,964	14,273
97,043	93,200	Gross expenses	282,181	276,150
34,998	34,602	Net earnings before taxes	114,451	103,222
18,955	18,741	Income tax prov. (credit)	61,978	55,906
$ 16,043	$ 15,861	Net earnings after taxes	$ 52,464	$ 47,316
$12,655,000	$12,550,000	Average deposits—Demand	$13,134,000	$12,650,000
979,000	1,100,000	Savings	986,000	1,057,000
55,000	55,000	Time	40,000	43,000
233,000	190,000	U.S.	213,000	183,000
13,922,000	13,895,000	Total	14,373,000	13,933,000
900,000	870,000	Average loans	775,000	827,000
5.82	5.76	Average loan rate	5.82	5.69
		Earnings rate on:		
4.08	3.95	Excess (borr.) funds	4.05	3.95
6.50	6.40	Savings deposits	6.46	6.40
26.5%	27.1%	Net earnings ratio (before taxes)	28.9%	27.2%
		Memo:		
—	—	Losses—before taxes	—	—
—	—	Recoveries—before taxes	—	—

Since salaries was the biggest single expense item, and the hiring and releasing of employees involved considerable cost, utmost care was required in budgeting this item. Branches were instructed to arrive at staffing requirements for the next year after a thorough examination of anticipated increases in productivity arising from mechanization or otherwise improved operating procedures, of anticipated changes in

EXHIBIT 3 Comparative Statement of Earnings, 1960 (Branch B)

3rd quarter			*January 1 through September 30*	
Actual	*Budget*		*1960 Actual*	*1960 Budget*
		Income:		
$ 951,617	$ 833,300	Interest on loans	$ 2,646,813	$ 2,202,750
7,015	7,400	Service chgs.—regular A/C's	24,020	21,900
8,211	7,600	Service chgs.—special ck.	23,384	22,600
2,049	2,100	Safe deposit rentals	6,712	7,100
9,202	9,478	Installment loans (net)	21,402	23,790
—	212	Special loans (net)	85	556
8,081	3,100	Fees, comm., other income	22,517	12,800
986,175	863,190	Total direct income	2,744,933	2,291,496
(191,650)	(121,960)	Interest on excess (borr.) funds	(430,444)	(121,493)
794,525	741,230	Gross income	2,314,489	2,170,003
		Expenses:		
69,308	62,633	Salaries	197,572	185,634
5,646	5,646	Deferred compensation	16,938	16,938
9,180	7,989	Employee benefits	25,833	23,967
27,674	27,775	Rent and occupancy	82,726	83,375
15,878	18,230	Interest on deposits	47,589	52,650
25,637	23,660	Other direct	86,112	71,400
17,232	17,072	Office administration	53,321	53,606
89,724	95,719	Service departments	290,082	283,531
22,406	18,001	Indirect and overhead	53,643	51,166
282,685	276,725	Gross expenses	853,816	822,267
511,840	464,505	Net earnings before taxes	1,460,673	1,347,736
277,212	251,576	Income tax prov. (credit)	791,100	729,934
$ 234,628	$ 212,929	Net earnings after taxes	$ 669,573	$ 617,802
$67,901,000	$70,000,000	Average deposits—Demand	$69,425,000	$72,667,000
2,354,000	2,700,000	Savings	2,328,000	2,600,000
74,000	90,000	Time	52,000	66,000
5,194,000	1,900,000	U.S.	4,086,000	1,733,000
75,523,000	74,690,000	Total	75,891,000	77,066,000
72,129,000	65,600,000	Average loans	67,446,000	57,666,000
5.25	5.10	Average loan rate	5.24	5.10
		Earnings rate on:		
4.08	3.95	Excess (borr.) funds	4.05	3.95
6.50	6.40	Savings deposits	6.46	6.40
64.4%	62.7%	Net earnings ratio (before taxes)	63.1%	62.1%
		Memo:		
—	—	Losses—before taxes	5,559	—
—	66	Recoveries—before taxes	798	—

the volume of activity, and of advantages and disadvantages of using overtime or temporary or part-time help. If the number of the required staff of a branch thus determined exceeded the number previously authorized by top management, the reason for the difference had to be thoroughly documented and substantiated to banking division headquarters and the budget committee. Top management was extremely critical of subsequent requests by the branches for staff increases which had not been reflected in the budgets.

In general, there were two types of income and expense items—those directly identifiable with a particular branch, and those not directly identifiable with a particular branch. Branches were instructed to budget only those direct expenses under their control. Indirect expenses were allocated to branches by the control division. In addition, the budgeting of certain direct expenses, such as depreciation of fixtures, employee benefits, and deferred compensation, was done by the control division because the branches had only secondary control over these expenses.

EARNINGS STATEMENT

The control division had encountered a number of serious problems in trying to produce an earnings statement that would be most useful for the branches and for the management of the banking division. The control division resolved some of these problems in the following ways.

Installment Loans

Record-keeping, issuance of coupon books, and part of collection work for installment loans generated by all branches were handled centrally by the installment loan department; and income earned from installment loans was therefore credited initially to this department. This income was in large part attributable to the branches that generated the loans and was therefore redistributed to them. The current procedure was to distribute gross operating income less the cost of "borrowed" funds and operating expenses of the department on the basis of the total direct installment loans generated by the branch during a revolving annual cycle.

An alternative basis that had been considered was to apportion the net income of the installment department according to the number of payments received by branches, since this measure of activity reflected the clerical time spent for coupon handling. This alternative was not adopted, on the grounds that it did not give branches enough motivation to seek more new installment loans, particularly since customers could make their installment payments at any branch they chose. An alternative basis considered was the amount of average loans outstanding. The controller thought this might be more equitable than the currently used basis, but he was of the opinion that the gain to be obtained from the adoption of the new basis was not large enough to offset the additional necessary record-keeping.

Interest on Excess (or Borrowed) Funds

Branches and other operating units, with funds available for investment in excess of their own requirements for loans, cash, and other assets, shared in the net earnings of the investment division, branches, and other operating units whose asset requirements exceeded their available funds and were charged for funds "borrowed." There was a wide variation in the ratio of deposits to loans among branches, and some branches were credited with the interest on excess funds in an amount higher than their direct income. An example of the calculation of this important income or charge item is shown in Exhibit 4.

EXHIBIT 4 Calculation of Interest Income on Excess Funds, Branch A (first three quarters of 1960)

Calculation of Excess Funds

	(000s)	
Total demand deposits	$13,134	
Less: reciprocal bank balances; float	(727)	
Plus: treasury tax and loan a/c	221	
Adjusted demand deposits	12,628	
Less: reserve at 18%	(2,273)	
Net demand deposits		$10,355
Savings deposits	1,026	
Less: reserve at 5%	(51)	
Net savings deposits		975
Net deposits available for investment		11,330
Less: loans, cash, other assets		(1,229)
Net excess funds		$10,101

Calculation of Interest Income on Excess Funds

	Principal		Annual rate		Three quarters		Interest
In special investment pool (63%)	$ 614,000	×	7.88%	×	¾	=	$ 36,270
In regular investment pool (37%)	361,000	×	4.05%	×	¾	=	10,962
Savings deposits (100%)	975,00	×	6.46%	×	¾	=	47,232
In regular investment pool—demand deposits	9,126,000	×	4.05%	×	¾	=	277,202
Net excess funds	$10,101,000						
Interest on excess funds							$324,434

As shown in the top section of Exhibit 4, the first step was to compute the amount of excess (or borrowed) funds for the branch. Funds were divided into two pools: (1) special pool—earnings from special long-term, high-yield municipal securities, which were considered as an investment of part of the savings and time deposits; and (2) regular pool—earnings from other portfolio securities investments, interest on certain loans, and sundry earnings. As a rule, the special-pool investments yielded a higher rate of return than the regular-pool investments.

Third, branches with savings deposits were credited at the interest rate of the special pool on the basis of their pro rata share of savings deposits. Net savings deposits in excess of the principal of investment in the special pool, together with excess funds other than savings deposits, received pro rata credit from the earnings of the regular investment pool. Branches that borrowed funds were charged at the regular pool rate. In summary, the two rates from the two pools were as follows:

Special pool rate:	Net earnings of special pool/special pool securities principal (part of total savings deposits)
Regular pool rate:	Net earnings from regular pool/excess funds less borrowed funds less special securities principal

For the first three quarters of 1960, the budgeted regular pool rate and special pool rate were 3.95 percent and 7.81 percent; the actual rates, 4.05 percent and 7.88 percent, respectively. Thus, for Branch A the interest on excess funds for the first three quarters was calculated as shown in the lower section of Exhibit 4.

Rent and Occupancy Cost

Some branches operated in leased space, whereas others operated in bank-owned buildings. The first group was charged with the actual rent paid, but the second was charged with the "fair rental value," which was determined by outside real estate appraisers. The practice was thought to put the two groups on the same footing. The fair rental value charges were internal bookkeeping entries offset by credits to real estate accounts and, therefore, indicated the profitability of each building. The determination of the fair rental value was not difficult, and there had been no significant controversies involving its calculation.

Advertising

General or institutional advertising was charged to other indirect expenses. (See below for the allocation of other indirect expenses.) Advertising related to a specific branch was charged directly to that branch, except that, when advertising was placed in mass media, such as radio, television, and newspapers with general circulation, 33 percent of the expense was allocated to other indirect expenses and 67 percent was allocated to the specific branches involved. The theory of the exception was that when mass media were used, the whole bank benefited to a certain extent.

Banking Division Headquarters and General Administration

All expenses of the banking division headquarters, including the salaries of officers in the division headquarters, were allocated to branches on the basis of their prior year's average gross deposits. The figure for average gross deposits was considered as the best single measure of branch activity.

The salaries of general administrative officers of the bank were first allocated among divisions on the basis of the time spent on problems of each division as estimated by each officer. The amount of general administrative salaries thus allocated to the banking division was, in turn, allocated among branches on the basis of gross deposits in the prior year. All other general administrative expenses were charged on the same basis.

Bookkeeping Department

Much of the bookkeeping work was centralized for the whole bank. However, since the central department had been established only in 1959, several offices continued to do their own bookkeeping in 1960. The expenses of the central bookkeeping department were, therefore, allocated only to the branches it serviced. There were eight functional cost centers in the bookkeeping department, and each cost center had its own basis of allocation. The bases of four of the cost centers are given below.

1. *Regular Bookkeeping Cost Center.* In the bookkeeping department, a permanent clerical staff was assigned to process the accounts of each branch. Allocations to branches were based on the salaries of this assigned staff, plus fringe benefits and related overhead cost.
2. *Bank Ledgers Cost Center.* Allocation was on the basis of debit and credit activity as determined by an analysis made from time to time. Inasmuch as the main activity of this cost center was the posting of transactions to ledger sheets, the number of debit and credit entries were preferred to any other basis, e.g., number of accounts. A new survey of debit and credit statistics was made by the analysis department whenever it was believed that there had been a material change from the prior survey period and, in any event, at least once a year.
3. *Special Checking Cost Center.* Same as 2.
4. *Special Statement Section.* Allocation was on the basis of a

number of accounts handled. The activity of the section was to send out special statements on customers' special requests.

Before adoption of the current method based on the cost center concept, weight of statements mailed out had been the basis of allocation for the expenses of the entire department. The current practice was regarded as more accurate, because there were very few temporary movements of staff and machine services from one cost center to another and because there was a significant variation in the activity measures of the cost centers.

According to the controller, the main controversy involving the expenses of the bookkeeping department was not with respect to the basis of allocation but, rather, with respect to the absolute level of expenses of the department. Complaints were heard from those branches serviced by the department to the effect that they were handicapped relative to branches that did their own bookkeeping, because the cost charged by the central bookkeeping department was considerably higher than the cost that would be incurred if the branch did its own bookkeeping. The controller thought branches that had this opinion failed to recognize that the bookkeeping expenses showed in the earnings statements of the branches with their own bookkeeping were only part of the true bookkeeping cost, because an appropriate portion of supervisory salaries, occupancy costs, supplies, etc., was not included in the item. When the bookkeeping was centralized for a branch, the benefit gained from relieving the supervisors of supervising bookkeeping activity usually appeared as increased loans and deposits, and better management generally.

Check Clearance Department

The total cost of this department was divided among 12 functional cost centers, based on the number of employees assigned to each and the volume of its work. The cost of each cost center was, in turn, charged to branches. Examples of the basis of allocation are given below.

1. *IBM proof machine operation—exchanges:* allocated on the basis of number of checks handled.
2. *IBM proof machine operation—deposits:* allocated on the basis of the number of deposit items.
3. *Check desk:* allocated on the basis of number of checks handled.
4. *Transit clerical:* allocated on the basis of number of deposit items.
5. *Supervision:* allocated to the various check clearance department cost centers in ratio to labor costs.

As was the case with the bookkeeping centers, the measures of activity (checks handled and number of deposit items) were based on periodic surveys and remained unchanged until significant changes in the relative activity of branches indicated the need for a new survey. Every cost center's activity was reviewed at least once a year for this purpose.

There were two important sources of trouble in allocation of the expenses of the check clearance department. One was that branches cashed checks issued by other branches; the other was that branches received deposits for customers whose accounts were in other branches. In the periodic activity analyses made to determine the basis of allocating cost, the "number of checks cashed" was the number of checks actually cashed in the branch, whether or not the account was located in the branch. Similarly, the "number of deposit items" was the number of deposits made in the branch. Although it had been believed that the effect of these interbranch services largely offset one another, a recent study by the control division indicated that they, in fact, resulted in distortions with respect to certain branches. The control division was currently working on a method of allocation by which the charge would be made to the branch that benefited most, that is, the branch in which the account was located.

Credit Investigation Department

Although most branches had their own credit analysis staffs, they often asked the central credit department to make investigations. The expenses of the central credit investigation department, therefore, were allocated to the branches that requested its service. The basis of allocation was the number of requests for credit investigation weighted by the typical time required for the analysis performed. The weight for the various types of investigation was determined by the analysis department on the basis of an actual time study.

Term Loan Department

Income from term loans was credited to the branches that generated the loans. Officers of the term loan department actively counseled the branches in negotiating terms with customers, in drawing up loan contracts, and in reviewing existing loans. It was therefore necessary that the expenses of the term loan department be allocated to the branches that used its service. The basis of allocation was the number of loans considered, the number of loans outstanding, and the number of amendments to existing loans, weighted by the unit handling time of each of three classes. In order to determine the weight, the analysis department asked the staff of the term loan department to estimate the time spent on each class.

Personnel Division

The expenses of this division were allocated to all operating units in the ratio of the number of employees in each operating unit to the total.

Other Indirect Expenses

Items of a general overhead nature, such as expenses of the accounting division (except the direct cost of examining a branch, which was charged directly), cost of the senior training program, general institutional advertising, contributions, etc., were included under this heading. The basis of allocation of these expenses among branches was the ratio of annual operating expenses (excluding other indirect and interest on deposits) of each branch to the total operating expenses of all branches.

Deposits and Loans

In the lower part of the comparative statement were shown the budgeted and actual loans and deposits outstanding. Both top management and branch managers exercised a close watch over these primary indicators of the level of the branch's operation. The controller, however, believed that the ultimate test of the office performance should not rest with these items but, rather, with earnings. He maintained that the effect of changes in deposits and loans should and would be reflected in the earnings statement.

CONTROLLER'S VIEWS ON ALLOCATIONS

The controller believed that some arbitrariness was inevitable in the allocation of the income and expense items described above. With dozens of branches, each with its own operating characteristics, it was impossible to have a "perfect" or "right" system for all of them. What was more important, according to the controller, was agreement on the part of the branch managers that the system was generally equitable. If managers agreed on the fairness of the system, he believed, it was likely to be a success. The controller, therefore, let it be known to branch managers that the system was always open for revision, and he encouraged them to make known any criticisms they had. After the control division had done its best to find a workable system, the initiative for suggesting changes was with the branch managers. The controller said that several changes had been made as a result of branch managers' suggestions.

He warned them, however, against a blind and apathetic acceptance; the acceptance should be positive and constructive. On acceptance of the system, branch managers should be concerned with the reported result and make necessary efforts to improve it. Thus, he said, branch managers were told clearly that the earnings statement was used to evaluate their performance. This, he thought, attached sufficient importance to the matter to prevent any possible indifference.

ATTITUDES OF BRANCH MANAGERS ON ALLOCATIONS

The managers of two offices, A and B, held different opinions about the system. The operating characteristics of these branches were different, as indicated by their comparative statements of earnings for the third quarter of 1960, reproduced in Exhibits 2 and 3. Branch A was relatively small and deposit-heavy, did its own bookkeeping and operated in a leased space, whereas Branch B was larger, loan-heavy, used the centralized bookkeeping department, and operated in a bank-owned building. Their annual earnings statements of recent years are shown in Exhibits 5 and 6.

Comment by Manager of Branch A

The statement is useful because I like to see, at least quickly, whether I am within the budget and what caused the deviations from it, if any.

The earnings of our branch are relatively low, because the volume of business is limited by the location. We have more deposits than our loan requirements; consequently, we get credit for the excess funds. In fact, as you see, for the first three quarters of 1960, interest on excess funds was more than four times the total direct income. The 4.05 percent rate on the excess funds seems fair enough, but we try always to increase our loans in order to increase our earnings. However, the location of our office is a limiting factor.

Since rent and occupancy is the actual rent paid to the owner of the building, we can't have any quarrel about that, but the service department charges are certainly too high. We don't have any control over these costs; yet we are charged for them. I am not complaining that this is unfair; on the contrary, I believe branches should share the burden. My only misgiving is whether those service departments are doing enough to cut down their costs.

About one half of the service department expenses charged to our branch is for check clearing service. Although I don't know the basis of allocation, I don't doubt that it is fair. Besides, even if I should have some questions about the basis, probably it wouldn't reach up there; the communication channel from here to the top is long and tedious.

At present, we do our own bookkeeping, but soon this will be centralized. I have heard some managers complain that the cost charged to them for the centralized bookkeeping is higher than the cost

EXHIBIT 5 Condensed Annual Earnings Statements, Branch A ($000)

	1960	1959		1958		1957		1956	1955
	Budget	Budget	Actual	Budget	Actual	Budget	Actual	Actual	Actual
Total direct income	$ 98	$ 93	$ 90	$ 87	$ 89	$ 99	$ 90	$ 99	$ 82
Interest on excess funds	409	364	381	327	316	299	287	263	355
Gross income	507	457	471	414	405	398	377	362	437
Expenses:									
Salaries	130	129	125	125	125				
Deferred compensation	12	10	10	8	9	140	147	132	114
Employee benefits	19	19	18	17	17				
Rent and occupancy	45	46	45	45	47	47	49	43	43
Interest on deposits	30	30	27	19	19	9	11	6	4
Other direct	32	29	31	30	30	*	*	*	*
Office administration	13	15	13	17	16	*	*	*	*
Service departments	70	58	61	57	57	67	69	62	44
Indirect overhead	18	18	21	19	16	*	*	*	*
Gross expenses	369	354	351	337	336	315	329	296	256
Net earnings before taxes	138	103	120	77	69	83	48	66	181
Average gross deposits	13,975	13,550	13,707	13,573	12,948	14,540	13,442	15,057	21,504
Average loans	820	820	810	746	737	990	927	1,139	1,093

* Changes in accounting procedure make these items noncomparable with later years.

EXHIBIT 6 Condensed Annual Earnings Statements, Branch B ($000)

	1960	1959		1958		1957		1956	1955
	Budget	*Budget*	*Actual*	*Budget*	*Actual*	*Budget*	*Actual*	*Actual*	*Actual*
Total direct income	$ 3,077	$ 2,725	$ 2,532	$ 2,214	$ 2,201	$ 2,338	$ 2,395	$ 1,959	$ 1,172
Interest on excess (borrowed) funds	(177)	157	222	154	263	73	(32)	209	556
Gross income	2,900	2,882	2,754	2,368	2,464	2,411	2,363	2,168	1,728
Expenses:									
Salaries	249	255	256	245	247				
Deferred compensation	22	19	21	17	18	250	264	236	232
Employee benefits	32	34	33	30	31				
Rent and occupancy	111	105	104	104	105	106	108	65	85
Interest on deposits	71	75	66	51	52	19	25	12	10
Other direct	95	93	108	84	86	*	*	*	*
Office administration	71	85	76	86	83	*	*	*	*
Service departments	379	383	360	356	345	361	380	315	224
Indirect overhead	65	64	72	60	51	*	*	*	*
Gross expenses	1,095	1,113	1,096	1,033	1,018	878	928	829	814
Net earnings before taxes	1,805	1,769	1,658	1,335	1,446	1,533	1,435	1,339	914
Average gross deposits	77,410	79,885	75,853	72,063	73,899	73,415	69,683	70,740	73,433
Average loans	58,000	56,000	49,702	48,971	47,095	50,000	49,945	44,460	28,378

* Changes in accounting procedure make these items noncomparable with later years.

when they did their own bookkeeping. However, such intangible gains as prestige and customer relations may justify a little higher cost. At any rate, we wouldn't have any choice if top management decides to centralize our bookkeeping. It may be better in the long run.

Although I don't know exactly what items are included in other direct and indirect and overhead expenses, I don't think they are excessive. The control division is trying to be fair.

In summary, I think the statement is useful, but there are many factors you should consider in interpreting it.

Comment by Manager of Branch B

The statement is a fair measure of how branches are doing. It is true that the location of a branch has a lot to do with its operation; in evaluating a particular branch, the location is an important element to be taken into account. To take the extreme case, you don't need a branch in a desert. If a branch can't show earnings after being charged with its fair share of all costs, perhaps the purpose of its existence is lost.

High volume and efficient operation have contributed to our high level of earnings. Our branch has more loans than can be sustained by our own deposits; thus, we are charged with interest on borrowed funds on the theory that we would have to pay the interest if we borrowed from outside. Of course, by increasing deposits we could meet the loan requirements and add to our earnings a good part of the interest on borrowed funds; indeed, we have been trying to lure more deposits to our branch. Quite apart from this special effort, however, we do not neglect to seek more loan opportunities, for loans increase earnings even after the interest charge.

Our office is in a bank-owned building, but instead of controversial depreciation and maintenance charges we are charged with the fair rental value. We are satisfied with this practice.

The bookkeeping of our branch is centralized. I believe we could do it for less money if we did our own bookkeeping; but competing banks have centralized bookkeeping departments, and we have to go along. I suspect there are some intangible benefits being gained, too.

If I really sat down and thoroughly examined all the allocation bases, I might find some things that could be improved. But the fact of life is that we must draw a line somewhere; some arbitrariness will always be there. Furthermore, why should our branch raise questions? We are content with the way things are.

Comments by Banking Division Headquarters

We call this report [Exhibits 2 and 3] our Bible, and like the actual Bible, it must be interpreted carefully. Many factors affect the performance of a branch that do not show up on the report. For example, in an area that is going downhill the manager of a branch has to work terribly hard just to keep his deposits from declining, whereas in a

EXHIBIT 7 Branch Office Report

1960

Location and Office No. A

	All Dollar Amounts in Thousands Unless Otherwise Stated		JAN.	FEB.	MAR.	APRIL	MAY	JUNE	JULY	AUG.	SEPT.	OCT.	NOV.	DEC.	YEAR AVERAGE	
	DEPOSITS - AVERAGE															
1	Demand - (Ind., Part., Corp.)	$	14 038	13 473	12 330	12 919	13 108	12 911	12 596	11 907	12 746	12 202				1
2	Demand - Banks	$	50	50	-	-	-	-	-	-	-	-				2
3	Special Checking	$	221	218	220	251	235	216	237	244	236	219				3
4	Treas. Tax & Loan Account	$	118	149	238	124	270	321	232	202	265	196				4
5	Savings	$	987	974	1 001	990	976	1 012	972	978	986	1 013				5
6	Christmas Club	$	15	23	30	35	41	46	51	55	60	63				6
7	Time	$	-	-	-	-	-	-	-	-	-	-				7
8	Total	$	15 429	14 887	13 819	14 319	14 630	14 506	14 088	13 386	14 293	13 693				8
	NUMBER OF ACCOUNTS															
9	Demand (Ind., Part., Corp.)		1 515	1 513	1 507	1 503	1 516	1 511	1 514	1 497	1 478	1 473				
10	Demand - Banks		1	-	-	-	-	-	-	-	-	-				
11	Special Checking		868	865	884	892	894	900	903	911	939	948				
12	Savings		585	587	593	589	587	591	593	587	621	645				
13	Christmas Club		540	536	534	538	533	530	526	519	516	511				
14	Time		-	-	-	-	-	-	-	-	-	-				
15	Total		3 509	3 501	3 518	3 522	3 530	3 532	3 536	3 514	3 554	3 577				
	LOANS														YEAR AVERAGE	
16	Total Loans - Average	$	723	755	720	627	672	773	841	889	971	961				16
17	Instalment Loan - Volume	$	20	24	36	31	35	22	25	34	27	39				17
18	Spec. Loan Dept. - Month End	$	-	-	-	-	-	-	-	-	-	-				18
	NUMBER OF BORROWERS															
19	Total Loans		48	58	50	49	51	54	55	60	62	63				
20	Instalment Loans - Made		24	37	46	50	32	30	28	45	44	39				
21	Special Loan Dept.		-	-	-	-	-	-	-	-	-	-				
22	Staff - Number of Officers		4	4	4	4	4	4	4	4	3	3				
23	No. of Employees - Auth. Budget		25	25	25	25	25	25	25	25	25	25				
24	Total		29	29	29	29	29	29	29	29	28	28			YEAR - TOTALS	
25	Overtime & Supper Money Payments (To nearest dollar)	$	276	135	273	93	496	123	536	370	350	220				25
	SERVICE CHARGES (To nearest dollar)															
26	Regular Checking Accounts	$	1 543	1 578	1 445	225	2 550	858	2 378	1 998	1 997	1 833				26
27	Special Checking Accounts	$	1 017	1 119	1 220	1 397	1 223	1 322	1 313	1 237	1 266	1 340				27
28	Total	$	2 560	2 697	2 665	1 622	3 773	2 180	3 691	3 235	3 263	3 173				28

Income and Expense By Quarters And Cumulative

To Nearest Dollar		1st Quarter	2nd Quarter	Jan. thru June	3rd Quarter	Jan. thru Sept.	4th Quarter	Jan. thru Dec.
Gross Income	$	133 060	131 531	264 591	132 041	396 632		
Gross Expenses	$	92 050	93 088	185 138	97 043	282 181		
Net Before Taxes	$	41 010	38 443	79 453	34 998	114 451		
Net After Taxes	$	18 799	17 622	36 421	16 043	52 464		

	1st Quarter	2nd Quarter	Jan. thru June	3rd Quarter	Jan. thru Sept.	4th Quarter	Jan. thru Dec.
Average Loan Rate	5.80	5.83	5.81	5.82	5.82		
Earn. Rate-Excess Funds	4.02	4.06	4.04	4.08	4.05		
Earn. Rate-Savings Deposits	6.52	6.55	6.54	6.59	6.55		

EXHIBIT 7 ***(continued)*** **Branch Office Report—Supplement**

1960

Location and Office No. A

	All Dollar Amounts in Thousands	JAN.	FEB.	MAR.	APRIL.	MAY	JUNE	JULY	AUG.	SEPT.	OCT.	NOV.	DEC.	YEAR TOTALS	
	Regular Checking Accounts - Number														
1	Opened - New	26	17	7	15	16	17	10	9	14	11				1
2	Opened - A/C Trans. within Office	-	1	1	1	4	-	1	-	-	-				2
3	Opened - A/C Trans. from other Off.	-	1	1	-	3	-	2	-	1	-				3
4	Total Number Opened	26	19	9	16	23	17	13	9	15	11				4
5	Closed	24	17	12	17	6	19	9	17	24	14				5
6	Closed - A/C Trans. within Office	-	2	1	2	2	-	-	8	6	1				6
7	Closed - A/C Trans. to other Offices	4	3	2	1	2	3	1	1	4	1				7
8	Total Number Closed	28	22	15	20	10	22	10	26	34	16				8
9	Net Opened or Closed	-2	-3	-6	-4	+13	-5	+3	-17	-19	-5				9
	Regular Checking Accounts Average Deposits Closed - Monthly														
10	Closed $	16	7	3	15	7	14	4	11	18	7				
11	Closed - Trans. within Office $	-	19	2	4	2	-	-	6	4	1				
12	Closed - Trans. to other Offices $	5	6	2	-	1	3	1	1	2	2				
13	Total Average-Closed Accts. $	21	32	7	19	10	17	5	18	24	10				
	Accounts Since Jan. 1st- Cumulated*														
14	*No. Opened (Line 1)	26	43	50	65	81	98	108	117	131	142				
15	No. Closed (Line 5)	24	41	53	70	76	95	104	121	145	159				
16	*Opened-Current Mo. Avg. (Line 14) $	83	191	162	143	120	102	120	109	114	127				
17	Closed-Total Avg. Bal. (Line 10) $	16	23	26	41	48	62	66	77	95	102				
	Business Development													YEAR TOTALS	
18	No. of calls - Customers	3	8	7	4	10	8	6	9	5	5				18
19	No. of calls - Prospects	3	4	4	4	1	4	2	6	5	5				19
20	Total	6	12	11	8	11	12	8	15	10	10				20
21	Spec. Checking Accts - Opened	26	21	31	21	19	22	15	33	37	29				21
22	Spec. Checking Accts - Closed	13	24	12	13	17	16	12	25	9	20				22
23	Spec. Checking Accts - Net	+ 13	- 3	+ 19	+ 8	+ 2	+ 6	+ 3	+ 8	+ 28	+ 9				23
24	Savings Accounts - Opened	17	9	22	9	15	24	15	9	52	39				24
25	Savings Accounts - Closed	21	7	16	13	17	20	13	15	18	15				25
26	Savings Accounts - Net	- 4	+ 2	+ 6	- 4	- 2	+ 4	+ 2	- 6	+ 34	+ 24				26
27	S.D. Boxes - New Rentals	9	6	3	9	3	6	5	6	4	-				27
28	S.D. Boxes - Surrendered	9	4	9	11	12	10	6	7	7	3				28
29	S.D. Boxes - Net	-	+ 2	- 6	- 2	- 9	- 4	- 1	- 1	- 3	- 3				29
30	No. of Personal Money Orders Sold	523	543	583	643	421	467	447	419	452	367				30

growing area, the manager can read the *New York Times* all day and still show an impressive increase in deposits. The location of the branch in the neighborhood, its outward appearance, its decor, the layout of its facilities—all can affect its volume of business. Changes in the level of interest rates, which are noncontrollable, also have a significant effect on income. At headquarters, we are aware of these factors and take them into account when we read the reports. The unfortunate fact is that some managers—for example, those in declining areas—may not believe that we take them into account. Such a manager may worry about his apparently poor performance as shown on the report, and this has a bad psychological effect on him.

One other difficulty with the report is that it may encourage the manager to be interested too much in his own branch at the expense of the bank as a whole. When a customer moves to another part of town, the manager may try to persuade him to leave his account in the same branch, even though the customer can be served better by a branch near his new location. We even hear of two branches competing for the same customer, which certainly doesn't add to the reputation of the bank. Or, to take another kind of problem, a manager may be reluctant to add another teller because of the increased expense, even though he actually needs one to give proper service to his customers.

Of course, the earnings report is just one factor in judging the performance of a branch manager. Among the others are the growth of deposits compared with the potential for the area; the number of calls he makes soliciting new business (we get a monthly report on this); the loans that get into difficulty; complaint letters from customers; the annual audit of his operations made by the control division; and, most important, personnel turnover, or any other indications of how well he is developing his personnel. Some of these factors are indicated in these statistics [see Exhibit 7], which are prepared at banking division headquarters.

Questions

1. The general question is: What are the strong and weak points of the budget-reporting-performance evaluation system of the bank in reference to its branch operations? What improvements would you suggest?

Examples of specific topics you should consider are:

a. What characteristics of banking make its management control system different from that of a manufacturing operation?

b. What is the relationship between the earnings statement and the branch office reports?

c. Would you recommend calculating a return on investment for each branch? If so, how would you determine the investment base?

d. Should noncontrollable costs be omitted from the earnings statement? If so, what items would be affected?

e. In comparing actual with budgeted interest on loans, should a noncontrollable variance be developed which represents the effect of changes in the general level of interest rates?

2. Bank of America, the largest bank in the United States, charges its profit centers for the use of money at current interest rates for obtaining funds of like maturities and risk. For example, if a branch makes a 90-day loan, it would be charged at the current rate that the bank pays on 90-day certificates of deposits.[1] Should Chemical Bank adopt this practice?

CASE 15–3
Emerson & Hamlin*

John Hamlin, the managing partner of Emerson & Hamlin, read with interest a description of the method of appraising and rewarding partners used by Rachlin & Company, as reported in *The Journal of Accountancy,* February 1975. He wondered whether the plan was sufficiently worthwhile to discuss seriously with his colleagues.

Emerson & Hamlin was a single-office public accounting firm which engaged in auditing, management services, and income tax practice. It had 20 partners and 45 other employees, and annual billings of approximately $3 million. Currently, partners were compensated by a relatively small salary plus a share of the partnership income. Each partner's share was determined by the number of "units" assigned to him, as a proportion of the total number of units for all partners. Each partner's units were agreed on between him and Mr. Hamlin. The total number of units increased over time for two reasons: (1) addition of new partners, and (2) rewards for additional responsibilities or performance of existing partners. The total units decreased as partners retired or left the firm, but there was usually a net increase from one year to the next because the firm was expanding.

Mr. Hamlin was 60 and planned to retire in the near future. Privately, he thought that each of the three senior partners (in charge of audit, management services, and tax, respectively) was capable of becoming managing partner. Mr. Hamlin spent approximately 20 percent of his time on billable work, and each of the three senior partners spent about 60 percent.

RACHLIN PLAN

The plan used by Rachlin & Company, as described in the article, is summarized below.

---

[1] Mary Pollack, "Profitability Management at Bank of America," *WBD Management Magazine,* November/December 1978, p. 8.

* This case was prepared by R. N. Anthony, Harvard Business School.

Each partner has a base draw (or "salary") and any profit remaining above the draws is divided on the basis of points. Points also are used as the basis for determination of a partner's payout in the event of death or retirement. The initial number of points is based on original contributions to the firm (in clientele and/or capital), or points are allowed to be purchased on admittance to partnership.

More points can be acquired from the firm by award in the following manner. At the end of each year the firm considers it has available one point for each $1,000 of annual volume and can award those points not already outstanding. If we assume an annual volume of $750,000 then

Points available (total authorized)	750
Total of partner's present points (issued)	525
Points available for distribution	225

The firm thus has 225 points available to distribute to present or new partners. They can be awarded (issued) or carried over to subsequent years, depending on the recommendation of the Points Committee.

At the partners' December meeting each year, two partners are selected (by secret ballot) to serve as the Points Committee. At the January partners' meeting the committee presents its recommendations as to awarding points. If there is no veto by 75 percent or more of the partners, then the recommendations of the Points Committee shall be effective for the year beginning January 1.

The first time the Points Committee met, it found it had no criterion for awarding the points. The initial committee awarded no points, but it did develop an "evaluation analysis." This analysis is based on a partner performance list which Carl S. Chilton, Jr., of Long, Chilton, Payte & Hardin, described in *The Journal of Accountancy,* December 1973, and on material presented by William R. Shaw, of Arthur Young & Company, at the Management of an Accounting Practice Conference sponsored by the Missouri Society of CPAs in October 1973.

The evaluation analysis was a one-page form on which each partner was rated on 31 criteria as follows:

A. *Work load, production and firm responsibility:*
1. Fees produced by partner's client responsibility.
2. Profitability of service for clients (considering hourly rates, markdowns, markups, and so forth).
3. Fees produced by partner individually.
4. Effectiveness in collecting client receivables.
5. Performance and up-to-date knowledge in basic areas of practice (what every partner is expected to know).
6. Performance and up-to-date knowledge in partner's specialized area.
7. Performance in contributing to the management of the firm.

8. Engagement planning and control.
9. Ability to get things done.
10. Ability to delegate and supervise.

B. Client relations:

11. Reputation for "attentive" service.
12. Ability to complete work promptly.
13. Availability to clients when needed.
14. Confidence in the individual and satisfaction with work.
15. Expansion of service to existing clients.

C. Personal development:

16. Participation in recruitment.
17. Participation in training programs.
18. Efforts to bring along subordinates.
19. Attitude toward employees.
20. Employee attitude toward person evaluated.

D. Standing in the community and profession:

21. Image in the community as a top-level citizen and professional person.
22. Positions of leadership in community organizations.
23. New clients brought in through individual contacts and efforts.
24. Standing within the profession (positions of leadership, and so forth).
25. Participation in professional activities.

E. General:

26. Self-motivation (initiative, drive, energy).
27. Leadership (ability to motivate others).
28. Stability and maturity (discerning what is important, reliability in crises).
29. Judgment (when to decide and when to consult).
30. Cooperativeness and team play.
31. Promotion of firm's standing.

On each criterion, a person was rated on the following scale:

1. Disappointing, needs improvement.
2. Erratic, less than expected.
3. Satisfactory, normal expectancy.
4. Excellent, unusually well done.
5. Outstanding, rarely equalled.
0. No basis for judgment.

With a maximum rating of 5 for each criterion, the maximum possible score was 155.

The "evaluation analysis" is prepared three times a year by each partner on himself or herself and each of the other partners. The analyses are submitted to the managing partner, who is authorized to review any deficiencies or "downward trends" with the subject partner. At the end of the year these forms are made available to the Points Committee as a basis for judgment in awarding points.

In addition to specific areas of judgment, the form also provides space for subjective comments on outstanding accomplishments, areas of weakness, and efforts to resolve weakness.

The Points Committee reviews the three evaluation forms on each partner for the purpose of awarding the 225 available points. Assuming that all 225 points were awarded, the results could be as shown in Exhibit 1.

EXHIBIT 1 Awarding Available Points

	Present			*New totals*	
Partner	*Points*	*Percent*	*Awarded*	*Points*	*Percent*
A	250	47.6%	50	300	40.0%
B	100	19.0	50	150	20.0
C	75	14.3	75	150	20.0
D	75	14.3	25	100	13.3
E	25	4.8	25	50	6.7
Total	525	100.0%	225	750	100.0%

There are three key ideas which make this system of awarding points effective:

1. It is a method of rewarding the younger partners on a regular (annual) basis, to keep their enthusiasm high, and it allows them to share in increased profits.
2. Points are awarded only out of growth of the firm (if the annual fees did not increase there would be no new points available).
3. Points are never taken away, once awarded, so that no one feels that he or she has surrendered anything.

Question

Should Emerson & Hamlin adopt the Rachlin plan or some modification of it?

CASE 15–4
Acton Life Insurance Company*

It was the third week in July 1975. The Quarterly Review Report for the southern region of the Acton Life Insurance Company (see Exhibit 1) had recently been distributed. William Bailey, sales manager of the

* This case was prepared by R. F. Vancil, Harvard Business School.

EXHIBIT 1 Quarterly Operating Review Report: Southern Region—Second Quarter, 1975

Branch	*First-year premiums*	*First-year expenses**	*First-year expense ratio*
Atlanta	$69,216	$28,596	41.3%
Birmingham	60,004	19,634	32.7
Charlotte	45,614	13,220	29.0
Nashville	91,692	22,292	24.3
New Orleans	95,446	20,800	21.8
Tampa	76,370	14,430	18.9
Averages: Region	73,057	19,829	27.0
Averages: Company	76,234	18,898	24.8

* The expenses associated with the acquisition of new business, including salaries of salesmen. In the full report, 12 additional columns were included, showing a breakdown of the total expenses of the branches and certain adjustments.

southern region, was visiting the home office in Boston for the purpose of discussing this and related reports with John McFarland, vice president of sales. Much of the discussion related to the performance of the six branch agencies in the southern region. Mr. Bailey had been sales manager of that region for five months; formerly he had been a branch manager in the eastern region. This was his first visit to the home office since he had assumed his new duties.

Mr. Bailey: Our Atlanta branch had the best performance this past quarter. Just look at the volume of business it put on the books over the last three months—over $5.5 million. This works out to about $1,100,000 per salesman, which is way ahead of the other branches.

Mr. McFarland: Bill, don't you remember our discussion on performance yardsticks during my visit to your office earlier this year? I made a particular effort to explain why we feel that sales volume is not enough, that we have to relate the value of these sales to the cost of making them. For some time now, we have been using the ratio of first-year expenses to the total of first-year premiums. This is what the Operating Review Report is all about. Looking at this report, we can see that the Tampa branch was your best branch last quarter. Your Atlanta branch was actually your poorest performer.

Mr. Bailey: That's not the way I understood it when I was a branch manager under Eddie Petanski. I had the impression that the volume of business we booked was the really important yardstick: Don't we pay branch managers commissions on the basis of volume? Aren't all the awards we hand out based primarily on volume—the million-dollar round table, the president's club, and so on? All the branch managers I ever knew felt this way. In fact, we went even further; when we got together to compare performance, we usually ended up by looking at the total amount of commissions we had earned. After all, the real test is how much the company pays us for our efforts.

EXHIBIT 2 Quarterly Profit Report: Southern Region—Second Quarter, 1975

				Average-size first-year premium			
Branch	*Face value of insurance sold (000)*	*First-year premiums*	*Average-size policy*	*Amount*	*Per $1,000 insurance*	*Premium collection frequency**	*Two-year lapse ratio†*
Atlanta	$5,526	$69,216	$17,470	$219.76	$12.53	6.2	8.4
Birmingham	3,176	60,004	13,212	251.20	18.90	7.0	5.2
Charlotte	3,400	45,614	28,776	387.50	13.42	4.6	13.6
Nashville	4,728	91,692	23,854	460.00	19.39	2.8	12.9
New Orleans	3,832	95,446	26,422	657.06	24.91	3.7	18.3
Tampa	5,014	76,370	18,812	180.14	15.23	4.7	6.8
Averages: Region	4,280	73,058	21,856	430.38	19.69	4.2	10.9
Averages: Company	4,620	76,234	25,040	575.02	22.96	4.9	5.3

* The average number of times per year that premiums were collected per policy.
† The fraction of the number of policies sold in a given 12-month period that lapsed during the following two-year period, computed as a running average.

Mr. McFarland: Well, we're supposed to be using this expense ratio. It was put in before I became VP, and I thought by now we were all using it. We are not even satisfied with this measure, however, and have been turning out another report to be used in conjunction with the Quarterly Operating Review Report to help interpret the expense ratio. This is the Quarterly Profit Report [see Exhibit 2] which you've also received . . . there it is, at the bottom of that pile of papers. This shows that even your Tampa branch didn't do as well as it appeared to on the basis of its expense ratio.

Mr. Bailey: Hold on, Jack, now you've really got me confused. I looked over the Quarterly Profit Report when I got it, and compared these profit factors with previous periods to spot trends, as you suggested. But I didn't use it as you did just now. In fact, I don't see how I can relate these five measures to the expense ratio and to sales volume accomplishments and come up with anything meaningful on performance. I'd just be shooting in the dark. And I'd bet this is true with the other sales managers.

Mr. McFarland: You're probably right. It's pretty difficult to relate so many factors together and come up with a meaningful appraisal of performance. What we've been trying to do is to get a better indication of profitability of the business booked by each branch than the expense ratio tells us. The best we've come up with so far is the set of five factors.

Mr. Bailey: Well, I can see what you're driving at, but I just don't think you can do it. What we have now doesn't seem to get us much closer and is much too complicated. Besides, as an ex-branch manager, I'd bet most of our branches believe that volume of business is the primary yardstick.

Mr. McFarland: Bill, I don't think there is much to be gained by pushing our review of performance any further at this time. Some of these same problems have been bothering me for some time now. I think what I'll do is discuss this performance appraisal problem with Mr. Runyan [president of the company] during our regular meeting on Friday. Your points will be very helpful in this discussion. Thanks for bringing them up.

BACKGROUND

Acton Life Insurance Company was a stock company, formed in 1909. It was licensed to do business in all the 50 states, the District of Columbia, and most of Canada. At the beginning of 1975, 56 branches served these areas. It had a total of about $9 billion of insurance in force, and its total sales volume in 1974 was about $1,300,000,000.

The lines of insurance offered by Acton Life consisted primarily of ordinary life, accident and health, group life, and various annuities. As of 1975, the company sold its entire line of insurance through independent brokers, approximately 20,000 in number. As independent brokers, they were not required to sell Acton policies exclusively. Many also sold policies of the same general types written by other insurance companies.

The basic organization of Acton Life followed the general pattern in the industry. This was a functional type, consisting of six departments: actuarial, legal, sales, investment, underwriting, and administrative services. At the head of each of these departments was a vice president who reported to the president.

The sales department was responsible for directing the operations of the various branches, through which relationships with the independent brokers were established and maintained. The company planned to expand the number of branches as rapidly as it could over the following few years in order to serve a larger number of brokers. The branches were grouped into eight geographical regions, each region having from 4 to 11 branches. For each region, there was a sales manager, who reported to the vice president of sales. The heads of two staff activities (agency secretary and management training) also reported to the sales vice president.

A manager was in charge of each of the branches. His primary responsibilities were the direction of the selling effort of his branch, selecting and developing salesmen, participating in negotiating contracts with brokers, and supervising the office personnel required to service the policies sold by these brokers. In general, a branch manager was paid entirely in commissions on the business booked through his branch. However, new branch managers were paid a fixed salary for a period of five years, or until the commissions they would otherwise receive consistently exceeded the salary.

The average number of salesmen working for a branch was four. The major activities of the salesmen were calling on and developing contracts with brokers, helping them to start making sales, and following up from time to time to make sure their sales efforts were satisfactory. Branch salesmen were paid salaries only; commissions for selling the insurance were earned by the independent brokers.

In all branches except a few of the smaller ones, there was an assistant branch manager. Each branch also had a small clerical staff.

MEETING WITH THE PRESIDENT

At his regular Friday morning meeting with Mr. Runyan, Mr. McFarland brought up the problem of measuring the performance of branch managers. He summarized the discussion he had had earlier in the week with Mr. Bailey.

Mr. Runyan said that of late he had become concerned with a closely related problem—the need for a more rational approach to the planning and control of branch operations. Recently, he had read a doctoral thesis in which the author proposed a solution to this problem. Mr. Runyan suggested that Mr. McFarland study this proposal and, if it looked sufficiently promising, discuss it with his sales managers. In any event, the president wanted Mr. McFarland's considered opinion regarding the utility of the proposal for Acton Life and his recommendations for a course of action. Mr. McFarland agreed to submit a report of his conclusions and recommendations by October 1.

EVALUATION OF THE PROPOSAL

Over the weekend, Mr. McFarland considered how best to reach a meaningful appraisal of the proposal. He finally decided to send an abstract of it to each of his eight sales managers and to ask for their reactions to the idea of its adoption by Acton Life, either completely or in a modified form. Accordingly, on Monday, July 28, he asked his assistant to prepare such an abstract and to have it ready by the end of the week. A copy of the abstract is shown in Appendix A.

After reviewing and approving the abstract, Mr. McFarland dictated a covering memorandum to his sales managers. In this memorandum, he asked them to read the entire abstract carefully and focus attention on the feasibility of its adoption by Acton Life. He also asked for written comments, both favorable and critical. In order to have the branch managers' point of view represented, he suggested that each sales manager discuss the proposal with one or two of the better managers in his region and incorporate their comments, appropriately identified, as part of the memorandum each would submit.

To ensure that the proposal would not be dismissed quickly as impractical, Mr. McFarland stated that in his opinion the concept of ECTP (expected combination to profit), around which the proposal was constructed, appeared to have considerable merit. Although use of the concept in a system for planning and controlling branch operations would constitute a novel and somewhat radical step for a life insurance company, the concept had sufficient possibilities, he thought, to be considered seriously and with an open mind. In order to give everyone sufficient time for study and discussion, Mr. McFarland set September 15 as the deadline for submission of comments.

As of September 16, Mr. McFarland had received memoranda from all eight sales managers. He immediately began to analyze the comments in terms of the principal arguments for and against the proposal. In the process, he prepared a summary, included here as Appendix B. Five reaction patterns are highlighted in the summary:

1. Cost of implementing and administering the proposed planning and control system.
2. Method of calculating the expected contribution to profit (ECTP).
3. Concept of a profit measure at the branch level.
4. Applicability of the proposal in practice.
5. Defense of the industry.

In reviewing this summary, Mr. McFarland noted that comments by 10 branch managers had been submitted in addition to those from the eight sales managers. The summary represented the opinions of 18 of his best managers.

With his summary before him Mr. McFarland pondered what recommendations he should make to the president. He wanted to be sure that they resulted from an objective weighing of the advantages and disadvantages of the proposal, including a realistic appraisal of the benefits to be derived by Acton Life and the problems likely to be encountered. He also wanted to accompany his recommendations with a summary of supporting arguments, together with an action plan for implementing his recommendations.

Questions

1. Disregarding the practical problem of obtaining acceptance, do you believe the expected contribution to profit approach is conceptually sound?
2. Assuming that the approach is sound, what steps should be taken next?

APPENDIX A
Summary of Proposed Planning and Control System for Branches*

SCOPE OF THE PROPOSAL

This proposal applies primarily to the administrative needs of the branch manager and higher levels of management in planning and controlling the operations of branch agencies within a life insurance company. It is anticipated that parts of the proposal will also have utility for various classes of decision problems, such as the establishment of insurance premiums, the setting of commission scales, and the design of incentive systems.

This proposal does not apply directly to the planning and control of central staff activities, such as the legal department or the actuarial department. However, the proposal is fully compatible with the more traditional practices for planning and controlling such staff activities.

OBJECTIVES SOUGHT BY PROPOSAL

The objectives this proposal seeks to achieve are as follows:

1. To provide a satisfactory basis for branch managers to use to relate the financial worth of results achieved to the costs incurred in order to realize these results.

* Abstracted from a doctoral thesis by James S. Hekimian.

2. To provide both top management and branch managers with an improved system for planning and controlling the operation of individual branches.
3. To motivate branch managers to do what is in the best interest of the company.

COMPONENTS OF THE PROPOSAL

The proposal consists essentially of two parts:

1. *Expected contribution to profit.* A measure of the worth to the company accruing from the sale of an individual policy calculated at the time of sale. Use of this measure makes possible the calculation of the contribution to the company's profit arising from the operation of any branch.
2. *Improved planning and control system.* An overall planning and control system for the management of branch agencies of life insurance companies that incorporates the above profit calculations.

EXPECTED CONTRIBUTION TO PROFIT

Nature of the Problem

A major obstacle in the way of improving systems for planning and controlling the operations of branches is the lack of an adequate measure of the worth of accomplishments or results generated by branches. Most of the measures used currently are related to the volume of policies sold, either expressed directly as the aggregate of the face value of these policies, or indirectly as premiums collected or as commissions paid. Usually, expenses of operating a branch are related to these sales figures in some way, often in the form of a ratio; the implication of this practice is that there exists a certain standard ratio (based on past performance, or a current average, or both) that indicates profitable or, at least, desirable performance. Some management personnel believe that sales volume accomplishments should not be the end-all, and that some better measure of the worth of accomplishments should be developed against which to weigh the cost of achieving these accomplishments. A few believe that the problem is one of trying to operate a profitable branch without any idea of what profits are.

Everyone interviewed agreed that the various types of insurance policies differed considerably as to their worth to the insurance company. For example, it was generally acknowledged that a company gained less from selling a $1,000 term policy than from selling a $1,000 endowment policy. However, no practical way had been found as yet to measure the difference in gain and to incorporate it into a system for planning and controlling sales effects.

Analysis

In many industries the worth of the accomplishments of a branch is measured in terms of the gross profit on the sales volume it generates; against this are charged the expenses of acquiring this gross profit in order to arrive at the amount contributed to net profit. For the life insurance industry, this approach had never seemed possible because of accounting practices pertaining to the time the profit from a policy was realized. However, this obstacle resulted from an accounting convention, and accounting *need not* stand in the way of developing an improved measure of worth to guide the internal management of an insurance company.

As a result of discussions with management personnel, it was decided that in order to be truly useful any measure of worth should meet the following criteria:

1. Reflect the worth to the company of the sale of a particular policy.
2. Do this in monetary terms.
3. Do this as of the time a policy is sold.

If such a measure could be developed, it would make possible the calculation of a form of "profit" accruing to the company from the operation of any branch. An examination of the practice of the industry in computing premiums and of the expectations of the industry regarding actual performance in the three areas making up this premium calculation suggested that such a measure could be developed.

Basically, every life insurance premium was developed from three separate factors: a projected mortality rate, a projected interest rate, and a projected loading charge. Realistically, also, companies considered competition in setting a final premium; in practice, this consideration usually resulted in an adjustment in the loading factor. Given the three factors, insurance actuaries calculated an approximate premium for any kind of policy the company cared to sell.

All three of these factors in practice were deliberately set conservatively. Because the projected mortality rate was based on the actual mortality rate during some *past* period, companies were, in effect, assuming that the mortality rate was higher than it actually would be. But the mortality rate actually had been decreasing steadily over the years, and this trend was expected to continue. Thus, with the collection of every premium, the company expected a gain from overestimating mortality.

In projecting interest rates, companies tended to be very conservative in their estimates of the rate of return they would earn on their investments. The actual return on investments usually was higher than the assumed return; thus, the premium resulted in a gain from the interest assumption.

Finally, companies tended to overestimate the total loading charge required, thereby creating a third expected gain. In a stock company, a profit allowance usually was included as an explicit element of the loading charge, whereas in a mutual company an equivalent result was produced by the deliberate overstatement of costs.

In sum, then, because of the current practices of computing life insurance premiums, companies expected a gain from savings from the allowance for mortality, excess interest earned, and the loading charge.

Proposed Solution

Therefore it was argued, there was built into every life insurance premium an expected contribution to profit (hereafter referred to as ECTP). This ECTP occurred *at the time of sale* of a policy. It was further argued that this ECTP could be calculated and that this figure could serve the purpose of a ''profit'' figure for a branch. These conclusions were valid because *at the time of sale,* for each policy sold, one could calculate:

1. The expected gain included in the mortality charge. This was the difference between the premium actually charged—based on the assumption that projected mortality experience would parallel past mortality experience—and the premium that would be needed to cover *expected* mortality. That is, the mortality rate actually experienced would not be so high as assumed, death benefits would not be paid out so soon as assumed, and, therefore, companies would have more of the insurance premiums left for contribution to profits. In computing annuity premiums, insurance companies actually employed mortality rates lower than those they employed in computing life insurance premiums. A company's expectations regarding future mortality experience would fall somewhere between these two sets of rates.

2. The expected gain from the interest charge. This was the difference between the premium actually charged—based on a conservative assumption as to interest earned on investments—and the premium that would be charged if it were based on *expected* interest earnings. For most companies, estimates of future earnings rates on their investments were regularly made by their investment departments.

3. The expected gain from the loading charge. This was the difference between the total amount of loading in a particular premium and the actual amount of variable expense of selling that policy (commissions, medical fees, taxes on premiums, and so forth). Although the separation of variable expenses might be difficult to make, it was generally considered to be feasible. Even if this separation could not be made with a high degree of accuracy, the resulting error would be constant for all policies, and thus its effect on the proposed planning and control system would be minor.

Thus, for each year a particular policy was expected to be in force, an expected gain could be calculated *at the time of sale*. The present value of this stream of expected year-by-year gains from each policy sold is the *expected contribution to profit*. This represents the additional *worth* to the company *now* of selling a particular policy.

Given this calculation of ECTP, a branch manager could exercise intelligent control over his responsibility for the acquisition of business. This would be accomplished by relating the total ECTP of a branch to its cost of acquiring business.

For example, consider a $1,000 term insurance policy with a life of 20 years sold to a man, age 35, with premium payments to be made over the first 10 years. Using the standard mortality table, normal interest rate, and normal loading for selling and administrative costs, the premium on this policy would be calculated as $11.99 per year. With the substitution of expected values, the same calculation would produce a cost of $5.51 per year, plus $14.87 for selling and administrative costs in the first year, and $1.08 per year for each of the other nine years of premium payments. The difference between the premiums and the costs, with allowance for mortality, discounted at the company's expected earning rate, came to a total of $27.98. This was the expected contribution to profit on this policy.

Use of ECTP

The suggested method of making an ECTP calculation provides a valid profit figure at the branch level. It measures the additional current worth to the company of the sales made by a branch. And it is available at the time decisions regarding selling efforts are being made.

Admittedly, this figure is not a precise measure of realized profits in an accounting sense. Since we must necessarily be looking to future in any such calculation, and since the figure is filled with uncertainties, the results of such a calculation must necessarily have a high likelihood of being different from the profit actually realized.

This fact is of no practical concern, however. The principal objective of the concept of ECTP is to make available as good a figure as possible for planning and control purposes. Certainly, the best profit figure available at the time a relevant decision is to be made (realizing that this may be something less than perfectly accurate) will be more useful than a perfectly accurate figure (if there is such a thing) that is not available until sometime after the decision has been made.

The concept of ECTP also provides a new tool for use in analysis of different types of policies. Most companies now rely on first-year premiums or face value of policies sold as a measure of accomplishment, and both branch managers and salesmen generally are motivated to achieve as high a volume of either one (or both) as possible.

IMPROVED PLANNING AND CONTROL SYSTEM

The core of the proposed planning and control system is the establishment of each branch agency as a profit center, with the branch manager as the responsible supervisor. The appropriate "profit figure" for a particular branch is the ECTP earned by the branch, minus the expenses incurred by that branch in generating this ECTP. Operating plans are expressed in terms of ECTP and the expenses needed to achieve that ECTP. Actual expenses are deducted from the ECTP actually generated by the branch to determine the profit contributed by the branch; this actual profit is compared to the planned profit. Deviations from planned performance are shown for each element of ECTP and expense. The analysis of these deviations and the taking of appropriate corrective action are vital elements in the proposed planning and control system.

In designing this system, two precautions are vital: to match with ECTP only those expenses incurred to generate ECTP; to limit the expenses chargeable to a branch to only those which are controllable at the branch level.

Looking at the second requirement first, an examination of the various kinds of expenses incurred in the operation of a branch agency indicates that all these expenses are controllable to a significant extent by the branch manager. Some are controllable only over a fairly long time period, while others are controllable to a considerable extent on a day-to-day basis. In recognition of this variation in controllability as a function of time, all branch expenses are segregated, under the proposal, into three classifications: long-range controllable expenses, annual controllable expenses, and day-to-day expenses. The expenses segregated in each of these categories are as follows:

Long-range controllable expenses	*Annual controllable expenses*	*Day-to-day expenses*
Rent	Management salaries	Clerical salaries
Depreciation:	Advertising	Postage
Furniture	Training	Stationery and supplies
Equipment	Net advances to salesmen	Telephone and telegraph
		Repairs and maintenance
		Travel
		Entertainment
		Loss on advances to salesmen
		Miscellaneous

The first requirement can be understood best by regarding the mission of a branch agency as consisting of two functions: (1) the acquisition function, or the job of selling insurance policies; and (2) the service function, or the job of maintaining insurance in force. The expenses incurred for the service function do not create, or result in, ECTP. Therefore, these service expenses should be excluded from the matching of branch expenses against ECTP.

These service expenses can be classified in the following three categories:

1. *Putting new business on the books.* Checking over the application and other forms to see that everything is in order, setting up the appropriate accounting records, and mailing out the policy.
2. *Collecting premiums.* Sending out bills, changing beneficiaries, arranging for loans, and other routine service that is provided to all policyholders.
3. *Paying claims.* Final disbursement of cash, closing the records, and other details involved in terminating a policy.

The procedure for excluding these service expenses from the determination of the profit contributed by a branch consists of the following basic steps. Clerical time standards are established for each of these service activities; this may be done on the basis of time-and-motion studies, although an average of actual past performance could serve the purpose. The number of units of work (e.g., number of premiums processed, number of new applications processed) actually handled by a branch is multiplied by the time standard for the particular unit, and the resulting number of standard hours is multiplied by the average clerical wage at a particular branch. The resulting dollar figure is an allowance or credit for the service work performed during a reporting period by the branch. This expense credit is deducted from the appropriate expense classifications, with the balance of these expenses charged to the acquisition function. Nonclerical service expenses (e.g., supplies) are credited in the same proportion that the clerical cost allowance bears to the total of clerical expense.

Example of Proposed Control Report

A sample of the control report to be employed in the proposed planning and control system is shown as Attachment A. The report relates to the operations of a particular branch and covers a full year (in the example, the calendar year 1975). The upper portion of the report presents the components of ECTP, identified by the individual salesmen who have generated the ECTP by their sales activities. The middle portion presents the various expenses of operating a branch, grouped by controllability classification. Right below the line for "Total Expenses" are three lines involving profits: "Branch profit," the difference between actual ECTP and the total of actual expenses; "home

ATTACHMENT A Hypothetical Life Insurance Company Profit Schedule, Branch A—Profit Schedule, 1975

	(a) Total	(b)	(c) Service	(d)	(e) Acquisition	(f)	(g)	(h)
	Budget	Actual	Budget	Standard allowance*	Budget	Actual	Variance	
Expected contribution to profit:								
Baker	$ 60,000	$ 72,000	$ —	$ —	$ 60,000	$ 72,000	$12,000	20%
Donovan	60,000	66,000	—	—	60,000	66,000	6,000	10
George	30,000	24,000	—	—	30,000	24,000	(6,000)	(20)
Henderson	10,000	8,000	—	—	10,000	8,000	(2,000)	(20)
Levin	70,000	62,000	—	—	70,000	62,000	(8,000)	(11)
Lannigan	120,000	130,000	—	—	120,000	130,000	10,000	8
Ramos	80,000	78,000	—	—	80,000	78,000	(2,000)	(2)
New hires—three	10,000	14,000	—	—	10,000	14,000	4,000	40
Total ECTP	440,000	454,000			440,000	454,000	14,000	
Controllable branch expenses:								
Long-range:								
Rent	13,200	13,200	—	—	13,200	13,200	0	0
Depreciation on furniture and equipment	800	800	—	—	800	800	0	0
Annual:								
Management salaries	34,000	34,000	—	—	34,000	34,000	0	0
Advertising	10,000	9,600	—	—	10,000	9,600	(400)	(4)
Training	2,000	1,500	—	—	2,000	1,500	(500)	(25)
Net advances to salesmen	5,000	7,200	—	—	5,000	7,200	2,200	44
Day-to-day:								
Clerical salaries	58,000	60,000	14,000	15,150	44,000	44,850	850	2
Postage	2,200	2,400	400	400	1,800	2,000	200	11
Stationery and supplies	3,000	3,200	700	800	2,300	2,400	100	4
Telephone and telegraph	6,800	7,200	—	—	6,800	7,200	400	6
Repairs and maintenance	1,000	200	—	—	1,000	200	(800)	(80)

Entertainment	3,000	2,800	—	—	3,000	2,800	(200)	(7)
Travel	5,600	6,000	—	—	5,600	6,000	400	7
Loss on advances	1,000	3,000	—	—	1,000	3,000	2,000	200
Miscellaneous	1,200	1,100	—	—	1,200	1,100	(100)	(8)
Total expenses	146,800	152,200	15,100	16,350	131,700	135,850	4,150	
Branch profit					308,300	318,150	9,850	
Home office support						300,000		
Net profit						18,150		
Lapse ratio					5.0%	4.7%		

* Service allowance:

	Number of units	Standard time	Average clerical salary	Standard clerical cost	Total clerical cost
1. Clerical salaries:					
PNBB	650	4 hours	\$3.00 per hour	\$12.00	\$ 7,800
Collecting premiums	1,300	1½ hours	\$3.00 per hour	4.50	5,850
Paying claims	500	1 hour	\$3.00 per hour	3.00	1,500
Total	2,450				15,150

2. Postage: \$0.16 × 2,500 units = \$400.
3. Stationery and supplies: 25.1% of \$3,200 = \$800.

Total—Budget and Actual: the total amount of ECTP generated by each component (i.e., salesman), and the total of each class of expense.

Service—Budget and Standard Allowance: the allowances credited to the branch for the performance of its service functions.

Acquisition—Budget: for each line item, the amount in the Total, Budget column less the *budgeted* amount for each service allowance.

Acquisition—Actual: for each line item, the amount in the Total, Actual column less the allowances (if any) in the Service, Standard column.

Variance, dollars: for each line item, the dollar difference resulting from the subtraction of the amount in the Acquisition, Budget column from the amount in the Acquisition, Actual column. Negative amounts are shown in parentheses. For components of ECTP, positive values are favorable variances and negative values are unfavorable variances. For elements of expense, negative values represent overspending and positive values underspending; whether these variances are favorable or unfavorable can be judged only in the light of the particular circumstances giving rise to the variance.

Variance, percent: the magnitude of the dollar variance shown in the preceding column expressed as a percentage of the amount in the Acquisition, Budget column.

office support,'' an allocation of the fixed expenses of running the home office; ''net profit,'' the amount remaining after the allocated home office expense has been deducted from the branch profit.

The reason for this deduction is simply that the branch profit figure otherwise will always seem ''high,'' both because it gives credit (through ECTP) for profit not yet realized and also because it is in fact only a contribution to profit. The purpose of this deduction is to make the manager aware of the amount of support he is receiving from the home office. (For other purposes, the branch profit or ECTP is the appropriate figure.)

APPENDIX B
Summary of Comments on Proposal

COST OF IMPLEMENTING AND ADMINISTERING THE PROPOSED PLANNING AND CONTROL SYSTEM

Six comments related to the cost consequences of adopting the proposal:

1. Four men felt that proposed system would be a lot more costly than what was being done now; there would have to be an ECTP figure for each policy, and new calculations would have to be made each year on basis of expected figures; present measures were really good enough.
2. One man felt that proposal might be more costly than what was being done now but that it would be worthwhile to devote some effort to checking this more carefully.
3. One man felt that cost of proposal might seem high; ''but people often don't realize how costly the present system really is.'' If proposal adopted, it would substitute in many instances for work now being done and would eliminate the need for doing some other work. Felt, however, that straight cost comparison was not valid; the important consideration was whether or not the proposed system would supply better information and thus make possible better decisions; in particular, the motivation of branch managers should be directed better.

Method of Calculation of ECTP

Eight comments related to the method of calculating ECTP.

All eight felt that calculation was headed in the right direction, assuming that some sort of profit figure at the branch level was wanted;

idea of gain from mortality, gain from interest, and taking present value of expected cash flow felt to be sound if one wanted to do this kind of thing (idea of earning a contribution to overhead not understood very well).

1. Three men wondered why there wasn't an expected gain from loading.
2. Two men said calculation made a lot of sense to them; for the first time, they had an idea of what actuaries did.
3. Three stated if calculation could be made, would have little trouble applying it pretty much as suggested in proposal.

Concept of a Profit Measure at the Branch Level

Sixteen comments pertained to the idea of employing a profit measure for the planning and control of branch operations.

1. Three men felt concept of profit was not appropriate in the life insurance business; life insurance companies, through their salesmen, should sell insurance on basis of people's needs; salesmen generally trained first to recognize a client's insurance needs and then to try to satisfy those needs with available funds of client; if profits became a matter of concern, salesmen and branch managers would be induced to try to sell the more profitable policies rather than to satisfy clients' needs.
2. Thirteen men believed concept was useful, with reactions ranging from limited to broad usefulness.
   - *a.* At one extreme—that of limited usefulness: comment of regional manager that he had asked the actuarial department to make this kind of calculation from time to time just to see how various branches were making out, but doubted that information would be useful to managers in general.
   - *b.* At other extreme: comment of branch manager that it was just the tool he needed to do his best job; if he could somehow relate his decisions to the effect they would have on company profits, he would make better decisions in the long run and would also have an easier time making them.
   - *c.* Comment made by several men: had always thought something like this should be done, but either hadn't pursued it or hadn't been able to convince others of the merit of the idea.

Applicability of the Proposal in Practice

Of the 13 men who had positive reactions, in varying degrees, to the concept of a profit measure at the branch level, 10 made comments on how well they expected the proposal would work in actual practice.

1. Five men felt it would work, with following qualifications:
   a. One suggested it be tried out on a few branches to see how it worked.
   b. One uncertain whether calculation could be made in practice.
   c. Three suggested proposal be reviewed by a committee.
2. Five men believed proposal could work, but wouldn't work in actual practice due to lack of acceptance; reasons for this opinion can be categorized as follows:

> *Tradition.* Sales volume has always been the accepted measure of accomplishment in the insurance industry; almost everyone has become accustomed to this orientation; trying to effect such a radical change as substituting a profit measure for a sales measure will take a long, long time.
>
> *Status.* Certain people have achieved positions of prominence, both within the company and within the industry in general, on the basis of these traditional volume measures, who would not have been promoted to such positions if their performance had been measured by their profit contribution: (best example provided by those who sell mostly group insurance); a number of such people are in key positions in top management; these people are not likely to act favorably on a proposal which as much as tells them that they aren't as important as they imagined, and probably shouldn't be in the positions of prominence they currently occupy.
>
> *Profit image.* A lot of people in the industry wouldn't like our men talking about the business as being profit-oriented; image of a life insurance company as a benevolent institution catering to the public good should not be risked.

Defense of the Industry

Three comments categorized best as a defense of current practices of the life insurance industry focused on the importance of being conservative in one's expectations about the future (e.g., mortality tables, interest assumptions, and loading expenses), especially in light of the public interest being served and the indefinite nature of the business.

CHAPTER 16

Nonprofit Organizations*

The management control process in nonprofit organizations is in many respects similar to that in profit-oriented organizations, but in important respects it is different. The similarities and differences are discussed in this chapter.

PROFIT-ORIENTED AND NONPROFIT ORGANIZATIONS

The dominant purpose, or at least one of the major purposes, of some organizations is earning profits. Decisions made by their managements are intended to increase (or at least maintain) profits, and success is measured, to a significant degree, by the amount of profits these organizations earn. (This does not imply that profit is the only objective, or that success can be measured entirely in terms of profitability; that would be an overly simplistic view of most businesses.)

Other organizations exist primarily to render a service. Decisions made by their managements are intended to provide the best possible service with the available resources, and the success of these organizations is measured primarily by the amount and quality of the service they render it. More basically, their success should be measured by how much they contribute to the public welfare. This type of organization is here labeled "nonprofit." Included in this category are government organizations, educational organizations, hospitals and other health care organizations, religious and charitable organizations, clubs and similar membership organizations, foundations, and a variety of other types. They employ approximately 30 percent of the American work force.

"Service" is a more vague, less measurable concept than "profit." It follows that the measurement of performance is more difficult in a nonprofit organization than in a profit-oriented organization. For the

---

* This chapter is based on Robert N. Anthony and David W. Young, *Management Control in Nonprofit Organizations*, 3d ed. (Homewood, Ill.: Richard D. Irwin, 1984).

same reason, making rational choices among alternative courses of action is also more difficult. In a nonprofit organization, the relationship between costs and benefits, and even the amount of benefits, are difficult to measure. Despite these difficulties, an organization must be controlled. Its management must do what it can to assure that resources are used efficiently and effectively. Thus, the central problem is to find out what management control policies and practices are useful, despite the limitations.

CHARACTERISTICS OF NONPROFIT ORGANIZATIONS

Certain characteristics of nonprofit organization affect the management control process in those organizations:

1. Their tendency to be *service organizations*.
2. The dominance of the *professionals*.
3. The absence of the *profit measure*.
4. Less dependence on *clients* for financial support.
5. Differences in *governance*.
6. Differences in *top management*.
7. Their tendency to be *political* organizations.
8. A *tradition* of inadequate management organizations.

The first two of these characteristics were discussed in Chapter 15. The other six are discussed below. Of these, the absence of the profit measure is the most important, and it affects all true nonprofit organizations. Each of the others affects many, but not all, nonprofit organizations. Also, they are tendencies, rather than pervasive characteristics. Furthermore, again with the exception of the profit measure, these characteristics are not peculiar to nonprofit organizations. Each of them exists in many profit-oriented organizations; however, these characteristics are important in the *typical* nonprofit organization, but only in the *exceptional* profit-oriented organization.

The Profit Measure

All organizations use resources to produce goods and services; that is, they use inputs to produce outputs. An organization's *effectiveness* is measured by the extent to which its outputs accomplish its objectives, and its *efficiency* is measured by the relationship between inputs and outputs. In a profit-oriented organization the amount of profit provides an overall measure of both effectiveness and efficiency. In many nonprofit organizations, however, outputs cannot be measured in quantitative terms. Furthermore, many nonprofit organizations have multiple objectives, and there is no feasible way of combining the measures of the several outputs, each of which is intended to accomplish one of these objectives, into a single number that measures the overall effectiveness of the organization.

The absence of a satisfactory, single, overall measure of performance is comparable to the profit measure is the most serious management control problem in a nonprofit organization. (It is incorrect to say that the absence of the profit *motive* is the central problem; rather, it is the absence of the profit *measure*.) In order to appreciate the significance of this statement, we need to consider precisely the usefulness and the limitations of the profit measure in profit-oriented organizations.

Usefulness of the Profit Measure

The profit measure has the following advantages: (1) it provides a single criterion that can be used in evaluating proposed courses of action; (2) it permits a quantitative analysis of these proposals in which benefits can be directly compared with costs; (3) it provides a single, broad measure of performance; (4) it facilitates decentralization; and (5) it permits comparisons of performance to be made among responsibility centers that are performing dissimilar functions. Each of these points is discussed below.

1. Single criterion. In a profit-oriented business, profit provides a way of focusing the considerations involved in choosing among proposed alternative courses of action. The analyst and the decision maker can address such questions as: Is the proposal likely to produce a satisfactory level of profits, or is it not? Is alternative A likely to add more to profits than alternative B?

The decision maker's analysis is not so simple and straightforward as the above might imply. Objectives other than profit usually must be taken into account, and many proposals cannot be analyzed in terms of their effect on profits. These qualifications do not invalidate the central point, namely, that profit provides a focus for decision making in many situations.

In most management science techniques, a single objective function must be specified, and in a profit-oriented situation this objective function is profit. Differences of opinion among decision makers in a profit-oriented firm are likely to reflect differing judgments as to the best means of achieving the profit objective; they are unlikely to reflect differing judgments as to the relative importance of several different objectives.

2. Quantitative analysis. The easiest type of proposal to analyze is one in which the estimated costs can be compared directly with the estimated benefits. Such an analysis is possible when the objective is profitability, for profit is the difference between expense and revenue, and revenue is equated to benefits. By contrast, when the "benefit" is something other than revenue, the analysis is necessarily much more subjective. When the objective is profit, those elements of the analysis which can be stated in monetary terms can be weighed and balanced against one another in terms of the common criterion—their effect on profits. For example, a proposal to introduce a new product involves such considerations as the estimated revenue, the marketing effort required, the physical facilities, the additional inventory, and the additional production requirements. If reliable estimates of the dollar amount of each of these elements can be made, they can be easily summarized in a single number, the estimated net profit.

3. ***Broad performance measure.*** Profitability provides a measure that incorporates many separate aspects of performance within it. The best manager is not the one who generates the most sales volume, or the one who uses labor most efficiently, or the one who uses material most efficiently, or the one who has the best control of overhead, or the one who makes the best use of capital. Rather, the best manager is the one who does best on all these activities combined. Profitability incorporates these separate elements. The key consideration is not the details of the income statement, but, rather, the "bottom line." This measure is valuable both to the managers themselves and to those who judge their performance. It provides managers with a current, frequent, easily understood signal as to how well they are doing, and it provides others with an objective basis for judging the managers' performance.

4. ***Decentralization.*** Because profit-oriented organizations have a well-understood goal, and because the performance of many individual managers can be measured in terms of their contribution toward the goal, top management can safely delegate many decisions to lower levels in the organization. The principal management control device associated with such delegation is the profit center, which is a division or other operating unit whose manager is responsible for both revenue and expenses. In recent years, most large companies and many small companies have decentralized decision making by creating profit centers.

5. ***Comparison of unlike units.*** Finally, the profit measure permits a comparison of the performance of heterogeneous operations that is not possible with any other measure. Assuming that the accounting rules used to measure profits are similar, and that the amount of assets employed is properly taken into account in measuring profitability, the performance of a department store can be compared with the performance of a paper mill in terms of the single criterion: which was the more profitable? Profitability, therefore, not only provides a way of combining dissimilar elements of performance within a company; it also provides a way of making valid comparisons among organizations that have the same objective, the objective of profitability, even though the size, technology, products, and markets of these companies are quite different from one another.

Source of Financial Support

A profit-oriented company obtains its financial resources from sales of its goods and services. If the flow of these revenues is inadequate, the company does not survive. The market dictates the limits within which the management of a profit-oriented company can operate. A company cannot (or, at least, should not) make a product that the market does not want; and it cannot dispose of its products unless their selling prices are in line with what the market is willing to pay.

Some nonprofit organizations also obtain all, or substantially all, their financial resources from sales revenues. This is the case with most general hospitals (as contrasted with teaching hospitals), with colleges and universities that depend primarily on tuition from students, and with research organizations whose resources come from contracts for specific research projects. Such organizations may be called *client-supported* organizations. They are subject to the forces of the marketplace in the same way as are profit-oriented organizations in the same industry; that is, such nonprofit colleges and hospitals are similar to proprietary colleges and hospitals, and such nonprofit research organizations (e.g., SRI International) are similar to profit-oriented research organizations (e.g., Arthur D. Little, Inc.).

Other nonprofit organizations receive a significant amount of financial support from sources other than revenues from services rendered. These may be called *public-supported organizations*. There is no direct connection between the amount of taxes that an individual pays to a municipality and a government unit and the amount of services rendered to that individual.

A profit-oriented company wants more customers. More customers mean more profit. In public-supported organizations there is no such relationship between the number of clients and the success of the organization. If the amount of its available resources are fixed by appropriations (as in the case of government agencies) or by income from endowment or annual giving (as is the case with many educational, religious, and charitable organizations), additional clients may place a strain on resources. In a profit-oriented organization, therefore, the new client is an opportunity to be vigorously sought; in some public-supported organizations, the new client may be a burden, to be accepted with misgivings.

This negative attitude toward clients gives rise to complaints about the poor service and surly attitude of "bureaucrats." Clients of client-supported organizations tend to hear "please" and "thank you" more than clients of public-supported organizations.

Competition provides a powerful incentive to use resources wisely. If a firm in a competitive industry permits its costs to get out of control, its product line to become out of fashion, or its quality to decrease, its profits will decline. A public-supported organization has no such automatic danger signal.

Because the importance of what the organization does is not measured by demand in the marketplace, managers of public-supported organizations tend to be influenced by their personal convictions of what is important. As a substitute for the market mechanism for allocating resources, managers compete with one another for available resources. The physics department, the English department, and the library, all try to get as large a slice as possible of the college budget pie.

In responding to these requests, top management tries to judge what services clients need, or what is best in the public interest, rather than what the market wants. In the public interest, Amtrak provides railroad service to areas where it is not economically warranted, and the U.S. Postal Service similarly maintains rural post offices.

Just as the success of a client-supported organization depends on its ability to satisfy clients, so the success of a public-supported organization depends on its ability to satisfy those who provide resources. A state university maintains close contact with the state legislature. A university may place somewhat more emphasis on athletics than the faculty thinks is warranted in order to satisfy contributors to the alumni fund. Furthermore, acceptance of support from the public carries with it a responsibility for accounting to the public.

Governance

Although the statement that shareholders control a corporation is an oversimplification, it is unquestionably true that shareholders have the ultimate authority. They may exercise this authority only in times of crisis, but it is nevertheless there. The movement of stock prices is an immediate and influential indication of what shareholders think of the management. In profit-oriented organizations, policy and management responsibilities are vested in the board of directors, which derives its power from the shareholders. In turn, the board delegates power to the president, who serves at the board's pleasure, acts as the board's agent in the administration of the organization, and who is replaced if there are serious differences of interest or opinion.

In many nonprofit organizations the corresponding line of responsibility is often not clear. In nongovernment organizations the presumably controlling body does not necessarily represent the source of the organization's power. Instead of being selected formally by those ultimately responsible for the organization, it may be self-perpetuating, selected by outside parties, or selected de facto by management. Its members are seldom paid for their services. They may feel little pressure from, or little responsibility to, outside groups.

In government organizations, the diffusion of power is also great. The bureaucracy is often insulated from top management by virtue of job security and rules, and career civil servants may know that they will outlast the term of office of the elected or appointed chief executive. Agencies, or units within agencies, may have their own special-interest clienteles whose political power is stronger than that of the chief executive of the agency (e.g., the relationship of shipping interests to the Maritime Administration; the relationship of tobacco growers to the Department of Agriculture). In some situations, there is no one person with authority over the whole entity that corresponds to the authority of the chief executive officer of a profit-oriented company. This is the case in those states where the expenditure authority is vested in committees of independently elected officials, and in local governments administered by commissions whose members each administer a particular segment of the organization (e.g., streets, public safety, welfare, education). In state and federal governments, there is a division of authority among executive, legislative, and judicial branches. There may also be a vertical division of authority among levels of government (federal, state, and local), each responsible for facets of the same problem. For example, the federal government finances all major highways and partially finances many minor highways, and state and local governments construct and maintain other highways.

Although the power exercised by the governing board in a nonprofit organization is usually less than that exercised by the board of a profit-oriented organization, the need for an active involved governing body is actually greater in a nonprofit organization. This is because the vigilance of the governing board may be the only effective way of detecting when the organization is in difficulty. In a profit-oriented organization, a decrease in profits provides this danger signal automatically. Boards of trustees and legislative oversight committees, therefore, should take this responsibility seriously, much more seriously than most of them do.

Senior Management

Most organizations have a Number One person, who is the boss, the chief executive officer. In some nonprofit organizations, the chief executive officer does not have such overall responsibility. The Secretary of State typically regards his responsibility as foreign policy, but not what is called the "administration" of the State Department. Presidents of universities may say that they are the leaders of a "community of scholars,'' and that they should not soil their hands by becoming involved in other aspects of university management, particularly the ''business'' aspects (although this attitude is much less prevalent today than it was a generation ago). The minister of a church may feel that it is inappropriate to become involved in temporal matters. The Number One person in a hospital may have the title of ''medical director,'' which has the implication of lack of involvement in nonmedical matters.

Political Influences

Many nonprofit organizations are political; that is, they are responsible to the electorate or to a legislative body that presumably represents the electorate. In government organizations, decisions result from multiple, often conflicting, pressures. In part, these political pressures are inevitable—and up to a point desirable—substitutes for the forces of the marketplace. Elected officials cannot function if they are not reelected. In order to be reelected, they must—at least up to a point—advocate the perceived needs of their constituents, even though satisfying these needs may not be in the best interests of the larger body which they are supposed to represent.

In a democratic society the press and public feel that they have a right to know everything there is to know about a government organization. In the federal government and in some states, this feeling is recognized by ''freedom of information'' statutes. Channels for distributing this information are not always unbiased. Although some media stories that describe mismanagement are fully justified, others tend to be exaggerated and to give inadequate recognition to the fact that mistakes are inevitable in any organization. In order to reduce the opportunities for unfavorable media stories, government managers take steps to reduce the amount of sensitive, controversial information that flows through the formal management control system. This lessens the effectiveness of the system. The number of problems to which formal analytical techniques are applied is reduced because such techniques result in reports that may be open to public inspection.

Tradition

In the 19th century, accounting was primarily *fiduciary* accounting; that is, its purpose was to keep track of the funds that were entrusted to an organization to ensure that they were spent honestly. In the 20th century, accounting in business organizations has assumed much broader functions. It furnishes useful information about the business both to interested outside parties and to management. Nonprofit organizations, especially state and local governments, have been slow to adopt 20th century accounting and management control concepts and practices. They tend to focus on whether funds are spent legally, rather than on whether they were spent efficiently and effectively.

MEASUREMENT OF PERFORMANCE IN NONPROFIT ORGANIZATIONS

By definition, the goal of a nonprofit organization is something other than earning profits. Thus, even if the outputs in such an organization could be measured in monetary terms (corresponding to "revenues" in a profit-oriented company), the difference between monetary outputs and inputs would not measure how well the organization achieved its goal. The goal of a nonprofit organization is not to widen the difference between outputs and inputs. Rather, its goal is to render as much service as possible with a given amount of resources, or to use as few resources as possible to render a given amount of service. In most situations, the desirable *financial* performance in a nonprofit organization is a *break-even* performance; that is, in general and over the long run, revenues should equal expenses.

Even in an organization whose outputs can be measured in monetary terms (for example, in a hospital, if one accepts the premise that patient charges are a good measure of output), the income statement must be viewed in a fundamentally different way from the income statement of a profit-oriented company. If a hospital's revenues exceed expenses, this is a signal that its prices are too high or that it is not rendering enough service for what it charges. If revenues are less than expenses, the hospital will go bankrupt (leaving out short-run fluctuations, of course, in both cases). The desirable hospital income statement is one that shows revenues equal to expenses, provided that expenses measure the actual costs incurred in operating the hospital. (Conventional hospital income statements do not provide for a return on the entity's own capital, and they may understate the cost of using assets; these are justifyable reasons for the modest excess of revenues over expenses as conventionally measured.)

Although revenue measurement is important and should be attempted in all situations in which it is feasible, the amount of revenues must be viewed differently in a nonprofit organization than in a profit-oriented company. The amount of tuition revenue in a college does not reflect the overall effectiveness of the college, at least in the short run. (In the long run, a decline in tuition revenue indicates that the college is ineffective; at least, it indicates that potential students perceive it to be ineffective and consequently are unwilling to attend it.)

The measurement problem relates to outputs, not to inputs. With minor exceptions, inputs (i.e., costs or expenses) can be measured as readily in a nonprofit organization as in a profit-oriented organization.

However, without good measures of output, use of cost information to evaluate performance is necessarily subjective.

PRICING

Although prices charged for services rendered are an important consideration in the management control structure, many nonprofit organizations have given inadequate attention to their pricing policies. To the extent that pricing of services is feasible, the following benefits can be achieved:

1. If services are sold at prices that approximate full cost, the revenue figure that is thereby generated is a measure of the quantity of services that the organization supplies. In the absence of such an output measure, it is difficult to measure either efficiency or effectiveness.
2. Charging clients for services rendered makes them more aware of the value of the service and encourages them to consider whether the services are actually worth as much to them as their cost. If revenues generated by full-cost prices are not sufficient to cover total expenses, there is an indication that the service is not valuable enough to its clients, and therefore to society, to justify the cost of providing it. The organization's costs may be higher than are necessary for the quality or quantity of service that it does provide, or the client's needs may be satisfied by a lower quality or quantity of services.
3. If services are sold, the responsibility center that sells them can become, in effect, a profit center. The manager of a profit center becomes responsible for operating the unit in such a way that revenue equals expenses. Such a manager is motivated to think of ways of rendering additional service that will increase revenue, to think of ways of cutting costs to the point where the corresponding price is one that clients are willing to pay, to become more vigilant in controlling overhead costs, and in general to behave like a manager in a profit-oriented company. (Even if the responsibility center is expected to earn revenues that are less than costs, the advantages of a profit center can be obtained by making a specific "subsidy" to the unit that is equal to the anticipated loss.)

Notwithstanding these advantages of charging for services rendered, there are many situations in which prices should not be charged.

The most important class of these is *public goods*. Public goods are services furnished for the benefit of the public in general, rather than for an individual client. Examples are police protection, as contrasted with a police officer who is hired by the manager of a sporting event; and foreign policy and its implementation, as contrasted with services rendered to an individual firm doing business overseas. In addition to the general class of public goods, prices should not normally be charged for services when it is public policy to provide the services (e.g., welfare investigations; legal aid services), when it is public policy not to ration the services on the basis of ability to pay, when the cost of collecting the revenue exceeds the benefits, or when a charge is politically untenable.

Full-cost pricing. As a general rule, prices in nonprofit organizations should equal full costs. Full costs may include an allowance for interest on assets employed and, in some circumstances, an allowance for growth and expansion. If contributions or endowment earnings are intended to help meet the cost of the services, the gross cost may be reduced by the amount of these offsets.

A nonprofit organization may or may not have a monopoly position. In either situation it should not set prices that exceed its cost, for to do so would be inconsistent with its nonprofit objectives or, if it is a monopoly, result in the organization taking unjustifiable advantage of its monopoly status. Neither should a nonprofit organization price below full cost unless competitive conditions require it to do so, because that would be providing services to clients at less than the services are presumably worth; this can led to a misallocation of resources in the economy.

A full-cost pricing policy should normally apply to services that are directly related to the organization's principal objectives, but it does not necessarily apply to peripheral activities. Prices for these activities should ordinarily correspond to market prices for similar services. For example, in a hospital, prices for hospital care, surgical procedures, laboratory procedures, X rays, and meals come within the general rule, but prices in the gift shop in the hospital should be market-based.

Although the pricing strategy should normally be to recover full cost for the organization as a whole, it may be desirable to price specific services above or below full cost. The relevant considerations are essentially the same as those that profit-oriented companies consider when they depart from full-cost pricing.

The pricing unit. In general, the smaller and more specific the unit of service that is priced, the better the basis for decisions about the allocation of resources and the more accurate the measure of output for management control purposes. An overall price is not a good measure of output because it masks the actual mix of services rendered. For example, a blanket daily charge does not provide as good a measure of output in a hospital as specific charges for room rental, use of the operating room, drugs, and so on. Separate charges for the day of admission (to cover "work up" costs), and for geriatric and infant patients as compared with other patients, are examples of opportunities to make the pricing unit even smaller.

This principle is subject to two qualifications. The first is the obvious one that, beyond a certain point, the paperwork and other costs associated with pricing tiny units of service outweigh the benefits. The second qualification is that the pricing policy should be consistent with the organization's overall policy. It is a fact that undergraduate English instruction per student costs less than undergraduate physics instruction, and it would be feasible to reflect these differences in cost by charging different prices for each course that a student takes. Nevertheless, a separate price for each course may cause students to select courses in a way the university administration does not consider educationally sound.

Prospective pricing. As a general rule, management control is facilitated when the price is set prior to the performance of the service, as contrasted with the alternative of reimbursing the actual amount of costs incurred, after the fact. When prices are set in advance, they provide an incentive for the organization to keep costs within the level of anticipated revenue; whereas no such incentive exists when the organization knows that, whatever the level of costs may be, they will be recouped. An organization that knows it is going to recover its costs, whatever they are, is not likely to do much worrying about cost control.

This principle can be applied, of course, only when it is possible to make a reasonable advance estimate of what the services should cost. For many research projects, for example, there is no good basis for estimating how much should be spent in order to achieve the desired result, and the reimbursement for such work is necessarily based on actual costs incurred.

Transfer pricing. Most nonprofit organizations have not given much attention to developing a sound policy on transfer prices, even though goods and services are transferred from one responsibility center to another to roughly the same extent as in profit-oriented organizations. The basic purposes of a transfer price are the same in both types of organizations: to measure the revenue of the responsibility center that furnishes the product and the cost of the unit that receives the product in a way that aids management decisions and motivates responsibility center managers to work in the best interests of the organization. The principles for transfer pricing in nonprofit organizations are similar to those in profit-oriented organizations, as discussed in Chapter 7.

OUTPUT MEASUREMENT

Revenues can measure output only in client-oriented organizations. In other organizations, and in many circumstances in client-oriented organizations, output must be measured in nonmonetary terms. Output measures can be classified in various ways. They can be subjective or objective; that is, they can be derived from a person's judgment, or they may be derived from numerical data. They can be quantitative or nonquantitative. They can measure either the quantity of output or the quality of output.

An important way of classifying output measures is according to what they purport to measure. Although many different terms are used in practice, they can be grouped into three categories: (1) results measures, (2) process measures, and (3) social indicators.

A *results measure* (also *outcomes measure*) is a measure of output expressed in terms that are supposedly related to an organization's objectives. In the ideal situation, the objective is stated in measurable terms, and the output measure is stated in these same terms. When this relationship is not feasible, as is often the case, the performance measure represents the closest feasible way of measuring the accomplishment of an objective that cannot itself be expressed quantitatively. The term for such a measure is *surrogate* or *proxy*. A results measure relates to the impact the organization has on the outside world.

A *process measure* relates to an activity carried on by the organization. Examples are the number of livestock inspected in a week, the number of lines typed in an hour, the number of requisitions filled in a month, or the number of purchase orders written. Process measures are useful in measuring current, short-run performance. They are easier to interpret than results measures because, usually, there is a close causal relationship between inputs (i.e., costs) and the process measure. Process measures relate to efficiency, not effectiveness. Because they are not directly related to the organization's goals, they are not useful in strategic planning. They are useful in preparing those parts of a budget in which work to be done can be related to the costs required to do it; that is, activities for which reliable unit costs can be constructed. They are useful in the control of lower-level responsibility centers.

The essential difference between a results measure and a process measure is that the former is "ends oriented," and the latter is "means oriented." Results measures relate to "accomplishment" and process measures to "effort." An ends-oriented measure is a direct measure of success or failure in achieving an objective. A means-oriented measure is a measure of what a responsibility center or an individual did. There is an implicit assumption that what was done helped achieve the organization's objectives, but this assumption is not always valid.

A *social indicator* is a broad measure of output that reflects the result of the work of the organization. Since it is also affected by exogeneous forces, it is at best only a rough indication of the accomplishment of the organization itself. Social indicators are often stated in broad terms (e.g., "the expectation of healthy life free of serious disability and institutionalization"). Such statements are generally not so useful as those expressed in more specific, preferably measurable, terms (e.g., infant mortality rates, life expectancy). Social indicators are useful principally for long-range analyses of strategic problems. They are so nebulous, so difficult to obtain on a current basis, so little affected by current program effort, and so much affected by external influences that they are of limited usefulness in day-to-day management.

Costs as a Measure of Outputs

Although generally less desirable than a true output measure, costs are often a better measure of output than no measure at all. For example, it may not be feasible to construct output measures for research projects. In the absence of such measures, the amount spent on a research project may provide a useful clue to its output. In the extreme, if no money was spent, it is apparent that nothing was accomplished. (This assumes that the accounting records show what actually was spent, which sometimes is not the case.) When costs are used as proxy output measures, care must be exercised to avoid undue reliance on them, and the organization should try to develop direct measures of output.

PROGRAMMING

In government organizations particularly, and also in other organizations in which important resource allocation decisions must be made, programming is an important process, more important and more time consuming than in the typical profit-oriented organization. Until the 1960s', the process was carried out informally; but with the development of the Planning-Programming-Budgeting System (PPBS) in the federal government, it has become increasingly formalized. Although the name PPBS is no longer used in the federal government, its essential concepts continue there, and are also being used increasingly in state and municipal governments.

The programming process described in Chapter 9 is generally applicable to nonprofit organizations. Only two aspects of it are discussed here: (1) the program structure, and (2) benefit/cost analysis.

Program Structure

Because of the absence of the unifying profit objective, the development of a sound program structure in a nonprofit organization is much more difficult than in a profit-oriented organization. In a business company, the programs are essentially product lines plus research/development and other staff activities, and these are readily identified. In a nonprofit organization, it is difficult to decide on the best way of classifying activities into a formal program structure.

Information from the program structure is used for one or more of the following purposes: (1) to facilitate decision making about programs, (2) to provide a basis of comparison of the costs and outputs of similar programs, (3) to set selling prices or provide a basis for reimbursement of costs. The structure should be designed to meet these needs.

The information needed for one of these three purposes may differ from that needed by others. In that case, compromises in designing the structure may be required. In most situations, one of these purposes is clearly dominant, however, and the structure can be designed primarily to provide information needed for that purpose. In public-oriented organizations, the use of information as a basis for making decisions on programs tends to be by far the dominant purpose; whereas in many client-oriented organizations, pricing considerations tend to be dominant.

The program structure consists of three "layers." At the top are a relatively few *major programs*. At the bottom are a great many *program elements;* these are the smallest units in which information is collected in program terms. In between are summaries of related program elements; *program categories*.

The primary purpose of the classification of major programs is to facilitate top management judgment on the allocation of resources. Similarly, the primary purpose of the classification into program categories is to facilitate middle management judgment on the allocation of resources within programs. The program structure, therefore, should correspond to the principal objectives of the organization. It should be arranged so as to facilitate making decisions having to do with the relative importance of these objectives. Stated another way, it should focus on the organization's outputs—what it achieves or intends to achieve—rather than on its inputs; that is, the types of resources it uses, or the sources of its funds. A structure arranged by types of resources (e.g., personnel, material, services) or by sources of support (e.g., in a university: tuition, legislative appropriations, gifts) is not a useful program structure.

The designation of major programs helps communicate the objectives of the organization. The development of the management control structure also may clarify organizational relationships and thus suggest improvements in the structure of the organization. Therefore, the program structure should not necessarily correspond to the *existing* categories on which decisions are based; rather, it should correspond to those categories which can reasonably be expected to be useful for decision making in the future.

If it is feasible to do so, program categories and program elements should be so structured that each can be associated with a *quantitative* measure of performance (i.e., of output). At the broad level of programs, however, no reliable measure of performance can be found in many situations.

Relation to responsibility. Although there are advantages in relating major programs and program categories to organizational responsibility, this criterion is less important than that of facilitating senior management judgments. Sometimes the system's designers try to change the organization structure so it fits the program structure. In general, this should not be done. The system exists to serve the organization, not vice versa. Changes in organizational responsibility should be made if, but only if, such changes help the organization get its job done better. Sometimes the system designer does uncover a situation which would be improved by a reorganization. Unless the system designer can convince management that the change is desirable, the system should be designed to fit the organization as it exists.

Although the program structure need not, and ordinarily will not, match the organization structure, there should be some person who has identifiable responsibility for each major program and program category. In some agencies, each program has its own program manager. This is the *matrix* type of organization, the matrix consisting of program managers in one dimension and functionally organized responsibility centers in the other dimension; it is discussed in more detail in chapter 17. Program managers may have other responsibilities, and they may have to call on other parts of the organization for most of the work that is to be done on their programs. The program managers are advocates of their programs and are held accountable for the performance of their programs.

Benefit/Cost Analysis

The idea that the benefits of a proposed course of action should be compared with its costs is not new. Techniques for analyzing the profitability of proposed business investments involve essentially the same approach. Some government agencies, such as the Bureau of Reclamation, have made such analyses for decades. Proposals to build new dams were justified on the grounds that their benefits exceeded their costs. Interest in the approach grew rapidly in the 1960s when the Department of Defense applied the concept to problems for which no formal analysis previously had been attempted. It then became fashionable to apply benefit/cost analysis to all sorts of proposed programs in nonprofit organizations. The results of these efforts have been mixed, and there is now considerable controversy about the merits of the approach for certain types of problems.

Although overexuberant advocates and outright charlatans do exist, and their works are properly criticized, there is no doubt that benefit/cost analysis has produced useful results. There are two essential points:

1. Benefit/cost analysis focuses on those consequences of a proposal which can be estimated in quantitative terms. Since there is no important problem in which *all* the relevant factors can be reduced to numbers, benefit/cost analysis will never provide the complete answer to any important problem.

2. Nevertheless, if *some* of the important factors can be reduced to quantitative terms, it is often better to do so than not to do so. The resulting analysis narrows the area within which management judgment is required, even though it does not eliminate the need for judgment.

Alternative approaches. In benefit/cost analysis the general principles are that (1) a program should not be adopted unless its benefits exceed its costs; and (2) as between two competing proposals, the one with the greater excess of benefits over costs, or the one with the lower costs if benefits are equal, is preferable. In order to apply these principles there must be some way of relating benefits and costs.

For many proposals in nonprofit organizations, it is possible to estimate both costs and benefits in monetary terms. These proposals are similar to the capital budgeting proposals for profit-oriented companies, and the method of analysis in nonprofit organizations is essentially the same. A proposal to convert the heating plant of a hospital from oil to coal involves the same type of analysis that would be used for the same problem in an industrial company. Problems of this type are numerous in nonprofit organizations. Unfortunately, they also are relatively unimportant. For most of the important problems, a reliable monetary estimate of the benefits cannot be made.

Even if the benefits cannot be quantified, a benefit/cost analysis is useful in situations in which there are two or more ways of achieving a given objective. If there is a reasonable presumption that each of the alternatives will achieve the objective, then the alternative with the lowest cost is preferred. This approach has many applications, simply because it does not require that the objective be stated in monetary terms, or even that it be quantified. All that is necessary is a judgment that any of the proposed alternatives will achieve the objective. We need not measure the *degree* to which a given alternative meets the objective; we need only make the "go/no-go" judgment that the results are adequate. Similarly, if two competing proposals have the same cost, but one produces more benefits than the other, it ordinarily is the preferred alternative. This conclusion can be reached without a measurement of the absolute levels of benefits.

Different objectives. A benefit/cost comparison of proposals intended to accomplish different objectives is likely to be worthless. An analysis that attempts to compare funds to be spent for primary school education with funds to be spent for retraining of unemployed adults would not be worthwhile, because such an analysis requires that monetary values be assigned to the benefits of these two programs, which is an impossible task. Also, some benefit/cost analyses implicitly assume that there is a causal relationship between the benefits and the costs, that is, that spending *$X* of cost produces *Y* amount of benefit. If this causal connection does not exist, such an analysis is fallacious.

BUDGETING

Budgeting is a more important process in a nonprofit organization than in a profit-oriented organization. In a profit-oriented organization, operating managers can safely be allowed to modify plans, provided that the revised plan promises to increase profits. Operating managers of nonprofit organizations, especially those whose annual revenue is essentially fixed, must adhere closely to plans as expressed in the budget. Budgeting is perhaps the most important part of the management control process, and in well-managed organizations much thought and time are devoted to it.

The first step in the budgeting process is to estimate the amount of revenue that the organization is likely to receive for operating purposes during the budget year. In ordinary circumstances, the next step is to budget expenses that equal this amount of revenue. This matching of expenses to revenue differs from the approach used in profit-oriented organizations, because in profit-oriented organizations the amount budgeted for marketing expenses can influence the amount of revenue.

As a general rule, a nonprofit organization should plan to incur expenses that are approximately equal to its revenue. If its budgeted expenses are lower than its revenue, it is not providing the quantity of services that those who provide the revenue have a right to expect. If its budgeted expenses exceed its revenue, the difference must be made up by the generally undesirable actions of drawing down endowment or other capital funds that are intended to provide services to future generations. If the first approximation of budgeted expenses exceeds estimated revenue, the prudent course of action usually is to reduce expenses, rather than to anticipate that revenue can be increased. (As exceptions to the general rule, an organization may plan a deficit in one year to be offset by a surplus in another year, or it may plan a surplus to provide for anticipated future requirements of capital, or it may deliberately plan a deficit with the realization that it will eventually cease to exist.)

The budget is structured in terms of responsibility centers. Budget estimates are prepared by responsibility center managers and are consistent with the approved program and with other guidelines prescribed by top management. Budgetees negotiate approval of these estimates with their superiors. Because time does not permit a more thorough analysis, the level of current spending is usually taken as a starting point in these negotiations. The approved budget is a bilateral commitment: the budgetee commits to accomplish the planned objectives within the spending limits specified in the budget, and the superior commits to regarding such an accomplishment as representing satisfactory performance.

Management by Objectives

In addition to estimates of monetary amounts, budgetees should also state, as specifically as possible, the objectives that they expect to attain during the budget year. This part of the budgeting process is relatively new, or at least the organized effort under the label "management by objectives" is relatively new; but it is being emphasized increasingly in the federal government, and is spreading to other types of nonprofit organizations.

If at all possible, the objectives should be quantified so that actual performance can be compared with them. Objectives are outputs. These statements of objectives take the place of the profitability objective, which is a key part of the budgeting process in a profit-oriented company. The appropriateness of the revenue and expense estimates in such a company can be judged in terms of whether or not they produce a satisfactory profit. In a nonprofit organization, such an overall yardstick of judging the estimates in the budget does not exist. In the absence of some substitute, the budgeted expenses can be judged in terms of what was spent last year; but this is not a very satisfactory basis for judgment. What the supervisor wants to know is what results will be obtained from the use of the budgeted resources. A statement of objectives that is related directly to the budgeted costs provides this information.

Some organizations use a "management by objectives" procedure that is quite separate from the budgeting process. This separation came about usually because the technique happened to be sponsored by persons who were outside the controller organization. The controller is usually responsible for the budgeting process. Such a separation is undesirable. In discussing plans for next year, both the expenses and the results expected from incurring these expenses should be considered together.

Fund Accounting

A unique feature of the accounting systems in nonprofit organizations is the use of what are termed *fund accounts*. Indeed, a study of accounting in such organizations is often called "fund accounting," as if this were the central feature of the system. Actually, the fund accounts play a relatively minor role in the management control process. A general understanding of their nature and purpose is nevertheless desirable.

In a business accounting system, the available resources for the whole company are, in effect, in one "pot"; that is, the balance sheet lists the assets for the whole organization. In a nonprofit organization, by contrast, the resources may be accounted for in several separate pots, each of which is called a fund. Each fund has its own set of accounts that are self-balancing, and each fund is, therefore, a separate entity, almost as if it were a separate business. The purpose of this device is to ensure that the organization uses the resources made available to each fund only for the purposes designated for that fund.

The principal funds are:

1. The *general fund,* which comprises the resources made available to operate the organization for a specified period of time, usually a year; that is, there is one operating fund for 1984, another for 1985, and so on.
2. *Special revenue funds,* which account for revenues that are restricted to some specified purpose, and to the expenses incurred for that purpose.
3. A *capital fund,* which provides for the construction or acquisition of approved capital assets.
4. An *endowment fund,* which holds money entrusted to an organization for endowment purposes. The principal is supposed to be held intact, usually forever, and the earnings on that principal are made available for current use.
5. *Working capital funds,* also called "revolving funds," which are used to finance inventories and other consumable assets. Their function corresponds to the function of the inventory accounts in a business, namely, to hold assets in suspense until they are consumed and hence become expenses.
6. *Enterprise funds,* which account for business-like activities carried on by the organization (such as an electric utility operated by a municipality).

To the extent that fund accounting forces a clean separation between operating transactions and capital transactions, it is a useful device, corresponding essentially to the separation between income statement items and other balance sheet changes in a business. Fund accounting may also be useful as an internal device to ensure that restrictions on spending are adhered to, although the same results may be obtained by appropriate management controls without the use of funds. However, formal financial statements that report the details of spending by each fund, although still prevalent in most municipalities and states and in many other nonprofit organizations, are more confusing than informative.

Many nonprofit organizations measure spending on an expenditure basis, rather than on an expense basis. This is an archaic practice. An expenditure basis measures the resources *acquired* in a period, while an expense basis measures resources *consumed*. The expense basis, which is universally used in profit-oriented companies, is the only valid way of measuring the resources used in the organization's operations (unless, of course, there is no material difference between expenses and expenditures, which may be the case in some small organizations.)

SUGGESTED ADDITIONAL READINGS

Anthony, Robert N., and **David W. Young.** *Management Control in Nonprofit Organizations*. 3d ed. Homewood, Ill.: Richard D. Irwin, 1984.

Gross, Malvern J., Jr., and **Stephen F. Jablonsky.** *Principles of Accounting and Financial Reporting for Nonprofit Organizations*. New York: Ronald Press, 1979.

Hay, Leon E. *Accounting for Governmental and Nonprofit Entities*. 6th ed. Homewood, Ill.: Richard D. Irwin, 1980.

Lynn, Edward C., and **Robert J. Freeman.** *Fund Accounting Theory and Practice*. 2d ed. Englewood Cliffs, N.J.: Prentice-Hall, 1982.

Ramanathan, Kavasseri. *Management Control in Nonprofit Organizations*. New York: John Wiley & Sons, 1982.

CASE 16–1
Metropolitan Museum of Art*

The "first cut" at the operating budget of the Metropolitan Museum of Art for fiscal year 1973 (i.e., the year ended June 30, 1973) indicated a substantial deficit. Management was considering what, if any, steps should be taken to reduce or eliminate this deficit.

The Metropolitan Museum was organized in New York City in 1870. In 1972 it had over 1 million works of art, the largest collection of its kind in the Western Hemisphere. It had an endowment fund of $150 million.

* This case was prepared by Richard E. Kopelman under the direction of Fred K. Foukes, Harvard Business School.

GOVERNANCE AND MANAGEMENT

The board. Fiscal authority for direction of the Metropolitan Museum of Art was vested in the Board of Trustees. The board was responsible for the broad direction and control of the Museum and for the establishment and approval of basic policies and plans. Meeting quarterly, it also considered important operational matters.

The director. The director was the museum's chief executive officer. He was responsible for formulating policies and programs for the board's consideration and for implementing decisions made by the board. In addition to being responsible for overall planning and administration of the Museum's affairs, he was also involved in fund-raising and negotiating major art acquisitions. He presided at rehearsals of presentations by the curators and was present at actual presentations made to the Board of Trustees Acquisition Committee. Since 1966, the director was Thomas P. F. Hoving. Dr. Hoving had achieved national recognition as the commissioner of parks of New York City, particularly for his campaign to make New York a "fun city." He earned a Ph.D. in Art History at Princeton in 1959, and was hired as curatorial assistant at the Cloisters, the medieval art department of the Metropolitan. In 1965 he became curator of the Cloisters.

Curatorial. The vice director, curator-in-chief was responsible for 17 curatorial departments and the Conservation Laboratory, with a curatorial staff of nearly 200 persons.

The 17 curatorial departments varied considerably in the size of their staffs and collections, and in the range of their activities. While all departments collected art objects, some were more active than others. In general the more active departments were those that collected works of art currently available in the open market.

In addition to collection and display, curatorial departments were responsible for maintaining relations with collectors and art dealers, for developing scholarly and general literature on the collection, and for answering inquiries from the public. Some members of the curatorial staff also taught courses and lectured at the Museum or at other institutions.

Education. The vice director of education had general responsibility for developing educational programs for students and for the general public. Included in his domain were five departments: the Library, the Junior Museum, Secondary and Higher Education, Community Programs, and the Photograph and Slide Library.

Finance and treasurer. The vice director for finance and treasurer was the chief financial officer of the Museum. Reporting to him were four financial administrators, each with his own staff and task assignment. The assistant treasurer was responsible for the physical receipt and payment of funds, accounts receivable, the payroll, and general accounting. The controller prepared the annual budget and was responsible for accounts payable. The registrar maintained catalog descriptions of all objects belonging to the Museum, recorded the physical movement of these objects in and out of the Museum, and obtained insurance and custom handling for art shipments. The city liaison officer was responsible for developing and maintaining good relations with the New York City administration, in particular those officials with whom the Museum had financial transactions.

Public affairs. The vice director of public affairs, a position that was at the time vacant, had overall responsibility for eight departments, each of which had direct contact with the public. These departments were as follows: public information, information desk, bookshop and reproduction, development and promotion (fund-raising), membership office, publications, exhibition design, and the auditorium.

Operations. The operating administrator had general responsibility for the provision of the Museum's many service functions. These included: guardianship, maintenance, cleaning, purchasing stockroom supplies, telephone and office services, photograph studio, and the several restaurant facilities. This large department employed approximately 400 of the Museum's 800 employees.

Staffing levels for these activities are given in Exhibit 1.

EXHIBIT 1 Staffing Levels: 1967–1971 (excluding auxiliary activities)

	1971	*1970*	*1969*	*1968*	*1967*
Director and several offices	27	23	22	21	20
Vice director–curator-in-chief	199	185	170	172	167
Vice director for finance and treasurer	51	48	46	42	42
Vice director for education	63	55	53	52	52
Vice director for public affairs	31	28	28	28	25
Vice director for operations	412	407	370	365	361
Subtotal	783	746	689	680	667
100th anniversary	19	21	—	—	—
Total	802	767	689	680	667

In the late 1960s there was increasing interest among professional staff employees in establishing a union to represent them. Apparently this interest had been increasing despite efforts by the Museum's administration to be responsive to the needs of the professional staff. The administration had a publicly announced goal of bringing curatorial salaries up to the level received by professors in leading colleges and universities. From 1967 to 1971 there was a 30 percent increase in curatorial salaries. The 1972 budget, prepared in the spring of 1971, called for additional salary increases of between 11.6 percent and 17.9 percent depending on the level of curatorial rank.

The administration had also attempted to increase the extent of participation by professional employees. In 1970 the curators, acting with the backing of the administration, established a Curatorial Forum, which comprised the entire curatorial staff, and had a representative on the Staff Policy Committee, the executive team which made recommendations to the director and conducted routine business operations.

By April 1972, it appeared to management that the unionization issue was no longer alive and that many of the specific changes that had been introduced had been well received.

FINANCIAL BACKGROUND

The Museum began to suffer operating losses in the late 1960s. Historical financial data are shown in Exhibits 2 and 3.

EXHIBIT 2 Financial Record: 1960–1972

*Fiscal year**	*Operating income*	*Operating expenses*	*Surplus (loss)†*
1960	$ 4,006,943	$ 3,618,197	$ 388,746
1961	4,328,603	4,042,561	286,042
1962	5,181,647	4,433,087	748,560
1963	5,066,399	4,605,688	460,711
1964	5,280,503	4,802,832	477,671
1965	5,807,116	5,278,279	528,837
1966	6,128,155	5,698,411	429,714
1967	6,496,767	6,236,532	260,235
1968	7,054,341	7,461,354	(407,013)
1969	8,393,332	8,531,833	(138,501)
1970	8,405,569	9,226,513	(820,944)
1971	11,363,519	11,773,117	(409,598)‡
1972 (budget)	12,415,600	13,128,793	(713,193)

* Fiscal year ends June 30.
† For fiscal years prior to 1970, Surplus (loss) is before extraordinary charges.
‡ Plus an accumulated Centennial deficit of $1,121,697.

The emergence of financial problems was not a condition unique to the Metropolitan Museum of Art; many museums were faced with similar situations. The Museum of Modern Art, for example, reported a record deficit of $1.2 million in 1970. Also in 1970, a study conducted by the American Association of Museums found that 44 percent of its members were operating at a loss. Furthermore, at the time of the study the AAM spokesman said that the dismal trend was expected to continue.

Two broad explanations were advanced for the growing disparity between revenues and expenses. First, museums, like other entities which relied on a relatively fixed income, suffered from the effects of inflation. Second, in order to adapt to a changing environment museums had incurred new types of expenses.

EXHIBIT 3 Sources of Income: 1960–1971

Sources (in 000s)	*1960*	*1961*	*1962*	*1963*	*1964*	*1965*	*1966*	*1967*	*1968*	*1969*	*1970*	*1971*
Unrestricted investment income	$2,737	$2,890	$3,591	$3,474	$3,621	$4,051	$4,174	$4,380	$4,461	$4,658	$4,670	$ 4,722
Transfer of unrestricted endowment funds*	0	0	0	0	0	0	0	0	0	0	0	844
Appropriation from City of New York	974	1,038	1,191	1,259	1,293	1,385	1,528	1,554	1,678	1,853	1,974	2,323
Grants	0	0	0	0	0	0	0	53	160	577	126	683
Memberships	180	205	234	252	267	289	314	399	415	453	419	1,057
Admission fees	0	65	72	0	0	30	15	0	45	353	390	821
Contribution for general purposes	62	66	20	16	18	17	18	19	181	151	191	204
Other†	64	65	73	66	81	71	81	91	113	137	278	260
Subtotal	4,007	4,329	5,181	5,066	5,281	5,807	6,128	6,497	7,054	8,183	8,021	10,914
Plus: Net income for auxiliary activities	0	0	0	0	0	0	0	0	0	210	385	449
Total	$4,007	$4,329	$5,181	$5,066	$5,281	$5,807	$6,128	$6,497	$7,054	$8,393	$8,406	$11,364

* In 1971 a fixed rate of return (5 percent) was used for the first time to determine endowment income.
† Includes income from slide and photograph sales, guide service, course fees, and special seminars.

One cause of the difficulty was the rapid increase in museum attendance. It was noted that the 1971 exhibit entitled the "Drug Scene" at the Museum of the City of New York drew more people in three months of 1971 than the entire museum did in all of 1970. However, the cost of contemporary exhibits was high. The American Museum of Natural History, for example, spent $526,000 for its centennial exhibit "Can Man Survive?"

Another relatively new cost was the emergence of vigorous demands by professional employees for higher pay and more job security. According to Ann R. Leven, assistant treasurer of the Metropolitan, this new demand reflected the fact that curators no longer came predominantly from the ranks of the wealthy. Many curators had to live off salaries which were traditionally quite low.

The Metropolitan took action in 1971 to combat the trend of increasing deficits. The actions taken can be grouped into two categories, those which reduced costs, and those which generated additional revenues.

One cost-cutting action was a curtailment in the hiring of new personnel. Mr. Daniel Herrick, vice director for finance and treasurer, instituted the policy of not filling a vacancy unless the position was deemed essential.

A second austerity measure was the decision to close the Museum one day a week (Monday) beginning in July 1971. Prior to this decision the Museum had remained open to the public seven days a week, 365 days a year. Consequently many maintenance activities had to be performed at odd hours: before the Museum opened and after it closed. These scheduling demands, coupled with ordinary absences, resulted in (1) having to pay guards and maintenance personnel overtime pay, and (2) having to hire temporary personnel on a per diem basis. The budget for 1971–72 estimated that Monday closings would save the Metropolitan nearly $200,000 in annual labor cost. Ten New York City art museums, including the Guggenheim and the Whitney, adopted this policy before the Metropolitan did.

Another cutback was the elimination from the operating budget of various projects which the Museum had planned to carry out. Among the postponed items were the following: (1) the publication of a catalog of the Museum's programs of research and education; (2) hiring of a specialist for foundation and government fund-raising; (3) installation of a public education gallery dealing with current events in the art world; (4) free acoustiguide equipment; (5) redecoration of the restaurant; (6) development of a computer program for an art catalog. Perhaps the biggest disappointment to many people was the curtailment of the final Centennial exhibition, "Masterpieces of Fifty Centuries." In the words of Mr. Hoving, "Our budget could no longer afford the expenses involved in the foreign loans that we planned for the last great

Centennial show, especially the cost of insurance, which has skyrocketed in the last few years.''

At the same time that these cost reduction activities were undertaken the Museum also initiated steps to increase its revenues. One approach was the introduction in 1970 of discretionary admission charges at the main building and at the Cloisters. Mr. Hoving commented that ''after investigating different ways of charging admission to the Museum, the pay-as-you-wish plan emerged as the most satisfactory for two reasons. It created no economic barriers for the public and it proved that income was higher than with a set admission fee.'' (*New York Times,* October 9, 1970.) After a five-month trial period the average contribution per visitor was 64 cents. One reason for the high average was that the Museum ''strongly hinted'' that $1 would be a ''very nice'' contribution for adults, 50 cents for youngsters. The 1971–72 budget estimated that total receipts from the voluntary admission contributions would approximate $1 million. (The Museum found out in 1971 after it purchased electronic counting equipment that the earlier handcounted records of attendance were about four times too high.)

The introduction of a discretionary admission fee provoked sharp criticism from several sources. Among them was Mr. Carter Burden, a New York City councilman, who noted that ''of the 15 institutions which receive city funds, with the exception of the Bronx Zoo, the Metropolitan was the only one with a general admission fee.'' He added, ''Our society should be going in the opposite direction.''

Another step taken to enhance revenues was the adoption of the fixed rate of return concept for endowment funds. Whereas in past years endowment income was limited to interest and dividends, beginning in 1971 the Museum recorded as income 5 percent of the average market value of unrestricted endowment funds for the three previous years. It was anticipated that over the long run actual capital appreciation combined with dividends and interest would result in an annual yield at least equal to the fixed rate. This approach had the added advantage of making endowment income a constant amount during the course of the fiscal year. (See Exhibit 3.)

Also beginning in 1970 the Museum undertook an energetic campaign to enroll new members. As a result of this campaign 8,667 new memberships were sold by April 1971, bringing in added receipts of $360,000. One spur to get new members was that beginning in April 1971, the prices of individual and family memberships were raised from $15 to $25 and $40, respectively. Because of the price increase the Museum expected only a small increase in memberships for 1972.

The recent history of membership growth, was marred by only one major downturn. This occurred in 1967 when prices were raised. However, there was a short downturn for a few months in the fall of 1968 as a result of the contemporary exhibition, ''Harlem on My Mind.'' One hundred and sixty-five members canceled their memberships and many others failed to renew. The two major criticisms were an anti-Semitic comment in the catalog, and the view that this exhibit was not "real" art.

Another approach to enhancing revenues were efforts to make the Museum's auxiliary activities more profitable. Additional merchandising operations were opened and prices on prints, books, and other items were set at levels to bring an optimum return. As a result of these changes the 1971–72 budget anticipated an increase in contribution on these activities from $415,000 to $615,000.

Still another revenue producing activity was the search for nontraditional sources of funds. In 1970 the state of New York broke new ground when it appropriated $18 million for support of the arts. The Metropolitan received a total of $418,500 of the appropriation in 1971, and expected continued support from the state. Another new source of funds was the federal government which, under the National Endowment for the Arts, was expected to make an initial contribution to the Metropolitan of $110,000 in 1972.

Yet by far the largest public contribution came from the City of New York, which gave $2.3 million in 1971 to cover the costs of guardianship and maintenance. While the city's contribution to the operating income had declined from 27 percent in 1959–60 to 21 percent in 1970–71, the amount contributed had increased. It was estimated, furthermore, that by 1976 the city would increase its annual commitment by an additional $585,000. (*The Wall Street Journal,* July 27, 1971.) Consequently, some administrators at the Metropolitan felt uneasy when elected city officials began to urge the city to reduce or even eliminate its contributions to the Museum.

CURRENT FINANCIAL SITUATION

During the 1971–72 fiscal year it became increasingly evident that the financial plans for the year were not going to be met. A deficit of $713,000 was originally budgeted compared to the preceding year's deficit of $1,531,000. The reduction had been planned to be accomplished by keeping 1972 expenditures near the 1971 level ($13.1 million in 1972 versus $12.9 million in the prior year), while revenue was to be increased by $1 million. However, by April 1972 it appeared that the actual deficit for the fiscal year ending June 30 would approximate $1.4 million. The chief reason for this turn of events was that revenue had not increased as planned.

Attendance in the Main Building was down approximately 25 percent from the year before, and admission income was one third below the budgeted figure of $930,000. Mr. Daniel Herrick, the vice director of finance and treasurer, attributed the falloff to several factors: a post-

Centennial slump in public interest, reduced hotel occupancies in New York, and a growing reluctance of New York City residents to go out at night. As a direct result of decreased attendance, the contribution to expenses provided by the restaurant and bookstores was reduced by $130,000.

Two additional factors contributed to lower than planned revenues. In fiscal 1970–71 the Museum undertook a special membership campaign whereby new individual and family members were encouraged to join at the old rates (before new, increased rates went into effect), and existing members were allowed to extend their memberships for an additional year at the old rates. The effect of this campaign was an extraordinary increase in memberships. From 1963 through 1968 membership fluctuated between 20,000 and 23,000 each year. In 1969 it rose to over 24,000; in 1970 to 27,000; and in 1971 to 37,760. However, in early 1972 as memberships began to expire, the renewal rates were lower than anticipated, mostly among the lower membership categories. In the single month of February, for example, 937 individual and family memberships were not renewed. As a result of this higher than anticipated lapse rate, membership income was about $90,000 below the budget. A final disappointment was the reduction in grants received by the Museum. New York State reduced its grant to $221,000 from $418,000 the year before, and the National Endowment for the Arts contributed $60,000 less than budgeted. Total grant income was $280,000 short of the budgeted level.

THE BUDGET FOR 1972–1973

The preliminary budget for the forthcoming year indicated that total revenue would decline slightly to $11.7 million, principally reflecting a further reduction in grants to the Museum. The budget report suggested that there were three principal options to be considered:

Option 1. Deficit $1 million. Across-the-board cut in expenditures of 10.3 percent. Staff cut of 36 (excluding auxiliary activities). Requires effecting efficiencies in all departments and certain cutbacks most notably in the Curatorial and Operations area. Reduce advertising. Reduce number of activities for members. Close Monday holidays, 11 A.M. to 1 P.M. Sundays, Friday evenings. Cancel employees' Christmas party.

Option 2. Deficit $500,000. Across-the-board cut in expenditures of 16.4 percent. Staff cut of 60. The effect falls heaviest on those departments with limited program money, cutting deeply into the Curatorial and Operating staffs. Allows for basic maintenance of collections; study rooms would close; conservation and research would stop; exhibitions would be severely limited. Reduce community education activities unless outside funding obtained. Close 83d Street entrance.

Option 3. No deficit. Across-the-board cut in expenditures of 22.5 percent. Staff cut of 91. Merely maintains the Museum as a repository for works of art. Requires a major functional reorganization of the staff. All cataloging ceases. Closes libraries during the summer, eliminates weekend and summer education programs. Consolidates Development and Membership offices.

When Mr. Herrick was asked whether the administration had considered the possibility of passing the hat among the trustees in order to make up operating deficits, he said:

> The days when a few wealthy contributors would ante up the money to cover a deficit are over. Even the richest person in the world doesn't have an inclination to keep giving money if you have continuing deficits of over $1 million a year. Furthermore, anteing up to fill a deficit is the least attractive type of donation from the viewpoint of most contributors. Philanthropists far prefer to donate money for works of art, buildings, or even endowed chairs before giving to cover operating losses.

Mr. Herrick continued discussing the financial problems of the Museum:

> We are reluctant to cut back expenses especially since the staff takes intense pride in what has been accomplished at the Metropolitan Museum. At a time when other aspects of New York City life are deteriorating, the Museum has been on a planned and vigorous course of greater service to the community in maintaining and communicating the meaning of its collection of works of art to the public.
>
> We have considered numerous alternative forms of retrenchment but because salaries comprise roughly 70 percent of our total costs [see Exhibits 4 and 5], there is virtually no way to avoid laying off people. Furthermore, this raises the difficult problem of deciding which people to release and how to handle the dismissals. We are even exploring the

EXHIBIT 4 Administration Expenses (as budgeted for the year ended June 30, 1972)*

	Personal service	*Other expense*	*Total*
Director and several offices	$ 404,095	$ 173,085	$ 577,180
Vice director–curator-in-chief	2,455,227	695,316	3,150,543
Vice director for finance and treasurer	555,561	355,910	911,471
Vice director for education	783,708	812,586	1,596,294
Vice director for public affairs	467,725	701,815	1,169,540
Vice director for operations	3,625,199	1,435,570	5,060,769
Benefits and allowances	1,764,170	—	1,764,170
Adjustments†	(566,295)	(156,478)	(722,773)
Total estimated operating expenses	$9,489,390	$4,017,804	$13,507,194

* As revised 3/31/72.

† Accounting deductions distributed among capital budget, auxiliary activities, the Cloisters.

EXHIBIT 5 Actual Administration Expenses

	1971	1970	1969	1968	1967
Personal service (including benefits and allowances)	$ 8,287,400	$ 6,909,700	$6,151,300	$5,422,000	$5,181,400
Other than personal service	3,138,000	2,086,500	1,971,300	1,398,600	1,119,300
Subtotal	11,425,400	8,996,200	8,122,600	6,820,600	6,300,700
100th Anniversary personal service	96,100	210,100			
Other than personal service	1,454,000	1,595,900			
Total	$12,975,900	$10,802,200	$8,122,600	$6,820,600	$6,300,700

possibility of converting to a four-day week, perhaps in lieu of salary increases.

The fact of the matter is that even if the Museum were to cut its expenditures to create a balanced budget in the forthcoming year, the same problem would recur again next year. As long as the Museum exists in an inflationary economy, where there is an inevitable upward push in terms of wages, fringe benefits, and operating costs, the Museum must seek some means of achieving an adequate and dependable source of funding to maintain the status quo at least.

POSSIBLE REPERCUSSIONS OF CUTBACKS

The administration was well aware of the possibility that cutbacks might lead to renewed interest in unionization among the professional staff. John Conger, the personnel manager, identified the immediate costs to the Museum of collective bargaining. First, more time would be spent in negotiating contracts. Second, there was a high probability that the final contract agreement would be more costly to the Museum.

Mr. Hoving stated that the union would have little overall impact on the Museum. "There are very few things they could bargain for. Salaries of curators are at the level of university professors, working conditions are excellent, as is the grievance procedure. A union would actually make management's position stronger. It would absolutely define the areas of bargaining as stipulated by the NLRB. The staff would have much less say on policy matters."

Mr. Herrick noted that "the chances are pretty good that if we decide to have layoffs there may be a professional union. But if there is, that wouldn't be the end of the world."

Question

What actions, if any, would you tentatively recommend as a means of reducing the budgeted deficit?

CASE 16–2
Boston Symphony Orchestra, Inc.*

For several years prior to 1982, Boston Symphony Orchestra, Inc. (BSO), operated at a deficit. For the four years 1978–81, the deficit totalled $4.5 million, an amount that had to be withdrawn from capital funds. Were it not for one special circumstance—a fund drive conducted in connection with BSO's 100th Anniversary in 1982—capital funds would have been exhausted within a decade if the deficit continued at the 1978–81 rate.

Background

BSO owned two properties. One was Symphony Hall in Boston. The orchestra performed there, except in the summer and when it performed in other cities. When Symphony Hall was not needed for performances, rehearsals, or recording sessions, it often was rented to other organizations.

The other property was Tanglewood, a large complex in the Berkshire Hills, about 130 miles from Boston. The orchestra performed there for nine weeks in the summer. Several hundred students participated in training programs at Tanglewood each summer. (The principal buildings at Tanglewood were not winterized and could be used only in the summer.) In the summer of 1982, attendance at Tanglewood totalled 308,000.

In 1981–82, in addition to Tanglewood, the orchestra gave 107 concerts, of which 13 were in foreign countries and 14 in other American cities. The Boston Pops Orchestra, formed from symphony orchestra players, gave 63 concerts in Symphony Hall and 7 free concerts at an outdoor concert shell in Boston, known as the Esplanade. At the July 4 Esplanade concert, a Boston institution, attendance was estimated at 200,000. Nearly all orchestra and Pops performances were sold out.

Management estimated that annual use of Symphony hall in the evenings was approximately as follows:

Symphony orchestra concerts	52
Pops concerts	70
Rentals to outside groups	33
Orchestra rehearsals	10
	165

* This case was prepared by Robert N. Anthony, Harvard Business School.

In the afternoons there were 22 symphony orchestra concerts and approximately 25 rentals to outside groups. The orchestra used the hall an additional 125 to 150 occasions annually for rehearsals, recording, or television sessions.

Proposed Plan

The "BSO/100" fund drive raised about $20 million of capital funds (primarily endowment) over a five-year period. Management recognized, however, that the special stimulus of the 100th Anniversary could not be counted on to provide the funds needed to balance the budget in the future. Alternative ways of financing operations were discussed, and the trustees eventually agreed on the plan given in Exhibit 1. In the BSO annual report for 1982 (i.e., for the fiscal year ended August 31, 1982), this plan was described as follows:

> As the orchestra embarks on the first decade of its second century, Trustees, Overseers, and Friends must make plans based upon the experience of the past and their best estimate of the economic climate in the years ahead. The single most important assumption in making such a projection is the rate at which "fixed costs" of maintaining the present organization and properties will increase due to inflation. Included in the Analysis of Revenue Contribution to Fixed Costs are projections based upon several assumptions:
>
> (1) that "fixed costs" will increase at a compound annual rate of approximately 7 percent through fiscal 1989–1990;
>
> (2) that management will be able to increase the percentage of "fixed costs" financed by concert activities by ½ of 1 percent per year;
>
> (3) that the Investment Committee and the Resources Committee working together will be able to increase the percentage of "fixed costs" covered by endowment income by ½ of 1 percent per year;
>
> (4) that the Resources Committee will be able to raise on average about $6,000,000 per year, of which $2,000,000 per year will be available to balance the budget; and
>
> (5) that the Buildings and Grounds Committee will be able to limit capital expenditures for depreciation, for necessary improvements, and for new facilities to $500,000 per year.
>
> Perhaps the most significant conclusions to draw from the projections in [Exhibit 1] is that, in the absence of some new source of revenue, ticket prices will have to continue to increase so that the marginal contribution from concert activities can increase from $5,709,000 in 1981–82 to $10,500,000 or 64.5 percent of "fixed costs" in 1989–90.

EXHIBIT 1 Analysis of Revenue Contribution to Fixed Costs For the Year Ended August 31, (in thousands)

	Actual				
	1978	*1979*	*1980*	*1981*	*1982*
Fixed costs:					
Artistic	3,902	4,243	4,514	5,176	5,608
Facilities	920	1,005	1,160	1,318	1,348
Administration	1,377	1,472	1,268	1,940	2,204
Total fixed costs	6,199	6,720	7,442	8,434	9,160
Results from operations:					
Operations:					
Concerts	2,666	2,986	3,161	3,827	4,006
Radio (BSTT)	125	145	160	185	185
Recording	320	384	510	543	827
Television	139	225	289	223	246
Occupancies	101	91	186	252	244
Education	(100)	(60)	(87)	(34)	(77)
Other income	—	12	32	35	278
Marginal contribution	3,251	3,783	4,251	5,031	5,709
% fixed costs	52.4	56.3	57.1	59.7	62.3
Operating (deficit)	(2,948)	(2,937)	(3,191)	(3,403)	(3,451)
% fixed costs	47.6	43.7	42.9	40.3	37.7
Endowment income	981	1,221	1,358	1,691	1,893
% fixed costs	15.8	18.2	18.3	20.0	20.7
Annual fundraising:					
Total annual gifts	1,133	1,121	1,211	1,334	1,786
Special-purpose gifts transferred to operations	(162)	(302)	(268)	(299)	(355)
General-purpose gifts	971	819	943	1,035	1,431
Net project revenues	176	209	229	264	723
	1,147	1,028	1,172	1,299	2,154
Fundraising expenses	(549)	(441)	(414)	(553)	(442)
Total	598	587	758	746	1,712
% fixed costs	9.7	8.7	10.2	8.8	18.7
Total endowment income and annual fundraising	1,579	1,808	2,116	2,437	3,605
% fixed costs	25.5	26.9	28.5	28.8	39.4
Surplus (deficit)	(1,369)	(1,129)	(1,075)	(966)	154
% fixed costs	22.1	16.8	14.4	11.5	1.7
Funding from (to) unrestricted capital	1,369	1,129	1,075	966	(154)
	-0-	-0-	-0-	-0-	-0-
Capital analysis:					
Added to endowment funds	$ 442	$ 1,750	$ 1,433	$ 1,308	$ 3,540
Added (charged) to special reserve					150
Funding of plant additions	433	980	493	1,641	326
Added to unexpended property fund balance					241
Funding of deficit	1,369	1,129	1,075	966	
	$ 2,244	$ 3,859	$ 3,001	$ 3,915	$ 4,257
Pooled investments:					
Cost	$10,343	$12,018	$13,850	$15,822	$19,465
Market	11,645	14,015	15,817	16,356	20,536
Endowment share unit value	12.54	13.20	13.67	13.78	14.19

EXHIBIT 1 (*concluded*)

			Projections				
1983	*1984*	*1985*	*1986*	*1987*	*1988*	*1989*	*1990*
$10,140	$10,850	$11,800	$12,425	$13,300	$14,225	$15,225	$16,300
6,160	6,675	7,325	7,775	8,375	9,025	9,750	10,500
60.8	61.5	62.0	62.5	63.0	63.5	64.0	64.5
(3,980)	(4,175)	(4,475)	(4,650)	(4,925)	(5,200)	(5,475)	(5,800)
39.2	38.5	38.0	37.5	37.0	36.5	36.0	35.5
3,865	4,175	4,475	4,650	4,925	5,200	5,475	5,800
38.1	38.5	38.0	37.5	37.0	36.5	36.0	35.5
(115)	–0–	–0–	–0–	–0–	–0–	–0–	–0–
1.1							
115							
–0–	–0–	–0–	–0–	–0–	–0–	–0–	–0–
$ 3,500	$ 3,500	$ 3,500	$ 3,500	$ 3,500	$ 3,500	$ 3,500	$ 3,500
(115)							
1,021	500	500	500	500	500	500	500
(241)							
$ 4,165	$ 4,000	$ 4,000	$ 4,000	$ 4,000	$ 4,000	$ 4,000	$ 4,000
$23,000	$26,500	$30,000	$33,500	$37,000	$40,500	$44,000	$47,500

During the past five years the orchestra raised a total of $20,000,000 for BSO/100 and $7,000,000 from Annual Fund Drives for a grand total of $27,000,000.

The goal of $6,000,000 per year, or $30,000,000 over the next five years, is challenging, but the task is not much greater than the task already accomplished during the period of the BSO/100 Campaign.

Contributions to Fixed Costs

The concept of "contributions to fixed costs" referred to in the above description was explained in the Annual Report as follows:

Each year the Trustees are faced with certain relatively fixed costs which are scheduled in the Analysis of Revenue Contribution to Fixed Costs report. These are primarily for the annual compensation of orchestra members, the general administration of the orchestra, and the basic costs of maintaining Symphony Hall and Tanglewood. Management earns a percentage of these "fixed costs" by presenting concert programs, through radio, television, and recordings, and through other projects which involve both direct expenses and related income from ticket sales, fees, and royalties.

Each program or activity, of which there are over 40, is expected to make a "marginal contribution" to "fixed costs." The marginal contribution" is the difference between direct income and direct costs of the particular program or activity. The orchestra continued to make progress toward its goal of increasing the percentage of "fixed costs" contributed from operation activities.

The "marginal contribution" from all operations in 1981–82 covered 62.3 percent of "fixed costs" as compared to 59.7 percent last year and 43.0 percent in 1971–72.

In fiscal 1981–82, the "fixed costs" amounted to $9,160,000, compared to $8,434,000 in 1980–81, an increase of 8.6 percent. Operations earned $5,709,000, compared to $5,046,000 last year, a 13.1% increase. This left an "operating deficit" to be funded from other sources, e.g., endowment income and unrestricted contributions, of $3,451,000 in 1981–82, compared to $3,403,000 last year.

Other Information

The 1982 Annual Report contained the following explanation of endowment income:

Investment Income reached an all-time high of $2,134,000 as compared to $1,838,000 in the prior year. Of this amount, $219,000 was used for restricted purposes, e.g., supporting the winter season programs ($35,000), providing fellowships for the Berkshire Music Center and other BMC activities ($101,000), supporting the Esplanade concerts ($47,000), underwriting the Prelude Series ($29,000), and other miscellaneous activities. An additional $22,000 went to nonoperational

EXHIBIT 2

BOSTON SYMPHONY ORCHESTRA, INC.
Balance Sheets
August 31, 1982, and 1981

Assets	*1982*	*1981*	*Liabilities and fund balances*	*1982*	*1981*
Current Funds					
Cash (including savings accounts of $49,835 in 1982 and $463,320 in 1981)	$ 119,888	$ 501,962	Accounts payable	$ 564,677	$ 591,559
Short-term cash investments	2,600,000	1,666,222	Accrued pension liability	221,116	187,775
Participation in pooled investments, at market	1,979,960	1,681,781	Accrued expenses and other liabilities	619,008	189,972
Accounts receivable—less allowance for doubtful accounts of $10,000 in 1982 and $32,000 in 1981	709,069	937,016	Advance ticket sales and other receipts	2,781,005	2,516,114
Grants and other receivables	285,900	291,071	Advance receipts—special events	137,983	803,015
Prepaid salaries and wages	343,962	345,195	Due to other funds	240,528	—
Deferred charges	163,893	40,111		4,564,317	4,288,435
Prepayments and other assets	491,605	506,858	Fund balances:		
			Unrestricted	150,000	—
			Internally designated	1,979,960	1,681,781
				2,129,960	1,681,781
	$ 6,694,277	$ 5,970,216		$ 6,694,277	$ 5,970,216
Property Funds					
Due from other funds	240,528	—	Fund balances:		
Properties and equipment at cost, less accumulated depreciation of $2,209,622 in 1982 and $1,956,005 in 1981	4,766,216	4,693,885	Unexpected balances	240,528	—
			Investment in plant	4,766,216	4,693,885
	$ 5,006,744	$ 4,693,885		$ 5,006,744	$ 4,693,885
Endowment and Similar Funds					
Cash management fund—annuities	$120,409	$179,390	Annuity payable	$ 67,778	$ 103,662
Real estate and other property held for sale	712,223	862,233	Fund balances:		
Pooled investments, at market	20,536,010	16,356,225	Endowment principal and income restricted	2,533,903	2,142,179
Less participation in pooled investments by other funds	(1,979,960)	(1,681,781)	Funds functioning as endowment—trustee designated	16,787,001	13,470,216
				19,320,904	15,612,395
	$19,388,682	$15,716,057		$19,388,682	$15,716,057

uses, leaving $1,893,000 for unrestricted use in support of operations. This compares to $1,690,000 in 1980–81, a 12 percent increase.

The Annual Report also explained how the budget for 1982 was balanced, as follows:

> The percentage of "fixed costs" that had to be provided by unrestricted gifts was reduced from 20.3 percent in 1980–81 to 17.0 percent in 1981–82, amounting to $1,558,000.
>
> The sources of the $1,588,000 required to balance revenues and expenses in 1981–82 were:
>
> (1) Annual Fund (net): $989,000, up $250,000 or 34 percent over the previous year.
>
> (2) Projects (net): $723,000, up $459,000 or 174 percent over the previous year.
>
> Since funds available from these two sources totaled $1,172,000, it was possible to transfer the excess gifts of $154,000 for other needs.

Exhibit 2 gives the balance sheet, taken from the Annual Report.

Questions

1. Do the plans for 1983–1990 seem reasonably attainable?
2. Speculate as to other possible ways that BSO should seek to balance its budget during this period?

CASE 16–3
U.S. Naval Supply Center*

The Naval Supply Center at Newport, Rhode Island, serviced the almost 300 fleet and shore units of the U.S. Navy based throughout New England, New York, and New Jersey. From its 85 buildings and five fuel tank farms stretched along five miles of the Narragansett Bay shoreline, the Center received, stored, and issued materials for its customers, whether at home base or deployed on the other side of the globe.

Although handling supplies was the Center's principal mission, it also provided a variety of services for other naval operations, including purchasing, accounting, data processing, disposal, and household goods shipment.

The center's 547 civilian employees at Newport were managed by 19 military officers who occupied the key positions, including com-

* This case was prepared by Joseph E. Kasputys, Harvard Business School.

manding officer and all department heads. All but one of the officers were members of the Supply Corps and many held graduate degrees in business administration. In addition to its Newport facilities, the Center had an annex at Bayonne, New Jersey, which employed another 85 civilians to supply ships operating from New York, and to make many of the Center's overseas shipments. The Center was also assigned 10 enlisted men for special functions, giving a grand total of 661 employees.

The annual operating budgets for 1974–77 are shown below. Although the budget had increased, the increases had not kept pace with inflation. Approximately 70 percent of the budget was for labor, and substantial pay increases were granted to federal employees annually. The 661 employees on March 31, 1977, was a reduction of 16 percent, or 127 people, from the fiscal year 1975 average employment of 788. About half of this reduction was due to a drop in work done by the data processing and comptroller departments on a reimbursable basis for other navy operations.

	Fiscal year			
*Net funds authorized**	*1974*	*1975*	*1976*	*Estimated 1977*
Operations	$6,177,000	$5,881,000	$6,259,000	$6,408,500
Facilities maintenance	601,000	545,000	395,000	435,000
Disposal	191,000	170,000	214,000	232,000
Data processing	388,000	419,000	395,000	395,000
Total	$7,357,000	$7,015,000	$7,263,000	$7,470,500
* Does not include reimbursables of:	$1,098,000	$1,120,000	$846,000	$528,000

The Center's annual operating budget did not finance the inventory. The customers "bought" items using funds from their own annual operating budgets, which money was then used to replenish the inventory.

INVENTORY

The material supplied by the Center covered a spectrum from fuel to electronic repair parts to frozen meats. Some 48,100 different items were carried in inventory, excluding fuel oil.

Principal categories	*Number of items*	*Value (millions)*
Personnel support (food, clothing, medical supplies)	3,550	$ 2.2
Technical items (repair parts)	37,050	15.5
Other material (forms, office supplies, housekeeping items, etc.)	7,500	7.4
Total	48,100	$25.1

For management purposes, the inventory was divided into two major categories:

> *"Push" material.* Material automatically sent to the Center for stock. Decisions on items and quantities to be carried were made by central offices that control navy-wide inventory levels for technical supplies, and were based on material usage rates and the anticipated requirements for new equipment being introduced into the fleet. "Push" material, which included all the 37,050 line items of technical supplies, accounted for approximately 90 percent of the dollar value of the inventory.
>
> *"Pull" material.* Material, including most personnel, general, and industrial supplies, that was ordered by the Center for stock from wholesalers, such as the Defense Supply Agency and the General Services Administration. The demands placed upon the Center by customers are used to determine the range (number of different items) and depth (quantity of each item) that are carried.

Prior to 1961, all customers had to submit requisitions to the Center and wait, often for several days, for processing and delivery of the material. Although high-priority requisitions did move through the system rapidly, customers often experienced costly delays when ordering material for lower-priority work. The SERVMART, a self-service "supermarket" of high-usage items, was developed at Newport to reduce this problem. The customers merely selected what they needed and "checked out" at a checkout counter, which saved the Center handling and delivery costs and put the material in the customers' hands when they needed it. The SERVMART accounted for 50 percent of the Center's issues. Due to budgetary restrictions, changing support patterns, and management improvements, the range of the Center's inventory had been steadily shrinking. As a result, an increasingly greater percentage of issues would be made through the SERVMART.

OUTPUT MEASUREMENT

Outputs for the Center's primary mission, its supply operation, were measured at three different levels—performance of the total Center, of each cost account, and of each different task.

Overall performance of the Center. The speed of delivery and the success of the inventory in satisfying customer demands were watched carefully by the Center's top management and Washington headquarters. The principal indicators used to measure these outputs were: *receipts* of wholesale supplies; *demands* for supplies; *issues* of invoices for shipment; and *shipment*. Receipts, issues, and shipment were measured in both line items and measurement tons, since they involved the actual movement of material. Customer demands were measured only in line items, since they may have to be referred elsewhere for issue.

Washington headquarters gave the Center an objective for each of the four areas. Exhibit 1 summarized these objectives and showed the Center's performance against them for the past four years. For receipts, the objective was to process 85 percent within seven days, so that they were taken up on the stock records and were in the proper storage location, ready for issue. It was felt that the amount of receipts in process should be kept at a minimum, since they represented unusable stock that tied up inventory dollars.

EXHIBIT 1 Objectives and Performance Measures for Supply Operations

	Objectives (percent)	*Monthly average by fiscal year (to 3/31/77)*			
		1974	*1975*	*1976*	*1977*
Receipts:					
Receipts (M/T)		9,800	9,520	10,935	9,577
Receipts (L/I)*		16,480	17,750	16,989	10,187
Receipt processing time (85% of all receipts processed through storage within 7 days)					
Regular receipts	85	N.A.	65.7	75.6	91.0
Material returned by customer	85	N.A.	25.7	57.8	76.0
Issues:					
Issues (M/T)		9,820	10,203	10,587	9,355
Issues (L/I)*		57,870	57,600	57,903	53,122
Warehouse refusal rate—less than	1	.40	.32	.45	.60
Shipped:					
Shipped (M/T) (includes Center issues and transshipments)		11,254	11,700	12,347	11,844
Shipped (L/I) (transshipments only)		3,650	2,865	4,187	4,888
Shipped on time (95% of all items shipped on time)	95	98.8	93.4	96.9	96.0
Demands:					
Demands (L/I)		108,426	89,568	87,780	77,211
Material availability:					
Gross:					
"Pull" material	None	N.A.	61.9	61.2	64.2
"Push" material	None	N.A.	54.9	37.1	39.9
Net:					
"Pull" material	94	93.5	91.6	92.2	92.2
"Push" material	75	73.1	73.6	75.2	74.7

N.A. = not available.
* The discrepancy in receipts and issues line items reflects the fact that the Center received in bulk and issued in smaller quantities.

The objective for issues was a warehouse refusal rate of less than 1 percent. Warehouse refusals occur when the computer indicates material is on hand and issues an invoice, but the material department cannot locate the material in the warehouse. The more common reasons for warehouse refusals are improper record-keeping or storing the material in the wrong location.

The "shipped on time" objective affected both issues and shipments. Each customer demand carried a priority assigned by the customer, which indicated the maximum time allowed for delivery, varying from one day for issue group 1 to twelve days for issue group 4. The Center's objective was to ship 95 percent of all issues within these times. Although the assignment of higher priorities did not cost the customer anything extra, there were clear rules governing their use that were policed by both the Center and operational commanders.

Finally, gross and net material availability measured how well the Center's inventory was meeting customer demands. Gross availability was measured against *all* demands received from customers and was a measure of (1) how well the items for the inventory were selected and (2) how well the selected items were managed. From the customer's point of view, gross availability represented the probability that a demand would be filled by the Center in a timely fashion. Given a particular set of items for the inventory, net availability showed whether these items were in stock when demanded.

Because of the differences in management, separate measurements were made for "Push" and "Pull" material. Although no specific goals were established for gross availability, the "Push" inventory always achieved poorer results than the "Pull" inventory, since only a fraction of all possible technical repair parts were carried in the Center's stocks. Although additional repair parts were carried at the largest Centers, such as the one at Norfolk, many parts were not carried by the supply system at all, and were purchased or fabricated when needed. The goals for net availability were 75 percent for the "Push" inventory and 94 percent for the "Pull" inventory. Since the Center determined neither the range nor depth of the "Push" inventory, meeting the goals for its gross and net availability was the responsibility not of the Center but of the Navy's central inventory control offices.

All of the output measures in Exhibit 1 were reported on the Weekly Operations Report Measurement Summary (WORMS). Exhibit 2 is a copy of this report, referred to as "WORMS" not only because of its acronym but also because of the problems it could reveal. The only parts of Exhibit 2 filled in are those that have been discussed or are self-explanatory. The report was used by Center management to evaluate the past week's performance and to anticipate problems due to backlogs for the coming week. Since the use of overtime was a principal means of reducing backlog, the status of overtime funds was also shown, as well as current and authorized employment (omitted from Exhibit 2). The only material availability figures that were reported to Washington were those without the SERVMART activity, since headquarters believes that the high volume but low dollar value SERVMART business would mask main supply performance.

EXHIBIT 2 Weekly Operations Report Measurement Summary

WEEKLY OPERATIONS REPORT MEASUREMENT SUMMARY
NSCNPT W400/6 (REV 12-69)

WEEK ENDING: 7 May 1977

PART I - CENTER BUSINESS

	PRIORITY/CATEGORY	CURRENT WEEK TOTAL	CURRENT WEEK %	PREVIOUS WEEK TOTAL	PREVIOUS WEEK %
REQUISITION INPUT	GROUP I	151	1.9	195	2.2
	GROUP II	2290	29.0	2388	26.8
	GROUP III	3184	40.3	4311	48.3
	GROUP IV	2272	28.8	2024	22.7
	TOTAL	7897	100.0	8918	100.0
	NSC BEARERS				
	ALLOW. LISTS.				
ISSUES	SERVMART	4495	52.4	5120	50.0
	MAIN SUPPLY	4086	47.6	5045	50.0
	W'HSE REFUSALS	34	0.4	57	1.0
	SHIPS PRESENT	PIERS 19	OTHER 6	PIERS 16	OTHER 6

PART II - PROCESSING TIME

PRIORITY/CATEGORY % SHIPPED ON TIME	CURRENT WEEK %	PREVIOUS WEEK %	MONTH TO DATE %
GROUP I	100.0	96.0	100.0
GROUP II	97.0	95.0	97.0
GROUP III	99.0	95.0	99.0
GROUP IV	100.0	100.0	100.0
OVERALL	98.0	97.0	98.0
REC. PROC. WITHIN 0-7 DAYS	CURRENT WEEK %	PREVIOUS WEEK %	MONTH TO DATE %
REG REC THRU STK RECORDS			
REG REC THRU STORAGE	97.0	90.0	97.0
MTIS THRU STK RECORDS			
MTIS THRU STORAGE	98.0	92.0	98.0

PART III - SERVMART INFORMATION

ISSUES (L/I)	REPLENISHMENT (L/I)	NOT IN STOCK (L/I)
4495	337	80

INVENTORY VALUE ($)	VALUE OF ISSUES ($)

PART IV - PURCHASE MEAN LEAD TIME

PRIORITY	OBJ DAYS	OVERALL	IN-DEPT	% PROC ON TIME	DOCS
GROUP I	2			100.0	4
GROUP II	8			52.0	152
GROUP III & IV	16			35.0	149

PART V - MATERIAL AVAILABILITY

POINT OF ENTRY

WEEKLY	TOTAL	PUSH	PULL
W/SERVMART	79.0		
W/O SERVMART	62.0	37.4	68.1
MONTH TO DATE	TOTAL	PUSH	PULL
W/SERVMART	79.0		
W/O SERVMART	62.0	37.4	68.1

NET EFFECTIVENESS

WEEKLY	TOTAL	PUSH	PULL
W/SERVMART	93.6		
W/O SERVMART	87.5	74.6	91.2
MONTH TO DATE	TOTAL	PUSH	PULL
W/SERVMART	93.6		
W/O SERVMART	87.5	74.6	91.2

WEEKLY	CURRENT WEEK	PREVIOUS WEEK
TECHNICAL COGS		
PERSONNEL COGS		
MONTH TO DATE	CURRENT WEEK	PREVIOUS WEEK
TECHNICAL COGS		
PERSONNEL COGS		

PART VI - MISCELLANEOUS

ITEM	INPUT	PRODUCTION	BACKLOG
STORAGE ISSUE L/I	4982	5434	953
STORAGE ISSUE M/T		514	
STORAGE RECPT L/I	1405	1609	69
STORAGE RECPT M/T		709	
SHIPPING L/I	1101	1632	335
SHIPPING M/T	211	211	59
DELIVERY - PALLETS			
PACKING L/I			
SCREENING L/I			

ITEM	INPUT	PRODUCTION	BACKLOG
RECEIVING			
HHG CONTRACT JOBS			
HHG CLAIMS			
DEMAND PROCESSING			
KEYPUNCH (DOCS)			
PURCHASE L/I			BUYER
PURCHASE DOCUMENT			TYPE
DISPOSAL			

THE RESOURCE MANAGEMENT SYSTEM

Outputs were also measured by cost account, as part of the resource management system (RMS) implemented throughout the Department of Defense in 1968. Under RMS, budgets were on an accrual basis and reflected expenses (the use of resources) rather than obligations (a government accounting concept reflecting essentially the purchase of resources) as in the past. As a result, responsibility centers were charged with all measurable expenses, as opposed to as little as 40 percent under former systems. This new system permitted managers to determine the true costs of specific missions, compare actual progess with planned progress, and, with accurate output measurement, relate resources consumed to work done. The RMS accounting techniques provided vastly improved data on inputs, which needed to be compared to equally reliable data on outputs.

Following RMS procedures, the Center collected all costs by job order, which uniquely identified both a responsibility center and a cost account. The cost account covered a function, such as incoming storage operations, keypunch operations, or bulk fuel distribution. Within the cost account, costs were segregated by type, such as military and civilian salaries, overtime, and material. Each month, costs were summarized by cost account within responsibility center to get total expenses, which were then compared to the responsibility center's budget. The Center was divided into some 50 responsibility centers and 115 cost accounts, 60 of which had an associated output measure. Each cost account and its related output measure, which was called a work unit, had been carefully defined.

Below is a sample definition for the "Bulk Issue" cost account, which was charged chiefly by the material department:

Cost Account 21B2, BULK ISSUE

a. Scope. The cost account includes all physical handling (including the operation of materials handling equipment) incident to the breaking out of material for issue from large- and medium-lot bulk stores and the loading of the material for movement to packing, preservation, bin location, shop stores, SERVMARTS, advance base assembly areas when no intermediate operations are necessary prior to consolidation of material being issued, and for delivery to central or marine terminals; and direct supervision of the foregoing operations. This cost account *excludes* physical movement of material from one bulk storage location to another; physical handling, selection or off-loading of material to and from preservation, packaging and packing areas or repair shops for minor repairs when such operations are incident to care of material in storage; physical handling of bulk stock from permanent storage location directly into transportation carrier; and physical movement of bulk stock to other work areas when the movement exceeds normal forklift truck travel distances.

b. Work unit. Measurement tons.

1. *Definition.* Measurement tons (1 M/T = 40 cubic feet) of material physically handled incident to the issue of material from storage for shipment or delivery including issues to SERVMARTS.

2. *Point of count.* In the land–air freight and water freight operations upon completion of the final loading of material onto carriers for

final shipment or delivery and in bulk issue for tonnage moved to shop stores and SERVMARTS.

3. *Backlog.* Will not be reported.

Several departments could charge the same cost account. For example, cost account 21AK, Incoming Storage Operations, was charged by the material department for all physical handling of material upon receipt. These costs, together with the output measure, which is measurement tons, were shown on the material department's monthly reports. At the same time, the data processing department charged this cost account for the operation of a remote computer terminal serving the incoming storage operation. These latter costs appeared on the data processing department's monthly reports with no related output measure. Thus, although 60 of the cost accounts did have related output measures, each measure was used for only one of the several responsibility centers that could charge the account.

At the end of the month, a report was prepared that gave budgeted and actual expenses and work units. To eliminate the effects of volume fluctuations, unit costs were calculated on an actual and budgeted basis and a standard unit cost was shown, if available. Backlogs were also reported, if required. This report, called "Local Performance Statement," was prepared monthly and cumulatively each fiscal year for each responsibility center. Exhibit 3 is a monthly report for responsibility center 310, the storage division of the material department. The Bulk Issue cost account described above appears on this report.

For further analysis, expenses were segregated by type for each cost account within a responsibility center, also on a monthly and cumulative basis.

THE MANPOWER UTILIZATION AND CONTROL SYSTEM

At the third and final level, output was measured by task for each worker and compared to a standard, using the manpower utilization and control system (MUACS). The standards, which had been set through time studies, were used for work load planning and budgeting, while the actual output was used to evaluate and control performance. The following sample monthly figures for the material department illustrate the four basic types of standards and man-hours earned against each one.

Type of standard	*Man-hours earned*
1. Engineered standard (ES)	17,764
2. Statistical standard (SS)	230
3. Engineered fixed allowance (EFA)	20,138
4. Statistical fixed allowance (SFA)	8,329
Total	46,461

EXHIBIT 3

Local Performance Statement—Monthly
(For Period Ending April 30, 1977)

				Expenses		Work Units		Unit Cost		Standard Backlog
LMC	FC	CA	Title	Actual	Budget	Actual	Budget	Actual	Budget	W/U
310										
	A5	21AJ	RECEIVING OPERS	1,384	757					
	A5	21AK	INCOMING STORAGE	2,822	3,331	3,943		0.72		0.87
	A5	21BA	LIGHT PACKING	895	625					
	A5	21B2	BULK ISSUE	7,801	7,686	3,762	4,020	2.07	1.91	1.91
	A5	21B3	BIN ISSUE	5,476	4,595	14,971	15,755	0.37	0.29	0.29
	A5	21B4	SHIPPING	866	1,109					
	A5	21B9	PKG ISSUE SUPPORT	9,397	8,087					
	A5	21C1	CARE MTL IN STORE	6,415	4,050		53	76.42	76.17	
	A5	21C2	REWAREHOUSING	3,617	2,680		87		30.80	30.80
	A5	21C6	INVENTORY	377	444	990	596	0.38	0.74	0.74
	A5	21D5	MTL SCREEN IDENT	84	399					
	A5	21H1	STOR & WARE SUPPORT	1,698	951					
	A5	21H3		221						
	A5	21	STGE WAREHOUSE OPERS	41,053	34,714					
	A5	22BA	SC REQUIRE DIV	314	124					
	A5	22		314	124					
	A5	2330	HOUSEHOLD GOODS	165						
	A5	23	TRAFFIC MANAGEMENT	165						
	A5		DIRECT PROD EXPENSE	41,532	34,838					
310				41,532	34,838					

Abbreviations:
CA—Cost Account
FC—Fund Code
LMC—Local Management Code
W/U—Work Units

Within each cost account, different standards were set for each type of material being handled. The reason for this can be found by examining the Bulk Issue (21B2) cost account, which is described above. While the RMS can ascertain the average cost of bulk issue per measurement ton, it does not account for the fact that issues of different materials require different amounts of time. Some of the standards MUACS used to make this discrimination were:

Type of material	*Hours per line item*
Gas cylinders	.0177
Electronic parts	.0832
General material	.0832
Paints	.0990
Clothing	.1242
Medical supplies	.1544
Metals, pipes, and cables	.4226

Supervisors recorded both labor hours and output for each worker and turned in reports biweekly, at the end of each pay period. To aid supervisors in using the system, the various tasks and associated standards were grouped together for each responsibility center and published in a manual, containing 97 closely printed pages.

Data furnished by the supervisors were used to produce a monthly production report showing performance against each standard, which was used to judge the efficiency of labor. A page from this report is shown in Exhibit 4. The LMC code of 3100 identifies the storage division in the material department. The second code, headed "MS," identifies the work area. Codes E, F, and G are unique to Building 12. Only some of the E codes are shown at the bottom of the page, with the remainder of the Building 12 information continued on additional pages. The sixth line from the bottom is job order 3105, which is bulk issue. Since 444 work units were completed and the standard was .4226 hours per work unit, Building 12 earned 188 man-hours. However, this work was accomplished with 157.50 man-hours, giving production efficiency of 119.4 percent. This means that 2.8 line items were issued for each man-hour in lieu of the 2.4 line items per man-hour anticipated by the standard. The report also shows that there was a backlog of 97 line items to be issued from Building 12, which, according to the standard, should require 41 man-hours.

REPORTS FOR HEADQUARTERS

Washington headquarters was periodically furnished reports on costs and outputs for all three levels—Center, cost account, and task. These reports, which were summaries of those used by the Center's

EXHIBIT 4

MUACS Production Report—Monthly
(Date: April 30, 1977)

LMC	M S	JOB ORDER	TYPE STD	EARNED/ AUTH MH	ACTUAL MH	PRD EFF/ VAR MH	PLANNED RATE	ACTL RATE	WU COMPLETED	WU BACKLOG	MH BACKLOG	PLANNED WORKLOAD	STD
3100	A	3102	SFA	148	126.00	22							6.73
3100	A	3103	SFA	148	146.00	2							6.73
3100	A	3105	ES	209	197.00	106.1	8.1	8.5	1,684			1,210	.1242
3100	A	3106	ES	209	18.00	94.4	20.5	19.4	349			559	.0476
3100	A	3107	ES	17	16.00	137.5	14.0	19.2	307			220	.0702
3100	A	3111	ES	22	67.00	143.3	2.9	4.1	274			220	.3518
3100	B	3108	EFA	96	93.00	38 -							2.50
3100	C	3103	EFA	55	90.00	218							14.00
3100	C	3104	ES	308	6.50	76.9	22.6	17.4	113			8,646	.0476
3100	C	3105	ES	5	86.00	83.7	12.1	10.1	869			880	.0832
3100	C	3106	ES	72	4.00	100.0	15.0	15.0	60			154	.0627
3100	C	3107	ES	4	4.00	50.0	26.0	13.0	52			132	.0314
3100	C	3108	ES	2	2.00	50.0	20.0	10.0	20			704	.0563
3100	C	3109	EFA	1	17.00	8 -							.40
3100	C	3111	ES	9	33.00	69.7-	7.3	5.1	169			154	.1342
3100	C	3112	ES	23	15.00	93.3	12.6	11.8	177			1,188	.0780
3100		3108	EFA	14	31.50	58							4.10
3100	E	3103	EFA	90	274.50	33							14.00
3100	E	3105	ES	308	157.50	119.4	2.4	2.8	444	97	41	653	.4426
3100	E	3106	ES	188	7.50	213.3	8.1	17.3	130			427	.1218
3100	E	3107	ES	16	5.00	320.0	6.3	20.0	100			150	.1639
3100	E	3108	ES	16	9.00	122.2	2.2	2.7	24			132	.4509
3100	E	3109	EFA	11	3.00	1							.20
3100	E	3110	SFA	4	9.00	9 -							.01

Abbreviations:
LMC—Local Management Code
EARNED/AUTH MH—Earned or Authorized Manhours
PRD EFF/VAR MH—Production Efficiency or Manhour Variance
WU—Work Units

management, were used to evaluate the Center and compare its performance to that of other supply centers.

Questions

1. Based upon the outputs and costs shown, how would you evaluate the Center's recent performance?
2. Were the output measurements taken at the Center adequate to assess effectiveness? Efficiency?
3. Were three separate levels of output measurement necessary? What advantages and disadvantages were there to this structure?
4. How did the externally imposed objectives affect the structure and operation of the Center? What is your opinion of this "management by objectives"?
5. Were the reports shown in Exhibits 3 and 4 useful management tools? What problems, if any, are evident in these reports?

CHAPTER 17

Management Control of Projects

In the preceding chapters, we tended to focus on the management control of ongoing operations. These are operations that go indefinitely, even though for reporting purposes they are divided into annual or other discrete time periods. In this chapter we discuss the somewhat different problem of the management control of projects.

A project is a set of activities intended to accomplish a specified end result, of sufficient importance to be of interest to management. The project ends when that result has been attained or, in some cases, when the attempt is abandoned. Common types of projects are the construction of buildings, roads, dams, or other works, and we shall use construction projects as illustrations throughout the chapter. Other examples are the production of motion pictures or television specials (as contrasted with nightly news programs); most research/development activities; engagements of law firms, consulting firms, and public accounting firms; the overhaul of ships, aircraft, and other major assets (as contrasted with regular maintenance); and the production of a major single asset, such as a large turbine.

CHARACTERISTICS OF PROJECTS

Projects have one characteristic that makes control easier and other characteristics that make control more difficult than management control of ongoing operations.[1] The characteristic that makes control easier is that the end product is defined. Management focuses on its completion, and the management function ends at this time. Managers in ongoing operations must consider how current decisions affect the foreseeable future, whereas managers of projects need not look beyond

[1] For an expanded discussion of this point, together with other aspects of the management control of projects, see William H. Lucas and Thomas L. Morrison, "Management Accounting for Construction Contracts," *Management Accounting,* November 1981, pp. 59–65. For a discussion of a quite different type of project, see Eileen Morley and Andrew Silver, "A Film Director's Approach to Managing Creativity," *Harvard Business Review,* March–April 1977, pp. 59–70.

the end of the project (except as the conduct of the project affects their reputation and suggests better ways of doing future projects).

Factors that make management control more difficult vary with the nature of the project. Performance on research/development projects is difficult to measure, and the artistic elements of motion picture production causes difficult control problems. For large construction projects, some of the characteristics that make project control more difficult than the control of production operations in a factory are: (1) the work tends to be less standardized, (2) the control systems tend to be less standardized, (3) the rhythm of the work is different, (4) the uncertainties are greater, (5) the environmental influences are greater, and (6) building satisfactory organizational relationships is more difficult.

Less Standardization of Work

Although some components of a construction project are similar to those in other projects, there are many differences, at least in detail, between one project and others. Consequently, the standards for project work typically are less reliable than those used for production operations. If the standard for a production operation is 100 pieces per hour, production of only 95 pieces per hour is usually cause for concern. This is not so likely to be the case in a construction project.

The lower reliability of the standards has implications for planning, for execution, and for evaluation. For planning, it means that the estimates of time required and of costs are subject to a larger margin of error than estimates of production time and costs; the plan must provide allowances for this margin of error. For execution, it means that judgments about deviating from the plan are more likely to be necessary. For evaluation, it means that the project manager has less confidence than the production manager that a difference between planned and actual results is significant.

In the production operation, the term *out of control* often has a precise meaning. If, for example, standard production in a certain process is 100 pieces per hour, statistical techniques can be used to establish a control limit, say 96 pieces. If actual output falls to 95 pieces per hour, there is a known probability that the process has gone out of control. (The deviation does not ordinarily signify poor management; usually, it means only that some unforeseen factor has affected the production process.) In a project, the standards are usually not reliable enough for statistically sound control limits to be specified.

Less Standardization of Systems

In a factory, once a satisfactory control system has been developed, it can be used for a long time. Unless there is a major change in the production process or a major development in systems technology (such as the introduction of computers), systems development work is primarily a matter of fine tuning. This not only reduces the cost and time required to develop systems but it also increases the likelihood that those who work with the system understand what the information means and how to use it.

In many construction projects, control systems must be developed to meet the requirements of the particular project. If the project is carried out by a single contractor who has done similar work previously, the contractor can use parts of systems used on the earlier projects. Even in these circumstances, the requirements of the client, the type of work done by subcontractors, the location of the job, and other considerations may require substantial modification of these systems.

Different Rhythm

In a factory, the production operation often is repetitive. Today's work is like yesterday's. Even in a job shop in which individual jobs are different, each job is done by executing a limited number of familiar production operations. A construction project, particularly a large project, has a quite different rhythm and tempo. In the early planning phase, the effort is small-scale. As planning becomes more concrete, the staff grows larger and experts with different skills are added. When construction starts, there is the process of mobilizing the work force, which has no counterpart in the typical factory. (Even when the plant is shut down for a model change or because of a slackening of demand, the hiatus is usually temporary, and essentially the same work force returns when production resumes.) Work then builds to a peak and, thereafter, tapers off in the final acceptance phase of the project. Moreover, personnel with different skills are involved in each stage of the project: first, conceptual planners; then, architects, engineers, and designers; and finally, personnel with the skills required for actual construction. The skill requirements of the latter group vary at different stages in the project.

Many production operations are repetitive, which permits a learning process to occur; the more times the operation is repeated, the greater the productivity. On the typical project, the operations are less repetitive, and the possibilities of improvements through learning are correspondingly less.

More Uncertainties

In a production operation, workers process materials with known qualities, fabricate metals with known specifications, and use machines with known capabilities. In a construction project, the knowns are typically much less, particularly if the project involves going beneath the earth's surface, as in mining, petroleum drilling, and excavation. Despite the best efforts to find out, the subsurface characteristics usually cannot be known precisely until work gets underway.

Production operations must cope with the uncertainties of demand for the product, of late deliveries of material or components, and so on. However, in a production operation, in-process and finished goods inventories can provide a buffer against the impact of these uncertainties. If on a given day one production operation does not complete the planned number of parts or components, succeeding operations can proceed by drawing parts or components from inventory. Although there are some opportunities to provide buffers on a construction project by rescheduling work, failure to complete one operation on time tends to delay the succeeding operations. Rescheduling manpower and equipment may be difficult, and unavoidable idle time often results.

Environmental Impact

In a factory building, the equipment, service facilities, and inventories are in fixed and known locations; the physical environment is usually controlled; and employees know where to report for work each day without being told. In a construction project, the work is done at a site removed from the organization's permanent facilities. Unless the project consists of constructing a single structure, the location of this site changes as work progresses. The environment at the site is usually not controlled; the influence of weather conditions can be estimated but never forecasted precisely. Personnel, materials, and equipment must be brought to the site when they are needed. Thus, the scheduling problems of construction projects are more complicated than those in most production operations, even those for assembly plants to which parts are shipped from fabricating plants.

Organizational Relationships

The employees in a factory may be members of the same responsibility center—the department or section—for a long time. In this environment, they learn what behaviors are acceptable and what are not, they learn the personalities of their supervisors and co-workers, and they learn many other things that constitute the organization's climate. Managers learn how best to work with their subordinates and with other managers. They learn the strengths and weaknesses of other people, how to get them to work together as a team, and how to motivate them to achieve the desired results.

By contrast, the team that does a construction project is assembled, does its job, and then is disbanded. At the beginning, the organizational relationships do not exist; they must be developed. The desired climate must also be created.

PROJECT ORGANIZATION

A project may be carried out by an in-house team (i.e., by company employees assigned to this work), by a contractor, by a new organization created for the purpose, or by some combination of these.

When the project is carried out in-house, a project manager is designated and other personnel are drawn from various functional parts of the organization. This results in what is called a "matrix organization," and its control problems are discussed in the next section.

If the project is assigned to an outside contractor, the client's control problem is to create and maintain the proper interface with the contractor. A contractor brings its own control systems to the job, and information from those systems is used by the client to the extent feasible; this is usually supplemented by information developed by the client's personnel assigned to monitor the project. Problems associated with various types of contractual relationships are discussed in a following section.

Creation of a new organization with responsibility for carrying out a project is appropriate for certain joint ventures (i.e., projects carried out for the benefit of two or more companies). When a new organization is created, appropriate control systems must be developed. Although some pieces of these systems may be developed by using the experience of the participating companies or of the contractors, much time and effort usually are required to develop systems that are appropriate for control of the particular project. Creation of a new organization requires an additional layer of control between the sponsoring companies and those who do the work on the project.

Matrix Organizations

There is no general agreement as to what type of organization qualifies as a "matrix organization."[2] Some people use the term to refer to any organization in which the manager who is responsible for the end product must obtain some resources from responsibility centers headed by other managers. In this broad sense, almost every large organization is a matrix organization because they have service and support units that provide maintenance, data processing, engineering, market research, and other services to the responsibility centers that

[2] For a full discussion of matrix organizations, see Stanley M. Davis and Paul R. Lawrence, *Matrix* (Reading, Mass.: Addison-Wesley Publishing, 1977).

are responsible for manufacturing and marketing products. Such a definition is too broad to distinguish matrix organizations from other organizations in a way that permits analysis of their special problems. We shall use a narrower idea, and define a matrix organization as one in which managers responsible for end products obtain a *substantial fraction* of the resources needed to do their jobs from other responsibility centers.

We also limit the discussion to the management of projects; that is, jobs that have a defined beginning and end. Some companies use the matrix form of organization for continuing activities. For example, some companies have product managers or brand managers who are responsible for a product line but who must rely on other responsibility centers to both manufacture and market the product. In Procter & Gamble, there is a brand manager for each product line, such as Ivory soap, but the plant that manufactures Ivory soap and the marketing organization that sells and distributes it is not under the control of that brand manager. The brand manager plans the promotional efforts for the product line and coordinates the manufacturing and marketing activities. This is a matrix organization, but not a project organization—because the brand manager's responsibilities are continuing.

The special problems of project control in a matrix organization arise both because the work is a project and also because the project manager must rely heavily on other responsibility centers for the resources required to do the work. At the extreme, the project manager may not have direct control over any resources except a personal staff. All the work is carried out in other responsibility centers, and the job of the project manager and the staff is to handle relations with the client for whom the work is done and to plan, coordinate, and troubleshoot the work of the other responsibility centers. This form of project management is used in aerospace companies for projects such as the space shuttle, guided missile systems, and communications satellites. It is also used by advertising agencies; the project manager, called the account executive, relies on other departments of the agency for most of the resources needed to plan and carry out an advertising campaign.

In another form of a matrix organization, the project manager assembles resources from functional responsibility centers. During the time they are working on the project, employees assigned to the job are responsible to the project manager, and equipment and other resources are also his or her responsibility. The project manager also draws on the services of shops and other responsibility centers. This is often the case in accounting firms, consulting firms, research/development firms, certain engineering and construction projects, and shipyards.

There are all sorts of variations on this general idea. In a research/development laboratory, a typical project has a nucleus of full-time people, it has part-time people "on loan" from other departments, and it uses computers, model shops, and other specialized activities when the need arises.

Behavioral problems. In projects carried out within a matrix organization, the special management control problems are the most severe. The essence of the problem is that the project manager has the *responsibility* for the project but does not have the corresponding *authority* over the resources used in the project. Put another way, employees who work on a project have two bosses: the project manager, for whom they work temporarily, and the head of the functional responsibility center that is their permanent home.

For example, in a shipyard, one dimension focuses on the projects—the various ship overhaul jobs—and the other dimension focuses on the responsibility centers, the functional shops to which the personnel are permanently assigned. Management control goes on concurrently in both these dimensions. The project manager may be the manager of one of the responsibility centers which work on the project, or he or she may not be associated with any of these responsibility centers. The interests of project managers often do not coincide with those of responsibility center managers. Project managers want full attention given to *their* projects, while responsibility center managers must take into account *all* the projects on which the center works. This conflict of interest is inevitable; it increases the complexity of control. A matrix organization creates tension. As Vancil says, there is "an atmosphere of constructive conflict in which managers in one function know they are working toward the same goal and must compete among themselves to cooperate with other managers.[3]

The larger the project, the more complicated the control problem becomes. When the TRW Company was working on the Apollo space program, for example, the project manager not only had a large office responsible for scheduling the project and dovetailing the operations of the many functional departments involved, but he also had full-time liaison people in each of these departments. They were responsible to the project manager for work related to the project; but each was also a member of the functional department, and his or her overall performance was judged by the head of the department.

Planning and scheduling. In a matrix organization, planning is complicated by the interrelationship between the project and the financial responsibility centers that provide resources for it. The functional units must plan to have available adequate work force and other resources to meet the needs of all the projects that will be worked on during the period, and must, therefore, find out what these needs are likely to be. Project managers often cannot anticipate their needs accu-

---

[3] Richard F. Vancil, "What Kind of Management Control Do You Need?" *Harvard Business Review*, March–April, 1973, p. 75.

rately, however. In scheduling, it is important that all available resources be employed on some project; but since needs cannot be entirely foreseen, it is to be expected that some slack time will exist. Moreover, there is the difficult problem of resolving conflicts when two projects request more resources than currently are available.

Contractual Relationships

When the work is performed by a contractor, the nature of the contract affects the management control problem. There are two general types of contracts—fixed-price and cost-reimbursement—with many variations within each. Each is appropriate for certain types of projects and is inappropriate for others. Each requires a different approach to management control.

Fixed-price contract. If the desired end product can be clearly specified, and if the cost of producing this end product can be reliably estimated in advance, a fixed-price contract usually is appropriate. Theoretically, the client should have no cost control problem with such a contract. If the end product meets specifications and, if it is completed on time, the fixed price is paid—and that is that. Theoretically, therefore, the client need not, and should not, be involved in controlling how the contractor incurs costs.

In many situations, however, control is not that simple. On a project of even moderate complexity (such as building a house or a single office building), writing specifications that describe the desired end product precisely is a difficult task. In evaluating the work, the client not only must assure that the product meets specifications, but also that the product actually meets the client's needs; some desirable aspects may have been omitted from the specifications.

Moreover, as the work progresses, unforeseen problems usually surface, and opportunities for improving the product are discovered. These may lead to changes in the specifications, and such changes usually require that the fixed price be renegotiated. Analyzing proposed changes and the associated costs can be complicated and time-consuming. Thus, the price eventually paid for the work often is not the "fixed price" specified in the contract.

Cost-reimbursement contract. If the end product cannot be clearly specified or if the cost of providing it cannot be reliably estimated, a cost-reimbursement contract is appropriate. In this type of contract, the contractor is reimbursed for reasonable costs incurred, plus a profit or fee (unless the contractor is a nonprofit organization). If the client requested bids on a fixed-price basis for work of this type, it could expect that bidders would include, in their calculation of the fixed price, a contingency allowance for the cost uncertainties, and this would likely make the final cost higher than it would have been if costs were reimbursed only to the extent incurred. If a fixed-price contract is awarded to a bidder whose price turns out to be low, because it was based on an inadequate contingency allowance, the contractor will try to "get well" by requesting change orders for the unforeseen events. In extreme cases, if proposed change orders are not approved, the contractor may "walk away from the job" or go bankrupt, and then there will be no end product.

Client/contractor relationships. In both fixed-price and cost-reimbursement contracts, the contractor's skill and reputation are the principal assurances that the job will be done properly. With a fixed-price contract, the client will tend to focus on technical quality and on-time completion, and the contractor is primarily responsible for the control of costs. With a cost-reimbursement contract, both parties have a significant interest in cost control.

With a cost-reimbursement contract, the contractor tends to be willing to accept changes in the work proposed by the client because the additional costs will be reimbursed. With a fixed-price contract, as noted above, proposed changes that affect costs require time-consuming negotiations.

Incentive contracts. An incentive contract rewards the contractor for performance that exceeds some specified target with respect to the quality of the work, the time required, or the cost, or penalizes the contractor for performance that is below these targets. Incentive contracts are effective only if reasonable targets can be arrived at in advance. If the incentive targets turn out to be so tight as to be unattainable, they provide no motivation. If they are too loose, the contractor might be paid more than would be the case with a cost-reimbursement contract.

THE MANAGEMENT CONTROL PROCESS

Management control of projects has a planning phase, an execution phase, and an evaluation phase. In each of these phases, attention must be directed to three aspects of the project: (1) its scope, (2) its time, and (3) its cost.

Scope refers to the technical specifications of the project (i.e., the desired end product). In the planning phase, the desired end product is described as specifically as is feasible; in the execution phase, the work required to produce this product is carried out; and in the evaluation phase, the actual quantity and quality of the work done to date are compared with the specifications and appropriate action taken.

In the planning phase, the *time* required for each part of the project is estimated and, if feasible, set forth in a schedule. The schedule guides the execution phase. In evaluation, the actual time taken for each activity is compared with the estimated time, and significant variances are identified and acted upon.

The *cost* estimate, or budget, for a project is prepared by costing-out the project specifications. The physical resources required—personnel, material, and so on—are estimated, and these are translated into costs. These requirements guide managers in procuring and using resources during the execution phase. In evaluation, actual costs are compared with budgeted costs or with other standards, causes of significant variances are identified, and appropriate action is taken.

As the project progresses, circumstances may suggest the desirability of revising any or all of the scope, time, or cost estimates.

Work Packages

Most projects are broken down into pieces, in order to facilitate control. These pieces are called "work packages." A *work package* is a measurable increment of work that can be related to a physical product, milestone, or other indicator of progress. One work package should require a relatively short time, it should have an identifiable starting point and completion point, and it should be performed by a single responsibility center.

Work packages always include the time and scope dimensions; they may or may not include cost information. Often it is not necessary to collect costs at the level of individual work packages; instead, costs are collected in aggregates of several work packages.

PROJECT PLANNING

The planning for a construction project usually starts with a rough, quite vague idea, which becomes increasingly definite on the basis of discussions, tests, various types of preliminary studies, negotiations between the client and the project management, and actual performance as the work progresses. Thus, planning is an iterative process. Rarely is there such a thing as "the" plan. Rather, there is a succession of plans, each presumably better than the preceding one.

Prior to project planning, the client has investigated the desirability of the project itself. In the structure used in this book, this is a strategic planning process, not a management control process. For this purpose, rough estimates are made of the time and costs required to produce the desired end product, or of several alternative end products. Cost estimates for constructing an office building, for example, may be arrived at simply by estimating the number of square feet of floor space and multiplying this by an estimated cost per square foot, with little attention being given to the characteristics of the specific building or to the special construction problems at the specific site. When the feasibility of a project is being explored, a rough cost estimate suffices. In any event, information required for a detailed estimate usually is not available at the early stages.

The planning phase, as such, begins after a decision has been made to proceed with the project. At this time the parties have agreed on the general nature of the desired end product, the approximate time required, and the approximate magnitude of the cost. These general plans are translated into specifications, schedules, resource requirements, and budgets, and these form the basis for project execution and evaluation.

Schedules, resource requirements, and budgets are prepared as close to the inception of work on the project as is feasible. If they are prepared earlier than is necessary, last-minute changes in the project specifications, newly acquired information about the nature of the work to be done, or more recent estimates of unit costs may require that the work be redone, with a consequent waste of some of the earlier effort.

Planning the Scope Dimension

After the specifications of the end product have been reasonably well established, the work packages required to produce the product are identified. Often, this is done by working backward from the product specifications to the specific jobs that must be done. Ideally, each work package should contain a statement of just what is to be done, but this is not always feasible. Unavoidable imprecision in the description of work packages complicates the problem of control.

Planning the Time Dimension

Several tools are available for constructing the time schedule for the project. They go by such acronyms as PERT (program evaluation and review technique), and CPM (critical path method). These techniques have three basic steps: (1) determining the time required for each work package, (2) identifying the interdependencies among work packages (i.e., the work packages that must be completed before a given work package can be started), and (3) calculating the critical path.

Collectively, these are techniques for *network analysis*.

A network diagram consists of *(a)* a number of nodes, or *events* (also termed *milestones*), each of which is a subgoal that must be completed in order to accomplish the project; and *(b)* lines joining these nodes to one another, which are *activities*. The estimated time to carry out each of these activities is shown on the network diagram. An activity connecting two events, say A and B, indicates that the activity cannot be started until event A has happened and that the completion of the activity results in event B. These activities are work packages. Thus, a network diagram shows the chronological sequence in which events must be completed in order to complete the whole project.

Critical path and slack. Computer programs are available for analyzing project networks. They identify the *critical path,* which is the sequence of events that requires the longest total time. The nature of the critical path is shown in Exhibit 17–1. In order to complete event B, event A must first be completed; this requires two weeks. A–B requires an additional five weeks. Then B–C, requiring an additional three weeks, is done in order to complete the project. This is the critical path, and it is 10 weeks long. Note that to complete event B, activity X–B must also be undertaken, with an estimated time of four weeks. However, activity B–C cannot be started until *both* A–B and X–B have been completed. Since X–A and A–B require a total of seven weeks, X–B, which requires only four weeks, can be performed any time during this period. Activity X–B is said to have three weeks of *slack.*

EXHIBIT 17–1 Critical path (heavy line indicates critical path)

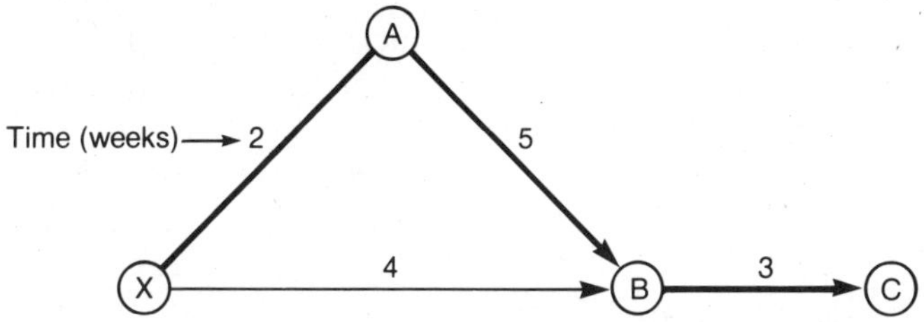

There are several management control implications in the concepts of critical path and slack. First, in the control process, special attention must be paid to those activities that are on the critical path, and less attention needs to be paid to slack activities (although not so much less that time is allowed to slip by and eat up the amount of slack; the activity then automatically becomes on the critical path). Second, in the planning process, attention should be given to possibilities for reducing the time required for critical path activities; if such possibilities exist, the overall time required for the project can be reduced. Third, it may be desirable to reduce critical path times by increasing costs, such as incurring overtime; but it is not desirable to spend additional money to reduce the time of slack activities.

Probabilistic PERT. As the PERT system was originally conceived, the estimated times required for each activity in the network were arrived at on a probabilistic basis. Three estimates were made for each activity: a most likely time *(m),* an optimistic time *(a),* and a pessimistic time *(b).* The optimistic and pessimistic times were supposed to represent probabilities of approximately .01 and .99 on a normal probability distribution. The most likely estimate was given a weight of 4, and each of the other estimates a weight of 1, and an expected time *(t)* for each activity was computed as

$$\bar{t} = \frac{a + 4m + b}{6}$$

It was soon discovered that this approach had serious practical difficulties. Engineers and others who were asked to make the three estimates found this to be a most difficult task. It turned out not to be possible, in most cases, to convey what was intended by "optimistic" and "pessimistic" in a way that was interpreted similarly by all the estimators. Furthermore, it was found that estimators tended to make symmetrical estimates; that is, their optimistic and pessimistic estimates were equal distances from the most likely estimate. When this happened, the resulting expected time ($\bar{t}$) was the same as the most likely time, so there was no gain in going through the probabilistic exercise. For example, if the estimates were 3 weeks for *a*, 5 weeks for *m*, and 7 weeks for *b*, the expected time was

$$\frac{3 + 4(5) + 7}{6} = \frac{30}{6} = 5$$

Thus, although probabilistic PERT is still referred to in the literature and in formal descriptions of the PERT technique, the probabilistic part is not widely used in practice.

Network analysis.[4] The approach to constructing and analyzing a project network, and the limitations of such an analysis, can be understood from the example in Exhibit 17–2. The example is for a simple situation, but the same principles apply for complex projects involving hundreds or thousands of activities and events.

The project is a simple construction task that consists of six events. Four employees are available to work on the project. In Section (A) of Exhibit 17–2, each of the six events (here called "jobs") is represented by a circle. The lines connecting the circles are activities. The number above each circle is the estimated number of days required for the activity involved in completing that job, and the number below the circle is the number of workers required for that activity. The "critical path" duration of this network, without considering resources, is eight days.

Section (B) shows the eight-day job sequence and the resulting daily work force requirements. It can be seen that the available work force constraint is exceeded on days three and four; thus, this eight-day schedule is *resource-infeasible* (assuming that the limit of four employees cannot be exceeded). In order to complete the project, job sequencing decisions are required, which will result in the shortest possible project duration, and involving not more than four workers each day.

[4] This section is adapted from material prepared by Edward W. Davis.

EXHIBIT 17–2 Example of Network Analysis

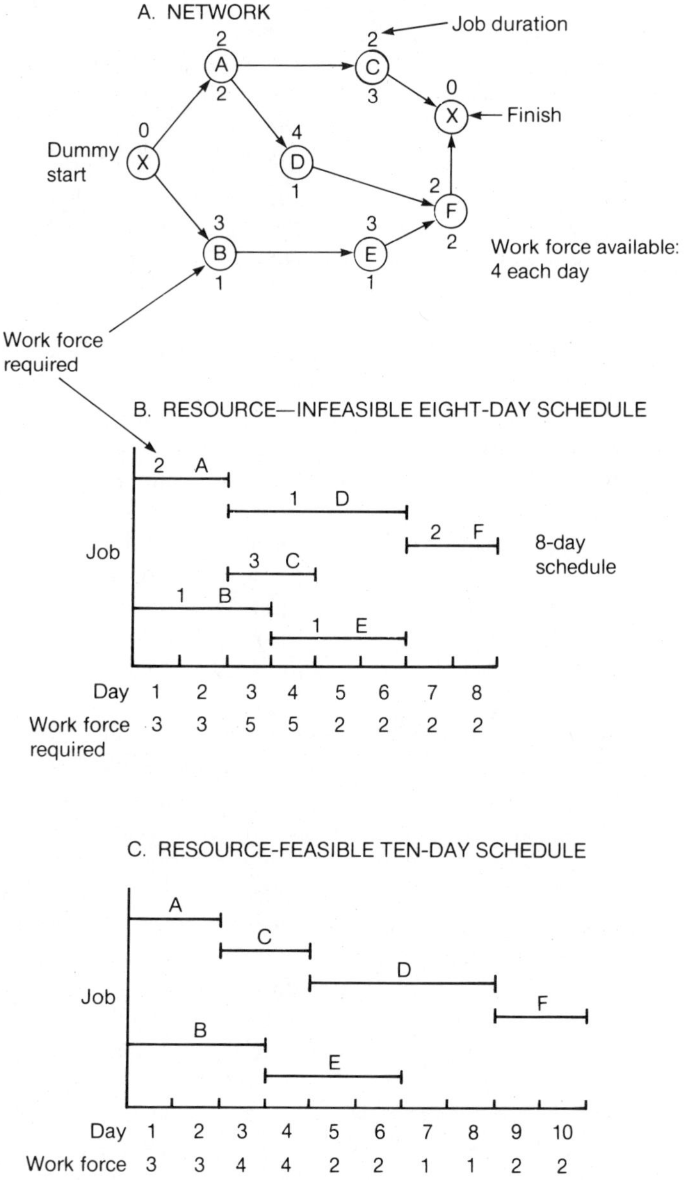

In what order should the jobs of this project be sequenced so as not to exceed the available limit of four workers, and yet minimize the increase in project duration? This is the crux of the issue in scheduling project networks under resource constraints.

In spite of this problem's apparent simplicity, there exists today no practical computational scheme for determining optimal solutions to problems of the size and complexity generally encountered in real-life situations. It should be noted that the simple example of Exhibit 17–2 involves only one work force type for the entire project. If each job required various amounts of several different work force types (e.g., carpenters, plumbers, electricians), and each type were limited in availability, the problem would be much more complicated—and more representative of what actually occurs in practice.

One approach to the simple one-resource problem described above is to sequence those jobs causing the resource conflicts according to some *heuristic* (rule of thumb) rule, such as the "shortest job first." Using this rule, job D of the sample problem would be delayed until after job C, and the resource-feasible schedule of 10 days' duration shown in Section (C) is obtained. The drawback of using such a heuristic approach is that we do not know if the resulting schedule is the shortest possible. Thus, there may well be a nine-day solution for this problem, which we *might* obtain by using a different sequencing heuristic.

Another approach to the problem would be to formulate it for solution as an integer linear programming problem. This approach will yield the optimal (shortest duration) schedule, but *(a)* the formulation is extremely cumbersome, requiring dozens of equations for small problems and *(b)* computation times to solution, even on the largest computers, are quite long.

A third approach—which would also yield the optimal solution—would be to enumerate all possible job sequences and choose the one producing the shortest project duration. This approach usually is impractical, because the number of possible job sequences increases exponentially with an increase in the number of jobs. Stated another way, the decision tree of possible job sequences grows quickly to unmanageable proportions. For example, the decision tree for this very simple problem contains more than 100 nodes, and the tree for a slightly larger example containing 11 jobs contains more than 200,000 nodes!

A fourth—and more recent—approach involves the techniques of *bounded enumeration*. As implied by the name, this approach involves enumerating and searching over only a portion of the decision tree for a given problem. The partial enumeration and search is conducted in such a fashion that the final solution is demonstrably optimal. Bounded enumeration has so far been successfully applied only to relatively small networks.

Because of its formidable combinatorial proportions, the bulk of effort on the resource-constrained network scheduling problem has been devoted to the development of *heuristic* solution procedures. Dozens of elaborate computer-based schemes have been developed in government and industry. Some of these computer programs will quickly produce a *feasible* solution to projects involving hundreds of jobs and many different resource types. The manager who uses these programs should be aware, however, that irrespective of their complexity—and despite the "best possible solution" claims of their marketers—the "goodness" of the final schedule (relative to the optimum) is generally unknown. Although some heuristic procedures are generally recognized as more effective than others, there is no one "heuristic" that will perform best, relative to other heuristics, in every given case.

Estimating Costs

For practical reasons, cost estimates are often made at a level of aggregation that incorporates several work packages. Resources used on individual work packages are controlled in terms of physical quantities, rather than costs, and, costing out each work package, therefore, would serve no useful purpose.

Cost estimates for construction projects tend to be less accurate than those for manufactured goods because projects are less standardized, and cost information that has been accumulated for similar work is therefore not as valid as an indicator. Nevertheless, if a contractor has performed similar work in the past, the costs incurred on these work packages provide a starting point in estimating the costs of the new project. For some work, industry norms, or rules of thumb, have been developed that are useful in estimating costs.

Obviously, no one knows what will actually happen in the future; therefore, no one knows what future costs actually will be. In estimating what costs are likely to be, two types of unknowns must be taken into account. The first are the *known unknowns*. These are estimates of the cost of activities that are known to be going to occur, such as digging the foundation for a house. The nature of the task is known; and the costs, although unknown, often can be estimated within reasonable limits on the basis of past experience. If unexpected rock or other conditions are encountered, however, these estimates may turn out to be far from the mark.

The other unknowns are the *unknown unknowns*. For these activities, the estimator does not know that they are going to occur, and obviously, therefore, has no way of estimating their cost. Work stoppages, destruction caused by storms or floods, delays in receiving materials, accidents, failure of government inspectors to act in a timely manner, are examples. In a fixed-price contract, the costs incurred by such events, if they occur, often are added to the fixed price; in the contract, these events are referred to as *force majeure*.

In using the cost estimates in the evaluation phase, it is essential that the impossibility of estimating the cost of unknown unknowns be recognized. Their actual costs may range from zero, if none of them actually occur, up to any amount whatsoever. There is no definable upper limit. The most the estimator can do is to include a contingency allowance for these cost elements.

Developing Control Systems

As part of the planning process, systems that will be used in the execution and evaluation phases are designed. These are systems for both task control and management control. Some of them, or some parts of them, may be brought to the project by the contractor. Others must be developed to fit the needs of the specific project.

Some task control systems used on construction projects are similar to, but more complicated than, corresponding controls in a factory. For example, the scheduling of resources so they will arrive at the proper place at the proper time is more complicated for a construction project than scheduling the flow of materials through a factory. Most task controls are nonmonetary. Reports show man-hours, rather than labor costs; yards of concrete, rather than dollar costs of concrete—and so on. These nonmonetary amounts can be obtained more quickly and more simply than dollar amounts, and they are all the supervisor needs to exercise day-to-day control.

As is the case in a factory, information in management control reports is basically a summary of information developed for task control purposes. Although managers at higher levels need cost reports (i.e., reports in monetary terms) in order to obtain a summary view of progress, turning the quantitative information in the task control reports into dollars usually slows down the reporting process. Since managers need information as quickly as possible, they often rely heavily on nonmonetary information. Cost reports are used subsequently as an overall check on the reliability of the nonmonetary information.

Planning Organizational Relationships

Planning the structure of the project organization and how it will operate is an important part of the process. Management control is exercised through people, not reports. Plans are developed for the ways in which managers are expected to act during the execution of the project. These include the delineation of lines of authority and responsibility; preparation of rules and guidelines on matters such as actions that managers can take on their own authority, contrasted with actions requiring higher approval; creation of organization units responsible for inspecting quality and monitoring costs; deciding on what meetings will be held to discuss progress and problems, who will attend, and how often they will meet; and any other aspects of the control process that can be worked out in advance. As is the case with other plans, all these arrangements are subject to change as the work progresses and as better information about needs and workable processes is developed.

These arrangements set the stage for the *control climate,* which is the general attitude toward control that managers will have during the execution phase of the project. As is the case with atmospheric temperature, the control climate is felt rather than seen; it is evidenced more by the nature of informal interactions than by formal documents.

PROJECT EXECUTION

In the execution phase (the phase in which the work is done), the principal control activities are those of task control. In this phase, managers, as distinguished from task supervisors, are involved in a variety of activities, some related to control and others not. Management cannot literally "control" the costs of a project. What management does—or at least what it attempts to do—is to control the actions of the people who are responsible for incurring these costs.

Their role in accomplishing the work involves coordination with other responsibility centers to break bottlenecks, resolving disputes within their own responsibility center, approving proposed actions that their subordinates cannot take on their own authority, suggesting the solution to problems, suggesting better ways of getting the work done, and, most important, enhancing the "control climate" by commending subordinates for good performance and criticizing or taking other appropriate action for unsatisfactory performance. These activities are essentially unsystematic, unforeseen, and unplanned. If execution is proceeding according to plan, the manager is not even needed.

PROJECT EVALUATION

In the evaluation phase, information on actual performance, time, and cost is compared with one or more standards. Possible standards include the estimates, past performance, performance of similar activities by others, or simply standards based on experience. These comparisons may be made either when a designated milestone in the project is reached or they may be made at specified time intervals, such as daily, weekly, or monthly.

The three aspects—scope, time, and cost—cannot be considered separately from one another, for trade-offs may be desirable. For example, overtime might be authorized in order to assure ontime completion, but this might add to costs; or conversely, additional overtime might actually reduce the total cost of the project by reducing the overall time required and, consequently, reducing those costs that are a function of time.

Nature of Reports

As is the case with production operations, information about what has happened on the project comes to management's attention from both informal sources and formal reports. The informal sources consist of conversations, memoranda, meetings, and personal observation. Since this information is not subject to the disciplines that are built into a formal reporting system, informal sources may not always provide accurate information. As mentioned in Chapter 12, in conversations and memoranda, subordinates naturally put the best light on their performance and tend to imply that other people or noncontrollable factors are responsible for their less-than-satisfactory performance; the manager must take these biases into account in evaluating such information. Subject to these qualifications, informal information can be extremely important. Indeed, formal reports alone are an inadequate control device on any except the most routine projects.

Analysis of Reports

As is the case with performance reports for ongoing operations, project reports often separate those unfavorable aspects of performance that seem to have been controllable from those that were noncontrollable. The person who is being reported on has a natural tendency to attribute as much as possible of unfavorable performance to causes that are noncontrollable or that are the responsibility of someone else. Readers of the report make their own judgment as to the validity of these claims.

It is important that actual costs be compared with the budgeted costs of the work done, which is not necessarily the same as the budgeted costs for the time period. The danger of misinterpretation is illustrated in Exhibit 17–3, which shows actual and budgeted costs for a project. As of the end of September, actual costs were $345,000, compared with budgeted costs of $300,000, which indicates a cost overrun of $45,000. However, the budgeted cost of the work actually completed through September was only $260,000, so the true overrun was $85,000.

If only direct costs are matched with work done, reports on indirect costs must be prepared separately. These reports measure costs in a different dimension than do reports on the direct costs of project work. In the case of direct costs, actual costs are compared with budgeted costs for the work actually accomplished. In the case of indirect costs,

EXHIBIT 17–3 Interpretation of Cost/Schedule Reports

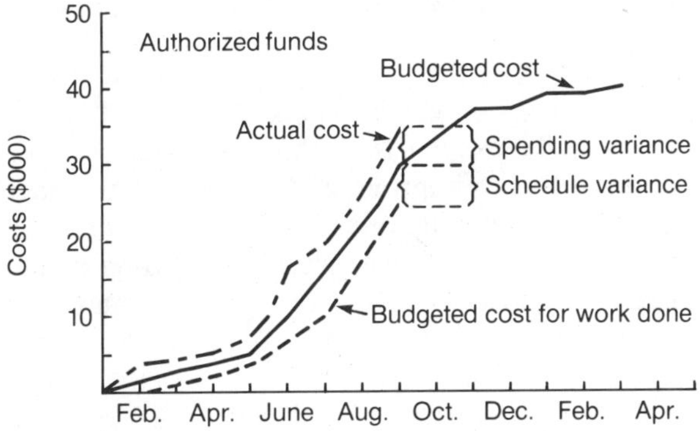

the actual costs for a period, such as a month, are compared with the budgeted costs for that same period.

Budget overruns. When actual costs exceed budgeted costs, there is said to be a "budget overrun." To some, this implies that actual costs were too high. An equally plausible conclusion, however, is that the budgeted costs were too low. If the higher costs resulted from changes in the scope of the project or from noncontrollable factors, the explanation is that there was an underestimate of costs, rather than excessive actual costs. Interpretation of the cost reports is complicated by the need to analyze both the budget and the actual costs.

A common error in analyzing costs is to assume that the budget represents what the costs should be. It does not. At best, the budget estimates what the cost should be *as based on the information that was available at the time it was prepared.* This information rarely is an accurate reflection of conditions that will be encountered on the project; and to the extent that it is inaccurate, the budget does not reflect what the costs should be. Moreover, budget numbers are estimates made by human beings who make them based, in part, on judgments and assumptions. Although reasonable people can differ in their judgments and assumptions, only one set of conclusions is incorporated in the budget.

Having identified the noncontrollable differences, attention is focused on the amounts not explained by these factors. These amounts were presumably controllable. As a starting point, but only as a starting point, there is a presumption that, if actual *controllable* costs were higher than budgeted costs, then the supervisor has not performed as well as was expected. As is the case in ongoing operations, this is a rebuttable presumption; the supervisor may have good explanations for such apparently unfavorable differences.

A fundamental point here is that control relates to desired results, which are not always the same as planned results. The basic job of management is to attain the project's goals. Plans are made with these goals in mind. Although in the normal course of events the plans indicate the results that the organization wants to attain, there are many circumstances in which rigid adherence to plans is not the best course of action. The supervisor who always plays by the rules may pass up opportunities to improve performance or to anticipate and correct incipient problems; the rules may not provide the best course of action in a given situation. For example, permitting unauthorized overtime to repair an inoperative piece of equipment may break the rules but may be worthwhile if it gets badly needed equipment back into operation quickly.

Cost to complete. As suggested by Exhibit 17–3, actual direct costs should be compared with the budgeted costs of the work actually done. Matching these two amounts is often difficult. Moreover, if the actual costs to date exceed budget or if the project is behind schedule, final costs may exceed the budgeted total by an even greater amount. A budget overrun may indicate that there are unanticipated difficulties that will affect later phases of the project. A schedule slippage indicates that costs, which are related to time (i.e., fixed costs), may be greater than the amount budgeted. This suggests that attention should be focused not only on the costs incurred to date but also on the current estimate of the total costs of the project. Exhibit 17–4 is a report incorporating this idea.

EXHIBIT 17–4 Project Cost Summary ($000)

Original budget		$1,000
Authorized revisions to date:		
For inflation		50
For specification changes		200
For time delays		60
For cost savings		(30)
Revised budget		1,280
Current estimate to complete		1,400
Variance		120
Explanation of variance:		
Material cost increases	$ 20	
Overtime	60	
Spending variances	40	
	120	

Action

The purpose of analyzing control reports is to provide a basis for action—if action is necessary. In many cases, of course, the report indicates that performance is satisfactory, and the only action required is to compliment the supervisor on doing a good job. In other cases, the formal report merely confirms what the manager has found out from informal sources, and he or she already may have taken corrective action based on the informal information. In some cases, the formal report leads to corrective action.

The report also may suggest the need to change the plan itself. In the case of a budget overrun, for example, the client might decide to accept the overrun and proceed with the project as originally planned; it might decide to cut back on the scope of the project, with the aim of producing an end product that is within the original cost limitations; it might decide to try a different way of producing the desired end product; or it might decide to replace the project manager or the contractor.

Revisions. The decision may lead to a revision of the project plan. If so, some managers favor tracking future progress against the revised plan. Others continue to track against the original plan, because of the danger that the revised numbers may incorporate inefficiencies. (When proposed revisions are not given hard-headed scrutiny, the revised budget is said to be a *rubber baseline*.) Still others track against *both* the original and the revised plan, as illustrated by the report in Exhibit 17–4.

Audit Functions

In addition to the control exercised directly by managers, others are involved in the control process: inspectors examine the quality of the work, and, on most large projects, there is an internal audit organization. One of the primary functions of the internal auditors is to investigate how well the control systems are functioning, suggest improvements in them, and call management's attention to failures to follow prescribed practices.

Timekeepers are responsible for records of hours worked, and storekeepers for records of material received and issued. At one time, auditors actually checked the validity of these records, and certified each voucher for payment. Although this practice is still followed in some organizations, most rely on an audit of the adequacy of the control system, including tests of a sample of records to confirm their validity, rather than on complete voucher checking. The philosophy is that a good system contains its own internal checks and controls, and that the auditor's function is to assure these are operating properly.

Auditing of costs is especially difficult when the contractor works simultaneously on several projects. Many defense contractors, for example, work on both cost-reimbursement defense contracts and on commercial projects. Some of them attempt to charge an unreasonable amount of overhead costs to the cost-reimbursement contracts, and this is a principal reason for cost disallowances on these contracts.

In recent years internal auditors have expanded their function into what is called "operational auditing." In addition to examining the adequacy of the control systems, they called attention to management actions they believed to be inadequate. Properly done, operational auditing can be useful. However, there is the great danger that the auditors, who, after all, are not managers, will second-guess the decisions that managers made in the light of all the circumstances—as they understood them—at the time the decisions were made. Using hindsight to evaluate management actions is unfair.

SUMMARY

Management control of projects is easier than management control in an ongoing organization in only one respect—the fact that a project has a defined end product. Its other characteristics make project control more difficult. Because an organization and the control systems, at least in part, must be developed for the specific project, control is more difficult than in situations in which organizational relationships have been well established and in which a control system already exists. Because most projects involve uncertainties and a succession of nonrepetitive actions, estimates of cost and time are a less satisfactory basis, both for planning and as a standard for evaluating actual performance. This is especially the case with a construction project that is conducted outside the controlled environment of a factory.

With these qualifications, the management control process for a project is basically similar to that for ongoing operations. It has three phases: planning, execution, and control.

The *planning process* is iterative; that is, there are a succession of plans, rather than a single document that can be labelled "the" plan. The *execution phase* is primarily the responsibility of first-line supervisors; management's responsibility is to assure that the climate in which they work is conducive to good control and that problems are identified and resolved promptly. In the *evaluation phase,* the primary reliance is on informal sources of information; but formal reports that compare actual technical performance, time taken, and cost with some standard are used to assure the completeness and accuracy of the informal information, and, in some cases, to provide a direct basis for evaluation.

SUGGESTED ADDITIONAL READING

Maciariello, Joseph A. *Program-Management Control Systems*. New York: Ronald Press, 1978.

CASE 17–1
Northeast Research Laboratory (*B*)

On a Friday morning in late December 1973, Sam Lacy, head of the Physical Sciences Division of Northeast Research Laboratory (NRL) thought about two letters which lay on his desk. One, which he had received a few weeks before, was a progress report from Robert Kirk, recently assigned project leader of the Exco Project, who reported that earlier frictions between the NRL team and the client had lessened considerably, that high-quality research was under way, and that the prospects for retaining the Exco project on a long-term basis appeared fairly good. The other letter, which had just arrived in the morning's mail, came from Gray Kenney, vice president of Exco, and stated that the company wished to terminate the Exco contract effective immediately.

Lacy was puzzled. He remembered how pleased Gray Kenney had been only a few months before when the Exco project produced its second patentable process. On the other hand, he also recalled some of the difficulties the project had encountered within NRL, which had ultimately led to the replacement of project leader Alan North in order to avoid losing the contract. Lacy decided to call in the participants in an effort to piece together an understanding of what had happened. Some of what he learned is described below. But the problem remained for him to decide what he should report to top management. What should he recommend to avoid the recurrence of such a situation in the future?

COMPANY BACKGROUND

Northeast Research Laboratory was a multidisciplinary research and development organization employing approximately 1,000 professionals. It was organized into two main sectors, one for economics and business administration and the other for the physical and natural sciences. Within the physical and natural sciences sector, the organization was essentially by branches of science. The main units were called divisions and the subunits were called laboratories. A partial organization chart is shown in Exhibit 1.

Most of the company's work was done on the basis of contracts with clients. Each contract was a project. Responsibility for the project was vested in a project leader, and through him up the organizational structure in which his laboratory was located. Typically, some members of the project team were drawn from laboratories other than that in which the project leader worked; it was the ability to put together a

EXHIBIT 1 Organization Chart (simplified)

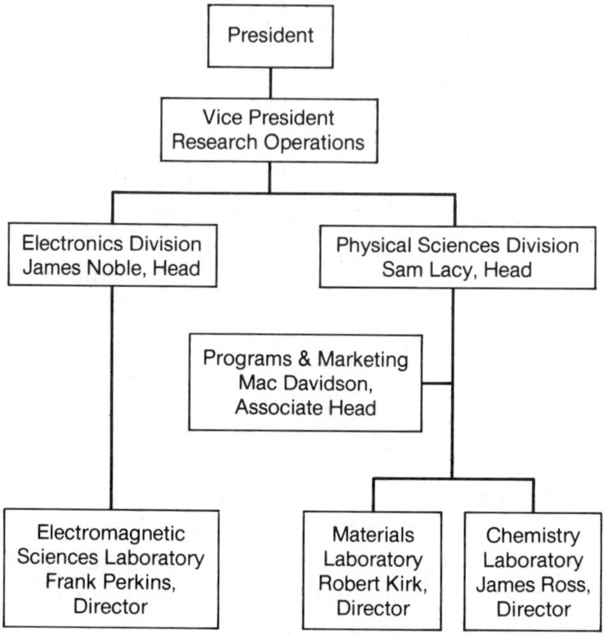

team with a variety of technical talents that was one of the principal strengths of a multidisciplinary laboratory. Team members worked under the direction of the project leader during the period in which they were assigned to the project. An individual might be working on more than one project concurrently. The project leader could also draw on the resources of central service organizations, such as model shops, computer services, editorial, and drafting. The project was billed for the services of these units at rates which were intended to cover their full costs.

INCEPTION OF THE EXCO PROJECT

In October 1972, Gray Kenney, vice president of Exco, had telephoned Mac Davidson of NRL to outline a research project which would examine the effect of microwaves on various ores and minerals. Davidson was associate head of the Physical Sciences Division and had known Kenney for several years. During the conversation Kenney asserted that NRL ought to be particularly intrigued by the research aspects of the project, and Davidson readily agreed. Davidson was also pleased because the Physical Sciences Division was under pressure to generate more revenue, and this potentially long-term project from

Exco would make good use of the available work force. In addition, top management of NRL had recently circulated several memos indicating that more emphasis should be put on commercial rather than government work. Davidson was, however, a little concerned that the project did not fall neatly into one laboratory or even one division, but in fact required assistance from the Electronics Division to complement work that would be done in two different Physical Sciences Laboratories (the Chemistry Laboratory and the Materials Laboratory).

A few days later Davidson organized a joint client–NRL conference to determine what Exco wanted and to plan the proposal. Kenney sent his assistant, Tod Denby, who was to serve as the Exco liaison officer for the project. Representing NRL were Davidson; Sam Lacy; Dr. Robert Kirk, director of the Materials Laboratory (one of the two Physical Sciences laboratories involved in the project); Dr. Alan North, manager of Chemical Development and Engineering (and associate director of the Chemistry Laboratory); Dr. James Noble, executive director of the Electronics Division; and a few researchers chosen by Kirk and North. Davidson also would like to have invited Dr. James Ross, director of the Chemistry Laboratory, but Ross was out of town and couldn't attend the pre-proposal meeting.

Denby described the project as a study of the use of microwaves for the conversion of basic ores and minerals to more valuable commercial products. The study was to consist of two parts:

Task A—An experimental program to examine the effect of microwaves on 50 ores and minerals, and to select those processes appearing to have the most promise.

Task B—A basic study to obtain an understanding of how, and why microwaves interact with certain minerals.

It was agreed that the project would be a joint effort of three laboratories: (1) Materials, (2) Chemistry, and (3) Electromagnetic. The first two laboratories were in the Physical Sciences Division, and the last was in the Electronics Division.

Denby proposed that the contract be open-ended, with a level of effort of around \$10,000–\$12,000 per month. Agreement was quickly reached on the content of the proposal. Denby emphasized to the group that an early start was essential if Exco were to remain ahead of its competition.

After the meeting Lacy, who was to have overall responsibility for the project, discussed the choice of project leader with Davidson. Davidson proposed Alan North, a 37-year-old chemist who had had experience as a project leader on several projects. North had impressed Davidson at the pre-proposal meeting and seemed well suited to head the interdisciplinary team. Lacy agreed. Lacy regretted that

Dr. Ross (head of the laboratory in which North worked) was unable to participate in the decision of who should head the joint project. In fact, because he was out of town, Ross was neither aware of the Exco project nor of his laboratory's involvement in it.

The following day, Alan North was told of his appointment as project leader. During the next few days, he conferred with Robert Kirk, head of the other Physical Sciences laboratory involved in the project. Toward the end of October, Denby began to exert pressure on North to finalize the proposal, stating that the substance had been agreed upon at the pre-proposal conference. North thereupon drafted a five-page letter as a substitute for a formal proposal, describing the nature of the project and outlining the procedures and equipment necessary. At Denby's request, North included a paragraph which authorized members of the client's staff to visit NRL frequently and observe progress of the research program. The proposal's cover sheet contained approval signatures from the laboratories and divisions involved. North signed for his own area and for laboratory director Ross. He telephoned Dr. Noble of the Electronics Division, relayed the client's sense of urgency, and Noble authorized North to sign for him. Davidson signed for the Physical Sciences Division as a whole.

At this stage, North relied principally on the advice of colleagues within his own division. As he did not know personally the individuals in the Electronics Division, they were not called upon at this point. Since North understood informally that the director of the Electromagnetic Sciences Laboratory, Dr. Perkins, was quite busy and often out of town, North did not attempt to discuss the project with Perkins.

After the proposal had been signed and mailed, Dr. Perkins was sent a copy. It listed the engineering equipment which the client wanted purchased for the project and described how it was to be used. Perkins worried that performance characteristics of the power supply (necessary for quantitative measurement) specified in the proposal were inadequate for the task. He asked North about it and North said that the client had made up his mind as to the microwave equipment he wanted and how it was to be used. Denby had said he was paying for that equipment and intended to move it to Exco's laboratories after the completion of the NRL contract.

All these events had transpired rather quickly. By the time Dr. Ross, director of the Chemistry Laboratory, returned, the proposal for the Exco project had been signed and accepted. Ross went to see Lacy and said that he had dealt with Denby on a previous project and had serious misgivings about working with him. Lacy assuaged some of Ross's fears by observing that if anyone could succeed in working with Denby it would be North—a flexible man, professionally competent, who could move with the tide and get along with clients of all types.

CONDUCT OF THE PROJECT

Thus the project began. Periodically, when decision arose, North would seek opinions from division management. However, he was somewhat unclear about whom he should talk to. Davidson had been the person who had actually appointed him project leader. Normally, however, North worked for Ross. Although Kirk's laboratory was heavily involved in the project, Kirk was very busy with other Materials Laboratory work. Adding to his uncertainty, North periodically received telephone calls from Perkins of the Electronics Division, whom he didn't know well. Perkins expected to be heavily involved in the project.

Difficulties and delays began to plague the project. The microwave equipment specified by the client was not delivered by the manufacturer on schedule, and there were problems in filtering the power supply of the radio-frequency source. Over the objection of NRL Electromagnetic Sciences engineers, but at the insistence of the client, one of the chemical engineers tried to improve the power supply filter. Eventually the equipment had to be sent back to the manufacturer for modification. This required several months.

In the spring of 1973, Denby, who had made his presence felt from the outset, began to apply strong pressure. "Listen," he said to North, "top management of Exco is starting to get on my back and we need results. Besides, I'm up for a review in four months and I can't afford to let this project affect my promotion." Denby was constantly at NRL during the next few months. He was often in the labs conferring individually with members of the NRL teams. Denby also visited North's office frequently.

A number of related problems began to surface. North had agreed to do both experimental and theoretical work for this project, but Denby's constant pushing for experimental results began to tilt the emphasis. Theoretical studies began to lapse, and experimental work became the focus of the Exco project. From time to time North argued that the theoretical work should precede or at least accompany the experimental program, but Denby's insistence on concrete results led North to temporarily deemphasize the theoretical work. Symptoms of this shifting emphasis were evident. One day a senior researcher from Kirk's laboratory came to North to complain that people were being "stolen" from his team. "How can we do a balanced project if the theoretical studies are not given enough work force?" he asked. North explained the client's position and asked the researcher to bear with this temporary realignment of the project's resources.

As the six-month milestone approached, Denby expressed increasing dissatisfaction with the project's progress. In order to have concrete results to report to Exco management, he directed North a number of times to change the direction of the research. On several occasions various members of the project team had vigorous discussions with Denby about the risks of changing results without laying a careful foundation. North himself spent a good deal of time talking with Denby on this subject, but Denby seemed to discount its importance. Denby began to avoid North and to spend most of his time with the other team members. Eventually the experimental program, initially dedicated to a careful screening of some 50 materials, deteriorated to a somewhat frantic and erratic pursuit of what appeared to be "promising leads." Lacy and Noble played little or no role in this shift of emphasis.

On June 21, 1973, Denby visited North in his office and severely criticized him for proposing a process (hydrochloric acid pickling) that was economically infeasible. In defense, North asked an NRL economist to check his figures. The economist reported back that North's numbers were sound and that, in fact, a source at U.S. Steel indicated that hydrochloric acid pickling was "generally more economic than the traditional process and was increasingly being adopted." Through this and subsequent encounters, the relationship between Denby and North became increasingly strained.

Denby continued to express concern about the Exco project's payoff. In an effort to save time, he discouraged the NRL team from repeating experiments, a practice that was designed to insure accuracy. Data received from initial experiments were frequently taken as sufficiently accurate, and after hasty analysis were adopted for the purposes of the moment. Not surprisingly Denby periodically discovered errors in these data. He informed NRL of them.

Denby's visits to NRL became more frequent as the summer progressed. Some days he would visit all three laboratories, talking to the researchers involved and asking them about encouraging leads. North occasionally cautioned Denby against too much optimism. Nonetheless, North continued to oblige the client by restructuring the Exco project to allow for more "production line" scheduling of experiments and for less systematic research.

In August, North discovered that vertile could be obtained from iron ore. This discovery was a significant one, and the client applied for a patent. If the reaction could be proved commercially, its potential would be measured in millions of dollars. Soon thereafter, the NRL team discovered that the operation could, in fact, be handled commercially in a rotary kiln. The client was notified and soon began planning a pilot plant that would use the rotary kiln process.

Exco's engineering department, after reviewing the plans for the pilot plant, rejected them. It was argued that the rotary process was infeasible and that a fluid bed process would have to be used instead.

Denby returned to NRL and insisted on an experiment to test the fluid bed process. North warned Denby that agglomeration (a sticking together of the material) would probably take place. It did. Denby was highly upset, reported to Gray Kenney that he had not received "timely" warning of the probability of agglomeration taking place, and indicated that he had been misled as to the feasibility of the rotary kiln process.[1]

Work continued, and two other "disclosures of invention" were turned over to the client by the end of September.

PERSONNEL CHANGES

On September 30, Denby came to North's office to request that Charles Fenton be removed from the Exco project. Denby reported he had been watching Fenton in the Electromagnetic Laboratory, which he visited often, and had observed that Fenton spent relatively little time on the Exco project. North, who did not know Fenton well, agreed to look into it. But Denby insisted that Fenton be removed immediately and threatened to terminate the contract if he were allowed to remain.

North was unable to talk to Fenton before taking action because Fenton was on vacation. He did talk to Fenton as soon as he returned, and the researcher admitted that due to the pressure of other work he had not devoted as much time or effort to the Exco work as perhaps he should have.

Three weeks later, Denby called a meeting with Mac Davidson and Sam Lacy. It was their first meeting since the pre-proposal conference for the Exco project. Denby was brief and to the point:

Denby: I'm here because we have to replace North. He's become increasingly difficult to work with and is obstructing the progress of the project.

Lacy: But North is an awfully good man . . .

Davidson: Look, he's come up with some good solid work thus far. What about the process of extracting vertile from iron ore he came up with. And . . .

Denby: I'm sorry, but we have to have a new project leader. I don't mean to be abrupt, but it's either replace North or forget the contract.

Davidson reluctantly appointed Robert Kirk project leader and informed North of the decision. North went to see Davidson a few days later. Davidson told him that although management did not agree with the client, North had been replaced in order to save the contract. Later Dr. Lacy told North the same thing. Neither Lacy nor Davidson made an effort to contact Exco senior management on the matter.

---

[1] Ten months later the client was experimenting with the rotary kiln process for producing vertile from iron ore in his own laboratory.

Following the change of project leadership, the record became more difficult to reconstruct. It appeared that Kirk made many efforts to get the team together, but morale remained low. Denby continued to make periodic visits to NRL but found that the NRL researchers were not talking as freely with him as they had in the past. Denby became sceptical about the project's value. Weeks slipped by. No further breakthroughs emerged.

LACY'S PROBLEM

Dr. Lacy had received weekly status reports on the project, the latest of which is shown in Exhibit 2. He had had a few informal conversations about the project, principally with North and Kirk. He

EXHIBIT 2 Weekly Project Status Report

PROJECT/ACCOUNT STATUS REPORT

ORG	PROJ/ACCT	SUB	W/O	WEEK ENDING DATE	TYPE	REV TYPE	PRICE	CLIENT		INT/DOM	NOTICES	PAGE
325	3273	000	000	12-22-73	PROJ	INDUS	SCA	YD		DOMESTIC		1

DIVISION	DEPARTMENT	SUPERVISOR	LEADER
PHYSICAL SCI	CHEMISTRY LAB	ROBERT KIRK	ROBERT KIRK

PROJECT TITLE: MICROWAVES IN CONVERSIO:: OF BASIC ORES AND MINERALS

INST	READY DATE	STOP WORK DATE	TERM DATE	BURDEN %	OVERHEAD %	FEE %
EXCO	11-06-72	- -	11-06-74	28.00	105.00	15.00

COST CATEGORIES	(OBJECT CODE)	DOLLARS PTD13WK1	DOLLARS TO DATE	LABOR HOURS ESTIMATE	LABOR HOURS TO DATE	LABOR HOURS BALANCE
SUPERVISOR	(11, 12)		560		36	
SENIOR	(13)	192	17986		1348	
PROFESSIONAL	(14)	150	16787		1678	
TECHNICAL	(15)	529	5299		1037	
CLER/SUPP	(16, 17, 18)		301		84	
OTHER	(10) (19)	72	72		12	
LABOR (S. T.)		943	41005		1644	
BURDEN		248	11481			
OVERHEAD		1227	55110			
OVERTIME PREM	(21)	160	1540			
OVS./OTH. PREM	(22-29)	242	476			
TOTAL PERSONNEL COSTS		2820	109612			
TRAVEL	(56-59)		776			
SUBCONTRACT	(36)					
MATERIAL	(41, 42)		3726			
EQUIPMENT	(43)					
COMPUTER	(37, 45)					
COMMUN	(62, 63, 70, 71)	2	507			
CONSULTANT	(74, 75)					
REPORT COST	(44, 47)					
OTHER M&S		54	99			
TOTAL M&S COST		56	5098			
COMMITMENTS			26847			
TOTAL LESS FEE		2876	141557			
FEE (15.00)		158	24376			
TOTAL		3031	165933			

	ESTIMATED	BALANCE
TOTAL LESS FEE	250435	108878
FEE (15.00)	37565	13189
TOTAL	288000	122067

LAST BILLING:	
DATE	11-30-73
AMOUNT	11350
ACCOUNT STATUS TO DATE:	
BILLED	154583
PAID	154583
TIME BALANCE %	39.4
COST BALANCE %	43.5
TIME BALANCE WKS.	41

COMMITMENT STATUS TO DATE

PO NO		OBJ	VENDOR/DESCRIPTION	TOTAL	CHARGES	BALANCE
A61289	11-21-73	41	MINNESOTA MINING	111	61	50
A61313	11-23-73	41	ALDRICH CHEMICAL	348		348
A95209	11-28-73	43	TENNECO CHEMICAL CO	5		5
A95093	11-15-73	41	UNION CARBIDE CORP	23194		23194
B 95104	11-19-73	37	SCIENTIFIC PRODUCTS	600		600
B 95232	11-25-73	41	VAN WATERS & ROGERS	2500		2500
018046	12-15-73	57	ROGER MD	300	150	150
						T 26847

TRANSACTIONS RECORDED 12-15-73 - 12-22-73

LABOR

ORG	ID	W/E DATE	T/S NO	OBJ	NAME	HOURS WEEK	HOURS TO DATE
322	02345	12-22-73	363073	13	KIRK	6.0	150
322	02345	12-22-73	363073	22	KIRK	6.0	
322	03212	12-22-73	363082	13	DENSMORE	8.0	25
322	03260	12-22-73	236544	14	COOK	15.0	30
325	12110	12-08-73	C30093	15	HOWARD	15.0	82
325	12110	12-15-73	236548	15	HOWARD	36.0	
325	12110	12-22-73	376147	15	HOWARD	8.0	
325	12357	12-22-73	376149	15	SPELTZ	15.0	68
325	12369	12-22-73	376150	15	GYUIRE	15.0	17
325	12384	12-22-73	R08416	15	DILLON	40.0-	44
325	12397	12-22-73	336527	15	NAGY	31.0	31
325	12397	12-22-73	336527	21	NAGY	15.0	
652	12475	12-22-73	236548	15	KAIN	8.0	20
652	12475	12-22-73	236548	21	KAIN	15.0	

	HOURS	DOLLARS
LABOR (STRAIGHT TIME)	117.0	943
PAYROLL BURDEN		248
OVERHEAD RECOVERY		1227
OVERTIME PREMIUM LABOR	30.0	160
OTHER PREMIUM LABOR	6.0	242
TOTAL PERSONNEL COSTS		2820 S

MATERIALS & SERVICES

PO NO	REF NO	OBJ		DESCRIPTION	REQUESTOR	
61289	54065	48	438	REA EXPRESS	KIRK	42
17234	87413	48	456	GED SUPPLY CO	COOK	10
	04461	71	448	P.T.&T. 326-6200	NAGY	2
				TOTAL M&S COSTS		56 S
				FEE		158
				TRANSACTION TOTAL		3034 T

had not read the reports submitted to Exco. If the project had been placed on NRL's "problem list," which comprised about 10 percent of the projects which seemed to be experiencing the most difficulty, Lacy would have received a written report on its status weekly, but the Exco project was not on that list.

With the background given above, Lacy reread Kenney's letter terminating the Exco contract. It seemed likely that Kenney, too, had not had full knowledge of what went on during the project's existence. In his letter, Kenney mentioned the "glowing reports" which reached his ears in the early stages of the work. These reports, which came to him only from Denby, were later significantly modified, and Denby apparently implied that NRL had been "leading him on." Kenney pointed to the complete lack of economic evaluation of alternative processes in the experimentation. He seemed unaware of the fact that at Denby's insistence all economic analysis was supposed to be done by the client. Kenney was most dissatisfied that NRL had not complied with all the provisions of the proposal, particularly those that required full screening of all materials and the completion of the theoretical work.

Lacy wondered why Denby's changes of the proposal had not been documented by the NRL team. Why hadn't he heard more of the problems of the Exco project before? Lacy requested a technical evaluation of the project from the economics process director and asked Davidson for *his* evaluation of the project. These reports are given in Exhibits 3 and 4. When he received these reports, Lacy wondered what, if any, additional information he should submit to NRL top management.

EXHIBIT 3 Technical Evaluation

By Ronald M. Benton
Director, Process Economics Program

Principal Conclusions

1. The original approach to the investigation as presented in the proposal is technically sound. The accomplishments could have been greater had this been followed throughout the course of the project, but the altered character of the investigation did not prevent accomplishment of fruitful research.
2. The technical conduct of this project on NRL's part was good despite the handicaps under which the work was carried out. Fundamental and theoretical considerations were employed in suggesting the course of research and in interpreting the data. There is no evidence to indicate that the experimental work itself was badly executed.
3. Significant accomplishments of this project were as follows:
   a. *Extraction of vertile from iron ore by several alternative processes*. Conception of these processes was based on fundamental considerations and demonstrated considerable imagination. As far as the work was carried out at NRL, one or more of these processes offers promise of commercial feasibility.
   b. *Nitrogen fixation*. This development resulted from a laboratory observation. The work was not carried far enough to ascertain whether or not the process offers any commercial significance. It was, however, shown that the yield of nitrogen

EXHIBIT 3 ***(continued)***

oxides was substantially greater than has previously been achieved by either thermal or plasma processes.

c. *Reduction of nickel oxide and probably also garnerite to nickel.* These findings were never carried beyond very preliminary stages and the ultimate commercial significance cannot be assessed at this time.

d. *Discovery that microwave plasmas can be generated at atmospheric pressure.* Again the commercial significance of this finding cannot be appraised at present. However, it opens the possibility that many processes can be conducted economically that would be too costly at the reduced pressures previously thought to be necessary.

4. The proposal specifically stated that the selection of processes for scale-up and economic studies would be the responsibility of the client. I interpret this to mean that NRL was not excluded from making recommendations based on economic considerations. Throughout the course of the investigation, NRL did take economic factors into account in its recommendations.
5. Actual and effective decisions of significance were not documented by NRL and only to a limited extent by the client. There was no attempt on NRL's part to convey the nature or consequences of such decisions to the client's management.
6. The NRL reports were not well prepared even considering the circumstances under which they were written.
7. It is possible that maximum advantage was not taken of the technical capabilities of personnel in the Electromagnetic Sciences Laboratory. Furthermore, they appeared to have been incompletely informed as to the overall approach to the investigation.
8. There was excessive involvement of the client in the details of experimental work. Moreover, there were frequent changes of direction dictated by the client. Undoubtedly these conditions hampered progress and adequate consideration of major objectives and accomplishments.
9. In the later stages of the project, the client rejected a number of processes and equipment types proposed by NRL for investigation of their commercial feasibility. From the information available to me, I believe that these judgments were based on arbitrary opinions as to technical feasibility and superficial extrapolations from other experience as to economic feasibility that are probably not valid.

Evaluation of Client's Complaints

Following are the comments responding to the points raised by the client management during your conversation:

1. *Client anticipated a "full research capability." He had hoped for participation by engineers, chemists, economists, and particularly counted on the provision of an "analytical capability." It was this*

EXHIBIT 3 ***(continued)***

combination of talents that brought him to NRL rather than [a competitor]. He feels that the project was dominated almost exclusively by chemists.

This complaint is completely unfounded. All the disciplines appropriate to the investigation (as called for in the proposal) were engaged on the project to some degree. In addition, men of exceptional capabilities devoted an unusually large amount of time to the project. The client never officially altered the conditions of the proposal stating that no economic studies should be performed by NRL and there was no explicit expression of this desire on the part of the client until near the project termination.

2. *The analytical services were poor. They were sometimes erroneous and there were frequent "deviations." Data were given to the client too hastily, without further experiment and careful analysis, and as a result a significant amount of the data was not reproducible. NRL was inclined to be overly optimistic. "Glowing reports" would be made only to be cancelled or seriously modified later.*

   There is no way of determining whether the analytical services were good or bad, but one can never expect all analytical work to be correct or accurate. Because the client insisted on obtaining raw data, they would certainly receive some analyses that were erroneous. With respect to the allegation that NRL was overly optimistic, there were no recommendations or opinions expressed in the NRL reports or included in the client's notes that can be placed in this category. Whether or not there were verbal statements of this kind cannot of course be ascertained.

3. *There were "errors in the equations and the client was not informed of the changes." This refers to the case of a computer program that had not been "de-bugged." It was the client who discovered the errors and informal NRL of the discrepancies. (The program was eventually straightened out by the Math Sciences Department.)*

   The client's complaint that they were given a computer program which had not been "de-bugged" is valid, but it is not certain that the project leadership gave them the program without exercising normal precautions for its accuracy. The program was developed by a person not presently with NRL and for another project. He transmitted it without any warning that "de-bugging" had not been conducted. It is even possible that the existence and source of error could not have been determined in his usage and would only appear in a different application.

4. *NRL told the client that the "vertile from iron ore" process could be handled commercially in a rotary kiln process and then was informed by his Engineering Division that this was completely infeasible. Plans were then shifted to a fluid bed process and much time and money had been wasted. Client claims that he was not warned that in the fluid bed agglomeration would probably take*

EXHIBIT 3 (*continued*)

place. Agglomeration did take place the first time this process was tried ("open boats") and the client was greatly upset.

It is unclear whether the original suggestion that a rotary kiln be used in the vertile process came from the client or NRL. In any event, it is a logical choice of equipment and is used for the production of such low-cost items as cement. Without the benefit of at least pilot plant experience that revealed highly abnormal and unfavorable conditions leading to excessive costs, no one would be in a position to state that such equipment would be uneconomic. It is true that a completely standard rotary kiln probably could not be employed, if for no other reason than to prevent the escape of toxic hydrogen sulfide gas from the equipment. At least special design would be needed and probably some mechanical development. However, it is rare that any new process can be installed without special design and development and it is naive to expect otherwise.

I do not know, of course, how much time was actually spent on the "elaborate plans" for the vertile process using a rotary kiln. I can, however, compare it with generally similar types of studies that we carry out in the Process Economics Program. For this kind of process we would expend about 45 engineering manhours, and the design calculations would be more detailed than the client's engineer made (his cost estimates incidentally reflected inexperience in this field). I doubt, therefore, that this effort represented a serious expenditure of money and would not have been a complete waste even if the process had been based on a partially false premise.

The contention that the client was not informed of the agglomerating properties of the vertile while the reaction was taking place seems unlikely. The client's representatives were so intimately concerned with the experimental work that it would be unusual if the subject had not been raised. Moreover, it is doubtful that the client would have been deterred by NRL's warning, in view of their subsequent insistence that considerable effort be devoted to finding means by which a fluid bed could be operated.

5. *The meetings were poorly planned by NRL.*

   There is no way of evaluating this complaint, but certainly the extreme frequency of the meetings would not be conducive to a well-organized meeting.

6. *Experimental procedures were not well planned.*

   Apparently this refers to the client's desire that experiments be planned in detail as much as three months in advance. Such an approach might conceivably be useful merely for purposes of gathering routine data. It is naive to think that research can or should be planned to this degree and certainly if NRL had acceded to the request it would have been a fruitless time-consuming exercise.

EXHIBIT 3 (*continued*)

7. *Economic support was not given by NRL.*
   As mentioned above, the proposal specifically excluded NRL from economic evaluations, but NRL did make use of economic considerations in its suggestions and recommendations.
8. *NRL promised to obtain some manganese nodules but never produced them.*
   Manganese nodules were obtained by NRL but no experiments were ever run with them. Many other screening experiments originally planned were never carried out because of the changed direction of the project. It seems likely, therefore, that the failure to conduct an experiment with manganese nodules was not NRL's responsibility.
9. *The client claims that he does not criticize NRL for failing "to produce a process." He says that he never expected one, that he wanted a good screening of ores and reactions as called for in the proposal, and that he had hoped for results from the theoretical studies—Task B. This he feels he did not get. We did not do what the proposal called for.*
   The statement that a process was not expected seems entirely contrary to the course of the project. There was universal agreement among NRL personnel involved that almost immediately after the project was initiated it was converted into a crash program to find a commercial process. In fact, the whole tenor of the project suggests a degree of urgency incompatible with a systematic research program. It is quite true that the theoretical studies as a part of Task B were never carried out. According to the project leader this part of the proposal was never formally abandoned, it was merely postponed. Unfortunately, this situation was never documented by NRL, as was the case with other significant effective decisions.

Additional Comments:

1. It appears that the first indication that the client expected economic studies or evaluations of commercial feasibility occurred during the summer of 1973. At this time the project leader was severely criticized by the client's representatives for having proposed a process (hydrochloric acid pickling) that was economically infeasible. The basis for this criticism was that hydrochloric acid pickling of steel had not proved to be economically feasible. It is totally unreasonable to expect that NRL would have access to information of this kind, and such a reaction would certainly have the effect of discouraging any further contributions of an economic or commercial nature by NRL rather than encouraging them.

   Actually it is patently ridiculous to directly translate economic experience of the steel industry with steel pickling to leaching a sulfided titanium ore. Nevertheless, I directed an inquiry to a responsible person in U.S. Steel as to the status of hydrochloric acid pickling. His response (based on the consen-

EXHIBIT 3 (*concluded*)

sus of their experts) was diametrically opposite to the client's information. While there are situations that are more favorable to sulfuric acid pickling, hydrochloric acid pickling is generally more economic and is becoming increasingly adopted.

2. The reports written by NRL were requested by the client, but on an urgent and "not fancy" basis. If such were the case, it is understandable that the project leader would be reluctant to expend enough time and money on the report to make it representative of NRL's normal reports. However, the nature of the reports seems to indicate that they are directed toward the same individuals with whom NRL was in frequent contact, or persons with a strong interest in the purely scientific aspects. The actual accomplishments of the project were not brought out in a manner that would have been readily understandable to client's management.

Recommendations

It is recommended that consideration be given to the establishment of a simple formal procedure by which high risk projects could be identified at the proposal stage and brought to the attention of the division vice president. There should also be a formal procedure, operative after project acceptance, in which specific responsibilities are assigned for averting or correcting subsequent developments that would be adverse to NRL's and the client's interests.

Some of the factors that would contribute to a high risk condition are insufficient funding, insufficient time, low chance of successfully attaining objectives, an unsophisticated client, public or private political conditions, and so forth. The characteristics that made this a high risk project were certainly apparent at the time the proposal was prepared.

EXHIBIT 4

MEMORANDUM

January 8, 1974

TO: Sam Lacy
FROM: Mac Davidson
RE: The Exco Project—Conclusions

The decision to undertake this project was made without sufficient consideration of the fact that this was a "high risk" project.

The proposal was technically sound and within the capabilities of the groups assigned to work on the project.

EXHIBIT 4 (*concluded*)

There was virtually no coordination between the working elements of Physical Sciences and Electronics in the preparation of the proposal.

The technical conduct of this project, with few exceptions, was, considering the handicaps under which the work was carried out, good and at times outstanding. The exceptions were primarily due to lack of attention to detail.

The NRL reports were not well prepared, even considering the circumstances under which they were written.

The client, acting under pressure from his own management, involved himself excessively in the details of experimental work and dictated frequent changes of direction and emphasis. The proposal opened the door to this kind of interference.

There was no documentation by NRL of the decisions made by the client which altered the character, direction and emphasis of the work.

There was no serious attempt on the part of NRL to convey the nature or consequence of the above actions to the client.

Less than half of the major complaints made by the client concerning NRL's performance are valid.

The project team acquiesced too readily in the client's interference and management acquiesced too easily to the client's demands.

Management exercised insufficient supervision and gave inadequate support to the project leader in his relations with the client.

There were no "overruns" either in time or funds.

CASE 17–2
Construction Associates, Incorporated*

Construction Associates of Syracuse, New York, did general construction work. In April of 1965, the company had three jobs in progress—a six-family apartment house, a gas station, and a four-store addition to a shopping center.

The owner of the shopping center, Mr. Mahara, had recently returned from Akron, Ohio, where he had discussed with the executives of a large tire company the possibility of opening a tire sales and service shop in his shopping center. Mr. Mahara decided that a tire

* This case was prepared by W. K. Holstein, Harvard Business School.

shop would be a profitable addition to his shopping center and on the morning of April 2, 1965, he decided to proceed at once to arrange for the construction of a suitable building to house the tire shop in one corner of the shopping center parking lot. He then called Mr. Heitman, the president of Construction Associates, to arrange a meeting to discuss plans for the building. During their meeting Mr. Mahara and Mr. Heitman agreed that a suitable building for the new tire shop would be a one-story frame structure somewhat similar in exterior design to the gas station that Construction Associates had under construction at that time.

Although the time was short, Mr. Mahara was anxious to have the tire shop building completed by the time the addition to the shopping center was completed. He felt that the grand opening of the tire shop should be tied in with the opening of the four stores in the new addition. The construction schedule for the addition, which was easily being met, indicated that the shopping center addition would be completed in 51 working days after April 2.

Following his meeting with the shopping center owner, Mr. Heitman spoke with Mr. Bevis, Construction Associates' planning specialist. Realizing time was short, Mr. Heitman asked Mr. Bevis to plan immediately the construction schedule for the tire shop building. Mr. Bevis was instructed to use the plans and costs of the gas station under construction as guidelines for his preliminary planning of the tire shop.

In his initial analysis of the problem Mr. Bevis noted the following construction relationships generally observed in construction of this type:

1. A preliminary set of specifications would have to be completed before work could begin on the set of blueprints and before the foundation excavation could begin. After the excavation was completely finished, the foundation could be poured.

2. The preparation of a bill of materials would have to be deferred until the final set of blueprints was prepared. When the bill of materials was completed, it would be used to prepare order invoices for lumber and other items. Construction of the frame could not begin until the lumber had arrived at the construction site and the foundation had been poured.

3. After the frame was completed, electric work, erection of laths, plumbing, installation of millwork, and installation of siding could begin.

4. Painting of the interior walls could not start until the electric work, plastering of the walls, and plumbing were completed. Plastering of the walls could not begin until the laths were erected.

5. The final interior decorating work could not begin until the interior walls were painted and the trim installed. Installation of trim could not begin until the millwork was completely installed.

6. Painting of the building's exterior could not proceed until the windows and exterior doors were installed. Installation of the window and doors, in turn, could not start until the siding was in place.

After studying the plans and construction schedule of the gas station under construction, Mr. Bevis developed an estimate of the time required to complete each step of the building of the tire shop. The estimates (Exhibit 1) were in most cases developed from the figures given Mr. Bevis by the foremen on the gas station job. Mr. Bevis had found in the past that figures of this type were usually quite accurate. One exception to this were the figures obtained from the carpenter foreman, who was sometimes a little too pessimistic about his estimates.

EXHIBIT 1

	Step	*Estimated time required to execute step (days under optimal cost conditions)*	*Days reduction*	*Cost*
A.	Prepare preliminary specifications	10	2	$ 10
			3	120
B.	Excavate foundation	5	1	200
C.	Pour foundation	6	1	180
D.	Electric work	5	2	200
E.	Lath work	2	1	20
F.	Plumbing	6	2	80
G.	Plaster walls	4	1	40
			2	100
H.	Paint interior walls	5	1	70
			2	150
I.	Millwork installation	10	2	200
			3	350
J.	Trim installation	8	2	90
			3	150
K.	Erect frame and roof	15	2	1,000
			4	2,500
L.	Final interior decoration	8	2	100
			4	800
M.	Installation of siding	7	1	100
			3	600
N.	Paint exterior	7	1	50
			2	150
O.	Blueprints finalized	5	2	70
			3	120
P.	Prepare bill of materials and order invoices	3	1	50
			2	170
Q.	Time required to receive lumber after order is sent	8	2	100
			4	290
R.	Window and exterior door installation	6	1	100

As he studied the time estimates he had put together for the tire shop job, Mr. Bevis realized that some of the steps would have to be rushed in order to complete the job in 51 days. To provide more usable information on the effects of rushing some of the construction steps, Mr. Bevis estimated the extra cost of reducing the normal time required for each step by one or more days (Exhibit 1). These costs would increase the cost of the tire shop over what might be called the cost under "optimal conditions" (i.e., the cost incurred if each step could be performed at normal pace without undue rushing, overtime, etc.). Realizing that any extra cost should be kept to an absolute minimum, Mr. Bevis tried to develop a construction schedule which rushed only those activities where the extra cost was not too high. After several hours of work, Mr. Bevis devised the following tentative construction plan.

Step	*Planned duration (days)*	*Step*	*Planned duration (days)*
A	8	J	5
B	5	K	15
C	5	L	6
D	3	M	7
E	1	N	6
F	4	O	3
G	3	P	2
H	4	Q	6
I	7	R	6

Deciding the plan needed further work, Mr. Bevis put all his notes on the tire shop job into his briefcase to do further work at home that evening.

Question

What schedule would you recommend?

CASE 17–3
Star Industrial Contractors, Inc.

"Laura, how are we doing on the C. W. Chemical Company job?" asked Stephen Elliott, the president of Star Industrial Contractors, Inc. "Well, it depends on how you look at it," was the rather cryptic response of Laura Ashley, the company's controller.

Star Industrial usually had about 15 contracts in process at any one time and had about $18 million a year in billings. Laura explained that in order to determine the status of a job she used two different approaches in analyzing the job data. One approach was based on generally accepted accounting principles, and the other was based on the economic nature of the job.

For financial reporting purposes, Star used the recommended GAAP method, percentage of completion, on its multiperiod construction contracts. This method assumes that the accomplishments of the firm, measured as revenues, are a function of its efforts, measured as costs; and further, that the relationship is constant for all cost factors and that all costs are fully defined. Under this method, Star's computation of its earned gross profit was simply:

$$\frac{a}{a + b} \times (c - d)(a + b)$$

where: a is the incurred cost to date,
b is the estimated future cost,
c is the contract price, and
d is the estimated total cost $(a + b)$.

However, the cost amounts did not include any allowances for future possible events until they could be specifically identified and quantified (i.e., until the possible future event met the GAAP requirements for contingencies). "As a consequence," Laura said, "I believe that this method misstates the status of the job throughout its duration. In the early periods, without all the contingencies being defined and all possible future costs estimated, the gross profit and the financial condition are overstated. In the last fiscal periods, when all costs become known, the jobs appear to have been mismanaged because of poor earnings or even losses."

Consequently, she used another method, based upon the economic nature of the contract, for feedback to management. The basic assumption in this method was that each cost factor in a lump-sum contract (i.e., labor, material, etc.) had its own markup, just like it would have in a cost-plus contract and, most importantly, that since the contractor had assumed all the risks for completing the project at a set price, an inherent part of the contract was the opportunity to make a true economic profit. The realization of this profit was dependent upon the contractor's ability to plan, to control, and to act in managing the risks undertaken. If the contractor was successful, then the amount included in the contract for the risk-taking became additional gross profit. If the contractor failed in handling risks (e.g., a concrete pour was lost because of an unexpected freeze) then he had to pay for the additional costs incurred because of these risks. As a result, his economic profit was reduced or eliminated.

Using this method, Laura first broke the contract down into its component cost factors and computed the earned gross profit on each factor. Specifically, the profit recognized on each factor in an interim period was equal to the gross margin on that factor, divided by the expected total amount of that factor, multiplied by the quantity of that factor delivered to the job. For example, the profit recognized on labor would be equal to the labor margin, divided by the estimated total labor hours, multiplied by the labor-hours used to date.

Two problems could occur under this method. Although the markup on a factor is budgeted when the job is bid, variances from budget can often occur. Each period a budget status report was prepared for each job, and the variances were computed. The variances became adjustments to the original margins budgeted. Cost overruns reduced the margin, and underruns increased it. However, if the overrun was greater than the original margin, then the entire difference became a reduction of the earned gross profit of the period.

The second problem was how to deal with the risks remaining on the job at the reporting date. If there were substantial risks in the remaining work on the project, then none of the contingency costs included in the contract price could be recognized as earned gross profit. Therefore, the amount to be treated as currently earned was the remainder of the original contingency amount after subtracting the estimated possible cost of the risks still on the job. If the amount of the risks was not highly predictable, then the total amount set up was deferred to future periods until the contingency was either removed or became controllable.

The budget summary for Job 78512 is shown in Exhibit 1. Each factor was budgeted for the respective parts of the job. A gross profit was computed for each factor of production, and, an estimated contingency cost was added in order to determine the bid price for the project. The contingency cost represents the total risks in the job.

The factor markups and their computation by the contract estimator for this job are summarized in Exhibit 2. The gross profit amount was shown to be a function of the resources that would be required. An important consideration in this particular bid was that the company needed the job to maintain its work force and, therefore, deliberately reduced its normal margins to assure being the low bidder. The contingency cost was added by management based on its experience and its estimate of possible adverse conditions or events that could occur with this project.

Each month a job status report was prepared for each job, analyzing the factors for the subparts of the job. The job status report at the end of the fiscal period to Job 78512 for materials is shown in Exhibit 3, and the status of the contract for all factors is summarized in Exhibit 4. Two items are obvious from these exhibits: there have been budget

EXHIBIT 1 Estimate Summary

ESTIMATE NO. 78512 **BY:** **DATE:** 12/15/82

OWNER: C. W. Chemical **PROJECT:** Sludge Belt Filter

Code	*Description*	*Hours*	*Labor*	*Material*	*Sub*	*Other*	*Total*
01	Site improvements						
02	Demolition						
03	Earthwork						
04	Concrete						
05	Structural steel	1,653	18,768	15,133			33,901
06	Piling						
07	Brick and masonry						
08	Buildings						
09	Major equipment	2,248	26,059	1,794			27,853
10	Piping	2,953	34,518	57,417	1,500	34,541	127,976
11	Instrumentation				33,000		33,000
12	Electrical				126,542		126,542
13	Painting				14,034		14,034
14	Insulation				4,230		4,230
15	Fireproofing			530	1,110		1,640
16	Chemical cleaning						
17	Testing						
18	Const. equipment					35,666	35,666
19	Misc. directs	1,008	10,608	2,050		2,000	14,658
20	Field extra work						
Subtotal direct cost		7,862	89,953	76,924	180,416	72,207	419,500
21	Tools—supplies			7,361			7,361
22	Payroll burden					16,580	16,580
23	Start-up assistance						
24	Insurance and taxes					5,268	5,268
5	Field supervision	480	7,200			2,038	9,238
6	Home office expense					2,454	2,454
7	Field emp. benefits					10,395	10,395
Total indirect cost		480	7,200	7,361		36,735	51,296
Adjustments							
Total field cost		8,342	97,153	84,285	180,416	108,942	470,796
8	Escalation						
9	Overhead & profit		8,342	5,057	9,021	10,190	32,610
30	**Contingency**						18,076
31	**Total project cost**						$521,482

EXHIBIT 2 Gross Profit Computations—Cost Code 29

Factor	*Basis*	*Quantity*	*Rate*	*Amount*
Labor	Man-hours	8,342	$1	$ 8,342
Material	Cost (net)	$ 84,285	6%	5,057
Subcontracts	Contract amount	180,416	5%	9,021
Equipment	Cost	35,666	14.04%	5,009
Other—direct.	Cost	36,541	14.18%	5,181
				$32,610

variances, both underruns and overruns, and the company still has a large exposure to risks in future periods on this job.

At the time the contract was awarded, the company and the client agreed upon an allowable billing schedule setting forth the items to be considered. Exhibit 5, a billing invoice, identified the billable items and the allowed amounts. The amount billed was determined by multiplying the base amount by the mutually agreed upon percentage of completion. On December 31 the company had billed out $280,424, or 53.8 percent of the contract.

The computation of the amounts to be presented in the year-end financial statements is shown in Exhibit 6. Using the percentage of completion method, the recognized gross profit was determined to be $25,118. Revenue was the $288,631 of cost plus earned gross profit. In addition, the evaluation of billings revealed that $288,631 was in excess of billing to date, $280,424, so that an additional current asset, Cost and Earned Gross Profit in Excess of Billings, of $8,207, would be shown on the balance sheet. Even though the company cut its margins for this job, the results to date, using generally accepted accounting principles, were reported as being satisfactory.

The alternative analysis for the year-end presentations for income and financial position evaluation is shown in Exhibit 7. The gross profit earned on the factors was only $15,952. Notice that the negative margin was reported in the year of occurrence, so the cost of overrun of $5,295 minus the budgeted gross profit of $5,057 resulted in a net loss on material of $238 for the current year. The other factors are simply the product of the margin rate times the factors supplied; for example, 4,251 labor-hours were provided, and the adjusted markup was $1.43 per hour, so the earned gross profit was $6,079. The adjusted rate of $1.43 is different from the budgeted rate of $1 because the total labor-hours decreased to 8,200. The new rate was computed as follows: original markup plus the variance ($8,342 + $3,418) divided by the new estimated total hours to be required. The variance on Other—Indirect Cost was included in this period's gross profit because it was deemed to be immaterial.

EXHIBIT 3 Job Cost Analysis—Material

JOB: 78512 **DATE:** 12/31/82

OWNER: C. W. Chemical **PROJECT:** Sludge Belt Filter

Code	Description	Budget	Total est. cost	Cost to date	Commit to date	Exposure	Variance
01	Site improvements						
02	Demolition						
03	Earthwork						
04	Concrete						
05	Structural steel	15,133	18,133	14,287	3,846		(3,000)
06	Piling						
07	Brick and masonry						
08	Buildings						
09	Major equipment	1,794	1,489	1,489			305
10	Piping	57,417	60,017	52,719	7,298		(2,600)
11	Instrumentation						
12	Electrical						
13	Painting						
14	Insulation						
15	Fireproofing	530	530		530		
16	Chemical cleaning						
17	Testing						
18	Const. equipment						
19	Misc. directs	2,050	2,050	987		1,063	
20	Field extra work						
Subtotal direct cost		76,924	82,219	69,482	11,674	1,063	(5,295)
21	Tools—supplies	7,361	7,361	1,853		5,508	
22	Payroll burden						
23	Start-up assistance						
24	Insurance and taxes						
25	Field supervision						
26	Home office expense						
27	Field emp. benefits						
Total indirect cost		7,361	7,361	1,853		5,508	
Adjustments							
Total field cost		84,285	89,580	71,335	11,674	6,571	(5,295)

EXHIBIT 4 Job Status Report of December 31

Factor	Budgeted cost	Total est. cost	Cost to date	Estimated future cost: Commitments	Estimated future cost: Exposure	Under (over)
Labor	$ 97,153	$ 93,735	$ 49,596		$44,139	$3,418
Material	84,285	89,580	71,335	$ 11,674	6,571	(5,295)
Subcontracts	180,416	182,568	73,759	108,809		(2,152)
Equipment	35,666	38,219	16,398	10,000	11,821	(2,553)
Other—direct	36,541	35,469	34,541		928	1,072
Other—indirect	36,735	36,530	17,884		18,646	205
Totals	$470,796	$476,101	$263,513	$130,483	$82,105	($5,305)

EXHIBIT 5 Progress Billing 78512–3

TO: My Client
Anywhere, USA

RE: Sludge Belt Filter
PO: CG 9473–N–457

Item	Base	Percent complete	Billing to date	Prior billing	Net billing
Supports	$ 52,000	40	$ 20,800	$ 15,600	$ 5,200
Equipment—machinery	104,000	25	26,000	10,400	15,600
Fabrication and piping	235,000	90	211,500	188,000	23,500
Electrical and instrumentation	104,000	20	20,800		20,800
Coatings	26,482	5	1,324		1,324
Total	$521,482		$280,424	$214,000	66,424
Less retainage—10%					6,642
Amount due this invoice					$59,782

EXHIBIT 6 Job 78512: Analysis of December 31

Description	Amount
Contract price	$521,482
Estimated cost:	
Cost to date	263,513
Estimated cost to complete	212,588
Estimated total cost	476,101
Estimated gross profit	45,381
Percent complete	.5535
Earned gross profit	25,118
Cost and gross profit to date	288,631
Billings to date	280,424
Cost and earned gross profit in excess of billing	$ 8,207

EXHIBIT 7 Job 78512: Analysis of December 31

Factor	*Original margin*	*Budget variance*	*New margin*	*Current estimated units*	*Adjusted margin rate*	*Units delivered*	*Earned gross profit*
Labor	$ 8,342	$ 3,418	$11,760	8,200	1.43%	4,251	$ 6,079
Material	5,057	(5,295)	(238)				(238)
Subcontracts	9,021	(2,152)	6,869	182,568	.0376%	73,759	2,773
Equipment	5,009	(2,553)	2,456	38,219	.0643%	16,398	1,054
Other—direct	5,181	1,072	6,253	35,569	.176%	34,541	6,079
Other—indirect	0	205	205				205
	$32,610	$(5,305)	$27,305				$ 15,952
Cost to date (Exhibit 4)							$263,513
Cost and earned gross profit to date							279,465
Billings to date (Exhibit 5)							280,424
Billings in excess of cost and earned gross profit to date							$ 959

"So, you have a choice in reviewing the contract status: either an earned gross profit of $25,118 with a net asset of $8,207; or, an earned gross profit of $15,952 and a net liability of $959," said Miss Ashley as she placed the worksheets back into the job file.

Questions

1. Be prepared to explain each item on Exhibits 6 and 7.
2. Which approach is more useful to management in controlling contract costs?

CASE 17–4
Sonic Aircraft Corporation

The U.S.A. still enjoys a good world-wide reputation for building modern weapons systems. Indeed, the sale of U.S. built weapons systems abroad has helped to lessen the dollar drain caused by the purchases of imported oil. Currently, Sonic Aircraft Corporation (SAC) is developing its F-69 fighter aircraft for sale to a host of O.P.E.C. nations. The F-69 will be a modern fighter using current state-of-the-art technology in order to provide an easily maintainable weapons system for use in the desert climate of the Middle East.

SAC has formed an F-69 project with Nicky St. John as the project manager. The president of SAC has made it crystal clear that the F-69 is their No. 1 project and that there will be no delays in the scheduled first flight test. That is crucial for the follow-on production contract of 100 F-69 aircraft at $8 million each.

The F-69 engine will be an existing jet engine model currently used on SAC's corporate jet aircraft—highly reliable and with adequate thrust for the F-69 fighter. However, this engine has to be modified to include an afterburner section, part of the specifications for the F-69 fighter. Time estimates are as follows: modification design (six months), engineering of the afterburner section to match the modified engine (four months), fabrication of modified engine and afterburner section (five months), prototype assembly and engine test-cell run (three months).

The airframe will be the basic SAC six-passenger corporate jet with the passenger compartment modified to a bomb bay and the nose baggage compartment modified for 7.62 mm machine gun installation. Time estimates are as follows: design airframe modification (seven months), engineering and wind tunnel testing (three months) and prototype fabrication and assembly of airframe (six months).

Subsystems, such as UHF radio, navigation units, autopilot, instruments, etc., will be "off-the-shelf" components; that is, subsystems in current use, with high reliability and ease of maintenance. There will be no radar subsystem because of its complexity. The F-69 fighter will be a daytime fighter/bomber only. There will be a simple lead computing sight subsystem for gunnery and manual bombing purposes, said subsystem also being "off-the-shelf" hardware. Time estimates are: request for bids on subsystems (four months), selection of subsystems (two months), award of contracts (two months), delivery of subsystems (six months), checkout and installation in prototype aircraft (three months).

Completion of the first F-69 will involve airframe/engine mating, a series of powered checks, taxi tests, etc., for one month—followed immediately by the first flight test. If all tests are successful, the F-69 prototype design and the specifications will be used for the production phase.

Questions

1. Using the Critical Path Method (CPM) technique, develop a network for the F-69 pre-production project.
2. What is the time in months for the first F-69 test flight?
3. What is the critical path?
4. Assume a one-month delay in obtaining bomb bay racks for the F-69 bomb bay. Would you request Nicky St. John to authorize the use of overtime to make up for this delay?
5. Assume a two-week delay in receipt of an alignment jig for aligning the center axis of the engine with the center axis of the afterburner section. Would you request Nicky St. John to authorize the use of overtime to make up for this delay?
6. Assume a strike at one of the subsystem vendors will delay delivery of the UHF radio unit by two months. Would you request Nicky St. John to authorize the formation of a second shift for the subsystem checkout and installation in the prototype aircraft activity?

Author Index

Subject Index

* Titles of cases are in italics.

This book has been set Linotron 202, in 10 and 9 point Times Roman, leaded 2 points. Part and chapter titles are 24 point Helvetica. Part numbers are 24 point Helvetica Light and chapter numbers are 12 and 24 point Helvetica Light. The size of the type page is 30 by 47 picas.